The Reconstruction of the International Economy, 1945–1960

The Growth of the World Economy

Series Editor: Nick F.R. Crafts
Professor of Economic History
London School of Economics, UK

The Reconstruction of the International Economy, 1945–1960

Edited by

Barry Eichengreen

Department of Economics
University of California at Berkeley, US

THE GROWTH OF THE WORLD ECONOMY

An Elgar Reference Collection
Cheltenham, UK • Brookfield, US

Published by
Edward Elgar Publishing Limited
8 Lansdown Place
Cheltenham
Glos GL50 2HU
UK

Edward Elgar Publishing Company
Old Post Road
Brookfield
Vermont 05036
US

British Library Cataloguing in Publication Data
Reconstruction of the International
Economy, 1945–60. – (Growth of the World
Economy Series; No. 5)
  I. Eichengreen, Barry II. Series
  330.9

Library of Congress Cataloguing in Publication Data
The reconstruction of the international economy, 1945–1960 / edited by
  Barry Eichengreen.
      p. cm. — (The growth of the world economy : 5) (An Elgar
  reference collection)
    Includes bibliographical references and index.
    1. Economic history—1945–1971. I. Eichengreen, Barry J.
  II. Series. III. Series: An Elgar reference collection.
  HC59.R32 1996
  337′.09′045—dc20   95–36672
                                                                                CIP

ISBN 1 85278 979 4

Printed in Great Britain by Galliard (Printers) Ltd, Great Yarmouth

Contents

Acknowledgements

The editor and publishers wish to thank the following who have kindly given permission for the use of copyright material.

American Economic Association for article: John G. Gurley (1953), 'Excess Liquidity and European Monetary Reforms, 1944-1952', *American Economic Review*, **XLIII** (1), March, 76–100.

American Historical Association for article: Charles S. Maier (1981), 'The Two Postwar Eras and the Conditions for Stability in Twentieth-Century Western Europe', *American Historical Review*, **86**, 327–52.

American Political Science Association for article: Donald C. Stone (1952), 'The Impact of U.S. Assistance Programs on the Political and Economic Integration of Western Europe', *American Political Science Review*, **XLVI** (4), December, 1100–116.

Banca Nazionale del Lavoro Quarterly Review for article: Robert Triffin (1954), 'International Currency and Reserve Plans', *Banca Nazionale del Lavoro Quarterly Review*, **VII** (28–29), January–June, 5–22.

Basil Blackwell Ltd for article: Rolf H. Dumke (1990), 'Reassessing the *Wirtschaftswunder*: Reconstruction and Postwar Growth in West Germany in an International Context', *Oxford Bulletin of Economics and Statistics*, **52**, 451–92.

Berg Publishers Inc. for excerpts: Werner Abelshauser (1991), 'American Aid and West German Economic Recovery: A Macroeconomic Perspective', in Charles S. Maier and Günter Bischof (eds), *The Marshall Plan and Germany*, Chapter 8, 367–409; Knut Borchardt and Christoph Buchheim (1991), 'The Marshall Plan and Key Economic Sectors: A Microeconomic Perspective', in Charles S. Maier and Günter Bischof (eds), *The Marshall Plan and Germany*, Chapter 9, 410–51.

Cambridge University Press for article: John S. Odell (1988), 'From London to Bretton Woods; Sources of Change in Bargaining Strategies and Outcomes', *Journal of Public Policy*, **8** (3/4), 287–315.

Diplomatic History for article: Alan S. Milward (1989), 'Was the Marshall Plan Necessary?', *Diplomatic History*, **13** (2), 231–53.

Duke University Press for article: Chiarella Esposito (1991), 'French International Monetary Policies in the 1940s', *French Historical Studies*, **17** (1), Spring, 117–40.

Economic History Association and Cambridge University Press for article: Moses Abramovitz (1986), 'Catching Up, Forging Ahead, and Falling Behind', *Journal of Economic History*, **XLVI** (2), June, 385–406.

Economic Policy for articles: Barry Eichengreen and Marc Uzan (1992), 'The Marshall Plan: Economic Effects and Implications for Eastern Europe and the Former USSR', *Economic Policy*, **14**, April, 14–75; Barry Eichengreen (1993), 'A Payments Mechanism for the Former Soviet Union: Is the EPU a Relevant Precedent?', *Economic Policy*, **17**, October, 310–53.

Elsevier Science Publishers BV for article: Albert O. Hirschman (1951), 'The European Payments Union: Negotiations and the Issues', *Review of Economics and Statistics*, **XXXIII** (1), February, 49–55.

International Finance Section of Princeton University for article: William Diebold, Jr. (1952), 'The End of the I.T.O.', *Essays in International Finance*, **16**, October, 1–37.

International Monetary Fund for article: J.J. Polak (1953), 'Contribution of the September 1949 Devaluations to the Solution of Europe's Dollar Problem', *IMF Staff Papers*, **2**, 1–32.

MIT Press Journals for article: G. John Ikenberry (1992), 'A World Economy Restored: Expert Consensus and the Anglo-American Postwar Settlement', *International Organization*, **46** (1), Winter, 289–321.

Richard N. Gardner for his own article: (1994), 'The Bretton Woods-GATT System After Fifty Years – A Balance Sheet of Success and Failure', *Sterling-Dollar Diplomacy: The Origin and the Future of the Bretton Woods-GATT System*, 1–25.

Richard T. Griffiths for his own excerpt: (1988), 'The Schuman Plan Negotiations: The Economic Clauses', in Klaus Schwabe (ed.), *Die Anfänge des Schuman-Plans*, 35–71.

University of California Press Journals for article: Michael J. Hogan (1984), 'Paths to Plenty: Marshall Planners and the Debate over European Integration, 1947–1948', *Pacific Historical Review*, **LIII** (3), August, 337–66.

In addition the publishers wish to thank the Library of the London School of Economics and Political Science, the Marshall Library of Economics, Cambridge University and the Photographic Unit of the University of London Library for their assistance in obtaining these articles.

Introduction

The reconstruction of the international economy was one of the great achievements of the post-World War II era. The starting point was the almost total cessation of normal international economic relations. The achievement was the most remarkable boom in international trade and lending the world has ever known. Between 1950 and 1965 the volume of world trade grew at a rate of nearly 8 per cent per annum. International lending recovered more slowly but by the second half of the 1960s was poised to explode. This buoyant expansion of international economic transactions did much to fuel the tripling of world output over the third quarter of the 20th century.

Looking back, it is tempting to characterize these trends as inevitable. Declining transportation costs, new modes of communication and advances in computer technology reduced the costs of undertaking international transactions. The interwar period of high tariffs and quotas came to appear as an aberration; normalcy was the fluid and integrated world economy of 1870–1913, elements of which were successfully reconstructed after World War II. On the output side, the industrial economies benefited from the scope for growth offered by 'catch up'. Europe had fallen far behind the United States due to the destructive effects of two wars and the depression-ridden interlude between them. Now it could grow by emulating the US example – by exploiting US technologies and restructuring work organization along American lines. Trade and growth could feed on one another in a virtuous circle.

It is the historian's responsibility to resist any argument that conveys a sense of inevitability. Thus, it is necessary to emphasize that, in the wake of World War II, it was by no means certain that events would turn out this way. There were widespread fears that the international economy would not be rebuilt. The industrial nations, concerned to insulate themselves from destabilizing impulses emanating from abroad and to secure the freedom to pursue ambitious programmes of economic planning, might decide to retain the commercial and financial controls imposed in the 1930s and exploited during the war. The disintegration of the international economy that had followed the onset of the Great Depression might become the norm. Moreover, the prevailing expectation in the wake of the war was not for a golden age of economic growth but for slump at least as severe as that which the world had suffered in 1920–21, which barring concerted action might fester and transform itself into another depression.

The achievement of the post-World War II era was a set of policy initiatives that contained these dangers. They completed the reconstruction of the international economy and inaugurated a golden age of economic growth. Some of these initiatives were premeditated, others spontaneous. Some benefited from years of planning while others reflected postwar policy-makers' ability to think on their feet. Together they provided a remarkably successful framework for the reconstruction of the international economy.

The most famous of these initiatives produced the Bretton Woods Agreement to establish the International Monetary Fund, the World Bank and the International Trade Organization. Since the collapse of the gold standard and the subsequent manipulation of exchange rates were seen as having greatly aggravated the economic problems of the 1930s, discussion centred on the Fund, the entity that would oversee the international monetary system. In one sense, creation of the Fund was a singular achievement. This was the first time the nations of the world had designed an international monetary system from scratch. The 19th-century gold standard had grown up spontaneously, while two international monetary conferences held earlier in the 20th century (at Genoa in 1922 and London in 1933) had come to naught.

A considerable literature, represented in this volume by John Odell and John Ikenberry (Chapters 1 and 2 respectively), explores why the Bretton Woods negotiations succeeded. Odell and Ikenberry emphasize 'expert consensus'. Both words are crucial. A *consensus* about the desirable features of an international monetary order developed in response to the turbulence of the interwar years and in the course of wartime dialogue between British and American officials. Such a system, in the prevailing view, should aspire to a balance of rules and discretion. It should be sufficiently rules based that nations would be prevented from engaging in destructive manipulation of their exchange rates and pursuing beggar-thy-neighbour policies. But it should allow for sufficient discretion that nations could avoid having to respond to balance-of-payments pressures with potentially disastrous policies of deflation. *Expert* opinion provided a basis for communication, articulated ideas and guided negotiations. Not surprisingly, popular histories of Bretton Woods are written as the tale of John Maynard Keynes and Harry Dexter White resolving their differences and bringing officials and politicians in their train.

Consensus there may have been, but there remained considerable disagreement between the British and Americans over the particulars of the Bretton Woods Agreement. And, as Chiarella Esposito attests in Chapter 3 of this volume, experts from other countries like Canada and France championed different ideas of their own. The final document may have had more in common with the White Plan than its rivals, but the American delegation had to offer significant concessions in order to secure the agreement of the other signatories.

Expert consensus alone was insufficient, moreover, to guarantee adoption and implementation of the agreement. A concerted campaign of political lobbying was also required. Divisions existed within governments over the merits of the document negotiated at Bretton Woods. Such schisms were evident in disagreements between the US State and Treasury Departments, for example. Getting national congresses and parliaments to ratify the agreement was an uphill battle. How this victory was won in the United States and how a combination of US pressure and domestic political manoeuvring combined to replicate it in other countries is a complex story deserving a volume of its own.

If there is a sense in which the establishment of the Fund and its sister institution, the Bank, was a singular success, there is also a sense in which it was a failure. The IMF played little role in international monetary affairs until the end of the 1950s. The quick transition to current account convertibility envisaged by the framers of the Bretton Woods Agreement never came to pass. Until 1st January 1959, international monetary relations over much of the world were regulated not by the IMF but by the European Payments Union, an arrangement for the multilateral clearing of inconvertible currencies that encompassed Western Europe, Europe's colonial dependencies and the British Commonwealth. Although the French had anticipated the need for a clearing union, nothing of the sort was negotiated at Bretton Woods. The World Bank, for its part, played little part in European reconstruction or, until the 1960s, in Third World economic development. It was crowded out by US bilateral aid, as described below. The third Bretton Woods institution, the ITO, was stillborn. The charter for an institution with far-reaching powers to monitor and coordinate national trade policies was never ratified. More than the agreement on exchange rates, the charter on trade incorporated the concerns of countries like Britain that governments should not be forced to deflate in order to maintain external balance, and of countries like France that the international regime should not hamper indicative planning. The ITO Charter featured clauses authorizing recourse to tariffs and quotas, permitting governments to support cartels and restrictive agreements, and strengthening host country control over foreign investment. As William Diebold describes in Chapter 13, the ITO was sunk by business opposition in the United States. It proved too interventionist and insufficiently free-market orientated for the American business community.

With US failure to ratify the ITO Charter, the General Agreement on Tariffs and Trade (GATT) was thrust into the breach. An interim arrangement intended to operate for three years until the ITO came into operation, the GATT became the permanent vehicle for efforts to liberalize trade. In contrast to the ITO, little, if any, legislative action and little direct support by business interests were needed in the participating countries. Difficult sectors such as agriculture and services were excluded. The ease with which signatories could withdraw heightened the fragility of the early GATT agreements, necessitating vigilance to sustain the precarious concessions negotiated in Geneva in 1947, Annecy in 1948 and Torquay in 1950. Yet throughout this period and into the 1970s, the GATT proved remarkably effective. Average tariff levels in the industrial countries were cut by half between 1940 and 1950 and by another 25 per cent by 1960.

What accounts for the fact that the Bretton Woods institutions, insofar as they functioned at all, took fully 15 years to come into operation? The explanation, as Richard Gardner demonstrates in Chapter 20 of this volume, lies in the Cold War and the responses it provoked. The Soviet threat tipped the balance between expedients and principles. The imperative for Western politicians became to initiate recovery and sustain growth even at the expense of heartfelt ideals, in order to restore political stability in Europe and halt the westward march of communism.

The Marshall Plan was the most important initiative developed in response. Between 1948 and 1951 the USA extended some $13 billion in aid, or roughly 2 per cent of recipient country GNP, to the war-torn economies of Western Europe. The economic and political consequences of the programme remain subjects of debate. Early histories of the Marshall Plan, written more often than not by persons present at the creation, trumpeted its economic benefits. Europe in 1947, these authors assert, was on the verge of starvation, economic chaos and political crisis. Marshall Plan funds played a critical role in restoring stability and paving the way for the resumption of growth.

Recent revisionism has challenged this view. Werner Abelshauser and Alan Milward, who in Chapters 4 and 6 of this volume summarize the arguments of longer books, insist that there is no evidence of economic crisis in 1947–48. Recovery from the war was under way. Annual measures of GNP rose without interruption. The Marshall Plan may have been a welcome gift from rich Uncle Sam, but there is no reason to think that Europe's recovery would have halted had this aid not been extended.

The obvious reason for insisting on the importance of the Marshall Plan is the external constraint. The threat to recovery in 1947 was the dollar shortage: European countries had no way of financing the inputs from the dollar area that recovery required. In Chapter 5 Knut Borchardt and Christoph Buchheim argue that the critical hard-currency imports were intermediate goods. The textile industry, for example, could not substitute away from imported cotton, negligible quantities of which were grown in Europe and no adequate substitutes for which existed. Only when Marshall aid came on stream were European producers able to rebuild raw material inventories to working levels.

The question about this argument is its generality. Cotton, obviously, is an extreme case. For other commodities, like coal, it was easier for industry to economize on their use by, for example, substituting water power. As my article with Marc Uzan, reprinted as Chapter 7, reports input–output analysis indicates that while the elimination of Marshall Plan-financed intermediate imports would have led to a noticeable decline in European production, that decline would have been a mere drop in the bucket compared with the expansion in European production over the Marshall Plan period of more than 50 per cent.

Milward argues that the external constraint on recovery was more likely to bind for investment goods than raw materials. Europe's postwar recovery was investment led. High levels of spending on imported capital goods had by 1947 all but exhausted Europe's hard currency reserves and outstripped its capacity to generate export receipts. In the absence of the Marshall Plan, governments would have had to cut back on investment. Whether growth would have just slowed or the negative multiplier effects would have plunged Europe into recession remains an unanswerable counterfactual.

Milward goes on to point out that prevailing levels of investment could have been maintained had governments compressed spending on other items, notably imported foodstuffs. Doing so was feasible technically; the question is whether it was viable politically. The issue was whose spending was to be compressed through income cuts, that of capitalists or of labourers. Each group understandably argued that the burden of adjustment should be borne by the other. Their refusal to concede tax increases or cuts in favoured public programmes led to budget deficits and to open and repressed inflation. This characterization suggests that the Marshall Plan may have operated most powerfully through political channels. By increasing the size of the distributional pie, American aid moderated the sacrifices in consumption necessary to sustain investment. It limited the concessions needed to balance government budgets and halt inflation. Budget balance and inflation stabilization were prerequisites for decontrol, which was itself necessary for the market economy to begin operating again. The role of the Marshall Plan, in this view, was to facilitate an end to the struggle over income distribution that had meant political instability, shortages and economic crisis.

The European Payments Union was another legacy of the Marshall Plan. Postwar monetary adjustments, including devaluation (see Polak, Chapter 8) and financial reform (see Gurley, Chapter 9), had gone a long way toward removing inflationary threats and structural payments problems. But even after these adjustments had taken place, policymakers remained sceptical of the feasibility of the quick move to current account convertibility anticipated by the framers of the Bretton Woods Agreement. Following the 1947 debacle when the UK, under pressure from the US, had attempted to restore current account convertibility but failed, Europe pursued a different course: a multilateral payments union. *De facto* current account convertibility was restored within Europe through multilateral clearing with credits, but discrimination against the dollar area remained.

In parallel with the literature on the Marshall Plan, there is a debate on the indispensability of the EPU. Early accounts by authorities such as Albert Hirschman and Robert Triffin, both of whom were involved in contemporary planning, insist that there existed no other option for multilateralizing Europe's trade. (See Chapters 10 and 11.) Recent scholarship, represented here by my article, suggests that there in fact existed a feasible alternative to inconvertibility, multilateral clearing and dollar discrimination, namely current account convertibility. Except for the UK and Ireland, where significant monetary overhangs remained, there was no technical obstacle to European countries moving more quickly to convertibility, perhaps as early as 1950.

The real argument for the EPU was not that convertibility was infeasible technically. Rather, it was that the EPU was more effective than unilateral convertibility for binding Germany into the international economy. Other countries were sceptical of Germany's commitment to openness, given memories of the Schachtian policies of the 1930s and the two world wars. Germany had been Europe's dominant supplier of capital goods and the single largest consumer of raw materials produced by other European countries. An arrangement which rendered credible Germany's commitment to intra-European trade would therefore go a long way toward reconstituting traditional patterns of comparative advantage, curing the dollar shortage and encouraging other countries to restructure their economies along export-orientated lines.

The EPU, together with the European Coal and Steel Community (negotiations over which are described by Richard Griffiths in Chapter 14), provided a solution to these commitment and coordination problems. As a condition for participating in the payments union, countries accepted a schedule for intra-European trade liberalization. By February 1951, less than a year after the EPU came into effect, all trade measures were to be applied equally to imports from all member countries. An EPU Managing Board, housed at the Bank for International Settlements and working hand in hand with the Organization for European Economic Cooperation, monitored compliance and imposed sanctions. For those concerned to solve this commitment problem, the EPU was preferable to unilateral convertibility, which lacked the multilateral surveillance and conditionality that rendered the EPU a credible institutional exit barrier.

Out of this nexus of policies grew the European Economic Community. While impetus for regional integration existed in Europe itself, the USA did much to encourage it, as Chapter 16 by Donald C. Stone shows. The Marshall Planners sought to encourage intra-European trade: they made progress on integration a condition for the extension of aid. As Michael Hogan and Charles Maier explain in Chapters 15 and 19, this reflected their understanding of the economic bases of America's international economic leadership at mid-century. Just as the USA benefited from the economies of scale and scope offered by a continental market, Europe could hope to keep pace only if it availed itself of an integrated market of its own. And, following the experience of two wars, it was desirable to use economic and ultimately political integration as an instrument to render war between France and Germany unthinkable.

These postwar initiatives combined to sow a fertile field for economic growth. While growth the world over was more rapid between 1950 and 1970 than in any comparable period before or since, the difference was most marked in Europe. The articles by Abramovitz and Dumke, reprinted as Chapters 17 and 18, both emphasize the technological gap that existed between Europe and the United States, providing scope for catch-up. But catching up was far from automatic, as Abramovitz's analysis makes clear. Countries had to possess the social capacity to absorb the advanced organizational forms pioneered by the United States and to adapt them to local circumstances. They had to activate the catch-up process by boosting saving, ploughing profits back into investment, and selling their products on an expanding international market. The various elements of the process had to be encouraged to feed on one another.

Here the international element was key. High levels of investment, supported initially by Marshall aid and subsequently by the savings generated by growing European incomes, augmented capacity and boosted productivity. The expansion of trade under the aegis of the GATT and the EPU allowed countries to specialize along lines of comparative advantage. The wage moderation that allowed profits to be ploughed back into investment could not have been sustained without the monetary reforms that ensured the restoration of price stability and the nominal anchor provided by the Bretton Woods international monetary system.

In the 1970s productivity growth slowed, and the golden age drew to a close. The final selection, Chapter 20 by Richard Gardner, suggests that this development can be attributed to widening divergences between the international structures created in the 1940s and the institutional requirements of the final quarter of the 20th century. The GATT proved less effective at liberalizing trade once tariffs had been reduced and the tangled undergrowth of non-tariff barriers was revealed. The Bretton Woods international monetary system broke down from a combination of structural flaws and mismanagement and was succeeded by a 'non-system' of managed floating that worked to no-one's satisfaction. International lending exploded in the 1970s but evaded the World Bank's efforts to regularize it. The absence of commodity-stabilization agreements of the sort Keynes had proposed at Bretton Woods was underscored by the two oil shocks of the 1970s.

It may never be determined how much of the post-1971 slowdown was attributable to strains in the international economy, and how much was due to exhausting the scope for catch-up and to growing domestic rigidities. But so long as historians and economists study this question, they will have to start with the 1945–1960 period which is the focus of this volume and with the topics under consideration here.

Part I
The Bretton Woods System

[1]

Jnl Publ. Pol., 8, 3/4, 287–315

From London to Bretton Woods; Sources of Change in Bargaining Strategies and Outcomes*

JOHN S. ODELL, *International Relations, University of Southern California*

ABSTRACT

Our most prominent theories of international bargaining miss elements essential for understanding national bargaining strategies and international outcomes. In particular they lack sufficient mechanisms of change over time. A focused contrast between the London economic and monetary conference of 1933 and the Bretton Woods conference of 1944 suggests three new dynamic hypotheses. (1) Changes, especially extreme ones, in national market conditions are likely to shift the state's bargaining strategy sharply even if its relative international position has not changed. A slump will produce a more exploitative strategy, while a boom will encourage either a passive or an expansive strategy. (2) Painful national experience running contrary to prevailing policy ideas is likely to discredit those ideas among politicians and officials, turn them toward alternative doctrines, and lead to corresponding strategy changes. The ideas most likely to spread politically are ones which had predicted the currrent problem, and those whose advocates mount the most sophisticated publicity campaign. (3) International technical disagreement can pose a decisive impediment to intergovernmental agreement, while in some conditions at least technical convergence facilitates official agreement.

* The author is grateful for helpful comments on previous drafts by Robert Aliber, Philip Converse, Barry Eichengreen, Jeffry Frieden, Robert Gilpin, Judith Goldstein, Randall Henning, Christopher Holloman, Leroy Laney, Robert Oliver, M. J. Peterson, Robert Putnam, Thomas Schwartz, Konrad Stenzel, and Thomas Willett. Versions of the article were debated at a University of Chicago seminar, the 1988 Claremont-USC Conference on International Financial Relations, the 1988 annual meeting of the American Political Science Association, and the 1988 Social Science Research Council Conference on Foreign Policy Analysis. Magid Matzinger and Eileen Rabach provided able research assistance. The preparation of the study benefited greatly from a fellowship granted by the Social Science Research Council and the Ford Foundation. None of these friends is to blame for the results.

288   *John S. Odell*

Our most prominent theories of international bargaining miss influences that are essential for understanding national bargaining strategies and international outcomes. Game theory and international structural realism, while they can contribute important insights, also obscure some of the most potent influences. They are notably weak in their dynamics, in specifying sources and processes of change over time.

A look at two contrasting historical cases suggests several new hypotheses worthy of further investigation. The 1933 World Monetary and Economic Conference in London ended in collapse, while a decade later another negotiation culminated in the Bretton Woods agreement that established long-lasting international monetary arrangements. These two bargaining outcomes differed sharply even though some of the circumstances were similar. In each case one or more states made proposals for a joint response to an economic problem. Many of the same leading states participated in both – Britain, France, and the United States especially. In fact, the same President and party governed America in both cases. Another key similarity will be discussed below.

Clearly a decisive reason for the difference was the changed behavior of the United States. Hence the two central analytical questions of this paper, as in much bargaining theory, are why state actors, concentrating on the US, have different preferences or follow different strategies in different cases, and why international outcomes vary between no agreement and agreement. This paper concentrates on the macro-monetary issues in these talks, largely setting aside aspects concerning trade barriers and international investment.

It might be helpful to clarify at the outset what is meant by international outcome and by state strategy. While the meanings of agreement and non-agreement are self-evident, analyzing these two particular cases will be clearer if some 1933 counterfactuals are made explicit. That is, if part of the question is why agreement was not reached in 1933, the answer depends on what particular potential agreement one has in mind. One candidate would be an agreement on terms favored at the time by the French or the British government in the absence of American leadership. France in 1932 was still wedded to gold-standard orthodoxy of the pre-depression era. The franc was convertible into gold and fixed, and the authorties were responding to the slump with spending cuts and monetary discipline. The real economy had not declined nearly as much as had the American. French prices, however, were steadily losing their world competitiveness, and threats to the franc were becoming worrisome. Britain had gone off gold in September 1931, and Roosevelt temporarily suspended the dollar's gold link as well in April 1933. Paris wanted above all to get London and Washington back to stabilizing the pound and the dollar in terms of gold.

Britain with its depreciated pound was seeing the beginnings of recovery at home. London's main financial concern was war debt payments to the Americans, which were continuing to absorb some 12 percent of Britain's export earnings (Clarke 1973, pp. 22–23). The proposal for a London conference had emerged out of the Lausanne meeting of 1932, where the European war victors agreed to accept an end to German reparations payments. They had conditioned implementation on a 'satisfactory settlement . . . between them and their own creditors' (quoted in Feis 1966, p. 20). Soon after Lausanne the British asked Washington whether it would participate in a broad world economic conference. When the US later also went off gold, Britain could of course agree with France on the need for American stabilization as well. Thus, if the US had simply agreed to European terms on financial issues, roughly speaking it would have stabilized the dollar in terms of gold and suspended war debts.

As seen with the benefit of hindsight a financial agreement along these lines would probably have broken down before long. To stabilize currencies in terms of gold in a lasting manner, given the profound imbalances and uncertainties prevailing in the world economy, would have required either large-scale international financing arrangements or provision for subsequent deliberate exchange-rate realignments, or both. As different national economies had declined to different degrees, had adopted different market controls, and were likely to recover at different paces, some lubrication would have been required between them. Neither form of lubrication was envisioned in these bargaining positions.

This is not to say, however, that the only alternatives available to the US were agreement on those terms or no agreement at all. America could have taken the lead. A very different counterfactual would have been an international agreement to reflate jointly, and to manage any resulting payments imbalances jointly by official credit or exchange-rate realignments. Such a deal is easily conceivable today, and it would clearly have benefited all the major parties, compared with no agreement. Unemployment and deflation were everywhere. In fact several such proposals circulated at the time. Keynes published a comprehensive, specific scheme for cooperative recovery in a series of London articles in *The Times* and *The News Statesman and Nation* in March and April 1933, offered for discussion at the coming world economic conference. His reasoning of course centered on the need for increased 'loan expenditure' at home to increase aggregate spending power, government taking the first step, which would require cheap bank credit as well. These measures would be possible, however, only if 'each Central Bank is freed from anxiety by feeling itself to possess adequate reserves of international money', in case of deterioration of its foreign balance. Competitive depreciations could

290   *John S. Odell*

not be a substitute for the world as a whole. 'We should attach great importance to the *simultaneity* (emphasis in original) of the movement towards increased expenditure' in many different countries. 'Combined international action is the essence of policy' (Keynes 1933).

Keynes proposed to allay those anxieties by creation of an international authority that would issue gold-notes to member countries in proportion to their 1928 gold reserves, for use only in official circulation, and backed by the member governments' guarantees. This radical plan would have enlarged world reserves instantly by that amount. States would have been required to eliminate offensive external practices like exchange controls in order to enjoy access to the international gold notes. Keynes felt some exchange stability would be preferable to free floating, and recommended that governments peg their currencies to gold, given the commitment to expenditure expansion. His scheme also provided, however, a five percent margin of flexibility between the gold points, and Keynes suggested the innovation that 'the *de facto* parity should be alterable, if necessary, from time to time if circumstances were to require, just like bank-rate, – though by small degrees, one would hope'. The British government also forwarded to Washington a less ambitious plan for an international monetary fund to help central banks remove barriers to international trade.' Some governments, including Japan and Sweden, did adopt large-scale deficit spending as a successful remedy for depression during this period.

Thus the first-level empirical question can be why some such international agreement was not adopted in 1933 while agreement was reached at Bretton Woods. The second-level variable is national bargaining strategy. Here some definitions may be in order. The 1933 American behavior exemplifies what could be called an *exploitative* or competitive strategy. With such an approach, the actor unilaterally grabs as big a piece of the common pie as possible, rather than proposing joint action that will expand the pie. In theory this strategy may include coercive or distributive tactics such as staking out commitments and demands, threatening negative sanctions if wishes are not granted, concealing true priorities and minimum needs, attempting to manipulate other parties' perceptions, and making secret deals.

The 1933 case does not present all these tactics. Washington blew hot and cold during the negotiations; at some stages some of its agents discussed agreements that would have met some of Europe's concerns. But all things considered, US behavior was heavily weighted in the exploitative direction. First, Washington did not take the initiative in promoting the conference of a monetary plan. Then the US went off gold in the midst of the preparations, while it had not a payments deficit but a strong position in international reserves and trade. In effect FDR and the

Democrats began 'talking the dollar down' before the conference, and afterwards he aggressively pushed it down much farther. In London the US, after having toyed with agreement, dramatically rejected even the most accommodating offers on behalf of joint gains. Roosevelt's scathing 'bombshell' telegram exploded the conference, for better or worse.

A decade later the same nation under the same President seized the initiative, devoted substantial resources to designing a global agreement in the common interest, accommodated some of the wishes of its chief interlocutor, Great Britain, and implemented its commitments after the conference, for better or worse. The 1943–45 American behavior illustrates what could be called an *expansive* or partly expansive bargaining strategy. There the actor proposes or agrees to measures that will benefit both or many parties, including itself. In theory the tactics most effective for expanding pies may be quite different from those used for competition. They may include open-ended search for technical problems common to both parties, unguarded exploration of alternative solutions, revealing one's true needs and priorities, and steps enhancing a climate of mutual trust.[2]

The 1944 case also fails to present a pure case of this second ideal type. In fact the Americans in 1944 were exploiting to some exent as well as 'expanding'. Parts of US proposals were designed to benefit or protect America in particular at the expense of other states, at least as the others saw them.

Even taken by itself, 'expansive' does not mean 'altruistic', or sacrificing national welfare for the benefit of foreigners. Such a concept would have relatively little empirical use in international relations. This second approach is a different means for advancing national welfare.

Parenthetically, interpretations of cases like 1933 sometimes come to rest showing only that the actor was not altruistic. We read, for instance, that the 1933 conference collapsed because America chose to favor domestic over international well-being. Such a statement is a truism that trivializes the problem. As between those two options, every government will choose the former every time. It also tempts us into the trap of explaining a change with a constant. The interesting problem is that policy is not constant; the same country used quite different strategies on different occasions.

Choosing between these two strategies always presents a dilemma. Either way, the actor will run some risks and pay a price in terms of self-interest. Exclusive devotion to expanding opportunities for joint gain runs the risk that one's partner will attempt exploitation. Yet an actor limited to the exploitative strategy is likely to realize only limited gain, especially over time, considering the undiscovered opportunities and retaliation.

292   *John S. Odell*

A third course could be called a *passive* strategy. The actor simply stays away from negotiations, or walks away, and avoids active measures that disadvantage others. Sometimes this stance coincides with a laissez faire policy. In economic affairs, governments always have the theoretical option in particular of 'leaving it to the market'. But a government might also decline a particular international bargain concerning a market with substantial existing regulation, or combine international passivity with national activism. In both 1933 and 1944, Americans also considered a passive strategy. Thus the second-level analytical problem is why bargaining states shift between exploitative, expansive and passive moves.[3]

The purpose of this study is not to develop a comprehensive understanding of this particular historical contrast, let alone to describe the events fully. Many accounts are available. Rather this is a focused comparison of two cases selected in order to generate hypotheses that might be useful, after further study, for application to other cases as well, outside as well as inside the monetary realm. The comparison focuses selectively on some variables and deliberately neglects others.

I. Problems with dominant theories

Game theory

The London–Bretton Woods contrast illuminates limitations of the theories of interstate bargaining that dominate our literature. The most popular formal approach by far has been game theory. Although there is dispute over whether game theory is really a theory or only a technique, it has certainly inspired a substantial research tradition. The contributions, have often been less, however, than its advocates think. Once we have mastered the technique we still have most of our problem before us. Game theory has not explained the contrast between London and Bretton Woods to my knowledge, and working further on such models is probably not the most urgent task. Doing so prematurely probably distracts attention from the most important variables.[4]

In political science, the most common applications have not used formal models themselves but have studied them for their heuristic value. In that way game theory has indeed proved to be stimulating, and concepts inspired by it have rightly entered into informal theories and interpretations of many events.

Often the more explicit game-theoretic analyses of interstate relations claim to offer explanations, but actually provide only post-hoc reconstructions of events in game language. The premises of the supposed explanations are not derived independently from the outcome to be explained.

From London to Bretton Woods   293

The Achilles' heel seems to be that states' preference orders are almost never derived from theory or from serious empirical investigation. The approach may be less problematic when the subject is the output of firms in a concentrated market. There we lose little in assuming that the actors' only goals are profits and that they prefer more to less. Since governments pursue multiple and often contradictory goals in international relations, however, and since their priorities are subject to influence, the technique inherently forces us to disregard much of what we know about the reality, or to compress it all into a single preference order. More than that, the game structure itself also assumes particular causal relations between state actions and outcome variables, relations that are also quite complicated in fact. As a result, even if the simplifying assumption is plausible as far as it goes, it is difficult to have great confidence in predictions about actual states made on this basis alone.[5]

Of course any modeling exercise works from assumptions and concentrates on elaborating their logical implications. Some purely theoretical game analyses are interesting in this respect and should be developed. In the future, models might be tested comparatively and develop empirically convincing explanations. Actual interpretations, however, often seem arbitrary and no more convincing than other interpretations that could be fitted to the data.

When we examine game-theoretic interpretations that address questions of policy change, the real 'action' in the interpretation is usually external to the model. The analyst is forced to go outside game theory to find the main insights behind change, and then restate them in game language (for instance, see Oye 1985).[6] Having begun an effort to escape ad hoc interpretation, the game analyst often ends relying centrally on ad hocery anyhow. Premature efforts to apply this approach, before we have established preference orders, divert our attention from the most important variables.

The usual assumption that preferences are fixed imposes a particularly severe constraint on an understanding of bargaining. This assumption obscures of the essence of the bargaining process – the parties' attempts to manipulate each others' perceptions and preferences. We are unlikely to arrive at a valid understanding of the difference between actual outcomes without delving into that process. The game theoretic approach might advance most by investing more in empirical study of the preferences of particular states regarding particular issues, in order to improve the quality of the 'inputs' driving the models' conclusions. The following sections take steps in that direction.[7]

294   *John S. Odell*

International power structure

The most influential informal theory of international bargaining attempts to infer state behavior and interstate outcomes from the international power structure. Specifically, we often say that the United States led the world to create the IMF in 1944 because it had hegemonic or overwhelming power over other states. Our literature exaggerates the importance of hegemony, however, and of power structures in general, and sometimes we confuse relative power with absolute or national conditions. Attention to power structures is necessary but not adequate. Anomalies for the hegemony argument in several periods have been acknowledged (Krasner 1976).

The reason the US did not take the lead in 1933 was not a lack of sufficient international power; America was already strong enough. Power refers to the resources that permit a state to influence actions abroad and to resist foreign influence attempts. Perhaps the most fundamental resource in the economic realm is production capacity, the ability to supply the rest of the world's needs and to survive blockades or overseas disruptions. Greater production capacity in turn permits greater accumulation of financial resources and credit power. America's share of estimated world manufacturing production rose steadily from 23 per cent in 1870 to 35 per cent in the period 1906–1913 (League of Nations 1945, p. 13). Presumably adding agricultural output would show an even larger US advantage. In terms of the output distribution, by World War I the United States was already a superpower, and the only one. For comparison, in 1950 the US share of world GNP was estimated at 39 per cent (US President 1971, vol. 2, chart 1).

In trade too, the US capacity to buy other nations' goods and to export already gave it a stronger basis for influence and leverage than any other country. The US share of world trade, which held steady at about 10 per cent over the decades prior to World War I, was almost 17 per cent in 1928. For comparison, the figure for 1950 was 16.7 per cent (Kuznets 1966, p. 308; Krasner 1976, p. 346. The data for 1928 are slightly overstated because they combine Canada and the US). Moreover, the fact that the country was so self-sufficient, that only a very small fraction of that huge output entered world trade, further strengthened its power in the 'net' sense. It was much stronger than Britain ever was, in the ability of its home economy to withstand overseas disruptions or foreign influence. The United States also became the world's leading international creditor after World War I. Fully 43 per cent of all the world's international investments in the 1920s came from this one country (Kuznets, p. 323).

If relative power defines interests, and if America had a major interest in creating an IMF in 1944, a strong case can be made that this interest was present long before then. A power analyst, focusing only on US potential gains relative to those of other states in 1933, would have expected the US to take the lead. A joint effort at expanding and stabilizing the world economy would have benefited American farmers, manufacturers, and foreign investors then as much as later. It is not far-fetched to imagine that if America had chosen to use its power quite differently, it could have brought about a comparable monetary agreement.[8]

Power structures certainly limit state actions and bargaining outcomes to some extent. World politics is far from an interaction among equally small units. American industrialization and the historic rise of US relative economic position from the 19th to the 20th centuries surely helped produce the agreement. But this rise is precisely why the contrast between these two historically decisive events is a puzzle.

US power did change somewhat between 1933 and 1944. The depression hit US production hard and drove the US share of world manufactures back down to 32 per cent in 1936–38. During wartime, the US position improved vis-à-vis the states participating in monetary negotiations. France was occupied, the Soviet Union and Britain were struggling for survival, and the latter badly needed American firepower, goods, and money. But this further improvement created surplus power, which was probably not necessary to produce the observed result.

The Achilles' heel of the power approach, analogous to that of game theory, is that power in itself is insufficient to identify the purposes for which states will use their power, or the direction in which policy will attempt to move. The typical application grafts on auxiliary assumptions about the purposes that would have been in the state's interest. The conclusions depend crucially on those assumptions, but realist theorists usually shun investigating them empirically. (For a prominent exception, see Krasner 1978.) This limitation again blinds the theory to powerful sources of change.

If these two prominent theories do not solve our problem, then, where should we turn? If key variables – the international power structure, national political institutions, and the party and the President in office – were basically held constant, why did US behavior change so drastically? Many ideas and facets of this history could be explored, but here I propose to highlight three arguments in particular. Each is a dynamic argument, highlighting processes that change bargaining situations over time.

II. *National market conditions and strategy change*

This historical contrast suggests, first, that if national market conditions change absolutely, especially if to an extreme degree, foreign economic

296   John S. Odell

strategy is likely to shift sharply, even if the state's relative interests given by the international system remain largely the same. Specifically, collapse makes an exploitative strategy more likely, and boom inclines the nation toward either passive or expansive behavior, other things being equal.

By 1933 the American national economy was in desperate condition, and it did recover, after all. In the four years after 1929, farmers and workers were thrown out of work by the millions until unemployment had expanded from 3 per cent to 25 per cent. Millions of others were working short hours at lower wage rates. The depression slashed away one-quarter of the average American's real disposable personal income. Farm prices fell so low, it is said, that a wagonload of corn would not pay for the shoeing of a pair of horses (Feis 1966, p. 10). Waves of financial panic hit banks, closing hundreds each year, which destroyed savings and in turn forced many businesses and individuals under. It was a time, wrote J. M. Blum, of want and despair, of despondency (Blum 1959, p. 35). The ship of state was listing severely, and many feared it might go to the bottom.

We often underestimate the degree of recovery registered by 1940, before the huge wartime fiscal deficits. By 1940 many Americans felt that something approaching prosperity was finally returning. The banking system was not on the verge of total collapse. Average real disposable income was at its 1929 level, and unemployment was down and falling rapidly, though still at 15 per cent. By the time the US launched the serious phase of bargaining over the monetary system in 1943, the home economy was booming. Gross national product was expanding at a 13 per cent annual rate, real personal income was up another 29 per cent since 1940, and unemployment dropped to 1.9 per cent (US Bureau of the Census 1966).

Oddly enough, our dominant theories of international bargaining entirely overlook absolute changes in domestic market conditions, which were probably necessary for this American shift from the exploitative to the expansive strategy. If domestic economic decline and fears anything like those of 1933 had prevailed in the early 1940s, the Bretton Woods initiative would have been just as unlikely, despite a further increase in US relative power. On the other hand, the actual recovery, together with other changes mentioned below, might well have been sufficient to free Washington to promote the IMF experiment even had US relative power declined slightly.

An intervening event, US agreement to the 1936 tripartite declarations stabilizing major currencies, adds support to this interpretation. The recovery was jagged, rising steadily to a peak in 1937, then falling again in 1938, then rising again. In 1937 real GNP equalled that of 1929, and personal income exceeded the 1930 level. By the end of 1935, in fact, Treasury Secretary Henry Morgenthau and the Federal Reserve were agitated about a risk of 'runaway inflation' (Romasco 1983, pp. 224). The fact that America's first hesitant turn toward international monetary arrangements also coincided with improved domestic circumstances is probably more than coincidence.

These cases suggest that some minimal level of politicians' confidence in the domestic economy is a prerequisite for international leadership. An international or expansive strategy is a means of improving one's country that works by first lifting the world economy, and such an approach depends on foreign governments to carry out their commitments. It also depends on international markets: US credit and cooperation must not fail to buoy foreign economies, and their increased spending must not flow entirely to producers outside America. While even purely national remedies carry uncertainties, international schemes have more. Any rational politician would need at least to see his way clear beyond short-term survival to be willing to commit his government to a strategy whose benefit depends on a longer causal chain and more time for its realization.

On this reasoning, if the 1933 Roosevelt Administration had been convinced, as it was not, that a policy of large-scale deficit spending would benefit the US economy in the medium run, it would still have been unlikely to propose or support an international monetary fund such as Keynes proposed, as long as the home economic situation remained extreme.

Whether the less extreme variations typical of more recent historical experience have analogous effects on state strategy requires further investigation. On the one hand, it seems logical to assume that the worse the national conditions, the more likely competitive behavior will be, regardless of external incentives, and the better they are, the more likely a state will follow either a passive or an expansive strategy. States may turn outward to some extent before home conditions are fully booming, as Morgenthau did. Investigations of nineteenth-century tariffs find that policies shift toward openness when national business cycles improve, and vice versa (McKeown 1983; Gallarotti 1985). Many recent observers have connected turns toward unilateralism in trade policy and deterioration of the GATT system to cyclical recessions (e.g., IMF 1978).

On the other hand, in the absence of extreme conditions, other influences might override this one. The 1982 recession was the worst in recent American experience, but given the welfare state's safety nets, its severity was far less than 1933. These conditions did not prevent the Reagan Administration's trade negotiators from attempting to initiate a new round of trade liberalization. Nor have less extreme oscillations seemed to correlate with the degree of cooperation achieved in Western economic summits (Putnam and Bayne 1987).

We might suppose that this business cycle effect on bargaining behavior would be less significant the smaller the country, in global economic terms. Following collective action theory, the small player would have less external incentive than the large to offer proposals to reform the international system. Thus it would be expected to confine itself to free-riding even when its economy is booming. Small size probably does inhibit expansive initiatives addressed to the entire world community. The smaller state, nevertheless, would have a greater incentive to make bilateral proposals to another state of its own size, or a regional community, where it would reap a more substantial share of the joint gains.

This first proposition might be made deeper and more precise by building in macroeconomics itself. To the extent that a macroeconomic model could forecast at least economies' future directions, if not their rates of change, then the enlarged argument might help in estimating, for example, the likelihood that official proposals to reform the exchange-rate regime will emerge and meet with approval. The disarray in macroeconomics today, however, complicates an effort to build in this direction.

III. Bad news, cognitive change, and bargaining strategy

The 1933/1944 contrast suggests, second, that changes in strategy and international outcomes depend, at least in some cases, on the displacement of powerful ideas blocking the way. Generally, if national experience contradicts prevailing policy ideas and their predictions, politicians are likely to shift to alternative ideas, pushing strategy and outcomes in corresponding directions. If prevailing ideas are discredited, officials will be likely to do the opposite the next time, attempting to refight the last war. Conversely, when the 'news' is good, the doctrine that is 'in' will become even more popular, and ideas already out of favor will remain so or decline further.

This hypothesis assumes that politicians' beliefs about policy will be partly independent of national interests defined objectively, and will shape and change bargaining strategies independently of the world power situation and game structures. This contrast also suggests conditions that favor some alternative ideas over others, and which therefore tell us something about the particular direction in which strategy and outcomes will shift.

Depression and popularity of the gold standard and floating rates

Until the Great Depression, gold standard orthodoxy had commanded genuine conviction, and not only among bankers. As is well known, this

From London to Bretton Woods

intense experience violently contradicted orthodox predictions, and badly discredited the bankers identified as the gold standard's chief advocates, in many countries. Careful social scientists rightly insist that correlation alone does not establish causation, but correlation is quite often enough to cement firmly-held beliefs among political leaders, especially if the experience is vivid and personal. The chaotic conditions also besmirched free trade, or at least made it seem infeasible in many countries. And yet the thirties turned out to be a way-station, a period after the discrediting had begun, but before an alternative theory and prescription for prosperity had attained widespread support among the governing classes.

In 1933, the most prominent advocates for an international agreement were identified politically with the seemingly bankrupt gold standard approach. Yet at the same time the conviction that governments had to balance their budgets every year was also still strong enough to block schemes like that of Keynes, at least in France and the US. In 1933 many leaders, including Franklin Roosevelt, were certain that a policy of large-scale deficit spending would be ruinous, or at least risky and distasteful. The orthodox belief held that if government restored balance to its budget, it would increase business confidence, and business would then prime the pump with increased investment spending. FDR's highly reluctant conversion to government 'spending for its own sake' was to wait until the economic relapse of 1938 (Stein 1969, chap. 6). Not one but two severe disconfirming experiences were necessary, but sufficient, in his case to shatter confidence in orthodoxy.

The chaotic international experiences of the mid- and later 1930s also limited the range of options likely to follow. Without following any particular alternative global doctrine, the world stumbled into surprising currency fluctuations, exchange controls, and discrimination. These coincided with the collapse of trade and incomes, which, along with episodes of the twenties, predictably discredited the idea of floating exchange rates for many years. In the US in particular, the international instabilities and cycles of fruitless neighbor-beggaring pointed expert thinking toward ways of removing these foreign obstacles to US exports and these self-defeating cycles.[9]

More open political economies had different experiences, of course, which led to some differences in the inferences drawn. Keynes and the British were especially keen to maintain the flexibility to protect their economy from future depressions that might originate abroad despite prudent British policy, and they wanted foreign financing to permit Britain to reduce discrimination and liberalize while national reserves were depleted. By extension, while the US was more concerned with stabilizing exchange rates, Keynes dwelled more on how to enable

300   *John S. Odell*

exchange rate adjustments to be made in an orderly manner (see Kahn 1976, p. 15).

Pearl Harbor and American isolationism

If the depression dealt a heavy blow to the classical strand of economic liberalism, a second world war virtually buried American political anti-war isolationism. This well-known fact, too, is typically overlooked when we think about Bretton Woods, however. Surely that sea-change in US political culture had something to do with the difference between 1933 and 1944, especially in the Congress.

After World War I, the isolationist voice remained dominant in America. Although some of Woodrow Wilson's followers carried on efforts to turn their countrymen to international organization, they did not win many converts among the public. The dominant doctrine held that the United States could best protect itself by neutrality legislation and isolation from foreign wars.[10]

However self-defeating it may seem today, genuine isolationist conviction specifically helped block 1933 US concessions on war debts, which would probably have been required in order to achieve a major financial agreement. Roosevelt rejected such concessions on the advice of the anti-war Raymond Moley, whom he designated his chief debt adviser, and others. In 1939 Moley still believed that this policy had:

maintained the integrity of the debts as living obligations which, from that day to this, have prevented the use of the United States as a war treasury by Europe and have done more to stave off a general war than a dozen alliances or a score of diplomatic notes. . . . It was a warning that the New Deal rejected the point of view of those who would make us parties to a political and economic alliance with England and France . . . seeking to enforce peace through threats of war (Moley 1939, pp. 78–79).

After 7 December 1941, defending the isolation recipe for US security was a bit awkward. Pearl Harbor in particular changed minds, from one idea defining the national interest to another, even on issues as technical as money. It is interesting, in fact, that before Pearl Harbor the State Department had negotiated and signed a convention with Latin American states to create an Inter-American Bank, largely in response to Nazi penetration of South America (Oliver, chap. IV). The Congress, however, had declined to ratify the agreement. Having worked on this ambitious bank plan, Harry White in the Treasury was also beginning to think about a still more comprehensive set of institutions. It was seven days after Pearl Harbor when Secretary Morgenthau formally directed his aide to draft an 'Inter-Allied Stabilization Fund' that would help allies, stabilize currencies after the war, and establish an 'international currency' (Eckes 1975, p. 46).

In the cauldron of another massive war, popular American sentiment surged to the alternative Wilsonian inferences from the first war and League failures, and US international bargaining behavior suddenly became much more expansive. In 1942 and 1943 Wilsonian lobbying groups and members of Congress increased organized public pressure for a concrete discussion of plans for after the victory (Divine 1967). Wendell Willkie's book *One World* sold many copies. Polls showed overwhelming support for a world peacekeeping organization. Even prominent isolationist legislators recanted publicly, and accepted the broad idea that improving the world as a whole would advance US interests most. This broader set of beliefs about international relations became the cognitive mold in which politicians thought about most international issues, including monetary ones.

American government executives came to identify the American failure to plan before the end of the first war as a cause of the inadequacy of the peace that followed. They inferred that poor handling of economic affairs had poisoned the peace. And they now had little doubt that US absence from the League had been a disastrous error (Gardner 1956, chap. 1). Given such a diagnosis, it is not surprising that they set to work on plans for the US to lead an international organization to smooth economic affairs after the war.

Broad beliefs about international relations specifically shaped the crucial, and controversial, American Congressional decision over whether to ratify or repudiate the 1944 monetary agreement. Among members of Congress, memories of America's past international security mistakes weighed heavily when they debated monetary ratification. Bretton Woods was the first international conference President Roosevelt had hosted as President, and this added to the need for it to be a success. Their vote on the Bretton Woods Agreements Act was taken in 1945 during the time of the San Francisco conference founding the United Nations. The technical financial agreement, set in these broader circumstances, presented political leaders with a powerful opportunity to symbolize America's determination to correct its terrible mistakes. Young Senator William Fulbright of Arkansas, speaking for ratification, distilled this diagnosis into an eloquent syllogism: 'We have tried self-sufficiency, and it has failed. Let us try cooperation and participation. It can be no worse' (quoted in Eckes, p. 201).

302   *John S. Odell*

Which alternative policy ideas will win?

If experience strongly contradicting the predictions of prevailing doctrine opens the way to alternative policy ideas, what determines which of the alternatives dominates politically? This political-intellectual process is not understood at all well,[11] but these and other cases hint at some of the determinants. Hypothetically, the ideas more likely to prevail are ones that had predicted the current failures, and those promoted by the more extensive and sophisticated publicity campaigns. Alternatives lacking these advantages are more likely to lose out politically, regardless of the merits intellectuals may find in them.

Cassandras and Candides

Keynes had been exhorting the world toward monetary reform since the early 1920s, and his warnings had turned out to be prophetic. His *Tract on Monetary Reform* (1923) launched a frontal assault on the gold standard itself, at a time when it was sacrosanct and unquestioned. 'But within a decade,' Harrod writes, 'Keynes' position had won the allegiance of at least half the world' (Harrod 1966, p. 339). For Keynes the actual choice was between managing money to keep foreign exchanges stable, or managing it to keep internal prices stable and employment high, and he came down for the latter, by altering the gold points if necessary. Almost alone, he attacked the Government mercilessly for the 1925 decision to restore sterling to its prewar parity, the decision Chancellor Winston Churchill himself later called the greatest mistake of his public life.

In 1933 and before, Keynes had warned that failure to cooperate internationally and to expand national spending would doom recovery, and subsequent miseries brought still more listeners to his lectures. The British government appointed him to the Treasury itself in 1940, the monarch made him a peer in 1942, and he represented his country as one of the two chief architects and negotiators at Bretton Woods. While other schemes for managing the monetary system might have had technical merit, it is hardly surprising that Keynes' proposals in particular should enjoy widespread public influence.[12]

A return to something like the traditional pre-1931 system was at least a theoretical alternative to the IMF agreement. In September 1944 Winthrop Aldrich, chairman of the Chase Bank, blasted the new regime just adopted at Bretton Woods. His ideal was an automatic system anchored to gold. He and other financiers favored a traditional ad hoc approach to currency stabilization, rather than creating a new universal intergovernmental organization. The British could borrow a temporary loan from the US Export–Import bank to help them reopen their economy (Eckes, pp. 174–75).

Many bankers supported an alternative international proposal, the so-called key currency plan published by Professor John H. Williams of Harvard University and the Federal Reserve Bank of New York, first in 1936 and again in 1943. Comparable to the 1936 tripartite stabilization arrangements between France, Britain, and the US, this plan would have had Britain and the US link their currencies to gold and cooperate somewhat more extensively than under prevailing practice. The plan would not have extended to many countries, however, not at least until later, and this discriminatory approach fatally tainted it in both the American and British governments (Horsefield, vol. I, p. 18). More generally, regardless of its prospects for successful technical operation after the war, this alternative idea probably was never in the running politically in the US, because of its association in the public mind with those Americans seen as most clearly responsible for the depression, the incorrigible antagonists of the popular New Deal.

Competing campaigns of persuasion

Alternative ideas will also tend to lose out if they concede an organized public struggle to establish a 'dominant cliche' or 'dominant metaphor' in public thinking about the issue.[13] When campaigns are undertaken via the mass media, they can imprint the public debate with a frame of reference, and at least at the margin such public intellectual struggle can help crystallize support for one policy direction rather than another. When rivals mount an equally extensive and sophisticated campaign of persuasion, the first idea is less likely to succeed.

Advocates of the more expansive, universalist monetary approach did mount a remarkable campaign of persuasion in the United States, and with telling effect. They reached out not only to the Congress itself, but to the nationwide mass public as well. They used sophisticated political techniques, including the repeated effort to identify Bretton Woods with the new approach to peace, in public thinking. Their rivals evidently did not match their comprehensive efforts among the mass public.

It was not at all obvious that US hegemonic interests would speak loudly enough by themselves to carry the day. Mass interest in international economic organization was much lower than in peacekeeping. Influential special interests and Republican legislators tried hard to prevent the ratification of the Bretton Woods agreements in the US. In Britain others had serious doubts. We tend to overlook domestic ratification struggles too, especially if we think only in game-theory or international-structure terms. Ratification probably would have failed in

304   *John S. Odell*

this case if it had been handled as some other cases have been handled.

In the first place, Roosevelt and Treasury Secretary Morgenthau personally chose the American delegates to Bretton Woods itself with a view to ratification. They formed their team with players who, if they themselves became convinced, would be especially able to persuade others to follow. The analogy of the Senate's repudiation of Wilson's League was on their minds. Doing the opposite of Wilson, they appointed members of Congress and representatives of diverse constituencies to the delegation itself. Fred Vinson was a former Kentucky Congressman who enjoyed the confidence of friends like Wright Patman in strategic positions on Capitol Hill. They found a banker in Chicago who was sympathetic, and could be a spokesman later in the midwestern isolationist heartland. They included the chairmen of the Senate and House Committees on banking and currency, which would vet any resulting legislation, and they also took a chance on the ranking Republicans on each committee.[14]

After the conference, the Treasury staff retained a New York public relations expert, and they orchestrated a stunning national campaign to 'stimulate public interest, crystallize public opinion, and make that opinion vocal.' They planned first to reach elite groups, which would then engage in 'aggressive "selling" of the idea'.

The advocates knew that the ordinary businessman or housewife had no clue to the technical issues, and might harbor suspicions of abstract, pie-in-the-sky New Dealers. So they stuck strictly to ordinary language anyone could understand. They helped a journalist prepare an article for *Colliers* magazine entitled 'Bretton Woods or World War III'. Secretary Morgenthau himself spoke in Detroit to the business elite, predicting the IMF and World Bank would translate into exports of a million cars per year. He went to Minneapolis to tout wheat exports. In the Red River Valley, he told farmers that 'discriminatory exchange rates squeezed agricultural income as much as if a farmer caught his hand in a threshing machine' (Eckes, p. 169). 'The Treasury organized informational luncheons for reporters and columnists; prepared radio scripts, pamphlets, and articles; and even subsidized short moving pictures'.

The Treasury also informally encouraged leading economists to speak out. Harvard Economist Seymour Harris, a prolific exponent of Keynesian ideas, lined up almost all living past presidents of the American Economic Association, and he reported that its diverse membership was almost unanimously behind Bretton Woods. The most prominent international economist in the country, Jacob Viner of Chicago, also urged passage, although he had some reservations (Eckes, pp. 170–71).

From London to Bretton Woods   305

The advocates lined up diverse constituency groups to testify before Congress in support, and they ghosted questions and speeches for congressional supporters to use. The other side, however, testified that a Fund was not needed and not workable. Most of the proposed member nations had adequate reserves, and the others would need more than the Fund could provide. The American Bankers Association favored some internationalist ventures, and they urged Morgenthau and Congress to modify the World Bank and reject the Fund, which they termed a compromise position (Eckes, p. 184). In March 1945 the House Banking committee chairman told Morgenthau that a majority on the committee were against the bill, and Aldrich of the Chase bank in New York was sure the opposition would prevail.

Over the next two months, however, the Treasury's publicity campaign shook much fruit from the trees. A hundred organizations were fanning out through the orchard. The American Federation of Retailers sent mailings to 1.8 million stores urging citizens to contact Congress on behalf of Bretton Woods and an end to war. The League of Women Voters left more than 100,000 pieces of literature in doctors' offices and beauty parlors. By mid-May the House Banking Committee alone had received 25,000 cards and letters in favor and only 42 against Bretton Woods (Eckes, pp. 195–96). The leading political adversary, Senator Robert Taft, would soon charge that Morgenthau had used tax dollars 'in one of the most completely organized propaganda efforts which this country has ever seen' (Eckes, p. 196). Congress quickly responded accordingly. As the bankers saw the tide turning, they signalled a willingness to compromise further.[15]

Morgenthau, again refighting Wilson's campaign in reverse, did not reject all Congressional efforts to change the legislation. He reluctantly agreed to small accommodations that would bring even adversaries aboard without necessitating additional international bargaining. The amendments urged that US representatives seek to have the World Bank make short-term loans, and they established a bureaucratic mechanism for coordinating US policymaking for the financial institutions. The ABA representative then swallowed hard and bravely told Congress this compromise was better than nothing. Moderate House Republican minority leader Jesse Wolcott, who had been a member of the delegation at Bretton Woods, now claimed that 'everyone is in favor of the bill except those who would vote against the Ten Commandments as part of our national policy' (Eckes, p. 198). (Raymond Moley's reply is not known.) With bipartisan support, the amended bill passed both the House and Senate with more than two-thirds support.

306   John S. Odell

Other cases

This relationship between discrediting experience, cognitive change, and policy change is not peculiar to these two historical cases. The Congress passed Smoot-Hawley after hearing confident assurances that it would not trigger retaliation. Subsequent events discredited that idea so dramatically that the symbol 'Smoot-Hawley' still intimidates American politicians today. Heavy deficit spending during the 1940s then coincided with the 'good news' of recovery from the depression, and thereafter Keynesian theory took root among politicians, eventually displacing the balanced-budget orthodoxy, although the process was slow.

The 1970s brought the phenomenon full circle with respect to domestic macroeconomic policy. Disappointing stagnation, actually due to complex causes including OPEC and industry investment decisions, helped discredit the belief that government regulation and spending help solve economic problems, then the most popular legitimating doctrine among politicians. This context helped bring the rival monetarism and the laissez faire view back in from the cold.

In the mid-1980s logic indicated very clearly to Washington that West German national interests would benefit if the German government would only accelerate its economy, but German authorities proved highly resistant to this unwelcome advice. This was particularly puzzling to a political analyst, unaccustomed to seeing political leaders fight to avoid having to cut their voters' taxes. It is reported that the Germans were refighting the 'last war' of 1978–80. At the 1978 Bonn summit meeting, the German government agreed to an American request to accelerate its economy, and subsequently Germany suffered the second oil shock, extremely high interest rates, and a slump (see Henning 1987).

More generally, since World War II changes in dominant American policy beliefs have had a predictable relation to changes in bargaining strategy on economic issues. When American politicians saw the world economy as benign, the US used expansive behavior; more recently a spreading perception of foreign unfairness stimulated increasingly competitive or exploitative action. On the one hand, the lessons of the interwar period imprinted themselves deeply, and America continued to use the more expansive approach, broadly speaking, until the late 1960s. The US led GATT rounds and reform of the international monetary system by proposing collective action, though not by ignoring special US interests, of course.

In 1970, though the economy did not return to a great depression, simultaneous increases in inflation and unemployment were followed by a deep plunge in the trade deficit in 1971. Leaders of the Nixon Administration then legitimated a change in strategy, at least temporarily, by declaring that US capacity to lead the world had declined, and that other countries were treating America unfairly. The decisions of August 1971 swerved dramatically away from expansive leadership. No plan for the monetary system was proposed; Washington simply demanded what the US wanted, and unilaterally imposed an import surcharge as a penalty until its demands were granted.

During the 1970s OPEC price increases, the seizing of the US Embassy in Teheran, and other events helped convince more American political leaders that the international system was hostile. Broad perceptions changed partly because of international economic developments, but partly also for other reasons. Washington continued, nevertheless, to practice both expansive and competitive behavior in international negotiations. American leaders pressed for further GATT negotiations in both the 1970s and 1980s, and used summit diplomacy to some extent to address global problems.

The unprecedented plunge in the trade deficit in the 1980s further challenged the 1940s worldview among politicians, and spread further the changed preference for conflict over perceived capitulation. To be sure, reality again gave rise to more than one diagnosis, and this spreading view was controversial, but spread it did. Accordingly diplomacy became more competitive or exploitative, emphasizing unilateral gains for the United States, relative to proposals for global rules in the collective interest. This could be seen in demands upon Asian countries for preferential increases in access to their markets, refusal to regulate the dollar or actions pushing it down despite other countries' objections, and adoption of extreme domestic fiscal and monetary policies without regard to the systemic consequences.

Theoretical basis for further development

Thus a small selection of examples certainly suggests that this hypothesis is worthy of further investigation, at least for the American case. Yet arguments about policy beliefs often seem ad hoc, even if developed though explicit concern for generalization and comparison. The present effort itself does not escape this problem entirely, and future study should attempt to strengthen this weak area.

Some fairly well-known social science premises provide a useful foundation for that effort. Such a theory assumes that international actors make decisions on the basis of bounded rationality.[16] They will choose those means likely to achieve their objectives with least cost, or tolerable cost, given the limits of their knowledge. This premise allows us to eliminate emotion and other irrationalities while also avoiding excessive simplicity. I assume that any theory hoping eventually to predict state behavior and bargaining outcomes, or even only to explain them adequately, will need to focus explicitly on the cognitive boundaries themselves. These include the objectives, the limiting and simplifying assumptions that decision-makers make, the beliefs that tell them in a given situation what policy options are thinkable, and their hunches about what will happen if each is chosen. Such a focus need not imply abandoning all concern with parsimony. Of course this is not all that such a theory will need; objective reality will matter as well.

This approach assumes that all decision makers use intellectual 'short-cuts'; they practice 'mental economics.'[17] When facing a problem, no leader will be able to engage in the full process of an idealized scientific method – posing several plausible hypotheses, gathering evidence from past experience through comprehensive, controlled comparisons, and rejecting the weaker hypotheses. Instead, he or she will attempt to find analogues or schemas already stored in memory, with which the current situation can be matched. Once an arguable analogy is identified, the decision maker will act rationally, given that this particular analogy is valid. He makes an inference identifying the cause of the past problem, and acts to correct the corresponding cause in the present situation. When the inventory of analogies or beliefs changes, policy will change accordingly. The content of these ideas may be especially important in determining which among several conceivable new policy directions is adopted, even when it seems clear that the situation would have caused any school of thought to abandon the old program.

Insights from cognitive psychology help narrow the range of likely dominant beliefs, and clue us to sources of change. Psychologists show that people are unlikely to act on the basis of analogies or lessons drawn at random from world history, but rather they use categories that are more 'available' cognitively. We may assume that political leaders will tend to apply the most recent analogy, not ones before that. They will be especially impressed with more vivid evidence and events, particularly those in which they participated first-hand. Deep economic depression and war are among the most vivid political-economic experiences. They are less likely to apply analogies from other countries' experience, and least likely to draw lessons from events that failed to occur.

Hence the historical observation that generals and diplomats tend to prepare to avoid or win the last war. They are preoccupied with either avoiding tactics that failed or repeating ones that succeeded in that one case. Military examples are familiar: the First World War analogy and the Maginot line; the Hitler analogy and Truman's response to North Korea; the near-explosion of the Cuban missile crisis and the first nuclear arms control agreements. The economic decisions discussed here seem clearly influenced by comparable 'last war' analogies, and thus are consistent with this framework.[18]

IV. International technical consensus and international outcomes

Finally, the London/Bretton Woods contrast suggests that technical dispute about the validity of key causal propositions can inhibit intergovernmental agreement, while consensus can facilitate it, for better or worse. The economic chaos of the early 1930s had thrown familiar economic principles into doubt, but no new theory had eliminated its rivals. Governments held different diagnoses of the depression and favored different prescriptions, the Belgians disagreeing with the French, the French with the British, and the Americans with the others.

No total theoretical victory had arrived by 1944 either. But by then many of the world's economists had converged on elements of a new monetary consensus, as indicated by the League of Nations 1944 report, *International Currency Experience: Lessons of the Inter-War Period*. This statement recognized that many governments now rejected the traditional gold standard rule of maintaining external payments balance even at the price of high unemployment at home. Exchange rate adjustments were considered appropriate in cases of fundamental domestic disequilibrium like that of Britain in the late 1920s. This was a striking change from the cacophony of 1933.

Furthermore, while in the twenties and thirties governments had often thought of exchange rate actions as purely national decisions to be taken separately, another lesson from experience held that a joint international mechanism for setting and adjusting rates could be much better for each country. The consensus certainly prohibited 'exchange dumping' or neighbor-beggaring devaluations, which were now better understood. Many also concluded that *freely* floating currencies would be damaging, by inducing speculative capital movements that would accentuate payments imbalances rather than offsetting them. 'Exchange stability should be the norm and exchange adjustment the exception'. (League of Nations, 1944, p. 225).

Currency controls were now considered acceptable to deal with temporary problems in certain circumstances, though their great potential for abuse was cause for caution. This statement also laid emphasis on the importance of adequate global international reserves, and on the dangers to the system of a single country amassing a large payments surplus. The proposition that domestic economic stability is a prerequisite of exchange stability, revived prominently in the 1970s and 1980s with reference to inflation more than unemployment, was also prominent in this 1944 report.

310   *John S. Odell*

As further evidence of this shift toward consensus, several monetary specialists outside the British and American governments also published or circulated proposals for a new, universalist international monetary regime, often intended to generalize the tripartite arrangements, and to allow for parity changes. Members of the governments in exile in London wrote informal papers. Authors of proposals included Johan Beyen, Camille Gutt, Zygmunt Karpinski, and Jacob Viner, as well as Herbert Feis of the State Department writing in his personal capacity (Horsefield, vol. I, pp. 16–17). In other words, while these particular new ideas helped Americans to dissolve their old conception of their national interest and adopt a new one, it was also not simply a case of the US forcing the scheme down the throat of a resistent world. Others were becoming convinced as well.

One of history's virtues is the perspective it gives on major changes in basic knowledge. Today we can see easily, for instance, that international agreement to control the spread of contagious diseases was delayed for at least fifty years because of confusion among scientists as to the causes of cholera and its propogation. 'Epidemiology in the nineteenth century was much like economics [and political science, it could be added] in the twentieth century: a subject of intense public interest and concern, in which theories abounded but where the scope for controlled experiments was limited' (Cooper 1986). Once research gradually eliminated the ambiguities of evidence and the world's scientists had agreed, governments coordinated with each other easily. Now we can also see more clearly the role that technical disagreement played in the interwar period in blocking economic agreements that seem beneficial to many experts in hindsight.

Today the technical disagreements among economists and among political scientists are quite wide as well, perhaps even wider than they were twenty years ago. Jeffrey Frankel concludes that the most serious obstacles to international financial coordination may lie in technical ignorance, especially regarding whether to ask foreign countries to expand or to contract their monetary and fiscal policies in order to improve the home economy's welfare. Leading econometric models disagree sharply as to whether a monetary expansion improves or worsens the domestic current account, and hence the foreign current account and output. Theory is largely unanimous in favor of a positive effect, but 8 of 11 models show a US monetary expansion worsening its current account (see Frankel in this issue and works cited there). Until economists can agree on the policy multipliers and more, it is easy to imagine the discord inside and between Bonn and Washington continuing, even if goals were identical.[19]

All three of these examples are cases in which different actors had a common interest, at least to some extent, and disagreed about the cause of the common threat or the effects of proposed measures to realize the interest. This disagreement impeded official negotiations to halt the spread of cholera, to reverse the world depression, and to reduce 1980s payments imbalances.

In other cases, however, technical disagreement can make governmental agreement more, rather than less, likely. If two actors have a conflict of interest, or so perceive their situation, diverging forecasts of policy effects, for example, can facilitate an agreement that at least one party would reject if they all agreed on the same forecast. If a seller is negotiating the possible sale of a building with a potential buyer, for example, the two have a pure conflict of interest over the price. But if the buyer forecasts a greater future increase of property values than the seller expects, the two might be able to agree on a price above the seller's minimum that would be out of reach if the buyer shared the seller's forecast.

Frankel also provides an international monetary example of this alternative possibility in an earlier work (1984; also see Henning 1987). In 1983 some US manufacturers and the US Treasury Secretary wanted Japan to upvalue its currency and thus cut its payments surplus with the United States. Secretary Donald Regan demanded that Tokyo reduce its controls over capital flows into and out of Japan, reasoning that capital liberalization would increase world demand for yen and push the yen upward. Presumably yen revaluation was not attractive to Japanese industrial exporters. To that extent there were elements of conflict of interest over exchange rate change. Japanese officials, however, evidently expected that the capital liberalization measures the Americans demanded would not raise the yen at all or would even depress it, since by their forecast, opening would spur greater Japanese capital outflow than inflow. In 1984 Tokyo agreed to take many of the measures Washington demanded, though partly for internal Japanese reasons. (In the short run the yen fell still further against the dollar; thereafter the yen rose substantially.)

Clearly, not all new knowledge will necessarily incline the world toward greater order and community. The discovery of atomic fission made international relations more precarious than ever before. Nor is technical or scientific knowledge the only, or even the most relevant, type of knowledge at issue. National politicians' ideas are the most proximate cognitive influence, and the relation between those and science is ambiguous. Scientists may change politicians' thinking directly or indirectly, as Keynes hoped. But politicians also shape scientific agendas, and they often use science selectively to legitimate policies chosen independently of scientific criteria (see, for example, King and Melanson 1972). Nor, finally, is it to say that cognitive consensus is more important than other conditions affecting international agreement; only that the

312   *John S. Odell*

difference between technical dissensus and consensus will matter, independently of national interests.

V. Conclusion

Our most prominent theories of international bargaining miss elements that seem essential for understanding national bargaining strategies and international outcomes, particularly if we are to grasp the sources of their dynamic change. While a given international power structure will make certain extreme outcomes highly unlikely, it will still permit a wide variety of different state behaviors and results. Game theory suggests valuable concepts, but it has little to say about the forces determining the state preference orders that drive its main conclusions.

This study does not exhaust the ideas that this historical experience might suggest, nor does it attempt to prove that other possible interpretations are inferior. For example, a sociologist might suppose that these US policy changes resulted from rising power in domestic politics of internationally-oriented segments of the US economy (see Gourevitch 1986 and Frieden 1988). In any case, however, such alternative answers have not been established for the present questions. Nor would adding them be sufficient by itself to show that the hypotheses proposed here are superfluous for this period or more generally.

This focused contrast between the London conference of 1933 and the 1944 Bretton Woods conference suggests three new dynamic hypotheses that seem worthy of further investigation. Changes, especially extreme ones, in national market conditions are likely to shift the state's bargaining strategy sharply even if its relative world position and external incentives have not changed. A national recession will make exploitative behavior more likely, and a boom will be more favorable for passive or expansive strategies. Second, painful national experience running contrary to prevailing policy ideas is likely to discredit those ideas among politicians and officials, turn them toward alternative doctrines, and lead to corresponding strategy changes. This political-intellectual dynamic does not require scientific proof that prevailing doctrine was the cause of the unfavorable experience. The alternative ideas most likely to spread politically are those that had predicted the current problem, and those whose advocates mount the loudest and most sophisticated publicity campaign. Finally, international dissensus among experts can pose a decisive impediment to intergovernmental agreement, while at least in some conditions technical convergence helps make official agreement more likely.

NOTES

1. Described in memorandum by Herbert Feis, 17 April 1933, *Foreign Relations of the United States 1933*, pp. 574–75.
2. This basic distinction is elaborated in the seminal study by Walton and McKersie (1965). Haskel (1974) advances an interesting international application.
3. These three strategy types are not meant to exhaust the logical possibilities.
4. The following section is confined to the use of game theory in explaining state policies rather than economic variables such as inflation or welfare. The approach may be an improvement over the theory of perfect competition for economic questions, but for state behavior this contention would be vanquishing a straw man. Representing the inequality of states as such does not require game theory.
5. For two of the more sophisticated and convincing applications of the genre, see Eichengreen 1985 and Lake 1983.
6. Related points are developed in Odell 1987 and Jervis 1988.
7. This plea parallels Herbert Simon's call (1987) for more empirical research to supplant the ad hoc premises about decision making on which prominent economists rely.
8. One might ask whether, even so, the events of the depression or other events did not depress Americans' *perception* of their international power. This distinction between power resources and perceptions is analytically crucial, and in fact is the basis for the next section of this article. If this question were valid, it would reinforce my general claim that analysts should separate the two and pay more attention to cognitive conditions emphasized there.
9. See, for example, the discussion of the White proposal's origins in Horsefield (1969), vol. I, chap. 1.
10. American bankers and certain other segments of society certainly ceased to be isolationist in their commercial activities during and after the first war, but the present point refers to political isolationism, both the attitude and the policy.
11. For an earlier attempt to lay out the dynamics of 'policy learning', see Odell 1982, pp. 367–74, as well as pp. 58–75.
12. Of course the United States forced Keynes and the British to compromise significantly, confirming the often mentioned role of relative national power in determining the location of the bargaining outcome within the zone of agreement.
13. I owe the term 'dominant cliche' to Morton Halperin. 'Dominant metaphor' appears in Haas *et al.* 1977, chap. 2.
14. Roosevelt was dead against the Republican Senator Charles Tobey: he was an isolationist, he was running for re-election and would gain publicity, and FDR thought he was 'a moron'. After weeks, Roosevelt nevertheless yielded to his advisers, still grumbling. Tobey attended, he did win re-election, and in 1945 the former isolationist spoke enthusiastically for ratification and international cooperation (Eckes, pp. 115–16). This section relies heavily on fine research by Eckes.
15. If politicians themselves had not been persuaded that Bretton Woods would contribute to peace and prosperity, but rather were merely coerced into line by superior political forces, then this case would not be ideal evidence for this cognitive argument. The case is supportive, however, to the extent that politicans themselves were also convinced. More detailed research would be necessary to establish this empirical point beyond all doubt, but it seems that quite a few politicans were convinced.
16 Herbert Simon's papers elaborating this approach are collected in his *Models of Bounded Rationality* (Cambridge, Mass.: MIT Press, 1982), esp. vol. 2, part VIII.
17. See Jervis 1976; Larson 1985, chap. 1; and Odell 1982, chap. 2, for reviews of the corresponding psychological theories and other applications to foreign and economic policy.
18. Recently several other scholars have been analyzing the effects of ideas on politics and policy, attempting to remedy weaknesses of previous studies in this genre. See Goldstein (1988), Hall (forthcoming), Ikenberry (1987 and 1988), Kingdon (1988), Marks (forthcoming), and Weatherford (1988).
19. On the issue of whether coordination in the presence of model uncertainty will help or hurt, Ghosh and Masson (1988) dispute Frankel's pessimism. For additional ideas on the role of economists' disagreements in making employment policy, see Rose (1987).

314   *John S. Odell*

REFERENCES

Blum, J. (1959) *From The Morgenthau Diaries: Years of Crisis, 1928–1938*. Boston: Houghton Mifflin.

Clarke, S. (1973) *The Reconstruction of the International Monetary System: The Attempts of 1922 and 1933*. Princeton Studies in International Finance No. 33. Princeton: Princeton University, November.

Cooper, R. (1986) International cooperation in public health as a prologue to macroeconomic cooperation. Discussion Papers in International Economics, No. 44. Washington Brookings Institution, March.

Divine, R. (1967) *Second Chance: The Triumph of Internationalism in America During World War II*. New York: Atheneum.

Eckes, A., Jr. (1975) *A Search for Solvency*. Austin: University of Texas Press.

Eichengreen, B. (1985) International policy coordination in historical perspective: a view from the interwar years. In W. Buiter and R. Marston (eds.), *International Economic Policy Coordination*. Cambridge: Cambridge University Press.

Feis, H. (1966) *1933: Characters in Crisis*. Boston: Little, Brown.

Frankel, J. (1984) *The Yen/Dollar Agreement: Liberalizing Japanese Capital Markets*. Policy Analyses in International Economics, No. 9. Washington: Institute for International Economics.

Frieden, J. (1988) Sectoral conflict and US foreign economic policy, 1914–1940, *International Organization*, 42, 1, 59–90.

Gallarotti, G. M. (1985) Toward a business-cycle model of tariffs, *International Organization* 39, 1, 155–188.

Gardner, R. (1956) *Sterling–Dollar Diplomacy*. Oxford: Clarendon Press.

Ghosh, A. R. and P. R. Masson (1988) International policy coordination in a world with model uncertainty, *IMF Staff Papers*, 35, 2, 230–258.

Goldstein, J. (1988) Ideas, institutions, and American trade policy, *International Organization* 42, 1, 179–218

Gourevitch, P. (1986) *Politics in Hard Times*. Ithaca: Cornell University Press.

Haas, E., M. P. Williams, and D. Babai (1977) *Scientists and World Order*. Berkeley: University of California Press.

Hall, P. (ed) (forthcoming) *The Political Power of Economic Ideas: Keynesianism across Nations*. Princeton: Princeton University Press.

Harrod, R. (1966) *The Life of John Maynard Keynes*. London: Macmillan.

Haskel, B. (1974) Disparities, strategies, and opportunity costs: the example of the Scandinavian economic market negotiations, *International Studies Quarterly* 18, 3–30

Henning, C. R. (1987) *Macroeconomic Diplomacy in the 1980s: Domestic Politics and International Conflict among the United States, Japan, and Europe*. Atlantic Paper No. 65. London: Croom Helm, for the Atlantic Institute for International Affairs.

Horsefield, J. K. (1969) *The International Monetary Fund 1945–1965*. Washington: International Monetary Fund.

Ikenberry, G. J. (1987) The spread of norms in the international system. Paper presented at the annual meetings of the American Political Science Association.

Ikenberry, G. J. (1988) Market solutions for state problems: the international and domestic politics of American oil decontrol, *International Organization* 42, 1, 151–178.

International Monetary Fund (1978). *The Rise in Protectionism*.

Jervis, R. (1976) *Perception and Misperception in International Politics*. Princeton: Princeton University Press.

Jervis, R. (1988) Realism, game theory, and cooperation, *World Politics* 40, 3, 317–349.

Lord Kahn (1976) Historical Origins of the International Monetary Fund, in A. P. Thirlwall (ed.), *Keynes and International Monetary Relations*. New York: St. Martins Press.

Keynes, J. M. (1933) *The Means to Prosperity*. London: Macmillan.

King, L. R. and P. H. Melanson (1972). Knowledge and politics: some experiences from the 1960s, *Public Policy* (Winter), 20, 1, 83–102.

Kingdon, J. (1988) Ideas, politics, and public policies. Paper presented at annual meetings of the American Political Science Association.

Krasner, S. (1976) State power and the structure of international trade, *World Politics* 28, 317–347.

Krasner, S. (1978) *Defending the National Interest*. Princeton: Princeton University Press.

Kuznets, S. (1966) *Modern Economic Growth*. New Haven: Yale University Press.

From London to Bretton Woods   315

Lake, D. (1988) *Power, Protection and Free Trade: International Sources of US Commercial Strategy 1887–1939.* Ithaca: Cornell University Press.

Larson, D. (1985) *Origins of Containment: A Psychological Explanation.* Princeton: Princeton University Press.

League of Nations (1944) *International Currency Experience: Lessons of the Inter-War Period,* Pub. 1944.II.A.4. Princeton: Princeton University Press.

League of Nations (1945) *Industrialization and Foreign Trade.* Princeton: Princeton University Press.

Marks, S. (forthcoming) Empirical analyses of the determinants of protection: a survey and some new results, in J. Odell and T. Willett (eds.) *Blending Economic and Political Analysis of International Trade Policies.*

McKeown, T. J. (1983) 'Hegemonic stability theory and 19th century tariff levels in Europe', *International Organization* 37, 1, 73–92.

Moley, R. (1939) *After Seven Years.* New York: Harper.

Odell, J. (1982) *US International Monetary Policy.* Princeton: Princeton University Press.

Odell, J. (1987) Constraints on international economic bargaining: theorizing via game models and beyond them. Prepared for the annual meetings of the American Political Science Association.

Oliver, R. (1975) *International Economic Co-operation and the World Bank.* London: Macmillan.

Oye, K. (1985) The sterling-dollar-franc triangle: monetary diplomacy 1929–1937, *World Politics,* 38, 1, 173–199.

Putnam, R. and N. Bayne (1987) *Hanging Together: Cooperation and Conflict in the Seven-Power Summits.* London: Sage Publications.

Rose, R. (1987) The political appraisal of employment policies, *Journal of Public Policy* 7, 3, 285–306.

Romasco, A. (1983) *The Politics of Recovery: Roosevelt's New Deal.* New York: Oxford University Press.

Simon, H. (1987) 'Rationality in Psychology and Economics,' in R. Hogarth and M. Reder (eds.), *Rational Choice. The Contrast between Economics and Psychology.* Chicago: University of Chicago Press. Also published in *Journal of Business* 59 (October 1986).

Stein, Herbert (1969) *The Fiscal Revolution in America..* Chicago: University of Chicago Press.

US Bureau of the Census (1966) *Long-Term Economic Growth, 1860–1965.*

US President (1971) *The United States in the Changing World Economy,* Report by Peter Peterson, 2 vols.

Walton, R. E. and R. B. McKersie. (1965) A Behavioral Theory of Labor Negotiations. New York: McGraw-Hill.

Weatherford, M S. (1988) The interplay of ideology and advice in economic policy making: the case of political business cycles, *Journal of Politics,* 49, 925–952.

[2]

A world economy restored: expert consensus and the Anglo-American postwar settlement
G. John Ikenberry

Even in the darkening days of World War II, British and American officials debated ideas about postwar order. Some proposals emphasized regional groupings, others sought to reinvigorate colonial empire, and still other proposals, championed by American officials, called for the building of an open international economy based on principles of liberal multilateralism. The most important differences in perspective over postwar order were those between American officials at the State Department, who wanted to reconstruct an open trading system, and British officials in the wartime cabinet, who wanted to ensure full employment and economic stability and were thus contemplating the continuation of the imperial preference system and bilateral trading. One vision was of a nondiscriminatory, multilateral trading system; the other, although not fully articulated, was of preferential economic groupings.

Despite their differences, Britain and the United States were able to reach watershed trade and monetary agreements during and after World War II, thereby setting the terms for the reestablishment of an open world economy—an accomplishment that was a bit astonishing given the ravages and dislocations of war and the multiple visions of postwar order. But the new system was different than anything that the capitalist world had seen before. The Anglo-American agreements established rules for a relatively open and multilateral system of trade and payments, but they did so in a way that would reconcile openness and trade expansion with the commitments of national governments to full employment and economic stabilization. Despite rapidly

Research for this article was supported by the Peter B. Lewis Fund and by the Center of International Studies at Princeton University. For their helpful comments and suggestions, I thank David Cameron, Peter Cowhey, Daniel Deudney, William Diebold, Jeff Frieden, Lloyd Gardner, Peter Haas, Robert Jervis, Peter Katzenstein, Robert Keohane, Stephen Krasner, David Lake, Craig Murphy, John Odell, M. J. Peterson, Thomas Risse-Kappen, and the participants of seminars held at Columbia University, the University of California at Los Angeles, Yale University, and the University of Southern California. I am also grateful to Geoffrey Herrera for his valuable research assistance.

International Organization 46, 1, Winter 1992

shifting global power capabilities, rising national economic vulnerabilities, and divergent and competing agendas within and between Britain and the United States, an innovative postwar agreement was engineered. Not surprisingly, the leading scholar of Anglo-American economic diplomacy characterized the postwar settlement as a "political miracle."[1]

Miracles aside, how do we explain this watershed agreement? Was the postwar settlement a straightforward expression of the prevailing distribution of power and interests at the end of the war, or do we need to dig more deeply into the political and intellectual foundations of the system? In its broadest outlines, the postwar settlement does reflect the interests and the overwhelming position of the United States after the war. If we are attempting to account for the fact that the postwar system was "open" rather than "closed," the structural variables are probably adequate. The distribution of power and interests within and among the United States, Britain, and countries in continental Europe set the broad limits on the shape of the postwar international economic order.

This structural explanation, however, leaves several issues unresolved. First, there was a range of postwar "orders" that were surely compatible with an American interest in an open world economy.[2] Indeed, a variety of designs for postwar order were advanced by officials within the American government. Why did the system take on the features it did, rather than a different set of features? To ask this question is really to ask why interests were defined the way they were by officials at the highest level of government. If the postwar order was a hegemonic system, why was it hegemony by consent (open but reciprocal and agreed upon rather than imposed)?[3] If American officials sought to build a postwar economic order that was deemed legitimate by other governments, how did this objective influence the choices they made?[4] More specifically, why did an American government with a State Department that

---

1. Richard N. Gardner, "Sterling-Dollar Diplomacy in Current Perspective," *International Affairs* 62 (Winter 1985–86), p. 21.
2. See Charles P. Kindleberger, "U.S. Foreign Economic Policy, 1776–1976," *Foreign Affairs* 55 (January 1977), pp. 395–417.
3. Maier argues that to understand the exercise of American power after World War II, it is necessary to appreciate power not only in terms of the ability to exert control over other countries' decisions but also in terms of the ability to create or sustain order. Power "usefully refers to the capacity to construct a higher degree, or alternative form, of political 'order' than would have existed in its absence." It is this form of American power, according to Maier, that is underappreciated in the postwar era. See Charles Maier, "An American Empire? Formative Moments of the United States Ascendancy After World War II," paper presented at the Shelby Cullom David Seminar, History Department, Princeton University, Princeton, N.J., November 1988, p. 2.
4. The ability of a hegemonic nation to generate shared beliefs in the acceptability or legitimacy of a particular international order—that is, the ability to forge a consensus among national elites on the normative underpinnings of order—is an important if elusive dimension of hegemonic power. See G. John Ikenberry and Charles A. Kupchan, "Socialization and Hegemonic Power," *International Organization* 44 (Summer 1990), pp. 283–315.

championed laissez-faire and free trade end up backing a system more concerned with safeguarding welfare capitalism?

Second, how did a transatlantic coalition in support of the Anglo-American settlement get cobbled together? The alternative to the settlement after World War II might not have been just another trade and monetary order; it might instead have been stalemate and disorder, which, after all, were the results of the attempt at a settlement after World War I. Agreement at Bretton Woods might have failed or gone the way of the Treaty of Versailles, a well-intentioned international agreement that fell prey to diverging national interests. How was agreement achieved amid the divergent and conflicting national and bureaucratic positions? What was the "glue" that kept the Anglo-American coalition—and the postwar settlement—together?

Answers to these questions will not emerge from an exclusive focus on the underlying conditions of power and interest. I argue that the policy ideas inspired by Keynesianism and embraced by a group of well-placed British and American economists and policy specialists were crucial in defining government conceptions of postwar interests, building coalitions in support of the postwar settlement, and legitimating the exercise of American power. By shifting the focus from trade issues, which were highly contentious, to monetary issues, about which there was an emerging "middle ground" created by Keynesian ideas, these experts helped overcome political stalemate both within and between the two governments. Put simply, this group of British and American experts intervened at a particularly fluid moment in history to help the British and American political establishments identify their interests, thereby creating the bases of postwar economic cooperation.

This argument contains a series of propositions (both historical and theoretical) about how and why these experts mattered in forging a postwar agreement.

(1) As deliberations on postwar order began during the war, divergent views within and between the British and American political establishments posed obstacles to agreement. The most important differences were between the British wartime cabinet's search for arrangements to secure postwar full employment and economic stabilization and the U.S. State Department's unalloyed free trade position.

(2) A community of policy specialists and economists assembled within and outside the British and American governments during the war articulated a set of ideas about monetary order and the organization of the postwar world economy that cut through these differences and moved their governments toward agreement. In effect, these experts identified a set of normative and technical positions that were later embraced by wartime British and American leaders.

(3) The Anglo-American monetary experts were a collection of professional economists and policy specialists who shared a set of normative and technical views which concerned "sensible" and "progressive" arrangements for the

postwar world economy and which distilled contemporary economic thought and lessons of recent economic history. In their commitments, assumptions, and expectations, these experts articulated a more or less coherent governing philosophy of postwar economic order: the philosophy that it should be a managed multilateral order, with monetary and trade practices subject to international agreement, and that the overall system would work to facilitate Keynesian economic policy and social welfare goals. The policy ideas of these experts were anchored in a common professional orientation, but they were not a set of causal scientific tenets or a simple economic doctrine.

(4) The British and American policy specialists came to form a loose transnational and transgovernmental "alliance" during wartime negotiations, and this alliance proved important in altering the sequence of Anglo-American negotiations. Initial negotiations on the postwar economic order, led by the State Department, dealt with trade arrangements and deadlocked without agreement. British and American Treasury Department officials shifted the negotiations to monetary arrangements, a less contentious issue, and agreement was eventually reached, undercutting the U.S. State Department's more conventional but also controversial free trade position.

(5) In the broader political setting, the ideas articulated by the community of experts played an important role in defining a "middle ground" between the old political divisions. In addition to offering an alternative to the old and contentious policies of laissez-faire and interventionism, the ideas on monetary order advanced by the British and American experts had the political virtue of opening up new possibilities for coalition building. What ultimately mattered in the ratification of the Bretton Woods agreement was not that it was based on the policy ideas advanced by an expert community but, rather, that the policy ideas resonated with the larger political environment. The ideas of the experts ultimately carried the day because they created the conditions for larger political coalitions within and between governments—coalitions which themselves reflected a more general postwar reworking of the sociopolitical order in Western capitalist democracies.

(6) The favorable reception of postwar economic "new thinking" within wider political circles was influenced by the long-term interwar evolution of mainstream public views about the role and obligations of governments in national economies and the proper goals of foreign policy. The Keynesian revolution and the reconstruction of internationalist thinking in American foreign policy were particularly consequential in creating a diffuse public "demand" for innovative postwar economic arrangements.

(7) Finally, the larger structural and historical setting in which the Anglo-American experts operated was important in that it simultaneously constrained and empowered them. The overwhelming position of the United States and the economic vulnerability of Britain together served to rule out postwar designs that each government might have found attractive. While the experts operated within very real political and economic limits, the larger structural setting also

served to give them unusual room for maneuver. The war provided a
"breakpoint" that made it necessary for governments to get into the business of
developing new rules of international economic and political order. This meant
that decisions would need to be reached. At the same time, political leaders in
both countries were generally dissatisfied with past monetary and trade
arrangements. This dissatisfaction as well as uncertainty over future conditions
elevated the role of the experts.

The group of economists and policy specialists involved in the postwar
settlement, however, did not fully constitute an epistemic community, nor did
the manner in which these experts influenced the terms of the settlement
conform to the strict logic of epistemic community influence that is proposed
elsewhere in this volume. First, the community of experts in this case was not an
independently existing scientific community; rather, it was a community
created by the process of Anglo-American negotiations. The economists and
policy specialists who eventually formed this transnational and transgovernmental community of experts were brought into government by policymakers such
as Secretary of the Treasury Henry Morgenthau. The expert community
emerged during the process of expert negotiations, and its members then
worked backed into their respective governments.

Second, the policy ideas that these experts shared—ideas concerning
monetary arrangements and the larger international economic order—were
anchored in a common professional orientation, but they were not a set of
causal scientific tenets or a common economic doctrine. Along this dimension,
the Anglo-American experts were, at best, a primitive epistemic community, a
collection of professional economists and policy specialists who shared a set of
general and technical views which concerned the proper functioning of the
world economy and distilled contemporary economic thought and lessons of
recent economic history.

Third, while policymakers defer to experts in some cases because the experts
are seen to possess indisputable scientific and technical knowledge, policymakers deferred in this case primarily because the ideas of the experts resonated
with the political needs of the moment and provided opportunities to bridge
old political divisions and build new coalitions. In the widest of political circles,
the influence of the experts was also strengthened because the economic
issues—particularly the monetary issues—were complex. It was difficult for
many politicians and groups to identify and articulate their interests during the
political debate. British and American experts were at an advantage in framing
the issues and resolving the disputes, and in this sense their shared professional
competence and knowledge mattered. But it was the political resonance of
their policy ideas that ultimately carried the negotiations to agreement.

The crux of the argument is that a transatlantic group of economists and
policy specialists, united by a common set of policy ideas and a shared view that
past economic failures could be avoided by innovative proposals, led their
governments toward agreement by identifying a set of common Anglo-

American interests that were not clearly discernible to others.[5] Structures of power and interests always matter. But at critical turning points, such as the end of a major war, uncertainties about power structures and unhappiness with past or current definitions of interests provide openings for rethinking. Moreover, at such moments, elites are interested in building institutions that have a measure of legitimacy, and this reinforces the value of authoritative policy ideas. For these reasons, it is necessary to search for the connections between policy expertise and underlying forces of power and interests.

I begin by sketching the characteristics of the Anglo-American postwar settlement and discussing the range of factors that are involved in any attempt at explanation. After identifying the group of experts that was active in shaping the monetary agreement, I situate the role of these specialists and their policy ideas within the larger structural setting. In subsequent sections, I trace the course of Anglo-American negotiations from early stalemate over postwar trade arrangements to the Bretton Woods settlement. Finally, I discuss the central ways that policy expertise mattered in shaping the Anglo-American agreement.

Explaining the Anglo-American settlement

The Anglo-American agreement on an international economic order, organized around a set of monetary and trade schemes, embodied a unique blend of laissez-faire and interventionism—of liberal multilateralism and the welfare state.[6] It allowed the operation of a relatively open system of trade and payments as well as arrangements to support domestic full employment and social welfare. This evolving synthesis of liberal economic and social welfare goals is captured in John Ruggie's notion of "embedded liberalism."[7] The international economic regimes of the postwar period were built on an historic political compromise: "Unlike the economic nationalism of the thirties, the

5. This argument would be undermined if it were established that British and American political leaders already had well-developed notions of postwar economic organization and simply called upon policy experts with similar views to refine and implement these views or if it were established that British and American leaders would have arrived at roughly the same settlement in the absence of the activities of the expert community. Empirical analyses of this sort require close attention to the sequence of events ("process tracing"), the use of counterfactuals, and, where possible, comparisons with similar historical episodes (in this case, the post–World War I settlement).

6. In this article, the specific outcome I am seeking to explain is the agreement signed at Bretton Woods in 1944. There was, of course, an entire sequence of "outcomes" that could be the object of explanation: the Anglo-American "Joint Statement of Principles," the agreement signed at Bretton Woods, the actual accord ratified by Congress and Parliament, the eventual monetary regime itself, and the larger set of political compromises. I focus on the Bretton Woods agreement because it provided the critical blueprint for the larger postwar economic order.

7. John Gerard Ruggie, "International Regimes, Transactions, and Change: Embedded Liberalism in the Postwar Economic Order," in Stephen D. Krasner, ed., *International Regimes* (Ithaca, N.Y.: Cornell University Press, 1983), pp. 195–231.

international economic order would be multilateral in character; but unlike the liberalism of the gold standard and free trade, its multilateralism would be predicated upon domestic interventionism."[8]

The forces that shaped this postwar settlement were obviously many and complex. A "first cut" would focus on the underlying structures of power capabilities.[9] According to this view, the postwar economic order reflected the efforts of the United States, as an ascending hegemonic power and victor in war, to build a system congenial with its interests. The most fundamental dynamic at work in the economic diplomacy of the 1940s, therefore, really involved attempts by the United States to break down the barriers to global economic openness, making compromises where necessary. As Charles Maier argues, "The central conflict defining international political economy from World War I until about 1950 was not that between American and Soviet alternatives, between capitalism and communism. . . . Viewed over the whole half century, the American international economic effort of the era of stabilization centered on overcoming British, Japanese, and especially German alternatives to a pluralist, market-economy liberalism."[10]

On the one hand, the commanding position of the United States and the resources available to it set the basic terms of the negotiations with Britain and influenced the direction of policy change in other countries. American efforts to recast the political and economic institutions of Japan and Germany after the war—efforts that in the years to follow had profound consequences for the stable functioning of a liberal multilateral order—perhaps reflected the ultimate exercise of hegemonic power.[11] On the other hand, hegemonic power has limitations as an explanation for the emergence of liberal multilateralism after the war.[12] American efforts to overcome European obstacles and induce acceptance of a liberal order in fact required a series of compromises and

8. See John Gerard Ruggie, "Embedded Liberalism Revisited: Institutions and Progress in International Economic Relations," in Emanuel Adler and Beverly Crawford, eds., *Progress in International Relations* (New York: Columbia University Press, 1991). For an excellent discussion of these political compromises and the economic lessons that informed them, see Richard Cooper, *The Economics of Interdependence: Economic Policy in the Atlantic Community* (New York: Columbia University Press, 1968).

9. Gilpin provides perhaps the most powerful and parsimonious explanation for the organization and reworking of international order. A prevailing international order is the reflection of the underlying distribution of material capabilities of states within the system. The distribution of power shifts over time, leading to ruptures in the system, hegemonic war, and an eventual reorganization of the international order that reflects the new underlying power capabilities. See Robert Gilpin, *War and Change in World Politics* (New York: Cambridge University Press, 1981).

10. Charles Maier, "The Two Postwar Eras and the Conditions for Stability in Twentieth-Century Western Europe," in Charles Maier, ed., *In Search of Stability: Explorations in Historical Political Economy* (New York: Cambridge University Press, 1987), p. 183.

11. See Ikenberry and Kupchan, "Socialization and Hegemonic Power."

12. See John S. Odell, "From London to Bretton Woods: Sources of Change in Bargaining Strategies and Outcomes," *Journal of Public Policy,* vol. 8, 1989, pp. 294–95. For a critique of hegemony as an explanation for U.S. postwar behavior, see John Gerard Ruggie, "Multilateralism in Theory and Practice," in John Gerard Ruggie, ed., *Multilateralism: The Anatomy of an Institution* (New York: Columbia University Press, forthcoming).

delays in the implementation of agreements, largely because of the economic and political vulnerabilities of a war-ravaged Britain and continental Europe.[13] Coercive efforts, such as those involved in the case of the British Loan, were less successful than often thought. Moreover, as discussed below, Britain and the United States together shaped the substantive content of the postwar system in ways that cannot be explained in terms of power considerations alone.[14]

In addition to focusing on hegemonic power, explanations might also trace the Anglo-American agreement to convergent shifts in underlying national economic interests. As I argue in a later section, there were underlying economic interests in both Britain and the United States that pointed in the direction of a relatively open system, particularly if protections and safeguards could be provided. What is missing in this explanation, however, is an account of how these structural conditions manifested themselves. This is particularly important because in both countries as economic planning and negotiations got under way during the war, there were substantial obstacles to agreement on even the most general outlines for postwar economic order.

Agreement on postwar monetary arrangements was fostered by a momentary community of experts who were engaged in negotiations and who, despite their many other differences, did share a view about the desirable organization of monetary relations and world economic order. As Alvin Hansen, a leading American economist in this postwar planning group argued, "Among the many contrasts between World War I and World War II nothing is more remarkable than the profound change in economic thinking." After World War I, the main purpose of postwar economic policy was to "reconstitute as rapidly as possible the automatic forces in economic life. The drive all around was a return, in the broad essentials, to laissez-faire."[15] By the late-1930s, Hansen argued, all of this had changed. A new social purpose infused postwar planning the second time around. Understanding how this "new thinking" got established and shaped government policy and the Anglo-American agreement is our task.

Postwar economic planners as a community of experts

Agreement between Britain and the United States on the shape of a postwar monetary system was fostered by the work of British and American policy

---

13. On the bargain struck between the United States and Europe after World War II over multilateralism and regional integration, see Benjamin J. Cohen, "The Revolution in Atlantic Economic Relations: The Bargain Comes Unstuck," in Wolfram Hanreider, ed., *The United States and Western Europe: Political, Economic and Strategic Perspectives* (Cambridge, Mass.: Winthrop, 1974), pp. 106–33.

14. For further elaboration of these arguments, see G. John Ikenberry, "Rethinking the Origins of American Hegemony," *Political Science Quarterly* 104 (Fall 1989), pp. 375–400.

15. Alvin Hansen, "Stability and Expansion," in Paul T. Homan and Fritz Machlup, eds., *Financing American Prosperity: A Symposium of Economists* (New York: The Twentieth Century Fund, 1945), p. 199.

specialists who shared a set of technical and normative views about the world economy and who were given remarkable discretion in developing policy proposals and negotiating on behalf of their governments. Although these experts shared a set of economic beliefs, it was only in the process of planning and negotiation that they came to possess a common identity and purpose. We can trace the contours of this assemblage of experts and situate it within the larger institutions of British and American government.

The Bretton Woods agreement is often seen as the result of the ideas and diplomacy of John Maynard Keynes and Harry Dexter White.[16] Indeed, these economists were pivotal figures in devising monetary plans, and they led their delegations in the celebrated Anglo-American negotiations during the war. But they were also part of a larger collection of economists and policy specialists who were located in the British and American Treasury Departments, in other government offices, and in universities and policy institutions. While many of the beliefs held by this loose community of specialists reflected the evolving views of professional economists, the community itself was given form by the demands of British and American governments to deliberate on postwar economic matters. The process of postwar planning on both sides of the Atlantic served to organize and stimulate the activities of these policy specialists.

In both Britain and the United States, most of the ideas that made their way into the Bretton Woods agreement were widely shared among what could be called liberal-minded international economists, whose views, more than anything else, reflected the lessons learned from recent historical experience as well as the ongoing evolution in professional economic thought. Among the group were many Keynesians, but group consensus was less the reflection of the common acceptance of a specific economic doctrine or theory than it was of a broader professional reaction to the recent upheavals and malaise in the world economy. Out of this reaction grew agreement on three aspects of a desirable postwar economy and the general policies and institutions that would sustain it.

First, the British and American experts held a common belief in the desirability of currency stability and the convertibility of currencies. Convertibil-

---

16. The definitive history of negotiations leading to the agreement remains Richard Gardner's *Sterling-Dollar Diplomacy: Anglo-American Collaboration in the Reconstruction of Multilateral Trade* (Oxford: Clarendon Press, 1956). In interpreting the events, Gardner places much more emphasis than I do on the differences between the American and British plans as they were advanced, respectively, by White and Keynes. While Gardner sees the Anglo-American negotiations more as a clash between officials representing different national interests, I see the expert negotiators as finding common cause in devising a plan that would reflect their economic thinking while also being capable of ratification by the American Congress. For a sophisticated political history of the events that also stresses the role of experts in promoting agreement, see Alfred E. Eckes, Jr., *A Search for Solvency: Bretton Woods and the International Monetary System, 1941–1971* (Austin: University of Texas Press, 1975). For a fairly straightforward and detailed history of the negotiations that relies primarily on British documents, see Armand Van Dormael, *Bretton Woods: Birth of a Monetary System* (London: Macmillan, 1978).

ity would be ensured by the abolition of exchange controls and restrictions. Disagreement could be found on the role of gold and other mechanisms for establishing stability in exchange relations, but currency exchange adjustments, when necessary to correct payments imbalances, were to be subject to international agreement. Behind the thinking of these specialists was the view that monetary arrangements must seek to avoid the political and economic instability of the interwar period. "In the interval between the wars," Keynes argued in an early draft of his monetary proposals, "the world explored in rapid succession almost, as it were, in an intensive laboratory experiment all the alternative false approaches to the solution."[17] The painful adjustments of the gold standard ruled out policy ideas of this sort. The currency fluctuations, exchange controls, and discriminatory policies of the 1930s also discredited ideas associated with floating exchange rates.[18]

Second, the British and American experts agreed that an international stabilization fund should be established to assist governments on a short-term basis and allow them to pursue multilateral and expansionary solutions to capital and trade imbalances.[19] As discussed below, while the experts disagreed over how generous this fund should be and over the obligations of creditor and deficit nations, these disagreements emerged more from divergent domestic circumstances than from divergent professional judgments.

Third, and most generally, the Anglo-American experts, some of whom were inspired by Keynes's pioneering work, agreed that new techniques of international economic management should be devised to reconcile the movement of capital and trade with policies that promote stable and full employment economies. Thus, although these experts generally favored an open world economy, it was also to be a managed world economy with new levels of international supervision of national monetary and trade policies. In this sense, the views of the experts differed from those of the State Department, which favored free trade. This difference was articulated by White in 1942: "The theoretical basis for the belief still so widely held, that interference with trade and with capital and gold movements, etc., are harmful, are hangovers from a nineteenth century creed, which held that international economic adjustments, if left alone, would work themselves out toward an 'equilibrium' with a minimum of harm to world trade and prosperity. It is doubtful whether that belief was ever sound."[20]

In short, rather than agreeing with Cordell Hull and the State Department, the experts agreed with White that international investment, capital movements,

17. John Maynard Keynes, "Post-War Currency Policy," in *The Collected Writings of John Maynard Keynes* (London: Cambridge University Press, 1980), vol. 25, p. 22.

18. Odell, "From London to Bretton Woods," p. 299.

19. Eckes, *A Search for Solvency.*

20. Harry Dexter White, March 1942 draft of the White plan, Mudd Library, Princeton University, Princeton, N.J.

exchange rate parities, and commodity prices were all potentially legitimate means for solving economic problems. An important purpose of the international stabilization fund and the other proposed postwar institutions was to separate legitimate from illegitimate economic practices.[21]

These views shared by British and American specialists reflected changing economic thinking, largely stimulated by the turmoil of the 1930s. But they also reflected a broader confluence of intellectual and political thought. The Keynesian policy revolution was still spreading in British and American policy circles, but its political consequences had already taken hold: politicians and government officials, equipped with modern tools of economic policy, were increasingly capable of managing national economies. As a consequence, they would need to attend, more than ever before, to policies that promoted full employment and social welfare—a responsibility formally accepted by the British government in May 1944 with the publication of the White Paper on Employment Policy.[22] Although innovations in economic and social policy allowed politicians to promise more to the electorate, the politicians encountered problems in delivering the socioeconomic goods.[23] The new socioeconomic goals of government were at odds with the deflationary discipline of the gold standard: contraction and unemployment were not a satisfactory solution for deficit nations. "Even if this policy [of gold standard discipline] had its advantages," Keynes wrote in 1944, "it is surely obviously out of the question and might easily mean the downfall of our present system of democratic government."[24]

The ideas of British and American monetary planners also resonated with the revival of American internationalism in the late 1930s, a process that involved the slow reorientation of American foreign policy. One benchmark of the earlier thinking came in the first year of Franklin Roosevelt's presidency. During the London economic conference of 1933, when Roosevelt declared that the "sound internal economic system of a nation is a greater factor in its well-being than the price of its currency," the message was that the United States would take little responsibility for developments within the world economy.[25] By the time the United States joined the war, official thinking had changed, and Roosevelt advanced the claim at the Bretton Woods conference in 1944 that "the economic health of every country is a proper matter of

21. Ibid.
22. See William H. Beveridge, *Full Employment in a Free Society* (London: Allen & Unwin, 1944).
23. See Robert Skidelsky, "The Political Meaning of the Keynesian Revolution," in Robert Skidelsky, ed., *The End of the Keynesian Era: Essays on the Disintegration of the Keynesian Political Economy* (London: Macmillan, 1977), pp. 33–40.
24. Keynes, "Memo to Sir Wilfred Eady and Richard Hopkins, 28 March 1944," in *The Collected Writings of John Maynard Keynes,* vol. 27, pp. 373–74.
25. Franklin Roosevelt, cited by Charles Kindleberger in *The World in Depression, 1929–1939,* rev. ed. (Berkeley: University of California Press, 1986), p. 216.

concern to all its neighbors, near and distant."[26] The change in Roosevelt's views reflected the renewal of internationalist thinking in American foreign economic policy.

The rise of Keynesianism and American internationalism, still under way as Anglo-American postwar planning began, provided a stimulus to that planning as well as a ready audience. As Jacob Viner, a leading American economist and postwar planner, stressed in 1942, the views held at this time contrasted sharply with those held after World War I: "There is wide agreement today that major depressions, mass unemployment, are social evils, and that it is the obligation of governments . . . to prevent them." Moreover, there is "wide agreement that it is extraordinarily difficult, if not outright impossible, for any country to cope alone with the problems of cyclical booms and depressions, . . . while there is good prospect that with international cooperation . . . the problem of the business cycle and of mass unemployment can be largely solved."[27] A remarkable sense of economic possibility and social purpose infused the thinking of Viner and the other American and British planners.

In the mid-1930s, under the leadership of Morgenthau, a group of international economists had been assembled within the Treasury Department to work on exchange rate stabilization. Viner and White had been leading members of this group,[28] and their early efforts had culminated in the 1936 Tripartite Stabilization Agreement, which established at least the principle of international monetary cooperation.[29] By 1941, White had risen in the Treasury Department to take overall responsibility for foreign economic policy. Soon thereafter, in December 1941, Morgenthau directed White to prepare a memorandum on the establishment of an inter-Allied stabilization fund—a fund that would "provide the basis for postwar international monetary arrangements."[30]

Although the origins of the proposals contained in the plan prepared by White are unclear, the ideas were ones generally shared by many of White's professional and departmental colleagues. In the late 1930s, newly trained economists, mostly from Harvard University and embracing Keynesian ideas, had begun to find places in the U.S. government.[31] The process of recruitment had been set in motion by several key officials in the Roosevelt administration,

26. Roosevelt, "Opening Message to the Bretton Woods Conference, 1 July 1944," in U.S. Department of State, *Proceedings and Documents of United Nations Monetary and Financial Conference* (Washington, D.C.: Government Printing Office, 1948), vol. 1, p. 71.

27. Jacob Viner, "Objectives of Post-War International Economic Reconstruction," in William McKee and Louis J. Wiesen, eds., *American Economic Objectives* (New Wilmington, Penn.: The Economic and Business Foundation, 1942), p. 168.

28. David Rees, *Harry Dexter White: A Study in Paradox* (New York: Coward, McCann & Geoghegan, 1973), p. 62.

29. John Morton Blum, *From the Morgenthau Diaries: Years of Crisis, 1928–1938* (Boston: Houghton Mifflin, 1959), pp. 131–34.

30. John Morton Blum, *From the Morgenthau Diaries: Years of War, 1941–1945* (Boston: Houghton Mifflin, 1967), pp. 228–29.

31. John Kenneth Galbraith, "How Keynes Came to America," in Andrea D. Williams, ed., *Economics, Peace and Laughter* (Boston: Houghton Mifflin, 1971), pp. 43–59.

including Marriner Eccles, who was chairman of the Federal Reserve Bank, and Lauchlin Currie, a Harvard economist whom Eccles had attracted to the Federal Reserve. Currie, in turn, had become an important conduit for the recruitment of Keynesian economists into the federal bureaucracy.[32] By the start of the war, Keynesians had come to occupy positions in the Bureau of the Budget, the Commerce Department, and the Treasury Department. During the war, they also assumed positions at the Office of Price Administration and on the National Resources Planning Board, which was also involved in postwar planning.[33] Although Morgenthau was not a Keynesian, other key posts within the Treasury Department came to be occupied by those who were.[34] When the department's work on postwar monetary proposals began, the experts surrounding White shared his basic views concerning the need for far-reaching and innovative economic proposals. After the White plan was drafted, interdepartmental technical discussions, primarily involving economists and lawyers (rather than business executives and bankers), provided a vehicle for expert deliberations within the government.[35]

This community of experts extended outside of government as well. Most of the important ideas that found their way into the White proposal were also discussed during the war at a series of expert planning sessions sponsored by the Council on Foreign Relations and attended by members of the Economic and Financial Group. This group, working under the auspices of the Council's War and Peace Studies Project and led by Alvin Hansen and Jacob Viner, provided an extraordinary vehicle for the concentration of expertise and planning.[36] The Economic and Financial Group also provided an important forum for discussions with British economists after monetary planning got under way in 1941.[37]

32. See Walter S. Salant, "The Spread of Keynesian Doctrines and Practice in the United States," in Peter A. Hall, ed., *The Political Power of Economic Ideas: Keynesianism Across Nations* (Princeton, N.J.: Princeton University Press, 1989), p. 40. See also Herbert Stein, *The Fiscal Revolution in America* (Chicago: University of Chicago Press, 1969); Alan Sweezy, "The Keynesians and Government Policy, 1933–1939," *American Economic Review* 62 (May 1972), pp. 116–24; and Dean L. May, *From New Deal to New Economics: The American Liberal Response to the Recession of 1937* (New York: Garland Publishing, 1981).

33. See Margaret Weir, "Ideas and Politics: The Acceptance of Keynesianism in Britain and the United States," in Hall, *The Political Power of Economic Ideas*, p. 56. See also Marion Clawson, *New Deal Planning: The National Resources Planning Board* (Baltimore, Md.: Johns Hopkins University Press, 1981).

34. Fred Block, *The Origins of International Economic Disorder* (Berkeley: University of California Press, 1977), p. 39.

35. Eckes, *A Search for Solvency*, p. 60.

36. Domhoff argues that the Bretton Woods proposals had their origin in the deliberations of the Council's War and Peace Studies Project and the Economic and Financial Group. See G. William Domhoff, *The Power Elite and the State* (New York: Aldine De Gruyter, 1990), chap. 6. For an earlier argument along these lines, see Laurence H. Shoup, "Shaping the Postwar World: The Council on Foreign Relations and United States War Aims During World War II," *The Insurgent Sociologist* 5 (Spring 1975), pp. 9–52.

37. Interview with William Diebold, Jr., New York, 14 August 1990. Diebold was research secretary for the Economic and Financial Group in 1941 and 1942.

Most of the experts who worked on postwar monetary planning, whether inside or outside of the Treasury Department, were associated in one way or another with the Economic and Financial Group. Viner played a key role in developing the rationale for the White plan, and Hansen, a leading Keynesian economist, was involved in revising the proposals.[38] The group also commissioned its own studies dealing with various dimensions of postwar reconstruction and international economic relations. In both the specific ideas related to monetary stabilization and the broader discussions of postwar economic reconstruction, the planners elaborated a vision of British and American cooperation.

The British community of economic experts concerned with postwar monetary planning was overshadowed by Keynes.[39] After World War I, Keynes had written a well known polemic, *The Economic Consequences of the Peace,* which harshly criticized the terms of the postwar settlement and forecast destructive trade and monetary policies and the eventual collapse of the European economy.[40] Two decades later, the prophetic nature of Keynes's views, along with the success of his own pioneering theory, left Keynes in a commanding position to influence British postwar policy. During the war, Keynes was given an office at the Treasury to work on wartime economic administration and financial negotiations.[41] As postwar planning began, other economists of a Keynesian persuasion, such as Lionel Robbins and James Meade, were actively involved in the deliberations.[42]

The British officials involved in planning, like the American economists in the Treasury Department, believed that currency stability must be anchored in international agreement. "Exchange depreciation," Keynes wrote to Viner in 1943, "is nothing like as fashionable as it use to be, and experience has taught many countries what a futile expedient it is except in quite special circumstances."[43] Yet the single most striking lesson that the British economists working on postwar monetary arrangements had learned was that currency exchange commitments must not undermine expansionary domestic policies. British economists (and many politicians as well) had by the mid-1930s come to believe that the return to the gold standard in 1925 had brought economic

38. See Domhoff, *The Power Elite and the State,* chap. 6.

39. See Hans Singer, "The Vision of Keynes: The Bretton Woods Institutions," in Erik Jensen and Thomas Fisher, eds., *The United Kingdom and the United Nations* (London: Macmillan, 1990), pp. 235–45.

40. John Maynard Keynes, *The Economic Consequences of the Peace* (New York: Harcourt, Brace, & Howe, 1920).

41. As discussed later in my article, however, Keynes's first negotiations with the American government during the war dealt with lend-lease and postwar trade relations.

42. See Weir, "Ideas and Politics," p. 55. See also Richard Gardner, "The Political Setting," in A. L. K. Acheson, J. F. Chant, and M. F. J. Prachowny, eds., *Bretton Woods Revisited* (Toronto: University of Toronto Press, 1972), p. 24; and Susan Howson and Donald Moggridge, eds., *The Wartime Diaries of Lionel Robbins and James Meade, 1943–45* (London: Macmillan, 1990).

43. Keynes, "Letter to Jacob Viner, 9 June 1943," in *The Collected Writings of John Maynard Keynes,* vol. 25, p. 323.

misery to the domestic economy and that the departure from this standard in 1931 had been associated with recovery.[44] The overriding view of the British economists in government during the war was that social welfare and economic management must dictate postwar international economic plans, rather than the other way around.

While planning experts formed independent communities in Britain and the United States, they also were connected as a transnational community. Interaction between British and American experts had several dimensions. First, White and Keynes and their associates were involved in official discussions held between 1942 and the Bretton Woods conference. Many of these discussions were technical in nature and took place after the British and American plans had been drafted.[45] The expert-oriented nature of the talks was anticipated by White in a July 1942 discussion with a British official who later related White's thoughts to Keynes:

> White talked at length but not very clearly on the necessity of getting agreement between experts on the objectives of Article VII before trying to bring in policy-makers. *If agreement could be reached between experts he would be fairly optimistic on the possibility of influencing the respective administrations,* but he was not so optimistic about the possibility of influencing Congress, although in this respect the chances would be better during the war than after it. At the expert level White thought that there should be no need to bargain because the long-term interests of the major countries are the same. He himself would hold no cards below the table and would hope that other experts would be in the same position. The long-term interest of each country lies in multilateralism.[46]

This captures White's views on the primacy of expert discussions, the common perspectives that these experts shared, and their role in shaping the views of the British and American governments.

Second, there were many informal discussions among the relevant British and American economists, several of which took place under the auspices of the Council's Economic and Financial Group. In these and other settings, it appears that Viner and Hansen played a vital role in facilitating cooperation. Viner was a close friend of Lionel Robbins, a British economist who who was an associate of Keynes and was also involved in postwar planning.[47] Hansen made an important visit to Britain in the autumn of 1941, presenting proposals for Anglo-American economic cooperation that differed markedly from those

44. See Stephen Clarke, "The Influence of Economists on the Tripartite Agreement of September 1936," *European Economic Review* 10 (December 1977), pp. 375–89. See also Peter Hall, *Governing the Economy: The Politics of State Intervention in Britain and France* (New York: Oxford University Press, 1986), pp. 49–50.

45. See Eckes, *A Search for Solvency,* chap. 4.

46. Cable from the British Embassy, Washington, D.C., to Keynes, 3 July 1942, T247/11, Public Records Office, London; emphasis added.

47. Interview with Diebold, New York, 14 August 1990.

being advanced by the State Department.[48] The discussions between British economists and members of the Economic and Financial Group, which were carried out in 1941 and 1942, provided useful communication between planners. In discussing British thinking on postwar economic problems, one member of the Economic and Financial Group noted in July 1942 that "economists in England are discussing things very similar to those which have formed the agenda of the Economic and Financial Group, and for the most part look toward similar solutions."[49]

There were monetary specialists who were not part of the expert community. American bankers, for example, were supportive of more traditional plans than those being fashioned in the American and British Treasury Departments. One of their proposals was for ad hoc stabilization agreements tied to gold, while another proposal, advanced by Professor John Williams, involved what amounted to an extension of the 1936 Tripartite Stabilization Agreement.[50] Regardless of their technical merit, specialists wielding proposals of this sort tended to be vulnerable within the Roosevelt administration, whose New Dealers were distrustful of the conservative banking community. It is revealing that these more conventional policy specialists were not part of the loop. Morgenthau's recruits to the Treasury Department were not just specialists; they were specialists with a New Deal planning orientation. Morgenthau did not like Keynesian fiscal thinking, but he had an even stronger dislike for the banking community. These considerations helped shape the character of the experts who were positioned close to the centers of policymaking within the Roosevelt administration.[51]

Unlike an epistemic community, the community of British and American economic planners that emerged during the war did not really stand alone outside of government. The efforts of government officials in Britain and the United States to get postwar planning started helped stimulate the thinking and give organizational form to the experts. The colonizing of parts of the British and American bureaucracies by Keynesian economists also strengthened the sense of community among these experts. Many of the views that the Anglo-American experts held, particularly those concerning past monetary experience, were also shared by a larger international community of economists and policymakers.[52] As discussed below, there were some differences of

48. See R. F. Harrod, *The Life of John Maynard Keynes*, pp. 527–28.
49. Minutes of the Thirty-Second Meeting of the Economic and Financial Group, 13 July 1942, p. 8, Council on Foreign Relations, New York.
50. For unofficial proposals, see J. Keith Horsefield, *The International Monetary Fund, 1945–1965: Twenty Years of International Monetary Cooperation* (Washington, D.C.: International Monetary Fund, 1969), vol. 1, pp. 16–18.
51. Interview with Diebold, New York, 14 August 1990. According to Diebold, John Williams was initially involved in the discussions of the Economic and Financial Group at the Council on Foreign Relations, but, perhaps reflecting his absence of agreement with the "new thinking," he soon dropped out.
52. See League of Nations, *International Currency Experience* (New York: League of Nations, 1944).

view among the British and American monetary planners, but these differences did not always cut along national lines. On the basic issues of postwar monetary order, the community of economic planners shared a core set of beliefs.

Situating the role of expert consensus

To locate a role for the community of experts that guided British and American negotiations during the war, it is important to appreciate the wide-ranging and frequently antithetical views on postwar order that spilled across the British and American political establishments. In the United States, the views ranged from those of the State Department, which favored the free flow of trade and capital, to those of the group of New Deal planners, which favored expanded government management of the economy. Lurking behind American wartime debates was a domestically minded and tightfisted Congress. In Britain, where the virtues of a liberal multilateral system were less apparent, the splits were even more profound. Conservatives were reluctant to abandon the imperial preference system, and many on the left saw an open economy to be a dangerous threat to economic planning and social welfare policies. Situated between these groups were the economic advisers to the wartime government. Although the advisers were not eager to return to bilateral trade and the preference system, they thought that such an option might be necessary to protect Britain's postwar payments balance and, in any event, might be used to extract concessions from the United States. In short, pursuing this option might make the United States agree to a more forgiving and expansionary system, which was precisely the "new thinking" that Keynes and his American counterparts were seeking to develop.

Before we examine these competing views and the initial deadlock in negotiations that they produced, it is important to establish a point made earlier: the underlying structures of power and interests set the broad parameters around which an agreement could be built, but they were not imperatives that inevitably produced the agreement.

The United States did have a basic and increasingly robust interest in an open system, and key American economic and political elites recognized this fact. In the 1930s, with the apparent collapse of the international economy and the emergence of German and Japanese regional economic blocs, American policymakers and intellectuals debated the plausibility of regional alternatives to an open world economy. Doctrines of this sort were long associated with German geopolitical thinkers such as Friedrich List and Friedrich Ratzel and were more recently associated with Karl Haushofer.[53] In the United States, as

53. See Andreas Dorpalan, ed., *The World of General Haushofer: Geopolitics in Action* (New York: Farrar & Rinehart, 1942). In particular, see the discussion of Gunther Scholders and Walter Vogel's *Economics and Space* in the Dorpalan volume.

306 International Organization

in Germany, the question concerned the size of an area that a nation would need to encompass or have access to in order to ensure industrial strength and meet the resource requirements for economic and military viability.[54] This question grew in importance in the early 1940s as political elites debated whether the United States should get involved in the war. Could the United States remain a going concern within a Western hemispheric bloc? The academic culmination of this debate came with the work of Nicholas Spykman, who articulated what was to become the conventional wisdom: a hemispheric bloc would not be sufficient to protect American economic and geopolitical interests.[55] Military planners in the War and Navy Departments during the war also began to conceive of postwar American strategic interests in global terms.[56] In 1941, similar views emerged among economic and political experts involved in the Council on Foreign Relations discussions concerning the nature of the Grand Area—that is, the core regions on which the United States depended for its economic viability.[57] The attack on Pearl Harbor only strengthened the evolving view that the United States would need to work with Britain to reintegrate as much of the world economy as possible. Moreover, in the two decades between the world wars, the internationally oriented sectors of the American economy had expanded considerably, increasing the nation's stakes in a wider capitalist world order.[58] These economic and national security debates and underlying economic shifts all pointed in the same direction and reinforced liberal international thinking among political elites.[59]

The underlying British interests are more difficult to specify. Fred Block argues that British participation in an American-sponsored system was not inevitable. According to Block, "national capitalism" was the central alternative to liberal multilateralism: "There is good reason to believe that after the war, there might have been substantial experiments with national capitalism among the developed capitalist countries." Nevertheless, he continues, this idea was not pursued, since "it became a central aim of United States foreign policy to prevent the emergence of national capitalist experiments and to gain widespread cooperation in the restoration of an open world economy."[60]

54. Brooks Emeny, *The Strategy of Raw Materials* (New York: Macmillan, 1934).

55. Nicholas John Spykman, *America's Strategy in the World: The United States and the Balance of Power* (New York: Harcourt, Brace, 1942).

56. See Melvyn P. Leffler, "The American Conception of National Security and the Beginning of the Cold War, 1945–48," *American Historical Review* 89 (April 1984), pp. 346–81.

57. See Council on Foreign Relations, "Methods of Economic Collaboration: The Role of the Grand Area in American Economic Policy," in *Studies of American Interests in the War and Peace*, 24 July 1941, E-B34. Council on Foreign Relations, New York.

58. See Jeff Frieden, "Sectoral Conflict and U.S. Foreign Economic Policy, 1914–1940," *International Organization* 42 (Winter 1988), pp. 59–90.

59. For a recent discussion of American international liberalism during this period, see Thomas J. McCormick, *America's Half-Century: United States Foreign Policy in the Cold War* (Baltimore, Md.: Johns Hopkins University Press, 1989), chap. 2.

60. Block, *The Origins of International Economic Disorder*, p. 9.

This view is invoked by those who argue that Britain and other European nations had political values and economic interests which might have led to alternative postwar arrangements if not for the hegemonic power of the United States. There remains an historical dispute on this matter, but the strong version of the argument, which states that Britain could have remained within its Commonwealth and imperial system, is probably incorrect.[61] On the one hand, it is true that the United States did confront considerable resistance to liberal multilateralism in Europe.[62] Indeed, reservations about a liberal economic order were part of the broader differences between the United States and the European countries over such matters as empire, spheres of influence, and regionalism.[63] On the other hand, it is less clear that the European countries had viable alternatives to participation in an American-sponsored system. For example, it would have been extremely difficult and costly for the British to have constructed an alternative system organized around bilateral trade and the imperial preference system, as the British Foreign Office admitted in a memorandum written in 1942: "Any attempt by the United Kingdom to make the British Empire a closed trading area, economically self-sufficient, will be stoutly opposed by the Dominions, if not also by India. Those countries are reaching economic and political maturity at the precise moment at which it is becoming clear to them that the United Kingdom has not the strength to defend them under modern conditions. It is in the highest degree unlikely that they will consent for long to be held within the narrow limits of an Empire trading and political order."[64]

British political elites were of divided opinion, but they had little choice but to cooperate with the United States. For those British officials who held this view, their tasks were to use what intellectual and political capacities that Britain had to shape the agreement in ways that served their socioeconomic goals and to find ways to secure that agreement within a conflictual and fragmented political landscape.

Underlying structures of power and interest provide enough information to explain the fact that the postwar system was more or less open. But this information is not enough to explain the character of that open system. Nor is it enough to explain, even if we agree that Britain and the United States had

61. See the contrasting views of Skidelsky and Rowland in Benjamin Rowland's *Balance of Power or Hegemony: The Interwar Monetary System* (New York: New York University Press, 1976).

62. See David Watt, "Perceptions of the United States in Europe, 1945–83," in Lawrence Freedman, ed., *The Troubled Alliance: Atlantic Relations in the 1980s* (New York: St. Martin's Press, 1983), pp. 28–43.

63. This is a theme of Charles Maier in "The Two Postwar Eras and the Conditions of Stability in Twentieth-Century Western Europe." On the British case, see William Roger Louis, *Imperialism at Bay: The United States and the Decolonialization of the British Empire, 1941–45* (New York: Oxford University Press, 1978).

64. British Foreign Office, "Cooperation Between Great Britain and the United States," memorandum, 1942, F0371/30685, Public Records Office, London.

common "objective" interests in a liberal multilateral system, how the many conflicting political positions were reconciled in reaching an agreement. It is useful to sketch these conflicting positions within and between the British and American governments and then trace the evolution of agreement between Keynes and the American negotiators.

Competing Anglo-American plans for postwar order

Economic and foreign policy elites in both countries ranged widely in their views about postwar economic order. The crucial antagonists in the debates were American officials, mostly in the State Department, who were intent on constructing an open and nondiscriminatory trading system, and British government officials, who for reasons of political expediency and economic vulnerability resisted the abandonment of the imperial preference system and the sterling bloc. The debates during the war were really a continuation of controversies that had emerged in the 1930s when the British government experimented with imperial trade and currency blocs and other governments experimented with regional blocs.[65]

Within the Roosevelt administration, the most vocal advocates of a system of free trade and multilateralism came from the State Department, led by Secretary Cordell Hull and his assistant, Leo Pasvolsky, and from the Division of Commercial Policy and Trade Agreements, headed by Harry Hawkins.[66] Throughout the Roosevelt presidency, Hull and other State Department officials consistently held the conviction that an open international trading system was central to American economic and security interests and was also fundamental to the maintenance of peace. This conviction was well anchored in American history and was given expression in the Atlantic Charter, signed by Roosevelt and Churchill during the war. The consistency of the State Department position could also be found in its ongoing opposition to the British imperial preference system. The 1932 Ottawa agreements, according to Hull, represented "the greatest injury, in a commercial way, that has been inflicted on this country since I have been in public life."[67] Hull believed that the bilateralism and economic blocs of the 1930s, practiced not only by Britain but also by Germany and Japan, were a root cause of the instability of the

65. Regarding this dispute in the 1930s, Rowland notes that "whether the blocs were a good in themselves, an unqualified 'bad,' or only a useful expedient on the way to recovery were questions on which there was little agreement either within the leading countries or among them." See Benjamin Rowland, "Preparing the American Ascendancy: The Transfer of Economic Power from Britain to the United States, 1933–1944," in Rowland, *Balance of Power or Hegemony*, p. 200.

66. Penrose, *Economic Planning for the Peace* (Princeton, N.J.: Princeton University Press, 1953), p. 15.

67. Cordell Hull, cited by Van Dormael in *Bretton Woods: Birth of a Monetary System*, p. 25.

period and the onset of war.[68] Charged with responsibility for commercial policy, the State Department championed tariff reduction agreements, most prominently in the 1934 Reciprocal Trade Agreement Act and the 1938 U.S.–British trade agreement.[69]

Another camp within the Roosevelt administration was composed of economic planners and New Dealers, including Harry Hopkins, Vice President Henry Wallace, and numerous Keynesian economists within the National Resources Planning Board. The officials in this group were interested in an expanded government role in managing the economy to promote full employment and social welfare. As Block argues, they had little sympathy with the State Department's multilateral vision: "They favored a world system made up of national capitalisms because of the priority they gave to the pursuit of full employment. They believed that the maintenance of high levels of employment and the development of national planning throughout the world should take precedence over the opening of economies to the free flow of investment and trade."[70] At the same time, these officials were not isolationists.[71] They favored international arrangements to foster expansionary domestic economic policies and institutions to channel capital to underdeveloped areas.[72]

In October 1942, the British ambassador to the United States summarized the ideas of the competing camps in the Roosevelt administration as follows:

Two kinds of general economic frameworks have been outlined by Administration with respect to international post war organization, one more clearly and persistently by the Hull group, other more vaguely and sporadically by

68. See Robert A. Pollard, *Economic Security and the Origins of the Cold War, 1945–1950* (New York: Columbia University Press, 1985), pp. 11–12.

69. Herbert Feis, the State Department's economic adviser, noted the continuity of the department's position when he argued during the war that "the extension of the Open Door remains a sound American aim." See Herbert Feis, "Economics and Peace," *Foreign Policy Reports* 30 (April 1944), pp. 14–19; cited by Lloyd Gardner in *Economic Aspects of New Deal Diplomacy* (Madison: University of Wisconsin Press, 1964), p. 263.

70. Block, *The Origins of International Economic Disorder*, pp. 36–37.

71. In ibid., p. 32, Block argues that the Treasury Department planners were "national capitalist" in orientation and favored increased government planning and social spending, while the State Department planners were "business internationalists" and favored unfettered free trade and an open world economy. According to Block, "It is one of the stranger ironies of international monetary history" that the Treasury Department planners began with national capitalist assumptions but ended up with plans that supported the business internationalists. I do not think this view can be sustained. Although White and his colleagues had a disdain for nineteenth-century laissez-faire ideas, the "new thinking" that they and Keynes were developing was clearly seen as an attempt to construct an open world economy, one that was built around a more sophisticated set of policies and institutions. The British and American architects of the Bretton Woods agreement were either alloyed or unalloyed internationalists. See Gardner, *Sterling-Dollar Diplomacy*, p. 15; and Eckes, *A Search for Solvency*, p. 4.

72. On the limits of the redistribution and expansionary dimensions of the Bretton Woods agreement, see Craig Murphy, *The Emergence of the NIEO Ideology* (Boulder, Colo.: Westview Press, 1984), chap. 1.

Vice-President and Milo Perkins group. . . . Cleavage on economic side is counterpart of well-known division between planners and their opponents in domestic affairs. Hull group believe that positive measures of Government control or guidance internally do not necessarily involve planning on grandiose scale advocated by planners nor do they believe that grandiose planning at home or internationally is necessary to attain a large measure of international collaboration. . . . This difference in outlook on planning will persist and will produce clashes on specific proposals in international sphere.[73]

These differences were perhaps understandable. Roosevelt's New Deal lacked an ideological core and consisted instead of a mixture of policy orientations.[74] It was also Roosevelt's management style to encourage bureaucratic and individual competition. The result, as characterized by Charles Maier, was a "stalemate of forces."[75] As described below, the split was eventually resolved when the sequence of negotiations was altered. After the Treasury Department group succeeded in reaching an agreement with the British on postwar monetary arrangements, the State Department group found its nineteenth-century style trade proposals essentially incompatible with these agreements.

Before World War II, British attitudes toward the imperial preference system split largely along party lines.[76] The core of the Conservative party favored the maintenance of empire and the continuation of the Ottawa preference system. As Ernest Penrose argues, they "valued the system of preferential duties on Empire goods as a force making for solidarity within the British Commonwealth of Nations."[77] The individuals in this group stressed the importance of Commonwealth ties and viewed them as a symbol of Britain's great power status. With respect to dismantling the preference system, Roy Harrod notes that "some resented the idea mainly on sentimental grounds that we should be asked to abrogate this valuable symbol of Commonwealth and Empire unity."[78] Moreover, it was the Commonwealth nations, such as Canada, Australia, and New Zealand, that had risen in support of a beleaguered Britain during the war. While the conservatives tended to identify British interests with

73. Memorandum from Ambassador Halifax to the British Foreign Office, 20 October 1942, F0371/31512, Public Records Office, London.

74. See Alan Brinkley, "The New Deal and the Idea of the State," in Steve Fraser and Gary Gerstle, eds., *The Rise and Fall of the New Deal Order* (Princeton, N.J.: Princeton University Press, 1989), pp. 85–112.

75. Charles Maier, "The Politics of Productivity," in Peter J. Katzenstein, ed., *Between Power and Plenty: The Foreign Economic Policies of Advanced Industrial States* (Ithaca, N.Y.: Cornell University Press, 1978), p. 28.

76. On the general schools of thought among British foreign policy elites, see D. Cameron Watt, *Succeeding John Bull: America in Britain's Place, 1900–1975* (Cambridge: Cambridge University Press, 1984), pp. 16–17.

77. Penrose, *Economic Planning for the Peace*, p. 19.

78. Harrod, *The Life of John Maynard Keynes*, p. 515.

those of the Commonwealth,[79] Churchill and his followers were sympathetic with the free trade position. According to Penrose, although Churchill "acquiesced in a certain degree of protectionism as a *fait accompli,* he still thought there was a general presumption on the side of free trade and felt no enthusiasm for the system of Empire preferences adopted at Ottawa."[80] His major consideration was to protect the unity of his ruling coalition and to push on with the war.

The forces of support and opposition to the imperial preference system began to change during the war. The deterioration of the country's economic position made the preference system more attractive to some British officials who otherwise would not support discriminatory trade practices.[81] These officials believed that the preference system might be a way to protect Britain's payments balance after the war, at least in the short term, particularly if the international economy fell into recession. They realized that turning away from multilateral trade and payments would mean relying on trade restrictions and currency controls. While this would split the world into blocs, the bloc system would insulate Britain from low-cost foreign competition and the deflationary effects of an American recession.[82] Alfred Eckes offered the following characterization of the coalition that favored this option: "In Britain an unlikely coalition of socialists and conservative imperialists favored this alternative— the socialists to achieve full employment and domestic reform, the imperialists to preserve traditional ties with the Commonwealth. But although these interests were articulate and enjoyed some support in the cabinet, where Churchill and Beaverbrook attached considerable importance to preserving the empire, the rigid restrictionist view had little appeal among official economists."[83]

Other British officials were more skeptical of bilateral trade and the preference system, even as a fallback option, but they saw threatening recourse to that option as a way of gaining bargaining leverage with the United States.[84]

79. See Penrose, *Economic Planning for the Peace*, p. 20. In discussing the views of the conservatives, Penrose states that "perhaps their most active and uncompromising member was Leopold Amery, who had great energy, high integrity, and keen political insight, but little facility in economic reasoning."

80. Ibid., p. 20.

81. Ibid., p. 14.

82. For a discussion of the relationship between British domestic economic problems (particularly those concerning employment) and an open international economic order, see Allan G. B. Fisher, *International Implications of Full Employment in Great Britain* (London: Royal Institute of International Affairs, 1946). Fisher also surveys various positions on multilateralism and its alternatives.

83. Eckes, *A Search for Solvency*, pp. 64–65.

84. According to Harrod, these officials believed that Britain "could not afford to abandon any device that might assist her to retain or enlarge her export trade. Such motives were honourable and not fundamentally inconsistent with what the State Department had in mind. Most of those who held such opinions would not have deemed it a wise long-run policy to push the system of

While they believed that the only real option was to cooperate with the United States, they wanted to do so in a manner that would allow Britain to achieve its economic objectives.[85]

In short, there were striking divisions between and within the British and the American governments. In Washington, the State Department articulated a remarkably unadorned vision of nineteenth-century free trade. In London, the wartime government, worried about the stability of its political coalition and the fragility of its impending postwar economic position, entertained notions of regional and managed economic arrangements. These differences became apparent in the earliest discussions of postwar order.

From trade stalemate to monetary agreement

The first exchanges on postwar economic questions between the United States and Britain were triggered in the summer of 1941 during negotiations over a lend-lease agreement. State Department officials wanted to use the occasion to secure a promise that the British would open up the imperial preference system. British officials resisted and sought to tie the dismantling of discriminatory practices to a larger program of postwar reconstruction that ensured economic expansion and employment stability. The principles and mechanisms of the larger program, however, remained obscure.

Discussions began in the summer of 1941 when Keynes, who had been appointed as adviser to the Chancellor of the Exchequer, arrived in Washington to negotiate the terms of the lend-lease agreement. But the visit only underscored the differences in official British and American thinking.[86] Disagreement centered on the proposed terms of Article VII, which set forth the framework for postwar settlement of mutual aid obligations. The article

---

Imperial Preference further and build a self-supporting British Empire *bloc.*" See Harrod, *The Life of John Maynard Keynes*, p. 515.

85. This was the position of most officials at the British Foreign Office and the Treasury. See the Foreign Office report, "Note on Post-War Anglo-American Economic Relations," 15 October 1941, F0371/28907, Public Records Office, London.

86. Keynes's initial thoughts on postwar policy were prompted by an invitation from the Ministry of Information to draft a response to the German propaganda campaign and its proposal for a "New Order." In the draft statement, Keynes argued that the British too could provide a new order in Europe, based on sterling and the larger resources of the Commonwealth and empire. Britain, Keynes argued, would not return to the prewar gold standard and the policies that produced severe unemployment and other dislocations. The Keynes memorandum stressed national measures to ensure employment and social welfare, and although it spoke of the need to restore European trade, there remained the implication that the British preference system would continue. The draft statement, sent by the British government in advance of the Keynes visit, showed a very different orientation than that which was emerging in the State Department. For the text of the statement, see *The Collected Writings of John Maynard Keynes*, vol. 25, pp. 11–16. See also Harrod, *The Life of John Maynard Keynes*, pp. 503–4; and Gardner, *Economic Aspects of New Deal Diplomacy*, p. 276. As Gardner notes, "American leaders were not quite sure how to take these ideas; to most of them Keynes's memorandum meant socialism if not something worse."

provided that, in meeting these lend-lease obligations, no conditions should be laid down to obstruct commerce and that measures should be taken to reduce trade barriers and eliminate preferential duties. In a meeting at the State Department, Keynes asked if this provision "raised the question of imperial preferences and exchange and other trade controls in the post-war period."[87] Assistant Secretary Dean Acheson acknowledged that it did, although it was not meant to impose unilateral obligations on Britain. According to Acheson, Keynes strongly objected to this provision: "He said that he did not see how the British could make such a commitment in good faith; that it would require an imperial conference and that it saddled upon the future an ironclad formula from the Nineteenth Century. He said that it contemplated the impossible and hopeless task of returning to a gold standard where international trade was controlled by mechanical monetary devices and which had proved completely futile."[88] Keynes argued that to maintain economies in balance without great excesses of imports or exports, countries in the postwar period would need exchange controls, precisely the types of measures that seemed to be prohibited by Article VII.[89]

The disagreement was clear and seemingly fundamental, and Keynes left Washington without conceding to the State Department position on Article VII. The economic planners at the State Department, however, were quite determined. During the Atlantic conference in 1941, Sumner Welles raised the issue of imperial preferences with Alexander Cadogan, a member of the British delegation. Welles told Cadogan that he "had unfortunately received the impression that Professor Keynes represented at least some segment of British public opinion which was directing its energies toward the resumption or continuation by Great Britain after the war of exactly the kind of system which had proved so fatal during the past generation."[90] The Atlantic conference merely papered over rather than resolved the conflict.

The difficulty of Anglo-American negotiations over Article VII led some British officials to reconsider the virtues of bilateral bargaining and imperial preferences. Leading economists in the British government voiced reservations

87. "Memorandum of Conversation, by the Assistant Secretary of State (Acheson)," 28 July 1941, in E. R. Perkins, ed., *Foreign Relations of the United States, 1941* (Washington, D.C.: Government Printing Office, 1959), vol. 3, p. 11.

88. Ibid., p. 12.

89. In *The Life of John Maynard Keynes*, p. 512, Harrod offers the following description of Keynes's position in Washington: "What he had in mind was the application with American assistance of Keynesian remedies for unemployment and trade depression on a world scale. He was not averse from breaking down the barriers to trade, but thought that the necessary pre-condition was a much more thoroughgoing policy of reconstruction. He had also in the forefront of this mind the appalling problems that Britain would face after the war in the matter of her own trade balance. It was, therefore, far from his thought that all could be set right by the mere elimination of 'discriminatory' practices from trade policy." Harrod confirms that the reports at the time were correct: Keynes had referred to the first draft of Article VII as "the lunatic proposals of Mr. Hull."

90. "Memorandum of a Conversation," in *Foreign Relations of the United States, 1941*, vol. 1, p. 353.

over bilateralism in late 1941. About this time, Keynes was also rethinking his views. An American official who knew Keynes during this period notes the change: "In his own mind, Keynes had dropped, or was on the verge of dropping, the argument that hard bilateral bargaining would have to be resorted to; and he was replacing it by a plan for an international institution to deal with balance-of-payments questions."[91] Throughout his career, of course, Keynes had been of two minds on the virtues of unrestricted trade and monetary arrangements. One mind showed itself after World War I when he argued that free trade was both an economic and a moral imperative. The other showed itself when Keynes argued that goods should be "homespun where it is reasonably and conveniently possible" and that "a greater measure of national self-sufficiency and economic isolation among countries than existed in 1914 may tend to serve the cause of peace rather than otherwise."[92] Keynes was capable of articulating both restrictionist and expansionist positions on postwar order. In the autumn of 1941, he moved vigorously in the expansionary direction. He came to the view that perhaps an agreement could be reached with the United States for a monetary order that would be expansionary and could keep the trading system open but safeguard against depression.[93] The search for a postwar settlement involving both a relatively open trading system and measures to ensure employment stability soon became the preoccupation of Keynes and other British planners.

On the American side, as we have seen, there were conflicts between the State Department and the Treasury Department over postwar planning. The stalemate on the postwar economic order, arrived at in the contentious Anglo-American discussions of trade arrangements, did not prevent Treasury Department officials from proceeding with monetary planning and, in the process, shifting the focus of negotiations to monetary arrangements.

A flurry of monetary planning broke out on both sides of the Atlantic. In Britain, Keynes listened to arguments from various quarters and retreated to the countryside, where he developed an ambitious plan involving mechanisms for both the orderly adjustment of exchange rates and the mobilization of credit that would prevent countries from resorting to deflation as a means to correct maladjustments.[94] According to the plan, an international clearing union would have the authority to create and manage $25 billion to $30 billion of a new international currency to correct payments imbalances.[95] It would also have the authority to tax the excess reserves of creditor nations and impose other

91. Penrose, *Economic Planning for the Peace*, p. 18.
92. Keynes, cited by Lionel Robbins in *Autobiography of an Economist* (London: Macmillan, 1971), p. 194. Robbins considered this view "a sad aberration of a noble mind"; see p. 156.
93. See Eckes, *A Search for Solvency*, p. 65.
94. The initial draft and subsequent versions of the Keynes plan are published in *The Collected Writings of John Maynard Keynes*, vol. 25, pp. 21–40.
95. As Eckes notes in *A Search for Solvency*, p. 66, this "distribution of new financial assets would allow members—particularly heavily indebted countries like Britain—to remove restrictions on all capital movements, maintain stable exchange rates, and pursue stimulative domestic policies without fear of an external payments crisis."

measures to ensure that payments imbalances would be corrected both in surplus countries and in deficit countries.

In the United States, monetary planning got under way in early 1942 under White's direction. White's plan was similar to Keynes's plan in its attempt to eliminate exchange controls and restrictive financial practices and in its provision of rules for alterations in rates of exchange. Although it provided relief for monetary authorities in international difficulties, it differed from Keynes's plan in that it proposed relatively modest resources for this purpose and severely limited the obligations of creditor nations to contribute to the relief fund. In contrast to the clearing union scheme, which obliged creditor nations to accept a clearing unit (Bancor) up to the limit of the established amount of this medium, the American plan restricted the obligation of creditors to the amount of their subscription with the fund.[96]

These two plans formed the basic framework of negotiations that followed throughout 1943 and up to the Bretton Woods conference. Many of the compromises were made in favor of the less ambitious White plan, but many of the British demands were also met. The capital was to be subscribed under the compromise plan; there would not be a new international currency. Moreover, the primary responsibility for restoring international equilibrium would be borne by the deficit countries and not, as Keynes had proposed, shared by deficit and surplus countries. The power of member nations to change their exchange rates was increased in the emerging agreement, which addressed the British interest in flexibility. Finally, Keynes's provisions designed to address short-term postwar financial problems were left out of the compromise plan. Wartime debts and reconstruction loans would be dealt with through other bilateral agreements and a development bank.[97]

The crucial breakthrough in Anglo-American negotiations occurred in September 1943, when the British agreed to abandon the idea of "unlimited liability" of creditor countries contained in the clearing union scheme. Lionel Robbins noted later that "once we had recognized the political unacceptability of the unlimited liability of the creditor, the rest was a compromise between essentially friendly negotiators."[98] After this concession, much of what followed involved practical adjustments to specific national interests and domestic politics.

Policy ideas and political coalition building

The "new thinking" embraced by the Anglo-American planners, with its synthesis of interventionist and liberal goals, had a political resonance within wider and more contentious British and American political circles. The Bretton

96. The White plan is published in *Foreign Relations of the United States, 1942*, vol. 1, pp. 171–90.
97. Penrose, *Economic Planning for the Peace*, pp. 55–60.
98. Robbins, *Autobiography of an Economist*, p. 200.

Woods ideas played a politically integrating role: they allowed political leaders and social groups across the political spectrum to envisage a postwar economic order in which multiple and previously competing objectives could be met simultaneously. The alternatives of the nineteenth century and of the interwar period suggested options that were much too politically stark. Outside the narrow transatlantic community of government economists, politicians were looking for options that could steer a middle course. In the end, the ability of policy experts to articulate ideas that spoke to the needs of practical British and American politicians was the most consequential aspect of their work.

Throughout their discussions with American officials, the British were looking for a middle ground between bilateralism and the imperial preference system on the one hand and laissez-faire on the other. This was noted by Ambassador Halifax in his cable to the British Foreign Office in October 1942, following a visit from John Foster Dulles, who at the time was a corporation lawyer in New York:

> The most interesting point on the economic side of the discussion was Mr. Dulles' exposition of the Cordell Hull school of free trade, and the place which it had in the plans of the Administration. I said to him that I thought that we did not clearly understand what the significance of the Hull policies was. There was a feeling in some quarters here that we were faced with two alternatives, either we must revert to a completely 19th century system of laissez-faire, or else we must safeguard our balance of payments position by developing a bilateral system of trade with those countries whose natural markets we were. It seemed to me that neither of these courses would work; the first was clearly impossible, the second might be disastrous. I asked Mr. Dulles whether there might not be some middle course which would take account of our special difficulties and which at the same time would satisfy Mr. Cordell Hull on the question of discrimination, preferences, etc.[99]

If we are looking for historical moments when political elites are open to the new ideas of intellectuals and policy experts, here is one. Later in the year, when Keynes and the British shifted negotiating partners and topics—from the State Department, focusing on trade policy, to the Treasury Department, focusing on monetary policy—opportunities for finding that middle ground emerged.

In both Britain and the United States, the onset of major war stimulated and widened political debate about the future world economic order. Even before the war, politicians and editorialists on the left and the right had staked out a wide range of positions on the proper direction of world trade and monetary order. The wartime views of American liberal and progressive circles, as seen, for example, in the pages of *The New Republic* and *The Nation*, affirmed the

99. Dispatch from Ambassador Halifax to the British Foreign Office, October 1942, F0371/31513, Public Records Office, London.

goals of full employment and economic planning and included calls for a postwar world economic federation and multilateral cooperation.[100] Liberal and progressive spokespeople stressed different goals: some advanced vague commitments to liberal internationalism, others favored the primacy of economic planning, and still others reaffirmed a commitment to free trade. While most commentators agreed that a new economic order must be built, there was little agreement on what that meant.

Once the Bretton Woods proposals were on the table, however, the various liberal and progressive commentators largely fell in line behind the agreement. Keynesian planners saw the agreement as an attempt to bring Keynesian management to the world economy; free traders saw it as a commitment to trade expansion; and internationalists now saw few alternatives to it. Indeed, it is striking how quickly the various alternatives to the Bretton Woods proposals disappeared from public debate after 1944. By this time, the opponents of the Bretton Woods proposals—including New York bankers, advocates of high tariffs, and isolationists—began to be seen as an odd bunch, outside the political mainstream.[101]

In Britain, the Bretton Woods proposals also played a politically integrating role. This can be seen by tracing the editorials that appeared during the late 1930s and the war period in *The Spectator,* a conservative free trade journal. There was no praise for economic planning and little discussion of British full employment policy. Commentary on the great tools of planning and ending the business cycle were absent. While the contributors to *The Spectator* supported free trade and a new economic order for Europe,[102] the Bretton Woods proposals seemed to meet their needs. In the two years leading up to the agreement, only favorable discussions of the White and Keynes proposals were offered.[103] As the war began, contributors to *The Economist,* another conservative free trade journal, stressed the need for postwar economic cooperation with the United States. During the war, their editorials were unclear in defining postwar economic problems and solutions.[104] In the end, they supported the Bretton Woods agreement but argued that its success would depend on all sorts

100. See periodic essays by economic editorialist George Soule in *The New Republic.* Soule argued that postwar economic planning must be handled carefully this time, since it was botched the last time. He called for economic planning at the national and international level, which together would constitute a new form of economic federation. Similar views were expressed by economist Keith Hutchison in a series of articles in *The Nation* during the war. Hutchison favored an economic bill of rights to guarantee jobs at a living wage, but he also supported world federalism to regulate tariffs and engage in reserve banking for investment and distribution of surplus savings. See "Economy for a New World," *The Nation,* 22 March 1941.

101. See, for example, "Support for Bretton Woods," *The Nation,* 16 June 1945, pp. 661–62.

102. See, for example, Mark Sterling, "Peace by Economists," *The Spectator,* 24 July 1941, pp. 79–80.

103. See, for example, "Currency and Trade," *The Spectator,* 9 April 1943, pp. 331–32.

104. *The Economist* clearly favored multilateralism to blocs and bilateral trade. By the end of the war, its editors argued that the world needed to move toward "managed free trade." See "The Multilateral Approach," *The Economist,* 22 January 1944, pp. 94–96.

318 International Organization

of other adjustments and changes in the manner that nations conduct their economic business.

In Britain and the United States, the Bretton Woods proposals represented a "middle way" that generated support from both the conservative free traders and the new prophets of economic planning. Wartime economic "new thinking" helped redefine the political mainstream, making it possible to form new coalitions. Like a piece of crystal, the Bretton Woods agreement had many different surfaces and projected different things to different groups. No other internationalist proposal could appeal to such a broad base of interests.

Conclusion

The above analysis helps shed light on several questions: How do we explain the Anglo-American settlement? Why did certain proposals become an effective basis for agreement between Britain and the United States? And how, given the divergent and conflicting national and bureaucratic positions, was agreement achieved within a wider and fragmented political setting? The argument presented here is that agreement was fostered by a community of experts composed of liberal-minded British and American economists and policy specialists who shared a set of technical and normative views about the desirable features of an international postwar monetary order and who were given remarkable autonomy to negotiate a deal. As discussed in further detail below, these experts fostered agreement by altering the political debate about postwar policy, by crystallizing areas of common interest between the two governments, and by elaborating a set of politically resonant ideas that served to build larger coalitions within and between governments.

Shaping government conceptions of interests

There are junctures or "breakpoints" in history when the possibilities for major change are particularly great and the scope of possible outcomes is unusually wide. In this century, the several years surrounding 1945 would surely be one such juncture. Nobody knew how the world order would be reorganized, but everybody believed that reorganization was inevitable. The ending of a major war or the aftermath of large-scale economic crisis alters the parameters of policymaking: dissatisfaction with past policy creates a new willingness by political leaders to reevaluate their interests, goals, and doctrines; the disruption or breakdown of rules and institutions creates a need for nonincremental decision making; and the collapse of old political coalitions requires a search for new coalitions. At these moments, the removal of obstacles of change occurs simultaneously with the surge of impulses to change. When this happens on a global scale, fundamental change is possible.

At these critical turning points, the interests and capacities of the dominant groups, states, and classes still matter, as they always do, but uncertainties about power structures and dissatisfactions with prevailing definitions of interests create opportunities for the recasting of interests. At the core of the postwar settlement were British and American political leaders who were open to the redefinition of national economic policy interests. Keynes, White, and the other "new thinkers" were particularly well situated to shape the resolution of these uncertainties: the transgovernmental "alliance" that they formed allowed them to shape the agenda, taking the initiative away from the free trade–oriented State Department; the complexity of the issues gave them a privileged position to advance proposals; and their ideas were particularly well suited to building winning political coalitions.

Building new political coalitions

The consensus among British and American monetary experts provided a basis for breaking through various layers of conflicts and deadlocks within and between the British and American governments. Most immediately, the consensus among Anglo-American experts cut through conflicts by shifting the ground of debate from trade to monetary issues. In a more general way, the monetary agreement served the purpose of political compromise by articulating ideas that created possibilities for new political coalitions. The "new thinking" embraced by Anglo-American experts provided a solid intellectual foundation for a political middle ground between an unregulated open system and bilateral or regional groupings. As Albert Hirschman emphasized with respect to Keynesianism, economic ideas "can supply an entirely new common ground for positions between which there existed no middle ground whatsoever."[105] It was Keynes and the British who were most intent on finding a middle ground—something that seemed so elusive in the early Anglo-American discussions over postwar trade arrangements. The Bretton Woods agreement articulated a middle position between a nineteenth-century style free trade system and regional or national capitalist arrangements. The policy views of the monetary experts were intellectually synthetic and politically robust: they not only provided a respectable position between extremes and set the stage for political compromise between the British and American governments, but they also foreshadowed and perhaps enabled a broader sociopolitical reordering of coalitions within postwar Western capitalist democracies.[106]

Policy ideas do more than simply "enlighten" political elites. They have a political as well as a cognitive impact. They offer opportunities for new

105. Albert O. Hirschman, "How the Keynesian Revolution Was Exported from the United States, and Other Comments," in Hall, *The Political Power of Economic Ideas*, p. 356.
106. The rise of postwar political coalitions around Keynesian social democracy has been widely discussed. For a good analysis of the rise and fall of Keynesian social democracy in Britain, see David Marquand, *The Unprincipled Society: New Demands and Old Politics* (London: Jonathan Cape, 1988).

coalitions of interests and give intellectual force or inspiration to those groupings. Ideas do change minds, but it is their practical value in solving political dilemmas which gives them a force in history.

Legitimating hegemonic power

American leaders certainly wanted to promote American interests, and they were willing to use the nation's power capabilities to do so. But one can also detect a desire on the part of many officials to promulgate a postwar system that would have a normative appeal to elites in other nations. American officials realized that building an international economic order on a coercive basis would be costly and ultimately counterproductive. This is not to say that the United States refrained from exercising its hegemonic power; it is to say that there were real limits to the coercive pursuit of the American postwar agenda. Historical records indicate that American officials wanted to avoid looking as if they were imposing policies on the Europeans. This general observation helps explain why American officials paid more than insignificant attention to the normative bases of the postwar settlement and why they were willing to make adjustments along the way to give the system a certain legitimacy. "Power needs ideas and legitimation," Reinhard Bendix has noted, "the way a conventional bank needs investment policies and the confidence of its depositors."[107] This phenomenon is really quite routine in history, although it is probably underappreciated in the study of international relations.

A question of timing

Finally, it is reasonable to ask why this community of experts did not emerge earlier and play a role in fostering international economic agreement prior to World War II. There are several reasons. To begin with, in the period following World War I, the range of legitimate policy views on monetary relations was much wider. The lessons learned by British economists and politicians from the disastrous return to the gold standard in 1925 were crucial in narrowing the range of expert views. Similarly, the experiences of the 1930s were crucial in discrediting monetary ideas associated with floating exchange rates.[108] In the subsequent period, British and American governments began actively recruiting economic planners, most of whom were trained in the "new thinking," and provided them with an opportunity for devising international rules and institutions in a way that was not fully available in the 1930s. The formation of an influential community of Anglo-American monetary experts had to wait for these developments.

107. Reinhard Bendix, *Kings or People: Power and the Mandate to Rule* (Berkeley: University of California Press, 1978), p. 16.
108. This is stressed by Odell in "From Bretton Woods to London."

Beyond these immediate factors, there were more diffuse shifts in thinking among British and American elites concerning the virtues and necessities of internationalism. Paradoxically, much of the new value attached to international institutions and much of the perceived necessity of striking a deal between Britain and the United States sprang from the progressive rise in the social obligations undertaken by the modern welfare state. During the early 1940s, the goals of full employment, economic stabilization, and social welfare repeatedly found their way into discussions about the postwar economic order and were the topics of major concern in popular journals, in congressional and parliamentary debates, and in Anglo-American planning deliberations. Nothing similar had been evident in 1918, when the rapid return to laissez-faire and the automatic forces of economic life were the order of the day. Between the wars, the sociopolitical underpinnings of the modern state had changed.[109] As a result, the elites who commanded the British and American governments in 1945 had a different set of perceptions and goals of postwar order than their predecessors had in 1918. In this sense, the "demand" for new ideas was greater the second time around. At the same time, the size of the Anglo-American sociopolitical coalition that would potentially favor internationalist solutions to problems of postwar reconstruction was also larger the second time around. What was needed was an intellectual and political basis for coalition building on a grand scale, and this is what the Keynesian "new thinkers" provided.

109. During the interwar period, the legitimacy of the modern industrial state began to hinge more and more on the provision of socioeconomic welfare. See T. H. Marshall, *Class, Citizenship and Social Development* (Garden City, N.Y.: Doubleday, 1964); Reinhard Bendix, *Nation-Building and Citizenship: Studies of Our Changing Social Order* (New York: Wiley, 1964), chap. 3; Karl Polanyi, *The Great Transformation* (New York: Farrar & Rinehart, 1944); and Gianfranco Poggi, *The Development of the Modern State: A Sociological Introduction* (Stanford, Calif.: Stanford University Press, 1978), chap. 6, especially p. 134.

[3]

French International Monetary Policies
in the 1940s

Chiarella Esposito

Much has been written about French economic policies in the 1940s, especially concerning the French modernization plans.[1] However, by and large these works have concentrated upon domestic economic issues, leaving the question of the economic relations of France with the rest of the world somewhat neglected.[2] This study tries to fill that gap partially through a survey of French international monetary policies in the 1940s and an analysis of how these policies related to the domestic economic objectives of the Fourth Republic. Indeed, domestic and foreign economic policies were intimately related. Thanks to their realistic approach, French authorities managed to adapt France's international monetary policies to the paramount national goal of economic overhaul. The French appear to have been more realistic and pragmatic than their Anglo-American allies, whose international monetary plans would dominate in the postwar world. France's plans were based on a correct forecast of the postwar disarray in international trade and payments and provided special measures for a transitional reconstruction period. The Americans, and to some extent the British, instead presumed a rapid return to a "normal" multilateral system of

Chiarella Esposito is assistant professor of history at the University of Mississippi. She is currently revising for publication her doctoral dissertation entitled "The Marshall Plan in France and Italy 1948–1950; Counterpart Fund Negotiations," SUNY at Stony Brook, 1985.

[1] See especially Richard F. Kuisel, *Capitalism and the State in Modern France: Renovation and Economic Management in the Twentieth Century* (New York, 1981); Jean Bouvier and François Bloch Lainé, *La France restaurée, 1944–1954: Dialogue sur les choix d'une modernisation* (Paris, 1986); Philippe Mioche, *Le Plan Monnet: Genèse et élaboration, 1941–1947* (Ph.D. diss., Université de Paris I, 1987); and some of the articles in Patrick Fridenson and André Straus, *Le Capitalisme français, 19e–20e siècle: Blocages et dynamismes d'une croissance* (Paris, 1987).

[2] Exceptions are Robert Frank, "Contraintes monétaires, désirs de croissance et rêves européens (1931–1949)," in *Le Capitalisme français*, 287–306; Frances M. B. Lynch, "Resolving the Paradox of the Monnet Plan: National and International Planning in French Reconstruction," *Economic History Review* 37, 2nd series (May 1984): 229–43.

French Historical Studies, Vol. 17, No. 1 (Spring 1991)
Copyright © 1991 by the Society for French Historical Studies

exchanges based on convertible currencies and, paying little attention to postwar problems, prepared plans for a definitive payments system. France's economic policy-makers would prove to be well in tune with postwar realities, vindicating their fame as able economic planners not only at the national but also at the international level.

It is important first of all to determine what the principal French economic goals for the postwar period were. It was quite clear that the French economy would be in extreme distress at the end of the war and that France would be faced with a large balance of payments deficit. The first goal, therefore, was simply economic recovery. That goal alone, however, would not satisfy the French public. For virtually all French political groups a major cause of the 1940 defeat was to be traced back to French economic backwardness in the interwar period. Both Vichy and Resistance planners agreed that a complete overhaul of the French economy was necessary if France were to have a prominent European and worldwide role again after the war.[3] Such economic overhaul would be achieved by establishing economic plans requiring large-scale investment by the government. Therefore, policies of economic expansion were on almost every political group's agenda as the key to rapid recovery and modernization. As a consequence, one question of foremost consideration to the French authorities was that of creating a new international payments system, which would allow France to modernize her economy *despite* a projected large balance of payments deficit and a badly damaged economic apparatus at the end of the Second World War.

In this connection it was a priority for the French to avoid the return to a traditional gold standard system as the chief regulator of international exchange.[4] In a gold standard regime, countries with a balance of payments deficit had traditionally been compelled to resort

---

    [3] Kuisel, *Capitalism and the State*, chaps. 5 and 6.
    [4] The following discussion about France's views and plans concerning the postwar international monetary situation is drawn from these sources: "Note sur le problème monetaire français," 21 May 1942, and "Suggestions Regarding an International Monetary System," undated, both in Ministère des affaires étrangères (MAE), Guerre 1939–1945, Alger CFLN-GPRF, 725; "Problèmes économiques d'après-guerre: Un Point de vue français," by Hervé Alphand, July 1942, and "Rapport préliminaire sur les questions économiques financières et sociales d'après-guerre," undated, both in MAE, Guerre 1939–1945, Londres CNF, 174; "Note," 8 October 1942, MAE, Guerre 1939–1945, Alger CFLN-GPRF, 1532; "Résumé du projet anglais et du projet américain," undated, MAE, Guerre 1939–1945, Londres CNF, 175; "Note - a.s.: De certains aspects des problèmes économiques de l'après-guerre," 1 October 1943, MAE, Papiers 1940, Bureau d'études Chauvel, 159; Keith J. Horsefield, ed., *The International Monetary Fund, 1945–1965: Twenty Years of International Monetary Cooperation* (Washington, D.C., 1969), 3:97–102.

to deflation and the shrinking of domestic demand in order to increase exports, cut imports, and return to an international payments equilibrium. The burden of readjustment toward an international payments equilibrium had been placed on debtor countries. If it was clear that France would have large balance of payments deficits at the end of the war, it was just as clear among French economic experts that the solution to the deficits could not be deflation: deflation would not only curtail the modernization effort, but it would also hinder the social reforms that were on the agenda of most Resistance groups. Consequently, the French abhorred a return to a traditional gold standard at the end of the war because of its deflationary bias. Some other system of international payments should be adopted, taking into account the enormous difficulties and the economic and political priorities of the reconstruction period.

The question was precisely, what new system of international trade and payments should be adopted if a return to the gold standard was to be excluded. That question was particularly hard to settle in view of the disruption to world trade that had occurred in the 1930s when, due to the depression, the gold standard had been abandoned. Lacking an international monetary standard, countries had then generally resorted to bilateral trade and payments agreements in order to maintain reciprocal exchanges in equilibrium. These bilateral treaties had resembled a sophisticated form of barter. Such agreements disrupted the ideal, "natural" system of free-trade international competition by putting emphasis on the necessity to balance bilateral accounts rather than on obtaining the best quality products at the lowest prices.

In the postwar period the international payments situation would be quite similar to that of the 1930s in one respect at least: most currencies would have no fixed value vis-à-vis gold and could not be used for international payments. International payments then could be effected only through gold or through currencies convertible into gold (primarily the U.S. dollar). But with gold and dollars in short supply, the only alternative would be bilateral payments agreements once again as in the 1930s. Unless some new international monetary system was created, international exchanges would not be conducted on a multilateral basis.

French economic experts, such as Jean Monnet, Hervé Alphand, and André Istel, were well aware of these problems. They anticipated economic losses larger than those caused by the First World War. All European countries, burdened by war debts and lacking gold and dollar reserves, would be unable to pay for the imports necessary for survival and reconstruction. In such a situation international trade might come to a standstill. Therefore a return to a multilateral system of trade and payments based on the gold standard would not only create enormous difficulties for French modernization, but it would be above all simply impracticable.

French experts were fully aware that the system of bilateral exchanges of the 1930s would be detrimental to the expansion of world trade and postwar recovery, and they favored a multilateral system of trade and payments regulated by an international exchange standard more flexible than the traditional gold standard. However, these French experts did not think that such a multilateral system could be introduced immediately after the Second World War. First, the European economy had to recover, then multilateralism could be reinstituted. The transitional period therefore would have to bring a temporary system of international trade that would allow each European country to import without exhausting all of its gold and hard currency reserves together with large amounts of international credits—where presumably the principal lender would be the United States of America—for relief and reconstruction purposes. As a consequence, all international monetary and trade plans would be judged by French authorities on the basis of how flexible they would be in coping with the problems of the reconstruction period and on how much international credit these plans would extend.

In the course of the transitional reconstruction period, French authorities expected to maintain or modify a number of wartime economic controls—as most other European countries would be compelled to do as well. There would be rationing of basic products and raw materials, controls on prices and exchange rates, and commercial treaties with several countries favoring the imports of relief items, the necessary primary resources for reconstruction purposes, and re-equipment items for modernization of the French economy. The volume and the type of imports would have to be established by the French government. French authorities expected that at the end of the war the French government would embark upon widespread economic management and that it would not resort to *laissez-faire* policies. Although this preference for *dirigisme* is well known with regard to French domestic economic policies, it is clear that the same attitude applied also to international economic relations.

Hervé Alphand and André Istel, two of the principal French economic experts, wasted no time in elaborating a plan for international payments and trade which should operate during the crucial reconstruction period. Alphand and Istel used as a basic model for their plan a payments and trade agreement stipulated by France and Great Britain in 1939, at the outbreak of the Second World War.

The 1939 payments and trade agreement with Britain had been conceived in a war emergency situation[5] and was therefore appealing as a model to cope with the foreseen postwar payments and trade difficulties. In 1939 France and Britain had agreed to fix their reciprocal exchange rates. There were provisions for reciprocal compensation in case of devaluations agreed to by both partners. Each country held a certain amount of the other country's currency to be used only for purchases within the French franc zone and the sterling zone respectively, not in third markets, unless both partners agreed to it. Nor could those francs or pounds be sold for gold without both countries' consent. Credit surpluses above the maximum amount of the other country's currency that a partner had agreed to hold would be covered by issuing low-interest treasury bonds, in the name of the creditor government, to be regularized at the end of the war. Prices within the two countries had to be maintained at similar levels in order to avoid speculation. A common trade policy toward third countries would be maintained, but both countries could depreciate their respective currency *vis-à-vis* third countries unilaterally.

One of the chief advantages of this agreement was considered to be the fact that credit balances would be expressed in the debtor country's currency, not that of the creditor's as in a gold standard system: the creditor countries would hold "an internal purchasing power" within debtor countries, that were bound by treaty not to "freeze" their own currencies held by their creditors. Instead, in a gold standard system, all a creditor held was a promise to be paid back, but in its own currency, a currency that a debtor might be unable to obtain.[6]

How could this 1939 agreement with Britain be modified in order to fit the postwar situation? The first step would be for all interested countries to sign similar bilateral trade and payments agreements with one another, thus creating an extended network of such treaties. Secondly, the French experts realized that the 1939 agreement allowed for virtually unlimited reciprocal credits between Britain and France. That feature, dictated by the war emergency, should be removed to

---

[5] "Note sur le problème monétaire français," 21 May 1942; "Problèmes économiques d'après-guerre," July 1942; "Suggestions Regarding an International Monetary System," undated.

[6] Horsefield, *The International Monetary Fund*, 3:99.

avoid the accumulation of excessive deficits.[7] Alphand and Istel indicated that there should be a ceiling on credit to be made available to each prospective partner. Exchange rates, as in the 1939 agreement, would be fixed according to mutual agreement or through an international conference among all countries adopting the French plan. Devaluations would take place only in agreement with bilateral treaty partners and would be followed by compensation for partners' losses (gold, foreign bills, raw materials).[8] International payments would be made by acquiring a specified maximum amount of each partner's currency and then using it for payments within that currency's zone. A surplus by a creditor country would therefore be denominated in the currency of the debtor country, as in the 1939 agreement with Britain. International cooperation would assure that central banks holding surpluses of foreign currencies would keep them blocked, or would "sterilize" them, in inflationary times. That was a key provision in order to forestall the potentially inflationary dangers embedded in a system where countries' debts were expressed in their own currency. Surpluses could not be sold in exchange for gold or at exchange rates different from the agreed ones in order to avoid speculation. A *Caisse internationale de compensation* would keep the accounts of all countries which subscribed to the network of bilateral treaties, and the *Caisse* could then transfer currencies to third countries as long as the currencies would be used by the purchasers within each currency's own monetary zone.[9] The *Caisse* would thus provide a sort of partial multilateral clearing. It would also monitor both temporary and structural payments disequilibria and encourage creditor countries to extend long-term loans to debtors or to sign commerical treaties favorable to the debtor countries.

Alphand and Istel defined this payments system as being merely a "mechanism" to be applied in order to activate international trade at the end of the war and certainly not as a definitive solution. Ideally, following the formation of the network of bilateral agreements, international cooperation would continue, and a satisfactory international monetary system would eventually be instituted thanks to such cooperation. Indeed, the French experts stressed the need for international

    [7] "Note sur le problème monétaire français," 21 May 1942; "Problèmes économiques d'après-guerre," July 1942; "Note sur les négociations relatives à l'établissement d'un plan monétaire international," 15 November 1943, MAE, Guerre 1939–1945, Alger CFLN-GPRF, 1194.
    [8] Horsefield, *The International Monetary Fund*, 3:100.
    [9] Thus, for instance, if Belgium had a French franc surplus and a lire debt, it could have its French franc surplus transferred by the *Caisse* to Italy, which would get paid therefore in French francs. Italy would then have to use those francs for imports from the French franc zone.

FRENCH MONETARY POLICIES

cooperation. They favored a form of international *dirigisme*, whereby countries would sign agreements concerning a host of issues, such as prices, transportation costs for goods, import and export policies in general, fair trade settlements, agreements that would take into account each country's resources, skills, production costs, and creditor or debtor situation. The ultimate goal was a fair apportionment of world resources and production from which all would benefit. A word used to describe such an international cooperation system was "concertée." Indeed such cooperation would be necessary to prevent a degeneration into the retrograde form of bilateralism of the interwar period with its inefficient use of world resources.

Some advantages of this "mechanism," the French claimed, were the possibility to apply the system immediately at the end of the war by many countries, whether they used exchange controls or not, and the system's flexibility. Also, the bilateral trade and payments treaties envisioned by the French were meant to be temporary, and their terms could easily be modified progressively as the international trade and payments situation evolved. The French scheme provided for fixed and therefore stable exchange rates and for the temporary elimination of international payments blockages caused by the widespread lack of reserves. It did this by creating a form of short-term financing of world trade that did not require immediate resort to either gold or hard currencies. Creditor countries would have to provide ample international credits during the reconstruction period for countries needing help beyond the limited resources provided by their bilateral accounts.

A role for gold was still envisioned by the French experts.[10] Although it was not acceptable to reinstitute a gold standard with all its deflationary perils, the French pointed out that the total world supply of gold had quadrupled since 1914 and that it could indeed still be used by countries to effect certain payments and as collateral. Actually the French went so far as to declare that given the great difficulties of creating an international exchange unit acceptable to all, gold could certainly become either the "fiduciary" or "international" currency of the future. The important point was that international monetary authorities would be empowered to modify the value of gold as well as of all currencies and that, at least in the reconstruction period, currencies should not be required to maintain a par value. Even though limited gold usage was thus welcomed by the French, gold should not regulate international trade and payments.

---

[10] "Suggestions Regarding an International Monetary System," undated; Horsefield, *The International Monetary Fund*, 3:100–101.

Finally, alongside the series of bilateral treaties, the French also envisioned the creation of customs unions in which participating countries would maintain low custom duties among themselves and higher ones toward non-customs union countries. There were suggestions concerning even a monetary union with a common central bank for all customs union countries.[11] The countries with which France sought to form customs unions were primarily Belgium,[12] the Netherlands, and Luxembourg. Such customs unions, it was pointed out, would not contradict the spirit of the bilateral treaties' network but were to be considered as steps toward expansion of world trade.

In short, the French considered that a modified and temporary form of bilateralism would be a practical and easily applicable system of international trade and payments to cope with the problems of the reconstruction period. Such a system would allow France to shelter her economy while modernizing and postponing the payment of her debts. A movement toward a new international monetary standard for multilateral exchanges, even though not a new gold standard, was certainly envisioned by the French, but it would have to be approached gradually, when the international economy had at least begun to recover, and through a high degree of permanent international management of the world economy.

By taking this position, the French experts were being more pragmatic, it appears, than their Anglo-American counterparts; the Americans, and to a lesser degree the British, would soon demonstrate their inability to provide a new international trade and payments system suitable to the economic disarray of postwar Europe. French pragmatism concerning these issues would in fact clash against the more comprehensive but less realistic plans for a new, definitive international monetary system put forth by the Americans and the British.

Because the Americans and British held much greater international prestige and political power than the Comité français de la Libération nationale (CFLN)—the French provisional government—the French plans were bound to be brushed aside. Indeed, the negotiations for the International Monetary Fund (IMF) in 1944 at Bretton Woods, N.H., were based almost exclusively on a compromise reached between American and British plans. The American and British plans have

[11] "Problèmes économiques d'après-guerre," July 1942; "Note - a.s.: De certains aspects des problèmes économiques de l'après-guerre," 1 October 1943; "Note," 25 March 1943, MAE, Guerre 1939–1945, Alger CFLN-GPRF, 1533.

[12] There are a number of documents concerning the strategic and economic importance of Belgium in French postwar international policy in MAE, Papiers 1940, Bureau d'études Chauvel, vol. 106.

been studied much more thoroughly than the French proposal, but a recapitulation of their most important features enables an assessment of how these plans contrasted with French views, how the French came to favor the British plan, and how the French would fare, later, once the IMF began its operations.

The American and the British plans had as their main objective the creation of a multilateral system of payments (and trade) in a situation of high or even full employment.[13] Both plans were also devised to operate, ideally, in "normal" international trade conditions; they were not designed to cope with the transitional reconstruction period, but rather to provide a permanent multilateral system of payments for the future. However, beyond the sharing of these basic principles, the American and the British plans presented some fundamental differences concerning the treatment of debtor and creditor countries, access to foreign exchange, total capital available to the new international monetary institution that would be created, devaluation procedures, and the possibility of maintaining exchange controls.

The American plan was prepared primarily by Harry Dexter White, a financial expert in the United States Treasury, and it called for the creation of an International Stabilization Fund.[14] The Stabilization Fund would operate with a capital of 5 billion dollars, contributed by the participating countries in different proportions. Exchange rates would be fixed at the outset, and later devaluations would be difficult to obtain: devaluing countries should demonstrate a vaguely defined "fundamental disequilibrium" and obtain a 4/5 favorable majority of votes at the Fund's governing agencies. Exchange controls, generally prohibited, could be adopted only through special permission by the Fund and on a strictly temporary basis. The Fund would have the authority to monitor and advise member countries and could curtail funds for debtors that were not following the fund's prescriptions to redress their deficits. The only restriction envisioned for creditors was the rationing of their currencies when these were in short supply. All in all, the responsibility to bring about international equilibrium was set upon debtor countries, especially considering that they would not be able to adopt exchange controls and would have to muster a 4/5 majority at the Fund's governing body in order to be able to devalue.

The British plan for an International Clearing Union was pre-

---

[13] Richard N. Gardner, *Sterling-Dollar Diplomacy in Current Perspective: The Origins and the Prospects of our International Economic Order*, new expanded edition with a revised introduction (New York, 1980), 71.

[14] Ibid., 72–77, 80–95.

pared by the famous economist John Maynard Keynes.[15] Keynes intended to create a multilateral payments system that would avoid the drawbacks of the gold standard. Keynes's system aimed to allow for constant worldwide economic growth with full employment—barred by the deflationary cycles of a gold standard—and for a progressive expansion of international trade.

The world's limited supply of gold, which could not keep up with the expansion of world trade and thus exerted deflationary pressures, induced Keynes to create a new international unit of exchange. This would be *bancor*, whose total supply would be flexible and proportional to the overall volume of world trade. All international accounts would be expressed in *bancor*. For instance, France's debts and credits in all currencies would be offset against one another using each currency's par value to *bancor*, and the remaining net surplus or deficit would be denominated in *bancor*. The Clearing Union would then operate much like an international central bank and provide a complete multilateral clearing mechanism. The Clearing Union would start with a capital of 26 billion dollars that would not come from countries' contributions. It would be created instead by opening overdraft facilities for each country proportional to each country's prewar share of world trade. The Clearing Union's total capital would increase with the expansion of world trade.

This system allowed for access to large credits so that most exchange controls—although permitted—might become unnecessary. It would allow countries to import and expand their economies at the same time, even if they started out with a deficit. Measures to correct deficits could be imposed on debtor countries, but because a country could not be declared in default until it had withdrawn 3/4 of the *bancor* allotted to it, this country could in fact run a very large deficit—much larger indeed than under the Stabilization Fund's scheme—before being checked by the Clearing Union authorities. A debtor country could also devalue up to 5 percent without consulting the Clearing Union. Therefore, all in all, the Clearing Union gave debtor countries very large room to maneuver before they would have to resort to any strict correctives on their domestic economic policies.

Creditor countries were instead dealt with in a stricter fashion. There was no real limit to a creditor country's liabilities. A creditor could keep accumulating *bancor* surpluses up to the amount of all

[15] Ibid., 77–95; Robert Triffin, *Europe and the Money Muddle: From Bilateralism to Near-Convertibility, 1947–1956* (London, 1957), 93–109.

other countries' overdraft facilities combined. For instance, because the United States would start with a 3 billion *bancor* account (equal to 3 billion dollars) and the remaining 23 billion *bancor* would be allotted to other member countries, the latter countries could theoretically contract debts toward the United States up to 23 billion *bancor*, a very large figure in the postwar period, with no American power to control the situation. One serious risk was that if the debtor countries' deficits were fueled by inflation of their domestic prices, indicating that these countries were living well above their national resources, the only way creditor countries could try to come to a balance of payments equilibrium would be by engaging in inflationary policies powerful enough to offset the inflation in the debtor countries. This was clearly not a sound remedy.[16] To make things even more difficult for creditor countries, a 2 percent interest rate would be charged on credit balances—the same as on debit balances. Creditor countries could also be advised by the Clearing Union to adopt any of the following measures: expand domestic markets, raise the value of their currency, lower tariffs, and use surpluses to make international loans. Thus most responsibility for readjustment toward an international payments' equilibrium was placed on creditor countries.

It is clear then that Keynes' plan had been devised in order to safeguard British interests, for Britain already had large payments deficits accumulated during the war and expected to be a debtor country in the reconstruction period. In this connection, it is important to note that the British Labour government had, as did the French, ambitious and expensive social and economic reforms in mind, which could not be enacted unless Britain could postpone the payment of her debts. The large overdraft facilities provided by the Clearing Union scheme, even though not designed to cope ideally with the transitional reconstruction period, certainly offered much greater capability to the war-ravaged countries of Europe to cope with their postwar payments problems.

It is not surprising therefore that the French experts expressed a marked preference for the Clearing Union plan.[17] As a debtor country France was in a position very similar to that of Great Britain. More-

[16] Gardner, *Sterling-Dollar Diplomacy*, 93–94.

[17] "Etude comparée des deux plans financiers de l'Amérique et de l'Angleterre pour l'après-guerre," May 1943, and "Rapport sur la conférence monétaire préliminaire tenue à la Treasury les 15, 16, 17 Juin 1943," both in MAE, Guerre 1939–1945, Alger CFLN-GPRF, 725; "Note sur les plans monétaires de MM. Keynes et White," 15 July 1943, MAE, Guerre 1939–1945, Alger CFLN-GPRF, 1194; "Résumé du projet anglais et du projet américain," undated.

over, the French experts proceeded to assess the American and the British plans in view of the French capability, in both hypothetical systems, to maintain export and import controls—such as the restriction of luxury items imports.

Actually the French found White's Stabilization Fund totally unacceptable. They found that it would impose far too rigid obligations on its members. According to White's scheme, France would be compelled to maintain a fixed exchange rate for the franc which it would not be able to change unless it proved that there was a "fundamental" problem with its present rate and unless it obtained a 4/5 majority of votes at the Fund's governing board. Exchange controls were not permitted, nor were bilateral trade and payments agreements. If that had not limited national independent policies enough, the Fund was also endowed with considerable power to modify debtor countries' domestic economic policies. In a Stabilization Fund scheme, the French would have to abandon their projected policies of high investment completely. Indeed it is hard to see how, from the French point of view, the Fund would have been much better than the gold standard itself.

The Clearing Union plan, on the contrary, was praised by the French for several reasons. Keynes's plan preserved independent national economic policies and allowed countries to resort to exchange controls as well. Devaluation up to 5 percent was permitted without consulting the Clearing Union authorities. Placing responsibility for readjustments on creditors was also considered a very positive feature. The creation of *bancor*, moreover, gave better guarantees of ending deflationary pressures in case of international payments disequilibria, with which the Clearing Union would be able to cope much more smoothly than the Stabilization Fund thanks to the Union's considerable capital. Finally, Keynes's position on the usage of gold was quite similar to French views. In Keynes's plan, gold could be used for payments, if a country desired to do so, and the Clearing Union would be obliged to accept it. However, creditors could not require payments in gold, but would be obliged to accept *bancor* instead. Thus Clearing Union obligations were considered much less burdensome by the French than those required by White's plan.

After publication of the British and American plans, there intervened a period of about one year, from the summer of 1943 to the summer of 1944, during which the Americans and the British started to work toward a compromise of their two plans. The French, on their part, simply prepared themselves to make their priorities very clear to their allies in prospect of a final international monetary agreement.

The CFLN assumed a generally conciliatory posture, while pursuing French interests on key issues.[18]

The CFLN decided first of all to do away with the Alphand and Istel plan. It is difficult to assess exactly why that decision was made. First, France still had a very weak international position between 1943 and 1944, so much so that in 1943 the French complimented themselves simply because they were being consulted at all by the Allies on such international monetary matters.[19] In this situation, trying to impose a French plan, which was totally different from both the British and American concepts, was unthinkable. Secondly, it would have been very difficult to counter the more comprehensive British and American monetary plans for a new and definitive international monetary system with the much more modest and transitory "mechanism" earlier proposed by Alphand and Istel.

However, having abandoned its plan, the CFLN certainly did not abandon its priorities. The French kept insisting that the resources of a new international monetary institution would have to be large, that access to the institution's resources should be expeditious, and that separate regional and bilateral trade and payments schemes should be allowed in the transitional reconstruction period. The French also pointed out that countries' quotas to enter a scheme such as White's Fund would have to be determined according to each country's resources only after immediate relief and reconstruction needs had been satisfied.

It must also be noted that, in the period before the international conference that established the International Monetary Fund (IMF) at Bretton Woods in the summer of 1944, the French had no illusions about the actual possibility of Keynes's plan being adopted. The Clearing Union plan appeared to be too onerous for the United States and, the French surmised, would never be accepted by the Americans. The French were indeed correct in this assessment. The institution that finally emerged, the IMF, turned out to be a modified version of the Stabilization Fund scheme. Fortunately for the French, Keynes managed to wrest several important concessions from the Americans. Because

[18] "Note sur la prochaine conférence monétaire internationale," by André Istel, undated, and "Projet d'instruction pour la délégation française à la conférence monétaire internationale," undated, both in MAE, Guerre 1939–1945, Alger CFLN-GPRF, 1194; "Rapport à Monsieur le Ministre des Finances fait par M. de Largentaye, Inspecteur des finances sur la conférence de Bretton Woods," August 1945, Ministère de l'économie et des finances, Archives économiques et financières (AEF), B 33284.

[19] "Rapport sur la conférence monétaire préliminaire tenue à la Treasury les 15, 16, 17 juin 1943."

the Clearing Union plan had been totally discarded, Keynes had, paradoxically, great leverage in obtaining major modifications of key Stabilization Fund provisions. At this point it is important to summarize briefly what shape the IMF, born of an Anglo-American compromise, finally took, because that is what determined the international environment in which France's international monetary policies would be formulated after the war.

The IMF called for participating countries' contributions amounting to a total of 8.8 billion dollars, with the United States' contribution set at 3.174 billion dollars.[20] A rather vague provision regulated the availability of the IMF funds: credits would be extended to member countries only in order to further the main purpose of the IMF itself, that is, in order to eliminate disequilibria. The vagueness of this provision assured that there would be no steadfast rule; rather each case would be judged separately. Because IMF resources were limited and would not allow countries to run large deficits, the British also asked for easier devaluation procedures. Thus it was established that countries could devalue up to 10 percent without IMF approval and more than 10 percent with IMF consent if a "fundamental disequilibrium" could be demonstrated. The IMF could criticize and advise persistent debtor countries, but it had no specific authority to influence a country's domestic economic policies; in this way national sovereignty was safeguarded. The White plan's provision about rationing currencies in high demand was reinforced. Scarce currencies would be rationed to borrowers while countries were allowed to adopt discriminatory controls in operations dealing with currencies termed scarce by the IMF. The small amount of IMF resources also meant that countries could not count on them in order to cope with the large deficits of the immediate postwar period. Thus the British asked and obtained that countries ravaged by the war would be able to maintain controls on payments and capital transfers for a period of five years, at the end of which there would be a consultation with the IMF about the maintenance of such controls in the future.

This concession by the Americans was indeed crucial because it allowed for the maintenance of controls for an indefinite period of time. Also, international exchanges would not become fully multilateral at the end of the war. Rather there would be a transitional period during which countries could sign separate bilateral or regional payments and

[20] Gardner, *Sterling-Dollar Diplomacy*, 110–21; Triffin, *Europe and the Money Muddle*, 109–38.

trade agreements, and there would also be regional custom unions in order to reach multilateralism gradually. The Americans in the end had to bow to the fact that in the postwar period special provisions should be allowed.[21]

From the French point of view, the final IMF agreement embodied some of the most important French priorities: relatively easy devaluation procedures, the power to maintain exchange controls, the ability to discriminate against scarce-currency countries and to sign regional and bilateral treaties during an indefinite period while moving slowly toward multilaterialism.

The Americans, however, had succeeded in limiting IMF funds. For the French, the greatest problem remained the scarcity of the Fund's resources, which were designed to cope with a "normal" pattern of international payments and not with the difficult reconstruction period. The credits which the IMF would extend to debtor countries were insufficient to help France reconstruct, expand, and modernize her economy while at the same time running a large balance of payments deficit. France tried unsuccessfully to obtain substantial loans from the United States. Large credits did not become available to France till the Marshall Plan was enacted in 1948. Before then, as we shall see, France had to circumvent that problem by adopting a series of measures—such as bilateral treaties and devaluations—without however resolving most of her economic problems. Only large international credits, as the French had maintained all along, could bring true recovery and growth.

France's IMF quota was originally set at 450 million dollars. Because the quota also determined total drawing rights, France tried to have it increased and managed to achieve that, although in small amounts, with an increase to 525 million dollars in 1946.[22] France also had to fight in order to obtain adequate voting power within the IMF governing bodies. In fact, the French representatives threatened complete withdrawal of France from the IMF scheme unless France could obtain better representation. Finally France was assigned a most important seat in the IMF executive committee. These early bouts of French independence *vis-à-vis* the American-dominated IMF, despite

[21] Gardner, *Sterling-Dollar Diplomacy*, 121.
[22] Telegram from Pierre Mendès-France's office (signed by Hoppenot) to General Charles de Gaulle and MM. Massigli and Giacobbi, No. 1696 Diplo-A96 Ficomi, from Algiers, 27 July 1944, MAE, Guerre 1939–1945, Alger CFLN-GPRF, 1533; Speech by the French minister of foreign affairs, 26 December 1945, MAE, Y - Internationale, 84; "Rapport à Monsieur le Ministre des Finances," August 1945; and Jean-Guy Mérigot and Paul Coulbois, *Le Franc, 1938–1950* (Paris, 1950), 376.

France's weak international position, actually prefigured more independent actions in the future.

The French began immediately to take advantage of IMF provisions allowing for the adoption or maintenance of exchange controls and for the stipulation of bilateral and regional trade and payments agreements during the transitional reconstruction period. First of all, the French government either adopted or maintained all sorts of controls concerning the volume and type of imports and exports, capital movements, and sales and purchases of foreign currencies. Gold transactions were altogether prohibited.[23] Secondly, the French had meant to sign bilateral payments and trade agreements ever since 1942 and proceeded to do so swiftly as soon as the IMF was established;[24] indeed, at the end of the war, resorting to bilateral payments and trade agreements was considered very important by the French government. France and its major trading partners in Europe all had large deficits. At the same time, France's principal export goods, immediately after the war, were luxury items such as liquors, wines, perfumes, and "articles de Paris."[25] In the absence of bilateral treaties, which compelled France's trading partners to buy an agreed amount of French goods, these luxury items could have been paid for only with gold or hard currencies. But most of France's trading partners would have refused to use their very scarce gold and hard currencies reserves to buy luxury items. Those scarce resources had to be used, as in France's own case, for vital relief and reconstruction imports mostly from the dollar area. Thus bilateral treaties were the only manner by which France could emerge from a virtual trading impasse and create a market for French franc exports. The franc, in this manner, would at least begin to reconquer an important position in international financial markets. France's trading partners were often in similar situations, because the variety and quantity of their exports were limited. As a consequence, Europeans all shared an interest in concluding bilateral accords with one another, extending that network of agreements as much as possible.[26]

[23] Ibid., 244–256.
[24] "Note sur les relations financières de la France avec l'étranger," 18 Feburary 1946; "Note sur les relations financières de la France avec l'étranger," 20 April 1946; Letter from the Ministry of Foreign Affairs to the Ministry of Finance, Brunet, 5 April 1946; Letter from the Ministry of Finance, Brunet to the Ministry of Foreign Affairs, Alphand, 20 May 1946; "Note No. 4 sur les accords de paiement," 1 June 1948; "Note sur les accord de paiement de la France avec les pays étrangers," June 1951; Memorandum without title, 15 June 1951; all these documents are in AEF, B 33854. See also "Note sur les négociations relatives à l'établissement d'un plan monétaire internationale," 15 November 1943.
[25] Letter from Ministry of Foreign Affairs to Ministry of Finance, Brunet, 4 April 1946.
[26] "Note - a.s.: Première session du Comité pour le développement du commerce extérieure de la commission économique pour l'Europe," undated, MAE, Y - Internationale, 86.

FRENCH MONETARY POLICIES   133

The French and other European governments were in fact following a path very similar to that originally suggested by Alphand and Istel, that is, the formation of a network of bilateral accords.

France concluded many such bilateral agreements. In general the accords called for the opening of reciprocal accounts, for France and each of her partners, at each respective central bank. For instance, Belgium would have an account opened at the bank of France whereby Belgium's surpluses with France were recorded as French franc credit balances. There was an agreed maximum of French francs that Belgium would accept as payment for yet unreciprocated exports; beyond that maximum surplus, France would then have to pay for her imports from Belgium with either gold or hard currencies. Each country guaranteed a fixed exchange rate for accumulated balances up to the agreed maximum surpluses. Generally there were also provisions regulating capital transfers for current account payments. These agreements, which began to be stipulated in 1944–45, were progressively enlarged, particularly after January 1947, by raising the maximum surpluses or deficits allowed to France and her partners and generally by increasing the categories of free capital transfers between partners.[27]

An extensive network of bilateral treaties therefore allowed France to begin postwar trade despite her large deficits. However, we must observe that there were serious problems concerning French domestic economic policies that made it extremely difficult for France to use the bilateral treaties as an effective stepping stone toward a balance of payments in equilibrium and toward a true multilateral system of payments. France's principal problem was caused by persistent domestic inflation and the consequent progressive depreciation of the French franc.[28]

French inflation since the end of the war was fueled by two principal forces. First of all, the supply of goods on the French markets could not keep up with demand. Demand, at the same time, was kept high by large public expenditures and by an upward movement of wages and prices. This situation reflected French political priorities at the end of the war: while wages had to be raised at the end of the hostilities, because they were low and for political reasons, the government assumed much of the burden of French reconstruction and modernization, perhaps the most important item on France's postwar agenda. As we have

[27] See *Committee of European Economic Cooperation: Report of the Committee on Payments Agreements, Second Meeting, October 15–25, 1947, Final Report* (London: His Majesty's Stationary Office, 1948), found in AEF, B 33854.

[28] Mérigot and Coulbois, *Le Franc*, 99–106, 112–23.

seen, deflationary policies that would slow down reconstruction were abhorred by French authorities. At the same time, production increases could not yet fill the gap between demand and supply—that could be done only through imports. As we have seen, France tried and succeeded temporarily in filling part of that "inflationary gap" through the bilateral treaties' imports. But such measures were insufficient; French prices kept rising steadily after the war, with only brief periods of respite. Rapid inflation, in turn, made French products thoroughly non-competitive, even for the bilateral treaties partners. This situation could be and was partially offset by devaluing the French franc. There were at least three major devaluations between 1945 and 1949, and some "alignments" of the franc that never were officially considered devaluations.[29]

The first major devaluation took place in December 1945, as France was to communicate the value of the French franc to the IMF. From the current official value of 49 francs to the dollar, France passed to 119 francs to the dollar. The 49-francs rate had been thoroughly unrealistic in France and in competitor countries, and the communication of a realistic rate to the IMF therefore provided the opportunity for this substantial devaluation.

The franc remained at its fixed rate of 119 francs to the dollar until January 1948. Thus throughout 1946 and 1947 France upheld her IMF obligation to maintain a fixed exchange rate. But if the official rate was stable, the black market rate of the dollar, which in many ways was more realistic, floated around 320–330 francs in the same two-year period. The franc still appeared to be overvalued. Although there was an improvement in France's balance of trade in 1946, the situation began to deteriorate anew in 1947, when French inflation picked up again. Between December 1945 and January 1948 most prices had either tripled or quadrupled. Once again that indicated an enormous depreciation of the franc and a totally unrealistic exchange rate when trying to promote French exports abroad. But even though a new, major devaluation might appear to solve the problem at one stroke, French authorities remained very cautious about resorting to devaluation. There were good reasons behind this hesitation. On the one hand the government feared that a moderate devaluation would turn out to be only a temporary solution, as prices might continue to mount, compelling a second devaluation later with all its negative psychological effects. On the other hand, a sizable devaluation might have been more realistic

[29] Ibid., 93–96, 175–77; 244–90.

considering French prices, but this risked depreciating the French franc to the point of damaging France's terms of trade more than necessary. That is, with a sizable devaluation French goods would indeed become cheap, but the necessary imports from all countries and especially from the dollar area would become prohibitively expensive. A sizable devaluation would also have triggered more inflation. Thus the French government was caught in a potentially vicious circle of "devaluation-inflation-devaluation" which would further weaken confidence in the franc and worsen France's terms of trade progressively.

As a consequence, in January-February 1948, the French government chose a graduated devaluation which would involve the adoption of multiple exchange rates and of discrimination against hard currencies, particularly the dollar. The 119 francs rate was abandoned completely. The dollar, the Portuguese *escudo*, and soon thereafter the Swiss franc were allowed to float in a "free market" in Paris. In this manner the value of the dollar oscillated, from January to October 1948, between 306 and 312 francs. The official exchange rate of the franc, used for transactions involving all other currencies, was raised from 119 to 214 francs to the dollar. However, all commercial transactions would be handled through an average rate of 261–263 francs, which was the calculated medium point between the official 214 francs rate and the floating "free market" rate of the dollar. The intended effect of this operation was to make French exports toward the dollar area almost three times cheaper, while maintaining better terms of trade with all other countries. At the same time French authorities hoped that the "free market" rate of the dollar would come close to the black market rate in order to decrease the number of black market transactions.

After the French government took these measures, the IMF authorities and the British protested against the adoption of multiple rates for the franc. They argued that the multiple rates might easily result in all kinds of speculations against currencies other than the dollar, the *escudo*, and the Swiss franc. The IMF, of course, could not endorse a measure that could damage IMF member countries, and the British feared speculations against their overvalued sterling pound. As a consequence the IMF decided to suspend France from access to all IMF funds.

France had taken a bold and controversial step by adopting multiple rates of exchange for the franc. It was clear that when IMF membership would be more a burden than an advantage, the French government did not fear to abandon the institution temporarily. But the French government's priority had to be to maximize exports to the dollar area while maintaining a stronger franc *vis-à-vis* most of the rest of the world. Moreover, such a graduated devaluation would limit much of the negative psychological effects of a large flat devaluation. In fact, the French government did not even define this operation as a devaluation. It termed it rather a "temporary measure" allowing the establishment, without major upheavals, of the "natural" rate of the franc, a rate that the government would eventually be able to adopt and maintain. It must also be observed, at this point, that the "free market" rate of the dollar actually was not really "free": all export and import operations had to go through the member states' financial institutions which themselves determined just how widely the "free market" dollar rate could actually float. It was in practice the minister of finance who decided what this rate would be. Therefore, nothing was left to chance, the whole scheme established a deliberate government control on the dollar rate.

In the course of 1948 this maneuver had the effect of improving France's balance of payments toward the dollar area, if by small margins, and, more important, diverting French importers to non-dollar markets, particularly the sterling area. What the maneuver could not achieve, however, was to stop the depreciation of the franc. French domestic prices began to mount again in the summer and early fall of 1948 so that France could still not manage to export sufficiently. In fact, the country was beginning to build up a large deficit toward the sterling area.

As a consequence a second operation was undertaken in October 1948. This restricted the employment of the official rate of 214 francs to the dollar, which had been used in dealing with the currencies not floating in the Paris "free market." The value of these currencies would now be calculated considering their value *vis-à-vis* the dollar and the average rate between the dollar's "free market" rate and the original 214 rate. Therefore, the most representative franc rate became about 264 francs to the dollar, a rate now applied to all transactions with all currencies except the dollar, the *escudo*, and the Swiss franc. This amounted to a devaluation of about 23 percent.

This second operation began to close the gap between the "free market" dollar rate, now about 312 francs, and the rate of the franc in relation to all other currencies. The operation drew praise from the IMF which, however, was not yet fully satisfied, because there was still no official fixed exchange rate for the French franc as there should have been according to IMF requirements.

The system created in October 1948 lasted for almost a year, until

FRENCH MONETARY POLICIES   137

September 1949, with only a minor change in April 1949, whereby the "free market" rate of the dollar was brought up to 329 francs and the rate for other currencies to 272 francs. Multiple exchange rates were eliminated only in September 1949. By then the French government could afford to do so; the French economy had recovered remarkably in the course of 1949. Inflation had been tamed, if temporarily, mainly by balancing the budget without resorting to inflationary financing and by maintaining stable wages.

This recovery undoubtedly owed much to American aid. The long-sought substantial international credits became available in 1948. The Marshall Plan had started that year and it had provided necessary reconstruction and modernization imports from the United States in the form of grants so that France would not need to pay for them with dollars or by other means. At the same time the Marshall Plan mechanism of counterpart funds had provided substantial capital with which the French financed their modernization plan, the so-called Monnet Plan.[30] All these factors combined also resulted in a spectacular increase of production in the course of 1949, which, in turn, helped fill the "inflationary gap" between supply and demand.

By September 1949, when the British suddenly and unexpectedly devalued the pound, France followed suit in order to remain competitive with Britain and devalued by 22 percent. But in doing so the French government took the opportunity to eliminate the multiple rates of exchange and adopt a single exchange rate of 350 francs to the dollar for all transactions involving all currencies. Other rates disappeared completely.

By 1949 it was also evident that the government's maneuvering with rates had helped—together with France's overall recovery—to reduce the gap between the dollar "free market" rate and the black market rate. At the end of August 1949 the black market rate of the dollar was about 50 francs higher than that in the "free market," a considerable success taking into account that the black market rate had been four times higher than the official rate in 1944 and almost three times higher throughout 1946 and 1947. Therefore, these monetary maneuvers had

[30] See Chiarella Esposito, "The Marshall Plan in France and Italy, 1948-1950: Counterpart Fund Negotiations" (Ph.D. diss., State University of New York at Stony Brook, 1985). The American position concerning how much aid should be extended to Western Europe changed considerably between 1944, when the IMF was instituted, and 1948, when the Marshall Plan started. There are numerous studies on this subject. The two most recent ones are Alan S. Milward, *The Reconstruction of Western Europe, 1945-1951* (Berkeley, 1987); and Michael J. Hogan, *The Marshall Plan: America, Britain and the Reconstruction of Western Europe, 1947-1952* (New York, 1987).

produced some positive results, and with the economic recovery of 1949 even the French balance of payments had begun to improve.

However, since 1948 it had become evident that the network of bilateral trade and payments agreements among European countries was no longer performing a positive function and that some sort of intra-European form of multilateral clearing was now necessary. The chief problem concerning the bilateral agreements was that most European countries had already reached their maximum deficits or surpluses vis-à-vis their bilateral partners as authorized by each separate agreement. Once the maximum was achieved, payments had to be made on a bilateral basis with gold or foreign currencies. In order to avoid the depletion of scarce reserves, the European countries had resorted to quantitative restrictions on those imports that would have required payment in either gold or hard currencies. Capital transfers had also been severely limited.[51] Thus the "enlightened" bilateralism of 1944–47 had become, by 1948, much more similar to its 1930s retrograde precursor.

In view of this problem, what did the French government and its partners propose to do? The French had declared all along that a multilateral system of exchanges could be achieved only gradually. First of all, they advocated, as we have seen, the progressive extension of a network of bilateral agreements. Secondly, they had also promoted the creation of small-scale, regional customs unions designed as early steps toward the adoption of larger, intra-European multilateral trade and payments institutions.[52] France's own principal partners in such schemes would be the Benelux countries and Italy. Early attempts at such unions, which were not very successful, were projects such as Finebel and Fritalux.[53] All these steps, however, had fallen short of establishing any effective system of multilateral exchanges.

Slightly more successful was the First Agreement on Multilateral Monetary Compensation between France, Italy, and Benelux, later joined by the other OEEC countries in October 1948 to form a 1948–49 Agreement for Intra-European Payments and Compensation, which

---

[51] "Note sur les accords de paiement de la France avec les pays étrangers," June 1951; Triffin, *Europe and the Money Muddle*, 146.
[52] "Problèmes économiques d'après-guerre," July 1942; "Note - a.s.: de certains aspects des problèmes économiques de l'après guerre," 1 October 1943; "Note," 25 March 1944; Comité d'action économique et douanière: Les Unions douanières, 20 February 1948, and circulaire N. 237 - IP, 15 September 1947, both in MAE, Z - Europe 1944–1949, généralités, 5; "Groupe d'étude pour l'union douanière Européenne," February 1948, MAE, Y - Internationale, 86; Communiqué de presse, 25 October 1947, AEF, B 33283.
[53] See Alan S. Milward, *The Reconstruction of Western Europe*, 306–16.

was then renewed for one year.[34] These were payments mechanisms that allowed for partial multilateral clearings among the OEEC countries. The agreements in fact covered only 25 percent of all transactions and they could work only under certain specific circumstances. For instance, if France had a surplus of 10 billion dollars with Italy and a deficit of the same amount with Belgium, and if Belgium in its turn owed 10 billion dollars to Italy, France would offset her debt to Belgium with her credit with Italy, and Belgium could pay Italy off with the 10 billion received by France. Unless such a triangular offsetting could be arranged, there would be no clearing.[35] Clearly this was not a true multilateral clearing mechanism, but just a partial one.

Another attempt at improving the intra-European payments situation was made through Marshall Plan "conditional aid," whereby a creditor country could receive Marshall Plan dollars in exchange for credits granted to one or more of its OEEC debtor countries.[36] This mechanism, however, did little to move the OEEC countries toward an intra-European multilateral system, because credits granted in exchange for Marshall Plan dollars were calculated on a bilateral basis, between the country expecting the "conditional aid" and its debtor.

The solution to these problems came only in 1950 with the creation of the European Payments Union (EPU).[37] The EPU constituted a true intra-European multilateral payments system. All bilateral credit and debit balances of all OEEC countries would be offset multilaterally against one another to leave only *net* credit or debit balances to be registered in the EPU's own accounting books. The maximum deficits allowed were determined by multilateralizing the maximum deficits allowed by the pre-existing bilateral agreements. Surpluses above the agreed maximum debit/credit balances would be paid off through gold and Marshall Plan dollars. The total EPU starting capital amounted to 350 million dollars granted to the EPU by the Americans through the Marshall Plan. This capital would be used for the EPU's normal operations and to extend special aid to countries with "structural" deficits.

As a consequence, when a form of multilateralism was achieved for the Western European countries, it was quite different from what

[34] Triffin, *Europe and the Money Muddle*, 147–60.
[35] Another authorized form of clearing allowed countries to substitute a debtor or a creditor with another. For instance, if France had a 10 billion dollar surplus with Italy and the same size deficit with Belgium, France could offset her surplus with her debt if Belgium accepted Italy as its 10 billion dollar debtor instead of France.
[36] Triffin, *Europe and the Money Muddle*, 153.
[37] Ibid., 161–69; and Milward, *The Reconstruction of Western Europe*, 320–34.

the Americans had sought through the IMF (and later in the context of the Marshall Plan). The Americans had worked all along for a comprehensive, permanent payments scheme through which they hoped to reintegrate the European countries into a world-wide multilateral system of international trade and payments. But the EPU was only a regional, not a worldwide, multilateral payments system. Moreover, it had sprung out of the previous bilateral agreements, to which it had been superimposed, making use of those bilateral agreements as a basis for all its offsetting operations and for defining maximum debit/credit margins. The EPU would, however, be financed through the Marshall Plan. Thus the French and the other Europeans were still financially dependent on the Americans, but that did not prevent them from maintaining considerable independence in devising their payments scheme.[38]

In France's case, successful and independent policy-making becomes ever more evident when we compare French wartime plans to the EPU. Even though the EPU had certainly no direct connection with the original Alphand-Istel plan, it embodied its basic principle: a gradual movement from a network of bilateral agreements toward some form of multilateralism where gold would not play a crucial role. One could even argue that, at least in principle, the EPU was not much different from the *Caisse internationale de compensation* envisioned by the wartime French monetary planners. It appears that the French had shown considerable foresight concerning postwar international monetary developments and had been, in that sense, much more realistic than the presumably more pragmatic Americans.[39]

More importantly, by the time of the creation of the EPU in 1950, France's economy had recovered in spectacular fashion. With the adoption of the bilateral agreements, with her complex system of exchange controls, with her controversial graduated devaluation of the franc in 1948, and with the help of the long-sought international credits in the form of Marshall Plan aid, France had been able to carry out an impressive recovery and modernization effort while at the same time running large balance of payments deficits throughout the period. The French economic experts had then managed to adapt, with their pragmatic and gradual approach, French international monetary policies to the national agenda requiring complete economic overhaul. Considering the initial odds against the Fourth Republic economic planners, that success was no small achievement.

[38] This interpretation is in agreement with Milward's argument in *The Reconstruction of Western Europe*. See especially chap. 10.

[39] Robert Frank's conclusions, with some minor differences, are quite similar to mine: Robert Frank, "Contraintes monétaires," 302.

Part II
The Marshall Plan

[4]

American Aid and West German Economic Recovery: A Macroeconomic Perspective

Werner Abelshauser

The Controversial Marshall Plan

The American aid programme for the reconstruction of Europe (ERP) is widely considered one of the great success stories of this century.[1] The Marshall Plan has become the byword for economic assistance. There is hardly a crisis anywhere in the world which in the view of the West ought not be solved by a sort of 'Marshall Plan'. Frequently the 'Marshall Plan' is also discussed in connection with the search for strategies to overcome the more recent lack of growth in the Western industrial nations. No better proof exists for the enduring effect of this decisive transatlantic undertaking than its present utilization as a crisis strategy for coping with international problems.

Even those who have viewed it sceptically from the very outset have come to accept this judgement of the Marshall Plan's positive *economic* effects. The shrill condemnation of the Marshall Plan as an instrument of 'dollar imperialism' by the Soviet Union and its Eastern European satellites served to underline the economic effectiveness of the plan even though they regarded it as an instrument of intervention in the sovereignty of the countries concerned. The Western European left also tended to view the economic importance of the Marshall Plan as crucial when it blamed the American initiative for being one of the principal causes for the collapse of

---

1. This was the conclusion of a more recent study by Immanuel Wexler, who praised the Marshall Plan as 'one of the great economic success stories of modern time', see *The Marshall Plan Revisited: The European Recovery Program in Economic Perspective* (Westport CT, 1983), p.255.

Werner Abelshauser

socialist-democratic plans for reordering the political system. The intervention of the United States and the resulting economic post-war recovery was made responsible for bringing an abrupt end to the 'Socialist century' which had begun with such promise in 1945.[2]

The US did not need its competitors in reordering the postwar political economy to tell it what it was doing right. From its very beginning the Marshall Plan was an exercise in public relations. Following the rule 'Do good and let everyone know about it!' the bilateral ERP treaties contained clauses requiring recipient countries to make every effort to 'promote understanding for common endeavors and mutual aid . . . by spreading information widely'.[3] Long before the arrivals of the first tonne of wheat and the first bale of cotton in Western European ports, the publics of the recipient countries were well informed about the potential blessings of the programme. Thanks to a modern multimedia 'blitz', expectations of the Marshall Plan far exceeded realities. By the beginning of 1949, however, the Marshall Plan had achieved only few 'immediately tangible economic results', the Adviser for the Marshall Plan in the Office of the bizonal *Oberdirektor* noted in his very candid confidential annual report.[4] On the other hand, the demands placed by the Americans on the bizonal German Marshall Plan section responsible for publicity were already 'quite considerable'.[5] The fact alone that the *Oberdirektor*, the chief of government in the Bizone, had two reports made – a glowing 'general report'[6] for the larger public and an unvarnished 'confidential report' – betrays the gap between image and reality in sources of this kind. Assessing such discrepancies is not an easy task for those historians who deal with the effect of the Marshall Plan on the West German economy.

It was not uncharacteristic for the public relations policy under the aegis of the Marshall Plan intentionally to misinform the people about the extent of American aid. Ludwig Erhard and other sup-

2. Werner Abelshauser, 'Wiederaufbau vor dem Marshallplan: Westeuropas Wachstumschancen und die Wirtschaftsordnung in der zweiten Hälfte der vierziger Jahre', *Vierteljahrshefte für Zeitgeschichte*, 29, 4(1981), pp.545–78.

3. See Article VIII of the Economic Cooperation Agreement between the governments of the United States and the Military Governors representing the American and British occupied zones in Germany, 14 June 1948, quoted from ECA-Deutschland (ed.), *Deutschland und das Europäische Wiederaufbauprogramm: Die Wichtigsten Dokumente* (Frankfurt, 1949), p.103.

4. Frankfurt, 27 January 1949, p.2, Bundesarchiv (Federal Archives) (hereafter cited as BA), B 146/189.

5. Ibid.

6. Frankfurt, 7 January 1949, BA, B 146/189.

American Aid and West German Recovery

porters of the social market economy saw the root of legends in those 'stories of the Marshall Plan' that falsified the essence of the successful resuscitation of the West German economy from the very beginning: 'As a result of an omnipotent propaganda campaign, deceptive statistics, thoughtless repetition or unexamined and incorrect claims . . . and above all a total misjudgement of economic correlations, public opinion remained uncorrected and so did the views of ministers and representatives who bear the responsibility.'[7] Just when ERP goods worth $99 million had been delivered, Dr Hermann Pünder, the chairman of the Administrative Council of the Vereinigtes Wirtschaftsgebiet, spoke of 'hundreds of millions of dollars', in his 1949 New Year's radio address, which under the Marshall Plan had already 'poured into our country in the form of goods'.[8]

The decisive factor for the high regard in which Marshall Plan-type programmes have been held both by the public and by historians, however, was the close connection between the unfolding of the ERP and the economic recovery of Western Europe after the crisis of 1947. The economic boom, of course, lasted way beyond the four years of the Marshall Plan. Particularly in the case of West Germany the time period from the announcement of the plan to its end in December 1951 ran parallel with Bizonia overcoming the crippling effects of the postwar collapse. During this time the Federal Republic both consolidated its economic recovery and regained its position in the world economy. These were precisely the explicit goals of the US Foreign Assistance Act of 1948, which the Organization of European Economic Cooperation (OEEC) translated into operational projections at the end of 1948. According to them, industrial production was scheduled to be raised 30 per cent, and agricultural production 15 per cent, above prewar levels in the course of the Marshall Plan; equilibrium should be achieved in the balance of payments.[9] In fact, West Germany, whose industrial production at that time was far below that of the other participating countries, considerably exceeded these targets. Moreover, foreign trade goals were realized in an impressive fashion

7. 'Dollar-Gift', Editorial, April 1951, L. Erhard, E. Hielscher, M. Schönwandt (eds), *Währung und Wirtschaft, Unabhängiges Forum für Wirtschaft-Wissenschaft, -Praxis, -Politik*, 2, 40(1951), p.437; see also 'Geschichte und Geschichten vom Marshall-Plan', ibid., no. 25/26, pp.93–8.

8. 'Die Fundamente sind gelegt', 5 January 1949, *Öffentlicher Anzeiger für das Vereinigte Wirtschaftsgebiet*, vol.2, no. 1 (Frankfurt, 1949), p.1.

9. OECE, Rapport intérimaire sur le programme de relèvement européen, Paris, 30 December 1948, vol.I, pp.52, 85, 242–3.

Werner Abelshauser

as well. Only agricultural production lagged behind the targets, but was still stepped up substantially during the ERP period. At the end of 1952 there was little doubt in people's minds that West Germany was economically 'viable' without foreign aid. This coincidence of goals and results, along with the apparent linkage of economic aid and economic growth, led most observers to believe that there was a close relationship between US financial assistance and the recovery of Western Europe in general and West Germany in particular: 'Both the phenomenal growth of GNP and the rapid rise in industrial production attest to the success of the Marshall Plan in helping to rebuild Europe's productive capacity and thereby induce a sizeable increase of Western Europe's total production.'[10]

In the case of Germany the goals of the Marshall Plan seemed to be better met than elsewhere: the transfer of resources from the United States was designed to get production going, provide the necessary investment capital for economic recovery and familiarize the German economy at the same time with the latest technological innovations and production methods; here, then, was an aid programme that permitted the German economy to start from scratch quantitatively ('production') and qualitatively ('productivity').

In the early summer of 1947, nobody in West Germany doubted that American aid was necessary to boost industrial production. The paralysing crisis of the winter of 1946–7 had not been overcome and had ruined the previous advances in reconstruction.[11] The recovery of bizonal industry had reached its limits in this harsh winter of 1947. The poor condition of the transportation system did not even allow modest production expansion. Although the crisis turned out to be particularly severe in Germany for various reasons, it was a general European phenomenon that boded ill for the US stabilization efforts. As a consequence, the economic and food crises of the winter of 1947 constituted the principal reasons for plans to preserve Europe from sliding into economic and political chaos by coordinating and expanding existing American aid.

In the autumn of 1947, only a few months later, prospects were improving markedly throughout Western Europe. In West Germany, contemporaries observed an astonishing and continuous process of economic recovery, lasting way beyond the period under examination here.[12] The 'timing' of the 'German economic

10. Wexler, *Marshall Plan*, p.252.
11. Werner Abelshauser, *Wirtschaft in Westdeutschland 1945–1948*. In: Schriftenreihe der Vierteljahrshefte für Zeitgeschichte, 30 (Stuttgart, 1975), pp.35–42.
12. Ibid., pp.45–51.

American Aid and West German Recovery

miracle' cast new light on the significance of the Marshall Plan for economic recovery. The more newly opened sources and archival materials economic historians started to use, the more they started to question the importance of the transfer of resources from the United States – after all, American aid started to flow slowly only one year *after* the process of German recovery had begun. Historians concentrated on different influences of the Marshall Plan and stressed the relatively favourable economic starting position of the Bizone. The material effects of Marshall Plan aid are now viewed with more sophistication in the European context as well. The Marshall Plan did not extricate Western Europe in 1948 from economic collapse; nor can one rule out today that the participating ERP countries (with the exception of France and the Netherlands) might have achieved an equally high level of capital formation without Marshall aid.[13]

Contrary to this view, Knut Borchardt and Christoph Buchheim have recently tried to reassess the effect of Marshall Plan aid on 'key areas' of the West German economy.[14] Their starting points are the presumably positive effects of the December 1948 announcement of cotton imports on the supply of goods offered by the textile industry, as well as the role of ERP counterparts in the financing of investments in the electricity industry, which, between 1949 and 1951, was starved of funds. In both these areas the effects of the Marshall Plan supposedly helped the currency reform of 1948 to succeed and contributed towards securing a free-market economy. Naturally, these aspects have not been overlooked by previous Marshall Plan scholarship. An older work, for example, has noted on the advance effects of the delayed ERP raw material deliveries:

> The announcement of raw material deliveries from the ERP programme – and even more the hope for a general resumption of foreign trade – led to the incorporation of raw materials and stocks into the production process, namely stocks that had been stretched or held back completely. Even though the effect of such methods on production cannot be quantified, they certainly had a crucial impact on the consolidation of the reconstruction process.[15]

The central importance for successful reconstruction of financing

13. These are two important conclusions of Alan Milward's work, see *The Reconstruction of Western Europe 1945–1951* (London, 1984), pp.465–70, and idem, 'Was the Marshall Plan Necessary?', *Diplomatic History*, 13, 2(Spring 1989), pp.231–53; see also Abelshauser, 'Wiederaufbau vor dem Marshallplan', pp.35–42

14. See their contribution in this volume, pp.410–51

15. Abelshauser, *Wirtschaft in Westdeutschland*, p.169.

Werner Abelshauser

the investments of the production goods industry, which had been handicapped by Erhard's economic reform programme, had been similarly emphasized in earlier works.[16]

The case studies by Borchardt and Buchheim are based on the conviction that the structural problems of the West German post-war economy must be examined in a specific perspective that cannot be provided by a macroeconomic approach. By pleading for a sectoral or 'bottleneck' approach they are in fact pursuing a method that some researchers have already favoured,[17] and which indeed remains promising. To be sure, a true microeconomic approach that examined the impact of the Marshall Plan not merely on the sectoral but the firm level would be promising and useful.

But why, when there is such a high degree of agreement in terms of methods and individual results, is there such disparity in the overall assessment of the economic effects of the Marshall Plan in Germany? One reason is that Borchardt and Buchheim concentrate their attention on the period after the 1948 currency reform, and on the significance of the ERP for the success of the currency reform and for securing the conditions for Erhard's liberal reforms. But the question I have sought to raise is not whether the Marshall Plan was significant looking from the vantage point of later prosperity, but whether the aid programme was significant for the take-off of recovery or might alternative resources have been tapped instead. This question is not intended to deny, but to qualify, the importance of the Marshall Plan for West German reconstruction.

Some disagreement remains on specific questions, for example over the issue of whether the so-called internal Marshall Plan should be seen as an addition to Marshall Plan aid. The apparently miraculous increase of biblical proportions in funds – which has since formed one of the permanent myths shrouding the US aid programme in Germany – depends upon adding the resources from both sources (i.e. American dollar credits and German counterpart

---

16. See, for example, Hans Adamsen, *Investitionshilfe für die Ruhr: Wiederaufbau, Verbände und Soziale Marktwirtschaft 1948–1952*. In: Düsseldorfer Schriften zur Neueren Landesgeschichte und zur Geschichte Nordrhein-Westfalen, 4(Wuppertal, 1981), esp. chapters 2 and 3; Werner Abelshauser, *Der Ruhrkohlenbergbau seit 1945: Wiederaufbau, Krise, Anpassung* (Munich, 1984), esp. chapter 2; see also Manfred Pohl, *Wiederaufbau, Kunst und Technik der Finanzierung 1947–1953. Die ersten Jahre der Kreditanstalt für Wiederaufbau* (Frankfurt am Main, 1973).

17. See, for example, Mathias Manz, *Stagnation und Aufschwung in der französischen Besatzungszone, 1945–1948*. In: Beiträge zur südwestdeutschen Wirtschafts- und Sozialgeschichte, 2(Ostfildern, 1985); Abelshauser, *Wirtschaft in Westdeutschland*; idem, *Ruhrkohlenbergbau*; Adamsen, *Investitionshilfe*; there is, however, no 'naive' form of a 'macroeconomic approach' in the literature.

American Aid and West German Recovery

funds) under the rubric of the Marshall Plan. Naturally, it can be argued that the deliveries of goods from the ERP released funds for investment that otherwise, by dint of greater exports to the dollar area, would have had to finance vital imports. But the net aid still remains the original credits, not the sum of credits and the German funds thus liberated for other purposes.

The following essay attempts to place the discussion about the effects of the Marshall Plan on the West German economy on a broader base. The first task is to look more closely at the industrial economy on the eve of the Marshall Plan and the steps that led to recovery. It is not sufficient to know that Marshall Plan aid influenced economic reconstruction and stimulated growth; one has to understand how this process took place. The second task, based on the records of the German and American Marshall Plan administration, will be to show the *via dolorosa* of the early phase of the Recovery Program. As part of this examination we must discuss the connection that Americans and Germans saw between the ERP and DM counterpart funds. Finally we shall examine the continuing effects of the Marshall Plan with a view to showing that the reconstruction of the economy was more significant than the goods deliveries themselves, which until now have remained the central point of interest.

Germany Before the Marshall Plan

US Economic Policy in Germany: Goals and Limits

Written in the aftermath of the dispute over the Morgenthau Plan, Military Government Directive JCS 1067 had a restrictive tenor. It flatly forbade the Military Governor to take measures promoting the economic recuperation of Germany or which had as their purpose strengthening the economy. But from the very beginning, the staff of the US government, impressed by the ruin and suffering on all sides, disliked the directive. Military Governor Lucius D. Clay demanded changes in it as early as May 1945 so that 'an affirmative program with respect to Germany should be developed as promptly as possible'.[18] The War Department and the Department of State agreed but felt it inopportune after the Morgenthau débâcle to resume public discussion of Germany's postwar economic treatment. The War Department let it be known that JCS

18. Robert R. Bowie, 'Memorandum for General Clay, Subj.: Report of Field Survey of Regional Government in Bavaria', 5 June 1945, WW II RC 10–3/I.

Werner Abelshauser

1067 gave Clay enough latitude to pursue his own policy. From the very beginning there was an 'affirmative' US policy towards Germany in practice, although the restrictive directives were not lifted until July 1947. In the meantime, the stipulations of the Potsdam Treaty replaced them.

Although French resistance undermined the most important provisions of the Potsdam Agreement – economic unity, central administration, planning of foreign trade – the US Military Government tried to act as if the agreement were reality, or at least might become reality. At first this constructive view of German revival was confined to Clay and his associates, most of them prominent businessmen in civilian life. But soon there were compelling material reasons to raise occupation costs within the American Zone itself. Later it became increasingly difficult for the War Department to secure Congressional appropriations because the Army only half-heartedly supported them. Although mainly pragmatic reasons were behind the encouragement of industrial reconstruction in the US Zone, the idea corresponded to the notion which took hold in Washington during 1947 concerning the role of Germany in the economic reconstruction of Europe.

At the end of 1946, the economic recovery under way ground to a halt. In December, industrial production in the US Zone fell for the first time since the beginning of the occupation. While seasonal factors were partly to blame, it soon became clear that the recovery was running into resistance (see table 8.1). Even though production had recovered to the levels of the previous year by the summer of 1947, the economy remained weak. The transportation system was unreliable, and the food situation worsened to the point that in the Ruhr demonstrations, disorder and strikes broke out threatening recent increases in coal output. A major American initiative seemed to be required to prevent certain deterioration of the economy in the future. The US Military Government therefore decided on its own to resume its policy of promoting industrial recovery.

The political context of the German problem had changed in the meantime. Before the summer of 1947, Washington subordinated policy towards Germany to its policy *vis-à-vis* the USSR and viewed France as the bridgehead of US stabilization policy. This prevented the Military Government from withholding the shipment of reparations goods in order to help German recovery, or from taking other independent initiatives to reduce German suffering.

American Aid and West German Recovery

Table 8.1 Industrial production in the German occupation zones, 1945–9[a] (1936=100)

Year/Quarter	American Zone	British Zone	French Zone	Russian Zone
1945				
III	12	15		
IV	19	22		22
1946	41	34	36	44
I	31	30	32	39
II	37	33	36	40
III	46	37	38	47
IV	50	37	38	50
1947	44[b]		45	54
I	34		39	41
II	44		46	48
III	46		48	
IV	50		48	
1948	63		58	60
I	54		50	
II	57		54	
III	65		61	
IV	79		67	
1949	86		78	68

(a) 1945–second quarter 1948, estimated figures.
(b) Joint British–American Occupation Area.
Sources: Abelshauser, *Wirtschaft in Westdeutschland*, pp.36, 39–40, 43, 57; Manz, *Stagnation und Aufschwung in der französischen Besatzungszone*, pp.25, 32–6; *Statistisches Jahrbuch für die Bundesrepublik Deutschland*, 1959, p. 264.

The Balance of Resources

The Military Government had long been aware that the German economy was far stronger than the desolate impression given by its destroyed central cities. Even before the war was over, a group of economists headed by John K. Galbraith had begun to study the effects of strategic bombing on the German arms industry. They soon discovered that most attacks on factories had been nothing more than 'costly failures'.[19] Even in 1944, the high point of the Allied air offensive, no more than 6.5 per cent of all machine tools had been damaged; among them only 10 per cent were totally

19. John K. Galbraith, *A Life in Our Times: Memoirs* (Boston, 1981), p.226.

Werner Abelshauser

Table 8.2 Gross industrial fixed assets in the British–American
occupation area, 1936–48 (1936=100)

Gross fixed assets* 1936	100
Gross industrial investment 1936–45 as % of 1936	+ 75.3
Depreciation 1936–45 as % of 1936	− 37.2
Destruction by war as % of 1936	− 17.4
Gross fixed assets 1945	120.6
Gross industrial investment 1946–8 as % of 1936	+ 8.7
Depreciation 1946–8 as % of 1936	− 11.5
Restitution 1945–8 as % of 1936	− 2.4
Dismantling 1945–8 as % of 1936	− 4.4
Gross fixed assets 1948	111.1

* Calculated in 1936 prices.
Source: Abelshauser, *Wirtschaft in Westdeutschland*, pp.116–21.

unusable. Only 16 per cent of the machines in the critical ball-
bearing industry had been damaged or destroyed. In the steel
sector, only some blast furnaces and installations had been damaged, and only one rolling mill had been put out of service completely. According to the May 1945 report of an American
economic adviser, the Ruhr mines had suffered only insignificant
damage and the conveyor belts were in good enough shape for full
production to resume within a few months.[20] Gross industrial
assets had in fact increased by 20 per cent since 1936 (see table 8.2).
The decade between the end of the Depression and the beginning of
the air offensive was one of unparalleled investment activity. From
1935 to the end of 1942 this trend accelerated from year to year.
Only in 1944 did bomb damage exceed total investment. By the
end of the war accumulated industrial investment totalled about 75
per cent of the total 1936 industrial investment, while over the same
period write-offs amounted to 37 per cent of 1936 capital assets.

This relatively positive balance of industrial assets looks even
better with respect of quality. By the end of the war the ratio
between net and gross industrial capital (*Gütegrad*) was the highest
since the First World War (see table 8.3). This was the predictable
result of the investment boom of the rearmament period. For the
same reason, the age structure of industry was considerably better

20. Report by M. Abramowitz (14.5.45), NA, 740.00119 Control (Germany)/
5–2345, p.226.

American Aid and West German Recovery

Table 8.3 Relationship of net to gross of fixed assets (*Gütegrad*) in industry (Federal territory)

Year	Mining and basic industries	Investment–goods industries	Industry (total)
1924	52.8	54.1	53.8
1929	51.4	52.1	53.1
1935	48.5	47.1	49.7
1939	54.4	51.4	53.5
1945	63.7	62.8	61.3
1949	56.3	57.4	55.7
1957	59.6	68.0	62.6

Source: Rolf Krengel, *Anlagevermögen, Produktion und Beschäftigung im Gebiet der Bundesrepublik von 1925, bis 1956*, Sonderhefte des DIW, 42 (Berlin, 1958), p.79.

Table 8.4 Age-structure of gross fixed assets in industry

Age groups (years)	1935	1945	1948
0–5	9	34	16
5–10	20	21	34
10–15 \ more than 15 /	71	6 39	12 38

Source: Krengel, *Anlagevermögen*, pp.52f.

in 1945 than in the 1930s (see table 8.4). The German economy entered the postwar period with a remarkably large and modern capital stock, especially in comparison to the extremely low outputs.

Labour was also far from being in short supply. Compared to the 1930s, the population of the British Zone had increased by 11.3 per cent, and the population of the American Zone by 17.1 per cent. Only in the French Zone, which was of minor importance in this respect, had the population decreased – by 4.1 per cent. Although 7 million refugees resided in the American and British zones in 1946, it was only after a resolution of the Control Council that the French would accept even 150,000 refugees.

The population growth was distributed unevenly. In Schleswig-Holstein, an agricultural area, population had increased by 6.3 per cent, while in North Rhine–Westphalia the figure was 1.8 per cent. Labour was abundant but not always located where it was needed. But with these qualifications, there existed a considerable labour potential (see table 8.5). A qualitative minus must be added, however,

Werner Abelshauser

Table 8.5 Size of potential workforce* in the British–American
occupation area, 1936–48

Year	Total (1000)	% Growth rates in relation to preceding date	1936–48
1936	20,610		
1939	21,247	3.0	
1946	22,780	7.3	
1947	23,822	4.6	
1948	24,249	1.8	17.7

* Men in age groups 14–65; women in age groups 14–60.
Source: Abelshauser, *Wirtschaft in Westdeutschland*, p.105.

to this quantitative surplus. Rates of employment fell sharply; the
percentage of young (and strong) workers declined while the
number of older (and weaker) workers increased. The growth in
total employment between 1936 and 1939 was due to increased
entry of women into the civilian labour market while 2 per cent of
the men actually left it. But in another important respect there was
no reduction in quality: skill levels may have increased; valuable
on-the-job experience was gained during the war; occupation mobility improved; and labour training became more widespread.[21]

Brakes on Recovery

There was a negative as well as a positive side to the German
balance of resources. Occupation costs and reparations weighed
heavily on zonal industry, and there was both an open and a hidden
drain of resources.

The Brussels Interallied Reparations Agency (IARA) reserved
1,800 manufacturing installations for reparations in the Control
Council's first Level of Industry Plan. The list was soon shortened
however.[22] The revised Level of Industry Plan of August 1947
contained only half as many plants, while the Petersberg Agreement of November 1949 kept only 38 per cent of the plants on the
original list. It is impossible to determine the exact amount of
reparations or their effect of the German economy. This is especially the case with the original 'unilateral dismantling' carried

21. John Gillingham, 'The "Deproletarization" of German Society: Vocational
Training in the Third Reich', *Social History* (March 1986).
22. Werner Abelshauser, *Wirtschaftsgeschichte der Bundesrepublik*, 5th edn (Frankfurt, 1989), pp.25ff. See also essays by Hogan and Schwartz, pp.148 ff., 184ff.

American Aid and West German Recovery

out independently in each zone of occupation until June 1946, when the first Level of Industry Plan was announced by the Control Council. Reparations are equally difficult to calculate during the following IARA phase, in which all goods destined for Western recipients were tabulated in Brussels. These figures do not adequately indicate the actual loss of West German industrial capacity. German estimates of the current value of the dismantled industrial installations run from three to four times as much as those of the Allies. The IARA estimated losses due to dismantling based on replacement costs as of 1938 and arrived at a figure of 3.1 per cent for Germany; the German reparations expert Harmssen, comparing 1936 with 1949, came up with a figure of 5.3 per cent.

In addition to the dismantling of industry, restitution (the removal of illegally acquired assets) also reduced the stock of postwar German capital goods. The total value of claims filed was about RM 1 billion (1936), of which half were from the industrial sector (see table 8.2). West German industrial capacity also fell because investment in the years from 1946 to 1948 did not offset losses due to inadequate write-offs. This reduced capital assets a further estimated 2.8 per cent by 1948. Even so, capital assets in 1948 remained about 11 per cent above 1936 levels, and both age structure and asset quality were better than in 1936, although after 1945 these trends turned downward (see tables 8.3 and 8.4).

While the effect of dismantling on production was largely psychological in character, 'hidden reparations' placed real limits on West German recovery. This was true for interzonal trade and especially for foreign trade. One cannot speak in the usual sense of 'foreign trade' until 1948. Imports and exports, which were under Allied control for the first three postwar years, were conducted only at government level. Neither JEIA (Joint Export–Import Agency) nor OFICOMEX (Office du Commerce Extérieur de la Zone Française d'Occupation) based their policies on the interests of Germany. The Control Council directive of 20 September 1945 governed West German trade with third countries. It required payments to be made in dollars and at world market prices. This made it impossible for Germany to trade bilaterally with her neighbours, which lacked dollars. Trade was limited to two kinds of deliveries – grain imports from the GARIOA aid programme to prevent 'disease and unrest', and reparations in the form of forced exports of raw materials.

Food imports reached levels nominally comparable to those before the war. It is impossible to approximate either food imports by the occupation authorities, or German exports prior to

–379–

Werner Abelshauser

mid-1946. In 1947, however, $659 million of foodstuffs were imported, compared with $718 in 1936. But the 1947 imports consisted almost entirely of low-quality grain, whereas previously fats and meats had been imported. The grain imports had minimum requirements which otherwise could not have been met because of Allied foreign trade controls. These remained unchanged throughout 1948. Industrial imports were insignificant until mid-1948; they totalled 8 per cent of overall imports during that year, or 4.4 per cent of 1936 industrial imports.

This did not impede the resumption of production in the Western zones. It was at a low level and directed towards goods such as coal, gas and electric current, which did not depend on raw materials. Although an export economy such as the German one could hardly thrive under these circumstances, foreign exchange earnings from exports provided more than enough to cover authorized industrial imports. Until 1948, the French Zone enjoyed an absolute export surplus. The French occupation element dictated the export of coal, lumber, electric current and scrap, even though far larger export earnings could have been made by finishing these products rather than shipping them out as raw materials. The German export structure was thus turned topsy-turvy. Before the war, raw materials comprised only 10 per cent of total exports, while manufactured goods accounted for 77 per cent. In 1947, however, 64 per cent of exports consisted of raw materials, and only 11 per cent were manufactured products. The suspicion that these 'exports' were little more than a form of hidden reparations is confirmed when the prices are considered. The Allies set $10.50 as the benchmark for a ton of coal, most of which they in fact bought for themselves – at a time when the coal price on the world market was $25 to $30. Hence, up till late 1947, the Western zones lost $200 million in export earnings, according to the bizonal Verwaltung für Wirtschaft. Losses were equally great in lumber products, which were exported at a third of world market prices. Between April 1945 and mid-1947, some 3 million tons of scrap was seized as war booty and as reparations; it was sold commercially at a third of the value of world market prices. The exports of electrical current resulted in further losses of $50 million from 1946 to 1948.

'Invisible exports' – that is payments to support the occupation authorities – had similar effects to those in the field of 'foreign trade'. In the fiscal year 1946/7, RM 5.5 billion were raised in the three Western zones (excluding Berlin), partly in direct payments, partly in goods taken out of production. By this means the occupation authorities laid claim to a sixth of the West German social

American Aid and West German Recovery

product, and this came in addition to reparations. The occupation costs were spread unevenly. During the fiscal year 1946/7, expenditures by the occupation authorities in the French Zone were 28 per cent (which surpassed even the 26.1 per cent spent by the Soviets), while they amounted to 15.9 per cent in the American Zone and 12.7 per cent in the British Zone. Above all, the removals of 10 per cent out of production between 1945 and 1947 impaired the German reconstruction effort seriously.

Not only France and the Soviet Union profited in this way: they merely did it openly. The Anglo-Americans took advantage of compulsory exports, export restrictions and other types of hidden reparations (though mostly for recovery and rehabilitation of the liberated countries). For instance, compulsory German deliveries to the post-exchange system in the US Zone (and all of Western Europe), which provided American soldiers with consumer goods and food, cost another estimated $100 million annually. The seizure of German patents and production processes (FIAT project) also came at the expense of the German economy. Clay self-critically admitted that these practices were comparable to French and Russian seizures.[23] The US taxpayer, unlike the French, compensated for much of this through aid and credit. Only in 1948 did the burden of occupation become lighter. Only then did foreign trade really begin again for the first time since the war.

Before 1948, when the first Marshall Plan deliveries arrived, West German revival depended largely on its own resources and energies. Yet the country had underlying strengths, as indicated by the value of its industrial assets and the potential of its labour force. West Germany was poor but by no means underdeveloped.

Once Germany had independent control of her own resources and the foreign trade situation became favourable, rapid economic growth should have been expected. These conditions started to emerge in 1947–8, less because of the Marshall Plan but rather because of more general changes of US policy towards Europe, in which the Marshall Plan was but one element, though doubtless an important one.

1947: The Year of Decisions

After the collapse in the winter of 1946–7, the Military Government abandoned the effort to distribute hardship evenly throughout

23. Jean Edward Smith (ed.), *The Papers of General Lucius D. Clay: Germany 1945–1949*, vol.1 (Bloomington and London, 1974), pp.305ff.

Werner Abelshauser

the economy; instead it concentrated resources in the critical bottlenecks. High priority was given to restoring the transportation infrastructure, organizing a system of premiums for coalminers (*Punktsystem*), introducing a central plan for home construction, putting into effect a programme for doubling electricity output in the British Zone and getting the necessary coal supplies to the iron and steel industry so that it could provide the raw materials needed to build up the railroads and critical industrial installations. The scene of this activity after 1 January 1947 was the Combined Economic Area, or Bizone. The zonal fusion was a necessary but not a sufficient cause for the economic turnabout. To break the transportation bottleneck, German and Allied planners used every relevant organizational concept in Speer's wartime repertoire. The 'top priority' (*Schwerpunktbildung*) given to the manufacture of Reichsbahn rolling stock resulted in production targets being surpassed by the autumn of 1947. This success was timely. Although by the summer of 1947 the transportation situation had somewhat improved, by October it had again become the main focus of the recovery problem, as had been anticipated all along. But this time it could not actually block recovery. Instead, the Ruhr mines were able to reduce coal stocks by 1.2 million tons over the winter months, and the iron and steel industry cleared up their shipment backlog. The solution of the transportation problem was surely one of the most important preconditions for economic recovery.

Once the transportation problem had become less acute, other planning priorities could be met. In the winter of 1946–7, coal was in increasingly short supply; but after January 1947, production took off. Early in that year the Military Government had introduced a system of production bonuses. Ruhr miner privileges – namely supplementary rations of bacon, coffee, cigarettes, sugar and *schnapps* – came initially at the expense of the average German consumer. Although these bonuses had little effect on subsurface productivity, they did reduce absenteeism and made mining sufficiently attractive to end labour shortages.[24]

But the food problem, with the exception of miners, became all the more important. Shortages in early 1947 in the Rhine–Ruhr area threatened to wreck the priority programme and seemed an omen of the catastrophe impending in the next winter, unless either production or imports could be stepped up. Neither actually ever happened. The much-feared food crisis none the less never materi-

24. Abelshauser, *Ruhrkohlenbergbau*, pp.36–43.

American Aid and West German Recovery

alized. The worst was prevented, thanks to tighter supervision of food supplies from the countryside and a reorganization of the food distribution bureaucracies. This made it possible to increase the rations of key personnel.

Three improvements had been made. The material requirements for recovery were slight. What was necessary was to concentrate resources on priority programmes, even at the expense of consumer-oriented branches of production. The October 1947 breakthrough to steadily rising rates of production was achieved without outside help. The Military Government had none the less laid the basis for this development by concentrating bizonal resources on reconstruction.

The American, the European and the German Marshall Plan

At approximately the same time as the American Army introduced the new DM currency in the Western zones and Ludwig Erhard's economic reforms were taking their course, the work of the Marshall Plan administration (ECA) in Frankfurt began to make itself felt. From the outset, General Clay viewed it with suspicion; he was concerned that it would develop into a second centre of power independent of OMGUS – threatening to become another branch of American government in West Germany. In order both to dispel these anxieties and to win the support of OMGUS, Paul G. Hoffman, the ECA administrator, and Averell Harriman, the special American ERP ambassador in Paris, offered Clay their services as 'investment bankers for recovery'.[25] Hoffman emphasized that the economic recovery of West Germany was a basic prerequisite for European reconstruction. He appealed to Clay's commitment to the economic reconstruction of Europe, requested his support in this work and promised that the ECA Mission would do everything possible to achieve the aims of the US military governor. Right in time for the large-scale monetary and political reorganization of the West German economy, the material resources, which were to safeguard this new beginning, appeared to be flowing into the country.

Only a few days later, however, disillusionment set in. In a long telegram to the Secretary of War, Kenneth Royall and his deputy

25. Hoffman to Clay, 23 June 1948, NA, Record Group [RG] 286, ECA, Germany, box 4.

Werner Abelshauser

Tracy Voorhees, Clay's deputy, General Draper, rang the alarm bells in Washington. It had quickly become apparent in Frankfurt that the planned procedure for ECA imports could not be carried out. In the view of the Bizonal Control Office (BICO), which was shared by Special Ambassador Harriman on an information visit to Frankfurt, the bureaucratic obstacles (if they could be negotiated at all) would delay the aid programme for such a long time as to make it 'relatively ineffective' in the end.[26] BICO had assumed, explained Draper, that the American ERP legislation wanted to promote private trade and private entrepreneurs. They had discovered, however, that the inefficient and bureaucratic regime of the Joint Export–Import Agency (JEIA) had become inflexible; a system of state export trade was being imposed on the bizonal authorities which, in the meantime, they had already started to dismantle successfully. Draper urgently requested that a man of the authority of the deputy ECA administrator, Howard Bruce, be sent to Frankfurt in order to initiate a radical renewal of procedures. He was convinced that 'controlling the mass of paper' was not enough to achieve 'true economic recovery'.

Draper's cry for help was dramatic enough to trigger strong reactions in Washington, and soon enough, in Paris and Frankfurt as well. From 2 to 12 August a series of conferences took place in Frankfurt attended by Voorhees and his staff from Washington as well as William C. Foster from Paris, the deputy chief of the ECA Mission in Europe. Clay, JEIA and BICO were consulted from time to time.[27] The 'Frankfurt Agreement', drawn up between Voorhees and Foster and without Clay's participation, called for a compromise between the interests of the Military Government and the Marshall Plan administration. While ECA funds were to be administered exclusively by the ECA representatives in Paris rather than by OMGUS, the respective procurement authorizations were no longer to be handled out of Washington but in Europe. But Clay was not prepared to agree with this outcome. He insisted on the competence of OMGUS, but under pressure from the War Department he was forced to withdraw his objections. The ECA in Washington, however, failed to cable its agreement, since Hoffman insisted on Washington retaining the power for issuing procure-

26. Confidential and personal (copy), Draper to Royall and Vorhees [*sic*], Frankfurt, 1 July 1948, NA, RG 286, Germany, box 4.
27. Notes on the Army–ECA Mission to the Bizone, 2 to 12 August 1948, E. T. Dickinson (ECA Director, Program Coordination Division), NA, RG 286, Countries – Germany, May–August 1948, Asst Administrator for Programs, Subject files, box 19.

American Aid and West German Recovery

ment authorizations. Consequently Voorhees had to admit that the negotiations had failed, and cancelled his planned visits to Vienna and London. He returned to Washington on 11 August to fight for the Frankfurt Agreement on the higher levels of decision making.

In fact, the non-stop negotiations only pinned down the extent of the crisis and pointed out some of its causes. Voorhees was deeply upset when he found out that to date not a single ECA delivery had arrived in Germany – not counting the ongoing emergency food aid from the US Army (GARIOA) and batches of baling twine. In spite of the fact that procurement authorizations amounting to about $90 million had been issued in Washington, not even one delivery contract had been concluded. The experts in JEIA, BICO and in ECA reluctantly admitting it agreed that the bureaucratic mess ('red tape, bureaucratic etc. requirements') of the Marshall Plan administration had to be blamed. ECA Washington could defend itself only by noting the narrow basis of decision making given to it by the Bizone for making the programme work.[28] JEIA also had to put up with being accused of a lack of initiative and a hesitancy to take on responsibility. The Allied export office, for example, had been sitting on cable authorizations from Washington because the actual 'green sheets' had not physically arrived. In this case, at least, it was possible to correct the situation 'on the spot'. General Clay was convinced that JEIA would be able to fulfil the ECA requirements and continue its working procedures only if its present staff of 150 was increased by several hundred.

The disagreements in Frankfurt and the Washington 'epilogue' in fact reveal the deeper disagreements between ECA and OMGUS concerning the order of priorities which the reconstruction of West Germany was to occupy within the framework of the Organization of European Economic Cooperation (OEEC). The American Military Government expected the ERP above all to deliver imports which would speed up the industrial reconstruction of West Germany ('recovery items'). It therefore put up a fight against the import of food and 'luxury goods' like citrus fruit and vegetables from Italy, or tobacco from Turkey ('relief items'). Clay argued that such imports might be good for Europe, 'but for Germany it was only a luxury and only a temporary shot in the arm'.[29] The mere fact that no goods had yet been imported which were

28. This was also clearly expressed as such in a letter from Hoffman to Royall, 10 September 1948, NA, RG 286, Countries – Germany, Asst Administrator for Programs, Subject files, box 19.

29. Notes on the Army–ECA Mission (see n.27); this is the verbatim record of Clay's statements.

Werner Abelshauser

critically important to the reconstruction effort and that only $20 million had been allocated for a first, urgently required 'long-range recovery program' comprising railway freight carriages, mining equipment, raw materials, etc. valued at $134 million, gave him reason to doubt whether ECA was a 'good buy' for West Germany. Moreover, Clay noted that the 5 per cent of strategic materials demanded out of West German ERP counterparts by Article V of the Economic Cooperation Agreement, was 'a high rate of interest'.

Even though the ECA recognized the central importance of West German reconstruction for the stabilization of Western Europe, it argued that this obliged the Bizone first and foremost to contribute to the economic recovery of Europe. As a consequence, Paul Hoffman rejected not only Royall's demand to increase the bizonal programmes in the first ERP year by $200 million – from the original $437 million to $637 million;[30] he also complained about the 'almost defiant attitude' of the bizonal representatives in the OEEC negotiations as well as Clay's refusal to cooperate in working out trade agreements with other European countries 'where the Bizone might have to give way a bit but where the benefits to Western Europe would be considerable'.[31] Only with considerable effort did Royall manage to prevent a planned reduction in ERP allocations to the Western zones to $364 million ('We intend to instruct General Clay . . . to make it clear that such an allocation could not be voluntarily accepted'), and to maintain the volume of the programme at a level of at least $414 million.[32]

The scope for reconstruction-related Marshall Plan aid for West Germany within the OEEC framework was rather limited. The British government in particular was insisting that the same distribution criteria be applied to all the participant countries.[33] However, the reference was not to the respective capital requirements for reconstruction but to the balance of payments deficit with the dollar area.[34] The attempt of the United States to get a special

30. This can be found in a letter dated end of August 1948, NA, RG 286, Countries – Germany, Asst Administrator for Programs, Subject files, box 19.

31. Hoffman to Secretary of the Army, undated draft (10 September 1948), see n.28.

32. See n.30.

33. Memorandum 'Bizonal share of ERP aid', British Embassy (Washington), 27 August 1948, NA, RG 286, Countries – Germany, May–August 1948, Asst Administrator for Programs, Subject files 1948–50, box 19.

34. From the German point of view, this was the decisive mistake ('*Konstruktionsfehler*') of the Marshall Plan, as *Ministerialdirigent* Dr G. Keiser, the ERP expert of the Verwaltung für Wirtschaft, repeatedly noted in no uncertain terms; see, for

American Aid and West German Recovery

ruling within the OEEC for the Bizone was turned down by Great Britain:

> It is not clear to His Majesty's Government whether the United States Authorities hold other views, or whether they feel that the Bizone's claim ought to be judged according to principles and standards other than those applied to the rest of the participating countries. In either case, His Majesty's Government should be bound to disagree, and could not, consistent with their convictions and their responsibilities in the OEEC, join with the United States in asking for a larger share of aid for the Bizone.[35]

In the view of the British, an American intervention in favour of the Bizone threatened to revive earlier fears about preferential treatment for German reconstruction; it would, above all, provide fuel for the Communist propaganda machine in France.

The Paris negotiations led to the conclusion on 11 October 1948 of the first Inter-European Payments Agreement. In keeping with the spirit of the leading group of countries within the OEEC, the Bizone unexpectedly found itself in the position of a 'net creditor country' *vis-à-vis* her European neighbours such as France, Austria and the Netherlands. This agreement (the 'small' or 'European' Marshall Plan) obliged potential surplus countries like Great Britain, Belgium and the Bizone(!) to grant economic aid to presumed deficit countries in order to fuel intra-European trade. Part of the economic aid from the 'big' (American) Marshall Plan, then, was given to the ERP countries as 'conditional aid' in the form of domestic resources.[36] Even though the donor of such drawing rights received the exchange value of the dollar aid, the net effect of the American foreign aid was reduced by the amount of the drawing rights in the national currency of the respective countries which had to be granted to the 'net debtor countries'. In the case of the Bizone, this unremunerated outflow of goods and services – in fact, a form of West German economic aid for Europe – amounted to $48.3 million during the first Marshall Plan year, way above the $9.4 million originally envisaged.[37]

---

example, 'Korreferat über das "Long-term Program und die amerikanische Politik"', 1/2 September 1949, BA, B 146/171.

35. British Embassy (Washington), see n.33.

36. Werner Abelshauser, 'Der Kleine Marshallplan: Handelsintegration durch innereuropäische Wirtschaftshilfe 1948–1950', in Helmut Berding (ed.), *Wirtschaftliche und politische Integration in Europa im 19. und 20. Jahrhundert (Geschichte und Gesellschaft,* Sonderheft 10) (Göttingen, 1984), pp.212–24.

37. The Bizone was supposed to give a net amount of $10.2 million (in DM

Werner Abelshauser

In the second year of the Marshall Plan, West German economic aid to Europe remained below the planned amount of $163.9 million and amounted to 'only' $49.9 million. At the same time, however, Washington decided to reduce ERP dollar aid. Baron Snoy, the President of the OEEC Council, and Robert Marjolin, its General Secretary, worked out a key whereby the West German reduction of 32 per cent lay markedly above the average reduction of 20 per cent. This meant that West Germany had to stomach the highest losses in total foreign aid among all participant countries, namely 42 per cent.[38] In addition, there was also the West German economic aid to Berlin (the 'German Marshall Plan'), which exceeded the entire ERP aid (excluding GARIOA) with its DM 1.5 billion in the second year of the Marshall Plan. For the 'unbiased observer' – as the German Marshall Plan office in Frankfurt viewed itself – the result was a 'grotesque picture': 'the Bizone, with the most serious war damage, with these cuts and drawing rights was cheated out of almost the entire ERP quota, while England and France received very high quotas, even though both these countries had been enjoying once again a flourishing economy and had suffered relatively little war damage'.[39] If the ongoing food imports from the GARIOA programme of the US Army are taken into account, the net position changes. We are still left with the overall picture of a foreign aid programme more geared towards Western European rather than West German economic reconstruction.

During those turbulent August days in Frankfurt, and even more so in the subsequent round of Washington negotiations, the Department of the Army was able to achieve short-term improvements in the organizational sphere; it did not succeed, however, in asserting itself against the ECA in the crucial questions. When John McCloy was preparing to take over both as High Commissioner for Germany and as head of the ECA Mission in Frankfurt, the daily operations of the Economic Cooperation Administration were even 'more chaotic' than before.[40] Yet the balance of power

counterparts), while the French Zone was to receive $0.8 million (in European currency). For the extent of the German economic aid for European 'deficit countries', see Abelshauser, 'Der Kleine Marshallplan', tables 3 and 4.

38. According to the original planning, which was not revised until December 1949, the overall reduction was supposed to have amounted to 63 per cent, see Länderrat des Vereinigten Wirtschaftsgebietes [VWG], M 1–1, Nr. 29/49, Die Aufteilung der Dollarhilfe und der innereuropäischen Hilfe für das Jahr 1949/50, 5 September 1949, BA, Z 14/41.

39. Dr Herbert Martini to Dr von Mangoldt (Bizonal ECA delegation Paris), 12 August 1949, BA, Z 14/46.

40. This was the assessment in a secret memorandum by Henry S. Reuss after an

American Aid and West German Recovery

within the American occupation authorities in Germany had shifted so much in favour of the ECA that Paul Hoffman was able to recommend to McCloy in an informal directive 'that the ECA should deal with the German Government at arm's length, that it should rely upon the ultimate economic sanction, not upon the political sanction available to an occupying power, and that the ECA mission should not participate so directly in forming the policy of the German Government that it becomes identified with the policy of that government'.[41]

The Marshall Plan was more than just the occupation statute; it had developed into the practical foundation upon which American policy in the Federal Republic of Germany was building. It linked West German reconstruction tightly with the general goal of Western European economic revival. It allowed the Federal Republic early on to export to the rest of the ERP countries – goods that otherwise could have been imported only from the dollar area. Although this meant that ECA transferred the hardest tasks in European reconstruction to West Germany, it did not allow the FRG any special privileges in the distribution of relief goods. The Western zones of Germany thus were the stepchildren of the Marshall Plan. While France received a total per capita aid of $21.7 in the second year of the Marshall Plan, Austria $36.2 dollars and the Netherlands $45, the West Germans received only $12 in per capita aid, including GARIOA aid.[42] Given these facts, it is even more significant that the core of German industry had not been left in a shambles at the end of the war. It offered good prospects in 1947–8 of becoming economically successful in the postwar era. As a consequence one has to direct one's attention away from the transfer of material towards different effects of the ERP.

Light and Shadow of ERP Practices

The failure of 'non-food ERP deliveries' to materialize had to be noticed sooner or later on the German side. On the occasion of his visit to Germany in August 1948, the Deputy Minister of War, Tracy Voorhees, informed the bizonal *Oberdirektor* Hermann

inspection trip, 27–8 September 1949, NA, RG 286, Germany, box 4.

41. Confidential letter, Paul Hoffman to John McCloy, 13 July 1949, NA, RG 286, Germany-Administrator, box 4. See also essay by Schwartz, pp.178ff.

42. Dr G. Keiser, Konstruktionsmängel des Marshallplans, table 1, BA, B 146/171.

Werner Abelshauser

Pünder about his efforts to simplify the import procedures.[43] He nevertheless was unable to promise any far-reaching changes as far as the composition of the relief goods was concerned. Consequently those hopes were dashed that saw in the Marshall Plan first and foremost an aid programme *additional to* the GARIOA programme (imports of Category A), different in form from those food deliveries by the US Army earmarked as 'preventing disease and unrest'. As late as February 1948, Ludwig Erhard still operated under the assumption that he could practically finance his entire investment programme for the Bizone out of the Marshall Plan, which would have allowed the German national income to go towards consumer products.[44] A depression of sorts replaced these euphoric expectations. During one of the inter-party discussions of the Economic Council concerning the Marshall Plan in September, Hermann Pünder only managed to paint 'a positive side to the unsatisfactory state of the actual aid deliveries' by acknowledging 'the foreign policy aspects of the Marshall Plan, which are frequently overlooked'. At the same time, however, he advised that 'these positive signs [be noted] with great caution since on the whole the outlook was also very uninspiring in Paris'.[45]

By the end of the year very little indeed had changed. Of the total goods delivered until then, valued at \$99 million, only \$22 million had been allotted to non-food products – two-thirds of which went towards cotton. This meant that only 27 per cent of the promised aid of \$367 million had actually arrived in the Bizone. Moreover, both the meagre amount of actual deliveries and their actual composition were increasingly subjected to public criticism. At the end of October, Erich Welter, the future editor of the *Frankfurter Allgemeine Zeitung* and a man with a generally positive view of the Marshall Plan, pointed out before the Wirtschaftspolitische Gesellschaft of 1947 that 'the amounts lost by the scandalous JEIA procedures [were] considerably larger than the amounts received by the ERP'.[46] There was also widespread criticism of an alleged American inclination 'to utilize the Marshall Plan as a tool to get rid of domestic overproduction, in spite of the fact that these surplus goods were not very high on the list of urgent European

43. Speech draft by *Oberdirektor* Dr Pünder before the ERP Committee, 7 September 1948, BA, Z 14/8.
44. BA, Z 32/10, fo. 83.
45. Confidential note on the inter-party ERP discussions, 7 September 1948, BA, Z 14/8.
46. 'Probleme um den Marshall-Plan', *Handelsblatt*, no. 61, 22 October 1948, p.2.

American Aid and West German Recovery

requirements'.[47] In a more extended and more balanced 1948 end-of-the-year summary, the *Handelsblatt* referred to 'the impressive fact that West Germany had recovered so well without much help from the Marshall Plan'; the danger was pointed out 'that the strengths and capacities which are ready for a real financial and productive recovery might be sacrificed to the forces of decay in Western Europe'.[48]

In contrast to the German public at large, which linked the Marshall Plan with the notions of free dollar grants, transfers of American technology and machinery, vehicles and plant, the economic experts held more realistic views about the ERP. As late as March 1949, the German Marshall Plan administration found it difficult to name typical 'Marshall Plan goods'. The Adviser for the Marshall Plan answered an enquiry in a radio interview about textiles, noting that they could not be considered a 'typical' ERP product. Textiles were largely produced from cotton that did not come through the ECA channels.[49] Except for black-market products, even the fashionable and highly valued 'extra fine' ladies' stockings came out of German production after the autumn of 1948 – and they were not made only out of ECA cotton! The machine tool producer Böhringer Brothers in Göppingen assembled the first two cotton machines, which had been developed by engineers from Saxony. The somewhat smaller machines by Schönemann in Wiesbaden could knit three pairs of 'German nylons' every twenty-five minutes.[50] There existed no plans for importing finished textile products.

At this early stage of reconstruction, West Germany could naturally make use of everything which would help boost the still awesome production apparatus and keep it going. On the whole, there was not so much a shortage of machines and plant, but of raw material imports putting the idle production capacities to use. To finance these raw material imports from the dollar area should therefore have been the central concern of the Marshall Plan.

When the first raw material imports worth mentioning finally reached the country in the first quarter of 1949, the importers did not exactly rush to get the ECA goods. On the contrary, importers under the Marshall Plan could be found only with great difficulty.

47. 'Schiffbruch-Gefahr des Marshallplans', *Handelsblatt*, no. 80, 31 December 1948, p.10.
48. Ibid.
49. 3 March 1949, BA, Z 14/85.
50. 'Cottonmaschinen in Westdeutschland', *Handelsblatt*, no. 25, 1 April 1949.

Werner Abelshauser

The payments for ECA allocations – given the exchange rate of 30 cents to the DM – were usually above world market prices. Whereas food imports were subsidized with budgetary funds down to domestic price levels, the exchange rate fully made its mark on prices for industrial imports. On top of that, the initial deliveries of ECA goods happened to arrive during a period of slackening in West German domestic markets. At the end of 1948 the rate of growth fell to half of that of the previous period, prices fell and unemployment jumped dramatically. It was also the case that delays in the issuing of purchasing authorizations hindered the smooth transfer of Marshall Plan goods into German hands. Many importers had helped themselves in many instances by taking over 'commercial' JEIA imports. In the case of the French Zone, they supplied themselves from the Bizone but did not make much use of the delayed ERP deliveries. Similar problems cropped up when orders from the Marshall Plan administration were centrally placed, often ignoring the requirements of the potential buyers – contrary to the advice of the German experts. Urgently as mining equipment was needed in 1949, under such conditions it could not be used 'on the spot' in a number of cases.[51]

In the spring of 1949 reports were piling up about unused ERP allocations and about difficulties in persuading importers to accept Marshall Plan goods.[52] On 11 March, the minister-president of the French Zone reported to General Koenig, the commander-in-chief, his 'worry and concern . . . with regard to the expiration of unused Marshall Plan credits on 31.3.1949'.[53] In his reply, the chief of the French Military Government pointed out the following facts: 60 per cent of a credit of $100 million had been released; but goods worth only 35 per cent of it had been received; 27–8 per cent of it was foodstuffs, which left 7–8 per cent for industrial products. But a commission had been sent to Washington which was applying American buying methods and was getting American agents involved (costing maybe 1–1.5 per cent more), but achieving much better results than the Bizone. There, 'with the greatest difficulty', only 25 per cent of the promised credits were used up.[54]

51. Complaints of this sort can be found in a letter from the Economics Minister of the French Zone to the chief of the ERP Department in the French Military Government, Colonel Halff, 28 May 1949, BA, Z 14/14b.
52. See, for example, the article 'Unausgenutzte Marshall-Gelder: Rund 250 Millionen Dollar unausgenutzt', *Allgemeine Zeitung* (Mainz), 31 May 1949.
53. Extract from the memorandum on the discussion in Baden-Baden, BA, Z 14/14b.
54. Ibid.

American Aid and West German Recovery

In the Bizone, worries centred increasingly around the sales rather than the procurement of allocated contingents and their utilization. On 30 June 1949 was the deadline affecting $202 million, out of which only $63 million were in serious danger of expiring without being used.[55] Hence Ludwig Erhard invited top representatives of the concerned branches of the economy, their trade associations and unions, as well as the President of the Bank Deutscher Länder (BDL) and other high officials to an emergency meeting. Erhard came out emphatically against 'measures with the characteristics of a planned economy or even the appearance of it'.[56] The approach of his Economic Administration was more pragmatic. They advised the industrial branches concerned to take the initiative and voluntarily give ECA allocations preference over so-called 'B' allocations (industrial imports financed by JEIA exports). In this way the burdens of the Marshall Plan were to be distributed more evenly among the participating importers. *Geheimrat* Vocke took up Erhard's appeal and promised that the BDL, by an added *engagement* in the credit sector, would make sure that no ERP aid would expire. But he was in no position to promise help 'in case import contacts did not materialize owing to risky prices or declining sales'.[57]

This, however, was precisely the problem in more than just a few sectors. The import of raw rubber and tyres started to slow down because of declining sales; in some cases sending products back to the US was seriously considered. The leather industry was confronted with a monthly surplus of c. 9,000 tons of leather, dropping out as a buyer for two whole months. The 'unreasonable international linkages' of the 'European' Marshall Plan were blamed; without success, advances from the bank of issue were demanded for middle- and long-term credits as the 'ignition spark'. The iron industry also pointed out a stagnation in sales. If this was the case with the present (projected figure) of an annual production of 9 million tons of raw steel, 'an allocated increase in annual production to the level of 11 million tons could not be justified'. In the case of vegetable and animal oils and fats, stocks of 85,000 tons (worth around DM 100 million) had been accumulated, which had been bought with payments 25 to 30 per cent above world market

---

55. Referat Marshallplan, Vermerk zur Frage des Ausnutzung des ECA-Hilfe (Vermeidung des teilweisen Verfalls der für das laufende ERP-Jahr genehmigten Kontingente), Frankfurt, 16 May 1949, BA, Z 14/17.
56. Ibid., p.3.
57. Ibid., p.1.

Werner Abelshauser

prices. If this 'mortgage' were to be written off, new ECA allocations could be absorbed. The textile industry alone regarded its
position 'in terms of receiving ECA allocations as relatively
favourable'.[58] As far as price and quality were concerned, the textile
industry did not spare the ERP from its criticism. Above all, the
stipulation that 22.5 per cent of the imports had to be accepted in
the form of 'low-grades' met with more and more resistance,
particularly as other ERP countries had to accept low-grade cotton
only for 13 per cent in their allocation.[59] Before the war, the
Germans had processed only very small amounts of low-grade
cotton, which meant that they did not have the suitable machines
and spindles. Producers also criticized the high prices of the ECA
goods that were centrally procured in the bulk purchasing
procedures.[60]

From the outset it was the textile industry that profited most
from the Marshall Plan. By the end of 1948 raw cotton accounted
for $16 million of the $22 million from the ECA. By March 1949
almost two-thirds of all cotton imports derived from the Marshall
Plan, compared with the almost negligible contribution before
November 1948. In addition, the announcements of newly delivered cotton in the trade press had already had an impact on the
textile industry's stocks. In November and December the spinning
mills used more of their raw material reserves than before. While
these facts are well known,[61] the Borchardt/Buchheim essay in this
volume also attributes the new buoyancy of the cotton industry to
the Marshall Plan contribution and identifies its ramifications on
prices as the key to the success of Erhard's policies.[62]

Indeed there is every reason to believe that this freeing of the
cotton market helped to prevent rationing from being reintroduced
into the textile industry (officially it had not yet been revoked). But
the Marshall Plan was not the only factor involved. The Bank
Deutscher Länder differentiated between the psychological and
objective reasons that lay behind the levelling off of cotton prices in
December 1948 (and then to their crumbling in January 1949) after
they had peaked in October and November.[63] Consumers and
suppliers evidently expected price cuts after they had been re-

58. All statements, ibid., pp.3–5.
59. Economics Minister in the French Zone (see n.51).
60. 'Baumwollversorgung unzureichend', *Handelsblatt*, no. 1, 21 January 1949,
p.2.
    61. Abelshauser, *Wirtschaft in Westdeutschland*, p.169.
    62. See the Borchardt/Buchheim essay in this volume.
    63. *Monatsberichte*, January 1949, p.12.

American Aid and West German Recovery

peatedly promised, and increased imports were announced for the spring of 1949. The Bank Deutscher Länder, however, credited the change in market behaviour more to objective factors. The end of government increases in the money supply that stemmed from the currency reform, credit restrictions on the part of the central bank, stricter tax enforcement and the temporary increase of state cash balances had notably reduced the purchasing power of some branches of industry. Warehousing had also become more expensive. In the boom phase following the currency reform, the interested outside observer was already finding it difficult to judge 'to what extent the stagnation of production was the result of real lack of raw materials and to what extent it was the result of reflections about future price increases'. In any case, so commentators publicly suggested, the textile industry was particularly ripe for this combination of factors.[64] The price reversal at the turn of the year 1948–9 caused these speculative market strategies to collapse, particularly when they coincided with the sharp increase in warehousing costs. But until we have studies at the entrepreneurial level, it will be difficult to decide what really brought about the turnaround in the textile industry.

The Inner Marshall Plan

When hopes for earmarking sizeable investment funds from the ERP for West German reconstruction became dimmer day by day, the German side began to concentrate on trying at least to use the Marshall Plan indirectly to mobilize German resources for investments. The DM counterpart funds were a starting point, namely the DM sums which importers had to raise in order to purchase ECA goods.[65] From the very beginning, however, there was considerable confusion about the goals for and the actual utilization of these DM counterpart accounts.

On 9 July 1948 the United States concluded bilateral Economic Cooperation Agreements with the French Zone and on 14 July with the Bizone. These were the legal and political frameworks for the aid programme with West Germany; they also stipulated a later reimbursement of the dollar aid in hard currency. Excepted from

---

64. 'Zwischenbilanz nach der Währungsreform', *Handelsblatt*, no. 36, 27 July 1948, p.1.
65. Such 'counterpart funds' were also raised in DM currency in connection with the sale of GARIOA and StEG goods.

Werner Abelshauser

this provision were only those counterpart funds which were to be put at the disposal of the United States for financing programmes 'which were not of direct use to the German economy'. The obligatory conversion of DM counterparts into US dollars had to come out of export earnings and 'at the earliest possible date that is compatible with the restitution of the health and tranquillity of the German economy' (Article I/3 of the respective agreements).[66] At the same time, Article 4 of both agreements stipulated that special accounts be established for the German counterparts to be used at the exclusive discretion of the US. According to Article 115(b) 6 of the US Foreign Assistance Act of 1948, such assistance was to be used only in the case of aid deliveries 'to a participating country on the basis of non-repayable allocations'.[67] As a logical consequence, the agreements with the other participating countries stipulated (if they had any special provisions) that part of the dollar aid extended as 'grants' rather than 'loans' be deposited into such special counterpart accounts. In such cases the United States donated the exchange value of the aid to the receivers. They reserved the moral (and contractual) claim, however, decisively to influence the allocation of the counterpart funds in the respective national currencies. The US thereby retained the power to influence the national economies of the recipient countries. The underlying intention was to combat inflationary tendencies in Europe by means of controlling the counterparts and to make sure, gently but firmly, that the participating countries did not neglect the reconstruction of their industries.

In the German case the right of disposal over counterpart funds diverged from the usual system. Avoiding the terms 'grant' and 'loan', the contract contained 'claims against Germany', which Paul Hoffman unmistakably interpreted as 'forward sales charged against the German economy'.[68] According to the customary ECA business practices, in the case of repayable allocations the counterparts were planned to go into the budgets of the recipient countries and be freely disposable without any further reference to the ERP. In fact, however, the United States demanded two things from the Germans for their aid: on the one hand they had to repay the aid in dollars – financed out of export earnings, and on the other hand Washington reserved for itself far-reaching powers in the allocation

66. For a printed version of the ECA Agreement see *Deutschland und das Europäische Wiederaufbauprogramm* (n.3).

67. Ibid., p.56.

68. '*Termingeschäfte zu Lasten der deutschen Wirtschaft*', see speech draft by *Oberdirektor* Pünder (n.43). See also the Schwabe essay, pp.248ff.

American Aid and West German Recovery

of the counterpart funds. The contract stipulated that once the Military Government's expenses had been deducted and after the funnelling of aid to Berlin, the counterparts had to be used for the purchase of raw materials by the US government and the ECA administration and for financing German investments. Hence, in return for allocating the funds the ECA kept all powers and control rights in its hands. In spite of the contradictions with the customary ECA practices, German politicians still clung to the hope 'that the United States in practice did not intend to abide literally by the rules of [the repayment conditions]'.[69]

Such hopes were further strengthened through hints dropped by American officials indicating that the term 'claims against Germany' was actually a means 'for preventing other countries from realizing claims against Germany in future peace treaties, while the US had accepted the fact that future repayment could not be expected'.[70] The ECA had indeed concluded in a study that West Germany would not be able to repay its Marshall Plan debts in the near future.[71] On the occasion of the renewal of the bilateral ECA agreement after the foundation of the Federal Republic of Germany, however, the US was not prepared to give legal confirmation of this interpretation in a secret note (*Begleitnote*). Neither would the US even exclude the sums withdrawn from the German counterpart funds for American occupation expenses from its 'claims against Germany'.[72] Hence the DM accounts had the principal task of accumulating the German currency needed for the time of repayment and their transfer into US dollars.

Within the OEEC the utilization of counterpart funds was handled

69. Ibid.

70. Confidential memorandum, Dr K. Albrecht (betrifft Bilateraler Vertrag, Besprechung mit Prof. Bode, ECA), 19 October 1949, BA, Z 14/173.

71. Staff Doc. no. 271, National Advisory Council, 'Western Germany's Capacity to Repay ERP Assistance', 26 August 1948, NA, RG 286, Germany no. 1, box 19.

72. Dr K. Albrecht, Bemerkungen zu dem amerikanischen Vorschlag für den bilateralen Vorschlag, Frankfurt, 3 November 1949, BA, Z 14/173. At the 1951 London debt conference the US insisted that $1.2 billion of the total $3.2 billion be repaid. $1.620 billion of this were GARIOA aid which the Germans had only conditionally ('dem Grunde nach') recognized. In German civil law such a qualification did not only apply to the amount of the claim but also explicitly allowed for 'a certain degree of objections, if a legal basis did not exist for obligations to repay'. Compared with the resulting German negotiating position, which recognized only part of GARIOA aid as 'economic aid' forwarded *after* the inception of the Marshall Plan, a relatively huge amount of American credits had to be repaid – certainly more than the one-third officially announced. See Der Bundesminister für den Marshall Plan, Memorandum über Nachkriegs-Auslandschulden, vertraulich, nur zur Unterrichtung der deutschen Delegation, 20 September 1951, BA, B 146/234.

Werner Abelshauser

in a number of ways. Two basic approaches can be distinguished. Countries with their own autonomous credit policy and/or functioning capital markets did not depend on the release of counterpart funds. Such countries either never touched the counterpart releases, or used the funds for repaying floating domestic national debts. The second group of countries requested the release of counterparts because they either had an inadequate capital market, or their own banking system did not have sufficient room to manoeuvre with credit or did not wish to use it. The first group included Ireland, Iceland, the Netherlands, Turkey, Greece and Austria, as well as Norway, Great Britain and Denmark, while France, Italy and West Germany made up the second group.[73]

Given the state of the West German money and capital markets and the urgent long-term capital requirements, the special ruling stipulating that the Western zones also had to set up counterpart funds for repayable credits hardly could mean much of an advantage. Nor did it constitute an additional source of ERP resources.[74] In their assessments on the 'Economic Cooperation Agreement', the German Office for Peace Questions,[75] and, albeit in a more guarded fashion, the Bank Deutscher Länder[76] discerned the real impact from the very beginning: 'This [special ruling] represents a considerable limitation of the Bizone's room to manoeuvre in its credit policy; it is even more regrettable if one is convinced that German allocations of counterpart funds derived from ERP imports would be more expedient than the decisions on their utilization by military governors and the US government.'[77] The German Office for Peace Questions concluded that the special

73. Portugal and Belgium held a special position inasmuch as they were not dependent on the release of counterpart funds for investment purposes, nor did they believe a blocking of counterpart accounts was useful for reasons of stability; see ERP-Gegenwertmittel und ihre Verwendung in den innereuropäischen Partnerländern, bearbeitet im Bundesministerium für den Marshallplan, September 1951, BA, B 146/227.

74. See the Borchardt/Buchheim essay in this volume.

75. The minister-presidents of the Bizone founded this office for the discussion of 'foreign policy' questions. When Clay vetoed it because of its bizonal character, it was established in Stuttgart as an institution of the minister-presidents of the American Zone on 15 April 1947; see H. Potthoff and R. Wenzel (eds), *Handbuch Politischer Institutionen 1945–1949* (Düsseldorf, 1983), pp.153ff.

76. Dr Vocke to the chairman of the Administrative Council of the Vereinigtes Wirtschaftsgebiet, betr. ERP-Vertrag Bizone – USA, 28 September 1948, BA, Z 14/173.

77. Deutsches Büro für Friedensfragen, NfD, 'Zum Economic Cooperation Agreement mit der Bizone', 14 July 1948, Stuttgart, 20 October 1948, Anlage I, Ein Vergleich des Economic Cooperation Agreement der Bizone mit den entsprechenden Abkommen des Vereinigten Königreiches, BA, Z 14/171.

American Aid and West German Recovery

ruling above all expressed the 'desire of the Americans . . . to exert a strong influence on the Bizone's credit policy with their disposition over the Special Account'.[78] As far as the utilization of DM counterparts was concerned, until mid-1949 they had a restrictive influence on the Bizone's credit policy. The top German administrators nevertheless emphasized the 'great importance' that 'these DM sums' might have, which the public at large often mistakenly termed Marshall Plan funds.[79] Ludwig Erhard, when he insisted on the allocation of counterparts, also argued that the GARIOA counterparts '[represented] a sort of invisible *German* savings activity' (emphasis added).[80] Contrary to such views, the Americans were determined at first to use the German counterpart funds as a 'stabilization fund'. They argued 'that some considerable part of this money can always be withheld from circulation as a deflationary pressure to offset unavoidable inflationary pressures that arise from other sources within a normal economy'. In so far as part of the money should get into circulation, those projects should be favoured 'which will bring the most immediate production increases to Germany'.[81]

These basic principles of the American Military Government could not be brought into accord with the German economic administration, whose time frame and substantive ideas were quite different. The Germans wanted the *immediate* release of the counterparts for the financing of *long-term* investments of their infrastructure. The first indication of an ongoing re-evaluation in Washington came in mid-1949 in Paul Hoffman's directive for John McCloy, the designated High Commissioner. Referring to 'the most recent sign of a deflationary trend', McCloy was asked to pay close attention to the linkage between the lack of long-term capital and unemployment in West Germany, and to make recommendations. At the same time, however, the Americans still believed that 'the establishment and maintenance of financial stability, of a sound banking system, and broadly conceived investment policies, are clearly essential'.[82] In the memorandum 'Monetary Policy in Western

78. Ibid.
79. Draft speech by *Oberdirektor* Pünder, 7 September 1948, BA, Z 14/8.
80. See the Meeting of the Military Governors with representatives from the Bizone in Frankfurt, 15 December 1948, in *Akten zur Vorgeschichte der Bundesrepublik Deutschland 1945–1949*, vol. 4, no. 108, p.1017. ECA counterparts were not available yet at this time, but the procedure for the GARIOA funds was a similar one.
81. Jack Bennett (financial adviser to the Military Governor), confidential to Howard Bruce (Deputy Administrator, ECA Paris), 25 September 1948, NA, RG 286, Bizone – Country Mission, box 4.
82. Confidential letter, Hoffman to McCloy, 13 July 1949, NA, RG 286, Germany – Administrator, box 4.

Werner Abelshauser

Germany',[83] which was consequently drawn up in Frankfurt, the DM counterparts played only a minor role. Instead, it suggested that as a preliminary measure, all legal provisions should be revised as soon as possible that might constitute obstacles to the expansion of credit. The experts in the American Military Government regarded the expansion of credit as necessary, if the situation on the labour market did not improve. In such a case the memorandum envisaged giving the Reconstruction Loan Corporation the statutory power to grant long-term credits itself, or to issue papers which the commercial banks should buy with a view to creating indirect credit. Given the 'deep concern' caused by the 'apparent stagnation in the West German economy' to the Military Government since January 1949, it was considered necessary to point out explicitly that the Marshall Plan legislation did not forbid the German government to combat deflationary tendencies with the tool of the expansion of public credit. Moreover, the Foreign Assistance Act of 1948 and its call for a balanced budget – 'as soon as practicable' – gave further support to such a policy.

In addition, the ECA Mission in Paris left no stone unturned to impress on the German side what it considered 'the key to the solution of the German economic problems': 'a stronger *expansion of credit while channelling concurrently the buying power into the direction of domestic products, in particular housing*'. ECA was convinced that it was possible 'to expand the entire part of the German economy dependent on domestic production to the limit of productive capacities'.[84] Such a position stood in stark contrast to the policies of Ludwig Erhard and the bank of issue. Both felt that a stimulation of the German economy by means of public works programmes was misconceived. They were convinced that programmes for the expansion of the domestic sector could not solve the unemployment problem, since it was 'structural'. On the contrary, the German balance of payments deficit would only be increased. The Germans successfully fended off American pressure until the spring of 1950, when they gave the appearance of capitulating to the ideas of the High Commission. Even though the American High Commissioner had been releasing partial amounts of DM counterparts since the autumn of 1949, he considered this only to be a means to move the government of the Federal Republic towards a com-

83. Confidential memorandum, 21 October 1949, NA, RG 286, Germany, box 4.

84. O. Emminger, Aktenvermerk über eine Unterredung mit Mr Ostrander an Averill [sic] Harriman, US Special Representative ECA Paris, 21 April 1950, NA, RG 286, Counterpart-Germany, box 4.

American Aid and West German Recovery

prehensive credit expansion programme: 'We shall continue to keep up our pressure for a more adequate employment program, but in order to do so, we must be in a position to contribute to the success of such a program with the timely release of counterpart funds.'[85] In the meantime, criticism of the investment policy of the German government in Washington had taken a turn towards a more basic reassessment. ECA in Washington and the State Department penned a joint memorandum expressing the conviction that the high degree of self-investment was above all damaging the construction of housing and the export trade; instead, it was promoting the expansion of 'luxury industries'.[86]

In the spring of 1950 a regressive tax structure had produced a low tax morale, while a serious maldistribution of purchasing power went hand in hand with conspicuous consumption of luxuries; an increasing balance of payments deficit was the result, which went against liberal American policies and produced an American perception of the 'sick man on the Rhine'. The Americans recommended the introduction of higher tax rates for upper incomes and heavy excise taxes on luxury goods. It was also suggested that tax allowances be granted to those people who invested their profits into long-term obligations of the Kreditanstalt für Wiederaufbau (KfW); moreover food subsidies should be cancelled. All these measures were intended to allow the Federal government and the Bank for Reconstruction higher investments without raising the spectre of inflation. The funds were designed to be poured into a comprehensive programme for the improvement of public highways (not the Autobahns!), as well as reclamation of coastal lands, and credits for small businesses and the refugees. The programme should be financed from all the sources customarily utilized by the government and the banking system: direct investment from the budget and the printing of money by the Bank Deutscher Länder. Last of all, the release of DM counterparts was also considered, but these credits should be limited to the construction of housing, small business loans and agriculture. For the time being, the electricity sector was to be left empty-handed, even though Franz Blücher, the minister for the Marshall Plan, brought it up. In terms of financial policy, the memorandum was based on a

85. Robert M. Hanes (Chief, Special Mission to Western Germany) to Averill [*sic*] Harriman (US Special Representative, ECA Paris), 21 April 1950, NA, RG 286, Counterpart-Germany, box 4.

86. E. T. Dickinson, Jr. (Director, Program Coordination Division) to Robert M. Hanes (Chief, ECA Mission to Western Germany), 23 February 1950, with the confidential memorandum 'German Economic Problems' attached, NA, RG 286, Germany no. 1, box 19.

Werner Abelshauser

clear decision of general principle which had been apparent since the summer of 1949: 'The inflationary potential of an increase in the money supply cannot be ignored. On the other hand, it seems clear that, at the present time, deflationary forces outweigh the inflationary in Germany. Consequently, some increase in the money supply for the purpose of stimulating productive investment and reducing unemployment is both permissible and necessary.'

Further memoranda followed, recommending again and again that the central bank should be allowed to expand credit 'with a clear conscience'; moreover the relationship between the government and the Bank Deutscher Länder should be clarified in this respect.[87] The American experts in the High Commission and the ECA tended to accuse the Germans of 'a certain amount of amateurishness' in their handling of the domestic credit policy.[88] The Americans (and British) discerned particularly amateurish behaviour in the fixation of their German partners on seeing the counterpart funds as the only source of long-term financing of investments. This was all the more incomprehensible since the Germans were not utilizing foreign resources for their investments but their own. The DM counterparts were nothing else but a mobilization of resources available in the domestic economy.

As long as these resources were idle – and 2 million unemployed are a strong indication that they were – such a mobilization was harmless from the point of view of financial policy. If they were put to other economic uses, however, such as the luxury consumption of which the Americans were so suspicious, a reallocation with the tools of monetary, fiscal and financial policy would have been required. The High Commission was prepared to revise all institutional limitations which had resulted from the currency reform and from the law on the Bank Deutscher Länder. The Federal government, however, did not accept this offer for political reasons. By failing to develop alternatives to the DM counterparts, the Germans did not only hold up the reconstruction of the raw material and production goods industries, they also threw most of the investment decisions in these areas into the arms of the High

87. See, for example, the memorandum by Eward A. Tenenbaum, 'Financial Program for Western Germany', 2 July 1948, NA, RG 286, Germany no. 1, box 19. In the early summer of 1948, Tenenbaum was the leader of operation 'Bird Dog' which prepared and executed the currency reform of June 1948.

88. See T. Ostrander (German expert in ECA, Paris), 'The problem presented by the year's ECA Aid Allotment to Western Germany', 13 February 1951, NA, RG 286, Special Representative in Paris, Central Secretariat, Country subject files 1948–52, Germany, box 3, Germany payments.

American Aid and West German Recovery

Commission and the ECA. In the stopgap programme for the year 1949 still financed from the GARIOA counterpart funds, BICO put a stop to planned investment credits for the ball-bearing industry, even though the $2 million allocated were negligible. With one exception due to its location, BICO also cancelled all energy projects in communal electricity utilities. The decisive factor in this case was presumably that one of the intentions of the American investment planners was to prevent 'municipal luxuries' *à la* Weimar; it was incorrectly assumed that municipal utilities belonged to this category.[89]

The Frankfurt ECA Mission did not hesitate to use their lever to correct Ludwig Erhard's neo-liberal course which appeared to them far too 'doctrinaire' and beholden to the ideology of *laissez-faire*.[90] Indeed, after the currency reform, the financing of investments from counterparts remained the last bastion of public control over investments. Although the middle ranks of the economic administration continued to believe in the cautious economic control of the state after the currency reform, the 'guidelines for investment planning' were employed only *sub rosa* in informal agreements between the Economics Ministry and the Bank for Economic Reconstruction, which had been established specifically to administer the counterparts.[91] The Americans, however, strongly desired that the counterparts must be employed only within the economic framework of a general investment plan. It does not come as a surprise, then, that Hermann J. Abs, the Director of the Bank for Reconstruction, discovered a small sector of West German 'economic planning' deeply embedded in the general neo-liberal experiment.[92] For the Economics Ministry the advantage of the counterparts lay also in the fact that they constituted a last reserve for the correction of misdirected capital flows in the market-place, while allowing Ludwig Erhard not to admit to such a fallback position.

In the years 1949 to 1952 the share of the German Marshall Plan counterpart funds amounted to 5.5 per cent of the financing of gross industrial investments – not a very significant proportion. But these funds were mainly used to remove bottlenecks in the

89. Pohl, *Wiederaufbau*, p.55; see also Bennett to Bruce, 25 September 1948, NA, RG 286, Bizone – country Mission, box 4.
90. See Werner Abelshauser, 'Ansätze "korporativer Marktwirtschaft" in der Korea-Krise der frühen fünfziger Jahre', *Vierteljahrshefte für Zeitgeschichte*, 30(1982), pp.717–21.
91. Adamsen, *Investitionshilfe*, pp.51ff.
92. See the epilogue by Hermann J. Abs in Pohl, *Wiederaufbau*, p.143.

Werner Abelshauser

infrastructural and production goods sectors; they also mobilized additional credits from the banking community. At first, the lion's share of the released funds was poured into investment in the coalmining industry, followed by spending on the federal railroads (Bundesbahn) and in the energy sector. After the outbreak of the Korean War the distribution was shifted towards favouring the iron and steel industries. Against the backdrop of increasing tensions on the international scene, the production restrictions of the Level of Industry Plan were lifted from heavy industry in the interest of 'defending the free world'. The very economic sectors that had fallen behind after the 1948 economic reforms now entered a period of increased economic activity. Whereas the consumer goods industries were in a position to finance their investments from their own resources, various branches of production goods industry such as coal mining, iron and steel, and energy production were still prohibited from meeting their own financial needs by means of adequate market prices. Here, then, the counterpart funds played a crucial if still inadequate role.

At the beginning of the 1950s the institutional association of the Marshall Plan with the promotion of domestic investment had also taken on a psycho-political meaning. This linkage calmed down the German public, which had a traditional and well-founded suspicion of public credit as the seedbed of inflation. Even if such a fear of inflationary financing of capital formation was unfounded, given unemployment and idle production capacity, such caution could be useful in getting rid of the still latent fears of inflation. Another aspect in favour of allocating credits from the counterpart accounts was the central bank's ability to turn down at any time the government's wishes to expand credit. This was frequently done 'for currency reasons' in spite of the fact that the narrowly defined legal framework would have allowed it. As far as occupation policy was concerned, these limits could have been stretched, but it was not desirable from the point of view of political economy. Even if it is undisputed that in the early phase of reconstruction promotion of investments by the state was crucial, its linkage with the Marshall Plan did not create any irreversible economic necessities. The utilization of counterpart funds for long-term economic investment was indeed 'not a central part of the machinery of the Marshall Plan', as a leading official in the Economics Administration put it critically.[93]

93. 'Weit vom Kern der Mechanik des Marshallplans'; see Keiser, 'Long-Term Program und amerikanische Politik', 1/2 September 1949, BA, 146/171.

American Aid and West German Recovery

Helping Those Who Help Themselves

The Marshall Plan did not provide the initial spark for the reconstruction of the West German economy. The American policy of stabilization for Europe, however, which had bred the Marshall Plan, stands at the beginning of German reconstruction. The United States could build on a broad West German resource base that had survived the war, but which carried the mortgage of the German reparations debt. Initially the pragmatic and self-interested Military Government in Frankfurt countered the restrictive measures of official occupation policy by *practising* a constructive approach to reconstruction. At the beginning of 1947, however, West Germany moved into the centre of American stabilization efforts for all of *Western Europe*. The German reconstruction process had begun long before the arrival of the first shipments of Marshall Plan aid and without the benefit of foreign resources.[94]

Such a conclusion does not ignore the extensive imports of foodstuffs, which had become critical to secure the physical survival of the West German population. But the inflow of aid has to be posited against the outflow of German resources in the form of looted war booty, open and 'hidden' reparations, as well as forced and 'invisible' exports. Added to this must be the imposed restrictions and bans on economic activity, the burdens of the occupation policies as well as the consequences of the division of Germany and the 'resettlement' of Germans from agricultural surplus areas into subsidized areas.[95] After the postwar restrictions on German resources, the imports of the GARIOA programme and the British contributions followed as a necessary consequence.[96]

94. Abelshauser, *Wirtschaft in Westdeutschland.*
95. All these items were listed in a letter of 15 January 1951. In this missive the Committee for the Occupation Statute and for Foreign Affairs of the Bundestag asked the Federal Chancellor to present these objections to the Allies at the London Debt Conference; the parliamentary Committee was convinced that 'the full extent of the economic aid had been mainly a result of the Allied policies'. The letter is attached to the confidential 'Memorandum über Nachkriegsschulden' ('Memorandum on Postwar Debts') of the Federal Minister for the Marshall Plan, 20 September 1951, pp.8f, BA, B 146/234.
96. The Federal Minister for the Marshall Plan argued that 'the GARIOA programme, the initial aid . . . [served] the mere preservation of the survival of the West German population, which was in the interest of the occupying powers', ibid., p.26. The notorious 'chicken-feed speech' ('the time has come for German politicians to refrain from expressing gratitude for the food subsidies', BA, Z 61/70) by Johannes Semler, the Director of the Verwaltung für Wirtschaft, before the CSU

Werner Abelshauser

The Marshall Plan relieved Germany of these burdens which had been holding back its economic potential since the end of the war. This was achieved by compensating the reparation creditors' demands, by ending the deliveries out of current production, by reducing the 'hidden' exports, thereby returning to Western Germany step by step the right to dispose of her own resources. The material conditions for postwar economic revival were not bad at all. True, the West German economy was disorganized, crippled by production and transportation bottlenecks, and weakened by hunger. But it had not been seriously damaged in its substance and certainly was not underdeveloped. This is not to say that recovery and economic growth would automatically materialize. The negative example of the Weimar Republic[97] shows clearly that a favourable economic and political climate was a prerequisite for realizing the given economic potential. The 'Marshall Plan' – not its material aid – created these conditions. For not even the goods available in the critical months after the currency reform came out of Marshall Plan deliveries. What the announcement of aid shipments did do, however, was to bring about the release of German stocks of raw materials and goods, thereby providing a cushion for the inflationary pressure on the new currency. This, along with the monetary interventions of the central bank, may in some cases have saved Erhard's market economy from the perils of price controls and production planning. The Marshall Plan, in other words, never stood in the centre of economic reconstruction, either at the time of gearing up production before the currency reform, or in the difficult period of introducing the market economy thereafter.

Hence it cannot come as a great surprise that Ludwig Erhard and his supporters disputed the value of Marshall Plan aid for Western Germany from the very outset, once their original expectations had been disappointed across the board:

> ERP and foreign aid have (incidentally and contrary to other Marshall Plan countries) not made *the least* contribution to the revival. During the first year, they saved the people of West Berlin from starving; in the

---

Landesausschuss in Erlangen on 4 January 1948, can therefore not be seen as the 'inadvertent slip' of an irresponsible politician for which he could have been rightfully removed from office by the Allies. On the contrary, it was nothing else but the official – albeit not prominently publicized – German attitude on this problem.

97. Werner Abelshauser and Dietmar Petzina, 'Krise und Rekonstruktion: Zur Interpretation der gesamtwirtschaftlichen Entwicklung Deutschlands im 20. Jahrhundert', in W.-H. Schröder and R. Spree (eds), *Historische Konjunkturforschung* (Stuttgart, 1980), pp.75–114.

American Aid and West German Recovery

second [year], they facilitated the expansion of supplies and the reconstruction of factories, without being able to increase the national product. The best that can be said is that they allowed an additional per capita monthly consumption of DM 2 (and this only at the expense of distorting prices, which affected increases in production and the national product). The economic recovery was achieved exclusively *by our own efforts*.[98]

In the estimate of Ludwig Erhard and his editorial board only c. 10 per cent of the added plant and supplies were a direct result of foreign assistance in the second Marshall Plan year – none during the first year.[99] This position was a correct description of the *material* transfer of resources, and was intended primarily to acknowledge the innovation in political economy as the basis of the West German recovery. Based on the same motives, however, it neglected the fact that for West Germany the crucial importance of the American reconstruction programme was to be found in its effects on occupation policy and the international (world markets) framework for recovery.

One important factor in this respect was that the Marshall Plan was supposed to create the conditions for the solution of the reparations problem. In particular 'hidden' reparations – until October 1947 the bulk of German exports were of this sort[100] – were threatening the American intention of strengthening West Germany economically and politically to such an extent that it no longer contributed to the destabilization of Europe. The Marshall Plan was designed to allow the Americans to stop reparations. The United States were determined to redeem the mortgage which the West German economy had been shouldering since Potsdam to the advantage of the United Nations and for the compensation of creditors. If France was not the only target of this policy, it certainly was the most important one.[101]

In the last quarter of 1947, Paris received credits amounting to $337 million in anticipation of the Marshall Plan; in addition, on

98. 'Zwei Jahre Wirtschaftswunder', editorial of late June 1950, L. Erhard, E. Hielscher, M. Schönwandt (eds), *Währung und Wirtschaft*, 20/21 (1945/50), pp.521–2 (emphasis in the original).
99. See 'Geschichte und Geschichten vom Marshall-Plan', BA, B 146/234.
100. See John Gimbel, *The Origins of the Marshall Plan* (Stanford, 1976), p.165. and Werner Abelshauser, 'Wirtschafts- und Besatzungspolitik in der französischen Zone 1945–1949', in C. Scharf and H.-J. Schröder (eds), *Die Deutschlandpolitik Frankreichs und die französische Zone 1945–1949* (Wiesbaden, 1983), pp.111–40.
101. Milward, *Reconstruction of Western Europe*, and Gimbel, *Origins of the Marshall Plan*.

Werner Abelshauser

2 January 1948, interim aid worth $280 million was promised to France. Through the Foreign Assistance Act of 1948 France was scheduled to receive another $998 million. The French Zone, which on 18 February 1948 had become a member of the OEEC, was to receive a further $100 million. By the end of the ERP programme, France had become the recipient of a bonanza of economic aid totalling $3,104 billion.

The involvement of France in the Marshall Plan made it easier for the government in Paris to back down from maximum political demands *vis-à-vis* Germany, demands which all three Allies in the anti-Hitler coalition had for some time been rejecting as excessive. France nevertheless managed to realize some of its goals, namely the economic annexation of the Saar territory, the establishment of the International Ruhr Authority and the signing of the Brussels Security Pact. Against the background of the emerging East–West division of Europe and the partition of the German Reich, Paris found it less difficult to agree to the economic union of the three zones and finally the founding of the West German state. The zone of occupation had become obsolete as a bargaining chip for political and economic security. *With* American economic aid the zone could no longer be maintained as an autonomous entity *politically*; and *without* the Marshall Plan it could certainly not survive *economically*.[102]

The Marshall Plan brought into existence new forms of international economic cooperation and trade policy regulations that facilitated the international rehabilitation of the Federal Republic of Germany and made it possible for Germany to return to the world markets on a short-term basis. The leadership role assumed by the Federal Republic in setting up the liberal, multilateral trading system as part of the Marshall Plan demanded heavy burdens and would not have been shouldered without OEEC pressure. Such goals could not have been successfully pursued without the backing of the ERP.

The heavy demands for German drawing rights encouraged the supporters of a more far-reaching liberalization of German foreign trade 'to take the risk and open the doors'. Precisely because under the special conditions of the postwar period such a step involved the risk of a balance of payments crisis, the umbrella of American economic aid offered favourable circumstances. The Germans viewed the 'European' Marshall Plan positively in spite of the fact

102. Abelshauser, 'Wirtschafts- und Besatzungpolitik in der französischen Zone'. See also the Poidevin essay, pp.351ff.

American Aid and West German Recovery

that it distributed the internal European burdens of economic aid unevenly.[103] The breakthrough towards self-supporting economic growth completed in 1952, however, was a consequence of the unrivalled expansion of foreign trade, which had been triggered by the world-wide Korean boom. Efforts to take a prominent part in this economic upswing were reinforced by the institutional safeguarding of the liberalization policy under the auspices of the Marshall Plan. At the end of this development an international economic system emerged that has been meeting the needs of West German industry for decades and greatly contributed to the rise of German prosperity.

The Marshall Plan was no less important for the reordering of the economic system introduced in West Germany.[104] The United States was not interested at all in the ideologies behind Erhard's programme of *Soziale Marktwirtschaft*. It was the political and economic stabilization of Western Europe that enjoyed Washington's undivided attention; the means employed were pragmatical ones. As far as West Germany was concerned, Erhard's neo-liberal course had the advantage that it could be realized without a complicated and disputed reorganization of the institutional framework. Once the Korean War broke out, the United States demanded increased contributions to the defence of the Western world. To achieve this end the very modifications of the market economy appeared to be necessary for which Washington had been clamouring since the spring of 1950.

It would be easy to add to the list of direct and indirect effects of the Marshall Plan on the West German economy, especially since the political factors *per se* should not be viewed in isolation.[105] At the core of its economic activity, however, the Marshall Plan helped Germany to help itself in the true sense of the word. It enabled West Germany to recover on the basis of her own resources and capabilities and contributed to the stabilization of Western Europe in the process.

103. 'Without a doubt the drawing rights are an immense step towards a European economic community', see G. Keiser, 'Long-Term Program und amerikanische Politik', BA, B 146/171.

104. See Abelshauser, 'Ansätze "korporative Marktwirtschaft"', pp.715–56.

105. See, for example, Manfred Knapp, 'Reconstruction and West Integration: The Impact of the Marshall Plan on Germany', *Zeitschrift für die gesamte Staatswissenschaft*, 137(1981), pp.515–33, and more recently Hans-Jürgen Schröder, 'Marshallplan, amerikanische Deutschlandpolitik und europäische Integration 1947–1950', *Aus Politik und Zeitgeschichte*, B 18/87, pp.3–33, and the various contributions in this volume.

[5]

The Marshall Plan and Key Economic Sectors: A Microeconomic Perspective

Knut Borchardt and Christoph Buchheim

Introduction

Only a short time after the June 1947 announcement of the Marshall Plan expectations of its political and economic importance had already reached the realm of the fantastic. Bold hopes and, on the part of opponents, the worst fears were attached to the execution of the plan; no one seemed to doubt that it would have profound effects.

In retrospect, it is very difficult to identify the propagandistic or polemical portions of those contemporary oral and written opinions. The numerous motives for all parties to extol the importance of the plan are obvious. Nevertheless, we have no reason to doubt the honest conviction of many who have called the plan simply the most decisive act in, and the very foundation of, West German economic recovery. 'Without the foreign aid granted to us, a constructive German economic policy would be impossible', was the February 1949 judgement of the Wissenschaftlicher Beirat, a panel of leading professors of economics attached to the bizonal Economic Administration.[1] One year later this same group wrote that 'the generous help of the Marshall Plan has made it possible to bring Germany's economic processes back into motion'.[2]

At that time judgements similar to those above required no further, more specific explanation. How else could the West German balance of payments problem have been solved? How else could the credit bottlenecks in key segments of the economy have been undone? Finally how else could West Germany have been

---

1. Der Wissenschaftliche Beirat beim Bundesministerium für Wirtschaft, *Sammelband der Gutachten von 1948 bis 1972* (Göttingen, 1973), p.29.
2. Gutachten, 26 February 1950, in ibid., pp.68ff.

The Marshall Plan and Key Economic Sectors

integrated into an orderly system of international economic relations? Both economists and historians of the postwar period, as well as contemporary observers,[3] considered the inclusion of West Germany in the Marshall Plan to be one of the three keys (along with the currency reform and the decision in favour of a market-oriented economy) to understanding the astounding post-1948 economic developments.

Since that time both the currency reform and the decision in favour of a market economy have been the objects of numerous research projects in the form of monographs and detailed investigations which closely examine these events and their consequences. In contrast, the economic history of the Marshall Plan has received little research attention. There is of course a substantial body of literature on the origins of and the conceptual impulses behind the Marshall Plan, especially in the contexts of the origins of the Cold War and the integration of Western Europe.[4] Yet for information on the execution of the plan, we continue to depend primarily on the official reports of the American and German Marshall Plan administrations.[5] The economic aspects of allegedly the 'most important postwar measure in Europe, and one which contributed substantially to the economic integration of the Federal Republic into the world economy'[6] have hardly been touched by monograph literature.[7] Even academic journals and edited collections rarely

3. The OMGUS surveys provide information about public opinion. According to the surveys, in August 1949 the great majority of those questioned stated that economic conditions had improved in the course of the past year. 'Foreign aid ranked second to currency reform as *a voluntarily stated reason* for this improvement.' See A. J. Merrit and R. L. Merrit (eds), *Public Opinion in Occupied Germany. The OMGUS Surveys, 1945–1949* (Urbana Chicago and London, 1970), p.313. One must, however, also consider the public relations activities of the Americans and British.

4. See the literature cited in the other articles in this volume, especially the essays in Part I.

5. Characteristic of this is F.-W. Henning's 'Wege und Wirkungen des Marshall-Plans in Deutschland', *Scripta Mercaturae*, 15(1981), pp.91–112.

6. Hermann J. Abs in the 'Epilogue' to M. Pohl, *Wiederaufbau, Kunst und Technik der Finanzierung 1947–1953. Die ersten Jahre der Kreditanstalt für Wiederaufbau* (Frankfurt am Main, 1973), p.142.

7. There are a few works on the American side or which deal primarily with American decision-making processes. These usually pursue the effects on the economic development of Germany only peripherally. See W. A. Brown and R. Opie, *American Foreign Assistance* (Washington DC, 1953); H. B. Price, *The Marshall Plan and its Meaning* (Ithaca, 1955); W. W. Kretzschmar, *Auslandshilfe als Mittel der Aussenwirtschafts- und Aussenpolitik. Eine Studie über die amerikanische Auslandshilfe von 1945 bis 1956 unter Berücksichtigung sowohl wirtschaftlicher als auch praktisch-politischer Gesichtspunkte* (Munich, 1964); T. A. Wilson, *The Marshall Plan* (New York, 1977); U. Daniel, *Dollardiplomatie in Europa. Marshallplan, kalter Krieg*

Knut Borchardt and Christoph Buchheim

contain articles on this specific topic.[8]

It is rather difficult to account for this noticeable research gap, since the material is not inaccessible and there should be no lack of interest in ascertaining exactly how the plan was transposed into reality. Perhaps the fact that virtually all studies which mention the Marshall Plan agreed on the political-economic importance of the plan for the fate of West Germany did not inspire further detailed studies. Yet this early consensus can explain the existence of a research gap only to the mid-1970s; from that time on there can be no talk of a consensus evaluation of the Marshall Plan.

In 1975 Werner Abelshauser summarized his opinion on the topic by stating that 'the importance of the currency reform and the Marshall Plan deliveries in fuelling the start of the "economic miracle" of the 1950s must be downgraded'.[9] Although originally confined to economic developments in the second half of 1948, his suggestions for revising the accepted evaluation of the Marshall Plan effects were quickly and positively received in connection with other questions as well.[10] Almost immediately, Abelshauser's ideas served to reduce the economic importance of the Marshall Plan in

und US-Aussenwirtschaftspolitik 1945–52 (Düsseldorf, 1982); I. Wexler, *The Marshall Plan Revisited: The European Recovery Program in Economic Perspective* (Westport CT, 1983). In contrast, A. S. Milward, *The Reconstruction of Western Europe 1945–1951* (London, 1984), includes a good deal on internal European developments, but necessarily treats the developments in each individual country in less detail. On the history, execution and effects of the plan in West Germany see P. Rogge, *Die amerikanische Hilfe für Westberlin. Von der deutschen Kapitulation bis zur westdeutschen Souveränität* (Tübingen, 1959); E. R. Baumgart, *Investitionen und ERP-Finanzierung. Eine Untersuchung über die Anlage-Investitionen als Wachstumsdeterminante des Wirtschaftsprozesses in der Bundesrepublik Deutschland und die wirtschaftspolitische Einflussnahme durch Investitionsfinanzierung aus dem ERP-Sondervermögen in empirischer Sicht von 1949 bis 1956* (Berlin, 1961); Pohl, *Wiederaufbau*.

8. The extensive bibliography, *Schrifttum zum Marshallplan und zur wirtschaftlichen Integration Europas*, im Auftrag und unter Mitwirkung des Bundesministeriums für den Marshallplan zusammengestellt von Dr Adolf Wittkowski (Bad Godesberg, 1953), contains almost no scholarly pieces.

9. W. Abelshauser, *Wirtschaft in Westdeutschland 1945–1948. Rekonstruktion und Wachstumsbedingungen in der amerikanischen und britischen Zone* (Stuttgart, 1975), p.168.

10. See G. Ambrosius, *Die Durchsetzung der Sozialen Marktwirtschaft in Westdeutschland 1945–1949* (Stuttgart, 1977), p.182; G. Müller, *Die Grundlegung der westdeutschen Wirtschaftsordnung im Frankfurter Wirtschaftsrat 1947–1949* (Frankfurt, 1982), p.220; U. Uffelmann, 'Wirtschaft und Gesellschaft in der Gründungsphase der Bundesrepublik Deutschland. Eine Bestandsaufnahme in didaktischer Absicht', *Aus Politik und Zeitgeschichte. Beilage zur Wochenzeitung Das Parlament*, B1-2/82 (9 January 1982), pp.6ff; Chr. Weisz, Introduction to *Akten zur Vorgeschichte der Bundesrepublik Deutschland 1945–1949*, vol.4, January–December 1948 (Munich, 1983), pp.24ff.

The Marshall Plan and Key Economic Sectors

its entirety.[11] Now that Abelshauser has followed up on his first suggestions[12] with further work, and E. Ott's theses have set off a lively controversy,[13] we can no longer speak of a 'dominant view' regarding the importance of the Marshall Plan.

However, this debate is based largely on interpretations and evaluations; new facts have not been brought out and the research gap described above has not been filled in. Most probably the open disagreement on the effects of the Marshall Plan cannot be bridged without new research. A portion of the debate could certainly be more clearly resolved by rechecking the factual assertions which lie beneath the conflicting interpretations. The purpose of this article is to make a contribution in that direction.

It is well known that even before the Marshall Plan contributions began, West Germany had received significant help, largely in the form of GARIOA deliveries and UK contributions (totalling some $2 billion from 1945 to 1948).[14] At that point West German exports brought in only very modest sums of disposable foreign exchange,

11. Most emphatically in E. Ott, 'Die Bedeutung des Marshallplans für die Nachkriegsentwicklung in Westdeutschland', *Aus Politik und Zeitgeschichte. Beilage zur Wochenzeitung Das Parlament*, B 4/80 (26 January 1980), pp.19–37. Heiner R. Adamsen, 'Faktoren und Daten der wirtschaftlichen Entwicklung in der Frühphase der Bundesrepublik Deutschland 1948–1954', *Archiv für Sozialgeschichte*, 18(1978), pp.231ff. bases his critical assessment of the Marshall Plan not only on Abelshauser's seminal contributions but also on an astounding miscalculation: 'At the end of 1948 only $142 million had been sent from the Marshall Plan to West Germany, by a straight calculation just 1 Pfennig per capita.' (Checking the sources, one finds that it was DM 9.80 per capita.)

12. W. Abelshauser, 'Die Rekonstruktion der westdeutschen Wirtschaft und die Rolle der Besatzungspolitik', in C. Scharf and H.-J. Schröder (eds), *Politische und ökonomische Stabilisierung Westdeutschlands 1945–1949* (Wiesbaden, 1977), pp.1–18; 'Wiederaufbau vor dem Marshall-Plan. Westeuropas Wachstumschancen und die Wirtschaftsordnungspolitik in der zweiten Hälfte der vierziger Jahre', *Vierteljahrshefte für Zeitgeschichte*, 29(1981), pp.545–87; and *Wirtschaftsgeschichte der Bundesrepublik Deutschland 1945–1980* (Göttingen, 1983), pp.54–63. Abelshauser recognizes the role of the Marshall Plan in integration policy, and emphasizes its political and psychological importance, but denies its central importance for reconstruction in West Germany even more emphatically than previously.

13. W. Link, 'Der Marshall-Plan und Deutschland', *Aus Politik und Zeitgeschichte. Beilage zur Wochenzeitung Das Parlament*, B 50/80, 13 December 1980, pp.3–18; similarly, M. Knapp, 'Deutschland und der Marshallplan: Zum Verhältnis zwischen politischer und ökonomischer Stabilisierung in der amerikanischen Deutschlandpolitik nach 1945', in C. Scharf und H.-J. Schröder (eds), *Politische und ökonomische Stabilisierung Westdeutschlands 1945–49* (Wiesbaden, 1977), pp.19–43 and in 'Reconstruction and West-Integration: The Impact of the Marshall Plan on Germany', *Zeitschrift für die gesamte Staatswissenschaft*, 137(1981), pp.415–33 also emphasizes the positive role of the plan in reconstruction.

14. Deutsche Bundesbank, *Deutsches Geld- und Bankwesen in Zahlen 1876–1975* (Frankfurt. 1976), p.341.

Knut Borchardt and Christoph Buchheim

but even providing the population with minimal subsistence diet required substantial imports. With a low level of German self-sufficiency in food (roughly 50 per cent at that time),[15] the Allies financed Category A imports (food, seeds, fertilizers, pharmaceuticals and fuel) worth $600 million in 1947 and $920 million in 1948.[16] Export earnings for the same years were a mere $196 million and $536 million respectively.[17] Even if Category A goods had been the only necessary imports (an assumption which is far from the truth), export earnings could have covered only one third or little more than one half of imports.

One can of course speculate that West German export earnings might have been greater had not the JEIA (the foreign trade monopoly of the British–American occupation forces) credited certain forced exports at relatively low prices and diminished German chances for increasing exports by applying bureaucratic controls to foreign trade.[18] This latter point is supported by the sharp rise in exports in 1949/50 after the JEIA had abolished most of these controls. This does not, however, mean that a more liberal export regime could have dispensed with foreign aid. Firstly, foreign aid and especially the Marshall Plan, which offered a different range of goods from the GARIOA aid, may have been a precondition for abolishing fixed prices and rationing and for limiting foreign trade controls; this idea will be more closely examined in the following section. Secondly, West Germany remained dependent on substantial balance of payments help through 1949 and 1950. The alternative – a drastic reduction of German imports to match the level of exports (with incalculable political results) – would have required a social and economic policy completely different from that pursued by both the Allies and the Germans.

Even those who downplay the importance of the Marshall Plan for West Germany's economic reconstruction proceed from the explicit or, more usually, implicit assumption that continued foreign aid was necessary. Surprisingly, then, they manage to reach the conclusion that the Marshall Plan's contribution to the 'economic

15. *Einwirkungen der Besatzungsmächte auf die westdeutsche Wirtschaft* (Institut für Besatzungsfragen, Tübingen, 1949), p.85; and 'Primat der Einfuhr?', *Handelsblatt*, no. 18, 29 April 1948.
16. *Einwirkungen der Besatzungsmächte* (see n.15, pp.114f.).
17. W. Abelshauser, *Wirtschaft in Westdeutschland* (see n.9, p.158).
18. 'Aussichten deutscher Handelspolitik', *Handelsblatt*, no. 51, 22 December 1947, and 'Noch keine Aussenhandelsfreiheit', *Wirtschafts- und Finanz-Zeitung*, no. 42, 22 October 1948.

The Marshall Plan and Key Economic Sectors

miracle' was quite small.[19] The main support for this assertion is seen in the relatively late arrival of Marshall Plan deliveries.

The next section of this paper will show that despite the late arrival of the first industrial raw materials financed by the plan, these materials had decisive importance for the expansion of commodity supplies during a crucial phase of the currency reform. Any explanation of how these deliveries contributed to both the success of the currency reform and to the stability of the market-oriented economic order must describe exactly the problems and decisions of the time as well as the chances of the delivered goods to affect them. The textile industry has been chosen for detailed examination since it then stood in 'the centre of public and therefore political interest'[20] and was a primary receiver of Marshall Plan aid in the form of cotton imports.

The second form of Marshall Plan aid was the counterpart funds. After the announcement of the Marshall Plan German economic planners pinned their greatest hopes on them.[21] These funds offered partial, though not complete, solutions to (1) the capital shortage problem and (2) the problem of directing the available investment capital to the points of greatest need.

In the third section, the example of the electric power industry will be used to describe how bottlenecks affected the West German economy. It will be shown that these bottlenecks can, in turn, be traced back to a shortage of capital. In contrast to the claims of others, we have reached the conclusion that the fundamental political decision to keep price controls in effect for the electric power industry left that industry with few other financing alternatives to the Marshall Plan counterpart funds. There remain however some reasons to hypothesize that an earlier transition to market economy rules in electricity supply might have made Marshall Plan counterpart funds less crucial to financing this economic sector.

The case studies presented here rest on the firm conviction that the structural problems of the West German postwar economy require a specific vantage point. One of the most important problems, perhaps *the* most important problem, of economic development, was the bottlenecks in production and financing;[22] *they* defined

19. See the titles listed in nn.9–12.
20. 'Textilwirtschaft am Scheideweg. Rückfall in die Bewirtschaftung', *Wirtschafts Zeitung*, no. 61, 22 December 1948.
21. This is described by Pohl, *Wiederaufbau*, in connection with the establishment of the 'Loan Bank', later the Kreditanstalt für Wiederaufbau; see also *Akten zur Vorgeschichte der Bundesrepublik Deutschland 1945–1949*, vol.4, pp.562, 606.
22. See R. Salomon, *Begriff und Problematik der wirtschaftlichen Engpässe. Dargestellt*

Knut Borchardt and Christoph Buchheim

both the actual performance and the chances for further development. Analyses which fail to consider the role of bottlenecks and which describe the economy primarily by means of macroeconomic indices, drawing from them their conclusions, are not appropriate for peculiarities of this special economic situation. They transmit a distorted picture of the economic reality.

A macroeconomic perspective based on describing stocks and flows in terms of aggregates (GNP, gross investment, imports, exports, etc.) may do very well for a developed economy with a free-market price-setting mechanism. The assumption then is that the measures of value used (prices) express, or at least indicate, the values to society, and that the structure of these stocks and flows corresponds roughly to the needs of production and consumption. Those conditions, however, did not yet apply to the period under consideration here. For that reason any measure of the importance of the Marshall Plan which compares that Plan's contributions with large aggregate indices remains inconclusive.[23] For that reason it is necessary, especially in an analysis of the Marshall Plan, to confront directly the problem of economic bottlenecks. This can be done only by examining specific industrial sectors, and occasionally only by using a microeconomic approach to examine individual enterprises.

The Role of Cotton Imports Financed by the Marshall Plan in the Bizone in 1948 and 1949

'The textile industry stands in the very centre of West German social, political, and economic events. The textile industry will decide the fate of West Germany's future economic policy.'[24] This was Erhard's assessment as presented at a conference of textile retailers in December 1948. In an article on the threatening 'Return of Rationing', the *Wirtschafts Zeitung* commented that Erhard's statement

may seem an exaggeration when one weighs the importance of the consumer goods industries in comparison to basic industries. However,

---

am Beispiel der Bundesrepublik Deutschland in den Jahren 1948–1952 (Kiel, 1954).

23. See E. Ott, 'Die Bedeutung des Marshall-Plans für die Nachkriegsentwicklung in Westdeutschland', in which the insignificance of the counterpart funds is deduced from the relatively small percentage of these funds in total investment.

24. 'Gebundener Warenverkehr', *Textil-Zeitung* (*TZ*), no. 60, 11 December 1948.

The Marshall Plan and Key Economic Sectors

the statement is momentous: it means no less than that the future course of our economic policy will depend on developments in the textile industry. Today the textile industry, along with food supplies, stands at the centre of public attention and therefore at the centre of political interest.[25]

Concern centred on the disturbing price increases for textiles and clothing[26] which had taken place since July 1948, when price controls[27] and most of the rationing regulations[28] had been lifted on consumer goods. These price increases caused great social worry, since the poorer members of society were in fact having increasing difficulties covering their most pressing needs. So in response to the question 'Has your standard of living improved since the currency reform?' (part of a public opinion poll conducted in August), 74 per cent of workers answered 'no'. In contrast, only 24 per cent of the better-earning white-collar employees and just 15 per cent of civil servants chose that response.[29] The call for a return to government price controls was growing louder and gaining broad political support. The situation in the textile industry, or more exactly in cotton textiles, where 'things are especially dangerous in social policy terms' as Erhard was forced to admit in the course of debate with Erik Nölting (SPD) in November 1948,[30] threatened to cut short the experiment with a market economy.

The price increases signalled that the supply of textiles was insufficient in comparison with pent-up demand. After the currency reform stocks were reduced[31] and production increased sharply (table 9.1), but not enough to satisfy the demand for these goods. In the course of the war, official rations of textiles had

25. 'Textilwirtschaft am Scheideweg. Rückfall in die Bewirtschaftung?', *Wirtschafts Zeitung*, no. 61, 22 December 1948.
26. Increases in the cost of living price indices from June to December 1948: food +18%, clothing +35%, household utensils +12%, heating and lighting +13%, *Statistisches Jahrbuch für die Bundesrepublik Deutschland 1952*, p.404.
27. Anordnung über Preisbildung und Preisüberwachung nach der Währungsreform vom 25.6.1948, *Gesetz -und Verordnungsblatt des Wirtschaftsrats des VWG*, no. 12, 7 July 1948. See also C. Seeger-Kelbe, 'Die Reste gewerblicher Bewirtschaftung', *Wirtschaftsverwaltung*, 1(1948), 8, p.7.
28. Anordnung Text. II/48 vom 18.6.1948, *Mitteilungsblatt der VfW des VWG* (VfWMBL) 1948, I, pp.197ff., and Seeger-Kelbe, 'Die Reste'.
29. *Ifo-Schnelldienst*, no. 6, 10 September 1948.
30. 'Deutsche Wirtschaftspolitik nach der Währungsreform'. Reprint of Ludwig Erhard's speech in the debate with Erik Nölting on 14 November 1948 in Frankfurt, contained in Ludwig Erhard Stiftung, *Orientierungen zur Wirtschafts- und Gesellschaftspolitik*, 18(April 1983), p.41.
31. 'Die Lage nach der Währungsreform', *Wirtschaftsverwaltung*, 1(1948), 4, p.19.

Table 9.1 Textile production and textile prices in the Bizone in 1948/9

	1.48	2.48	3.48	4.48	5.48	6.48	7.48	8.48	9.48	10.48	11.48	12.48	1.49	2.49	3.49	4.49	5.49	6.49	7.49	8.49
1. Production index (excluding artificial silk and rayon staple) per working day (6.48=100)	89	105	104	108	105	100	128	147	156	164	168	172	185	199	219	226	237	224	217	235
2. Index of producers' prices (1938 = 100)						175	200	209	218	222	221	220	219	217	216	215	213	212	211	210
3. Index of retail prices (7.1949–6.1950 = 100)						107	112	118	124	130	135	135	129	124	120	116	112	108	106	104

Source:　Line 1 calculated from *Wirtschaft und Statistik*, NF 1 (1949).
Line 2 calculated from: *Statist.Jb.f.d.Bundesrep.Dtld.* 1952.
Line 3 calculated from: W. Moritz, *Die Entwicklung der westdeutschen Textilindustrie seit 1948* (Berlin, 1954), p.23.

The Marshall Plan and Key Economic Sectors

steadily decreased, and in 1945/6 virtually no textiles were offered. As late as 1947 the volume of textiles released for civilian consumption was equal to just 4 per cent of the per capita supplies of Germany in 1936. The situation improved somewhat in the first half of 1948, but it nevertheless remained rather bleak as per capita consumption of textiles reached only 20 per cent of 1936 levels.[32] It is no wonder that the demand for textiles expressed itself powerfully in the period following the currency reform.[33] A substantial portion of any consumer money which was not required for food now went primarily for textiles and clothing. In higher-income groups textile purchases made up as much as 30 per cent of total household expenditure.[34]

Even the formal continuation of textiles rationing in the form of the end-user points (Endverbraucherpunkte) could not prevent this sudden concentration of demand from driving prices sky-high. Since the currency reform, liquidity had become vital to industry, and purchase rights for textiles were given out freely in order not to constrict the flow of cash from consumers through retailers to producers.[35] Textiles were often sold without the necessary points,[36] and those who needed additional points in order to make a purchase could obtain these on the black market.[37] Once the system of money and prices had begun to function, it tolerated no additional rationing mechanism.[38] The demand boom allowed producers to pass the increased costs of textile production along to

32. *Erster Bericht der Deutschen Bundesregierung über die Durchführung des Marshallplans* (Bonn, 1950), Appendix no. 16; 'Bessere Versorgung der Textilindustrie', *Handelsblatt*, no. 58, 12 October 1948, and 'Zwischen Soll und Ist', *Neue Textil-Zeitung* (*NTZ*, predecessor to Textil-Zeitung), no. 15, 9 April 1948.

33. Compare the results of several public opinion surveys: 'Nach süddeutschem Muster', *NTZ*, no. 26, 25 June 1948, and 'Reactions to Currency Reform in the U.S. Zone of Germany', in A. J. Merrit and R. L. Merrit, *Public Opinion*. While 11 out of 25 Bavarian retail sectors showed in August 1948 declines in sales from July levels, textile and clothing sales continued to soar; *Ifo-Schnelldienst*, no. 9, 1 October 1948.

34. 'Textilkonsum nur ein Drittel des Vorkriegsstandes. Interessante Ergebnisse einer gewerkschaftlichen Erhebung', *TZ*, no. 53, 6 July 1949; see also W. Moritz *Die Entwicklung der westdeutschen Textilindustrie seit 1948* (DIW Sonderhefte, NF, 29) (Berlin, 1954), pp.45f. For the much lower percentages of the prewar years compare *Statistisches Jahrbuch für das Deutsche Reich 1930*, pp.342ff.

35. 'Die Lage nach der Währungsreform', *Wirtschaftsverwaltung*, 1(1948), 4, pp.8, 10f.; 'Verkaufsfreudigkeit in Württemberg', *NTZ*, no. 27, 2 July 1948, and 'Punkte nur zu 33 Prozent eingelöst', *TZ*, no. 12, 12 February 1949.

36. 'Stabilisierung in Sicht?', *Wirtschaftsverwaltung*, 1(1948), 7, p.26; 'Fortschreiten des Gesundungsprozesses', ibid., 11, p.22, and 'Kritik in Württemberg', *NTZ*, no. 29, 16 July 1948.

37. 'Die Lage nach der Währungsreform', *Wirtschaftsverwaltung*, 1(1948), 4, p.21.

38. Compare 'Preisspiegel', *Deutsche Wirtschaft*, no. 67, 30 August 1948: It was a mistake to think that price increases could be prevented by the continuation of

Knut Borchardt and Christoph Buchheim

consumers. (The establishment of the Mark's exchange rate at 30 cents in May 1948 had tripled cotton prices.)[39] The shortage was so pressing that retail prices rose as strongly as did producers' prices, leaving the retail mark-up as a percentage of the price undiminished and leading to sharply rising retail profits.[40]

Yet instead of leading to increased supplies of textiles, the price increases paradoxically produced the opposite effect. This was caused firstly by uncertainty about future supplies of raw materials. As a result of the 'import boom' in the first six months of 1948,[41] the JEIA had depleted its dollar reserves (including obligations incurred through letters of credit),[42] and had ordered a buying stop.[43] Secondly, having covered their immediate liquidity needs, textile producers and retailers began withholding supplies in the expectation of further price increases. As early as July 1948[44] one can see the first indications of this; delivery times were extended[45] and demands for counter-trade reappeared.[46] These processes also showed up at the textile trade fairs. As a result of the tumultuous demand, 'old customers' of suppliers were given priority and even these often received only 20–30 per cent of their requested amounts or were required to provide material in compensation.[47] The *Neue Textil-Zeitung* summarized the situation as follows: 'Almost all of the manifestations which one had hoped to bury following the currency reform are on the move again.'[48] In effect, market forces in the textile sector risked being neutralized by conditions which

rationing to some degree. 'The developments in the textile and leather sectors, where producers and sellers quickly found out how much money was in fact available, prove this.'

39. See '30 Cents endgültig in Kraft', *NTZ*, no. 24, 11 June 1948.

40. 'Weder Strukturschäden noch Störungen', *Wirtschaftsverwaltung* 1(1948), 6, p.22. According to an Emnid survey the majority of those questioned placed (partial) responsibility for textile price increases on the sellers, especially wholesalers. See 'Da tut Aufklärung not!', *Die Zeit*, no. 48, 25 November 1948.

41. Abelshauser, *Wirtschaft in Westdeutschland 1945–1948*, p.163; see also '222.5 Mill. Dollar Importverträge', *Die Welt*, no. 56, 13 May 1948, and 'Zwischen Soll und Ist', *NTZ*, no. 15, 9 April 1948.

42. 'Das unzweckmässige Importverfahren', *Handelsblatt*, no. 28, 29 June 1948.

43. 'Baumwoll-Versorgung gefährdet?', *NTZ*, no. 35, 27 August 1948.

44. 'Die zentrale Preisfrage', *NTZ*, no. 31, 30 July 1948; 'Die Lage nach der Währungsreform', *Wirtschaftsverwaltung*, 1(1948), 4, p.12, and 'Folgen verspäteter Preiskorrekturen', *Handelsblatt*, no. 35, 23 July 1948.

45. 'Die Lage nach der Währungsreform', *Wirtschaftsverwaltung*, 1(1948), 5, p.20.

46. 'Stabilisierung in Sicht?', *Wirtschaftsverwaltung*, 1(1948), 7, p.30, and 'Baumwolle aus der Türkei', *NTZ*, no. 36, 3 September 1948.

47. 'Wünsche und Möglichkeiten in Köln', *NTZ*, no. 39, 24 September 1948; on the Frankfurt fair see *NTZ*, no. 41, 6 October 1948; 'Die Disposition leicht gebessert', *Wirtschaftsverwaltung*, 1(1948), 9, pp.23f.

48. 'Faktor Zeit', *NTZ*, no. 42, 2 October 1948.

The Marshall Plan and Key Economic Sectors

they themselves had created. There was in certain aspects a 'voluntary' return to some of the practices of the rationing period, with the resulting symptoms of a hidden inflation. Any lengthy continuation of these circumstances was an obvious threat to the success of the currency reform.

The decisive bottleneck – and on this point there was general consensus – was the supply of raw materials, especially for the textile industry. The Munich-based Institut für Wirtschaftsforschung (Institute for Economic Research) accurately forecast in its very first bulletin on 20 July 1948 that 'the start [of the currency reform] is very positive. Yet the victory will depend on credit policy and, above all, on future supplies of raw materials'.[49] Reaching the same conclusion, the German Economic Administration of the Bizone decided to change its own supply policy. It applied to the ECA for permission to change the originally proposed distribution of upcoming Marshall Plan imports. Now instead of allocating 65 per cent of those imports for foodstuffs and agricultural goods, they proposed a reduction to 35 per cent, and conversely an increase to 65 per cent for imports necessary to manufacturing. 'The situation on the consumer goods market requires increased emphasis on industrial supplies; especially as no imports of industrial raw materials took place in the first quarter of the Marshall Plan.'[50] The head of the German bizonal administration, *Oberdirektor* Pünder, communicated the following message to the Military Government: 'The success of the currency reform depends primarily on our ability to offer sufficient quantities of industrially produced consumer goods and thereby to eliminate or at least to reduce current tensions in price developments and consumer supplies.'[51]

Certainly the textile market was not the only problem area during these months, yet it was undoubtedly an especially sensitive sector in terms of both economic and social policy. As the situation worsened, the disputes became more acrimonious,[52] accompanied by buyers' strikes,[53] demonstrations and violent riots.[54] The trade

49. *Ifo-Schnelldienst*, no. 1, 20 July 1948.
50. Assistant Secretary Keiser speaking at a Directors' meeting in Frankfurt on 24 August 1948, *Akten zur Vorgeschichte der Bundesrepublik Deutschland*, vol.4(1983), pp.759f.
51. Ibid., p.760.
52. For the following compare: Ambrosius, *Durchsetzung*, pp.184ff.
53. 'Öffentliche Hand muss sparen', *Wirtschaftsrevue*, no. 33, 13 August 1948, and 'Aktion gegen Preiswucher!', *Der Bund* (Nordmark Ausgabe), no. 17, 19 August 1948.
54. 'Zwischenfälle in Stuttgart', *Die Welt*, no. 128, 30 October 1948.

Knut Borchardt and Christoph Buchheim

unions called for a general strike on 12 November.[55] They demanded the imposition of an economic state of emergency and the
institution of temporary emergency measures (including the establishment of a Price Commissioner), thereby repeating, as the *Neue
Zürcher Zeitung* expressed it, 'the worst mistakes of the years 1931
and 1932'.[56] Over the course of these months the number of those
who believed in the success of the liberal market policy declined
steadily.[57] Some feared a wage–price spiral with a new round of
inflation and the collapse of the currency;[58] others feared Erhard's
downfall.[59] In the Economic Council the SPD placed two unsuccessful motions for the dismissal of the Economic Director, one on
17 August and a second on 10 November. The Länderrat, including
the CDU premiers, stood in opposition to the economic policies
coming out of Frankfurt. On 18 November that body passed a
resolution which contained the following passage:

> The Länderrat is unanimously of the opinion that the current situation
> necessitates a fundamental change in price policy. It is further of the
> opinion that the attempt to institute a functioning market economy in
> areas with critical shortages of supply must be considered a failure
> because the preconditions for this policy have not been realized. The
> situation is so serious that unquestionably some measures must be taken
> to create bearable price levels.[60]

Even in the Verwaltungsrat Erhard's policies were criticized; Hans
Schlange-Schöningen (Director for Nutrition, Agriculture and
Forests) suggested the creation of an independent Office of Prices.[61]

Under these circumstances, Erhard saw himself forced to take
public opinion into account; he needed, at the very least, to demonstrate that he was prepared to take direct and effective action against
rising prices and the ominous growth of barter and counter-trade
transactions. However the principle that prices must function as
indicators of shortages and as means of adjustment was to be

55. Compare: Müller, *Grundlegung*, pp.168ff.
56. 'Preispolitische Probleme Westdeutschlands. Gefährdung des Regimes Erhard?', *Neue Zürcher Zeitung* (*NZZ*), no. 331, 1 December 1948.
57. 'Klippen', *Allgemeine Kölnische Rundschau*, no. 21, 27 October 1948.
58. 'Preis-Löhne', *Die Welt*, no. 96, 17 August 1948; 'Besprechungen über
Kleider und Schuhe', *Hamburger Allgemeine Zeitung*, no. 80, 13 September 1948, and
'Besorgnis wegen einer Preis-Lohn Spirale', *Wirtschafts Zeitung*, no. 40, 1 October
1948.
59. See nn.56 and 57.
60. *Akten zur Vorgeschichte der Bundesrepublik Deutschland*, vol.4, p.985, n.5.
61. Cf. ibid., pp.53ff.

The Marshall Plan and Key Economic Sectors

preserved. Leonhard Miksch, one of Erhard's closest associates, explained the idea that prices must adjust to the stepped-up demand, 'if a new accumulation of pent-up purchasing power is to be avoided. That under the present circumstances would be especially dangerous since the entire population is still used to illegal recourse, which means that new corruption of the economic processes would immediately set in.'[62]

In September 1948 the first price guidelines for textiles and shoes were published, providing indices based on standard prices, and thereby contributing to some market transparency. The guidelines were to be visibly displayed in all stores.[63] At the same time the Economic Administration, together with the textile industry, began to elaborate the so-called 'Jedermann-Programm'. Using the English 'utility goods' as a model, the programme established a plan for production and distribution of reasonably priced quality goods,[64] and this started in November.[65] In October a bill sponsored by the Economic Administration took effect as the Law Against Profiteering (Gesetz gegen Preistreiberei) which penalized 'incommensurate charges'.[66]

Although these measures were initiated as a means of defending the market orientation of current economic policy, they contained in themselves some objectionable features in terms of market policy, and that did not escape immediate commentary.[67] They might ultimately prove to be signposts on the way back to a system of rationing and official price controls. During the most intense phase of pricing policy, at the end of 1948 and the beginning of 1949, this was in fact partially the case. In December Erhard announced the extension of the Jedermann-Programm to 70–80 per cent of textile production,[68] which in effect would have removed this sector from the market economy. Charging prices beyond those of the price guidelines was in itself sufficient cause for the price authorities to investigate whether the Law Against Profiteering

62. L. Miksch, 'Die Preisentwicklung', *Wirtschaftsverwaltung*, 1(1948), 7, p.4.
63. Anordnung PR no. 105/48, *VfWMBl* 1948, II, p.158, and 'Das sind die "Normalpreise"', *NTZ*, no. 38, 17 September 1948.
64. Cf. copy of 22 September 1948 letter from the VfW to the State Economic Offices, Bundesarchiv, B 102/629.
65. 'Die Jedermann-Höchstpreise', *TZ*, no. 53, 17 November 1948.
66. Gesetzblatt der Verwaltung des VWG, no. 20, 11 October 1948, p.99, and G. Müller, *Grundlegung*, pp.158ff.
67. 'Sozial geschützte Zone', *Industriekurier*, no. 23, 29 December 1948.
68. *Die Welt*, no. 143, 9 December 1948, and 'Gebundener Warenverkehr', *TZ*, no. 60, 11 December 1948.

Knut Borchardt and Christoph Buchheim

had been broken.[69] The next step was then the unanimous decision of all price-controlling organs to set maximum prices, beyond which charges would regularly be considered 'incommensurate'.[70] Finally, a renewal of the Law Against Profiteering abandoned the principle that shortage might influence price, and used instead production cost as its measure of what were commensurate charges.[71]

In view of these events, for which the developments in the textile industry served as a primary catalyst, the question remains why the relapse into a government-controlled economy did not take place. The answer is clear. As table 9.1 shows, average retail prices for textiles remained constant in December 1948 and then began a steady decline in the new year, falling below their June 1948 starting level. 'The change in the price curve [fell] so to speak, right in the middle of the Christmas shopping season',[72] and by year's end the general business community had the impression that prices had passed their peak.[73] The intensification of price control policy, with its potential to destroy the system, remained without effect because, in light of the changing trend, the Economic Administration refrained from further direct measures.[74] There was no further talk of the Jedermann-Programm; maximum prices were no longer set.[75] In April 1949 the obligatory display of price guidelines in shops was withdrawn;[76] in May the obligatory points for textile sales to consumers were formally abolished.[77] That summer the *Wirtschafts Zeitung* ran an article called 'Uninteresting Prices' which stated that 'the discussion about price developments has died out'.[78] Other problems such as capital shortage and unemployment became the new priorities.

Even today we do not completely understand what caused the

69. 'Überwiegend Ermässigungen', *NTZ*, no. 43, 13 October 1948.
70. '"Grenzpreise", ein neuer Preisbegriff', *Wirtschafts- und Finanz-Zeitung*, no. 2, 14 January 1949.
71. Gesetz gegen Preistreiberei of 28 January 1949 (*Gesetzblatt der Verwaltung des VWG*, no. 3, 5 February 1949, p.11): 'As a rule, incommensurate charges are those which do not consider the declining costs of replacement or of renewed production.'
72. 'Vor einer Senkung der Preise', *Wirtschaftsverwaltung*, 2(1949), p.43; see also *Monatsbericht der Bank Deutschen Länder* January 1949, pp.11f., and 'Auf welchen Stand pendeln die Preise aus?', *TZ*, no. 63/4, 23 December 1948.
73. 'Wirtschaftspolitischer Wochenkommentar', *Hamburger Freie Presse. Wirtschafts-Correspondent*, no. 52, 30 December 1948.
74. 'Preisstabilisierung als erstrebtes Ziel', *Handelsblatt*, no. 14, 22 February 1949.
75. 'Keine Grenzpreise mehr', *Die Welt*, no. 7, 18 January 1949.
76. Anordnung PR No. 36/49, 27 April 1949, *VfWMBl* 1949, II, p.55.
77. Anordnung Text II/49, 4 May 1949, *VfWMBl* 1949, I, p.70.
78. *Wirtschafts Zeitung*, no. 68, 24 August 1949.

The Marshall Plan and Key Economic Sectors

sudden reversal in the movement of prices, and thereby at the same time contributed to the success of the currency reform and the stabilization of the market-oriented economic order. The direct cause of the price trend reversal was presumably a weakening in consumer demand[79] which, in contrast to normal seasonal influences, had already begun to manifest itself before Christmas 1948. For the first time since the currency reform, the purchasing power of the mass of consumers was now limited to their current incomes, since most had spent their per capita quota of new money and the bulk of their converted savings.[80] The measures taken by the central banking system to limit the growth of credit in November 1948[81] may also have had a moderating influence on textile prices. These policies encouraged a more cautious pattern of consumption by the self-employed,[82] while an increase in finance costs of stocks accelerated the flow of goods on to the market. One might doubt whether any of the price-calming measures taken by the Economic Administration had any significant effect on the cooling off of prices, although this certainly did not prevent Erhard himself from expressing his satisfaction with the success of these measures in response to questioning from the SPD in the Economic Council. They were, after all, measures which he had ultimately supported.[83] Yet the early December date of the price reversal should, by itself, be a signal not to give too much weight to these acts.

In contrast, developments in the production of politically sensitive goods deserve much more attention than they have received in scholarly literature to date. Especially in textiles the stabilization of prices cannot be attributed to a slackening demand causing an 'overproduction' and hence downward pressure on prices. On the side of producers, demand held steady even after the reversal in retail prices and despite continuously increasing production. Manufacturers' prices reached their peak in October/November 1948 and declined only slightly in the following months (see table 9.1). This is confirmed by a February 1949 report on the economic situation:

79. *Monatsbericht der BdL*, January 1949, p.12.
80. Ibid., pp.24ff., and *Geschäftsbericht der BdL für 1948 und 1949*, p.7.
81. H. Möller, 'Die westdeutsche Währungsreform von 1948', in Deutsche Bundesbank, *Währung und Wirtschaft in Deutschland 1876–1975* (Frankfurt, 1976), pp.467f.
82. The demand for luxury goods in any case declined in December: 'Vor einer Senkung der Preise', *Wirtschaftsverwaltung*, 2(1949), p.42.
83. *Wörtliche Berichte und Drucksachen des Wirtschaftsrates des Vereinigten Wirtschaftsgebietes 1947–1949*, Institut für Zeitgeschichte und Deutscher Bundestag, vol.3 (Munich, 1977), p.1352 (31. Vollversammlung, 19 January 1949).

Knut Borchardt and Christoph Buchheim

'Demand continued greatly to exceed supplies for both raw materials and for yarn in the report period. The wholesale demand on the spinning, weaving and knitting industry continued, although somewhat diminished because of financial factors, with supply on the whole still insufficient.'[84] In fact the trade and the clothing industry seemed to be under pressure now, because consumers no longer uncritically bought everything offered. Stocks of older, overpriced goods of relatively inferior quality threatened to remain unsold. Yet the newer products from spinning and weaving mills moved without problems.[85] Any decrease in new production or even the chance of a decrease would presumably not have reduced hoarding[86] but rather would have stimulated it at every point in the industry. Supplies would not have been mobilized, and a decline in consumer prices would not have occurred, especially as final demand, e.g. for material sold by the metre, still could not be satisfied.[87] For the demand side alone to account for the price reversal in textiles would have required inducing a genuine deflation crisis with high levels of unemployment, which probably would not have made the success of the liberal market policy any more secure. The reason for events not taking that course lay in securing raw material deliveries through Marshall Plan imports.[88]

Imports, and especially imports of cotton, were crucially important for supplying the Bizone with the raw materials for textiles. Almost half of the yarn, including rayon, produced in the Bizone in 1948 and 1949 (January to September) came from cotton-spinning

84. *Wirtschaftsverwaltung*, 2(1949), p.221. Compare also 'Gesunde Textilproduktion. Die Krise rationalisiert den Verteilungsapparat', *Wirtschaftsrevue*, no. 6, 11 February 1949.
85. 'Gesunde Textilproduktion', ibid., and 'Schwarzer Peter', *TZ*, no. 29, 13 April 1949.
86. *Geschäftsbericht der BdL für 1948 und 1949*, p.7.
87. 'Textilwirtschaft im Aufstieg', *Wirtschafts- und Finanz-Zeitung*, no. 14, 7 April 1949; 'Mangelware', *TZ*, no. 35, 4 May 1949, and *Monatsberichte der BdL*, February 1949, pp.13f.
88. Developments were similar in the shoe industry, which also had come under critical crossfire because of rising prices at a time of widespread, urgent demand. Here the Marshall Plan in the first half of 1949 financed almost all of the leather imports and half of the imports of skins (with foreign supplies covering 70 per cent of the industry's needs); see F. Pfeiffer, 'Die Rohstoffversorgung der Lederwirtschaft', *Wirtschaftsverwaltung*, 2(1949), pp.160f.; *Das Europäische Wiederaufbauprogramm*, Amerikanische und Britische Besatzungszone Deutschlands, 1 January 1949 bis 31 März 1949 (= Gemeinsamer Bericht der Militärgouverneure der Vereinigten Staaten und des Vereinigten Königreichs, no. 3), 1949, pp.62f.; JEIA, *Monatsberichte April–Juni 1949* in conjunction with *Monatliche Aussenhandelsstatistik des VWG*, January–June 1949.

The Marshall Plan and Key Economic Sectors

mills.[89] In view of the relatively small volume of yarn imports, domestically produced cotton yarn constituted the single most important production input for the weaving mills. In 1950 almost 60 per cent of the fabrics woven in Germany consisted predominantly or completely of cotton.[90]

Table 9.2 shows that from the currency reform onwards well into 1949 cotton yarn production rose fairly steadily, with strong increases in production per working day. Both workers' productivity and the total number of hours worked increased rapidly.[91] In contrast, cotton imports fell off sharply after July 1948 at the time when the JEIA ordered its buying stop for the financial reasons already discussed. Raw material inventories at the spinning mills fell off accordingly. One may assume that the data in column (6) of table 9.2 present a reasonably accurate picture of total stocks as well because at the beginning of 1948 'OMGUS-Cotton', the first major postwar cotton import,[92] had been widely used up.[93] But then the renewed decline in inventories from September 1948 showed that the stocks of spinning mills, which had just reached the minimum level required for orderly production,[94] were melting away again. Added to this were low levels of current imports and a still insufficient number of new import contracts. Taken as a whole, one might understand the fears in the cotton industry which reached their peak and led to pessimistic predictions in August and September of 1948.[95]

Aside from the resumption of purchases by the JEIA,[96] the permission and realization of cotton imports financed with ERP funds was the single biggest reason why disruptions of cotton yarn

89. *Wirtschaft und Statistik*, NF 1(1949).

90. *Die Textilindustrie in der Bundesrepublik Deutschland im Jahr 1950*, Textil-Statistik GmbH, Frankfurt, pp.16f.

91. 'Bessere Versorgung der Textilindustrie', *Handelsblatt*, no. 58, 12 October 1948. Similar developments in other sectors brought about, as we have said, a complete change in VfW raw material planning.

92. Conversation with Dr Wiehenkel, former employee at the textile department of the VfW, in Garmisch-Partenkirchen, 14 January 1984; see also *Bericht der Handelskammer Bremen über die Jahre 1945/47*, pp.19f.

93. 'Textil-Produktion in der Doppelzone', *Wirtschaftsrevue*, no. 8, 21 February 1948.

94. There are various estimates for this, ranging from 1.5 to 4 times the monthly consumption. 'Zwischen 30 Cents und ACSC-Kredit', *NTZ*, no. 25, 18 June 1948; 'Baumwollversorgung gefährdet?', *NTZ*, no. 35, 27 August 1948, and 'Textil-Produktion in der Doppelzone', *Wirtschaftsrevue*, no. 8, 21 February 1948.

95. Compare e.g. 'Baumwollversorgung gefährdet?' (see n.94), where, because of the cotton shortage, threatening disturbances are mentioned 'which could have critical effects on the currency situation and on the development of price levels'.

96. 'Nötiger Sukkurs', *NTZ*, no. 37, 10 September 1948.

Table 9.2 Production and raw material consumption in the bizonal cotton spinning mills (in 1000 metric tons)

Month	Yarn production total (1)	Yarn production per working day (2)	Cotton consumption (3)	Net imports of cotton (4)	of which: % ERP financed (5)	Change in spinning mill inventory, cumulative since 1.48 (6)
1.48	6.2	0.24	5.5	9.3	—	3.6
2.48	6.5	0.27	5.7	3.3	—	0.5
3.48	7.2	0.29	6.4	5.7	—	-0.6
4.48	7.7	0.3	6.8	11.5	—	5.4
5.48	6.2	0.28	5.5	7.1	—	6.2
6.48	7.1	0.27	6.3	12.7	—	11.8
7.48	8.1	0.3	7.1	13.5	—	17.3
8.48	9.1	0.35	8.0	5.4	—	13.8
9.48	10.1	0.39	8.9	9.8	—	13.6
10.48	11.3	0.43	10.0	8.0	—	11.8
11.48	11.1	0.44	9.8	5.0	64	6.2
12.48	12.0	0.46	10.6	28.4	⎱	24.2
1.49	12.4	0.5	10.4	6.5	⎰	19.8
2.49	12.9	0.54	10.9	23.2	63	29.7
3.49	15.8	0.59	13.3	11.9		29.5
4.49	14.3	0.6	12.1	11.4	9	27.1
5.49	16.4	0.66	13.8	14.3	16	29.1
6.49	14.6	0.6	12.3	19.5	52	35.9
7.49	15.1	0.58	12.7	13.0	37	34.1
8.49	17.6	0.65	14.8	13.5	54	31.5
9.49	19.1	0.73	16.1	13.0	30	

Sources: Column 1: *Wirtschaft und Statistik*, NF, 1 (1949).

Column 2: Calculated from ibid.

Column 3: Calculated from column 1 on the basis of 15% waste in the spinning process in 1948 and 11% in 1949, and rayon staple constituting 25% of spinning-mill raw materials. These percentages were given to the authors in a letter from Mr Reiner Ott of the Industrial Association of Yarn Producers in Frankfurt. Compare also O. Pungs, 'Die Baumwollspinnereien im Aufschwung', in *Baumwollindustrie, Der Volkswirt*, 4(1950), 49, p.28.

Column 4: *Monatliche Aussenhandelsstatistik des Vereinigten Wirtschaftsgebiets.*

Column 5: Value proportions; ibid., in conjunction with *Das Europäische Wiederaufbauprogramm* (see n.88), pp.62ff.; JEIA, *Monatsberichte April–Juni 1949*, and *Status Reports* or *Berichte* (on ERP imports), BA B146/94–96.

Column 6: Calculated as cotton consumption (column 3) subtracted from the cotton imports of the previous month (column 4), whereby the resulting values were summed up. The column shows to what extent, under the stated consumptions, stocks at the end of each month had changed relative to January 1948. The one-month lag period between cotton imports and their arrival at the spinning mills is estimated from: Bremer Baumwollbörse, *Monatsberichte*. According to this publication between November 1948 and January 1949, the monthly imports of Bremen cotton traders were always roughly equal to warehouse inventories in Bremen at the end of that month. The results would not be substantially different if the lag period were disregarded.

Knut Borchardt and Christoph Buchheim

production were avoided. The developments in this respect were closely noted in the trade journals.[97] And at the beginning of December the *Textil-Zeitung* ran an article 'New Cotton Purchases in Sight' (from ERP funds) which declared that these imports 'would secure employment in the cotton industry through the winter months, a fact which will calm all members of the textile branch'.[98]

The certainty that new supplies were under way and that competition would therefore grow quickly meant that any hesitation now might later prove to be a dangerous mistake. These facts pushed the spinning mills toward a radical reduction of stocks in November and December.[99] Even before the first raw material deliveries had actually arrived, the Marshall Plan thus was already affecting production precisely at the time when price developments in the textiles market were playing a decisive role in the success or failure of Erhard's liberal market policies. For that reason it is not right to consider exclusively the period of actual delivery arrivals, and therefrom to conclude that the ERP deliveries played a relatively minor role in stabilizing the currency and economic policy reforms.[100] In addition, we can confirm that without the cotton imports financed by the Marshall Plan, which made up two-thirds of the total cotton imports into the Bizone from November 1948 to March 1949 (column 5, table 9.2), the production of the textile industry would not have been sufficient to achieve any retail price reductions in textiles. Finally, the development of stocks in 1949 shows that, despite fluctuations in cotton imports and in the percentage of ERP imports in the total, the raw material conditions for continuous production had been established.[101]

97. '95,000 Ballen US-Baumwolle', *NTZ*, no. 41, 6 October 1948; 'Die ECA-Baumwolle', *NTZ*, no. 46, 23 October 1948, and 'Erster ECA-Baumwolldampfer', *TZ*, no. 53, 17 November 1948. Very significant in this context is the somewhat erroneous comment by General Clay made in a conversation about the threatening supply crisis on 15 September 1948: 'Significant amounts of cotton and skins are underway to Germany.' See: *Akten zur Vorgeschichte der Bundesrepublik Deutschland*, vol.4, p.790. ERP status reports (BA B 146/94–96) show the first contract for a shipment of ECA cotton at 27 September 1948.

98. *TZ*, no. 59, 8 December 1948.

99. See also 'Früchte des ERP', *Die Neue Zeitung*, no. 39, 2 April 1949, and *Das europäische Wiederaufbauprogramm* (see n.88), p.35.

100. As do e.g. Ott, 'Die Bedeutung des Marshall-Plans', pp.34f., and Chr. Weisz (see n.10), pp.24f.

101. Cf. 'Das Leistungsbild der Textilindustrie', *TZ*, no. 103/4, 31 December 1949: 'The basis for the positive production development in 1949 has been the generous Marshall Plan help.' And 'Du und der Marshallplan!', *Der Bund (Nordmark Ausgabe)*, no. 20, 26 September 1949: 'Without ERP help there would not be large

The Marshall Plan and Key Economic Sectors

The Importance of Counterpart Funds in Ensuring Electricity Supplies in Western Germany

Although by 1948 electricity generation in West Germany had – in contrast to industrial production – already surpassed the 1936 level, the supply situation was far from satisfactory. The technological developments in factories and homes which demanded the use of 'refined energy' had progressed. The coal shortage as well caused consumers to use electricity to cover heating and power needs wherever possible. Although generation had made possible a 19 per cent increase in consumer electricity use from 1948 to 1949,[102] this was no indication that shortages had been overcome. Numerous consumer restrictions remained in force: reduced frequencies and voltage, bans on the use of certain appliances, shifting industrial production to night hours, and power shut-offs.[103] Bavaria especially suffered from electricity shortages.[104] The Electricity Committee of the OEEC heard a February 1949 report that estimated the electricity deficit for the Bizone at 8 billion kWh, with a then current generation of 30 billion kWh. The report went on to state that considering the superannuation and the susceptibility to trouble of the existing power plants, the shortage in fact amounted to a full half of the available 6,000 MW capacity.[105]

Beyond these immediate problems, the long-term prognosis in 1948/9 was also a cause for concern. The hoped-for rapid growth of industrial production might be seriously inhibited by energy supply bottlenecks. General Clay expressed his conviction 'that the only limit on the future development of industrial production would be in electricity'.[106] Similarly, the journal of the bizonal Economic Administration stated, 'The precondition for an increase in industrial production is a progressive increase in energy availability.'[107]

---

imports of cotton, wool, jute and leather. There would be fewer textiles for sale today than during the rationing system.'

102. *Statistisches Jahrbuch für die Bundesrepublik Deutschland 1953*, p.269.

103. 'Memorandum über die Lage der Elektrizitätsversorgung in der Bundesrepublik Deutschland vom 28.1.1950, pp.1f.; BA, Z 14/62.

104. W. Hartmann, 'Die öffentliche Elektrizitätsversorgung in Bayern', *Elektrizitätswirtschaft*, 48(1949), p.194.

105. 'Bericht über Sitzungen des Arbeitsausschusses des Electricity Committee der OEEC vom 10.2.1949', pp.1f.; BA, Z 14/62.

106. General Clay in a conversation with the premiers on 29 October 1948: *Akten zur Vorgeschichte*, vol.4, p.914.

107. 'Strommangel begrenzt Produktionsentwicklung', *Wirtschaftsverwaltung*, 1(1948), 13, p.5.

Knut Borchardt and Christoph Buchheim

The Korean War boom, and especially the winter of 1950–1, showed how correct these concerns about inadequate electricity generation capacity had been. The delivery abilities of the power plants remained far below the demand placed on them. The resulting electricity crisis led to drastic administrative restrictions. Industrial customers with an average weekly consumption of more than 2,000 kWh were forced to accommodate to a one-quarter cut in electricity allotments beginning on 15 January 1951. It is true that this reduction was relaxed in February and completely removed in March,[108] but in the following winter power shut-offs still could not be completely avoided.[109]

The most conspicuous cause of these difficulties was the coal shortage of the electrical power stations.[110] This in turn, however, was largely caused by inadequate capacity, i.e. by a shortage of efficient electricity generating plants. As late as 1953 demand was met only by continuing to employ plants which consumed twice as much coal as the average,[111] although investment had already done much to improve the average thermal efficiency. The hard coal consumption of public power plants fell from 0.66 SKE per kWh produced in 1948 to 0.52 SKE in 1952, a decline of 21 per cent.[112]

Taken together, current facilities, new construction and expansion of existing plants could hardly keep pace with the rapidly increasing demand for electricity and the burden of the coal shortage in the years immediately following 1948. It was not till 1953 that limitations on electrical consumption were phased out, and this was made possible only by employing very uneconomical plants. For that reason none of the power plants built partially with counterpart funds in the years

108. W. Abelshauser, 'Korea, die Ruhr und Erhards Marktwirtschaft: Die Energiekrise von 1950/51', *Rheinische Vierteljahrsblätter*, 45(1981), pp.288f.; see also *Börsen- und Wirtschaftshandbuch 1952* (Frankfurt, 1952), p.21.

109. 'Die Elektrizitätsversorgung in der Bundesrepublik Deutschland im Jahr 1951', *Elektrizitätswirtschaft*, 51(1952), p.357.

110. H. R. Adamsen, *Investitionshilfe für die Ruhr. Wiederaufbau, Verbände und Soziale Marktwirtschaft 1948–1952* (Wuppertal, 1981), p.101.

111. Kreditanstalt für Wiederaufbau, *Jahresbericht 1953*, pp.26f., and 'Die Elektrizitätsversorgung in der Bundesrepublik Deutschland im Jahr 1953', *Elektrizitätswirtschaft*, 53(1954), p.534.

112. 'Die Elektrizitätsversorgung' (see n.111), p.545. Important in this was the adaptation of the power plants for high temperature steam and the introduction of turbines connected in series; for this see *Gutachten über die Kosten- und Ertragslage der Elektrizitätswirtschaft im Bundesgebiet*, for the Bundesministerium für Wirtschaft written by H. Krönke et al. (Frankfurt, 1952), pp.48ff., and *Das Gemeinschaftswerk Hattingen und seine wirtschaftliche Vorrangstellung in der öffentlichen Energieversorgung* (1948), pp.15ff.

The Marshall Plan and Key Economic Sectors

prior to 1953 can be regarded as dispensable.[113]

That 'the expansion of power plant capacity [is] the most pressing task of the German economy'[114] was a widely held conviction. And indeed those persons responsible for the disposition of the Marshall Plan counterpart funds did justice to this conviction. It even appears that for some periods the representatives of the Military Government gave the electricity industry still higher priority for the reception of counterpart funds than did the German administration.[115] The result was that this industry received about one-quarter[116] of the DM 3.2 billion in original counterpart funds, which until 1952 were administered by the Kreditanstalt für Wiederaufbau (KfW) (Reconstruction Loan Corporation). That amount exceeded the amount given to any other industrial sector, including basic industries such as coal and iron, which, like the electricity industry, were subject to price controls and were thereby limited in their financing possibilities after the currency reform.

The following analysis of the expansion and financing of electricity generating capacity is limited for the most part to those electricity companies which provided power for public consumption. The material does not allow an investigation of the separate financing of private industrial plants. But in view of our interest in assessing the role of the Marshall Plan, the exclusion of the industrial power plants is not a serious cause for concern. In the official energy programmes, ERP loans to public power plants far exceeded loans granted to industrial companies for the purpose of expanding their power generating capacities. By the end of 1952 the KfW had used the original counterpart funds (including about DM 90 million in GARIOA counterparts but without loans from the ERP Interest and Repayment Fund) to grant DM 729 million in loans to public electricity companies; by contrast industrial power plants had received just DM 50 million.[117]

Table 9.3 provides a summary of the annual gross capital investment by public electricity companies and the increase of

113. Cf. also E. Baumgart, *Investitionen und ERP-Finanzierung* (=DIW Sonderhefte, NF, 56) (Berlin, 1961), pp.76f.
114. Cf. Institut für Wirtschaftsforschung, Munich, *Die Industrie Westdeutschlands. Jahresrückblick, Stand, Aussichten für 26 Industriezweige* (Munich, February 1950), p.16
115. *Akten zur Vorgeschichte*, vol.5, p.1057.
116. Pohl, *Wiederaufbau. Kunst und Technik der Finanzierung 1947–1953*, pp.200f.
117. KfW, *Darlehenskontenblätter*.

Knut Borchardt and Christoph Buchheim

Table 9.3 Gross capital investment and credits from the original counterpart funds to public electricity companies in West Germany (excluding West Berlin) (in million DM)

	1949	1950	1951	1952
1. Gross capital investments	890	1150	1260	1440
2. Increase in counterpart loans outstanding at year's end over the previous year*	174	345	152	57

* The corresponding numbers from the annual reports of the KfW are: for 1949, 203; for 1950 (including preliminary financing), 354; for 1951 (conflicting data), either 230 or 212; for 1952, 48 or, on the basis of the smaller value for the previous year, 66; a total therefore for the years 1949 to 1952 of DM 835 million as opposed to DM 729 million in the table. The difference arises from the fact that KfW annual reports on the one hand include loans for industrial power plants and, on the other hand, put down only for loans paid out, whereas in the table these have been balanced with repayments. A third and different set of figures is provided by Baumgart, who also works from loans paid out. Except for discrepancies in individual years (non-inclusion of preliminary financing?), his sum of DM 872 million up to 1952, not including industrial power plants (c. 50 million), including ERP interest and repayment funds (62 million) is not very far from the KfW annual report figures. Here we are working with the data presented in the table, since the public electricity companies had only loans of this amount at their middle-term disposal, which therefore could in fact serve as help in financing plant investment.

Sources: Line 1: E. Baumgart, *Investitionen und ERP-Finanzierung* (DIW, Sonderhefte, NF 56, Berlin, 1961), p.71

Line 2: KfW Darlehenskontenblätter (1949 and 1950 including DM 14 million in FINAG loans to electric companies in the French Zone, which were later taken over by the KfW).

outstanding loans provided by the counterpart funds at year's end.

Accordingly, loans from counterpart funds had their greatest importance in the years 1949–51, when, as we shall see, they were also most desperately needed. In the first two years those loans increased to 20 and 30 per cent of annual gross capital investment, and thereby, even if one includes later loans from the ERP Interest and Repayment Fund and the investment help (about DM 250 million over several years),[118] reached a level which remained unmatched in the following years.[119]

The loans supported primarily seven large companies: Bayernwerk AG, Energie-Versorgung Schwaben AG, Hamburgische Elektri-

118. Adamsen (see n.110), p.264.
119. Compare Baumgart, *Investitionen und ERP-Finanzierung*, p.71; KfW, *Jahresberichte 1951–*.

The Marshall Plan and Key Economic Sectors

zitätswerke AG, Nordwestdeutsche Kraftwerke AG, Preussische Elektrizitäts-AG(Preag), Rheinisch-Westfälisches Elektrizitätswerk AG (RWE) and Vereinigte Elektrizitätswerke Westfalen AG (VEW). This group held DM 156 million of the outstanding loans at the end of 1949, while the choice made by the Military Government meant that municipal power plants received nothing that year. Even at the close of 1952 some 70 per cent (DM 511 million) of the total of DM 729 million in loans had gone to those companies, DM 241 million to the RWE alone.[120] Since these big companies were the most important generators of power, this allocation of counterpart funds among the electricity industry indicates that the major policy emphasis lay in boosting electricity *generation*.

A look at the list of supported projects confirms this. With only a few exceptions, counterpart funds were granted to electricity companies only for construction of new, or expansion of old, power plants.[121] Investments in networks had to be financed by other means, usually by the company itself. This does not, however, mean that those investments were any less urgent. Although the prewar network had been built with a substantial reserve capacity, increased consumption had swallowed this capacity by the beginning of the 1950s, with the result that the amount of electricity being produced could hardly be properly distributed.[122] Take as an example a letter from the VEW to the West German Federal Ministry for the Marshall Plan:[123] 'In some areas both industry and other customers can no longer be adequately supplied because of an overburdened power supply grid. It is extremely difficult today to connect new customers.'

At the end of 1950 the investment required to guarantee the necessary reserve capacity in the power network was estimated to be far in excess of the means required for creating the necessary reserve of power generating capacity: DM 1.6 billion versus DM 0.4 billion.[124] This leads us to the conclusion that without the availability of counterpart funds for the electricity industry, investments in the network would have received priority over expansion

120. KfW, *Darlehenskontenblätter*; see also Pohl (see n.6), p.55.
121. Projekte der Elektrizitätswirtschaft im Rahmen der II. Tranche (DM 1150 Mio Programm) aus Counterpart Funds, BA, B102/684, and Projekte der Elektrizitätswirtschaft im Rahmen der III. Tranche (1500 Mio Programm) aus Counterpart Funds (temporary list), BA, B 102/15924.
122. *Gutachten über die Kosten- und Ertragslage der Elektrizitätswirtschaft*, p.182.
123. BA, Z 14/62, letter of 9 January 1950.
124. 'Reservehaltung in Kraftwerken und Leitungsnetzen in der westdeutschen Elektrizitätsversorgung', *Elektrizitätswirtschaft*, 51(1952), pp.95ff.

Knut Borchardt and Christoph Buchheim

of generating capacity with the inevitable consequence of continued power-saving policies and even deeper power cuts. An official memorandum on the electricity supply situation in the Federal Republic from 28 January 1950 outlined that domestic capital was needed especially for construction of lines and transformer substations.[125] Indications of how the capital shortage in the wake of the currency reform had left the electricity companies with very few options for financing new power plant construction can also be found in the completed questionnaires to the Marshall Plan administration of spring 1949 (although one must consider a certain self-interested one-sidedness on the part of the reporting companies). One can read there about arrested contracts due to capital shortages, about the danger of work stoppages on the construction of new power plants and about project completion dates dependent on credit clearances.[126] Table 9.4 provides a first impression regarding the importance of counterpart funds for the growth in capacity of the West German electricity industry.

Between 1948 and 1952 70 per cent of the increased electricity generation capacity of West German public utilities was at least partially financed by original counterpart funds. In terms of the entire West German electricity industry, including private industrial facilities, the funds helped to finance almost three-fifths of increased capacity.[127] The table shows further that from 1946 to 1948 the growth in capacity installed at public power plants was largely the result of repair work, but that after that time new construction played the primary role. Measured in terms of capacity, the volume of new construction was six times as great in 1949 as in 1948. Three-quarters of that was partially financed by counterpart funds. This percentage increased over the following years, reaching 100 per cent in 1951 before falling back below 50 per cent in 1953 and to just 8 per cent in 1954. Altogether, ERP funds at least partially financed four out of every five *newly* installed megawatts in the West German public electricity industry.

At this point a first attempt can be made to estimate the overall economic importance of these counterpart funds. The upper limit for the macroeconomic effect of ERP loans to the electric power industry results from the following hypotheses: (1) With-

125. BA, Z 14/62.
126. BA, Z 8/1520–4.
127. About 300 MW of the increased capacity of the private plants was also partially financed with counterpart funds. Bericht über Sitzungen des Electricity Committee der OEEC vom 8.7.1949, p.6, BA, Z 14/62 in conjunction with the project lists (n.121); see also *Elektrizitätswirtschaft*, 50(1951), p.30.

Table 9.4 Installed capacity of West German power plants (excluding Berlin) in MW

	1946	1947	1948	1949	1950	1951	1952	1953	1954
1. Industrial power plants, total at year's end	–	–	3.951	–	4.281	4.754	5.231	5.567	6.117
2. Public utilities, total at year's end	5.414	5.759	5.956	6.282	6.901	7.822	8.686	9.094	9.832
3. Net increase achieved by:	336	345	197	326	619	921	864	408	738
4. Repairs	225	342	150	68	35	25	–	–	–
5. New construction, expansion	111[a]	–	49	301	574	793[b]	872	453	903
of which:									
6. Partially financed with original counterpart funds	–	–	–	230[c]	485	805[b]	585	207	68

(a) Of which 18.5 MW from the transfer of an industrial power plant.

(b) 'Die Elektrizitätsversorgung in der Bundesrepublik Deutschland im Jahr 1951', *Elektrizitätswirtschaft*, 51(1952), p.358: adding the individual new gains in table 4 of that source results in 823 MW, whereas table 3 reports total new gains of 793 MW. The contradiction could not be resolved, but does explain the figure of 805 MW in line 6 of our table 9.4.

(c) Estimate: in 1949 and 1950 the total increase in capacity partially financed by the counterpart funds was 830 MW, of which 110 MW were in West Berlin (*5. und 6. Bericht der Deutschen Bundesregierung über die Durchführung des Marshallplans* (Bonn, 1951), pp. 43–5). Considering that for 1950 alone the figure was 485 MW (see table) and the fact that new industrial power plants in general were operational only in the following years, the reported number, about 230 MW, results.

Sources: Line 1: Statistisches Bundesamt, *Die industriellen Stromerzeugungsanlagen 1948–1954* (Die Industrie der Bundesrepublik Deutschland, Sonderheft 19), Stuttgart, 1956, pp.9f.

Lines 2–5: 'Die Elektrizitätsversorgung in der Bundesrepublik Deutschland', in *Elektrizitätswirtschaft* 49ff., 1950–

Line 6: The most plausible values which can be extracted from the data; see ibid. in conjunction with project lists (footnote 121); KfW, *Darlehenskontenblätter*, questionnaires (footnote 126); progress reports and correspondence, BA B102/681–4.

Knut Borchardt and Christoph Buchheim

out the counterpart funds those public and industrial power plants which received financial aid would not have been constructed. (2) Power capacity would then have grown until 1952 by some 2,400 MW less, with the same proportional reduction in electricity generation and consumption. (3) Electricity productivity, i.e. the ratio of electricity consumed to gross domestic product, remains constant. Under these conditions and without ERP loans for power plant construction, the gross domestic product in 1952 would have reached only 83 per cent of its actual level. In other words, in 1952 GDP (and industrial production measured in constant prices) would have barely increased from 1950 levels.[128] This must be considered the upper limit of our estimate since some of the projects partly financed by the ERP loans would have been built even without ERP money. In that sense hypothesis (1) is unrealistic.[129] Of course we cannot reliably state what the volume of new construction would have been without the counterpart funds. However we can estimate the total costs of power plant construction, which was partially financed by Marshall Plan means, and then compare with them the loans granted through the counterpart funds.

From data on the replacement values of power plant equipment and on the capital required for the amount of increased power plant capacity considered necessary,[130] we can construct the average cost in DM of each kW:[131]

DM per kW additional capacity in steam power plants   440

128. Statistisches Bundesamt, *Lange Reihen zur Wirtschaftsentwicklung* (Stuttgart, 1973), p.154.

129. In contrast, the other assumptions, taken together, seem very plausible because in view of the missing reserves, a parallel development of capacity expansion and amount generated is not improbable, and the total economic electricity productivity actually declined by 6 per cent between 1950 and 1952. There would indeed have been a certain compensation for reduced electricity use in the form of reduced fuel consumption by the power stations themselves. The rest of the economy therefore could have received larger coal allocations. However one must consider that the efficiency of the public electricity companies improved by 10 per cent from 1950 to 1952 precisely because of the introduction of new power plants ('Die Elektrizitätsversorgung in der Bundesrepublik Deutschland im Jahr 1953', *Elektrizitätswirtschaft*, 53(1954), p.545)

130. 'Reservehaltung in Kraftwerken und Leitungsnetzen in der westdeutschen Elektrizitätsversorgung', *Elektrizitätswirtschaft*, 51(1952), p.96.

131. Compare to this another estimate (values in the same order): 450, 1,400, 1,000 (F. Stiegler, 'Investitionshilfe und Strompreise', ibid., p.25). In contrast, the KfW gave a unified estimate for RWE of DM 400/kW (KfW, Kreditabteilung, Akte 1546 alt 1, note of 7 May 1956).

The Marshall Plan and Key Economic Sectors

DM per kW additional capacity running water power plants   1,640

DM per kW additional capacity reservoir power stations   770

Multiplying the capacity of the power plant projects partially financed by counterpart funds 1949–52 by average costs per kW produces a total cost for these projects of DM 1,340 million[132] compared to 729 million in ERP loans. A straight calculation thus shows that more than half of the capacity of power plants supported by the Marshall Plan was financed by counterpart funds, i.e. over 1,200 MW (including private industrial plants). Based on our calculation above, this means a contribution to the domestic product of roughly 9 per cent of the 1952 level. Had Marshall Plan financing for the construction of power plants not been available, the growth in real domestic product between 1950 and 1952 would have been 9.4 per cent instead of 20 per cent.

Even if one considers the possibility that building fewer new power plants would have meant that some of the investment in the power grid could also have been spared and thus theoretically more than 1,200 MW in power plant capacity could have been financed exclusively by German means, the calculation seems to be a reasonable, perhaps even a minimum, value of the effect of the counterpart funds channelled into the electricity industry. For it was exactly the large companies, i.e. the most important generators of electricity, who had the least means of their own for use in additional power plant construction. At the RWE, for example, new power plant construction in the fiscal years 1948/9 to 1952/3 totalled DM 288 million,[133] while at the end of 1952 the amount of outstanding original counterpart fund loans was, as already noted, DM 241 million, which had already been deployed in projects of 517 MW additional capacity. That means that almost the entire new

132. According to a similar calculation, all public utility power plant construction which came on line between 1949 and 1952 would have cost about DM 1.5 billion. This sum appears small in comparison to the gross plant investment given in table 9.3. Yet one must consider that grid equipment is very expensive. For example, the 1950 replacement costs of the West German power plants was placed at DM 4 billion and that of the power grid at DM 8.2 billion ('Reserverhaltung' (see n.130), pp.96f.). On average then, the investment in the power grid must have been twice that of investment in generating facilities. Using this for the years 1949–52, then the data in table 9.3 no longer appear incompatible with our calculations. See also *Elektrizitätswirtschaft*, 50(1951), p.30, where costs for the *total* building programme partially financed by ERP means are DM 1.33 billion. However, this sum must apply to the original plans from the years 1949–50, and these were, because of the increased costs (see K. W. Roskamp, *Capital Formation in West Germany* (Detroit, 1965), p.72), not kept.

133. KfW (see n.131).

Knut Borchardt and Christoph Buchheim

power plant capacity of this company was financed through ERP means. Had a credit shortage prevented the construction of that new capacity, smaller electricity companies certainly would not have installed an additional 250 MW either. This in turn shows how unrealistic the assumption is that a discontinuation of ERP loans and the consequent reduction of financial means by one half would have caused only one half of the power plant projects not to be built.

Of course this argument is only valid if the counterpart funds did in fact plug a financing gap, and if that gap could not have been filled by other means. So in the following pages we shall attempt to estimate the size of the financing deficit. Thereafter, on pp.444–9, we shall consider whether additional means for self-financing were available and/or whether other sources of appropriate external financing could have been tapped.

The balance sheets of the RWE, which again serve as our example, reveal the following concerning the financing deficit (Table 9.5):

In the year 1948/9 physical investments could have been financed by available long-term means even without the small loan from KfW. Significant, however, is the very small addition in power plants in that year. As this increased sharply in the following three years, the situation changed dramatically. Now the ERP loans filled an otherwise gaping financing deficit for the greater part of power plant construction in these years. In contrast, beginning in 1952/3 the gross investment in physical plant could be financed practically without the loans of the KfW. In fact by 1953/4 there was a large excess of financing means; thus financial investment jumped to DM 100 million.

The development of deductions explains the turnaround in the financial situation of the company. These shot up from DM 73 million in 1950/1, past DM 130 million in 1951/2, to DM 183 million in 1952/3. Line 5 of table 9.5 shows how the renewed special deduction possibilities given to basic industry in the Investitionshilfegesetz (IHG) (Investment Assistance Law) of 7 January 1952 made themselves felt. Yet these possibilities would probably have remained as ineffectual as the general permission for special deductions in paragraph 7a of the Income Tax Law which was valid until the middle of 1951, if the Economics Ministry had not used its powers according to paragraph 37 of the IHG to grant the electricity companies permission to set higher prices.[134] Even after the permission for special deductions had expired in 1956, the financial

134. See n.135.

Table 9.5 Financing capital investment at RWE (million DM)

						Year					
	1948/9	49/50	50/1	51/2	52/3	53/4	54/5	55/6	56/7	57/8	58/9
1. Net addition of physical assets (including those under construction) of which:	90	150	188	188	248	291	347	377	235	271	209
2. Additions of power plants	7	55	55	133	37	54	163	–	–	–	–
3. Net financial investment	–	–	–	–	21	101	18	73	6	-1	61
4. Total deductions on physical assets of which:	68	68	73	131	183	212	217	201	248	213[a]	178[a]
5. Special deductions	6	9	15	86	125	146	146	93	120	–	–
6. Additional long-term indebtedness of which:	13	64	70	70	69	123	50	41	-33	-21	54
7. KfW loans[b]	9	57	65	75	45	50	–	–	-13	-16	–
8. Increase in share capital	–	–	–	–	–	–	–	182	–	–	–
9. Other long-term resources	16	14	14	-3	25	72	53	227	32	112	24
10. Stated profit	1	4	10	12	14	19	22	39	42	54	55
11. Total long-term financial means, incl. profits	98	150	167	210	291	426	342	690	289	358	311
12. Total long-term resources, excl. KfW loans	89	93	102	135	246	376	342	690			

(a) Including deductions on financial investments.
(b) As of 1951, loans from the original counterpart funds supplemented by the ERP interest and repayment funds and the Investment Help; at the end of 1952, however, still 80 per cent of all KfW loans to electricity companies were original counterpart funds (KfW, *Jahresberichte*).

Sources: Annual balances, published in the *Bundesanzeiger*; KfW Credit Division, file 1546 alt 1.

Knut Borchardt and Christoph Buchheim

difficulties of the electricity companies did not return. On the one hand, the level of deductions remained rather high as a result of the non-linear deduction method which had in the meanwhile been allowed.[135] On the other hand, the increased profitability of the electricity industry, brought about by the deregulation of prices,[136] meant that recourse to the capital market now proved possible. This is clearly shown by the increase of 1955/6 in share capital and the successful borrowing of DM 75 million in 1958/9.[137]

In the period 1949 to 1952, however, the loans from the original counterpart funds were in fact decisively important for the construction of RWE's power plants. Since the situation in the other large companies was at that time quite similar,[138] the conclusions drawn from the RWE experience reflect the situation at large in public electricity supply. It was, in any case, not possible for these companies to finance the power plant construction of 1949–52 from their own resources.

This was a result of the low profitability of electricity generation in the years immediately following the currency reform – a consequence of the price freeze of 1936. Government price setting powers were applied quite differently to the production inputs of the power plants and to electricity sales. Over the years, the price of coal had been successively increased to more than twice the 1936 level,[139] but the electricity industry was allowed to pass along only a portion of the resulting cost increases.[140] Since the coal cost in the thermal power plants constituted half of the costs of producing electricity,[141] the profitability of these plants was greatly impaired. In addition, increases in the costs of other production factors such as wages, freight rates, material and interest were also not allowed

135. Compare H. Lilienfein, 'Die wirtschaftliche Entwicklung der Elektrizitätsversorgungsunternehmen im Spiegel der Bilanzen 1948 bis 1955', *Elektrizitätswirtschaft*, 56(1957), p.55.

136. See 'Probleme der bayerischen Elektrizitätsversorgung', *Elektrizitätswirtschaft*, 49(1950), p.286; 'Strompreise', ibid., 50(1951), p.31, and 'Die Elektrizitätsversorgung der Bundesrepublik Deutschland im Jahr 1957', ibid., 57(1958), p.412.

137. In 1958 a member of the executive board of the KfW stated publicly that the capital market was now productive enough for all electricity companies and that the use of counterpart funds was superfluous (compare *Elektrizitätswirtschaft*, 57(1958), p.159).

138. *Gutachten* (see n.112), pp.168, 184.

139. *Statistisches Jahrbuch für die Bundesrepublik Deutschland 1953*, p.488.

140. Anordnung PR 53/48 zur Änderung der Preise für elektrischen Strom of 21.6.1948, *Mitteilungsblatt der VfW*, 1948, II, p.94. Compare also 'Strompreise', *Elektrizitätswirtschaft*, 50(1951), p.30.

141. *Gutachten* (see n.112), p.116.

The Marshall Plan and Key Economic Sectors

Table 9.6 Costs and returns of two companies delivering to contract buyers 1950/1 (Pfennig per produced kWH)

	I	II
Production costs	5.94	5.09
Costs of sales and administration	1.81	1.97
Return from sales to distributing companies	5.49	4.54
Return from sales to special buyers	5.86	3.31

Source: Gutachten über die Kosten- und Ertragslage der Elektrizitätswirtschaft im Bundesgebiet, dem BMW erstattet von H. Krönke u.a. (Frankfurt, 1952), Appendices 523.0. 523.2, 53.

to be passed on to electricity purchasers.[142] Compare the 1950/1 costs and returns per kWh *produced* of two of the large companies given in table 9.6.

In both cases the average returns do not cover even average production costs. The effect of this on profits was somewhat reduced since both companies were able to obtain cheaper electricity from other sources (for 3.84 and 4.08 Pf./kWh respectively). The practical effect of the price freeze had placed producers of electricity at a disadvantage *vis-à-vis* resalers. It is then hardly surprising that with only one exception, of all of the firms covered in an inquiry into the electricity industry, only a few municipal works which did not have their own production were able to cover costs and even show a profit.[143]

Naturally, a situation in which electricity producers operated at a loss while demand for electricity grew quickly was in the long run untenable. The profitability of the producing companies would have to be improved, at the very latest after the large counterpart fund loans, which were not granted on the basis of private profitability, dried up. This is in fact what took place. Using paragraph 37 of the IHG, the Economics Minister on 26 March 1952 issued a directive through which the price-changing clauses of producer–resaler and producer–special buyer contracts were reinstated.[144] These clauses permitted the producers to adjust their sale prices to accommodate changes in the price of production inputs. Recent improvements in the thermal efficiency of power plants, however, meant that the nominal limits of price increases as set in these

142. P. Reichel, 'Strompreisgestaltung', *Elektrizitätswirtschaft*, 48(1949), p.33; 'Strompreise', n.140.
143. *Gutachten* (see n.112), Appendix 53.
144. VO PR 18/52, *Bundesanzeiger* (BAnz), 28 March 1952.

Knut Borchardt and Christoph Buchheim

clauses had in fact hardly to be fully used to reach profitability. The result was that, in effect, prices from then on were deregulated.[145] Barely one year later, the base prices for smaller industrial and agricultural customers, which had been set by the 1938 Rate Schedule for Electricity (Tarifordnung für elektrische Energie), were also deregulated.[146] By these means both the profitability and the credit-worthiness of electricity producers were restored. In conjunction with the generous deduction rules, there were no financing problems in the electricity industry any more, as the RWE example clearly shows.

It has therefore to be admitted that one alternative to the counterpart funds was available, i.e. a loosening of the price freeze on electricity some time before 1952. In that case special deduction opportunities for the electricity industry would not have been necessary since, as mentioned above, more general and wide-ranging rules for increased deductions were in effect until the middle of 1951. It is of course understandable why the electricity price freeze was not loosened in the second half of 1948. But in 1949/50, in the phase of falling retail prices, it would have been thinkable to allow electricity prices to adjust to changing production costs. For the mass of consumers this price increase would presumably have been only marginally noticeable, especially if the household rates had been left unchanged, as they were even in 1952/3. It is thus possible that the availability of the counterpart funds and the temporary relief they brought to the financial problems of the electricity industry actually had a retarding effect on reform of the electricity market.

Excluding the price deregulation scenario just sketched as an alternative to the use of counterpart funds for the construction of power plants, it is certain that the ERP loans closed a financing gap and contributed decisively to the growth of West German production. Is it, however, possible to strengthen this conclusion? Is it right to say that only because the counterpart funds were available, could the capacity for electrical power production be expanded to a significant degree? The accuracy of that statement depends on how one evaluates the probability that other financing possibilities would have been available for this purpose.

Up to now no one has asserted that normal capital market

145. K. Sachs, 'Aktuelle Fragen aus dem Preisrecht', *Elektrizitätswirtschaft*, 51(1952), pp.468ff., and Sachs, 'Strompreise und Preisänderungsklauseln im Spiegel des Preisrechts und des Währungsgesetzes', ibid., 53(1954), pp.438ff.
146. VO PR 3/53, *BAnz*, 31 March 1953.

The Marshall Plan and Key Economic Sectors

resources were available in sufficient quantities for these projects. In fact the shortage of exactly these types of funds was an obvious feature of 1949 and thereafter. At that time the electricity companies, in conjunction with the KfW, brought out subscriptions on DM 215 million worth of loans in order to cover the first ERP tranche. Of that amount only DM 29 million could actually be raised in 1949, DM 10 million in 1950 and much smaller sums in each of the following two years. The remaining portion ended up in KfW deposits, and in return the KfW gave book credits to these companies.[147] This failure caused the Kreditanstalt to cease demanding the issue of further bonds through the electricity companies.[148]

Offering inadequate interest rates was not the reason that the electricity companies failed to gain sufficient financing through the capital market. The return on their bonds was, at 6.5 per cent[149] on a twenty-year maturity,[150] in fact quite good in comparison to the older bonds which were still in circulation.[151] Yet there was no large-scale shift away from older bonds. Because of market imperfections, potential buyers of electricity company bonds faced very high price risks in any shift away from older bonds. For that reason, new offers, even with relatively good terms, could be absorbed only slowly.[152] There was very little first-time money looking for investments in the capital market, partly because of government intervention in that market. In addition, the savings rate on personal disposable income was low,[153] and private investors understandably still shied away from securities after their earlier experiences with inflation.[154] Corporations were using any free capital to cover their own investment needs.[155] And we must

---

147. KfW, *Jahresbericht 1949*, p.22, and *Jahresbericht 1952*, p.55.

148. KfW, proposal of 6 March 1952 for the 12. Kreditbewilligungsausschuss (KBA)-Sitzung; proposal of 20 June 1952 for the 13. KBA-Sitzung.

149. KfW, *Jahresbericht 1949*, p.22.

150. In any case at RWE; see Auszug aus dem Bericht des Vorstandes über das Geschäftsjahr 1947/48, BA, B102/684, p.3.

151. *Statistisches Jahrbuch für die Bundesrepublik Deutschland 1952*, pp.328f., and 1953, pp.410f.; see also e.g. *Börsenzeitung*, 1 February 1952. Industrial bonds from the prewar and war years with similar maturities often had less than 6 per cent return.

152. *Monatsberichte der BdL*, July 1949, p.7; November 1949, p.12; December 1949, pp.9f.; *Geschäftsbericht der BdL für das Jahr 1953*, pp.19f.

153. Deutsche Bundesbank, *Deutsches Geld- und Bankwesen in Zahlen 1876–1975* (Frankfurt, 1976), p.356.

154. *Monatsberichte der BdL*, March 1950, p.9; see also KfW *Jahresbericht 1949* p.34.

155. Baumgart, *Investitionen*, p.21, believes that even without preferential tax treatment for self-financing, this would have been the case.

Knut Borchardt and Christoph Buchheim

also not forget that the capital market normally draws a substantial sum of money out of annual interest returns, but that disposable capital had been largely destroyed in the currency reform. Further, unlike the post-1923 situation, foreigners invested little in Germany until after the London Debt Agreement of 1953.[156]

With a total sale of industrial shares and bonds of barely DM 870 million between the middle of 1948 and the end of 1952,[157] it is obvious that the capital market was in no way a substitute for the counterpart funds. Even at a higher rate of return on securities, the result would hardly have been much different, as we have seen. In addition, one would also have to consider that the electricity companies were incapable of earning any interest on their capital.[158] All in all, there was no alternative to the counterpart funds to be found on the capital market.

Even contemporary observers had already raised the question of whether the pressing investment needs could be financed through the resources of the central banking system.[159] Since that time Werner Abelshauser has emphasized that the counterpart funds were DM amounts 'which in contrast to the dollars of the Marshall Plan . . . could have been raised through credit expansion in the central banking system'.[160]

This opinion seems to have some basis in fact since the Bank deutscher Länder had helped the KfW with the preliminary financing of some power plant construction and had for this purpose brought central bank money into circulation.[161] However, this activity clearly remained a matter of preliminary financing, i.e. of the creation of a very limited amount of money by the central bank which was to be repaid as soon as possible from the counterpart funds as these funds became available. The central bank could justify this action in 1949/50 because the counterpart funds which had been collected up to that point had in fact been drawn out of domestic circulation and had thereby created a deflationary pressure. Central bank credit was therefore not an alternative to the counterpart funds for investment financing. On the contrary, cen-

156. *Deutsches Geld- und Bankwesen in Zahlen* (see n.153), p.343.
157. *Geschäftsbericht der BDL für das Jahr 1953*, p.53.
158. *Gutachten* (see n.112), p.169.
159. See, among others, Gutachten des Wissenschaftlichen Beirats bei der Verwaltung für Wirtschaft, 'Investitionspolitik', 12 June 1948, *Gutachtenband* (see n.1), pp.7ff., and KfW, *Jahresbericht 1950*, p.37.
160. 'Wiederaufbau vor dem Marshallplan' (see n.12), pp.568ff. and similarly at other points.
161. KfW, *Jahresbericht 1950*, p.44.

The Marshall Plan and Key Economic Sectors

tral bank credit had as its precondition the certainty that the counterpart funds would be made available for investment purposes.

It is not quite as easy to pass judgement on Abelshauser's opinion that central bank financing of power plant expansion would have been possible in the absence of the Marshall Plan and the temporarily inactive counterpart money. In any event without the Marshall Plan the world would have been so different in so many respects that no one can assert his ability to judge the imaginable political and economic alternatives with any scholarly validity. Presumably the social market economy would not have been established (see above, p.192ff. and passim) which means that any investment in the electric power industry would have had to be made on a completely different basis.

The major reason which prevented the responsible authorities in Germany from considering the theoretical possibility of financing desperately needed investments through additional credit in the narrow sense was expressed in the 1950 KfW annual report:

> The thought of using the central bank system's resources to satisfy the most pressing investment needs was, under the present circumstances, excluded by considerations of monetary policy. Considering the bottlenecks in the production of basic materials, the precarious situation of West Germany's balance of payments . . ., the considerable price increases on the world market and the shortages of certain international raw materials, any increase in the money volume would endanger the wage and price structure in the Federal Republic, and would clearly hurt the real incomes of the broad masses thereby destroying confidence in the stability of the currency.[162]

The Allies also very much considered currency stability a problem in Germany. In a March 1949 letter to the chairman of the Executive Council of the Bizone, BICO referred to a portion of the Economic Cooperation Act of 1948 which was subsequently included in the 1949 agreement on economic cooperation between the Federal Republic and the United States.[163] BICO stated clearly

---

162. Ibid., p.37.
163. *Bundesgesetzblatt (BGBI) 1950*, pp.10ff. Art. II explains the responsibility of the Federal Government 'to do its utmost to stabilize the currency, to obtain or preserve a valid exchange rate, to balance the budget as soon as possible, to create or preserve stable internal financial conditions, and to restore and preserve confidence in the currency system in general'. Daniel (see n.7), p.58 and Wexler (see n.7), p.30 show that this agreement was not a special rule for West Germany, but rather was a primary interest of the Americans and a motivation for the whole Marshall Plan.

Knut Borchardt and Christoph Buchheim

that[164] 'the importance of promoting or maintaining financial stability cannot be exaggerated. The Military Governors will only approve requests for the release of counterpart funds in the light of the general economic and financial situation existing in the Bizone at the time when the requests are received.' In general, currency considerations seem to have been the reason that the Americans were inclined to keep the counterpart funds inactive for a longer rather than a shorter period.[165]

Confidence in the new currency was the key to everything else. The events of the second half of 1948 had shown that this confidence initially was not particularly strong. The devaluation in the autumn of 1949, and especially the Korean crisis of 1950–1, caused new rounds of buying and bank withdrawals with their inherent inflationary pressures.[166] Equally indicative of the fragile confidence in the DM was public unwillingness to invest in securities, as mentioned above. If one could save, then savings deposits were chosen, since one could always use these without any loss in quoted value.[167] The free foreign exchange markets were also signalling potential dangers to the currency. For example, in July and August 1948 the DM was traded for about 30 Rappen in Zurich (official exchange rate = 1.29 Sfr[168] at the end of 1948). By the end of November the DM had sunk to under 20 Rappen.[169] The DM rebounded thereafter, but as late as May 1951, the DM was traded in Zurich with a 15 per cent discount.[170]

Even Abelshauser has considered the counterpart funds advantageous because they 'calmed the general public, which traditionally considered state credit creation to be the seed of inflation'. But in this regard the counterpart funds can only be considered a useful placebo, since fears of inflation were unfounded 'in view of the mass unemployment and unused production capacity'.[171]

It is really not possible at this point to continue discussing the

164. BA, Z 14/146.

165. Conversation with Dr Günter Keiser, retired Assistant Secretary, 10 February 1984 in Munich.

166. *Monatsberichte der BdL*, October 1949, p.5, *Geschäftsbericht der BdL für das Jahr 1950*, pp.8ff., for 1951, p.10; *4. Bericht der Bundesregierung über die Durchführung des Marshallplans* (Bonn, 1950), p.9.

167. KfW, *Jahresbericht 1949*, p.34.

168. *Statistisches Jahrbuch für die Bundesrepublik Deutschland 1952*, p.330.

169. 'DM-Notierung im Züricher Freiverkehr', *Wirtschaftsverwaltung*, 2(1949), p.174.

170. *5. und 6. Bericht der Deutschen Bundesregierung über die Durchführung des Marshallplans* (Bonn, 1951), p.149.

171. *Wiederaufbau* (see n.6), p.569.

The Marshall Plan and Key Economic Sectors

possibilities and risks of increasing the money supply. In any event, the counter-thesis should be presented, i.e. that the fears associated with increasing the money supply were not unfounded. The factors which spoke against financing investment through money creation were not imaginary, especially in view of the billions necessary for this at a time when the total cash in circulation was just DM 11.3 billion (end of 1952).[172] At the beginning of the 1950s one could not exclude the possibility that strong upward pressures on prices, if left unchecked, could combine with recent memories in the public mind and lead to a cumulative ruin of the currency. If, however, central bank loans to the electricity companies had not been additional credit, i.e. had not expanded money circulation, correspondingly less credit would have been available at other points in the system. If certain technical (and legal) conditions had been established, this redistribution of credit in favour of the electricity companies certainly could not have been criticized from the point of view of monetary policy. What other consequences such a credit redistribution might have had is almost impossible to judge without concrete information on where credit to other economic sectors would have been restricted. Before the middle of 1951 it seems that only *one* period might have been appropriate for a policy of somewhat quicker money supply expansion, namely the six months before the outbreak of the Korean War.[173] In contrast to that short period stood a long-term, *continuous* need for financing of crucial investment projects in the electricity and other primary industries. For that reason, an expansion of the money supply on the part of the central bank was not a real alternative to the counterpart funds.

Conclusion

Our examination of the Marshall Plan differs from others, essentially in two features:

(1) It is a 'micro–economic' analysis of two key sectors of industry.
(2) It seeks to explain the significance of the Marshall Plan by an examination as precise as possible of its effects, including the assessment of conceivable alternatives.

---

172. *Deutsches Geld- und Bankwesen* (see n.153), p.4.
173. At that time the Americans also demanded from the Federal government an investment programme financed by credit creation; Adamsen (see n.110), p.82.

Knut Borchardt and Christoph Buchheim

We come to the conclusion that the first cotton supplies under the Marshall Plan, although they arrived relatively late, constituted an important contribution to the success of the currency and economic reform. It is then shown that the Marshall Plan (counterpart funds) significantly accelerated the capacity build-up of the power plants, and thereby contributed to rapid growth in overall economic production.

The identification of the real problems in economic development policy at the time plays a major role in the accurate assessment of the Marshall Plan. Our position, though it is not possible for us to provide detailed justification here, is based on the well supported fact that there was, in the postwar period, a surplus of labour and at the same time considerable underutilization of existing capacity. However, there was not a full correspondence in the availability of means of production across all sectors. Whilst there existed overcapacity in some areas, others were suffering severe bottlenecks. The supply of (domestic and foreign) primary and intermediate products was particularly critical, and their availability was a decisive determinant of the overall economic performance and the possibilities for development. Additional supplies of goods in great shortage and the increase in production capacity in those areas unable to meet demand were the key to better utilization of the existing potential.

There is no standardized procedure for the assessment of the importance of such 'key products'. It is certainly insufficient merely to measure recorded values of additional deliveries or investments and then compare this with the size of population (DM per inhabitant), the level of GNP or total investment. At a time when the official exchange rate of the Deutschmark to the dollar reflected anything but the dollar shortage, indeed when, for the most part, dollar goods could be acquired only by spending foreign aid, the 'shadow prices' of these goods had to be far higher than those actually charged, which results in the curious fact that, in 1949 for example, the Marshall Plan supplies had a value of only DM 30 per inhabitant. At the time it was correctly assumed that the Marshall Plan funds had a far greater effect than can be accounted for on the basis of invoice prices.

In our paper we do not attempt to determine these 'shadow prices'; rather we seek to describe exactly some effects of Marshall Plan aid. Naturally judgements as to the role of the Marshall Plan are dependent on one's own conception of the possible course of West German history without it. Such an idea unavoidably prompts speculation. A course of history which did not take place can at best be made plausible, but it cannot be scientifically jus-

-450-

The Marshall Plant and Key Economic Sectors

tified. The scientific discussion of the Marshall Plan would benefit greatly, however, were one more prepared than has previously been the case to use the method of 'counterfactual thought'. Here one has to specify as precisely as possible which methods, other than those actually observable at the time, could have solved the problem in question, with what conceivable primary and side-effects, and at what cost. The evaluation of hypothetical history can be fruitfully discussed only when it can be described with a precision similar to that possible for factual history. In our case study we have expressly included consideration of alternatives, i.e. of the 'counterfactual history'. From these the significance of the observed Marshall Plan achievements is adduced. Admittedly each counterfactual argument must consider certain facts as given. We leave it to the reader to decide whether he finds our assumptions plausible or prefers to replace them with others.

It is most important that attention be drawn to the limits of our method of judgement. In our sectoral analyses we have dealt only with the assumption that the specific Marshall Plan inputs had not been available. However, the total data configuration which we have used comes, of course, from a history characterized by the Marshall Plan. But without the Marshall Plan, neither the cotton deliveries examined in our first case study nor the counterpart funds examined in our second would have existed; the whole history of Western Europe would have been quite different, and numerous (positive) parameters of our case studies would have been affected. Thus it appears to be justified to consider the sectoral effects which we observed, even if they should be too favourable in some detail, underestimating rather than overestimating the overall effect of the Marshall Plan.

[6]

FEATURE REVIEW*

Was the Marshall Plan Necessary?

ALAN S. MILWARD

Michael J. Hogan. *The Marshall Plan: America, Britain, and the Reconstruction of Western Europe, 1947–1952*. New York: Cambridge University Press, 1987. xiv + 482 pp. Notes, bibliography, index. $34.50 (cloth). $15.95 (paper).

With the publication of Michael Hogan's book we now have the first full diplomatic history of the Marshall Plan. The work is large in size and scope and as accurate and comprehensive in its coverage as could reasonably be expected. To my knowledge there are no relevant archival materials the author has left unexplored in the United States and the United Kingdom and he has used them well. He has overcome as far as possible the limitations which its confinement to sources in English has imposed on his work by combing all the accessible literature about the role of France and by having parts of the manuscript read by German historians. The book merits the compliments which it has so far attracted, not least the award of the Stuart L. Bernath Memorial Book Prize for 1987. By taking issue at several points with my own earlier work it opens a serious debate about the nature of the Marshall Plan and its outcome.[1] This debate has now been joined by other American scholars who do not exactly agree either with my own work or that of Hogan. Because Hogan's work can only command respect and because it represents historical controversy in the best tradition, learned, inquisitive, and courteous, this seems to be the moment to establish a useful map of these controversies, eliminating useless avenues of exploration while indicating more clearly the roads into the as yet unknown which lie so enticingly before us.

---

*The editor wishes to thank Professor Waldo H. Heinrichs. As senior member of the editorial board at the time, Professor Heinrichs made the arrangements for this review.

[1] Alan S. Milward, *The Reconstruction of Western Europe, 1945–1951* (London, 1984).

231

The core of Hogan's argument is, simplifying for heuristic purposes, that the Marshall Plan represented the transfer to Europe by diplomacy of the politico-economic compromise of the American New Deal as amended by the war. In doing so it brought the foreign policy of the United States into harmony with the underlying evolutionary trends of state and society in America. By enhancing the force and encouraging the evolution of similar trends in Western Europe it produced the stability and prosperity there which made the postwar peace settlement so conspicuously successful, thus fulfilling the Marshall Plan's most important objective.

At the start of his argument lies an account of the way American foreign policy after the First World War responded to changes in corporative attitudes and structures within the United States after 1880, the shift toward allocation of economic resources through a more organized and bureaucratized concentration of private economic power. "If," however, "the Marshall Planners succeeded where the Republicans failed," Hogan tells us, "this success was due in part to policy innovations growing first out of the New Deal and then out of the Cold War" (p. 19). These innovations were the outcome of the New Deal coalition, "a bloc of capital-intensive firms and their allies among labor, farm, financial, and professional groups" (p. 427). It was this coalition which was represented by the Economic Cooperation Administration (ECA), the agency created to administer the Marshall Plan, immediately represented in the sense that many of the leading personnel in the ECA had actually been architects of the New Deal coalition in the 1930s. The ECA then succeeded in translating the "neo-capitalist" (one of Hogan's favorite words) structure of American politics and society into a neocapitalist diplomatic program for the effective reconstruction of Western Europe. Its essential elements were "the patterns of corporative collaboration that had become a standard feature of public administration in the United States," thus "protecting private enterprise and public order against the dual dangers of bureaucratic statism and class conflict"; the promotion of "natural market mechanisms"; the restoration of a multilateral trade-and-payments network; and "a shared commitment to economic growth" as the key to the preservation of political democracy based on the kind of capitalism which had evolved in the United States (p. 428). The economic conclusion of this program would be found in the integration of Western Europe into one big market, like the United States. At this point some in the ECA went further and joined forces with ambitious dreamers in the State Department who hoped to guarantee the security of the United States and at the same time bring the boys back home by politically uniting the West European states. More moderate and more effective, says Hogan, were those in the State Department and the ECA who saw the political and economic integration of Western Europe as a long-term process which the Marshall Plan would initiate. Hogan believes it did so, leading ultimately to the Treaty of Rome.

He does not, though, argue that the whole of this diplomatic program was achieved. He argues that the Marshall Plan did lead, albeit by a more tortuous and slower rate than many earlier accounts have suggested, to the

WAS THE MARSHALL PLAN NECESSARY?   233

eventual implementation of the Bretton Woods accords. He concludes also that although the contribution of American capital to West European economic recovery was only marginal, this was, nevertheless as Schuker had earlier argued, the "crucial margin" that made recovery possible.[2] Without this contribution there would not have been the twenty-year era of peace and prosperity which followed the war. West European economic and political union will, he seems to imply, in the long run gradually come about—just as those whom he regards as the more realistic architects of the Marshall Plan supposed. But he maintains also that the neocapitalist political coalitions of the New Deal were no more than a part of the political model on which postwar Western Europe was built. Western Europe, he implies, was not short of political ideas of its own and the neocapitalist stability of the postwar world has been due, he suggests, as much to European as to American political models. Indeed, in a cryptic conclusion he tells us that in this last regard "America was made the European way" (p. 445).

As all readers of this journal will perceive, the force of these arguments lies in the way they relate diplomatic history to perceived patterns of economic and social change. Much of the revival of diplomatic history in the last ten years has been due to the belated recognition that it is superficial stuff unless it relates to what is actually happening inside countries. Although this process has not yet gone far enough to be intellectually satisfying, a weakness still apparent in Hogan's book, his conclusions demonstrate that he has certainly gone far enough in this direction to link his diplomatic history to the mainstream of historical analysis of the postwar world, the attempt to explain its prosperity and stability. How far are his conclusions proven?

With what Hogan has to say about the relationship of the ECA and of American policies under the Marshall Plan to the trends in postwar politics there can be no quarrel. Other scholars working independently on more detailed areas have also demonstrated that what the Marshall Plan supported in Western Europe was the politico-economic stance which was soon to be called "Keynesian"; a conscious effort to regulate the level of demand in the economy by fiscal adjustments, supplementary countercyclical policies to maintain high and stable levels of employment, the pursuit of higher levels of welfare both as a good in themselves and as a way of sustaining demand, and, the aspect on which Hogan lays the greatest emphasis, a corporatist association of government and industry in the pursuit of what was thought to be the common welfare.

These were the kinds of action which the ECA urged on European governments, sometimes threatening to recommend the suspension of aid if they were not taken. The Italians were berated excessively in 1948 for piling

---

[2] Stephen A. Schuker, "Comment on Charles S. Maier's 'The Two Postwar Eras and the Conditions for Stability in Twentieth-Century Western Europe,'" *American Historical Review* 86 (February 1982): 353–58. Maier had shown that the contribution of investment from the European Recovery Program counterpart funds to total capital investment in West European countries was very small. Schuker and Hogan emphasize rather the importance of imports from the United States as well as liquid capital.

up reserves instead of using their surplus earnings for investment, even at a time when investment levels were high and the effects of the monetary restrictions of 1947 on production were wearing off. The Norwegian national budgets, one of the first public expressions of Keynesian economics in action, were held up to admiration in the United States as a model by an ECA official.[3] Monnet, the apostle of indicative planning, was an ECA friend and ally, the Americans' man in Europe as some French politicians thought him. Far from being deterred by the battery of controls which supported the first French Plan for Modernization and Reequipment, and which made the French economy of all the Marshall Plan economies the one that most closely resembled an East European economy in its workings, the ECA sympathized openly with Monnet's objectives. Where there was no overall plan but only isolated and partial policies of modernization and national development, the ECA singled these out for financial support and favorable propaganda.[4] In Denmark it supported the efforts of the minority Social Democratic government to encourage industrialization and to reduce the dominance of agriculture over the economy.[5] Even when, by the autumn of 1948, the reduction of inflation had become a priority objective, this priority was combined with efforts to reform taxation systems to make them more suitable instruments of economic policy. Thus when the Queuille government in France in November 1948 was being pushed hard to reduce public expenditure, it was being pushed equally hard to reform the tax structure in a more progressive direction.[6]

Although Cold War denunciations of the Marshall Plan, that it reasserted a reactionary capitalism and a deflationary economics, stifling in the process hopes of radical social and economic change, can still, it seems, be made even on a foundation of historical research, they have an air of willful eccentricity.[7] The kind of capitalism for which the ECA wanted to make the world safe often had as many opponents in European countries on the right as on the left. At this level of generalization, therefore, Hogan's arguments stand; there were, to put it at its lowest, close affinities between the political and economic policy choices of postwar European governments and the policies upheld by American diplomacy through the ECA. When Hogan's judgments about the eventual results of the Marshall Plan are

---

[3] Alice Bourneuf, *Norway: The Planned Revival* (Cambridge, MA, 1958).

[4] David W. Ellwood, "Il Piano Marshall e il processo di modemizzazione in Italia" [The Marshall Plan and the process of modernization in Italy], and Pier Paolo D'Attore, "Aspetti dell'attuazione del Piano Marshall in Italia" [Aspects of the implementation of the Marshall Plan in Italy], in *Il Piano Marshall e l'Europa* [The Marshall Plan and Europe], ed. Elena A. Rossi (Rome, 1983), 163–80.

[5] Vibeke Sørensen, "Social Democratic Government in Denmark under the Marshall Plan, 1947–1950" (Ph.D. diss., European University Institute, 1987).

[6] Gérard Bossuat, "L'aide Américaine a la France après la Seconde Guerre Mondiale" [American aid to France after the Second World War], *Vingtième Siècle* [Twentieth Century] (January–March 1986).

[7] Annie Lacroix-Riz, *Le Choix de Marianne: Les relations franco-américaines de la Libération aux débuts du Plan Marshall (1944–1948)* [Marianne's choice: Franco-American relations from the liberation to the beginning of the Marshall Plan] (Paris, 1985).

WAS THE MARSHALL PLAN NECESSARY?   235

looked at with closer attention, however, it emerges that the widespread historical agreement about the nature of the ECA's policies which recent research has generated is not really taking us far toward a historical understanding of postwar stability.

Hogan believes, to take the first of his main conclusions, that it is correct to see the Marshall Plan as achieving what the American government claimed to be one of its principal objectives, enabling the Bretton Woods agreements on a multilateral international trade-and-payments system to be eventually brought into operation. This is a conclusion also recently reasserted by William Diebold.[8] The Bretton Woods agreements were of course supposed to make the common pursuit of postwar economic stability more possible by establishing a liberal trading system and stable exchange rates, which would be adjusted by orderly international agreement. Even at the outset of the Marshall Plan, however, doubts appeared in the United States and Europe about whether the Bretton Woods rules would prove compatible with the sort of domestic policies the ECA advocated and European countries pursued. Charles Kindleberger in a recent essay denies this, claiming that there were no differences of principle between on the one hand the ECA and the State Department, the two departments responsible for the Marshall Plan, and on the other hand the Treasury Department and the new postwar international financial agencies created by Bretton Woods.[9] It is as evident from Hogan's work as from my own that there were. The point at issue was that the Treasury was far from convinced that providing dollar aid to West European countries against deficits on their dollar balances of commodity trade, which was all that the complicated committee machinery of the ECA and the Organization for European Economic Cooperation (OEEC) managed to achieve by way of allocation, was a way of closing the dollar gap in world settlements. The Keynesian reply from the ECA and some, not all, European governments, that providing aid for otherwise unpurchasable imports from the United States would increase productivity by increasing output and thus enhancing economies of scale became part of the ideology of the Marshall Plan and of the 1950s. Only higher productivity in Western Europe, it was argued, could restore equilibrium to world trade and payments and allow the multilateral payments system conceived at Bretton Woods based on long-run exchange rate stability actually to function to the mutual benefit of America and Europe.

It is difficult to know exactly what the opinions of the U.S. Treasury were when faced with this intellectually fashionable reply because its postwar records are for all practical purposes of research into this question still closed, so its opinions appear only from occasional memoranda and letters in American archives of a different provenance, in *Foreign Relations of the United States*, or in foreign archives. But the issue did not go away. It burst out again in full force on the conclusion of the European Payments

---

[8] William Diebold, Jr., "The Marshall Plan in Retrospect: A Review of Recent Scholarship," *Journal of International Affairs* 41 (Summer 1988): 421–35.

[9] Charles P. Kindleberger, *Marshall Plan Days* (Winchester, MA, 1987), 252.

Union (EPU) agreement and again in 1952 when the agreement was renewed. The EPU as created in 1950 and renewed in 1952 was an institution partly financed out of Marshall aid for financing on generous terms deficits in intra–West European trade. The Treasury saw this as a device for allowing European countries to pursue expansionist economic policies on the basis of foreign credits when they should have been reducing expenditure and clearing their balance-of-payments deficits, the only way in its view that the Bretton Woods agreements could be made operable.

The evidence is accumulating that in this they were representative of finance ministries and treasuries elsewhere, whose attitude not infrequently was one of gloomy acceptance of Keynesian policies as erroneous but regrettably unavoidable in postwar circumstances, combined with a growing feeling that they made the Bretton Woods settlement unworkable unless its rules were changed. When the new British government in 1951 decided that the convertibility of the pound sterling at the earliest possible date was one of its highest priorities, government, Treasury, and central bank alike wanted to abandon the principle of fixed exchange rates on the grounds that they were incompatible with postwar domestic economic policies which they could not abandon. By 1954 the U.S. Treasury in no less a guise than Treasury Secretary George Humphrey and his deputy Randolph Burgess tended to agree with the British that flexible exchange rates, by which they meant a margin of 3 percent on each side of the Bretton Woods par rate, would have advantages in allowing countries to cope with the financial consequences of Keynesian policies at home, and that fluctuations within that kind of band were not the same as the competitive devaluations of the interwar period which Bretton Woods had proscribed. In the Federal Republic of Germany, Ludwig Erhard and his officials also much preferred flexible rates. So did the Belgian Ministry of Finance during the Marshall Plan and, when Maurice Petsche was minister in 1950, the French Ministry of Finance as well.[10] The view of all of them was that maintaining fixed exchange rates when deflationary reductions in public expenditure could not be made placed too great a strain on currency reserves and that an international payments system based on these principles would be inflationary and insecure.

There was in fact no economic consensus after the start of the Marshall Plan that the Bretton Woods rules were a good idea, much less that they were inviolable. The more successful arguments for retaining them once the general convertibility of West European currencies against the dollar would again have been reestablished were usually diplomatic ones. Fixed exchange rates, it was argued, would make West European integration easier. This was why John Foster Dulles and Konrad Adenauer wanted them. Why that was the system eventually chosen in 1958 after the establishment of general

---

[10] For Petsche's position see Richard T. Griffiths and Francis M. B. Lynch, "L'échec de la 'Petite Europe': les négociations Fritalux/Finebel, 1949–1950" [The demise of "Little Europe": The Fritalux/Finebel negotiations], *Revue historique* [Historical review] 274 (July–September 1985): 159–93.

WAS THE MARSHALL PLAN NECESSARY?   237

legal convertibility of West European currencies against the dollar is too early to know for certain. But the likelihood is that the Treaty of Rome and even more so the Franco-German agreements which were its foundation were as much a determining factor as the character of domestic economic policies. In this respect, however, foreign policy may have been closer to the "Keynesian" politics which brought German politicians their votes than to the economic critique of these policies from inside the government. Whatever the case, it would be wiser for historians not to borrow the concept of a "Bretton Woods System" from economists in order to define the period and surely wiser not to assume that the period 1948–1958 was only a journey back to that system.

The political consensuses of the postwar world were more the outcome of shifts of political power which imposed policies on frequently reluctant politicians and civil servants than the outcome of changes of intellectual outlook by policymakers or of any coordinated international attempt to overcome the manifest weakness of the international economy. There were great similarities between different countries in these shifts, but also important differences of nature and timing. There is little in Hogan's work to suggest that he would disagree with this, but it remains to specify more fully what these shifts of power were. "Neo-capitalism," no matter how large an aura of meaning it trails, is only a word, not a historical explanation. This is a point also made by Diebold, who finds unconvincing Hogan's brief account of what the New Deal coalition was and is even less convinced by Hogan's account of the ECA as Hoover's "associative state" come to fruition.[11] What exactly were these postwar coalitions which brought stability and how similar were they in Europe and the United States?

To answer this question it is necessary first to explore the correctness of Hogan's conclusion that without the Marshall Plan the economic recovery in Western Europe and thus the favorable conditions for the continuation of these coalitions would not have been possible. Did their success depend on support from the United States? Was the Marshall Plan necessary? This is a question which for a long time would have seemed pointless because the standard history and economic texts all explained the Marshall Plan in part as a response to a severe economic crisis in Western Europe and an impending collapse of West European economies. The official view, still loudly shouted by official American agencies throughout 1987 in a round of commemorative conferences in West European capitals and echoed in a blandly conformist radio program by the BBC, was that the Marshall Plan had "saved" Europe. Beneath this public conformity, however, the discussion had begun about whether the official line was true and from what, if anything, Europe had been "saved."

My own work argued that the alleged economic crisis of the summer of 1947 in Western Europe did not exist, except as a shortage of foreign exchange caused by the vigor of the European investment and production

---

[11] Diebold, "The Marshall Plan."

boom. This boom was sustained even in the face of rapidly worsening international payments balances in 1947 in several countries, notably in Italy, the Netherlands, and the United Kingdom. These were circumstances which in the interwar period would have provoked deflationary action. Because European governments were the prisoners of a shift of political power which imposed new policies on them, they could no longer respond in this way except in Italy and even there only briefly and, as some would now argue, ineffectually.[12] They were unable to arrest the boom without losing political legitimacy. An analysis of the international commodity trade figures shows that the *increase* in dollar imports into Western Europe in 1947 over 1946, before Marshall aid began to flow, was mainly in capital goods. This appears to rule out the earlier view that the summer of 1947 witnessed a crisis of confidence in Western Europe originating in economic dislocation, distress, and hunger.[13] It follows that Marshall aid did not revive the economy of an area vital to America's security; rather, it sustained a powerful investment boom already under way for two years by providing the dollars for a continued high level of capital-goods and industrial raw material imports from the dollar zone. This, of course, would be compatible with Hogan's argument that the Marshall Plan was the vehicle through which American diplomacy expressed support for the new political consensus in Western Europe after the war. But he cannot accept it, because for him the Marshall Plan still saved Western Europe from economic collapse. Kindleberger asserts this more stridently: "I think that Marshall Plan dollars did save the world."[14]

---

[12] Vera Zamagni, "Betting on the Future: The Reconstruction of Italian Industry, 1946–1952," in *Power in Europe: Great Britain, France, Italy and Germany in a Postwar World, 1945–1950*, ed. Josef Becker and Franz Knipping (Berlin, 1986), 283–300, shows how weak is the evidence for Italy's deflationary policies over the period 1947–1950 in such works as George H. Hildebrand, *Growth and Structure in the Economy of Modern Italy* (Cambridge, MA, 1965). At the same time she has brought together the evidence of consistent support for industrial development policies, especially for industries which would contribute to technological modernization and the growth of exports. In her work, Italy ceases to be the one European exception to the general rule in the Marshall Plan period that European governments pursued costly, even if selective, policies of expansion. The evidence for these elements of an expansionist industrial policy in Italy can be found in Piero Bairati, *Vittorio Valletta* (Turin, 1983); Franco Borelli, ed., *Acciaio per l'industrializzazione: Contributi allo studio del problema siderurgico italiano* [Steel for industrialization: Contributions to the study of the problem of Italian metallurgy] (Turin, 1982); Ruggero Ranieri, "L'espansione alla prova del negoziato: L'industria italiana e la Comunità del carbone e dell'acciaio, 1945–1955" [Growth under the test of negotiations: Italian industry and the coal and steel community] (Ph.D. diss., European University Institute, 1988); and Mariuccia Salvati, *Stato e industria nella ricostruzione: Alle origini del potere democristiano (1944–1949)* [State and industry in reconstruction: Origins of Christian Democratic power] (Milan, 1982).

[13] This was the interpretation of Joseph M. Jones, *The Fifteen Weeks: An Inside Account of the Genesis of the Marshall Plan* (New York, 1955), and Harry B. Price, *The Marshall Plan and Its Meaning* (Ithaca, 1955), both of which, although they should be seen as semiofficial State Department accounts, have been widely accepted by historians.

[14] Kindleberger, *Marshall Plan*, 247.

WAS THE MARSHALL PLAN NECESSARY?   239

The question must therefore be answered, whether the European boom could have continued had there been no Marshall Plan. To try to answer this question I undertook a sequence of counterfactual calculations.[15] The first was to assume that, had there been no Marshall aid, the West European countries would have foregone any increase in food imports beyond the 1947 level and any increase in food consumption measured by calorific intake beyond the level of the summer of 1947 and would have used the whole of their international dollar/gold earnings to continue to buy only capital goods, steel, vehicles, and industrial raw materials (not food) from the dollar zone. Of the six largest West European importers of capital goods under Marshall aid authorizations in 1949, four, by adopting this alternative policy, could in fact have paid for these imports from their exports to the dollar zone. Only two, France and the Netherlands, could not. This hypothesis, however, was far too drastic because it assumed no other source of dollar/gold earnings than commodity exports to the United States and Canada. I therefore constructed a second counterfactual in which, had there been no Marshall aid, the same European countries would still have had the dollar/gold resources to obtain half the value of their total dollar imports during the Marshall Plan period. Had the commodity distribution of their imports remained unchanged as this calculation assumes, this would have necessitated a 34 percent increase in imports of machinery and vehicles from nondollar sources, in effect from Western Europe itself, which was clearly impossible. Once again France and the Netherlands were the core of the problem. From this I proceeded to a third counterfactual. Suppose these six countries still to have had sufficient dollar/gold resources, even had there been no Marshall aid, to have been able to obtain half the value of the dollar imports which they actually purchased, but not to have increased their level of food consumption beyond the level of the summer of 1947. What then would have been the situation?

The outcome of this calculation was that the West European countries, again with the exception of France and the Netherlands, would have been able to obtain the same supply of capital goods and vehicles from the dollar zone as they did under Marshall aid and within the same period of time. In France and the Netherlands the period of time over which these imports were obtained would have had to be lengthened, in the Dutch case perhaps by as much as two years, so that the investment and output boom in those two countries would have been slowed down accordingly, at least until the reentry of Germany onto world markets as a capital-goods supplier. Even for France and the Netherlands, however, these conclusions hardly point to economic collapse had the U.S. government not come forward with the dollars.

It is this conclusion which Hogan refutes. He insists that, had there been no Marshall aid, there would have been "a serious crisis in production that would have come with the collapse of critical dollar imports" and that "signs of this were apparent early in 1947" (p. 431). What signs? He offers

---

[15] Milward, *Reconstruction of Western Europe*, 104ff.

none, other than the reiteration by advocates of some kind of aid program
that this would happen and the reiteration by European politicians that they
would like more dollars in order to avoid the unpleasant political choices
they could see ahead. I cannot find any economic indications of an
impending production crisis. There was only the mounting difficulty of
paying for dollar imports, to which governments might have responded with
a variety of policies, only some of which would have brought a production
crisis. Hogan argues that a payments problem must be a production problem
because of the subsequent effect on imports. But with all the inherent
weaknesses of counterfactual history, it does seem to me to have had the
methodological advantage in this instance of demonstrating that a reduction
of imports was not inevitable; with other policies they could still have been
obtained. Although there are discrepancies in foreign trade statistics which
economists, who seldom use them in detail, overlook and historians should
try to overcome, the margin of error cannot be so great as to cast any
serious doubt on a conclusion which, within the confines of statistical
analysis, ultimately rests not on counterfactual hypotheses but on the
measured movement of physical commodities.

The weakness of the counterfactual method lies rather in the assumptions on which it has to be constructed and the variables which it
omits. Knut Borchardt and Christoph Buchheim in a different counterfactual
approach explore the impact of dollar imports on the West German textile
industry in the Marshall Plan period. They argue that in this case Marshall
aid was indeed crucial to recovery, not so much because the imports would
not otherwise have been obtained but because of the confidence which it
gave to entrepreneurs to acquire stocks and to commit themselves to long
production runs.[16] The textile industry must be almost the least satisfactory
industry, however, from which to generalize such an argument because
cotton was the prime example of a dollar raw material import which could
not be substituted by supply from elsewhere and which was particularly
favored by the Marshall Plan. Indeed there are sometimes suggestions that
Germany would have preferred other imports. Nor does the method of
analysis used in this case convincingly demonstrate that the increase in
stocks was related to the Marshall Plan. We may safely assume that the
Marshall Plan increased confidence in the future, but the evidence is that
confidence was already very high. Nevertheless this microeconomic approach
does show that what may not be captured by one counterfactual argument
can sometimes be brought into the reckoning by a different counterfactual
approach, for which indeed Borchardt and Buchheim make a plea.

The argument that by maintaining food consumption at 1947 levels
Western European countries could have dispensed with dollar aid is a quite
different argument within the legitimate confines of statistical demonstration

---

[16] Knut Borchardt and Christoph Buchheim, "Die Wirkung der Marshallplan-Hilfe in
der deutschen Wirtschaft" [The impact of Marshall Plan aid on the German economy],
Vierteljahrshefte für Zeitgeschichte [Contemporary history quarterly] 35 (July 1987): 317–
47.

WAS THE MARSHALL PLAN NECESSARY?　　　241

from the same argument when set in what Hogan appears to regard as the only worthwhile confines, those of complex historical political reality. In the first place, the statistical data on food consumption are much less firm than for foreign trade. They refer to average rations or average consumption and all historians know that the number of people who consumed the average ration was only a small part of the population. Furthermore, they are expressed in calories as a device for standardization, and calories are not the same as food for purposes of judging the historical validity of the argument. Diet matters and foodstuffs are not perfectly substitutable, especially when we are calculating the possibility of surviving close to the margin of necessary calorific intake for sustained labor. But it is not only the conceptual weaknesses of the way the data are expressed and of the assumptions which have to be made in drawing conclusions from them which present difficulties, it is also the conceptual jump from this method of historical analysis to conclusions which embrace all the variables, the jump to what Hogan would regard as real history. Diebold and Kindleberger take exception to the necessary caution of the language in which these statistical conclusions are set out in my book. Hogan sweeps the whole statistical effort aside as no more than a conjuring trick, "analytical legerdemain" (p. 431).

With all respect for Hogan's own historical skills, it seems to me that this attitude imposes unnecessary limitations on diplomatic history. If diplomatic history has been revived by its newly found attention to economic diplomacy, how can it reject a methodology which helps in assessing the merits of that diplomacy? To leave that to another field of enquiry, perhaps called economic history, seems like willful self-castration. Let us take only one example directly relevant to the central issue at stake. Allowing for all the conceptual and statistical weaknesses of the counterfactual method in answering the question posed in the title of this essay, it has nevertheless eliminated one argument which was always to be found in the earlier historiography of the Marshall Plan. This was the argument that the extremely poor European harvest of 1947 was a major cause of Europe's growing deficit on dollar trade and of Europe's hunger, and thus of the alleged economic crisis and of the U.S. government's decision to initiate the aid program. Kindleberger insists that this earlier view is correct, arguing that agricultural bureaucrats would have been aware of the poor harvest in advance and would have purchased large imports in the summer of 1947.[17] Since the statistical evidence is firm that the increase in European dollar imports from the dollar zone both in 1947 and in 1948 over the previous year was not due to an increase in food imports, this argument seems merely perverse. The advantage of this methodology is clear in another direction, too. It measures and demonstrates the fundamental importance of the elimination of German manufactured goods as a cause of the postwar trade-and-payments imbalances, and so elevates the German problem to its just importance in the Marshall Plan.

---

[17] Kindleberger, *Marshall Plan*, 252.

Hogan sweeps aside every conclusion from these counterfactual and statistical attempts to measure the necessity of the Marshall Plan. For him still Western Europe in the summer of 1947 was in deep economic crisis in which hunger and falling living standards had as their outcome "a demoralized workforce" and "a pervasive sense of pessimism" (p. 30). To describe in these terms a time when, in every West European country except Germany, investment was higher absolutely and as a ratio of GNP than in any year since 1919, and when production was rising more rapidly everywhere than it had for twenty years, seems absurd. Perhaps Hogan would use the same word privately to describe the methodology by which my work claims to reveal this absurdity. But in that case he would simply have to turn to the plainer statistical account, which avoids these polemics, of Imanuel Wexler.[18] He ignores that, too, and the consequence is that what he would regard as the real-life history of the Marshall Plan is on this point seriously wrong.

Hogan does, though, make a second and stronger refutation of the statistical demonstration that the Marshall Plan may not have been necessary. It is one which goes right to the heart of the question with which we are faced. Even if, he claims, the statistical calculations which demonstrate that Europe was not saved from economic collapse by the Marshall Plan are valid, the alternative policy options which the absence of the Marshall Plan would have made necessary were "not available to the fragile coalitions that presided over many of the participating countries, none of which could retreat from already low levels of consumption and hope to survive" (p. 431). This argument needs to be emended in one respect where Hogan has perhaps not understood the statistical implications of the contrary argument. No government needed to *reduce* the levels of food consumption of 1947 to implement the alternative policies, and most could have increased them. Of the six countries in question, four could still have obtained dollar capital goods and raw material imports in the same value as under the Marshall Plan and have had a margin of extra gold/dollars for food imports above the 1947 level. Only France and the Netherlands would have had to stay at that level. With that emendation in mind, would alternative policies have been possible?

One way of testing Hogan's categorical assertion that European political consensuses could not have survived such policies is to look at government discussions on implementing them should they have proved necessary. Every government in Western Europe had to ask itself what it would do if the conditions attached to Marshall aid should prove unacceptable. But the problem is to know how much weight to attribute to the answers. In spite of the initial hostile reaction of the European countries to the American conditions for aid, these were soon shown in the bilateral negotiations as well as in the negotiations with the Committee on European Economic Cooperation (CEEC) to be less menacing to individual national

---

[18] Imanuel Wexler, *The Marshall Plan Revisited: The European Recovery Program in Economic Perspective* (Westport, CT, 1983).

WAS THE MARSHALL PLAN NECESSARY?   243

sovereignties than had at first been thought. In these circumstances a thorough discussion of alternative policies soon took on a hypothetical air only.

The British cabinet was presented with a Treasury paper in June 1948 which considered the eventuality of refusing Marshall aid if American conditions became such as to pose a genuine threat to the maintenance of the sterling area and its related foreign and economic policy priorities. Treasury calculations demonstrated that it would be possible to prevent reserves of gold and foreign currency falling below the danger level, which for this argument was set at £500 million ($2,100 million), and still maintain the predicted import surplus over the financial year 1948–49 without dollar aid. But it would mean no food imports from the dollar zone other than Canadian wheat and no tobacco imports from the same origin. There would be a general reduction of 12 percent in raw material imports and oil imports would be reduced by more than this. This might lead, it was suggested, to a return to interwar unemployment, amounting to as many as one and a half million workers, while the basic rations of tea, sugar, butter, bacon, and cheese would have to be reduced so that food consumption would be about 10 percent below the average of the prewar period.[19] The paper was clearly designed to persuade ministers to cast aside all idea of rejecting Marshall aid. The United Kingdom was much the most dependent of West European countries on Marshall aid for its food imports; the other major European food importers from the dollar zone, the Allied occupation zones of Germany, received more than half their dollar food imports under the GARIOA relief programs. To this extent it was harder for Britain to refuse the terms of the European Recovery Program. Nevertheless the Treasury calculations, in the light of the situation in other European countries, appear alarmist and exaggerated. The whole discussion was in any case by this date artificial, the decision had effectively been taken. Otherwise it might simply be concluded that if the Labour Government in the United Kingdom, which was far from being one of the "fragile coalitions" of Hogan's argument, could not contemplate refusing Marshall aid, surely none of the five other main Western European importers could have done so.

From what we now know of the debate in other governments, there was in fact a variety of opinion on the inevitability or even the desirability of accepting Marshall aid. Erik Brofoss, the Norwegian minister of commerce at the time and a member of the Norwegian delegation to the CEEC, has related that Norway stood ready to refuse American terms as presented to the CEEC but changed its mind when the United Kingdom accepted them in their amended form.[20] This, though, is refuted by a Norwegian historian who explains Norway's change of heart by a deterioration in its balance-of-payments position, without, however, producing the documentation which

---

[19] "Economic Consequences of Receiving No European Recovery Aid," 23 June 1948, Cabinet Paper CP (48) 161, CAB 129/28, Public Record Office, Kew, England.

[20] Erik Brofoss, "The Marshall Plan and Norway's Hesitation," *Scandinavian Journal of History* 1 (1976).

would clinch the argument.[21] Switzerland did refuse the American terms, but this tells us very little because whereas Switzerland did not need or take Marshall aid the United States needed to have Switzerland as a functioning member of any general trade-and-payments framework in Western Europe.[22] A further advantage of the counterfactual method is that it shows that the two countries that obviously matter most in trying to answer this crucial question are France and the Netherlands.

The French postwar reconstruction plan assumed from the outset that France would reconstruct with either German resources or American aid. In the spring of 1947, Monnet did face the possibility that American aid would be inadequate and that German resources might be unavailable. Once interim aid and Marshall aid were made available, however, the Monnet Plan was fundamentally revised to take account of them, U.S. aid was incorporated as an essential and integral part of French reconstruction expenditure, and there is universal agreement that the achievements of the Monnet Plan depended on it.[23] Dependence on American credits pushed France's foreign policy in risky European directions it was scarcely ready to take and also influenced domestic policies. It led, for example, to the modification of fiscal policies in late autumn 1948 in the face of overt ECA threats that otherwise aid would be reduced. From the start of interim aid this dependence on the United States for the fulfillment of an ambitious program was accepted. But it was also deliberately exaggerated in dealings with Washington. Interim aid allowed France to maintain for the first three months of 1948 the import programs envisaged by the reconstruction plan. Were this not to be followed by a further three months of interim aid and then by Marshall aid, so the French officially told Washington in January 1948, this would mean after 30 June a cut in coal allocations to the economy of 25 percent, in oil allocations of 50 percent, and in the sugar ration of nearly 30 percent. There would be thousands of unemployed, the risk of social revolt, and finally of a Communist takeover.[24] But what else were they likely to say if they wanted the aid? In fact over the whole period of Marshall aid France spent a larger proportion of it on machinery and vehicles than any other recipient, while going to great lengths to switch its food imports to the franc zone. The main contribution of Marshall aid was to goods for supporting industrial modernization rather than for staving off hunger, social revolt, and political

---

21 Helge Ø. Pharo, "Bridgebuilding and Reconstruction: Norway Faces the Marshall Plan," *Scandinavian Journal of History* 1 (1976): 125–53.

22 Antoine Fleury, "La situation particulière de la Suisse au sein de l'O.E.C.E.," in Raymond Poidevin, ed., *Histoire des débuts de la construction européenne, mars 1948-mai 1950* [The history of the beginnings of European construction, March 1948–May 1950], ed. Raymond Poidevin (Brussels, 1986).

23 Gérard Bossuat, "Le poids de l'aide américaine sur la politique économique et financière de la France en 1948" [The influence of American aid on the economic and financial policies of France in 1948], *Relations internationales* [International relations] 37 (Spring 1984); Robert Frank, "The French Dilemma: Modernization with Dependence or Independence and Decline," *Power in Europe*, 263–80.

24 Bossuat, "Le poids de l'aide américaine."

WAS THE MARSHALL PLAN NECESSARY?   245

collapse. In the spring of 1947, when it looked as though American aid would be ending and that German resources might not be at France's disposal, Monnet was in fact considering plans to limit dollar imports solely to capital goods and indispensable raw materials.

The evidence either way is not strong enough to say what would have happened had the European Recovery Program not been announced. Monnet, it should be noted, was able more or less to defend the investment priorities of his plan throughout the Marshall aid period against rival policies in France. On the other hand, so Hogan might argue, spending the Marshall aid dollars in that way liberated other funds for staving off social revolt and political collapse. All sources of capital were in effect fungible, which makes it impossible to arrive at any definitive conclusion on this question. It also makes it impossible, though, to assert that Marshall aid was the critical marginal quantity, other than by the macroeconomic methods whose inherent weaknesses have already been discussed.

In the Netherlands the minister of finance as early as September 1946 had refused to agree to the program of dollar purchases which had been drawn up. The reduced program which subsequently emerged, it was argued by Minister of the Economy Huijsmans, apparently with much cabinet support, was an absolute minimum in the sense that any further cuts in it would provoke an unbearable fall in consumption. Even so, by April this new program of dollar purchases had in fact effectively been reduced by providing credit approvals for only three-quarters of it.[25] Anything lower than this, the cabinet was again told, might mean an economic debacle. In the autumn of 1947 the Central Planning Bureau prepared two versions of its overall economic indicators for 1948, grandiosely called a plan: one was based on the assumption that Marshall aid would be available; the other, roughly the equivalent of what Huijsmans had declared to be the minimum possible, was based on the assumption that it might not be available or might even be refused. Without Marshall aid the shortage of foreign exchange for the year 1948 was estimated at 1,500 million guilders ($565 million) if the existing import programs were maintained. It would be possible to reduce this to 600 million guilders ($226 million) by reductions of between 10 and 14 percent in consumption and by as much as 26 percent in capital goods.[26] Before the arrival of Marshall aid, Finance Minister Pieter Lieftinck did in fact impose an emergency program to reduce dollar imports below the level on which the first forecast was based. Yet once the aid was certain to flow, but before any had arrived, the government pushed through the massive electrification programs of 1948, which depended heavily on imports, in spite of all Lieftinck's objections in the cabinet. "When business itself is willing to invest," Johannes Van den Brink, the

[25] Richard T. Griffiths, *Economic Reconstruction Policy in the Netherlands and Its International Consequences, May 1945–March 1951*, European University Institute Working Papers No. 76, 1984, p. 18.

[26] P. van der Eng, *De Marshall-Hulp: Een Perspectief voor Nederland 1947–1953* [Marshall aid: The perspective from the Netherlands] (Houten, 1987), 53ff.

minister for economic affairs, told his colleagues, "then government should not put obstacles in the way." To do so, he argued, would be to create another and worse kind of inflationary pressure, the need to finance unemployment pay.[27]

The evidence from the real and not the counterfactual historical world provides no clearer an answer to the question whether Marshall aid was necessary in France and the Netherlands. Politicians remained committed to expansionist policies, did not know whether they would still be possible without aid, and would have persisted with them until they had found out the answer, finally deciding their reactions from pragmatic political standpoints. It is particularly striking that there could be this range of discussion in the Netherlands, for that was the country, with the possible exception of Austria, whose economic recovery would have been most seriously set back in contrast to what actually occurred had there been no European Recovery Program. Van der Eng by another counterfactual also offers some figures about the extent of the difference which the absence of Marshall aid would have made to the Netherlands. There would have been, he suggests, a delay of one year in achieving the levels of national income growth that were attained, and of 5.6 years in achieving the levels of per capita consumption.[28] This calculation, though, depends on holding commercial and supply conditions steady in their 1947 circumstances throughout the period, whereas of course they greatly changed. Especially they changed with the expansion of German foreign trade, an expansion which was a powerful force for growth in the Dutch economy. The initial stages of this Dutch-German economic symbiosis were achieved under bilateral trade and did not depend on the ECA's trade liberalization program. Ultimately the best measure of whether Marshall aid was necessary for the Dutch recovery is perhaps the test of whether it was necessary for the German recovery and whether without it the Federal Republic would have been so closely integrated into the network of intra–West European trade and exerted the powerful force for expansion on its neighbors which it did.

The expansionary force of the Federal Republic was exerted in three ways: through its own high growth rates of national income; through its low tariffs, which offered rapidly expanding markets for specialized manufactures from its smaller immediate neighbors; and through its capacity to substitute for American exports. There seems no reason to argue that the commercial policy of the Federal Republic would have been different had there been no Marshall aid; it is impossible to think of any satisfactory way forward for West Germany in 1948 other than by way of an export expansion which necessarily implied commercial concessions to its neighbors. Because of the structure of the country's industry, reinforced by the pattern of expansion between 1933 and 1944, and because of the nature of external demand, this export expansion was bound to be skewed toward capital goods, a tendency reinforced by the initial low levels of personal

---

[27] Griffiths, *Economic Reconstruction*, 21–22.
[28] Van der Eng, *De Marshall-Hulp*, 169. The calculation is explained on p. 249.

disposable income on the domestic market. British protectionism provided a
further force for the integration of the Federal Republic into an expanding
intra–West European trade circuit. The question remains whether German
national income growth rates would have been so high without Marshall
aid.

In an unpublished paper Werner Abelshauser has described the
contribution of the Marshall Plan to German economic recovery as "hardly
noticeable."[29] As late as September 1948, Marshall aid had financed no
deliveries to an industrial recovery which was strongly under way. Even so,
by the end of 1949, when Marshall aid was financing 16 percent of the
Federal Republic's imports and other forms of American aid a further 21
percent, Abelshauser's comment is surely an exaggeration. Like Britain, the
Federal Republic was a food importer, especially a grain importer, and
unlike Britain and France had no source of food imports within its own
currency zone. Either its deficit on dollar trade would have been
unmanageable in 1949 or its food imports would have had to be much lower
had there been no Marshall aid. We are back to the question of whether
European populations could have continued to live and work at the low level
of food consumption of the spring of 1948. That level was particularly low
in Germany, at the best 2,000 calories per head on average, a figure lower
than in Italy.

The question of food consumption returns us to that of political
stability. In what did the stability of postwar West European politics
consist, and how far did it depend on the Marshall Plan? These are questions
almost wholly unexplained by historians. In an extended essay Maier has
considered the meaning and importance of stability in the postwar world and
tried to explain some of its origins.[30] He places the main emphasis on the
entry of organized labor into postwar governing political coalitions and the
changes this brought in economic policies. Hogan, like Maier, sees this as
an important element in the corporative "neo-capitalism" which the
Marshall Plan exported. Both place much weight on the role of trade unions
in the ECA and their efforts to promote the official ideology of productivity.
Others have confirmed that the ECA did consciously seek to bring European
trade unions into a consensus based on the belief that constant productivity
improvements would replace class conflict.[31] Although the situation was
much more complex in France, it is generally true that in Western Europe,

---

[29] W. Abelshauser, "The Economic Role of the ERP in German Recovery and Growth
after the War: A Macroeconomic Perspective," paper presented to the conference "The
Marshall Plan and Germany," Washington, October 1984.

[30] Charles S. Maier, *In Search of Stability: Explorations in Historical Political
Economy* (Cambridge, MA, 1987).

[31] Pier Paolo D'Attore, *ERP Aid and the Politics of Productivity in Italy during the
1950s,* European University Institute Working Papers No. 159, 1985; Anthony Carew,
*Labour under the Marshall Plan: The Politics of Productivity and the Marketing of
Management Science* (Manchester, 1987); Federico Romero, *United States Policy for
Postwar European Reconstruction: The Role of American Trade Unions,* European
University Institute Working Papers No. 311, 1987.

even more than in the United States, organized labor did become a part of the postwar political consensus. But in many countries, the United States included, organized labor was only a small part of the total labor force. The changes in economic policy favorable to labor in general, such as full-employment policies and more extensive welfare provision, were the outcome of direct democratic political pressures through the electoral system from which organized labor became the beneficiary just because it was organized. Although trade unions became an instrument of economic management in what Hogan calls neocapitalism and others like Maier prefer to call neocorporatism, the roots of this change are to be found not in changes of ideas but in a shift of political power which altered the parameters within which politicians could maneuver after 1945.

It is this mixture of greater sensitivity to popular demands arising through the electoral system on the one hand, and the persistence and in some directions the extension of the corporatist interest-group representational politics of the interwar period on the other, which characterizes post-1945 European government. It was anything but the mere extrapolation of the corporatist trends of the 1930s, as Hogan and Maier argue; it represents a sharp break in political practice characterized by a much greater responsiveness to the mass of the electorate. The reason for this, I would suggest, is not hard to seek. The restored national governments in Western Europe were weak and desperate for political legitimacy in the reconstruction period. The political consensuses which they created were the result of concessions intended to produce political stability. The massive money wage increases of 1944 and 1945 in countries like Belgium and France, the immediate welfare improvements offered, in the most unpropitious economic circumstances possible, in countries like Belgium, the United Kingdom, and, soon thereafter, Italy, all fall into this category. The acceptance of organized labor as a part of the government managerial machine was part of this process as well as an extension of what Hogan and Maier delineate as the managerial ideas of the interwar period.

If we were to look for a group whose position was even stronger, in the sense that it gained even more concessions, and whose inclusion in the new political consensus was virtually universal and almost unquestioned, we would find it at once and everywhere in the agricultural sector. Except for the largest and most efficient, farms were in effect transferred to the public welfare sector in return for votes. Massive agricultural protection was the order of the day in every European country, and a framework of regulation like that on a large state enterprise was imposed on the agricultural sector everywhere. This was a response to the circumstances of the interwar period, when sudden increases in the gap between agricultural and industrial incomes had placed insupportable strains on democracies. The outcome here too was a mixture of corporatist interest-group management and an extension of direct parliamentary democracy. An organization like the *Federation Nationale des Syndicats des Exploitants Agricoles* or the *Deutscher Bauernverband* exercised power not only through its association with official policy formulation (in the German case it staffed the Ministry of

WAS THE MARSHALL PLAN NECESSARY?   249

Agriculture) but also through the number of deputies elected to parliament who were its members or officials.

Not all industry by contrast was brought into the consensus. Governments encouraged the industries they wanted. In the mixed economy of post-1945 Europe, moreover, industries which were managed by government or received state help were an assortment of allegedly dynamic manufacturers whose role was to promote technological modernization and exports, like Fiat in Italy, and industries taken under government protection to solve particular social and political management problems, like coal mining in Britain. Within this selective framework of "industrial policy," it also became part of the postwar consensus that industry was a crucial component of national welfare. This was seen most clearly in the widespread national support for the successive modernization plans in France.

The welfare state as it evolved everywhere was another vital element in the postwar consensus. It cemented the consensus together by extending a common political interest to an ever-increasing number of middle-income and lower-income voters. The continual extension of welfare "rights" to particular social categories provided the ideal vehicle through which politicians could continue to respond to direct electoral demands. Furthermore, the development of large government insurance funds, sometimes virtually indistinguishable from the national taxation revenue, strengthened the capacity of the state to pursue the fiscal policies which Keynesian economics suggested were necessary to maintain demand and high employment and so preserve stability.

Lastly, the impact of rearmament on demand from 1950 onward also helped to preserve stability. When military expenditure settled on one of its brief plateaus between 1954 and 1958 it had been raised by NATO rearmament and the Korean War to a point where in most West European countries it was twice the proportion of the gross domestic product (GDP) it had been for most of the interwar period. In France military expenditure was 7.3 percent of GDP, the same proportion as under the rearmament drive in 1938. In the United Kingdom it was 8.8 percent, more than in 1938, when large-scale rearmament began. Countries which before the war had relied on diplomacy or declarations of neutrality to defend their independence now also committed themselves to armed forces on a large scale. Military expenditure was 6 percent of Dutch GDP in 1954, 5 percent of that of Norway, and 3.2 percent of that of Denmark. These proportions of public expenditure were constant until 1968 except for the decline in the 1960s in France. What this meant from 1949 onward was that some large West European economies were sustaining the levels of military expenditure which had generated the recovery from the downturn of 1938 and which had imposed such organizational strains on their economies. The persistence of these strains was a constant argument for maintaining some forms of central guidance and control over the economy, of which industrial policy was one example. Armaments industries always were thought of as an important aspect of industrial policy and this had the further effect of bringing into the

consensus manufacturers and research organizations that depended on the
defense sector, as well, of course, as the armed forces themselves.

Even when sketched out in this rudimentary way, and allowing for the
certainty that subsequent research will surely reveal different kinds of
European consensus created at different dates, in Sweden or Norway as early
as the 1930s, it can be seen that West European post-1945 political
coalitions were not simply the extrapolation of trends in the United States
during the New Deal. Neither perhaps were American post-1945 political
coalitions. Nor were these European political coalitions in any way the
consequence of the Marshall Plan. And the evidence is that politicians would
have persisted with them had there been no Marshall Plan.

How did the ECA react to them? Hogan's picture of the ECA drawing a
moderate managerial line in alliance with its European friends between free-
enterprise market economics and state control, justified in an industrial
perspective, has no place in any account of European agriculture. Europe
firmly exempted agriculture from the ECA's pressure for trade liberalization
and the one big market. Not even General Clay and the military
government, not even High Commissioner McCloy when the Federal
Republic was still in tutelage, could prevent the new liberal Germany from
being as protectionist in the agricultural sector as the Third Reich, because
on that the political future of the CDU and the coalition depended. In similar
circumstances in freely sovereign countries the ECA could do even less. By
1949, when the bogeyman of social revolution could not be used to
frighten, the ECA's main effort was devoted to curbing what it saw as the
inherently and excessively inflationary tendency of postwar political
consensuses. It did so unsuccessfully, however, because these consensuses
had a life of their own for which Marshall aid had provided a temporary life-
support system which by 1949 was no longer necessary, even if it may have
been so in one or two cases earlier. With the Korean war and rearmament,
the ECA was more concerned to slow down the acceleration of military
expenditure when several European governments were already seeing its
economic and political advantages.

In another way, too, the postwar European coalitions had a life of their
own which brought them into fundamental conflict with the ECA. This lay
in the obvious fact that these coalitions were based on nationalistic
objectives to be achieved by a bold reiteration of the nation-state as an
organizing principle. This can be seen in disputes over industrial policy.
Hogan can avoid this problem because so much of his book is about
American-British relationships. The British stayed out of arguments on
industrial policy by not using Marshall aid counterpart funds for industrial
investment and so not having to ask the ECA to approve the projects.
Where countries chose the opposite course they sometimes encountered
opposition from the ECA. To them this did not much matter because they
could always get the money from somewhere else, but the disputes show

WAS THE MARSHALL PLAN NECESSARY?   251

how divergent long-run ambitions were.[32] The ECA did not want a national
Norwegian steel industry created, especially near to the Arctic circle; it
wanted a rationally integrated European steel industry. It did not want the
French government to expand its petroleum refineries for purely national
reasons and would have greatly preferred more workers' housing to some of
the industrial investments in technological modernization. National
industrial policies in the reconstruction period, like the extension of national
welfare states and like agricultural protectionism, were erecting barriers to
integration more rapidly than the ECA was reducing them.

Here, the ECA was the prisoner of its own economic ideology. Keynes
was surely one of the great nationalists of the twentieth century and it is
easy for us now to see the many fundamental contradictions between
Keynesian economics and the economic integration of medium-sized
European states. Once national welfare states, national industrial policies,
and national agricultural protection had been added to the concept of national
budgets and national accounts, integration could only be more difficult.
Belgium never began any intra-European negotiation around which the
concept of integration was flickering without demanding that all other
negotiating partners raise their level of wages and social security payments
to those prevailing in Belgium. France never entered a similar negotiation
without first thinking of some demand which would mean that other
countries would have to raise their prices. Luxembourg would not even
countenance implementation of the Benelux agreements unless its entire
battery of agricultural protection was exempted from them before the talking
began. In this light it seems wrong to argue as Hogan does that the
Marshall Plan had any significant influence in the creation of the stable
political consensuses of postwar Western Europe. And to argue that the
Treaty of Rome was in some sense the eventual result of the Marshall Plan
seems equally wrong.

The final argument for integration was another magic word of the same
period, productivity. The politics of economic growth, the belief that it was
in the power of government to bring stability by policies designed to
produce constant increases in per-capita national income, were central,
Hogan argues, to generating the postwar political consensus on both sides
of the Atlantic. In this he elaborates the argument of Maier, whose phrase
"the politics of productivity" seems to have served a whole generation of
historians as an explanation of the postwar consensus.[33] It seems to me that
this too is an error of historical interpretation; it puts ideas before the events
that generated them. When did West European governments accept the

---

[32] There is a comprehensive account of the negotiations over the use of counterpart
funds in Chiarella Esposito, "The Marshall Plan in France and Italy, 1948–1950:
Counterpart Fund Negotiations" (Ph.D. diss., State University of New York at Stony Brook,
1985).

[33] Charles S. Maier, "The Politics of Productivity: Foundations of American
International Economic Policy after World War II," in *Between Power and Plenty: The
Foreign Economic Policies of Advanced Industrial States*, ed. P. Katzenstein (Madison,
1978).

political ideology of increases in productivity as a public good, branding all those who did not subscribe to it as "extremists"? Was it not first in the middle and late 1950s? And did not this ideology become accepted because it justified the coalitions and policies resulting from the shifts in real political power which had taken place? Was it not merely the intellectual proof that the consensus had become a firm one, rather than an element in the construction of the consensus? And, indeed, may not the same argument apply to the widespread acceptance of the ideas of Keynes as an important new level of truth, when their weaknesses were as apparent as those of the economics they replaced?

Hogan is clearly justified in basing the central argument of his book on the observation that a deep intellectual harmony joined the creators and administrators of the Marshall Plan and successful postwar West European politicians. This suggests that the shifts of political power on both sides of the Atlantic which these ideas justified had many similarities. There is a long program of research ahead to determine what the similarities and the differences were.[34] But this perspective in itself reduces the importance of the claims made for the Marshall Plan. It is obviously better that foreign policy should be in accordance with the long-run trends of political and economic development in both the subject and the object countries of that policy, and the Marshall Plan can deservedly be cited as a resounding success in that respect. But was it actually necessary? On balance the answer must be that, eminently successful policy though it was, the postwar European world would have looked much the same without it. More drastic foreign trade and exchange controls would have lasted longer in Western Europe. There would not have been the brief period of semiliberalization before the effects of the Korean War were felt and thus no model to go back to after 1953. Social conditions in some countries, France, the Netherlands, and the Federal Republic, would have been harder and in France and the Netherlands the growth of national income would have been at a lower rate before 1950. But there is no indication that economic objectives in these countries would have been altered, nor that the political coalitions which governed them would have collapsed: their roots were too deep and too strong.

That the Marshall Plan should raise such fundamental historical questions is nevertheless a proof of its importance and value as a subject of historical study. Hogan's work matches this importance in the scope of its discussion as well as in the immense effort of research on which it is based. The debate on the causes of the uniquely long period of prosperity after the Second World War has been advanced further, and also the debate on why it could not endure. Whereas economists have failed to provide entirely convincing explanations of either of these phenomena, historians could probably do so. Hogan's work will remain important to their search. It

----

[34] For Scandinavia the discussion is advanced further in the stimulating Gøsta Esping-Andersen, *Politics against Markets: The Social Democratic Road to Power* (Princeton, 1985).

WAS THE MARSHALL PLAN NECESSARY?   253

shows what can be contributed to contemporary debate by historical research. It is a reassertion of the superior value of historical research to contemporary comment, for most of the works on U.S. policy published at the time of the Marshall Plan and just afterward are now made to look superficial. Finally, it leaves us with a program for future research which emerges from Hogan's dialogue with other works published over the last few years. We need to know in historical detail how political consensus was formed, how it was maintained for so long, how relative adjustments within the consensus were maintained, and why they eventually proved impossible in some countries. The task must be an exciting one, for no other period of modern history presents the same aspect of constantly increasing income and welfare in the developed countries as that which began in 1945 and lasted to the end of the 1960s, in some countries even longer. It would not normally have been within the scope of diplomatic history to contribute part of the answer to questions of this kind and it is not the least of Hogan's contributions that he has made it do so. I hope that the many disagreements I have with *The Marshall Plan* are as constructive as the book itself.

[7]

The Marshall Plan: economic effects and implications for Eastern Europe and the former USSR

Barry Eichengreen and Marc Uzan
University of California at Berkeley and Harvard University

1. Introduction

The Marshall Plan is hailed as one of the great foreign economic policy achievements of the 20th century. Between 1948 and 1951 the US transferred \$13 bn. to the war-torn economies of Europe. (The Administration requested \$14.2 bn., Congress authorized \$13.4 bn., and \$12.5 bn. was ultimately made available. The \$14 bn. figure frequently cited includes appropriations for economic assistance in Asia, mostly to colonial dependencies of the European participants.) This timely and generous programme of aid is said to have solidified US leadership of the Western alliance, buttressed moderate elements in Western European politics, smoothed Europe's labour-management relations, and checked the westward march of communism (Kolko and Kolko, 1972; Patterson, 1973).

Less transparent are its economic effects. Qualitative discussions typically credit the Marshall Plan with a significant impact on Europe's recovery.[1] After stagnating through much of 1947, European growth

Much of the research for this paper was undertaken during Eichengreen's visit to the Research Department of the International Monetary Fund, whose hospitality is acknowledged with thanks. Eichengreen received financial support from the Center for German and European Studies of the University of California at Berkeley, Uzan from the Caisse de Depots. Many colleagues have provided helpful comments. We are especially indebted to Alessandra Casella and Brad De Long, on whose collaboration we have drawn (we hope not too) liberally. We gratefully acknowledge conversations with Jeremy Bulo, Daniel Cohen, Ishac Diwan and Dale Henderson. For comments on the paper we are grateful to our discussants at the Economic Policy Panel meeting, Nick Crafts and Martin Hellwig, and to Michael Bordo, Peter Garber, Douglas Irwin, Charles Maier, Torsten Persson and Charles Wyplosz. We thank Pamela Fox for logistical support.
[1] Views to this effect include Brookings Institution (1951), Ellis (1950), Tinbergen (1954), Mayer (1969), Arkes (1972) and van der Wee (1986). Arkes (1972), for example, asserts that Marshall Plan assistance was 'critical at the margins' and that it had a 'multiplier effect of three or four times its value', but he does not specify the model in which this result obtains. Wallich (1955) similarly concludes that, while several factors contributed to German economic revival, 'by providing key commodities at a critical time foreign aid probably helped to increase output by a multiple of its own value'.

accelerated in 1948, coincident with the release of Marshall aid. The
continent then embarked on two decades of sustained high growth.
The concurrence of Marshall Plan inflows with the quickening of growth
has encouraged observers to attribute European prosperity to the
American programme.

Quantitative discussions (e.g. Collins and Rodrik, 1991) are more
sceptical. Marshall aid averaged only 2.5% of the combined national
incomes of the recipient countries over the period it was in effect. Even
at its height it could have financed no more than 20% of their capital
formation. There is no obvious correlation across countries between
the magnitude of Marshall Plan allotments and the pace of economic
growth. Germany grew most quickly during the Marshall Plan years,
but its share of American aid was not large. Given the existence of
alternative explanations for Europe's rapid growth – notably post-war
reconstruction and scope for catching up to the US – there is no *a priori*
case for attaching particular weight to the Marshall Plan (Milward,
1984).

In this paper, we challenge this new conventional wisdom. We find
that the Marshall Plan's economic effects had a significant impact on
Europe's recovery from World War II. The recipients of large amounts
of Marshall aid recovered significantly faster than other industrial
countries. Strikingly, however, the obvious channels through which the
Marshall Plan could have affected European recovery – stimulating investment in plant and equipment, augmenting capacity to import, and
financing public investment on infrastructure repair – were relatively
unimportant. Post-war Europe's crisis was not a crisis of insufficient
investment, inadequate capacity to import raw materials, or inability
to repair devastated infrastructure. Rather, Europe was suffering a
'marketing crisis', in which producers refused to bring goods to market,
and workers and managers limited the effort they devoted to market
activity. Political instability, shortages of consumer goods and fears of
financial chaos led them to hoard commodities and withold effort. The
Marshall Plan facilitated the restoration of financial stability and the
liberalization of production and prices; this was its crucial role. The
Marshall Plan thereby allowed Europe to return to its underlying growth
path more quickly than would have been possible otherwise. Indeed,
one can imagine, had the Marshall Plan not been forthcoming and had
the post-war crisis deepened, that democratic institutions and the commitment to the market might have broken down, preventing Europe
from returning to that growth path at all.

These conclusions have obvious implications for Western aid to the
successor states of the USSR ('the Republics' for short), where uncertainty about the pace of liberalization and about the prospects for

16   *Barry Eichengreen and Marc Uzan*

monetary stability have given rise to shortages of consumer goods and financial chaos resembling those which plagued Western Europe after World War II. In the absence of a social contract, struggles over income distribution threaten to swamp efforts to raise productivity. Western aid could facilitate solutions to these problems. Equally, there are important differences between the two settings. Compared to Europe a half-century ago, the Republics today possess less experience with and commitment to the market. The institutional infrastructure that is a prerequisite for an aid-instigated acceleration of economic growth is not yet in place. Not even the outlines of a social contract are evident. These considerations militate against a Marshall Plan for the East.

2. Background

European economic recovery from the conclusion of hostilities to the inauguration of the Marshall Plan falls into two phases: six quarters of rapidly rising output achieved mainly through repair of infrastructure and productive capacity, followed by six more difficult quarters when the gains of the preceding period had to be consolidated.

2.1. Recovery before the Marshall Plan: the first phase (mid-1945 through 1946)

The first 18 months of the pre-Marshall Plan period, from mid-1945 through the end of 1946, were marked by rapid output increases. Industrial production had fallen to 30–40% of pre-war levels in Belgium, France and the Netherlands, and to less than 20% in Italy and Germany. The slump in industrial output reflected not the wholesale destruction of capacity, however, but disruption to the channels for obtaining inputs and distributing outputs. In Italy, for example, no more than 20% of industrial capacity had been destroyed by fighting, bombing, sabotage and the removal of plant and equipment to Germany (Grindrod, 1955). The low level of output reflected rather the difficulty of obtaining raw materials, transporting goods and distributing food. The majority of the continent's freight cars were damaged or destroyed. Blocked waterways and lack of barges and tugs crippled water transportation. At the time of liberation, only 5% of France's inland waterways were open to navigation. Roads, bridges and rail links were out of commission.

These conditions provided scope for rapid output growth through the reconstruction and repair of infrastructure. European industrial production (including mining, manufacturing, building and construction) rose quickly, to 83% of 1938 levels in the fourth quarter of 1946. Sectors producing final goods were fastest to expand. Resuming the

The Marshall Plan   17

Table 1. Indexes of industrial production in Western Europe (1938 = 100)

Country	1947	1948	1949	1950	1951	Percentage increase 1951 over 1947
Turkey	153	154	162	165	163	7
Sweden	142	149	157	164	172	21
Ireland	120	135	154	170	176	46
Denmark	119	135	143	159	160	35
Norway	115	125	135	146	153	33
UK	110	120	129	140	145	32
Belgium	106	122	122	124	143	33
Luxembourg	—	139	132	139	168	—
France	99	111	122	123	138	39
Netherlands	94	114	127	140	147	56
Italy	93	99	109	125	143	54
Greece	69	76	90	114	130	88
Austria	55	85	114	134	148	269
Germany (Federal Republic)	34	50	72	91	106	312
All participating countries	87	99	112	124	135	55
All participating countries exclusive of Germany (Federal Republic)	105	119	130	138	145	37

Source: US President, *First Report to Congress on the Mutual Security Program* (31 December 1951), p. 75. Drawn from Brown and Opie (1953), p. 249.

fabrication of finished goods required only the repair of some machinery. Manufacturers found a ready market. Often, however, raw material supplies were a binding constraint. Except in Germany, European forests had been overcut during the war, limiting supplies of timber. Coal production remained depressed due to manpower shortages and the destruction of mines. The output of iron and steel recovered only slowly, due in part to the lack of coal. In countries like Germany, the shortage of spare parts for industrial equipment was acute.

The incidence of recovery was uneven. As Table 1 shows, those parts of Europe remote from the main theatres of the war – the UK, Ireland and much of Scandinavia – were most successful at quickly surpassing pre-war levels of industrial activity. Italy, Greece and the Netherlands, along with Germany, in contrast, failed to match pre-war levels of manufacturing. Compared to industry, agriculture recovered slowly from the war. In 1946 European agricultural production was still less than two-thirds that of 1938. (Industrial production outside Germany,

18   *Barry Eichengreen and Marc Uzan*

in contrast, had already matched its 1938 peak.) Grain and potato
output recovered quickly, that of meat and dairy products less so.
Wartime slaughtering of livestock, destruction of farm machinery and
inadequate use of fertilizers all hampered European agriculture. Even
where capacity could be restored swiftly, many crops required a 6- or
12-month harvest cycle and livestock a comparable gestation period.
Considerable delay consequently ensued before the appearance of an
output response. Price controls on foodstuffs were kept in place longer
than other price ceilings, discouraging the expansion of production.
Fertilizers and machinery required by agriculture were in particularly
short supply.

2.2. Recovery before the Marshall Plan: the second phase (1947 through mid-1948)

The second phase of the pre-Marshall Plan period, from the beginning
of 1947 to the release of Marshall aid, was marked by mounting difficulties. According to World Bank experts, 'no further progress was made
in 1947' (IBRD, 1948). Leaving aside Germany, industrial output in
1947-III was no higher than at the end of 1946. The fourth quarter
of 1947 was marked by a growth spurt, with industrial output rising
by 8%. Then, however, stagnation set in again: output in 1948-III was
essentially unchanged from a year before. Europe's recovery seemed
in jeopardy.

We regard this view as overly pessimistic. There is no indication that
the growth process had petered out. Annual averages show, notwithstanding temporary set-backs, expansion throughout the period. Taking
annual averages, European industrial production (excluding Germany)
was 14% higher in 1947 than in 1946. Observers may have been
generalizing from more serious problems in agriculture. Measured
agricultural output was 3% lower in 1947 than in the preceding year.
Unseasonable weather in the winter and spring of 1947 depressed
yields. Winter frost damaged plants and trees; spring and summer
drought then hindered their recovery.

Pessimism may have also stemmed from developments which bode
ill for the future. Increasingly pervasive shortages threatened to create
disruptive bottle-necks. The fuel shortage associated with the cold winter
of 1947 limited energy supplies to manufacturing and transport. Thaw-
ing snows flooded coal mines, and summer drought reduced supplies
of hydroelectric power. Iron and steel shortages disrupted fabricating
industries requiring metals as inputs. Shortages of industrial raw
materials became increasingly prevalent. Except in the UK, the scarcity
of special-purpose machine tools emerged as a serious problem. The

The Marshall Plan   19

dearth of foodstuffs limited caloric intake and labour productivity. These developments may not yet have brought growth to a halt, but they threatened to do so.

Such difficulties were thought to reflect three problems: the slump in international trade which tightened the foreign exchange constraint; inadequate fiscal capacity which limited infrastructure repair; and low levels of income which constrained domestic savings. Following an overview of economic growth in the Marshall Plan years, we consider these problems in turn.

2.3. Economic growth in the Marshall Plan years

Discussions of the economic effects of the Marshall Plan (Berolzheimer, 1953; Kirman and Reichlin, 1991) typically compare industrial production at the start and end of the programme. Between 1947 and 1951 industrial output in the participating countries rose by 55%. (See Table 1.) Growth ranged from 7% in Turkey to 269% in Austria and 312% in the FRG. More typical were Denmark, Norway, the UK, Belgium and France, in each of which industrial production rose between 30 and 40% over the four years. Excluding Germany, the rise in industrial production averaged 37%. This was remarkably rapid progress.

The question is how much of this performance is attributable to the Marshall Plan. Variations in the rate of growth of industrial production provide few hints. Europe's industrial output rose by 15% between 1946 and 1947, by 16% between 1947 and 1948 and by 14% between 1948 and 1949.[2] In the aggregate, then, there is essentially no variation in the period spanning the inauguration of the Marshall Plan. Europe's agricultural output also rose impressively over the Marshall Plan years, by 37% in the OEEC countries (Table 2). Again, however, variations in the rate of output growth provide few hints about the role of the Marshall Plan. Measured production rose by 19% between 1945/46 and 1946/47, declined marginally between 1946/47 and 1947/48, but then rose strongly, by 17% between 1947/48 and 1948/49 and by 10% the following year. Unless the rebound from the bad harvest of 1947/48 is attributable to the Marshall Plan, its effect is not obvious.

Nor do cross-country variations in the rate of economic growth strongly support the existence of a Marshall Plan effect. Figure 1 juxtaposes Marshall Plan allotments as a share of GNP against the growth rate. There is considerable variation in the generosity of American aid. Austria and the Netherlands received Marshall transfers

---

[2] These figures exclude the USSR. (UN, 1949a, 1950).

Table 2. Index of total agricultural output for human consumption of OEEC countries (Pre-war = 100)

Country	% of pre-war total European production (a)	1947–48	1948–49	1949–50	1950–51
Austria	1.63	53	66	79	88
Belgium–Luxembourg	2.09 (b)	83	93	116	119
Denmark	1.93	84	92	113	126
France	15.72	78	100	103	111
Germany (Federal Republic)	10.61 (c)	60	76	96	106
Greece	1.21	83	79	110	93
Ireland	1.50	89	88	95	103
Italy	8.42	85	95	103	109
Netherlands	2.58	79	93	116	119
Norway	0.62	86	92	112	120
Sweden	2.08	101	111	115	116
Switzerland	1.38	95	98	98	104
Turkey	2.33	96	120	94	106
UK	5.89	95	111	114	122
All member countries	N.A.	81	95	104	111

Source: OEEC *Statistical Bulletins* (Paris, May 1952), Table II, 1, p. 66. Drawn from Brown and Opie (1953), p. 253. Also UN (1948), p. 11.
Notes: (a) Europe excluding USSR; (b) Belgium only; (c) Three Western Zones.

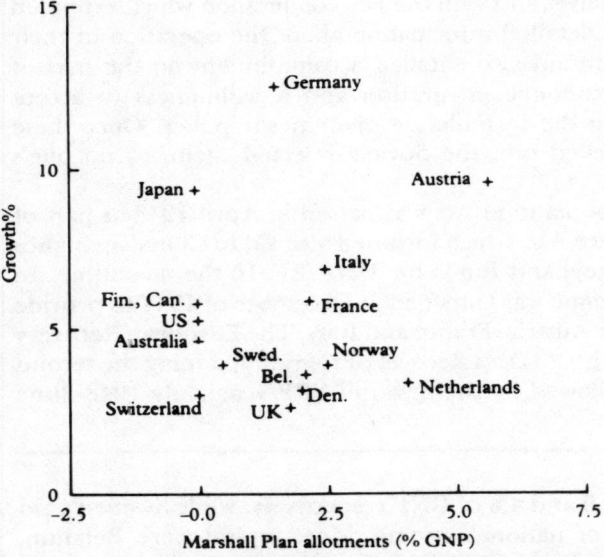

Figure 1. Annual rate of GDP growth and Marshall Plan allotments as a share of GNP, 1948–51

Box 1. The origins of the Marshall Plan

George C. Marshall traced the origins of the plan that bears his name to the failure of the UK and US in the spring of 1947 to win Soviet support for German industrial reconstruction. The Truman Administration was convinced that American prosperity required buoyant export markets, which hinged in turn on European recovery. The 1947 crisis convinced Marshall and other US officials that a viable European economy required a prosperous Germany at its core. Holding down German industrial production limited German imports from the rest of Europe and hindered the continent's recovery. Reversing the policy of limiting German production was necessary to stimulate European growth. Secretary of State Marshall and British Foreign Secretary Ernest Bevin put these points to the Soviets at the Moscow Foreign Ministers Conference of March–April 1947. Soviet resistance was interpreted as a ploy to radicalize Western European politics by destabilizing the continent's economy. This in turn provided the impetus for Marshall's aid proposal.

His June 5th Harvard address offered to include 'everything up to the Urals' so as not to antagonize European governments wishing to avoid a confrontation with the USSR. It seems unlikely that the US was serious about including the USSR. Washington made it clear that the offer was contingent on close cooperation by the participating governments among themselves and with the US, cooperation which extended to the disclosure of detailed information about the operation of their economies. American aid also entailed a commitment on the part of the recipients to economic integration and a willingness to accept American input into the formulation of domestic policy. Once these conditions were spelled out, the Soviets rejected them, to no one's surprise.

The Economic Cooperation Act was passed in April 1948 as part of the Foreign Assistance Act, which included also aid to China, assistance to Greece and Turkey, and funds for UNICEF. In the meantime, an Interim Aid Programme was launched in December of 1947 to provide modest assistance for Austria, France and Italy. The European Recovery Program opened with a 90 Days Recovery Program spanning the second quarter of 1948, followed by the first full ERP year (July 1948–June 1949).

amounting to nearly 6 and 4% of GNP respectively, while Sweden's aid was less than 0.5% of national income. More typical were Belgium, Denmark, France, Italy, Norway and the UK, all of which received about 2% of GNP. The figure suggests at best a weak positive correlation between the growth rate and Marshall Plan receipts as a share of national income. A regression of growth on a constant and on Marshall Plan allotments as a share of GNP fails to turn up a statistically significant relationship.

The foreign trade of the participating countries rose even more strongly than their domestic production, in contrast to the preceding depression in intra-European and intercontinental trade. Total exports in constant prices rose at an annual rate of more than 20% between 1947 and 1950. Europe's imports expanded more slowly than its exports, as was desired by those who wished for a strengthening of its current account.

By all three criteria, then – industrial output, agricultural productivity and trade – Europe's economic performance was admirable, absolutely and relative to the preceding period. The problem is to identify the contribution of the Marshall Plan.

3. Short-term effects

We turn now to this problem, concentrating in this section on short-term effects in the period when the Marshall Plan was in operation. Traditional accounts emphasize saving, imports of industrial inputs and public investment as constraints on economic growth. In Appendix A we develop a three-gap model which shows that foreign aid which supplements domestic saving, augments imports of industrial inputs and allows increases in public investment can have a major impact on current levels of output. In fact, however, it turns out that these were not the principal channels through which the Marshall Plan stimulated European economic growth.

3.1. The savings-investment gap

Was investment a significant short-run constraint on European economic growth? Did the Marshall Plan, by boosting investment, significantly raise the level of output? Although qualitative accounts typically answer both questions positively, systematic analysis gives grounds for scepticism.

The notion that the savings gap bound in the aftermath of World War II is implicit in accounts suggesting that the residents of many European countries were living close to subsistence. A physically active man requires 3,200 to 5,500 calories daily, depending on the nature of his work. In 1946 UN experts figured that more than 140 mn. Europeans were receiving fewer than 2,000 calories daily, while an additional 100 mn. Europeans were receiving fewer than 1,500 calories.

The Marshall Plan   23

**Table 3. Savings rates in the aftermath of
World War II and the 1950s (%)**

Period	1946–51	1948–51	1952–60
Australia	16	20	21
Austria	na	12	23
Belgium	na	na	17
Canada	16	20	21
Denmark	15	23	25
Finland	14	24	27
France	na	18	20
Germany	na	19	27
Italy	15	18	19
Japan	15	18	24
Netherlands	na	20	27
Norway	28	35	34
Sweden	17	21	22
Switzerland	na	10	23
UK	9	13	16
US	14	17	18

Source: Mitchell (1975, 1983).
Note: Saving rates are calculated as the sum of investment
and the current-account surplus.

In Germany, where the official ration was 1,550 calories, the actual
ration as late as 1948 was as little as 1,000 calories. The implication,
according to N. H. Collision, Deputy Chief of the European Cooperation
Agency (ECA) Mission to the Bizone, was that there was 'little savings
in Germany' (US House, 1949). Table 3 shows saving rates following
the war and compares them with those prevailing in the 1950s. That
savings rates were highest in countries with relatively high per capita
incomes is consistent with the view that people living close to the margin
of subsistence were unwilling or unable to defer consumption to the
future. For every European country but Norway, moreover, savings
rates were lower prior to 1952, when low incomes and inadequate
nutrition were a particular problem. Low recorded rates of saving and
investment may also reflect the post-war surge of consumer durables
spending, which in reality was a component of investment but showed
up in the statistics as consumption. But the implications were the same:
less domestic income was left for other forms of capital formation.
Strikingly, however, savings rates also were low in the US, Canada and
Australia, where they were hardly constrained by low levels of income.
The US was pegging interest rates at low levels until the Fed-Treasury
Accord of 1951; it could be that low interest rates affected savings
propensities. More than low levels of income seem to have contributed,
then, to Europe's low savings rates.

24   *Barry Eichengreen and Marc Uzan*

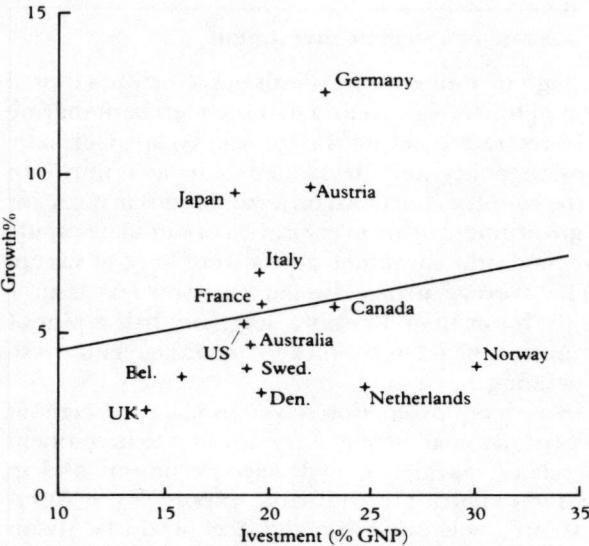

Figure 2. Growth and investment rates, 1948–51

Moreover, just because savings and investment rates were low, it does not follow that growth had to be significantly constrained. Figure 2 juxtaposes investment rates in the Marshall Plan years against rates of economic growth. The investment ratios of the high growth countries, Austria and Germany, were unexceptional. Other countries, notably Norway and the Netherlands, placed an even greater emphasis on investment (see Price, 1955). The relationship between the investment share of GNP and the growth rate is weak. Rigourous estimates are obtained from the analysis presented in Appendix B (multivariate regressions linking Marshall Plan allotments to investment) and C (regressions linking investment and growth). We find that Marshall Plan inflows were positively (and significantly) associated with subsequent investment, even after controlling for other determinants of capital formation. Transfers equal to 2% of GNP raised investment by 0.7% of GNP in the following year. We also find that the rate of GDP growth was positively related to investment – although the magnitude and significance of the effect depend on the specification. Excluding the special case of Norway (see Box 2), it appears that raising the investment share of GNP by 0.7% would have raised the growth of domestic output by 0.3%.

That $1 of Marshall Plan aid raised domestic investment by as much as 40 cents is striking when it is recalled that the vast majority of

Box 2. The peculiar case of Norwegian investment

In Figure 2, Norway's high investment rate stands out. Norway's capital
stock had been devastated by the war. Nearly half the merchant marine
fleet had been sunk. In retreating before the Russian Army, Germany
adopted a scorched-earth policy and devastated Norway's northern
regions. In response, the country embarked on an ambitious investment
programme, with the government using every device to stimulate capital
formation. Rations of food and consumer goods were kept at exceptionally low levels. The average urban dweller received less than 1
pound of meat a month, fewer than 30 eggs a year, and half a pint of
milk a day. Cabinet ministers bicycled to work to encourage citizens to
economize on their spending.

Norway's policy of investment promotion stayed in place throughout
the 1950s. Large shares of national income were devoted to investment
in rebuilding the merchant marine, in hydroelectric power, and in
industries producing for export. The principal exports were forest
products, fish products, ore, metals and iron and steel products. Metals
and engineering accounted for more than a third of Norwegian gross
investment in industry in 1947 (UN 1949b, p. 52). Investments in
rebuilding the merchant marine were particularly important. The transportation sector accounted for 40% of Norwegian investment in 1947
and 1948, a larger fraction than for any of the other 11 countries for
which UN (1949a, p. 50) provided sectoral breakdowns. The UN (1964)
devoted an entire subsection of its report on European economic growth
in the 1950s to the low productivity of investment in Norway. Norway's
investment rate was shown to be higher than for any other European
country but Ireland. UN (1964, Chapter IV, pp. 17–22) cited a combination of factors to account for this disappointing performance. Capacity
utilization in Norwegian industry declined between 1948 and 1959,
which reduced measured productivity. The country was said to have
invested in the wrong industries, like herring oil and meal. Investment
in the engineering industry significantly exceeded the availability of
labour with the relevant skills. Agricultural machinery was under-
utilized. Investments in transport and hydroelectric power yielded
significant increases in output only after an exceptionally long gestation
period, and government's efforts to bias investment toward the northern
regions of the country exacerbated these tendencies.

aid-financed imports took the form of food and raw materials. Equally,
that an additional percentage point of GNP devoted to investment
raised the growth rate by more than a third of a percentage point is

26   *Barry Eichengreen and Marc Uzan*

striking when one observes that we are considering a period as short as a year.[3] Yet even accepting these upper-bound estimates, the combined impact on European economic recovery was small. Marshall aid in the amount of 2.5% of recipient GDP, operating through this channel, would have raised the growth rate by only half a percentage point. While helpful, this is hardly the dramatic stimulus trumpeted by champions of the Marshall Plan.

3.2. The foreign exchange gap

Was capacity to import a significant constraint on European economic growth? Did the Marshall Plan, by providing additional foreign exchange, alleviate bottle-necks that otherwise would have stifled production? Again, while qualitative accounts emphasize the importance of the foreign exchange gap, more systematic analysis challenges the notion that it was a significant constraint on growth.

Imported raw materials were important to the operation of European industry. Cotton for the textile industry was in short supply.[4] So was the coal needed to provide power for manufacturing and to refine petroleum for transportation. The output of Ruhr coal, which 'provided the basis for much of the industrial development on the European Continent', had recovered to only 65% of pre-war levels by the end of 1947 (Federal Reserve Board, 1948). Western European coal production as a whole was still only 80% of pre-war. The current-account gap ostensibly bound not only for intermediate inputs but for foodstuffs as well. The American and British zones of Germany produced less than two-thirds of the modest food ration permitted by the occupation authorities. The rest had to be imported. Paul Hoffman, the ECA administrator, told the Senate Foreign Relations Committee that 'In

---

[3] Romer (1989) and Cohen (1991) find a virtually identical coefficient on the investment share in equations they estimate to explain growth in a cross section of countries, but both authors consider longer time horizons.

[4] As Paul Hoffman described the situation, 'I found last year that supplying cotton, for example, for mills that did not have cotton, was just as much a recovery item as perhaps machine tools to some company that needed machine tools.' Winks (1960) recounts the story of a Dutch bicycle firm saved from having to shut its doors by a mere $1,200 of Marshall Plan aid. Lauritz Hensen, President of Hede Nielsen Ltd., explained that he had the cash to buy bearings, but could not do so where kroner were acceptable currency. He appealed to his government and the $1,200 of ball bearings were flown from the US on an emergency order. Compare the recent story of a sock-making factory in the USSR with 50 'gleaming Italian sock-making machines purchased last year for about $15,000 each by the Soviet Ministry of Light Industry. For much of the time they stand idle because of a shortage of needles that sell in the west for a few cents. 'The ministry paid hard [Western] currency for these machines, and we paid them back in rubles [in the words of the plant manager]. But now they are saying that they don't have enough hard currency to buy the necessary needles and spare parts. As a result, we've already had to stop these machines on the evening shift and will soon have to stop the day shift as well.' Dobbs (1991).

The Marshall Plan   27

some cases I think the very No. 1 recovery item is a little more food to get a little more work out of people' (US Senate, 1949).

The current-account constraint bound only if reserves were depleted and foreign borrowing was precluded. In fact, reserves had been exhausted in the first post-war quarters, and foreign capital (mainly direct investment) supplemented domestic savings only modestly once aid fell off in 1947 (Table 4). American investors' unsatisfactory experience with foreign lending after World War I surely helped to shape these trends. Two-thirds of the foreign dollar bonds floated in the US in the 1920s lapsed into default in the 1930s, and more than a few remained in default following the war. The disorganization of the European economy and of its finances reinforced US investors' caution.

Figure 3 shows the current-account balances of 16 countries. Austria, Denmark, France, Germany, the Netherlands and Norway all ran substantial current-account deficits. There is a strong positive relationship between the current-account deficit and Marshall Plan receipts. A regression analysis suggests that increasing Marshall aid by 1% of GNP allowed a country to increase its current-account deficit by 0.9% of GNP. This simple correlation exaggerates the impact of the Marshall Plan on the current account, since causality also ran in the other direction: countries with larger current-account deficits received more

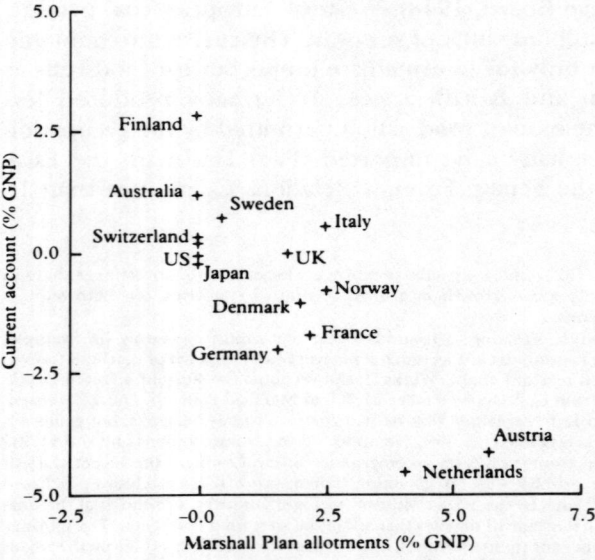

Figure 3. Average annual current-account balance and Marshall Plan allotments, 1948–51

Table 4. The financing of Europe's overseas deficit (billion current US$)

Item	1947 US	1947 Other overseas countries	1947 Total	1948 US	1948 Other overseas countries	1948 Total	1949 US	1949 Other overseas countries	1949 Total	1950 US	1950 Other overseas countries	1950 Total
I. Balance on goods and services and other transactions making up the deficit:												
Balance on goods and services	-5.6	-1.8	-7.4	-3.4	-1.5	-4.9	-3.2	-0.6	-3.8	-1.6	-0.9	-2.5
Private donations	+0.4	—	+0.4	+0.4	-0.1	+0.3	+0.4	-0.1	+0.3	+0.3	-0.1	+0.2
Private capital movements	+0.3	-1.1	-0.8	+0.2	-0.1	+0.1	-0.1	-0.4	-0.5	-0.1	-0.1	-0.2
Special official financing (debt settlements, specific investment projects etc.)	-0.6	-0.1	-0.7	-0.2	-0.3	-0.5	+0.2	-0.4	-0.2	+0.5	-0.3	+0.2
Total deficit to be financed:												
Unadjusted	-5.5	-3.0	-8.5	-3.0	-2.0	-5.0	-2.7	-1.5	-4.2	-0.9	-1.4	-2.3
Adjustments	-0.3	—	-0.3	—	-0.1	-0.1	-0.2	+0.7	+0.5	-0.1	+0.5	+0.4
Adjusted	-5.8	-3.0	-8.8	-3.0	-2.1	-5.1	-2.9	-0.8	-3.7	-1.0	-0.9	-1.9

Continued overleaf

Table 4 (cont.)

II. Official financing of a compensatory nature:												
Government grants	+1.0	—	+1.0	+3.2	—	+3.2	+4.1	—	+4.1	+2.7	—	+2.7
Long-term capital movement	+3.8	+0.9	+4.7	+1.1	+0.5	+1.6	+0.7	-0.5	+0.2	+0.2	—	+0.2
Financing by International Institutions	+1.1	+0.1	+1.2	+0.3	—	+0.3	—	—	—	—	—	—
Movement in sterling balances	—	-0.6	-0.6	—	-0.2	-0.2	—	-0.5	-0.5	-0.2	+0.9	+0.9
Movement in US dollar balances	+0.8	—	+0.8	-0.3	-0.3	-0.3	-0.1	-0.1	-0.1	-0.2	-0.4	-0.2
Gold movement	+1.9	-0.2	+1.7	+0.9	-0.4	+0.5	+0.2	-0.2	—	-1.3		-1.7
Total compensatory official financing	+8.6	+0.2	+8.8	+5.2	-0.1	+5.1	+4.9	-1.2	+3.7	+1.4	+0.5	+1.9
III. Multilateral settlements in US dollars:												
ERP reimbursement for European countries outside the US	—	—	—	-0.8	+0.8	—	-1.0	+1.0	—	-0.7	+0.7	—
Other dollar settlements by European countries outside the US	-2.8	+2.8	—	-1.4	+1.4	—	-1.0	+1.0	—	+0.3	-0.3	—
Total multilateral settlements in US dollars	-2.8	+2.8	—	-2.2	+2.2	—	-2.0	+2.0	—	-0.4	+0.4	—

Source: UK (1950), p. 116; UN (1951), p. 118.

30   *Barry Eichengreen and Marc Uzan*

American aid. Multivariate regression analysis (controlling for simultaneity and for other determinants of the current account) confirms
that recipients of Marshall Plan aid were able to run larger current-
account deficits, but the incremental effect turns out to be small. Countries receiving $1 of Marshall Plan aid increased their current-account
deficits by 12 cents. That current-account deficits did not widen further
reflects the fact that one goal of US policy was to produce current-
account balance between Europe and the US. The conditions attached
to American aid thus may have worked to limit the growth of European
trade deficits.

Even if ability to run larger current-account deficits had a major
effect on growth by relaxing resource bottle-necks, the growth effect
of the Marshall Plan, operating through this channel, still would have
been small because the change in current accounts was small. In fact,
the regression analysis in Appendix C suggests a negligible relationship
between current account balances and growth once other determinants
of the change in GDP are controlled for. The explanation for these
small effects is that resource bottle-necks had only a small impact on
production.[5] For example, coal was critical for the generation of electric
power, which in turn was required for the operation of a wide range
of industrial sectors. But over the Marshall Plan years, Europe imported
only about 7% of its apparent coal consumption. If half of European
production took place in sectors that were coal-burning and unable to
substitute other sources of fuel, 7% of that half would have had to shut
down. European output would have fallen by 3.5%.

This back-of-the-envelope calculation neglects indirect effects and
general equilibrium repercussions. One can imagine, for example, a
small decline in coal consumption producing a large decline in steel
output, which in turn provoked an even larger fall in output in sectors
where steel was an essential input. De Long and Eichengreen (1991)
use input–output analysis as a check on these calculations. Utilizing an
input–output table for Italy in 1950, they eliminate all Marshall-Plan-
financed coal imports and assume that all uses of coal would have been
proportionately reduced in the absence of Marshall Plan imports.[6] They
find that industrial production would have fallen by 6.8% and the supply

---

[5] We owe this argument to Brad De Long. Points made in this paragraph are elaborated in De
Long and Eichengreen (1991).
[6] Coal, according to American observers, was 'the major bottleneck of production' in Italy. See
Federal Reserve Board (1947). The country imported three-quarters of its coal in 1950. The
input–output table used, from Mutual Security Agency (1953), is disaggregated to 16 sectors.
Each element in the vector of final demands is reduced by the same proportion until the coal
constraint is just binding. The exercise assumes that all resources made slack would have remained
idle rather than being redirected to other sectors.

of transportation services by 7.3%, but that agriculture and services would have been unaffected. Since industry and transport account for less than half of national output, the latter would have fallen by 3.2%, close to the previous estimate.

Moreover, in the absence of the Marshall Plan, adjustments in the allocation of foreign exchange would have lowered the need for imports of consumption goods, coal and other intermediate products. Insofar as firms could have adopted less energy-intensive techniques in response to the coal shortage, the decline in production would have been moderated further. Thus, the estimated 3% output decline should be regarded as a generous upper bound on the Marshall Plan's contribution through the elimination of bottle-necks.

3.3. The fiscal gap

Was the capacity to finance spending on infrastructure repair and other public programmes a significant constraint on European recovery? Did the Marshall Plan, by providing governments with additional resources, stimulate growth by relaxing this constraint? While qualitative accounts emphasize this channel, once again systematic analysis refutes the notion that it was a significant constraint on growth.

We do not deny the existence of fiscal problems. Budget deficits in 1946 approached 10% of national income in the UK, Italy and France, and exceeded that threshold in Belgium. Dutch deficits were probably larger still. Given foreigners' unwillingness to lend and the dearth of domestic savings, these budget deficits were financed largely through monetization. Where they were closed, this was accomplished by reducing the government-expenditure share of GNP. The share of public investment in national income was forced to decline. Of 14 European countries, this share rose between 1947 and 1948 only in Belgium, Finland, Italy and Poland. Nor can one deny the destructiveness of the war. In France, 4,000 km of railway track and more than half of all rail yards had been destroyed. In Belgium, France, the Netherlands and Poland fewer than half of all steam locomotives remained in serviceable condition. Vital bridges had been destroyed in operations culminating in the invasion of Germany. It hardly paid to invest in plant and equipment or to produce for the market where roads and railways remained in disarray and goods could not be transported to ports or mercantile centres.

Yet the worst of this damage was repaired before the Marshall Plan came on stream. Railway track and locomotives were quickly restored. By the last quarter of 1946, nearly as much freight was loaded onto railways in Western Europe as had been transported in 1938. In the

32   *Barry Eichengreen and Marc Uzan*

British zone of occupied Germany, where only 1,000 km out of
13,000 km of track was usable at the war's end, 12,000 km were back
in operation by June 1946. (If ton-kilometres rather than tonnage are
used, recovery is faster still.) Water systems and electricity supply were
quickly restored. The implications for production were immediate.
Excluding Germany's three Western zones, by the fourth quarter of
1946 Europe's industrial output nearly matched 1938 levels.

Regression analysis (Appendix B) lends no support to the notion that
the Marshall Plan operated through this channel. There is no indication
in that Marshall Plan inflows allowed for increased levels of government
spending. Nor is there evidence that government spending in 1948 and
after had a significant impact on the rate of economic growth.

3.4. Combined effects

To estimate the combined effects of the Marshall Plan operating through
the investment, current account and public spending channels, we
simulated a system of four equations: a growth equation determining
the percentage change in GDP and three equations determining investment, the current account and government spending respectively.[7] The
Marshall Plan affects investment, the current account and government
spending with a lag; in turn these variables affect economic growth. To
isolate the impact of the Marshall Plan, we simulate the equations using
historical values of the exogenous variables, and then set the Marshall
Plan variables to zero and compute counterfactual values for GDP
growth. The difference between the predicted and counterfactual simulations is the Marshall Plan effect.[8] This effect is shown in Figure 4.
The sum of three small numbers is still a small number. Marshall Plan
allotments have raised GDP in the recipient countries by an average of
less than 0.1% in the two years following its implementation when it
should have had its largest effects. The change is largest in Austria
and the Netherlands, which received the most aid, and smallest in

---

[7] Investment, the current balance and government spending are all expressed as shares of GNP.
The growth equation used was the first equation from Appendix Table C2. In conducting the
counterfactual simulation, we allowed only the linear terms in investment (including the separate
term for Norway), the current account and government spending to operate. The interactive
terms and the direct effect of the Marshall Plan were not allowed to operate. See, however, the
simulations below.

[8] It would be possible to add a fourth equation endogenizing Marshall Plan allotments. Given the
structure of our model, the current year's Marshall Plan allotment depends on the current
balance and other determinants. American aid then affects the subsequent year's current balance,
investment and government spending ratios and through them as well as via its direct effects
the subsequent year's GDP growth. In theory there exists feedback from the induced change in
the current balance to the Marshall Plan allotment; in practice, the coefficients in question are
so small that they can be ignored.

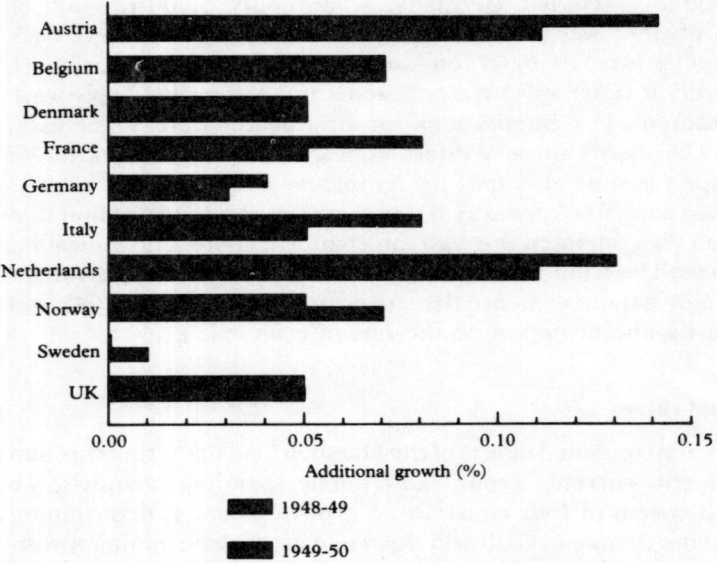

Figure 4. Additional output growth due to the Marshall Plan, including only investment, current account and government spending linkages

Sweden, which received the least (because of the linearity assumed for all equations).

3.5. Is something missing?

Is it correct to assume that the Marshall Plan operated exclusively through the savings, current account and fiscal gaps? To explore the possibility that other channels were also operative, the growth equations have been re-estimated with two modifications. The first one is to include the Marshall Plan allotment directly, to capture other effects of the Marshall Plan not operating through investment, the current account and public spending. The second modification is to interact (i.e. pre-multiply) investment, the current account and government spending with the Marshall Plan allotment. This allows for the possibility that these additional effects opeated most powerfully where investment was low, the current-account deficit was large, or government spending was constrained. The first modification resulted in statistically significant effects: countries receiving large Marshall Plan allotments grew faster, even after controlling for investment and other determinants of growth. The second modification further shows that this direct effect was largest

34   *Barry Eichengreen and Marc Uzan*

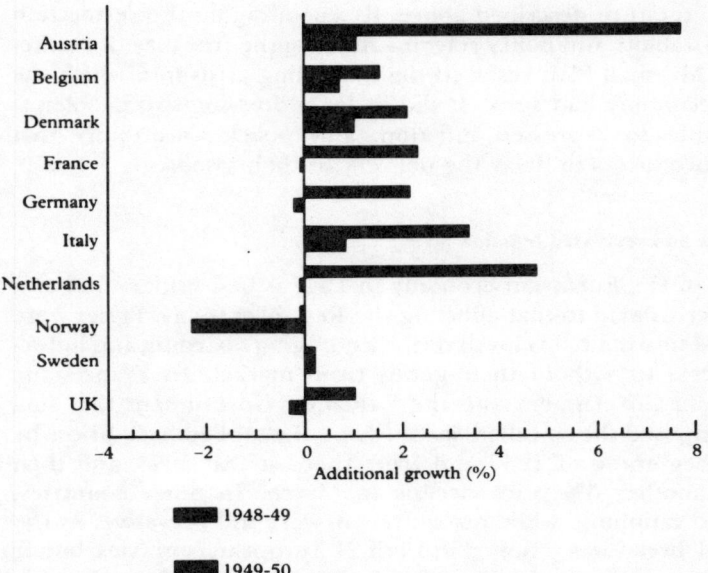

Figure 5. Additional output growth due to the Marshall Plan, including
investment, current account and government spending linkages and
interaction effects

where investment, the current-account surplus and government spending as shares of GNP were low. The conclusion is that the Marshall
Plan mainly operated by means other than altering levels of investment,
the current account and government spending.

Figure 5 shows the results of simulations when all channels are allowed
to operate. The effects of the Marshall Plan, especially in 1948–49, are
an order of magnitude larger than before. Austria, which received
Marshall aid equalling 7% of GNP in 1948, grew as a result by an
additional 7 percentage points between 1948 and 1949. In Austria,
France, Germany, Denmark and the Netherlands, the rate of return
on US aid in 1948 was on the order of 100% even if none of the effects
lingered! These simulations suggest very large effects of the Marshall
Plan. But if those effects did not operate by changing the levels of
investment, the current account or public spending, what did they
reflect?

4. The Marshall Plan and the marketing crisis

The association of the Marshall Plan with this dramatic burst of growth
reflected contributions neglected by the three-gap model and the

The Marshall Plan   35

traditional literature described above. By encouraging the restoration
of financial stability and policy reforms allowing the free play of market
forces, the Marshall Plan resolved the marketing crisis into which the
European economy had sunk. It did so by addressing two problems:
shortages due to repressed inflation, and policy uncertainty that
prompted producers to delay the delivery of their goods.

4.1. Shortages and repressed inflation

The plight of the European economy in 1947 is best understood as a
marketing crisis akin to that afflicting the Republics today. Prices were
controlled at unsustainably low levels, encouraging hoarding and inducing producers to withold their goods from market. In France, the
interim Blum Government and the Ramadier Government that succeeded it imposed the so-called *baisse Blum*: they rolled back prices by
5% at the beginning of 1947 and froze them at that level, and then
mandated another 5% price decline in March. In other countries,
controls and rationing, while not universal, were still pervasive. At the
end of 1948, bread was rationed in 14 of 21 European countries, butter
in 15, meat in 15, sugar in 15, coffee in 12, tobacco in 5, coal in 11,
textiles in 11 and gasoline in 14 (UN, 1950). While prompting the
growth of black markets, controls discouraged transactions at official
prices. The monetary overhang, resulting from the fact that money
supplies had increased more rapidly than prices, threatened renewed
inflation at any time. With budget deficits deep in deficit, investors
were hesitant to purchase government bonds. Inflation consequently
threatened to become an explosive spiral rather than a one-time event.
Anticipating that prices were soon to rise and that financial assets might
lose their purchasing power, producers had every incentive to hoard
commodities rather than delivering them to market. Farmers refused
to market their produce so long as prices were restricted to artificially
low levels. With their receipts vulnerable to inflation, they were better
off feeding grain to their livestock. The post-World War II food shortage
in many European countries reflected not just bad weather in 1947 but
the reluctance of farmers to deliver food to the cities.[9] The manufactured goods farmers might have purchased remained in short supply.
Industrial enterprises had the same incentive to hoard inventories. So
long as these shortages persisted, workers had little reason to devote
their full effort to market work. There is no better way to substantiate

---

[9] Compare the *Financial Times* on 21 August 1991, describing the situation in the USSR. 'The
state and cooperative farms, learning from last year, are now keeping their grain in store until
the state is willing to pay almost any price to get it.' Lloyd (1991).

36   *Barry Eichengreen and Marc Uzan*

this point that to quote a neglected passage from Marshall's (1947) Harvard speech itself:

> 'There is a phase of this matter which is both interesting and serious. The farmer has always produced the foodstuffs to exchange with the city dweller for the other necessities of life. This division of labour is the basis of modern civilization. At the present time it is threatened with breakdown. The town and city industries are not producing adequate goods to exchange with the food producing farmer ... The farmer or the peasant cannot find the goods for sale which he desires to purchase. So the sale of his farm produce for money which he cannot use seems to him an unprofitable transaction. He, therefore, has withdrawn many fields from crop cultivation and is using them for grazing. He feeds more grain to stock ... Meanwhile, people in the cities are short of food and fuel ...'

Many other examples could be cited on 5 January 1947, the *New York Times* noted that 'It has been a fact for some time that [French] peasants have not been delivering their products to market because of lack of confidence in the money they would get for them.' In its issue of 1 March 1947, *The Economist* commented that the 'main enemy' of French policy-makers was the French farmer, 'whose distrust of his currency makes him loth [sic] to send his produce to market – or at least to the controlled market.'[10] Its issue of 18 October 1947 reported that:

> 'For more than two months now Parisians have been eating yellow bread. Despite the substantial tonnages of wheat imported into France since the autumn of 1946 and the long prewar years of development towards a position of self-sufficiency in wheat, France has not been forced to turn to maize, and the French officials are seeking large imports of cereals again during the next twelve months ... One reason for this position is found in the weather of last winter and spring; another in the shortage of tractors, horses and implements. But perhaps the most important reason lies in French policies on prices and control of marketing during the last few years.'

The article then discusses how French wheat prices were kept below world price levels, how the policy of controlling the prices of consumer goods had greatly increased the nominal purchasing power of working-class wages, but how this caused foodstuffs to be in short supply. 'The

---

[10] *New York Times* (5 January 1947); *The Economist* (1 March 1947). For a French government account to a remarkably similar effect, see INSEE (1958).

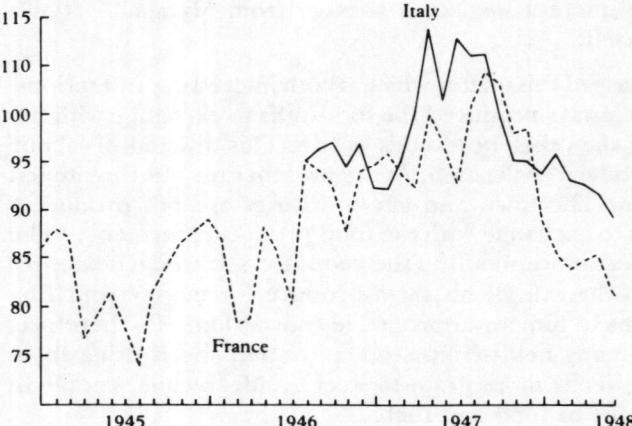

Figure 6. Relative price of food in Italy and France, January 1945–June 1948

Notes: August 1946=100. Wholesale prices for France, retail prices for Italy.

peasant, unable to purchase consumer goods and losing confidence in the currency, eats more himself and feeds wheat to his animals.'[11]

Four separate bodies of evidence support this interpretation. First, the behaviour of food prices is consistent with the view that producers were withholding goods from the market. Farmers, as described above, had exceptional scope for responding to shortages of consumer goods and the threat of inflation by holding back produce and feeding it to their livestock. In both France and Italy the relative price of foodstuffs consequently rose during the period of shortage and financial chaos, but fell during the stabilization. Figure 6 shows that much of the rise in food prices in France occurred *before* the cold winter of 1946–47, as if the problem was more hoarding than prospects of a poor harvest. In both countries the relative price of food fell following the announcement of the Marshall Plan, even though it is hard to find any evidence of 'news' about the harvest.

Second, the recovery of perishable and nonperishable agricultural products supports the interpretation. Grain and potato supplies recovered more quickly than those of meat, as farmers held off slaughtering their livestock. The output of meat remained depressed, even

---

[11] *The Economist* (26 July 1947). Or, as the *New York Times* (1 January 1949) had put it at the beginning of the year, expectations that prices would have to rise 'caused peasants to withold non-perishable products from the market, and led consumers to spend recklessly in anticipation of further price rises'.

though by early 1947 over much of Europe cattle were as numerous as before the war.[12]

Third, though the prevalence of controls was greatest on foodstuffs, other prices were also controlled, leading firms to hoard stocks. In Italy, the value of inventories rose by 2 bn. lire in 1946 and by 9 bn. lire in 1947, but declined by 1 bn. lire in 1948 (Casella and Eichengreen, 1991, Table 4). In France and Britain inventories of virtually every major good for which data on stocks are available declined following announcement of the Marshall Plan.[13]

Fourth and finally, governments' own policies substantiate the picture of unsustainably low prices giving rise to shortages. In France, Ramadier attacked speculators who were hoarding stocks and withholding goods from the market. He attempted to use the National Council of Credit, a body controlling the nationalized banks, to deny loans to holders of excessive stocks.

4.2. Policy uncertainty and the value of waiting

A dramatic change in the economic environment was imminent, but uncertainty about its nature remained pervasive. The immediate post-war period in many European countries was marked by protracted disputes between the Centre–Right and Left. In Italy, for example, the Liberals and Christian Democrats favoured fiscal discipline and abolition of subsidies and price controls, while the Socialists and Communists favoured capital taxation and extensive social spending. Italian government was by coalition, and until May 1947 Communist ministers controlled the budget. This did not make likely cuts in social spending to balance the budget. At the same time, parliamentary representatives of the propertied classes had sufficient leverage to block initiatives designed to balance the budget through confiscatory capital taxation.

In France, coalition governments were 'perpetually subjected to both political and economic pressures from different sections of the population, whose demands were often equally urgent and at the same time

---

[12] As the *New York Times* reported of the situation in France on 3 February 1947, 'It is said that cattle are now as numerous as before the war but the situation is such that the producers do not wish to sell. In the first place, they are dissatisfied with controlled prices. Second, as fodder is abundant, they can keep their stock. Third, they have lost confidence in the currency. The uncertainty on future prices and the lack of fertilizer and farm machinery cause the peasant to keep his animals or sell to the black market.'

[13] The only noteworthy exception is stocks of virgin copper. Data on British inventories are from the CSO's *Monthly Business Statistics* (various issues). Data for France are from Bournay *et al.* (1978).

totally irreconcilable' (Pickles, 1953). Having won 185 seats in the 1946 elections, the French Communists were the single largest party in the Assembly. The Socialists occupied an intermediate position between the Communists on the one hand and the Radicals and the clerical party, the Mouvement Republicain Populaire, on the other. Like their Italian counterparts, the French Socialists were 'committed to a directed economy and increased wages for hard-hit workers, while the Radical Socialists have campaigned for moving as rapidly as possible toward freedom of enterprise. . . .' (US Department of State, 1948a). To balance the budget, the left-wing parties favoured a capital levy, their more moderate counterparts cuts in social spending.

Uncertainty surrounding the outcome of this struggle increased the option value of waiting. Investors were reluctant to buy securities, not knowing whether they would be taxed away. Creditors were reluctant to loan money for any length of time, not knowing whether its value would be inflated away. Workers were reluctant to commit to training or apprenticeship programmes or to accept positions in which compensation was deferred, not knowing whether the structure of pay would be changed and job security would be threatened. Absenteeism was rampant.

Alexander (1991) documents the debilitating effects of policy uncertainty in Germany. In the immediate post-war years, uncertainty emanated from the policies of the Allied occupiers, whose goals included dismantling factories that had been integral to Germany's war effort and breaking up the cartels and combines that had been central to the highly-concentrated industrial sector. Until it was known which factories would be dismantled and which firms would be 'deconcentrated', investors held back. Moreover, until it was known whether the lead in the Bizone would be taken by the free-market-oriented US or by the British, whose Labour Government was nationalizing industry at home, property rights remained uncertain. Until the blockade of Berlin, there was even the possibility that Germany's post-war reconstruction would take place only after the four occupied zones had been reunited, which would have spread Soviet influence to the Western zones and lengthened the shadow over private property. Subsequently, however, uncertainty emanated from the clouded political outlook. The largest single German political party, the Social Democrats, advocated nationalization and the maintenance of controls. Its principal opponent, the Christian Democratic Union, preferred a market economy with a social safety net. Which party would dominate was far from clear. As American officials observed, this uncertainty about the nature of the regime created 'a general hesitancy to make any decisions at all' (cited in Alexander, 1991).

40   *Barry Eichengreen and Marc Uzan*

4.3. Resolving the crisis

Solving the crisis was straightforward. Prices had to be decontrolled to coax producers to bring their goods to market. Inflation had to be halted for the price mechanism to operate smoothly. Wage demands had to be moderated to relax the profit squeeze on firms and remove demands for government subsidies. Budgets had to be balanced to reduce inflationary pressure. With financial stability restored and market forces given free rein, individuals could direct their attention to market work.

If the solution was clear, why then was it not adopted? The economic model that best answers this question is the war-of-attrition model of Alesina and Drazen (1989). The idea is as follows. Suppose that the sum of notional demands for the national income exceeds 100% and that government is the residual claimant for money income. Demands for transfers exceed the taxes the government can collect. The budget deficit is financed by printing money, and open or repressed inflation results. Now assume that the burden of stabilization, in the form of policies reducing some group's share of the national income, is unevenly distributed. The group conceding first incurs the larger share of the costs. If rival factions differ in their ability to shoulder the costs of inflation and shortages, yet are uncertain about the cost-bearing capacity of the others, each will refuse to concede, hoping to outlast the others. Over time, the costs of inflation and/or shortages rise, and with them the perceived probability that the other factions are in fact more patient. Ultimately, those least able to bear the costs concede, and stabilization occurs. Even if inflation is finally halted by the adoption of policies identical to those deemed unacceptable initially, delay is rational. Different groups still have an incentive to hold out as long as the costs of stabilization are borne unevenly and there is uncertainty about the staying power of their rivals. Until they concede, the probability that others will concede first and bear the costs of stabilization is sufficient to justify the ongoing loss from inflation and shortages.

The distributional nature of the post-war crisis is clearest in the case of France. Successive strike waves punctuated calendar year 1947. When the *baisse Blum* failed to hold, a strike broke out in the Renault works, attracting the support first of the CGT and then of the Communist Party. When the Communist ministers urged the Ramadier Government to reverse its opposition to the strikes, Ramadier dismissed them. The critical question was whether the Socialists would also oppose the policy of pressure for wage moderation, or agree for the first time to support a government that did not include the Communists. Having suffered inflation and financial turmoil for nearly two years, they finally gave in. Real wages then fell continuously through 1950 and unemployment rose, together reflecting labour's acceptance of a smaller distributional share.

Similarly, by the spring of 1947 Italian political leaders agreed that open and repressed inflation were out of control, but they disagreed on policies with which to redress it. The Left favoured credit controls to squeeze the speculators regarded as responsible for the inflation, while the Right favoured fiscal austerity. In April–May 1947 Alcide de Gasperi, the Christian Democratic leader and Italian premier, dissolved the existing coalition and formed a minority government that survived with the support of the small parties. This new government represented a clear shift to the right. The Communists moderated their opposition, hoping that they might be able to re-enter the government in the future. de Gasperi imposed a variety of austerity measures, and unemployment rose dramatically, again reflecting the extent to which the costs were borne by the Left.

Thus, solving the marketing crisis was a problem of political economy, not just a problem of economics. As *The Economist* put it in a discussion of the crisis in France, 'Strictly speaking, the economic answer to all these problems is known – to increase taxation, to ensure investment, to cut state expenditure, to balance the budget and to restore confidence in the franc. But the political answer is one that has eluded Frenchmen for the last 30 years' (*The Economist*, 26 July 1947).

The Marshall Plan played a critical role in ending the war of attrition. It did not obviate the need for sacrifice. But it increased the size of the pie available for division among competing interest groups. Two-and-a-half percent – Marshall aid as a share of recipient-country GNP – was not an overwhelmingly large change in the size of the pie. But if the sum of notional demands exceeded aggregate supply by 5 or 7.5%, Marshall Plan transfers could reduce the sacrifices required of competing distributional interests by a third or a half. They could significantly reduce the costs of compromise relative to the benefits.

In both France and Italy, announcement of the Marshall Plan was accompanied by the exit of Communist ministers from the governing coalition and by the adoption of tax increases and expenditure reductions designed to move the budget toward balance. Subsidies on consumer goods were reduced. Workers moderated their demands for higher wages and government transfers. With the elimination of repressed inflation, goods returned to the market. This role for the Marshall Plan was acknowledged by contemporaries. In July 1947, less than two months after Marshall's Harvard speech, *The Economist* (26 July) noted that the workers were tiring of political strikes and that the unions of the Left were showing new signs of moderation:

'In theory, the economic assistance possible under a Marshall Plan might turn the scale between stability and further disintegration next winter. American assistance could pursue a double policy in attacking the basic problem – lack of confidence in the franc. The provision of dollars or gold could underpin the currency and imports of consumer goods, could begin to create a corrective process by tempting food and goods [to] market, restoring the purchasing power of wages and increasing the incentive to produce more.'

It was not inevitable, of course, that the nations of Western Europe would accept this bargain. Marshall aid was offered to Eastern Europe and even to the USSR. Moscow's rejection of the offer can be understood as unwillingness to allow the US to sidetrack its progress along the road of central planning. It is critical to acknowledge that the prices the US charged for its aid was a price that Western Europe might have paid for its own sake in any event. Support for the market was already widespread; the Marshall Plan only tipped the balance.

5. The role of conditionality

The conditions attached to American aid maximized the likelihood of this outcome. Yet some conditions were more effective than others. American demands that European governments meet specific fiscal and monetary targets were less successful than pressure for price liberalization and economic integration. A number of techniques were used to achieve these ends. First, each recipient was required to sign a bilateral pact with the US agreeing to balance government budgets, restore internal financial stability and stabilize exchange rates at realistic levels. Second, each expenditure of Marshall Plan funds had to be negotiated with the American authorities, a process which afforded the ECA opportunity to influence domestic policy. (For example, the Americans reacted to increasing British government involvement in housing construction by cutting Marshall Plan lumber imports.) Third, for each dollar of Marshall aid, the recipient government was required to place a matching amount of domestic currency in a counterpart fund to be used for purposes approved by the US. Each dollar of Marshall Plan aid thus gave the donor control over two dollars' worth of real resources. In many instances, the US insisted that these funds be used to buttress financial stability by retiring public debt. (See Table 5.) In others, the US authorities prevented the European government from making any use of its counterpart funds at all.

US pressure also operated informally. Marshall Plan administrators took a variety of *ad hoc* steps to encourage price decontrol and

Table 5. MSA/ECA approvals for withdrawal of European Counterpart Funds available for country use, by purpose and country, cumulative, 3 April 1948–30 June 1952 (Dollar equivalents of local currencies, in mn. US$).

Country	Total for production	Promotion of production					
		Electric, gas and other power	Transportation and communications	Agriculture	Manufacturing	Mining	Other production
Total	4,466.3	1,025.5	957.5	817.6	681.7	481.8	502.2
Denmark	62.4	0.6	2.8	11.2	6.7	—	41.1
France	1,925.6	738.4	294.2	234.1	249.2	340.6	69.1
Germany	753.7	182.6	86.8	70.7	218.7	91.8	103.1
Italy	823.8	1.0	348.9	204.8	22.6	—	246.5
Netherlands	212.8	—	13.6	166.5	32.3	—	0.4
Norway	8.4	—	2.7	—	—	5.7	—
Turkey	51.0	0.6	13.9	15.2	8.0	14.7	4.6
UK	2.2	—	—	0.2	—	—	2.0

Country	For other purposes				Total approved for withdrawal
	Monetary and financial stability	Housing and public buildings	Construction production procurement	Other	
Total	2,583.3	767.5	460.9	373.3	8,651.3
Denmark	130.1	—	9.4	2.2	204.1
France	171.4	314.4	283.9	7.5	2,702.8
Germany	—	97.7	—	157.7	1,009.1
Italy	—	172.7	—	45.9	1,042.4
Netherlands	197.4	88.1	46.3	3.0	547.6
Norway	292.7	—	—	—	301.1
Turkey	—	—	60.4	11.0	128.4
UK	1,706.7	—	47.5	6.4	1,762.8

Adapted from Table C-12, p. 13, Mutual Security Agency, *Report to Congress*, December 1952 (seven smaller countries' approvals not shown). Drawn from Mayer (1969), p. 87.

Box 3. The mechanics of the Marshall Plan

The bill passed by Congress authorized US assistance to Europe for four years but insisted that appropriations take place annually. The package authorized $5.3 bn. for the first year, which approximated the Administration's request of $6.8 bn. for 15 months. Congress specified that assistance could take the form of either grants or loans, but placed a ceiling on the loan component of the programme ($1 bn. in the first year). Subject to these limitations, the European Cooperation Agency (ECA) Administrator, heading an independent agency, was authorized to procure commodities and services from all sources for countries in need and to defray the cost of their transportation. The Administrator was instructed to curtail the procurement of American goods in short supply and to encourage the use of surplus stocks. In the case of surplus agricultural commodities, procurement was restricted to the US. When requesting the shipment of foreign merchandise, governments or nationals of the participating countries submitted procurement authorization requests to the ECA. Applications were reviewed to determine whether or not they exceeded the country's allotment, whether they satisfied the criteria set down by the Act, and for their effect on the US economy. Upon approval the ECA issued a letter of commitment to a cooperating bank guaranteeing ECA reimbursement of the credit extended. After the recipient of the merchandise, usually a government agency deposited a matching amount of local currency to a so-called counterpart account, it was able to draw on the credit established in the US.

The US State Department set the interim allocations for the first two ERP quarters (April–September 1948) but insisted that participating governments do so subsequently. For 1948 two US government studies had estimated the dollar deficits of European countries at $5.3 bn. The participating countries, when polled, objected that this figure understated their prospective deficits. In the event, it soon became apparent that Congress would appropriate only $4.9 bn. The OEEC was instructed to reduce country requests so as to produce a total not to exceed the appropriation. That it was able to submit recommendations in September 1948 that were accepted by all member countries but Greece and Turkey was a remarkable achievement. The excess dollar deficit was eliminated by shifting planned imports from the US to non-dollar sources. Priority was given to aid requests that would finance imports of consumption goods needed to keep living standards at 1947 levels, of raw materials needed to keep industry running at existing levels, and of capital equipment and raw materials that would stimulate the

The Marshall Plan   45

production of dollar-earning or dollar-saving commodities. In preparing the second set of allocation requests for 1949–50, the OEEC asked participating countries to assume a reduced level of funding. Its January 1949 submission requested $4.4 bn. Congress appropriated $3.7 bn. In August 1949 the OEEC appointed a committee to distribute the shortfall. ECA allotments were cut for all countries except Sweden and Iceland, with some participants (Germany and Belgium) suffering disproportionately. The negotiations were sufficiently difficult that it was decided to divide aid for the third year in the proportions established by the second allocation.

In the early stages of the programme most countries used ECA funds to import foodstuffs and other essential materials. This conformed to American wishes: the ECA's April 1948 order on operating policies and procedures specified that initial procurement should concentrate on food, fuel and fertilizer. But it had also urged participating countries to emphasize the procurement of commodities needed to facilitate industrial and agricultural production. With the recovery of domestic production, ECA aid was used increasingly to finance the importation of capital equipment for investment projects.

---

discourage nationalization. For example, they viewed with alarm British schemes for unifying and nationalizing the coal industries of the Ruhr, then part of the British zone of occupation. Such schemes were dropped once ECA administrators made their opposition known. Similarly, Hoffman lobbied against the nationalization of the British steel industry and at least delayed this eventuality. Washington, D.C. also pressed continuously for economic integration. Each aid recipient was required to develop a schedule for liberalizing its foreign trade. The recipient governments were forced to decide among themselves the international allocation of US aid and to coordinate their national recovery programmes so as to ensure that their combined current-account deficits *vis-a-vis* the dollar area did not exceed the aid the US was willing to make available. Their discussions, in conjunction with US pressure, led to the formation of the CEEC and the OEEC, way-stations along the route to the Schuman Plan, the European Payments Union and the EEC.

The question is how successful US conditionality ultimately proved to be. While much of the older literature (e.g. Price, 1955; Arkes, 1972) uncritically accepts the importance of conditionality, some recent revisionists (e.g. Esposito, 1985, Wall, 1991) dismiss it as ineffectual. In part, this dispute reflects the different countries and issues upon which these authors focus. That there were limits on what could be achieved by conditionality is apparent even from the bilateral agreements that

Table 6. US conditionality in France, 1948–50

Quarter	American demand	French response
1948-I	Refrain from inflationary finance.	Fix 200 bn. franc ceiling on Bank of France advances.
1948-II	Eliminate budget deficit, end use of Bank of France advances to cover budget deficit.	None.
1948-III	Eliminate budget deficit, end use of Bank of France advances to cover budget deficit.	Increase taxes on tobacco, and income, increase postal rates, impose credit controls.
1948-IV	Pass balanced budget for 1949, maintain credit controls.	Reduce ceiling on Bank of France advances to 175 bn. francs, limit government expenditure.
1949-I	None.	None.
1949-II	Eliminate prospective 100 bn. franc budget deficit.	Increase gasoline tax.
1949-III	None.	None.
1949-IV	Eliminate prospective 120 bn. franc budget deficit, do not increase ceiling on Bank of France advances.	New taxes imposed, capital controls maintained, advances ceiling left unchanged.
1950	Invest 20 bn. francs in low cost housing.	20 bn. francs invested in low income housing.

were a prerequisite for the receipt of aid. These agreements were the subject of protracted negotiations. London and Paris acceded to American demands to control the allocation of counterpart funds but resisted giving Washington control over their monetary and fiscal policies. An American-authored provision allowing the IMF to veto European exchange rate changes was eliminated. So was a provision that would have given the US first call on strategic materials possessed by the recipients. American demands for measures to balance budgets and restrict domestic credit creation also led to extended negotiations and, sometimes, political crises. Repeatedly, the US demanded tax increases, expenditure reductions and new restrictions on domestic credit creation. It threatened to impound counterpart funds unless these steps were taken. Table 6 shows the course of Franco-American negotiations over French macroeconomic policies. Strictly speaking, the US failed to achieve its stated targets. Not only was there no quarter in which the US target was fully met, but there was no quarter in which release of counterpart funds was actually suspended.

Yet if the ECA's stated target is viewed as the opening bid, there is reason to think that conditionality still had some effect. Stated targets were not achieved, but concessions were obtained. French budget deficits were smaller and monetary policies were less inflationary than they would have been otherwise. Analysis of a variety of episodes leads to this conclusion. For example, in the autumn of 1948, when the US threatened to withhold counterpart funds, Prime Ministe⁻ Henri Queuille moved to impose new taxes and to raise the prices of transport, postage and tobacco. The *loi des maxima* of December 1948 did much to stabilize the French public finances (Wall, 1991). Although the Americans were not fully satisfied with the outcome, it is likely that more movement in the direction of budget balance occurred than would have in the absence of American intervention.

In other countries, American conditionality operated more powerfully. In Italy, counterpart releases were delayed. Italian economic policy was modified. As James Clement Dunn, the American ambassador to Italy, put it, 'He who controls the so-called lire fund will control the monetary and fiscal, and in fact the entire economic policy of Italy' (cited in Hogan, 1987). In Greece, the US withheld the release of counterpart funds because it felt that the economy was operating under excessive pressure of demand. American control over economic policy was extensive. The treaties signed in conjunction with the extension of Marshall aid explicitly gave the US supervisory powers over domestic as well as foreign resources. The treaties 'ensured that no economic or military decision of any consequence could be taken by the Greek Government without the prior approval or consent of the US Administration or its representatives in Athens' (Freris, 1986).

What accounts for these different outcomes? American conditionality was least effective in countries that were strong fiscally and large economically. France and the UK were in a stronger fiscal position than Greece. France's fiscal position was more tenuous than the UK's, but her economy was large and therefore critical to European recovery. French officials, aware of this fact, played this card to their advantage. The UK's fiscal position was sufficiently secure that she required no counterpart releases for investment in housing or industrial investment. Brown and Opie (1953) conclude that countries like the UK utilizing counterpart funds to retire public debt eluded the influence of the ECA, but that for other countries counterpart releases gave US administrators significant leverage. Regression analysis supports this speculation. We added to the basic growth equation estimated in Appendix C counterpart funds withdrawn for 'productive purposes' (the ECA term for funds spent on investment or the purchase of inputs). We found that a Marshall Plan allotment of 2% GNP would have raised output by 4.6% in the next year if and only if the matching 2% of GNP was withdrawn from the counterpart accounts for use in production.

Otherwise, output would have risen not by 4.6% but by 0.3%.[14] Clearly, US decisions regarding the counterpart accounts mattered for recipient-country welfare and endowed US policy-makers with leverage.

Where political support was closely divided between Left and Right, extreme monetary and fiscal austerity might undermine Socialist support for moderate governments, leading to their downfall and playing into the hands of the Communist Party. This was especially true when austerity measures could be blamed on American interference. French politicians invoked this danger repeatedly. They warned that acceptance of American demands would lead to the government's downfall, and the Americans moderated their demands. In contrast, in countries where centrist governments were more firmly entrenched, the threat that conditionality would create political instability was less credible.

If the overall record of conditionality regarding fiscal and monetary policy was mixed, informal pressure for market liberalization and economic integration was more successful. These more abstract principles were less intimately connected to the public purse. Their distributional consequences were less transparent. Hence they were less likely to occasion a government's downfall or provoke complaints of American intervention. As a condition for receiving Marshall aid, each country was required to develop a programme for removing quotas and other trade controls. Even where domestic markets were highly concentrated, competition could be injected via international trade. Government intervention and other efforts to interfere with the operation of markets would be disciplined by foreign competition. American insistence that aid recipients coordinate their national recovery programmes led to regular meetings of the OEEC and to increasingly frequent bilateral consultations. They culminated in the creation of the Coal and Steel Community and the European Payments Union.

6. Enduring effects

The evidence presented so far indicates that the Marshall Plan *initiated* Europe's recovery from World War II earlier than otherwise. Less certain is whether US aid had a *permanent* impact on the level of output. In principle, both outcomes are possible. In traditional growth theory (in the tradition of Solow) diminishing returns to capital imply that it is impossible to increase permanently the capital/labour ratio. The steady-state level of output per capita depends exclusively on parameters

---

[14] This example considers, for simplicity, a country whose investment, current account and government spending ratios are zero. Some of this growth would have been given back in the succeeding year: see Appendix C for further details.

like the population growth rate, the rate of time preference and the rate of technological change. Since there is no reason why an injection of foreign aid should affect any of these parameters, there is no reason why it should permanently affect the level of output. If the aid arrives when the capital/labour ratio is below normal levels, then the fact that some part of the transfer is invested will allow the capital/labour ratio and output per person to rise toward their steady-state values faster than otherwise. But since their ultimate destination is unchanged, faster growth initially implies slower growth subsequently. The impact of aid on the *level* of output is temporary. In contrast, in endogenous growth theory (following Romer, 1990) there are no diminishing returns to capital so that a one-time injection of foreign aid may raise permanently the capital/labour ratio, and therefore output and savings proportionately. The higher capital/labour ratio can be fully financed with higher savings, so that the level of output can remain higher permanently. A temporary injection of foreign aid can have a positive initial impact on growth without being subsequently reversed.

To separate out these two hypotheses, we analysed quarterly data on industrial production and receipts of US foreign aid from 1948 through 1955 for the 10 principal beneficiaries of the Marshall Plan. The time pattern of foreign aid effects is captured by three lags. The results showed a positive impact effect followed by a negative subsequent effect. The three lagged terms summed to zero.[15] According to this evidence, recovery commenced earlier than it would have otherwise, but the Marshall Plan did not have enduring effects.

Still, one wonders whether American aid had enduring effects of a subtler nature. Perhaps the Marshall Plan permanently affected European economic growth in ways that did not materialize at the time of foreign aid receipts. (If so, its enduring effects would not be captured by our econometric techniques.) This would be the case, for example, if the Marshall Plan provided the solution to a coordination problem.

---

[15] Industrial production was expressed in logs, foreign aid in real terms by converting it into local currency and deflating it by the consumer price index. The countries were Austria, Belgium, Denmark, France, Germany, Italy, the Netherlands, Norway, Sweden and the UK; the sample period was 1948Q4 through 1955Q4. The coefficients on the three lags of foreign aid were constrained to be the same across countries but the constant and three lags of industrial production were allowed to differ across countries. A typical estimate (for Austria) was (with t-statistics in parentheses):

$$IP = 0.56 + 0.74\ IP(-1) + 1.58\ IP(-2) - 1.44\ IP(-3)$$
$$\quad\ (0.12)\ (0.28) \qquad\quad (0.59) \qquad\quad\ (0.62)$$

$$\quad\ + 0.22\ FA(-1) - 0.17\ FA(-2) - 0.02\ FA(-3)$$
$$\qquad\quad (3.23) \qquad\quad\ (2.78) \qquad\quad\ (0.42)$$

$$DW = 2.00$$

50   *Barry Eichengreen and Marc Uzan*

Imagine that European labour and management were faced with choosing between two equilibria after World War II. In one – the interwar equilibrium – each faction tried to maximize its current share of national income. Intense distributional struggles would have produced wage inflation, a profit squeeze, low levels of investment and lagging productivity. In the other – the post-war equilibrium – all parties agreed to trade current compensation for faster longer-term growth and ultimately for higher living standards. Workers deferred their wage demands, management its demands for higher profits. Higher investment and faster productivity growth ensued, ultimately rendering everyone better of.[16] The second equilibrium may not arise without some form of coordination. Indeed if workers press for higher wages, management has little incentive to plough back earnings in expectation of higher future profits. If management fails to plough back profits, workers have little incentive to moderate wage demands in return for the promise of higher future living standards. If workers and management in some sectors refuse to follow policies of moderation, reducing the supply of investible funds to the economy, those in other sectors have less incentive to do so.

The Marshall Plan could have shifted Europe from one equilibrium to the other. Until 1948, European labour-management relations were conflictual. Pressures for real wage increases were intense. At that point, the Marshall Plan administrators urged European unions and governments to focus on raising productivity rather than current compensation (Maier, 1977). They pressed governments to adopt a variety of investment-friendly policies (Esposito, 1985). European nations had an incentive to shift to the high-investment, deferred-compensation equilibrium in order to obtain Marshall aid. Once there, they had no reason to deviate.

The two most prominent features of the dramatic acceleration in European growth that began in 1948 and lasted for more than two decades – high investment rates and wage moderation – are consistent with this interpretation. The investment share of GNP in Europe was nearly twice as high as it had been between the wars (Table 7). Labour's share of national income was stable or falling. Workers consciously allowed real wage increases to lag behind productivity to provide the incentives and resources for investment. In Britain, for instance, the Trades Union Congress cooperated with management and with the

---

[16] This is how some historians view the high growth of the first post-World War II decades. For example, Maier (1981) concludes, 'For society as a whole, the politics of productivity meant simply the adjournment of conflicts over the percentage of national income for the rewards of future economic growth.'

Table 7. Non-residential fixed investment as percent of GNP at current prices

		Average of ratios for years cited	
	1920–38	1950–60	1960–70
Austria	6.1[a]	16.4	20.2
Belgium		12.4	15.5
Denmark	8.9	14.0	16.9
Finland		19.6	20.0
France	11.8	13.7	17.4
Germany	9.7	16.1	19.3
Greece	7.5[b]	11.7	18.2
Ireland		13.1	15.1
Italy	13.6	15.1	14.5
Netherlands		18.0	20.3
Norway	12.4	23.7[c]	23.8[c]
Sweden	10.5	15.5	17.3
Switzerland		14.1	20.0
UK	5.7	11.6	14.2
Average for Western Europe	9.6	15.4	18.1

[a] 1924–37.
[b] 1929–38.
[c] Includes some elements of repair and maintenance excluded by other countries.
Source: Maddison (1976), p. 487.

Conservative governments that ruled from 1951 through 1964, deliberately moderating their wage claims (Flanagan *et al.*, 1983). In the Netherlands, unions allowed wages to lag behind productivity in the 1950s 'so that industry could earn profits which would pay for expansion and modernization of the productive apparatus' (a quote from a *union publication*, cited in Windmuller, 1969). Industrial relations specialists like Barkin (1983) lay great stress on this growth-oriented consensus. Of course, other explanations exist for the high investment rates and labour-market flexibility that characterized Europe's first two post-war decades.[17] But the fact that dramatic shifts in the pattern of investment and in labour market conduct both surfaced during the Marshall Plan years lends credence to the idea that the American programme contributed to solving a coordination problem.

[17] International monetary stability and the absence of major supply shocks are two popular explanations for high investment in this period (Boltho, 1982). Similarly, the availability of elastic supplies of underemployed labour in Europe's rural sector, in conjunction with the influx of refugees from Eastern Europe and guestworkers from the Continent's southeast, may have enhanced labour market flexibility (Kindleberger, 1967).

52   *Barry Eichengreen and Marc Uzan*

7. Implications for Eastern Europe and the former USSR

Are conditions like those that made the Marshall Plan a success present
in Eastern Europe and the Republics today? Consider first the Republics' predicament. As in Europe in 1947/48, ceilings on food prices are
discouraging cultivators from bringing their produce to market.[18]
As in Europe in 1947/48, the traditional division of labour between
town and country has broken down; not just the fuel, fertilizer and
tractors required for agricultural production but the televisions and
refrigerators offered as incentives to farmers have not been made
available. Shortages of consumer goods are increasingly pervasive, as
enterprises hold back stocks in anticipation of higher prices once controls are relaxed. Workers hold back effort until policy uncertainty is
resolved.[19] Excess liquidity and government budget deficits create the
spectre of rampant inflation.

As in post-war Europe, foreign aid could help in principle to resolve
these problems. Support for living standards could contain public
opposition to economic reform if output falls during the transition
to a market economy. Hard currency would enable the Republics
to import much-needed equipment from the West or, better still,
from its Eastern European neighbours. Reserves of foreign exchange
would enable the authorities to stabilize the ruble once it is rendered
convertible.

On the other hand, very important differences weaken – in our view,
seriously – the case for a Marshall Plan for the Republics. In post-war
Europe there existed widespread support for the market economy. The
Marshall Plan only tipped the balance. The social contract upon which
the subsequent generation of prosperity was based was a compromise
between positions that were only a moderate distance apart. Hence a
modest side payment could make the difference between chaos and
stability. The same is not true of the Republics today. Powerful elements
in government and the military – certainly not all of which were eliminated by the failure of the August 1991 coup – oppose serious economic
reform. Much of the public understands only dimly what a free market
entails. The choice is not between a heavily regulated mixed economy
and a lightly regulated mixed economy, or between a distributionally
neutral fiscal system and a moderately redistributive fisc, but between

---

[18] 'It is the farmers' decision to hang on to their grain, rather than any absolute shortage, which
as much as anything underlies the latest US estimates that the Soviet Union will this year need
to import 37 mn. tonnes of grain.' Nicholson *et al.* (1991).

[19] Consider the following first-hand description of the situation in Lithuanian agriculture. 'Since
independence nobody at the Kolkhoz wants to work. Everyone is waiting. Production is falling.
We do not know what is going to happen.' (Ignatieff, 1991).

public and private property and between prices and commands. With the cleavage between views so pronounced, it is unlikely that a limited amount of foreign aid would significantly speed the emergence of a consensus favouring rapid liberalization. In post-war Europe, the administration of US aid encouraged the reductions in government spending needed for financial stability. It is far from certain that aid for the Republics would have the same effect. Aid transfers could place additional resources in the hands of the very individuals most opposed to scaling back the public sector, accelerating privatization and creating a market economy.

For those committed to aid, these arguments highlight the need for conditionality and specifically for conditioning aid on actions rather than promises. An area in which there exists a special opportunity for conditionality is relations among the Republics. Disputes among them threaten to derail the reform process. Free trade among the Republics will speed reform; otherwise comparative advantage will be squandered, local monopolies will gain power and traditional economic relationships will be disrupted.

Intervening in this process through the administration of aid might be regarded as meddling in the domestic politics of another country. Recall, however, that after World War II the US laid down as a condition for aid that the recipients collectively decide on the allocation of the funds. Trade liberalization and economic integration were explicit conditions of Marshall Plan aid. The OEEC and the EEC – two examples of the type of loose federations to which the Republics aspire – were established in response to this impetus. What worked once could work again. There is no reason why the US and the EC could not require the Republics to negotiate the formula according to which foreign aid would be allocated. The donors could make free trade among the Republics a condition for the receipt of Western aid, or press for establishment of a fiscal system like the US and other federal entities possess.

More specific forms of conditionality are more problematic. In principle, quarterly targets could be set for number of farms and firms privatized, number of goods freed from tariff or quota and progress on the fiscal and monetary fronts, with the release of aid conditioned on whether those targets are met. America's experience with the Marshall Plan indicates that such conditionality, while sure to produce controversy, can also produce results. But experience with the Marshall Plan suggests as well that aid conditioned on nuts-and-bolts issues of everyday politics is more likely to provoke a firestorm of protest and to backfire on the donor than is aid conditioned on high principles like openness and integration. A lesson of the Marshall Plan is that specific monetary and fiscal targets are especially difficult to impose on a large country to which the prosperity of an entire region is linked.

In Eastern Europe, the situation is simpler. In most cases, the central government remains a logical recipient of the foreign aid. In some countries a commitment to liberalization and meaningful reform already exists. But hard times threaten to fuel opposition. We believe that there exists a strong case for foreign aid to Eastern European countries precisely in order to minimize this danger. So long as reform continues, aid to solidify support for current programmes by easing the transition, however slightly, can only help. Its extension must be made contingent upon conditions, but if this is done it is hard to see how aid could be counterproductive.

One final caution. In post-war Europe, foreign aid could promote adjustment and growth because Europe had experience with markets and possessed the institutions needed for their operation. Property rights, a bankruptcy code and courts to enforce contracts, not to mention generations of accumulated entrepreneurial skills – were all in place. None of this is true today of the successor states to the USSR, and as yet it is true of only parts of Eastern Europe. Even under the best circumstances the donors should therefore not expect that the impact on economic growth will match that of the Marshall Plan.

Discussion

Nicholas Crafts
University of Warwick and CEPR

This is a very welcome and useful contribution on a topic neglected for too long by economists. I find myself agreeing with many of the conclusions though it might be useful to develop a wider historical perspective.

The approach through a three-gap model gives a good way of addressing the historical literature and quantifying arguments made by Maier, Milward and others to the effect that the impact directly on investment and the balance of payments of the grants under the ERP was modest. The econometric analysis also says that these peter out in a Solovian world, a result which does not surprise me. The authors are ingenious in supplementing this conventional analysis, which does not account for the revealed importance of the ERP, by suggesting its main effects came through solving a marketing crisis and/or by aiding the resolution of conflicts between capital and labour. Both these channels of influence might matter to Eastern European countries struggling with the political economy of transition.

The Marshall Plan   55

In terms of perspective, I would argue for something of a shift of emphasis. First, the Marshall Plan was part of a grander American design or foreign policy strategy. The end result of this was greater European integration to which European governments were credibly committed. Such commitment surely had a significant impact on subsequent rent-seeking (see Adams, 1989, on France). American leverage came from its German occupation, not from the Marshall Plan *per se*, and the outcome was not completely controlled by the US (c.f. Milward 1984). Second, in terms of the post-war dollar gap, it seems odd that the 1949 devaluations are not integrated into the tale more explicitly. Third, more might be made of the contrasts with Allied policy toward Germany in the early 1920s.

Mention of these aspects suggests there is a complementary account of the Marshall Plan impact, which is hinted at several times here, but could be drawn out more fully. This would involve explicitly linking the ERP – and more importantly American policy overall – to the optimal sequencing of reform in the transition from war to peace. This would seem a useful further exercise if lessons for Eastern Europe are to be learnt.

Finally, I have two doubts about the findings of the paper. First, I think the argument about ERP's role in solving the 'coordination dilemma' is oversold. Isn't this more a story about the changes in the natural rate of unemployment than about growth? Moreover, productivity and growth depend on bargaining structures: for Germany it may be that achieving (Olson-like) industrial unions was an important outcome from the war – but it was not a result of the ERP. Again, the American achievement through its 'Pax Americana' in destroying protectionism may be at least as important and was at least as clear an *ex-ante* objective. Second, the paper says relatively little about how Marshall Aid was allocated. In the growth equations, is it conceivable that 'Catch-Up' and 'Reconstruction' are not adequately normalized for and that 'Marshall Plan' is a surrogate for these variables? I think some further sensitivity analysis may be in order.

To conclude, this paper is highly informative and very nicely argued. It takes the literature on the Marshall Plan forward substantially.

Martin Hellwig
University of Basel

The paper by Eichengreen and Uzan presents an impressive and comprehensive assessment of the economic effects of the Marshall Plan. According to the authors, the Plan's direct economic effects were significant, but not overwhelming. Instead, they suggest that the Plan's

56   *Barry Eichengreen and Marc Uzan*

secular importance stems from its impact on the political process in Western Europe: by tipping the balance of political discussion, the plan set the stage for a new social consensus which in turn provided the basis for the sustained growth of the 1950s. By and large, I agree with the authors' assessment. Even so, there are a few points where the analysis could be sharpened.

First, I am uneasy about the role of macroeconomic aggregates in the analysis. In particular, I wonder whether the foreign exchange problems of the time are adequately captured by aggregate export, import and balance-of-payments data. After all, apart from the Swiss Franc, European currencies were not freely convertible, and trade was covered by multiple bilateral agreements with only limited credit agreements (which had largely been exhausted by 1947; see Kaplan and Schleiminger, 1989, p. 23). For a country like Belgium, the shortage of dollars to pay for raw materials from outside Europe was not alleviated by its exports of coal and steel to other European countries. Italy's surplus in its trade with the UK could not automatically be used to finance its deficits with other European countries or the US. In contrast, Marshall Plan aid came in a currency that was fully convertible and everybody wanted to have. To assess the significance of this advantage, a more disaggregated analysis of international trade relations in the late 1940s is needed.

Second, while I share the authors' views about the indirect, political effects of the Marshall Plan, I find it difficult to identify these effects (separating them, for instance, from the effects of changes in US military stance at the onset of the Cold War). If the political situation in Western Europe did change in the late 1940s, it is hardly possible to distinguish the effects of the Marshall Plan from the effects of the Cold War or, more vaguely, the effects of the American commitment not to leave Europe alone. Even in terms of direct economic consequences, in the case of Germany, it is difficult to determine the effects of the Marshall Plan from the effects of currency reform and economic reform – including the abandonment of the immediate post-war deindustrialization programmes.

A distinct role of the Marshall Plan is evident in the creation of the European Payments Union (EPU), the multilateral trade and payments agreement that replaced various bilateral agreements in 1950, providing for trade liberalization as well as multilateral clearing with certain credit facilities. Throughout the negotiations that eventually led to the EPU, the Marshall Plan administration played a leading role. Marshall Plan money provided a large part of the initial reserve of the EPU. Perhaps even more importantly, Marshall Plan money was instrumental in buying off British resistance against the move from bilateral to multilateral clearing (Kaplan and Schleiminger, 1989). To the extent that European growth in the 1950s is ascribed to the growth in intra-European trade, this effect of the Marshall Plan is important. Conditionality here was even more concrete than Eichengreen and Uzan's discussion suggests.

In contrast, I am sceptical about a more general linking of European integration to the Marshall Plan. To be sure, closer cooperation within Europe was one of the objectives which distinguished the Marshall Plan from earlier forms of American aid to Europe. However, the institutions of the OEEC – and later the EPU – were fairly weak, reflecting British insistence on national sovereignty rather than a substantial move towards integration (Monnet, 1976, pp. 321ff, 329ff). The creation of supranational institutions, which are the hallmark of the European Communities, seems to have had little to do with the Marshall Plan. Indeed, if we follow the account of Monnet (1976, pp. 341ff), the immediate motivation for the Schuman Plan came from a fear that the emancipation of Germany, which followed the onset of the Cold War, might re-establish national institutions and national patterns of behaviour, which reinforce old animosities and disadvantage French industry (see also Schwartz, 1986, pp. 716ff).

Third, it is not clear that the economic and political changes induced by the Marshall Plan were actually *sufficient* to propel Europe into the sustained growth of the 1950s. The German experience suggests that up to 1951 the situation may have been quite fragile. To be sure, the 'economic miracle' of 1948/49 solved what Eichengreen and Uzan call a 'marketing crisis' and led to a drastic increase in production. At the same time though, unemployment also rose drastically, reaching 9.5% in 1950, with a fair amount of social and political unrest. Later in 1950 and in early 1951, the problem was compounded by a balance-of-payments crisis, induced by panic buying of raw materials after the beginning of the Korean War (Stolper *et al.*, 1964, pp. 263ff). Policy advice to Germany in these years reads like a rehearsal for later 'go–stop–go . . .' routines, and the situation was anything but settled. The improvement in 1951 owed a lot to the Korean War boom and the concomitant increase in exports of final products i.e. a new and largely exogenous event. (The liberalization of intra-European trade through the EPU may have played a role as well.) Would the economic and political situation have been stabilized without the additional impulse from the Korean War?

To conclude my comment, I want to endorse the authors' warnings about any comparison of Eastern Europe or the former USSR today with Western Europe in the late 1940s. Eichengreen and Uzan stress the difference in the political constellations then and now. To this

58   *Barry Eichengreen and Marc Uzan*

concern, I would like to add the observation that Western Europe in the late 1940s had firms with well-defined property rights and a functioning legal and fiscal system as well as the managers, lawyers and administrators required to run these systems. In Eastern Europe today these preconditions of a functioning market economy are lacking. Also, if aspiration levels are guided by the comparison with Western standards of living, distributional conflicts in Eastern Europe today may be rather harder than in Germany in 1950 where people were happy merely to get out of the rubble of the war and its aftermath.

One aspect of the Marshall Plan that does seem relevant today is its limited time horizon. Accounts of the period give the clear impression that the limited duration of the Marshall Plan provided people with a sense of urgency. The idea that by 1951/52 Western Europe would have to stand on its own without Marshall Plan aid seems to have dominated people's thinking, sparked their imagination and increased their willingness to accept institutional reforms.

General discussion

Discussion focused both on the historical analysis of the paper and on the lessons for Eastern Europe today. Angus Maddison thought the authors underestimated the role of the Organization for Economic Co-operation, which reduced pressures for beggar-my-neighbour policies. He also thought it was easy to forget how many governments had been inclined towards highly dirigiste approaches to recovery, and thought that US pressure for more liberal policies had been of great though unquantifiable importance. Richard Portes found the evidence that the Marshall Plan ended a war of attrition weak; he also stressed the importance of the Korean War in changing the outlook for Germany. Maurice Obstfeld argued that policy-makers had indeed perceived a liquidity crisis and had proceeded cautiously as a result; the Marshall Plan had helped to change their behaviour even if the direct evidence for a liquidity crisis was now hard to discern.

There was disagreement about the effects of the European Payments Union. Georges de Menil thought that even with deeper devaluations it would still have been needed. Maurice Obstfeld was convinced that, despite its evident faults, the EPU had helped with settlements and promoted trade. Jeffrey Sachs argued that, though it had represented a major advance on earlier institutions, the EPU remained a poor model for the present day. This led on to a discussion of the lessons of the Marshall Plan for present-day Eastern Europe and the former USSR. Sachs pointed out that the problem with all major structural reforms lay in winning enough time for their beneficial effects to come through. Every successful structural reform had passed through a precarious phase (he mentioned the Japanese general strike of 1947). The point of a present-day Marshall Plan, which he strongly supported, was not so much to create present growth but to win time, to create the necessary institutions to enable future growth. This was made more urgent by the very high aspiration levels characterizing Eastern European societies.

Other panellists drew attention to important respects in which Eastern Europe today differed from Western Europe after the war. Richard Portes thought that, while there might be evidence of a marketing crising in the former USSR and perhaps in Bulgaria and Romania, it was irrelevant to Poland, Hungary and Czechoslovakia. Charles Wyplosz pointed out that international capital markets were much better developed now than in the 1940s; furthermore, private institutions were good at making conditionality credible. John Black stressed that conditionality was crucial: the scale of the problem was so great that aid could make no difference unless there was additional associated leverage: aid should consequently be linked to trading access. Petr Aven pointed out serious dangers in conditionality; they might be difficult to enforce, and if the policies failed might elicit a xenophobic response. However, both he and Jan Svejnar urged the need for a modern Marshall Plan. Svejnar argued that the present accommodating response of the trade union movement to the reforms could not be expected to last indefinitely. Aven said that it was hard to overestimate the psychological impact of Western aid upon the patience of those undergoing reforms. Michael Burda agreed that the distributional conflicts in Eastern Europe were very significant, and that the potential value of aid in buying time was extremely important.

Appendix A: A three-gap model for analysing the macroeconomics of foreign aid

To analyse the macroeconomics of foreign aid, we utilize the two-gap model of Chenery and Bruno (1962), as extended by Bacha (1990) to incorporate fiscal constraints on public capital formation. Our formulation has much in common with the treatment of McKinnon (1964).

We start with the savings-investment identity for an open economy:

$$S - I = X - M \qquad (1)$$

where S is saving, I is investment, and X and M are exports and imports of goods and services. Imports are of two types: consumption goods M_c and capital goods M_k.[20] (Abstracting from changes in relative prices, we set all prices to unity.) The balance of payments, which is the current account plus net capital transfers F, must equal zero. (We treat net transfers interchangeably with foreign aid because significant foreign borrowing was not possible in the immediate post-war years.)

$$X - M_c - M_k = -F \tag{2}$$

Domestic production is a function of the capital stock:

$$Y = \alpha K \tag{3}$$

A fixed fraction of investment requires imported capital goods:

$$M_k = m_k I \tag{4}$$

where I is investment. In addition, a fixed fraction of investment must take the form of public capital formation G_k:

$$G_k = g_k I \tag{5}$$

where g_k (like m_k) is taken as less than one.

To keep the model simple, we adopt the following functional forms for the behaviour of the household and government sectors. Aggregate savings S is a linear function of national income in excess of consumption necessary for subsistence:

$$S = s(Y + F - C) \tag{6}$$

where s is the savings rate and C is subsistence consumption. Total tax revenues T depend on the tax rate on income above subsistence t_y and the share of foreign aid accruing to the government t_f:

$$T = t_y(Y - C) + t_f F \tag{7}$$

The government budget constraint is:

$$G_k + G_c = T + D \tag{8}$$

G_c is the exogenous level of government consumption and D is the exogenous level of government spending financed from sources other than current taxation. For simplicity, we set $D = 0$.

Equation (1) can be solved for the relationship between the rate of growth γ ($\gamma = I/K$) and foreign aid as a share of GDP (denoted f, $f = F/Y$):

$$\gamma = [\alpha/(1 - m_k)][-x + s(1 + f - c) + m_c] \tag{9}$$

---

[20] The model is easily generalized to incorporate imports of intermediates used by industry. See Bacha (1984).

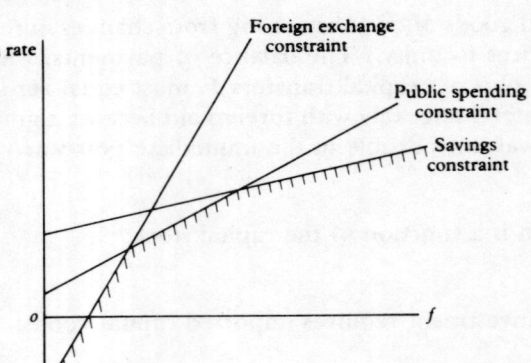

Figure A1. Three-gap model of constraints on growth

where x is the export share of GDP ($x = X/Y$) and c is subsistence consumption relative to GDP ($c = C/Y$). This relationship has a positive slope ($\alpha s/(1 - m_k)$) and intercept as depicted in Figure A1. It shows the familiar McKinnon-style relationship between aid and growth in an economy whose growth is constrained by a low level of saving. The innovation here is that the intercept can shift, and with it the likelihood that the savings gap binds, as the economy moves further from subsistence. If the savings gap binds, then $\partial\gamma/\partial f = s\alpha/(1 - m_k)$.

Similarly, Equation (2) can be solved for the relationship between growth and aid:

$$\gamma = (\alpha/m_k)[x - m_c + f] \tag{10}$$

This is the relationship between growth and aid in an economy constrained by the availability of imported capital goods. Equation (10), the foreign exchange constraint, is steeper than Equation (9). Its intercept is negative if $m_c > x$, which is appropriate to our circumstances. If the foreign exchange constraint binds, then $\partial\gamma/\partial f = \alpha/m_k$. This is larger than in the case where the savings constraint binds, under the plausible assumptions that the savings propensity is small and that only a minority of capital goods are imported. Then foreign aid has a larger growth effect in a foreign-exchange-constrained economy than in one that is savings-constrained because only a fraction less than one of foreign aid is saved, while all of f can be used to finance additional imports.

Finally, Equation (8) can be solved in a similar fashion:

$$\gamma = (\alpha/g_k)[-g_c + t_y(1 - c) + t_f f] \tag{11}$$

This is the relationship between aid and growth in an economy constrained by public capital formation. The likelihood that this constraint

62   *Barry Eichengreen and Marc Uzan*

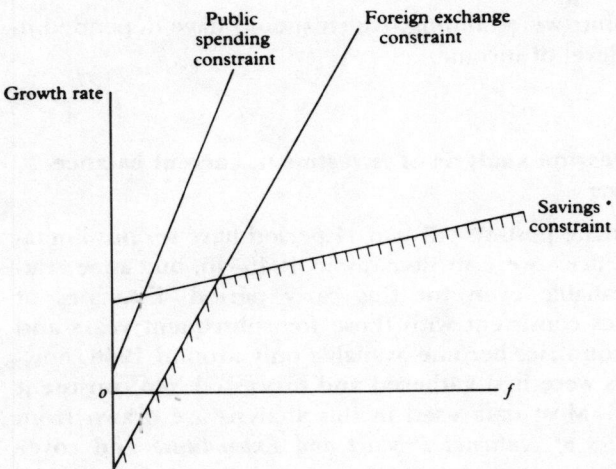

Figure A2. The case where only two constraints bind

will bind depends both on the intercept (and hence on proximity to subsistence c) and on the slope of $\partial \gamma / \partial f$ (namely $\alpha t_f / g_k$). The growth effect of foreign aid may be larger or smaller than in savings- and foreign-exchange-constrained economies. If $t_f > g$, which is plausible for the Marshall Plan period, and if m_k and g_k are small, then the effect of foreign aid in a public-spending-constrained economy will be larger than that in a savings-constrained economy. There is no obvious presumption about the relative size of the effect in foreign-exchange and public-spending constrained economies, which depends mainly on the relative magnitude of g_k and m_k.

Figure A1 shows the case where g_k is large relative to m_k, for a poor economy (one just above subsistence in the absence of foreign aid). The foreign exchange constraint cuts the public spending constraint from below. Additional foreign aid produces progressively smaller increments to growth, depending on whether the foreign exchange, public spending or savings constraints bind. Figure A2 shows the case where g_k is small relative to m_k. Here public spending is never a binding constraint.

How does the level of income influence the growth effects of foreign aid? As c declines from unity (the economy moves away from the margin of subsistence), the savings and public-capital-formation constraints shift up. For a given range of foreign aid, it becomes more likely that the foreign exchange gap binds, implying a large growth effect. Thus, the effects of the Marshall Plan should have depended in part on which of these three constraints were binding, which should have depended in turn on the initial level of income.

Appendix B. Regression analysis of investment, current balance and public spending

Data for the immediate post-World War II period have serious limitations. Statistical agencies were in disarray in 1945–46, but some scattered data are available even for this early period. Estimates of economic aggregates consistent with those for subsequent years and compatible across countries become available only around 1948, however, when statistics were first gathered and processed into consistent form by the OEEC. Most data used in this analysis are drawn from the OEEC's *Statistics of National Product and Expenditure* and cover the period 1948–55. The major exceptions are the rate of growth of GDP and Marshall Plan allotments.[21] Marshall Plan allotments were drawn from Mutual Security Program (various issues). We include funds made available in 1951–55 under the provisions of the Mutual Defence Assistance Program.[22] Data on the growth of GDP are from Maddison (1982), who drew figures from national sources and adjusted them for consistency. Maddison's sample therefore defines the 16 industrial countries forming our international cross section: Australia, Austria, Belgium, Canada, Denmark, Finland, France, Germany, Italy, Japan, the Netherlands, Norway, Sweden, Switzerland, the UK and the US.[23]

Investment, the current account and government spending are all assumed to depend on the economy's underlying rate of growth, proxied by per capita GDP relative to the US and by GDP growth since 1938. In addition, they are determined by the rate of population growth, the rate of consumer price inflation and the openness of the economy.

---

[21] Using the growth of GDP rather than the growth of GDP per capita as the dependent variable made no difference for any of the empirical results. We replicated the regressions reported below using GDP per capita, and found only the slightest changes in point estimates and levels of statistical significance.

[22] The MDAP was established by the Mutual Security Act of 1951, passed by the US Congress in response to the outbreak of the Korean War. For 1951–52 Congress authorized $4.92 bn. in military assistance and $1.02 bn. in economic and technical assistance (known as 'defense support'). Our data for foreign economic aid include only economic and technical assistance.

[23] For the non-European members of this group, ancillary variables were gathered from other sources. These came from Butlin (1962) for Australia, Ohkawa and Rosovsky (1975) for Japan, and Mitchell (1983) for Canada and the US, supplemented by the IMF's *International Financial Statistics* for later years. Annual population estimates for all countries were drawn from Liesner (1989).

64   *Barry Eichengreen and Marc Uzan*

Table B1. Channels linking the Marshall Plan to growth, 1948–54

(Dependent variables expressed as shares of GDP)

	Investment	Current account	Government spending
Constant	0.21	−0.16	0.37
	(5.42)	(3.16)	(2.84)
GDP relative to US	−0.10	0.17	−0.28
	(2.42)	(3.20)	(2.11)
GDP growth since 1938	0.10	−0.05	0.01
	(6.79)	(2.41)	(0.29)
Terms of trade	−0.01	0.01	0.01
	(1.98)	(0.37)	(0.34)
Pop growth	1.08	−0.24	1.95
	(2.42)	(0.39)	(1.25)
CPI inflation	0.06	−0.55	−0.13
	(2.73)	(1.63)	(1.75)
Openness	−0.03	0.48	−0.01
	(0.64)	(7.35)	(0.03)
Marshall Plan lagged	0.36	−0.12	−0.31
	(2.53)	(2.28)	(0.63)
n	122	113	125
S.E.	0.02	0.02	0.06

Source: See text.
Note: *t*-statistics in parentheses. Country dummy variables are included in all equations.

Marshall Plan allotments are entered with a one-year lag to minimize simultaneity.[24]

The first column of Table B1 reports the results on the determinants of investment. Investment ratios were higher in countries with rapidly growing populations, which had already restored output to 1938 levels, and which were far from the technological frontier as defined by the US. There is no indication that monetary stabilization, openness or the terms of trade (export prices relative to import prices) had a strong impact on investment.[25] In contrast, Marshall Plan transfers equal to 2% of GNP raised investment by 0.7% of GNP in the subsequent year.

---

[24] We experimented with a second lag of Marshall Plan allotments but found that it had a small coefficient, was uniformly insignificant and had no discernible impact on the other terms, including the first lag of Marshall Plan transfers. Hence we report only equations including the first lag. To test the exogeneity of lagged Marshall Plan receipts, we added the fitted value from a first-stage regression designed to explain Marshall Plan receipts. The fitted value consistently displayed a *t*-statistic smaller than unity.

[25] The result for openness is in contrast to Romer's (1990) finding for 90 countries over the period 1960–85, that more open economies had higher investment rates. The contrast may be explicable in terms of the slower and more troubled growth of international transactions immediately after World War II.

The Marshall Plan   65

This suggests a significant impact of the Marshall Plan. The second column reports results for the current-account balance. Relatively poor countries (those with per capita incomes far below America's) and countries that succeeded in restoring output to 1938 levels tended to run current-account deficits. Openness is associated with current-account surpluses. High inflation countries ran current-account deficits, which is plausible insofar as inflation signals excess demand. There is evidence, moreover, that Marshall Plan inflows permitted the maintenance of larger current-account deficits. Transfers equal to 2% of GNP were associated with an additional current-account deficit equal to 0.25% of national income in the subsequent year. The third column reports results for government spending. This is the least robust of the three equations. Marshall Plan receipts enter with a negative coefficient, suggesting declines in the public spending share in countries receiving US aid. This may be plausible insofar as the US pressured recipients to reduce government spending and to the extent that some countries, notably Britain, used counterpart funds to retire public debt, reducing debt service charges. In any case, the evidence on government spending provides little support for the notion that the Marshall Plan operated by bridging the fiscal gap.

Appendix C. Regression analysis of growth

Table C1 reports the simplest possible convergence and catchup regressions that might be used to analyse the Marshall Plan. These are descriptive correlations rather than tests of a particular model. The growth rate for each year from 1948 through 1954 is regressed on per capita GDP relative to the US, the GDP growth rate since 1938, and Marshall Plan allotments as a share of GNP in the current and immediately preceding years. Faster growth is exhibited by countries farther from the technological frontier as defined by the US, and by countries whose output had fallen most from pre-war levels.[26] Marshall Plan effects are substantial and significant at the 95% level; the negative lagged term is about half the size of the positive contemporaneous one. (Subsequent lags never approached statistical significance.) A coefficient

---

[26] Since 1938 was a recession year, we reran all regressions substituting GDP growth since 1936 for GDP growth since 1938. This substitution reduced the *t*-statistic on the change in output since the late 1930s below two in the third equation in Table C1 (without changing the magnitude or significance of any of the other variables). But in none of the subsequent regressions reported in this paper did this substitution alter the magnitude or statistical significance of the variable discernibly.

**Table C1. Catchup and convergence regressions
(dependent variable is growth rate of real GDP)**

	(1)	(2)	(3)
Constant	0.08	0.06	0.07
	(9.04)	(7.94)	(9.02)
GDP relative to US	−0.06		−0.09
	(3.38)		(3.91)
GDP growth since 1938		−0.01	−0.03
		(0.74)	(2.04)
Marshall Plan	1.29	1.43	1.41
	(4.55)	(4.73)	(4.92)
Marshall Plan lagged	−0.67	−0.59	−0.67
	(2.44)	(2.08)	(2.46)
n	126	126	126
S.E.	0.04	0.04	0.04

Source: See text.
Note: *t*-statistics in parentheses.

of unity suggests that a transfer of 2% of GDP raised the growth rate
of domestic output by two percentage points in the same year.

A reason to hesitate before drawing such inferences is the possible
endogeneity of Marshall Plan allotments. To test for this possibility,
using a procedure suggested by Hausman (1978), we added to the third
equation in Table C1 the fitted values of Marshall aid (current and
lagged one year) derived from regressing it on the current balance and
per capita GDP.[27] While the lagged value of Marshall aid had a small
t-statistic, that on the current value was significantly greater than zero
at the 95% confidence level, supporting our suspicion of the endogeneity
of Marshall Plan allotments.

---

[27] The Marshall Plan allotment was expressed as a share of GNP, as was the current account
balance. Consistent with specifications reported below, per capita GDP was expressed as a
proportion of US per capita GDP, where all income estimates were converted to US dollars
using Summers and Heston's purchasing-power-parity exchange rates. The equation, estimated
only on the subsample of countries receiving ECA aid, was:

ECA Aid = 0.035 − 0.313 Current balance/GNP − 0.067 Relative per cap GDP
        (7.02)   (5.74)   (4.94)

$R^2 = 0.48$ $N = 73$

with *t*-statistics in parentheses. For countries not included in the subsample, fitted values were
taken as zero.

**Table C2. Additional growth regressions for 1948–52
(dependent variable is growth rate of real GDP)**

	(1)	(2)	(3)	(4)	(5)	(6)
Constant	0.08	0.09	0.10	0.08	0.09	0.07
	(8.81)	(7.85)	(1.99)	(5.02)	(4.89)	(1.00)
GDP relative to US	−0.09	−0.10	−0.09	−0.09	−0.10	−0.05
	(5.24)	(5.25)	(1.44)	(4.72)	(3.61)	(0.66)
GDP growth since 1938	0.05	0.05	0.04	0.04	0.05	0.02
	(4.61)	(4.13)	(1.79)	(3.76)	(3.61)	(0.67)
Openness	−0.10	−0.10	−0.15	−0.10	−0.11	−0.09
	(3.98)	(3.99)	(1.78)	(3.26)	(3.30)	(0.86)
Export growth	0.05	0.04	0.04	0.05	0.04	0.04
	(4.72)	(2.99)	(3.66)	(4.27)	(2.76)	(3.18)
Marshall Plan lagged	0.59	0.85	0.38	0.58	0.73	0.38
	(2.85)	(3.10)	(1.47)	(2.52)	(2.48)	(1.39)
Marshall Plan lagged twice	−0.41	−0.83	−0.45	−0.49	−0.78	−0.58
	(1.95)	(3.09)	(1.88)	(2.18)	(2.69)	(2.29)
Investment				0.01	0.01	−0.01
				(0.20)	(0.16)	(0.28)
Current account				−0.05	−0.03	−0.06
				(0.47)	(0.30)	(0.44)
Government spending				0.01	0.01	0.02
				(0.06)	(0.35)	(0.29)
Year dummies		×			×	
Country dummies			×			×
n	112	112	112	112	112	112
S.E.	0.03	0.03	0.03	0.03	0.03	0.03

Source: See text.
Note: *t*-statistics in parentheses.

Table C2 therefore lags Marshall Plan aid one and two years to redress
problems of simultaneity.[28] In addition, it augments the basic regression
with measures of economic structure and policy, a la Barro (1989) and
Romer (1989). GDP per capita relative to the US continues to enter
with a negative sign, as if countries far from the technological threshold
had the greatest scope for growth subsequently, but GDP growth since
1938 no longer exhibits a negative sign. Openness, measured as exports

---

[28] In some early regressions we included also the current year's Marshall Plan allotments,
instrumenting them with the current balance and per capita GDP. In no case was the coefficient
on the current value significantly different from zero. Thus, it appears that aid affected growth
only with a lag. We therefore dropped the current value from subsequent regressions. We also
conducted Hausman tests of the hypothesis of exogeneity of the remaining (lagged) allotment
variables by adding their fitted values to the various equations reported in Table B1. In no
case did the fitted values have *t*-statistics as large as unity. We also experimented with additional
lags, but in no case was the coefficient of Marshall Plan allotments lagged two years statistically
different from zero at standard confidence levels.

68   *Barry Eichengreen and Marc Uzan*

as a share of GNP, enters negatively, indicating slower growth in more open economies (which plausibly suffered most from bilateral clearing arrangements, non-tariff barriers and the slow recovery of trade). As in previous studies like Michaely (1977), the growth rate of exports (in constant prices) enters positively. The coefficients on Marshall Plan allotments lagged one and two years both differ from zero at the 95% confidence level. Those on Marshall aid lagged one year are between 0.5 and 1, suggesting that allotments equal to 2% of European GNP raised European output by 1 to 2 percentage points in the subsequent year. Now, however, the coefficient on the second lag is as large in absolute value as the coefficient on the first. (We cannot reject the hypothesis that the two coefficients are equal and opposite in sign at the 95% confidence level.) This suggests that the effect of the Marshall Plan was temporary. The last three columns add investment, the current-account surplus and central government expenditure as shares of GNP. None appears to have had a statistically significant impact on growth.

A possible explanation for the small and statistically insignificant coefficients on investment, the current account and government spending is simultaneity bias. We tested for the endogeneity of these variables using the Hausman test described above, adding the fitted values for investment, the current account and government from the equations reported in Table B1 to the growth equations just reported, together and separately. In no case did the fitted values have t-statistics as large as one, supporting our treatment of these variables as exogenous with respect to growth.

Our three-gap model suggests that aid transfers to countries with low levels of investment, large current-account deficits and limited capacities to finance additional government spending may have had a disproportionately large impact on growth. To test this hypothesis, Marshall Plan allotments as a share of GNP lagged one year were interacted with the investment, current account and government spending ratios. (We also interacted Marshall Plan allotments lagged two years with the investment, current account and government spending variables, but the second lags were not statistically significant.) The estimated equations are reported in Table C3. The coefficient on Marshall aid lagged one year is now significantly greater than zero at the 99% confidence level. That on Marshall aid lagged twice differs significantly from zero at the 95% level in one of the three cases; in all three equations it is significantly smaller (at the 95% level) than the coefficient on the first lag. The interaction terms often display coefficients significantly different from zero at the 95% level. Their negative coefficients accord with the intuition provided by the three-gap model. That on the Marshall Plan

The Marshall Plan   69

**Table C3. Growth equations with interactive Marshall Plan
effects, 1948–54 (dependent variable is growth rate of real GDP)**

	(1)	(2)	(3)
Constant	0.06	0.06	0.07
	(3.29)	(3.24)	(1.15)
GDP relative to US	−0.08	−0.09	−0.09
	(4.28)	(4.45)	(1.43)
GDP growth since 1938	0.04	0.04	0.01
	(3.32)	(3.35)	(0.48)
Openness	−0.10	−0.10	−0.23
	(3.25)	(3.33)	(2.30)
Export Growth	0.04	0.03	0.03
	(3.98)	(2.51)	(2.67)
Marshall Plan lagged	2.86	2.96	5.36
	(2.43)	(2.39)	(4.12)
Marshall Plan lagged twice	−0.26	−0.54	−0.23
	(1.18)	(1.91)	(0.92)
Investment	0.10	0.11	0.35
	(1.40)	(1.48)	(1.96)
Current account	0.09	0.12	0.25
	(0.89)	(1.11)	(1.74)
Government spending	0.02	0.03	0.04
	(0.49)	(0.74)	(0.75)
Investment* Marshall Plan	−6.91	−7.29	−9.16
	(2.10)	(2.21)	(2.64)
Current account* Marshall Plan	−14.35	−14.69	−15.12
	(2.61)	(2.67)	(2.78)
Government spending* Marshall Plan	−5.83	−5.29	−16.50
	(1.48)	(1.27)	(3.49)
Year dummies		×	
Country dummies			×
n	112	112	112
S.E.	0.03	0.03	0.03

Source: See text.
Note: t-statistics in parentheses.

interacted with investment suggests that American aid provided the
least stimulus to growth in countries where investment was already
high. That on the Marshall Plan interacted with the current-account
ratio suggests that it boosted growth least in countries whose current-
account position was strong. That on the Marshall Plan interacted with
government spending suggests that American aid stimulated growth
least in countries where government spending was already high. This
supports the notion that the Marshall Plan had the largest impact on
growth in countries for which the savings, current account and fiscal
gaps were binding.

Table C4. Growth equations distinguishing counterpart funds used for production

	(1)	(2)	(3)	(4)	(5)	(6)	(7)	(8)	(9)
Constant	0.06	0.06	0.05	0.08	0.08	0.05	0.05	0.06	0.04
	(3.28)	(3.27)	(0.91)	(4.65)	(4.61)	(0.72)	(0.84)	(1.06)	(0.61)
GDP relative to US	-0.08	-0.09	-0.08	-0.08	-0.09	-0.04	-0.08	-0.09	-0.04
	(4.09)	(4.18)	(1.25)	(4.43)	(4.52)	(0.59)	(1.27)	(1.44)	(0.06)
GDP growth since 1938	0.04	0.04	0.01	0.04	0.04	0.06	0.01	0.01	0.01
	(3.18)	(3.10)	(0.24)	(3.42)	(3.29)	(0.22)	(0.13)	(0.13)	(0.08)
Openness	-0.09	-0.09	-0.21	-0.09	-0.09	-0.09	-0.21	-0.24	-0.10
	(2.81)	(2.82)	(2.05)	(2.78)	(2.74)	(0.91)	(2.08)	(2.39)	(0.94)
Export growth	0.05	0.03	0.03	0.05	0.03	0.04	0.03	0.03	0.04
	(4.08)	(2.51)	(2.83)	(4.30)	(2.62)	(3.29)	(2.89)	(2.74)	(3.31)
Marshall Plan lagged	3.74	3.62	5.75	2.30	2.40	1.53	5.58	5.05	1.65
	(2.93)	(2.71)	(4.02)	(4.10)	(4.03)	(2.29)	(3.93)	(3.91)	(2.49)
Marshall Plan lagged twice	-1.05	-0.97	-1.48	-1.62	-1.74	-2.26	-1.43	-0.32	-2.26
	(1.74)	(1.45)	(2.30)	(3.29)	(3.30)	(4.08)	(2.23)	(1.29)	(4.13)
Investment	0.09	0.09	0.39	0.04	0.04	0.19	0.42	0.40	0.24
	(1.31)	(1.31)	(2.21)	(0.66)	(0.59)	(1.06)	(2.42)	(2.25)	(1.36)
Investment for Norway	—	—	—	—	—	—	-1.35	-1.60	-1.57
							(1.54)	(1.85)	(1.70)

Continued overleaf

Table C4 (cont.)

	(1)	(2)	(3)	(4)	(5)	(6)	(7)	(8)	(9)
Current account	0.08 (0.72)	0.10 (0.93)	0.22 (1.54)	0.02 (0.18)	0.02 (0.22)	0.04 (0.31)	0.22 (1.56)	0.25 (1.76)	0.04 (0.26)
Government spending	0.02 (0.49)	0.03 (0.73)	0.04 (0.76)	0.01 (0.18)	0.01 (0.40)	0.02 (0.39)	0.04 (0.85)	0.04 (0.87)	0.03 (0.50)
Investment*	-5.57 (1.62)	-5.77 (1.65)	-8.64 (2.39)	—	—	—	-7.96 (2.20)	-8.61 (2.51)	-8.64 (2.39)
Marshall Plan	-8.24 (1.25)	-10.55 (1.55)	-8.31 (1.29)	—	—	—	-9.67 (1.50)	-16.16 (2.99)	—
Current account*	-5.22 (1.29)	-5.24 (1.22)	-14.72 (3.07)	—	—	—	-14.53 (3.05)	-15.78 (3.38)	—
Marshall Plan									
Government spending*									
Marshall Plan									
Counterpart for production	1.37 (1.74)	1.08 (1.29)	0.90 (1.07)	2.16 (3.34)	2.13 (3.19)	1.57 (2.12)	0.97 (1.15)	—	1.70 (2.30)
Marshall Plan	-0.62 (1.01)	-0.20 (0.30)	-1.35 (2.08)	-0.99 (1.81)	-0.77 (1.29)	-1.87 (3.00)	-1.15 (1.74)	—	-1.69 (2.71)
Counterpart for production									
Marshall Plan lagged									
Year dummies	—	—	—	—			—	—	
Country dummies	×	×	×	×	×	×	×	×	×
n	112	112	112	112	112	112	112	112	112
S.E.	0.03	0.03	0.02	0.03	0.03	0.03	0.02	0.02	0.03

Source: See text.

Notes: *t*-statistics in parentheses.

72   *Barry Eichengreen and Marc Uzan*

To test whether the use of counterpart funds had a significant impact on growth, we added counterpart withdrawals for productive purposes (investment and purchases of intermediates). Since counterpart authorizations followed Marshall Plan allotments with a lag of several quarters, we used the current year's authorizations rather than authorizations lagged. To make the effect of counterpart funds as transparent as possible, we defined the variable as counterpart withdrawals for production minus Marshall Plan allotments lagged. Table C4 reports the results. Both Marshall Plan allotments and counterpart withdrawals have economically important and statistically significant effects. But with the addition of measures of the use of counterpart funds, the interaction terms introduced in Table C3 matter less than before. Their coefficients are uniformly smaller and only the interaction terms involving the investment and government spending ratios in the equation with country dummy variables differ significantly from zero at standard confidence levels. Given the insignificance of the majority of these terms, we excluded the interactions from the equations reported in the middle three columns of Table C4. The coefficients on Marshall Plan allotments remain statistically significant. The same is true of the first lag of counterpart withdrawals. Evidence on the second lag on counterpart withdrawals is mixed. The results in the fourth column suggest that a Marshall Plan inflow of 2% of GNP raised output in the next year by 4.6% when a matching amount of counterpart funds were withdrawn for productive purposes. When counterpart funds were used for other purposes, however, the impact on output growth was only 0.3%. About two-thirds of the first year's output growth was given back in the second year. The fifth equation, which includes dummy variables for years, is essentially identical. Once again, however, the equation including dummy variables for countries (in the sixth column) tells a different story. A Marshall Plan allotment raises the growth rate in the first year after which it is received but reduces growth by a matching amount in the second subsequent year. This is true regardless of the disposition of counterpart funds.[29]

Thus, these results support the view that the Marshall Plan had important economic effects. Conditionality played an important role in shaping the effects of American aid. To determine the robustness of the results, we undertook a number of sensitivity analyses. We first reestimated the model containing counterpart effects but omitting interaction terms (the fourth equation of Table C4) eliminating each observation in turn. In no case did the omission of a single observation produce

[29] We tested for the equality, in absolute value terms, of the coefficients of Marshall Plan allotments lagged once and twice and of counterpart withdrawals lagged once and twice, and were unable to reject the hypothesis of equality at standard confidence levels.

a noticeable change. Next we explored whether the results were driven by the observations for a particular country. In no case did the omission of a single country have much impact on the coefficients on Marshall Plan allotments and counterpart withdrawals. (That the results survive Germany's exclusion reassures us that they are not picking up the effects of American occupation or of currency reform.) A potentially troubling aspect of these equations is the small size and statistical insignificance of the investment ratio. Our scatter plot of investment and growth suggests that the absence of a relationship may be due to the exceptionally high investment rate in Norway. We therefore added to our growth equations the product of the investment ratio and a dummy variable for Norway – which allowed the investment rate for this country to differ. The relevant regressions are shown in the last three columns of Table C4. This greatly increased the magnitude of the investment coefficient for the remaining countries. When the interaction term for Norway was included along with the vector of country dummy variables, the investment rate was generally statistically significant at the 95% confidence level. The coefficient on the investment rate, now in the neighbourhood of 0.4, is similar to those obtained in other recent studies. Of the other coefficients, the principal change is in the magnitude of the current-account ratio. This now has a larger effect and in one case is statistically significant at the 90% level. The other coefficients remain essentially unchanged. In particular, the effects of the Marshall Plan and counterpart withdrawals are no different than before.

References

Adams, W. J. (1989). *Restructuring the French Economy.* The Brookings Institution, Washington, D.C.

Alesina, A. and A. Drazen (1989). 'Why Are Stabilizations Delayed'? unpublished manuscript, Harvard University and Tel Aviv University.

Alexander, L. (1991). 'Radical Economic Reform in Germany, 1948 and 1990: Similarities, Differences, and Lessons for the Soviet Union', unpublished manuscript, International Finance Division, Board of Governors of the Federal Reserve System.

Arkes, H. (1972). *Bureaucracy, the Marshall Plan and the National Interest,* Princeton University Press, Princeton.

Bacha, E. L. (1984). 'Growth with Limited Supplies of Foreign Exchange: A reappraisal of the Two-Gap Model', in M. Syrquin *et al.* (eds.) *Economic Structure and Performance,* Academic Press, New York.

—— (1990). 'A Three Gap Model of Foreign Transfers and GDP Growth in Developing Countries', *Journal of Development Economics.*

Barkin, S. (1983). 'The Postwar Decades: Growth and Activism Followed by Stagnancy and Malaise', in Barkin (ed.) *Worker Militancy and its Consequences,* Praeger, New York.

Barro, R. (1989). 'A Cross-Country Study of Growth, Saving and Government Spending', NBER Working Paper no. 2855.

Berolzheimer, J. (1953). 'The Impact of U.S. Foreign Aid Since the Marshall Plan on Western Europe's Gross National Product and Government Finance', *Finanzarchiv.*

Boltho, A. (1982). 'Growth', in A. Boltho (ed.) *The European Economy,* Clarendon Press, Oxford.

Bournay, J., O. Maigne and G. Laroque (1978). 'Comptes trimetriels 1949–1959' *Collections de l'INSEE.*

Brookings Institution (1951). *Current Issues in Foreign Economic Assistance*, The Brookings Institution, Washington, D.C.

Brown, W. A. and R. Opie (1953). *American Foreign Assistance*, The Brookings Institution, Washington, D.C.

Butlin, N. G. (1962). *Australian Domestic Product, Investment and Foreign Borrowing*, Cambridge University Press, Cambridge.

Casella, A. and B. Eichengreen (1991). 'Halting Inflation in France and Italy After World War II', in Michael Bordo and Forrest Capie (eds.) *Monetary Regimes in Transition*, Cambridge University Press, Cambridge (forthcoming).

Chenery, H. and M. Bruno (1962). 'Development Alternatives in an Open Economy: The Case of Israel', *Economic Journal*.

Cohen, D. (1991). 'Slow Growth and Large LDC Debt in the Eighties: An Empirical Analysis', CEPR Discussion Paper No. 461.

Collins, S. and D. Rodrik (1991). *Eastern Europe and the Soviet Union in the World Economy*, Institute for International Economics, Washington, D.C.

Committee of European Economic Cooperation (1947). *General Report*, U.S. Department of State, Washington, D.C.

De Long, J. Bradford and B. Eichengreen (1991). 'The Marshall Plan: History's Most Successful Structural Adjustment Program', in R. Dornbush, R. Layard and W. Nolling (eds.) *Postwar Reconstruction 1945–9: Implications for Eastern Europe* (forthcoming).

Dobbs, M. (1991). 'In Moscow, Running out of Socks: Factory's Woes Reflect Breakdown of Soviet Economy', *Washington Post* (22 June).

Economic Cooperation Administration (various years), *Report*, GPO, Washington, D.C.

Ellis, H. (1950). *The Economics of Freedom*, Harper and Row, New York.

Esposito, C. (1985). 'The Marshall Plan in France and Italy, 1948–1950: Counterpart Fund Negotiations', Ph.D. dissertation, State University of New York at Stony Brook.

Federal Reserve Board (1947). 'France and Italy: Patterns of Reconstruction', *Federal Reserve Bulletin*.

—— (1948). 'Recovery in Western Europe', *Federal Reserve Bulletin*.

Flanagan, R. J., D. W. Soskice and L. Ulman (1983). *Unions, Economic Stabilization, and Incomes Policies*, The Brookings Institution, Washington D.C.

Freris, A. F. (1986). *The Greek Economy in the 20th Century*, Croom Helm, London.

Grindrod, M. (1955). *The Rebuilding of Italy*, Royal Institute of International Affairs, London.

Hausman, J. A. (1978). 'Specification Tests in Econometrics', *Econometrica*.

Hogan, M. J. (1987). *The Marshall Plan: America, Britain and the Reconstruction of Western Europe, 1947–1952*, Cambridge University Press, Cambridge.

Ignatieff, M. (1991). 'In the New Republics', *New York Review of Books* (21 November).

INSEE (1958). *Situation Economique de la France, 1944–57*, INSEE, Paris.

International Bank for Reconstruction and Development (1948). *Summary of the United Nations Economic Commission for Europe Report Entitled 'A Survey of the Economic Situation and Prospects of Europe'*, Economic Department, GdeF/cstp, IBRD, Washington, D.C.

International Monetary Fund (1949), *Balance of Payments Yearbook, 1938, 1946, 1947*, IMF, Washington, D.C.

—— (various years). *International Financial Statistics*, IMF, Washington, D.C.

Kaplan, Jacob J. and Günther Schleiminger (1989). *The European Payments Union*, Oxford University Press, Oxford.

Kindleberger, C. (1967). *Europe's Postwar Growth*, Oxford University Press, London.

Kirman, A. and L. Reichlin (1991). 'The Marshall Plan', in J.-P. Fitoussi (ed.) *A L'est en Europe: Des Economies en Transition*, Presses de la Fondation Nationale des Sciences Politiques, Paris.

Kolko, J. and G. Kolko (1972). *The Limits of Power: The World and United States Foreign Policy, 1945–54*, New York.

Liesner, T. (1989). *One Hundred Years of Economic Statistics*, Economist Publications, London.

Lloyd, J. (1991). 'Triple Panic that Sparked Kremlin Putsch', *Financial Times* (August 21).

Maddison, A. (1976). 'Economic Policy and Performance in Europe, 1913–1970', in C. Cipolla (ed.) *The Fontana Economic History of Europe*, Vol. 5, Pt. 2, Fontana, London.

—— (1982). *Phases of Capitalist Development*, Oxford University Press, Oxford.

Maier, C. S. (1977). 'The Politics of Productivity: Foundations of American International Economic Policy After World War II', reprinted in *In Search of Stability*, Cambridge University Press, Cambridge (1987).

—— (1981), 'The Two Postwar Eras and the Conditions for Stability in Twentieth-Century Western Europe', *American Historical Review*, reprinted in *In Search of Stability*, Cambridge University Press, Cambridge (1987).

The Marshall Plan   75

Marshall, G. C. (1947). 'European Initiative Essential to Economic Recovery', *Department of State Bulletin* (15 June).

Mayer, H. C. (1969). *German Recovery and the Marshall Plan, 1948–1952*, Atlantic Forum, Bonn, Brussels and New York.

McKinnon, R. (1964). 'Foreign Exchange Constraints in Economic Development and Efficient Aid Allocation', *Economic Journal*.

Michaely, M. (1977). 'Exports and Growth: An Empirical Investigation', *Journal of Development Economics*.

Milward, A. (1984). *The Reconstruction of Western Europe, 1945–51*, Methuen, London.

Mitchell, B. R. (1975). *European Historical Statistics*, Macmillan, London.

—— (1983). *International Historical Statistics*, Macmillan, London.

Monnet, Jean (1976) *Mémoires*, Fayard, Paris.

Nicholson, M., C. Freeland and G. Tett (1991). 'A Long and Hungry Ride to Market', *Financial Times* (1 October).

Ohkawa, K. and H. Rosovsky (1975). *Japanese Economic Growth*, Stanford University Press, Stanford.

Organization for European Economic Cooperation (1957). *Statistics of National Product and Expenditure*, vol. 1, OEEC, Paris.

Patterson, T. G. (1973). *Soviet-American Confrontation: Postwar Reconstruction and the Origins of the Cold War*, Johns Hopkins University Press, Baltimore.

Pickles, D. (1953). *French Politics: The First Years of the Fourth Republic*, Royal Institute of International Affairs, London.

President's Committee on Foreign Aid (1947). *European Recovery and American Aid* GPO, Washington, D.C.

Price, H. H. (1955). *The Marshall Plan*, Cornell University Press, Ithaca, New York.

Romer, P. (1989). 'Cross-Country Determinants of the Rate of Technological Change', unpublished manuscript, University of Chicago.

—— (1990). 'Capical, Labor and Productivity', *Brookings Papers on Economic Activity*.

Schwartz, Hans-Peter (1986). *Adenauer: Der Aufstieg 1876–1952*, Deutsche Verlags-Anstalt, Stuttgart.

Stolper, Gustav, Karl Hauser and Knut Borchardt (1964). *Deutsche Wirtschaft seit 1870*, J. C. B. Mohr Siebeck, Tübingen.

Tinbergen, J. (1954). 'The Significance of the Marshall Plan for the Netherlands Economy', in Ministry of Finance, *Road to Recovery: The Marshall Plan, its Importance for the Netherlands and European Cooperation*, Ministry of Finance. The Hague.

United Nations (1948). *A Survey of the Economic Situation and Prospects of Europe*, UN. Geneva.

—— (1949a). *Economic Survey of Europe in 1948*, UN, Geneva.

—— (1949b). *World Economic Report, 1948*, Lake Success, UN, New York.

—— (1950). *Economic Survey of Europe in 1949*, UN, Geneva.

—— (1951). *Economic Survey of Europe in 1950*, UN, Geneva.

—— (1964). *Some Factors in the Economic Growth of Europe During the 1950s*, UN. Geneva.

United States Department of State (1948a). *The European Recovery Program: Introduction to Country Studies*, US Department of State, Washington, D.C.

—— (1948b). *Foreign Relations of the United States in 1947*, GPO, Washington, D.C.

United States House of Representatives (1948). *Final Report on Foreign Aid*, Select Committee on Foreign Aid, GPO, Washington, D.C.

—— (1949). *Hearings Before the Committee on Foreign Affairs*, 81st Congress, 1st Session, on H.R. 2362, A Bill to Amend the Economic Cooperation Act of 1948, Part 1, GPO, Washington, D.C.

United States Mutual Security Agency (1953). *The Structure and Growth of the Italian Economy*, MSA, Rome.

—— (various years). *Report to Congress*, GPO, Washington, D.C.

United States Senate (1948). *Administration of United States Aid for a European Recovery Program*, Report to the Committee on Foreign Relations, 80th Congress, 2nd Session, GPO, Washington, D.C.

—— (1949). *Hearings on the Extension of ERP*, Foreign Relations Committee, 81st Congress, 1st Session, GPO, Washington, D.C.

van der Wee, H. (1986). *Prosperity and Upheaval*, University of California Press, Berkeley.

Wall, I. M. (1991). *The United States and the Making of Postwar France, 1945–1954*, Cambridge University Press, Cambridge.

Wallich, H. (1955). *Mainsprings of the German Economic Revival*, Yale University Press, New Haven.

Windmuller, J. P. (1969). *Labor Relations in the Netherlands*, Cornell University Press, Ithaca, New York.

Winks, R. W. (1960). *The Marshall Plan and the American Economy*, Holt, Rinehart and Winston, New York.

Part III
Postwar Monetary Adjustments

[8]

Contribution of the September 1949 Devaluations to the Solution of Europe's Dollar Problem

J. J. Polak *

B Y THE MIDDLE OF 1951, the "dollar problem" had come much nearer to solution than most observers had considered possible not many months earlier. Some of the more recent improvement in the dollar position of countries outside the United States is due to the rapid acceleration of U.S. imports after the middle of 1950 in connection with the hostilities in Korea. But even before this, the change in the situation had been very pronounced. The surplus on account of goods and services in the U.S. balance of payments, which had been at an annual rate of $7.6 billion in the first half of 1949, was reduced to an annual rate of $3 billion in the first half of 1950. In transactions with the OEEC countries in Europe alone, the U.S. surplus decreased from $3.7 billion to $1.9 billion (annual rates). Measured by the amount of grants from the United States and the use of dollar balances and gold sales to the United States, the improvement in the position of the European countries was even more striking, with the U.S. surplus vis-à-vis these countries dropping from $5.2 billion to $1.9 billion (annual rates).

Between these two periods occurred the greatest adjustment of exchange rates that ever took place in so short a period. Countries accounting for 65 per cent of world imports devalued their currencies, most of them by about 30 per cent. The question naturally arises, therefore, of the connection between progress toward the solution of the dollar problem and the widespread devaluations. To this question the present paper is directed; for practical reasons, its scope is limited to changes in the position of the European devaluing countries.

Ideally, an appraisal of the effects of the devaluations, which obviously had not fully materialized by the middle of 1950, should be based on observations drawn from as long a subsequent period as possible. But while it is difficult to disentangle the effects of the devalua-

* Mr. Polak, Assistant Director of the Research Department, is a graduate of the University of Amsterdam. He was formerly a member of the League of Nations Secretariat, Economist at the Netherlands Embassy in Washington, and Economic Adviser at UNRRA. He is the co-author, with Professor Jan Tinbergen, of *The Dynamics of Business Cycles,* and is also the author of several other books and of numerous articles in economic journals.

1

tions from those of other factors in the first nine months after September 1949, it becomes nearly impossible to do so for the period after June 1950. It is necessary, therefore, to be satisfied with whatever reasonable conclusions can be drawn from the experience of a limited period. The findings of the analysis which follows may be summarized briefly:

After the devaluations the dollar value of exports to the United States from the devaluing countries in Europe recovered from the low levels of the second and third quarters of 1949, but this recovery, which restored exports in the first half of 1950 approximately to the 1948 level should be attributed in large part to the recovery in the U.S. economy rather than to the devaluations. Apparently the devaluations increased the volume of exports to the United States by an amount little more than enough to offset the fall of about 15 per cent in dollar export prices. It may be further estimated that the devaluations were responsible for a 10 per cent increase in the dollar value of Western Europe's exports to other markets in the Western Hemisphere, in Canada and Latin America.

Between the first half of 1949 and the first half of 1950, Europe's dollar imports declined by one third. Most of this decline occurred, however, between the second and third quarter of 1949, that is, before the devaluations. Part of the total decline can be attributed to the intensification of restrictions in the United Kingdom; but the greater part appears to be attributable to the improved European supply position. Thus between the third quarter of 1949 and the first half of 1950, Europe's imports of foodstuffs and coal declined sharply, although a rise might have been expected because of seasonal factors. A comparison of other imports over the same period shows that, apart from sharp seasonal movements in cotton and tobacco, these other imports declined very little in the aggregate (4 per cent) and for a number of countries increased. The effect of the devaluations on imports is therefore not found in the statistics. This is not surprising, and does not imply that there was no effect. With imports generally controlled, the effect of the devaluations appeared much more in the reduction of pressure on the control authorities, the substitution of the price mechanism for at least part of the controls as barriers to imports, and the consequent more rational allocation of the relatively scarce dollars among different uses and different users.

Outward capital movements played a considerable role in worsening Europe's position before the devaluations, and their subsequent reversal accounted for a large part of the increase in reserves which followed the devaluations.

To study the effects of the devaluations at a time when many other factors were also changing, it is important to have "control observations," which may be assumed to be subject to most of the other factors but not to the one special factor of devaluation. If a large number of countries had devalued and a large number had not, the second group of countries could have been used as a "control." There was in fact only one major European trading country which did not devalue, Switzerland, and it would be undesirable to take as a standard of reference data from one country only. Since, however, Italy and Belgium devalued only a little (8 and 12 per cent, respectively), these three countries together may be compared with the other devaluers and, for convenience, may be described as the "non-devaluing countries," or "non-devaluers."

There are two main limitations to the use of the experience of these three countries as a yardstick by reference to which the effects of the devaluations can be measured. One is that the export prices of the non-devaluers fell rather considerably, though not so much as those of the devaluers and not so much for exports to the United States as for exports in general. The price reductions, however, gave the "non-devaluers" the opportunity to increase the volume, though not necessarily the value, of their exports to the United States. The second limitation to the use of the experience of the "non-devaluers" is that both they and the devaluers export to the United States many of the same types of commodity, and therefore part of the increase in the volume of exports of the latter may have been achieved at the expense of the exports of the former. While it cannot be assumed that the errors in opposite directions to which these two limitations give rise canceled each other out, it appears reasonable to use the experience of the "non-devaluers" as a yardstick.

1. Changes in Value of Exports to United States

The changes in the value of dollar exports from the main European countries to the United States are summarized in Table 1. Minor countries have been omitted since fluctuations in their trade tend to be relatively large. These fluctuations, however, are likely to be due to chance factors and therefore are of minor significance in the general picture.

Two sets of figures have been used in this table: U.S. data on imports from the countries concerned and export data of the exporting countries themselves. For each group as a whole the differences are quite small; they may easily be due to minor differences in recording or to the difference between the time when goods set out as exports and the time when they arrive as imports. There is no particular reason to consider either

TABLE 1. VALUE OF EXPORTS OF EUROPEAN COUNTRIES TO THE UNITED STATES, FIRST HALF OF 1949 AND OF 1950

Exporting Countries	U.S. Import Statistics				Countries' Export Statistics				
	First Half 1949	First Half 1950	Change	Percentage Change	First Half 1949	First Half 1950	Change	Percentage Change	Average of Percentages
	(million U.S. dollars)				*(million U.S. dollars)*				
Devaluers									
United Kingdom	112.1	126.2	+14.1	+13	111.9	130.0	+18.1	+16	+14
France	30.5	40.5	+10.0	+33	26.9	36.1	+ 9.2	+34	+34
Germany	27.1	31.0	+ 3.9	+14	31.6	26.2	− 5.4	−17	− 2
Netherlands	27.4	25.9	− 1.5	− 5	19.7	17.0	− 2.7	−14	−10
Norway	20.5	19.4	− 1.1	− 5	15.0	16.8	+ 1.8	+12	+ 3
Sweden	23.6	35.3	+11.7	+50	24.0	28.6	+ 4.6	+19	+35
Six devaluers	241.2	278.3	+37.1	+15	229.1	254.7	+25.6	+11	+13
Non-Devaluers									
Belgium	55.6	58.8	+ 3.2	+ 6	53.5	59.8	+ 6.3	+12	+ 9
Switzerland	45.3	44.2	− 1.1	− 2	44.1	46.9	+ 2.8	+ 6	+ 2
Italy	34.5	40.5	+ 6.0	+17	21.8	25.2	+ 3.4	+16	+16
Three non-devaluers	135.4	143.5	+ 8.1	+ 6	119.4	131.9	+12.5	+10	+ 8
Difference between Groups				+ 9				+ 1	+ 5

Source: *Direction of International Trade* (United Nations, International Monetary Fund, and International Bank for Reconstruction and Development), January–June 1950 and January–July 1950.

set as more reliable and the analysis is, therefore, based on a combination of the two.

The table shows that the gain of the devaluers between the first half of 1949 and the first half of 1950 in exports to the United States was small, measured at $37 million or $26 million according to the statistics used, that is, 15 or 11 per cent. During the same period the non-devaluers did nearly as well, gaining either $8 million or $12.5 million, that is, 6 or 10 per cent. Either set of statistics shows a reduction in exports for two of the six devaluers, while of the three non-devaluers, one, according to one set of statistics, showed a reduction. This comparison between the two groups seems to indicate therefore that only part of the small improvement in the devaluing countries' exports to the United States—perhaps an improvement of 5 per cent—can be attributed to the devaluations.[1]

Since the possible effects of devaluation on a country's exports are often discussed in terms of certain relevant elasticities, it may be useful to express the data in this form. When this is done, two reservations must be made. First, it should not (as is sometimes done) be assumed that the only relevant elasticity is the elasticity of demand for the country's exports abroad; the statistics available do not necessarily give a clue to the magnitude of that particular elasticity. Other elasticities, such as the elasticity of supply in the exporting country, and the elasticity of supply of competing commodities in the importing country, also enter into the picture.

A single figure expressing the effects of all these various elasticities on the dollar proceeds of export sales is given by the elasticity of the supply of dollars with respect to the dollar exchange rate,[2] i.e., roughly the ratio of the percentage change in the proceeds from dollar exports

---

[1] The data in Table 1 may be used to compute not only the average percentage change in each group but also the standard error of this average and the difference between the two groups and the standard error of this difference. In this calculation an *unweighted* average of the percentages (considering the observations on each country as of equal validity as an indicator of the effects of devaluation) is used rather than the *weighted* average shown in Table 1. This computation shows the following percentage changes in exports to the United States:

	U.S. Data	Exporting Countries' Data
Six devaluers	16± 9	8±8
Three non–devaluers	7± 6	11±3
Difference	9±11	−3±9

Depending on the data used, this table shows that the devaluers did either 9 per cent better or 3 per cent worse than the non-devaluers, both figures being subject to a large margin of error.

[2] See F. Machlup, "The Theory of Foreign Exchanges," reprinted in *Readings in the Theory of International Trade* (Philadelphia, 1949), pp. 104-58.

6   INTERNATIONAL MONETARY FUND STAFF PAPERS

to the percentage change in the dollar value of the currency.[8] This elasticity is shown in Table 2.

The calculation of any elasticity does not imply that this elasticity is necessarily a fixed constant and that a new change of exchange rates, in a different situation, could be expected to produce a proportional result. One particular feature of the devaluations under discussion was that they were undertaken simultaneously by a large number of countries. A devaluation of the same magnitude undertaken by one of

TABLE 2. APPARENT ELASTICITY OF SUPPLY OF DOLLARS FROM EXPORTS TO THE UNITED STATES WITH RESPECT TO THE EXCHANGE RATE, FIRST HALF OF 1949 TO FIRST HALF OF 1950

Exporting Countries	Percentage Increase in Value of Exports to United States	Percentage Decrease in Dollar Value of Currency	Apparent Elasticity [1] of Supply of Dollars
United Kingdom	14	30	0.4
France	34	22	1.3
Germany	− 2	21	−0.1
Netherlands	−10	30	−0.3
Norway	3	30	0.1
Sweden	35	30	0.8

[1] The data in this column have been computed on the assumption of a constant elasticity curve, and therefore they are slightly different from the ratio of the figures shown in the two preceding columns.
Sources: Table 1, last column, and Table 3.

these countries alone would probably have had a greater effect on that country's competitive position and hence on the increase of the dollar income it might have obtained from this devaluation.

The table refers to *apparent* elasticities, for the reasons indicated above and because no allowance has been made for the effect on exports of changes in income in the United States (see discussion below). If correction were made for this, the elasticities would be somewhat lower. The elasticities are also qualified by reference to a particular time indication, viz., changes from the first half of 1949 to the first half of 1950, in order to make clear that they refer only to the relatively short-run results of the devaluations.

2. Changes in Quantities Exported to United States

No direct information is available, in either export or import statistics, on the quantum of exports from individual countries to the United States. Therefore inferences on changes in the quantum of ex-

[8] In situations where the foreign elasticity of demand is the only relevant elasticity, the elasticity of supply of foreign exchange equals the foreign elasticity of demand less unity.

THE SEPTEMBER 1949 DEVALUATIONS   7

ports must be based on value data, combined with such price information as is available. The shift between the first half of 1949 and the first half of 1950 is indicated by Table 3, which shows the changes in the unit value or price index of exports for the most important devaluers and non-devaluers, together with the measure of devaluation of

TABLE 3. INDICES OF DOLLAR EXCHANGE RATES AND UNIT VALUE INDICES OF EXPORTS IN TERMS OF DOLLARS, FIRST HALF OF 1950

(First half of 1950 as per cent of first half of 1949)

Exporting Countries	Dollar Value of Currency	Export Unit Value Index in Terms of Dollars
Devaluers		
United Kingdom	70	72
France	78	84
Germany	79	64
Netherlands	70	71
Norway	70	66
Sweden	70	75
Average [1]	72	73
Non-devaluers		
Belgium	88	74
Switzerland	100	95
Italy	92	82
Average [1]	93	83

[1] Weighted by exports to the United States in first half of 1949.
Source: *International Financial Statistics* (International Monetary Fund).

each country's currency. The indices refer to total exports of which exports to the United States are only a small proportion; they do not, therefore, necessarily indicate that the prices of these countries' exports in U.S. markets declined by the percentages shown.

The U.S. Bureau of Labor Statistics has collected information for the ECA on price quotations of imports from various European countries shortly before the devaluations and in the nine months following. These data, which have not been published, indicate that the fall in U.S. prices of imports from devaluers was less in proportion than the devaluations. For imports from the United Kingdom and Italy, the number of quotations is sufficient to compute a weighted average percentage change in the U.S. import prices (in terms of dollars), which is fairly representative of a substantial part of U.S. imports from these two countries. A comparison of quotations in the first half of 1950 with those in the beginning of September 1949 shows that the prices of U.S. imports from the United Kingdom seem to have fallen by about 15 per

8   INTERNATIONAL MONETARY FUND STAFF PAPERS

cent, or about half of the degree of depreciation. If whiskey, the price of which remained constant in U.S. dollars, is excluded, the decline works out at about 20 per cent. Such information as is available on imports from France, Germany, the Netherlands, Norway, and Denmark also indicates that the fall in the prices of many imports from these countries was much less in proportion than the devaluations. On the other hand, prices of U.S. imports from Italy declined roughly by the same percentage as the lira was devalued against the dollar.

It is impossible to arrive at a precise indication of the dollar price change of imports into the United States from the devaluing countries, but the average decline may probably be put without much error at about 15 per cent. For the group as a whole, therefore, the 11 to 15 per cent increase in the dollar value of exports after the devaluations may be assumed to indicate an increase in quantity of about 30 to 35 per cent.

3. Factors Other than Devaluation Affecting Exports to United States

Business Conditions in United States

The most important factor other than the devaluations affecting European exports to the United States was the change in business conditions in the United States. There was a minor recession in the United States in the first half of 1949, which had passed by the first half of 1950. In the first half of 1950, U.S. national income was 2 per cent, and gross national product 3.5 per cent, above the first half of 1949. Usually, changes in U.S. national income are associated with somewhat larger relative changes in the value of imports. On this account, a change in imports of perhaps 3 to 5 per cent could have been expected. But the effect of short cycles, such as that of 1949-50, on imports appears to be proportionately more than the effect of longer cycles. Thus, from 1937 to 1938, when national income declined by only 8 per cent, the value of total U.S. imports fell by 31 per cent and that of U.S. imports from Europe by 33 per cent, indicating a short-run income elasticity of import demand of 3.5 to 4 as against 1.5 to 2 over longer cycles. A somewhat similar rather sharp decline in imports in response to a very minor decline in income appears to have occurred in 1949.

The parallelism between the value of imports and the business situation in the United States in short cycles is clearest if imports are compared with the index of industrial production. Such a comparison on a quarterly basis is provided by Chart 1, where the import figures have been roughly adjusted for seasonal variation on the basis of the average of the 1947 and 1948 seasonal patterns, which, incidentally, was almost the same as the average seasonal pattern for 1934-38.

THE SEPTEMBER 1949 DEVALUATIONS   9

CHART 1. U.S. Imports from Europe and Industrial Production

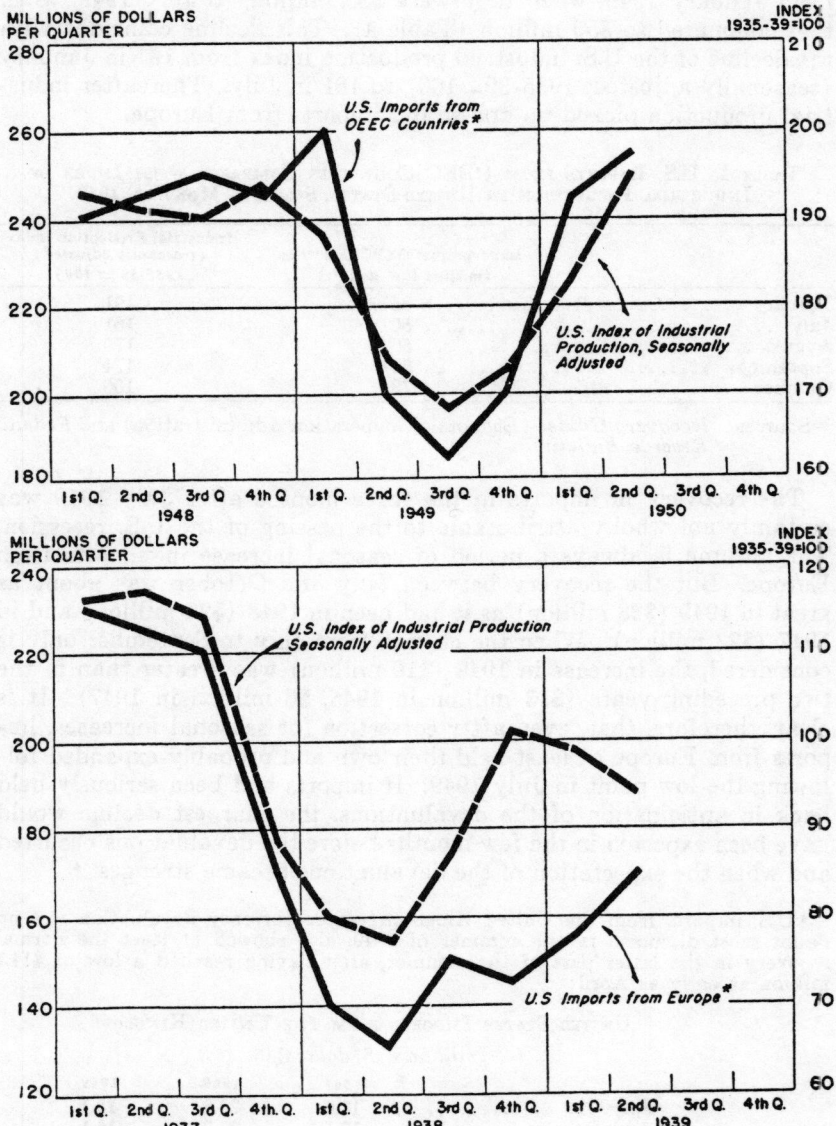

* Roughly adjusted for seasonal variation.

U.S. imports from OEEC countries declined more or less continuously from January 1949, when they were $85 million, to July 1949, when they amounted to $50 million (Table 4). This decline coincided with the decline of the U.S. industrial production index from 191 in January (seasonally adjusted, 1935-39=100) to 161 in July. Thereafter industrial production picked up and so did imports from Europe.

TABLE 4. U.S. IMPORTS FROM OEEC COUNTRIES COMPARED WITH INDEX OF INDUSTRIAL PRODUCTION IN UNITED STATES, SELECTED MONTHS, 1949

	Imports from OEEC Countries (*million U.S. dollars*)	Industrial Production Index (*seasonally adjusted; 1935-39 = 100*)
January	85	191
July	50	161
August	56	170
September	69	174
October	73	166

Sources: *Recovery Guides* (Economic Cooperation Administration) and *Federal Reserve Bulletin*.

The recovery in imports in the three months after July 1949 was certainly not wholly attributable to the passing of the U.S. recession. The autumn is always a period of seasonal increase in imports from Europe. But the recovery between July and October was about as great in 1949 ($23 million) as it had been in 1948 ($26 million) and in 1947 ($22 million). When the change from July to September only is considered, the increase in 1949 ($19 million) was greater than in the two preceding years ($13 million in 1948, $6 million in 1947). It is clear, therefore, that, even after correction for seasonal increases, imports from Europe at least held their own and probably expanded following the low point in July 1949. If imports had been seriously held back in anticipation of the devaluations, the sharpest decline would have been expected in the few months before the devaluations occurred and when the expectation of the devaluations became strongest.[4]

[4] U.S. imports from the United Kingdom, whose currency devaluation was no doubt most discussed in the summer of 1949, also showed at least the normal recovery in the latter part of the summer, after having reached a low of $14.1 million as early as April:

UNITED STATES IMPORTS FROM THE UNITED KINGDOM

(*million U.S. dollars*)

	1947	1948	1949
July	18.6	23.6	15.1
August	17.1	23.7	16.1
September	15.7	21.5	20.6
October	18.4	27.1	18.9
Change: July to September	−2.9	−2.1	+5.5
July to October	−0.2	+3.5	+3.8

As indicated in the lower section of Chart 1, the same parallelism between imports and industrial production in the downswing is shown by an earlier short U.S. cycle, from 1937 through the middle of 1939. The import figures for this period have, again, been roughly corrected for seasonal variations. The smallness of the recovery in late 1938 and 1939 was probably attributable to the impact of the impending war situation in Europe which affected the export supply situation.

In the first half of 1950, when U.S. industrial production had recovered to about its 1948 level, there was a similar recovery in U.S. imports from OEEC countries. For the first half of 1950 as a whole, imports from the non-devaluers, and also U.S. industrial output, were 2 per cent below the 1948 level, while imports from the devaluers were 3 per cent above the 1948 level.[5] These data would indicate, therefore, that the devaluers as a group had improved their position by something like 5 per cent, measured either against industrial production or against the non-devaluers. This figure is also in rough correspondence with the findings in section 1.

The conclusion to be drawn from these data, therefore, is that the main determinant of the fluctuations in the value of U.S. imports from OEEC countries in the period from 1948 through the middle of 1950 was the state of the U.S. economy, and that the recovery in imports which started in the middle of 1949 and continued in 1950 was attributable in large part to the continued improvement in the economy. Imports into the United States from the devaluing countries in the first half of 1950 were 3 per cent above 1948, 15 per cent above the first half of 1949, and 25 per cent above the third quarter of 1949 (all figures seasonally corrected). The part of the increase attributable to the devaluations may be put at the order of magnitude of 5 per cent.[6] Reductions of imports from Europe in anticipation of the devaluations were not of such magnitude as to stand out clearly against the broad downswing in the first half of 1949 and the upswing in the second half.

Other factors

If, however, all increases in U.S. imports from Europe which are not related to changes in U.S. business conditions are attributed to the devaluations, the effects of the devaluations will be overestimated since a number of other factors also tended to increase European exports to the United States.

Ever since the end of World War II, the inflationary domestic

---

[5] All figures seasonally corrected, and with the same rough correction coefficients used for both devaluers and non-devaluers.
[6] The equivalent increase in the volume of imports attributable to the devaluations would be roughly 20 per cent.

markets in Europe had been a factor limiting exports to the United States. Gradually, in one country after another, as inflationary conditions were brought under control, the export supply situation tended to ease. In the period under consideration, from 1948 to 1950, the general tendency in this direction continued. The increase in U.S. imports from Germany, for instance, from $10 million in the first half of 1948 to $31 million in the first half of 1950, probably must be attributed in part to the improvement of economic and financial conditions in Germany.

Some European countries, most notably the United Kingdom, engaged in "export drives" toward dollar markets both before and after the devaluations, and some of the efforts of these drives made in 1948 or 1949 may have come to fruition only in 1950. But it would be very difficult to assess the importance of this.

One particular measure to stimulate exports to the United States may well be mentioned here. Early in September 1949, just before the devaluations, the Netherlands granted exporters to the United States the right to retain for their own use 10 per cent of their dollar proceeds.[7] These dollars can be used for import transactions and thus create an implicit rate for this 10 per cent substantially above the official buying rate which applies to the remaining 90 per cent of the export proceeds. In practice, therefore, this measure constitutes an additional degree of devaluation on exports [8] to the United States and Canada. On the basis of very approximate information concerning the implicit rates applying to these "export dollars" in the Netherlands, the additional depreciation would appear to be about 5 per cent, so that the actual effective devaluation for the Netherlands (as far as exports to the United States and Canada are concerned) should be put at about 35 per cent rather than 30 per cent.

U.S. Imports Following Outbreak of Korean Hostilities

The developments in U.S. imports after the middle of 1950 cannot be expected to give much evidence that is relevant to estimating the effects of devaluation. The very sharp upsurge of imports from all countries after that date was related primarily to rearmament and the accumulation of inventories and, as the following figures [9] show, was far in excess

[7] A similar system had been in operation in France for a long time prior to the devaluations and was instituted in Germany in the middle of 1950 (and repealed in March 1951). Only in the Netherlands, however, could the effects of the introduction of this system obscure the effects of the September 1949 devaluation itself.

[8] As dollar imports are far larger than dollar exports, the corresponding additional devaluation on the import side may be considered as negligible.

[9] The quarterly data are corrected for seasonal variation. For imports, the 1950 data given are annual rates.

THE SEPTEMBER 1949 DEVALUATIONS   13

of what would have been expected on the basis of the increase in U.S. industrial activity alone:

	1948	1949	1950 I	II	III	IV
U.S. industrial production						
(*1935-39 = 100*)	192	176	183	195	205	216
Imports from OEEC countries						
(*million U.S. dollars*)	977	842	980	1020	1360	1600

In such a market situation, relative prices are likely to account for little of the change, possibilities of immediate purchase and anticipations of future price rises for much more. It may be instructive, nevertheless, to show how imports from individual European countries in the second half of 1950 compared with those in the second half of 1949. As indicated by Table 5, there was an average increase of imports into

TABLE 5. VALUE OF U.S. IMPORTS FROM OEEC COUNTRIES, SECOND HALF OF 1949 AND OF 1950

Exporting Countries	Second Half 1949	Second Half 1950	Percentage Change
	(*million U.S. dollars*)		
A. Devaluers			
United Kingdom	114.6	208.6	182
France	30.5	90.8	298
Germany	17.7	72.7	411
Netherlands	32.2	58.2	181
Norway	11.0	21.3	194
Sweden	30.9	35.9	116
Six devaluers	236.9	487.5	206 [1]
B. Non-devaluers			
Belgium	39.1	80.8	207
Switzerland	47.7	65.7	138
Italy	36.3	68.8	190
Three non-devaluers	123.1	215.3	175 [1]
C. A + B	360.0	702.8	195 [1]
D. All OEEC Countries	402.4	777.3	193 [1]
Ratio, devaluers to non-devaluers			$\frac{206}{175} = 1.18$

[1] Weighted average. The unweighted arithmetic averages are 230 for the devaluers and 178 for the non-devaluers. But in view of the large relative changes it is preferable to use *geometric* unweighted averages, if unweighted averages are used at all; they are 212 and 176, respectively, yielding a ratio of 1.20.

Source: Economic Cooperation Administration, *26th Report for the Public Advisory Board* and U.S. Bureau of Census. All figures are U.S. import figures.

the United States from OEEC countries of nearly 100 per cent, the devaluers' increase being 18 per cent larger than the non-devaluers. But it is doubtful whether this difference can be regarded as significant when the movement in the same direction of the two group figures, and the spread of the components around the average, are so large.

4. Exports to Other Western Hemisphere Markets

Changes in European exports to other countries in the Western Hemisphere may usefully be considered in this paper together with changes in exports to the United States. The Western Hemisphere is a concept wider than the "dollar area," and the meaning of the "dollar area" varies for different European countries.[10] It is, nevertheless, proper to examine here the course of European trade with the Western Hemisphere as a whole, because even the countries outside the "dollar area" are important suppliers of raw materials and foodstuffs for Europe which can be substituted for imports from the United States.

The movements of Europe's exports to Canada and the rest of the Western Hemisphere, and, as a standard of comparison, the exports of the United States to the same markets, are shown by the data in Table 6. The substantial increase of Germany's exports stands out most strikingly. In some individual markets, imports from Germany increased by several hundred per cent, usually from a very low initial figure. These increases reflected the recovery of markets lost by Germany during the war, and they were to be expected in the light of the rapid increase in Germany's industrial production. There is no reason to believe that somewhat similar increases would not have occurred without any depreciation of the German currency. If Germany is omitted, the exports of the devaluers to other Western Hemisphere markets would show a decrease of $18 million.

Even disregarding Germany, however, it appears that in the Western Hemisphere the devaluers on the whole did better than the non-devaluers. Germany excluded, the devaluers' exports decreased by only 3 per cent, while those of the non-devaluers decreased by 24 per cent and those of the United States by 15 per cent. The total of the devaluers reflects, moreover, primarily the United Kingdom's exports, which amounted to over 70 per cent of the total of the group in the first half of 1949. An unweighted average of the percentage changes of six countries, excluding Germany, gives +24 per cent, while the unweighted average of the percentages for the non-devaluers was −21 per cent.

[10] See Fernando A. Vera, "A Note on Payments Relations Between Latin American and EPU Countries," *Staff Papers*, Vol. I, pp. 465–70 (April 1951).

TABLE 6. VALUE OF EXPORTS OF WESTERN EUROPE AND UNITED STATES TO WESTERN HEMISPHERE OUTSIDE UNITED STATES, FIRST HALF OF 1949 AND OF 1950 [1]

Exporting Country	Importing Country or Area	First Half 1949	First Half 1950	Difference	Percentage Change
		(million U.S. dollars)			
A. Devaluers					
United Kingdom	Canada + Latin America	486	422	− 64	− 13
	Canada	159	161	+ 2	+ 1
	Latin America	327	261	− 66	− 20
Denmark	Canada + Latin America	6	9	+ 3	+ 51
France	"	89	127	+ 38	+ 43
Germany	"	16	49	+ 33	+ 206
Netherlands	"	27	27	0	0
Norway	"	8	11	+ 3	+ 40
Sweden	"	43	45	+ 2	+ 5
Seven devaluers	Canada + Latin America	675	690	+ 15	+ 2
	Canada	174	173	+ 1	0
	Latin America	501	517	+ 16	+ 3
Devaluers, excl. Germany	Canada + Latin America	659	641	− 18	− 3
B. Non-devaluers					
Belgium	Canada + Latin America	80	60	− 20	− 25
Switzerland	"	53	49	− 4	− 7
Italy	"	110	75	− 35	− 32
Three non-devaluers	Canada + Latin America	243	184	− 59	− 24
	Canada	21	18	− 3	− 13
	Latin America	222	166	− 56	− 25
C. United States	Canada + Latin America	2,613	2,228	−385	− 15
	Canada	1,044	929	−115	− 11
	Latin America	1,569	1,299	−270	− 17
D. A + B + C	Canada + Latin America	3,531	3,102	−429	− 12

[1] For convenience, the term "Latin America" is used here to describe all countries in the Western Hemisphere except the United States and Canada.

Source: *Direction of International Trade* (United Nations, International Monetary Fund, and International Bank for Reconstruction and Development), January–June 1950 and January–July 1950.

16   INTERNATIONAL MONETARY FUND STAFF PAPERS

In trying to isolate the effect of the devaluations on exports to markets in the Western Hemisphere outside the United States, allowance must also be made for other factors. One factor is the change in general import demand. In the absence of data on national income or industrial production such as were used for the United States—and such data, even if available, might not be good short-run indicators of import demand—probably the best indicator of fluctuations in total import demand is the value or the volume of imports from the United States plus Europe.

As shown by Table 6, total imports of the area from Europe and the United States decreased by 12 per cent in value terms between the first half of 1949 and the first half of 1950. After adjustment for price changes,[11] the decline in the volume of imports would be about 5 per cent. It appears reasonable to assume that the shift in the demand curve for imports, as distinguished from the actual reduction in the quantity of imports, was somewhere between 12 per cent and 5 per cent. To the extent that demand for imports was regulated on the basis of available foreign exchange, the value percentage would appear to be the significant indicator. To the extent that it was determined by market demand, the volume figure would constitute a minimum estimate of the decline in demand, the decline in import prices having kept the volume of imports somewhat above what it would have been at unchanged prices. On balance it seems reasonable to conclude that import demand in the area was about 10 per cent less in the first half of 1950 than in the same period in 1949.[12] In the absence of any special factor, imports from the United States and from Europe might have been expected to be affected in the same way and therefore to have fallen by 10 per cent. Imports from the devaluers actually declined by 3 per cent, if Germany is excluded and rose by 3 per cent, if Germany is included. Thus, an improvement in export value from 7 to 13 per cent may therefore be attributed to the devaluations (together with any other factors).

It cannot, however, be taken for granted that all shifts in trade in the period considered were due to changes in relative prices. Where, between 1949 and 1950, the importing country intensified its restrictions against imports from the United States, the resulting increase in imports from Europe may reflect the inability to obtain licenses for im-

[11] Assumed at a reduction of roughly 15 per cent for imports from Europe, 5 per cent for imports from the United States.
[12] It is beyond the scope of this paper to seek an explanation of this reduction in demand for imports. It may be associated in some countries with changes in export proceeds; in others with changes in monetary policies, or with the completion of certain large investment programs. Intensified import restrictions may also have been a factor.

ports from the United States rather than the increased attractiveness of European prices. During the period, Brazil, Chile, and Peru appear to have intensified discrimination against the United States; but Colombia, and possibly Argentina, seem to have relaxed their restrictions. While these changes naturally affected the import demand in each of these markets, their effects do not seem to have been such as to invalidate altogether the general conclusions suggested above. Specifically, it does not appear that all, or substantially all, the improvement of the position of the European devaluers in Latin America relative to the United States should be attributed to increased discrimination. Thus the non-devaluers, against whom discrimination was not nearly so generally directed as against the United States, on the whole did worse than the United States; and the following data on the percentage changes from the first half of 1949 to the first half of 1950 in the dollar value of exports from the United Kingdom and the United States to five markets which did not practice discrimination [13] show that the United Kingdom improved its position relative to the United States in four of them, and that the relative decline in the fifth market was negligible:

Importing Markets	From United Kingdom	From United States
Mexico	+ 28	− 11
Cuba	+ 15	+ 2
Netherlands Antilles	+ 21	− 14
Venezuela	− 33	− 32
Panama	+240	+110

In some countries in Latin America, imports were greatly affected by positions under payments agreements. It is impossible without a much more extensive study to appraise the effect of this factor and to isolate it from those of the devaluations. But it is probable that the violent changes, for instance, in trade with Argentina shown by the United Kingdom, France, and Italy reflect primarily changed positions under trade and payments agreements rather than changes in relative prices. U.K. exports to Argentina fell by 36 per cent, French exports tripled, and Italian exports were halved. For France and Italy the changes in the trade with Argentina were larger in dollar value than the changes with all other Western Hemisphere countries (outside the United States) combined, and in the opposite direction. Thus France's trade with this area excluding Argentina showed a decline, Italy's an increase. For the devaluers as a whole, however, the percentage change

[13] The figures for Canada (which, while practicing discrimination against imports from the United States, probably did not change the intensity of its restrictions during the period) show the same tendency: United Kingdom + 4 per cent, United States − 9 per cent.

18   INTERNATIONAL MONETARY FUND STAFF PAPERS

would not be greatly affected if exports to Argentina were excluded (from +3 per cent to +1 per cent), and the estimates derived above for the effects of devaluation on exports to this area, rough as they are, do not appear to need adjustment on this account.

5. Dollar Imports of Europe

Imports from United States

Attention must next be given to the effects of the devaluations on the imports of Europe from the Western Hemisphere. For this purpose,

TABLE 7. VALUE OF U.S. EXPORTS TO OEEC COUNTRIES, FIRST HALF OF 1949 AND OF 1950

Importing Countries	First Half 1949	First Half 1950	Difference	Percentage Change
		(million U.S. dollars)		
Austria	88.2	68.2	− 20.0	−23
Belgium	159.6	140.8	− 18.8	−12
Denmark	51.4	28.7	− 22.7	−15
France	327.9	195.8	−132.1	−40
Germany	445.4	239.5	−205.9	−46
Greece	68.9	63.6	− 5.3	− 8
Iceland	4.9	2.7	− 2.2	−45
Ireland	31.5	21.9	− 9.6	−31
Italy	305.2	206.0	− 99.2	−33
Netherlands	153.8	132.9	− 20.9	−14
Norway	56.1	38.3	− 17.8	−32
Portugal	34.4	21.0	− 13.4	−39
Sweden	45.3	45.4	+ 0.1	0
Switzerland	84.1	55.2	− 28.9	−34
Turkey	39.9	44.0	+ 4.1	+10
United Kingdom	391.2	244.0	−147.2	−38
Total	2,287.8	1,548.0	−739.8	−32

Source: Economic Cooperation Administration, *26th Report for the Public Advisory Board.*

it seems reasonable to compare imports before and after devaluation and to select for this comparison data for periods sufficiently near the devaluations and preferably in such a manner as to eliminate seasonal fluctuations. The choice of the first half of 1950 compared with the first half of 1949 is, therefore, logical. Data covering U.S. exports to OEEC countries in these two periods (Table 7) show a decline of about $740 million (equal to an annual rate of $1.5 billion) or 32 per cent, for the total value of imports from the United States to the OEEC countries of Europe. Is this decline attributable to the devaluations?

The suggestion is often made that the decline may have been due

THE SEPTEMBER 1949 DEVALUATIONS 19

largely to the intensification of restrictions; this intensification was, however, practically limited to the sterling area, and the United Kingdom, Iceland, and Ireland account for only one fifth of the total decline. The percentage declines are, moreover, strikingly similar for countries with very different economic conditions and trade policies. In order of magnitude, the following percentage declines are all within a narrow range: Germany 46 per cent, Iceland 45 per cent, France 40 per cent, Portugal 39 per cent, the United Kingdom 38 per cent, Switzerland 34 per cent, Italy 33 per cent. Obviously this general movement cannot be ascribed to increased restrictions.

It is also striking that the percentages for the countries which did not devalue much or at all are not particularly out of line with those for the devaluers. Switzerland and Italy are close to France and the United Kingdom, Belgium close to the Netherlands and Denmark. But this fact in itself would not necessarily invalidate the hypothesis that the change in all countries was due to the devaluations. It is conceivable that in each country the main effect of the devaluations was to make imports from the United States relatively more expensive than imports from the devaluers—not more expensive than domestic commodities. If that were true, the total volume of imports would not change much, the main substitution being between imports from the United States and imports from the devaluers rather than between imports from the United States and home goods. Since the change in the relative prices of imports was felt by all countries whether they devalued or not, the percentage decline in dollar imports due to devaluation could have been the same in both devaluing and non-devaluing countries.

But if this were the explanation of the similarity of the movements in imports from the United States, the recovery of exports by the devaluers to other OEEC countries would be expected to have been more pronounced than that of the exports by the non-devaluers; indeed, the exports of the latter to Western Europe might be expected to have declined just as much as U.S. exports to Western Europe, or more, because they included a lower proportion of essential, low elasticity imports than the imports from the United States. But as the figures in Table 8, column 1, show, there was no such contrast between the movements of intra-European exports of devaluers and non-devaluers. All increased their exports to OEEC countries, most of them by substantial percentages. While exports from the United States to all OEEC countries combined declined by 32 per cent in value and at least 25 per cent in volume, Italy increased its exports by 39 per cent in volume, in this respect doing better than two thirds of the devaluers. Switzerland, which did not devalue at all, improved its exports by 15 per cent, and Belgium, though nearly at the bottom of the list, still increased its exports to OEEC countries by 13 per cent. While the three "non-devaluers" did not, on the average, do quite so well as the other OEEC countries, their exports did not suffer in absolute terms and, indeed, showed substantial increases.

TABLE 8. CHANGE FROM FIRST HALF OF 1949 TO FIRST HALF OF 1950 IN EXPORTS FROM TWELVE [1] OEEC COUNTRIES TO NORTHWESTERN AND SOUTHERN EUROPE [2]

Exporting Countries	Percentage Change in Volume of Exports [3] (1)	Percentage Change in Export Price Index [4] (2)
Germany	+78	−36
Netherlands	+61	−29
Denmark	+42	−35
Italy	+39	−18
France	+26	−16
Sweden	+26	−25
United Kingdom	+23	−28
Norway	+22	−34
Switzerland	+15	− 5
Austria	+15	−33
Belgium	+13	−26
Ireland	+ 5	−29
Total	+33	−24

[1] Comparable data not available for Iceland, Portugal, and Turkey.
[2] Area covered includes Spain but figures are not significantly affected by this.
[3] Value figures from *Direction of International Trade* (United Nations, International Monetary Fund, and International Bank for Reconstruction and Development) adjusted for export price changes shown in column 2.
[4] Export price index expressed in terms of dollars. Data are based on indices in *International Financial Statistics* (International Monetary Fund).

It has been observed above (section 2) that the differences in the export price levels of the various European countries were, by the middle of 1950, by no means in line with the changes in the gold values of their currencies. The decline in the export price level in terms of dollars given in Table 3 is, therefore, shown in column 2 of Table 8, to see whether the development in the volume of exports in intra-European trade may perhaps be explained *not* by differences in the degree of devaluation, but rather by differences in the ultimate change in the export price level. The comparison is unrewarding. Large price declines are found both at the top and at the bottom of the list, and in other respects, too, there is little correlation between the two series of figures.

At this stage, therefore, the conclusions are (a) that the increases in intra-European trade were not significantly associated with changes in the relative prices of the exporting countries; (b) that the general and sharp decrease of imports from the United States was not, or at least not solely, attributable to the relative rise in prices of imports from the United States compared with prices of imports from European sources of supply; and (c) that the decrease in imports from the United States cannot, except for a fraction, be explained by increased restrictions.

CHART 2. U.S. Exports to OEEC Countries, January 1947–June 1950

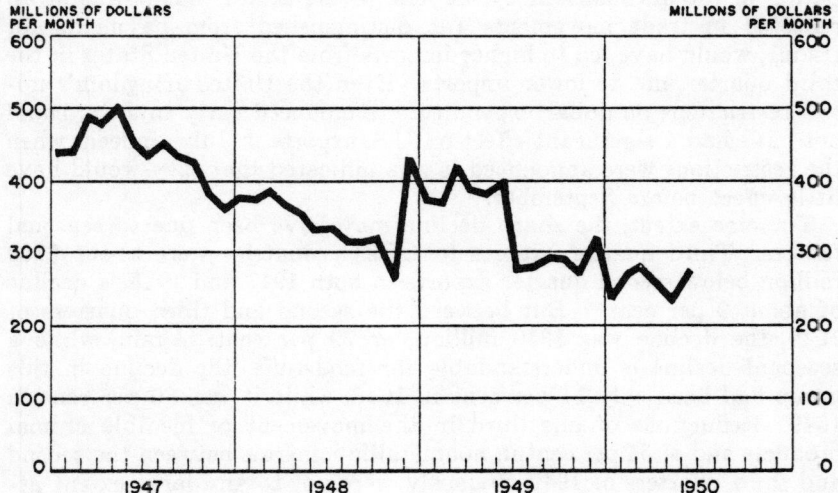

This means that the comparisons between the first half of 1949 and the first half of 1950 do not provide a satisfactory explanation of the decline in U.S. exports to Europe. It may be well to turn to statistics covering a somewhat longer period, i.e., the monthly value of U.S. exports to the OEEC countries for a period of $3\frac{1}{2}$ years (Chart 2). The pattern of the curve appears striking. From early 1947 through the fall of 1948, and again from the middle of 1949 on, these exports showed a very smooth decline which seemed to slow down gradually. But the figures for December 1948 (a month affected by the November maritime strike) and the first six months of 1949 were exceptionally high. It would appear that what requires explanation is not so much the level of exports in 1950 as the high rate prevailing in the first half of 1949.

The tendency for U.S. exports to OEEC countries to be higher in 1949 than could be expected on the basis of the 1947-48 trend is not surprising in general. While the European Recovery Plan had started

22　　　INTERNATIONAL MONETARY FUND STAFF PAPERS

in the spring of 1948, it was gathering force only toward the end of that year. It was also natural that, with ECA help gradually declining, exports in the fiscal year 1950 would be less than in the fiscal year 1949. But while these factors could explain some gradual changes, they do not seem to give any explanation of the marked plateau in the first six months of 1949 or the abrupt fall (from $400 million to $274 million) between June and July of that year.

Nor again can this fall be attributed to the devaluations which occurred less than two weeks before the end of the third quarter. Anticipation of the devaluations by traders, to the extent that it was at all reflected in trade movements (as distinguished from payments for trade), would have led to higher imports from the United States in the third quarter, not to lower imports. Even the United Kingdom's initial restrictions on dollar expenditure, announced early in July, could not have had a significant effect on U.S. exports in July; indeed, when the restrictions were announced it was indicated that they would have little effect before September.[14]

To some extent, the sharp decline may have been due to seasonal factors. Third quarter exports to OEEC countries were about $100 million below second quarter exports in both 1947 and 1948, a decline of about 9 per cent.[15] But between the second and third quarters of 1949, the decline was $350 million, or 29 per cent. Again, while a seasonal decline is understandable for foodstuffs, the decline in this group had been only 11 per cent in 1948, while it was 30 per cent in 1949. Reductions of one third in the movement of inedible animal products and of 54 per cent in nonmetallic minerals between the second and third quarters of 1949 obviously were not to any large extent attributable to seasonal factors.

The abrupt decline in exports in July may have been due in part to uncertainty in the spring of 1949 as to the magnitude of the ECA program for 1949–50, which made governments hesitant in granting import licenses and thus led to a reduced rate of imports in July. Whatever the explanation, the first half of 1949 clearly cannot be used as a base period from which to judge the effects of the devaluations.

The only possible course is therefore to measure the post-devaluation rate of Europe's imports in relation to imports in the third quarter of 1949. These data (Table 9) show a decline of only $134 million, or 8 per cent, between the two periods compared. Six of the 14 countries show increases rather than decreases in their imports from the United States.

[14] *The Times,* London, July 7, 1949. But restrictions may have been tightened in practice some time earlier.
[15] It is doubtful whether even these declines were seasonal. Half of the 1948 decline, for instance, was accounted for by reduced exports of merchant vessels.

THE SEPTEMBER 1949 DEVALUATIONS   23

Before this change can be related to the depreciations, a further analysis is required from two points of view. First, account should be taken of seasonal factors; secondly, it would be desirable to eliminate any part of the reduction that was clearly due to the improved supply position in Europe made possible by increased production. On the first point, it should be noted that cotton exports have a normal seasonal low in the third quarter of the year and tobacco exports a seasonal

TABLE 9. VALUE OF U.S. EXPORTS TO OEEC COUNTRIES, THIRD QUARTER OF 1949 AND FIRST HALF OF 1950

Importing Countries	Third Quarter 1949 [1]	First Half 1950	Difference	Percentage Change
		(million U.S. dollars)		
Austria	44	68	+ 24	+35
Belgium	153	141	− 12	− 9
Denmark	35	29	− 6	−21
France	150	196	+ 46	+23
Germany	382	240	−142	−59
Greece	104	64	− 40	−62
Ireland	27	22	− 5	−23
Italy	126	206	+ 80	+39
Netherlands	126	133	+ 7	+ 5
Norway	41	38	− 3	− 8
Portugal	17	21	+ 4	+17
Sweden	44	45	+ 1	+ 2
Switzerland	57	55	− 2	− 4
United Kingdom	312	244	− 68	−28
Total	1,680	1,546	−134	− 8

[1] Multiplied by 2 to give a half-yearly rate.
Source: Economic Cooperation Administration, *26th Report for the Public Advisory Board*.

high. Foodstuffs exports may also have a tendency to be low in the third quarter. Changes in foodstuffs supply conditions appear, however, to outweigh the effects of this seasonal tendency. Finally, the European coal supply became sufficient in 1950 virtually to eliminate the need for imports. The changes in these various categories are shown in Table 10, together with the residual change in all other exports, which was $36 million, or 4 per cent.[16]

[16] The procedure followed of eliminating cotton and tobacco precludes any inference on the effect of the devaluations on the imports of these two commodities. The following data for the first half of 1949 compared with the first half of 1950 indicate that the total decline for these two goods was only 4 per cent:

	First Half of 1949	First Half of 1950	Difference
		(million U.S. dollars)	
Cotton	339	337	− 2
Tobacco	64	48	−16
	403	385	−18

24   INTERNATIONAL MONETARY FUND STAFF PAPERS

Of the $175 million decline in foodstuffs exports, $153 million was accounted for by grains and grain preparations. This reduction in grains was not due to the devaluations. The price elasticity of demand for grains is negligible. The increased local currency price of grains could not in so short a period after the devaluations produce any increase in supply. The reduced import demand for grains was due to the improvement in European grain crops and would have occurred

TABLE 10. VALUE OF U.S. EXPORTS OF SELECTED COMMODITIES TO OEEC COUNTRIES, THIRD QUARTER OF 1949 AND FIRST HALF OF 1950

(In millions of U.S. dollars)

Commodities	Third Quarter 1949 [1]	First Half 1950	Difference
Cotton	139	336	+197
Tobacco	151	48	−103
Foodstuffs	528	353	−175
Coal	18	2	− 16
All other	828	792	− 36
Total	1,664	1,531	−133

[1] Multiplied by 2 to give a half-yearly rate.

Source: Economic Cooperation Administration, *26th Report for the Public Advisory Board*. Totals are slightly below those in Table 8 owing to apparent slight differences in coverage.

without the devaluations. The exports of wheat and rye to the OEEC countries from the Western Hemisphere and Australia show the following pattern during 1949 and 1950: [17]

	1949	1950
	(million metric tons)	
1st Quarter	3.8	2.4
2nd Quarter	4.2	2.6
3rd Quarter	3.1	2.1
4th Quarter	2.6	1.9

Value figures corresponding to these quantity figures are not available. Computed very roughly at a price of $80 a ton, these figures would indicate a reduction in value of $250 million between the first half of 1949 and the first half of 1950.

The residual decline of $36 million for all other commodities shown in Table 10 no doubt still contains some reductions for certain commodities that were due to supply factors. The decline in the export of steel mill products ($46 million, or more than the total residual

[17] Data are from Food and Agriculture Organization, *Monthly Bulletin*. They cover exports of wheat, wheat flour in wheat equivalents, and rye from Argentina, Australia, Canada, and the United States.

THE SEPTEMBER 1949 DEVALUATIONS 25

decline), for instance, is closely related to the increase in Europe's steel output.

Imports by countries of the commodities listed in Table 10 are not available for each OEEC country, but they may be obtained for the major countries, which account for 80 per cent of OEEC imports from the United States (Table 11). The two typically seasonal components

TABLE 11. CHANGES FROM THIRD QUARTER OF 1949 [1] TO FIRST HALF OF 1950 IN VALUE OF U.S. EXPORTS TO MAJOR OEEC COUNTRIES

(In millions of U.S. dollars)

Importing Countries	Cotton	Tobacco	Food	Coal	All Other	Total
Belgium	+ 10	—	− 31	—	+ 6	− 15
France	+ 39	− 2	+ 1	− 9	+17	+ 46
Germany	+ 34	− 8	−190	—	+16	−148
Italy	+ 53	+ 1	—	− 2	+28	+ 80
Netherlands	+ 14	+ 1	+ 12	− 1	−19	+ 7
Sweden	+ 4	—	+ 2	− 3	− 1	+ 2
Switzerland	—	− 1	+ 1	—	− 2	− 2
United Kingdom	+ 33	− 91	+ 15	—	−22	− 65
	+187	−100	−190	−15	+23	− 95
All other countries (residual figure)	+ 10	− 3	+ 15	− 1	−59	− 38
Total	+197	−103	−175	−16	−36	−133

[1] Multiplied by 2 to give a half-yearly rate.
Source: U.S. Department of Commerce, *Export and Import Trade with Leading Countries, January–June 1950,* and data in Table 8.

in Table 11 show consistent signs, high positive figures for cotton and, with two negligible exceptions, negative figures for tobacco. Food shows a number of increases, which may be seasonal, but they are far outweighed by the large decline shown by Germany. For coal all changes are, as might have been expected, negative. Attention should finally be concentrated on the "all other" column. Here, three countries (Belgium, Sweden, and Switzerland) show small changes, while the five other countries show three increases (France, Germany, and Italy) and two decreases (the Netherlands and the United Kingdom), the changes in each of these five countries being of the order of about $20 million. For the eight main countries combined, there is a slight increase of $23 million in the "all other" category, leaving a proportionately large decline ($59 million) for the "all other" category for the eight smaller countries combined.

The increase in imports of "other" goods in a number of countries and the smallness of the decrease in most other countries does not, of

TABLE 12. VALUE OF IMPORTS OF MAJOR OEEC COUNTRIES FROM WESTERN HEMISPHERE EXCLUDING THE UNITED STATES, FIRST HALF OF 1949 AND OF 1950

Importing Countries	Imports from Canada				Imports from Latin America			
	First Half 1949	First Half 1950	Difference	Percentage Change	First Half 1949	First Half 1950	Difference	Percentage Change
	(million U.S. dollars)				(million U.S. dollars)			
Belgium	21.8	18.2	− 3.6	−17	79.5	71.6	− 7.9	− 10
Denmark	2.4	0.3	− 2.1	−88	15.4	8.5	− 6.9	− 45
France	24.4	13.4	− 11.0	−45	125.7	142.9	+17.2	+ 14
Germany	7.1	4.1	− 3.0	−42	38.7	78.6	+39.9	+103
Italy	6.7	2.5	− 4.2	−63	88.5	82.7	− 5.8	− 7
Netherlands	6.0	4.1	− 1.9	−32	80.5	67.5	−13.0	− 16
Norway	6.1	4.7	− 1.4	−23	23.8	21.5	− 2.3	− 10
Sweden	2.9	1.7	− 1.2	−41	58.7	63.0	+ 4.3	+ 7
Switzerland	13.2	10.2	− 3.0	−23	39.0	44.9	+ 5.9	+ 15
United Kingdom	389.7	245.0	−144.7	−37	488.9	449.9	−39.0	− 8
Total	480.3	304.2	−176.1	−37	1,038.7	1,031.1	− 7.6	− 1

Source: *Direction of International Trade* (United Nations, International Monetary Fund, and International Bank for Reconstruction and Development), January–June 1950 and January–July 1950.

course, indicate that the devaluations were not effective in restraining demand for these goods. Before the devaluations there was in most European countries a large unsatisfied demand for dollar goods, which were kept out of the market by import restrictions. The devaluations, by raising the prices of dollar goods, reduced this excess demand. For some commodities they may just have eliminated it, thus rendering unnecessary the continuance of restrictions on their import. For others, where the excess demand was small or the price elasticity high, the devaluations may have reduced total demand below the level of the actual imports before the devaluations and thus released dollars for the import of other commodities. For the remaining commodities, finally, the devaluations made possible a reduction of the intensity of restrictions on two counts: first, because the higher prices of imports eliminated part of the demand, and second, because reduced imports of other goods made it possible to satisfy a greater proportion of the remaining demand.

Imports from other Western Hemisphere countries

Data on imports from Canada (Table 12) show on the whole percentage changes very similar to those found for imports from the United States (Table 7). It seems reasonable to assume, therefore, that in general the same factors were operative. Moreover, as much as four fifths of the imports from Canada, and as large a proportion of the reduction, were accounted for by the United Kingdom and should, therefore, be attributed to increased restrictions rather than to the devaluations. The decline for all the other major OEEC countries of imports from Canada was only $31 million, part of which was again not attributable to the devaluations.

The changes in imports from the rest of the Western Hemisphere show a rather close correlation with the changes in exports to that area (see Table 13), which suggests the probable effects of bilateral arrange-

TABLE 13. CHANGES FROM FIRST HALF OF 1949 TO FIRST HALF OF 1950 IN VALUE OF TRADE OF MAJOR OEEC COUNTRIES WITH LATIN AMERICA

(In millions of U.S. dollars)

Country	Changes in Exports	Changes in Imports
United Kingdom	−53.8	−39.0
France	+38.7	+17.2
Germany	+32.5	+39.9
Sweden	+ 2.2	+ 4.3
Belgium	−16.2	− 7.9
Switzerland	− 5.6	+ 5.9
Italy	−34.1	− 5.8

Source: See Table 12.

ments. For all countries combined, imports declined by only $7.6 million, less than one per cent, between the two periods.

6. The Role of Capital Movements

There are many indications that the deterioration of the trade position of the sterling area in the first half of 1949 was aggravated by movements of capital, despite the tight exchange control practiced by members of the sterling area.[18] This exchange control could not, in any case, be effective in preventing exporters from keeping export proceeds abroad for a short time, or importers from acquiring short-run foreign exchange positions. Exchange control will see to it that export proceeds are delivered (not without some leaks) within a reasonable time of the export of the goods, and that imports come into the country within a reasonable time after the exchange has been made available. But the flexibility afforded by these moderate time spans is sufficient to build up considerable balances abroad over a short period, and an outward movement of capital of this kind is likely when devaluation appears probable in the near future. There must, moreover, have been other possibilities of taking capital out of the United Kingdom, which were used more intensively when the devaluation of sterling appeared imminent.

It is not easy to find statistical evidence of the magnitude of the capital outflow in 1949. There are no quarterly balance of payments statistics for the United Kingdom, and the half-yearly data hide the deterioration between the first and second quarter and, even more important, the sharp reversal between the third and fourth quarter of 1949. The only evidence available, therefore, is (a) the quarterly data on the United Kingdom's gold and dollar reserves, (b) contributions to these reserves from ECA, the Canadian Loan, and Fund drawings, (c) the quarterly balance of payments of the United States with the

---

[18] "Of course, when people saw that our reserves were falling rapidly they began to wonder if their confidence in sterling was well placed. Talk had started last spring about our exchange rates in a way which led to doubt as to whether they were not too high. Once it was suspected that a lowering might take place, people tried to turn pounds sterling into gold and dollars by all sorts of devices. That is a very difficult thing to stop, and there has been a good deal of it going on latterly. With low reserves we can't afford losses of that kind. We had to take some steps to stop it.

"That was one reason which convinced us of the need to lower the sterling rate of exchange to a new rate which would stop this drain on our reserves."

From speech by Sir Stafford Cripps, on September 18, 1949, announcing the devaluation of sterling (*Financial Times*, London, September 19, 1949).

sterling area, and (d) scattered data on trade between the sterling area and the dollar area. These data are presented in Table 14.

Attention should be focused on column 5 of this table, entitled "other." It is derived as a residual from a comparison of the financing items to the right and the known trade items (United States and Canada) and invisibles and known private capital movements (United States only) to the left. This column shows that the United Kingdom paid out about $300 million a quarter in gold and dollars in 1948 to settle the net positions of the whole sterling area with the rest of the dollar area and to make payments to Europe and other countries. It is unlikely that at that time the figure included any abnormal hidden outflow of capital to the dollar area. The net gold and dollar outpayments covered in this residual category declined to $196 million in the first quarter of 1949, but then increased to $329 million in the third quarter. The sudden sharp reversal to a net receipt of $94 million in the fourth quarter points in particular to the presumption of an outflow of capital in the third quarter, followed by a reflux in the fourth quarter.

It is hazardous to derive from these figures any estimate of the magnitude of the speculative capital movement, because the figures contain also some current items (such as trade of the whole sterling area with the dollar area in Latin America) and ordinary capital movements with Canada and Latin America, as well as all errors and omissions. In some quarters, the fluctuations in these other factors may well have been larger than the total changes shown by the figures in column 5, of which they form a part.

The break between the third and fourth quarter of 1949 (about $425 million)[19] is, however, so sharp that speculative capital movements must be responsible for a large part of it. The improvement in current items included in this change is not likely to have exceeded, say, $50 million. This would leave some $375 million attributable to unrecorded capital movements (including unrecorded capital movements with the United States) and gold and dollar payments outside the dollar area. In the second half of 1949, the United Kingdom paid $118 million in gold and dollars to countries outside the dollar and the sterling areas. Under the assumption that practically all these payments occurred in the third quarter and that there was no significant reflux of gold or dollars from these countries in the fourth quarter, there would remain some $250 million due to uncovered capital movements with the dollar area, roughly from − $150 million in the third quarter to + $100 million in the fourth quarter. This might have been represented by an outflow of $150 million in the third quarter, offset by a reflux of $100 million

---

[19] Close to the total improvement which was $537 million (col. 6) and the reversal in the reserve position, $488 million (col. 9).

TABLE 14. ELEMENTS OF STERLING AREA BALANCE OF PAYMENTS WITH DOLLAR AREA, 1948-SECOND QUARTER OF 1950

(In millions of U.S. Dollars)

Quarters	Trade with U.S. and Canada			Other Known Transactions with U.S. (4)	Other [1] (5)	Total Surplus or Deficit (−) (6)	Gold and Dollar Financing		
	Exports (1)	Imports (2)	Balance (3)				Outer sterling area gold sales [2] (7)	Aid received [3] (8)	Change in U.K. reserves [4] (9)
1948: Average	490	764	−274	− 6	−328	−608	185	367 [5]	56
1949: I	488	722	−234	6	−196	−424	102	378	− 56
II	427	863	−436	−23	−274	−733	108	363	262
III	352	701	−349	27	−329	−651	124	302	225
IV	406	613	−207	−1	94	−114	95	282	−263
1950: I	440	472	− 32	42	− 26	− 16	65	248	−297
II	514	483	31	100	− 40	91	96	251	−438

[1] Includes the following transactions: (1) U.K. non-trade transactions with Canada and all U.K. transactions with dollar area outside the United States and Canada; (2) U.K. gold and dollar payments to (−), or receipts from, non-dollar, non-sterling countries; and (3) other sterling area non-trade transactions with Canada and all transactions with dollar area outside United States and Canada.

[2] Outer sterling area gold sales to the United States and the United Kingdom. Quarterly figures on sales to the United Kingdom estimated from available half-yearly figures on basis of sales to the United States and changes in Union of South Africa gold reserves.

[3] ECA aid (net of counterpart funds), drawings on Canadian loan, and drawings on International Monetary Fund.

[4] A minus sign indicates an increase.

[5] Includes South African Gold Loan to United Kingdom in 1948.

Sources: *United Kingdom Balance of Payments, 1946 to 1950* (Cmd. 8065, October 1950); U.S. Department of Commerce. *Survey of Current Business*, June 1950; Dominion Bureau of Statistics, *Canadian Statistical Review.*

THE SEPTEMBER 1949 DEVALUATIONS   31

in the fourth quarter, if residual current items were in balance in the fourth quarter, or, say, by an outflow of $125 million and an inflow of $125 million, if there was a debit on account of residual current items of $25 million in the fourth quarter.

It is by no means inconceivable that an outflow of capital of, say, $150 million could have occurred in the third quarter of 1949 as a

TABLE 15. IMPROVEMENT BETWEEN NINE MONTHS ENDED SEPTEMBER 1949 AND NINE MONTHS ENDED JUNE 1950 IN STERLING AREA BALANCE OF PAYMENTS WITH DOLLAR AREA

(In millions of U.S. dollars)

	United Kingdom	Other Sterling Area	Total
Increase in exports	−49	142	93
Decrease in imports	326	392	718
Trade balance	277	534	811
Other known transactions with U.S.	....	....	131
Other	....	....	827
Total improvement	....	....	1,769
Reduction in sterling area gold sales	....	....	78
Reduction in aid	....	....	262
Change in movement in U.K. reserves	....	....	1,429 [1]
	....	....	1,769

[1] From decline of $431 million in first period to increase of $998 million in the second period.
Source: Table 14 and sources given there.

result of nothing but adjustments on the part of traders of leads and lags in connection with trade payments. Total trade of the sterling area with the United States and Canada in the third quarter was at a rate of $350 million a month. Thus, a capital movement of $175 million from the sterling area to the dollar area could be brought about by a two-week shift in payment practices, paying imports two weeks earlier than was customary and receiving payment for exports two weeks later.

If somewhat longer periods are compared, by using three quarters rather than one before and after the devaluations, the extent to which changes in "other" items should be considered as capital movements is less certain; but it is still clear, as Table 15 shows, that (a) more than half of the improvement is to be found outside the main section of trade with the United States and Canada; (b) nearly nine-tenths of the improvement in the trade position vis-à-vis the United States and Canada was due to decreased imports; and (c), that while the reduction

32   INTERNATIONAL MONETARY FUND STAFF PAPERS

in imports was about equally divided between the United Kingdom and the rest of the sterling area,[20] there was a net decrease in U.K. exports, offset by a larger increase in exports by the rest of the sterling area.

[20] On a percentage basis, the similarity in the decline was even more striking: 30 per cent for the United Kingdom, 33 per cent for the rest of the sterling area.

[9]

EXCESS LIQUIDITY AND EUROPEAN MONETARY REFORMS, 1944-1952

By John G. Gurley*

During the early postwar years in this country, there was much discussion concerning the probable effects of large liquid asset holdings on consumption and private investment spendings. Some economists, reasoning along strictly Keynesian lines, visualized these assets as influencing private spending only through changes in the interest rate. Many others, however, felt that excess liquidity would have a *direct* inflationary effect on the spending habits of both households and business firms. Nevertheless, few economists at this time were willing to argue that the conventional anti-inflationary measures were either unworkable or unfeasible in the face of so much excess liquidity. What was needed to turn aside the forces of inflation, it was argued, was a substantial government surplus[1] coupled with tight credit controls; many also urged the continuance of direct controls over prices and wages until these forces had subsided. The existence of excess liquidity was largely taken for granted with the result that, except for a few digressions, the discussion centered around the question of how inflationary these holdings would be and not around the question of how to rid the economy of them.

However, in many areas of Europe at this time, the second question commanded more interest than the first, primarily because it was generally agreed that there was imminent danger of hyperinflation if the volume of liquid assets were not drastically reduced.[2] Further, a wide-

* The author is assistant professor of economics at Princeton University. He is indebted to W. J. Baumol, E. O. Edwards, and P. J. Strayer, all of whom offered valuable comments on earlier drafts. He also wishes to acknowledge the aid received in Europe during the summer of 1951 as a result of discussions with numerous individuals, too many to be listed here. The study was made possible by a grant from the Merrill Foundation, which the author gratefully acknowledges.

[1] Actually, of course, if one is free to alter both government expenditures and tax rates, there are many government deficits that would be just as deflationary as any given surplus.

[2] The difference in attitude between U.S. and many European economists on this question was due partly to the fact that the liquid asset-national income ratio was substantially higher in most European countries than it was in the United States after the war. However, whatever this ratio, quantity theorists tended to stress more vigorously the direct inflationary threat of these assets than did Keynesian theorists. In this connection it is interesting to note that where Keynesian doctrine in Europe was particularly strong—in England and the Scandinavian countries—either no steps to reduce excess liquidity were undertaken or else only token gestures in this direction were made.

spread feeling existed that if the assets were allowed to remain in the system they would undermine any monetary-fiscal program aimed at deflation. Through European eyes, the presence of large liquid asset holdings created a serious stumbling block in the path leading to inflation control. As a consequence, one of the principal anti-inflationary weapons used in this area of the world was monetary reform[3] which, in one way or another, swept away large portions of liquid assets accumulated by the public in the course of war and occupation. Many of these programs were designed to slow down the course of inflation and to prepare the way for the utilization of more orthodox anti-inflationary programs.

A study of the European monetary reforms, therefore, should throw some light on the broad topic of "the economics of excessively liquid economies." In this paper it is the intention of the author to consider: (1) the various ways in which the large liquid holdings of the European population were swept away, (2) the factors that induced many European countries to center their attacks on these holdings, (3) the degree of success attained by the programs, and (4) the conditions under which the monetary reform became a necessary part of any broad anti-inflationary program. It is hoped that this study will focus the attention of economists on a relatively neglected aspect of anti-inflationary policy, and that it will prove useful in further analysis of the rôle of liquidity.

I. *The Extent and Nature of the European Monetary Reforms*

The monetary reform was used widely throughout Europe during the post-World War II period. In fact, several countries in eastern Europe[4] relied upon this monetary device more than once, the most recent repeat performances taking place in Poland (October 1950), Rumania (January 1952), and Bulgaria (May 1952).

It was, however, a western European country, Belgium, which opened the attack on inflation in this manner by introducing a monetary reform program as early as October 1944, several months before the fighting within her borders terminated. Within a year, four other western European nations had followed suit, and these reforms were matched, or were soon to be matched, by a host of similar measures elsewhere.[5] Altogether, there were twenty-four monetary reforms in

---

[3] The expression, "monetary reform," has been used in the literature to describe a variety of monetary and banking programs. In this paper, however, it refers to those particular measures that reduced, or partially blocked for periods ranging from a few days to several years, the large liquid asset holdings of households and businesses.

[4] For the purposes of this paper, eastern Europe includes Finland, Greece, and all European countries (including the USSR) which now have communist governments.

[5] As we shall see, though, some of these programs were not designed primarily as anti-inflationary weapons.

Europe from the fall of 1944 to mid-1952. Some countries, such as Great Britain, Sweden, and Italy, did not utilize this technique at all; the majority employed it only once during the early years of the postwar period; and several, as mentioned above, used it two or three times.

The monetary reform, at one extreme, swept away the major portion of liquid holdings during the first few days of the program. At the other extreme, no reduction in the supply of liquid assets took place; instead, a small portion of the assets was blocked for a short period of time and then released to its owners. Inasmuch as the liquid assets affected by the programs generally comprised only banknotes and bank deposits—sometimes government and other securities were included—the monetary reform was at times similar to a capital levy applied to an extremely narrow base. It was a once-and-for-all "tax" on claims to wealth; however, in most cases no tax receipts accrued to the State, since the face values of the assets were written down, and to this extent a portion of the assets completely disappeared from the economy. When the assets were blocked (and not swept away), the reform was a "forced asset-holding" scheme, analogous to a program of forced saving out of current income. Finally, it was a "reform" in the sense that new banknotes were always issued for the old ones; in some instances, the unit of account was changed along with the entire price and wage structures.

II. *The Principal Types and Provisions of European Monetary Reforms*

Despite the almost endless array of provisions contained in the monetary laws, it is possible to group these programs into three general types, based on the manner in which the various countries dealt with the excessive supply of liquid assets in their economies. There were, first, those monetary reforms that reduced the supply of liquid assets at the outset without blocking any portion of this supply. This "mopping-up" operation was accomplished through the compulsory exchange of old banknotes and "old" bank deposits for new ones at rates of exchange which effectively reduced the outstanding volume of these assets. Each family and business firm was permitted to exchange its holdings of banknotes and deposits for new ones at the established conversion rate, say, three-to-one as in the 1947 Austrian program. Occasionally, however, some basic amount was allowed exchange rights at par, and other par exchanges were sometimes made for emergency cases or for favored groups. Once these exchanges were consummated, though, the program's initial objective was realized: individuals and businesses owned a smaller volume of liquid assets, but they were free to spend whatever remained.

The second type of monetary reform embodied no immediate reduction in the supply of liquid assets, but instead provided for the immobilization of a portion of this supply in the form of blocked deposits at banks. Again, banknotes were called in and bank deposits were declared by their owners during a specified period of time. In this case, each family and business firm was permitted to convert its old assets for new ones at a one-to-one ratio, but only a certain amount of new money was turned over to it for free use. The "excess assets" were placed in special bank accounts which in general could not be drawn upon for the purchase of current goods and services. In short, individuals and businesses retained in full their prereform holdings of these assets, since these holdings were all converted at par, but they were permitted to spend only a certain portion of them.

The third type combined the primary features of the other two. Currency and bank deposits were, first of all, converted into new money at deflated rates of exchange, but a portion of the amount remaining was in turn frozen in blocked accounts. One thousand units of a currency, for example, would be exchanged for five hundred new units, and, of this amount, two hundred and fifty of the new units would be tied up in accounts not usable for current transactions.

In all three types, the monetary provisions often called for the registration of securities, life insurance policies, personal property, and other forms of wealth. The authorities' primary interest in doing this was to survey the distribution of these holdings for the purpose of later capital levies or capital increment taxes. Only occasionally was the supply of financial assets, other than currency and deposits, reduced or partially blocked. In a few cases, though, government bonds were converted at deflated rates, and in one instance the public debt was cancelled by the monetary law.

Using the above classification as a guide, Table I lists the European monetary reforms in chronological order and classifies each as either Type One, Two, or Three. Since a series of two or even three reforms occurred in some of the countries, the successive reforms for any one of these countries are identified with Roman numerals after the name of the country.

The table records twenty-four separate monetary reforms from October 1944 to May 1952. Of this total, eight were of Type one, twelve of Type Two, and only four of Type Three. One-half of the reforms were introduced before the end of 1945, and since mid-1948 there have been only three reforms, all of them taking place in eastern Europe. Further, of the last seven reforms, five were undertaken in eastern Europe and only two—those of West Germany and France—occurred in west European locales.[6] The countries of western Europe

---

[6] The French program involved no more than a temporary blocking of the 5,000 franc banknotes.

TABLE I.—CLASSIFICATION OF EUROPEAN MONETARY REFORMS

Country	Month and Year of Reform	One	Two	Three
Belgium	Oct. 1944		x	
Greece	Nov. 1944	x		
Poland I[a]	Dec. 1944		x	
Yugoslavia	Apr. 1945			x
France I	June 1945		x	
Austria I[b]	July 1945		x	
Denmark	July 1945		x	
Norway	Sept. 1945		x	
Netherlands[c]	Sept. 1945		x	
Czechoslovakia	Oct. 1945		x	
Austria II	Nov. 1945		x	
Hungary I	Dec. 1945	x		
Finland	Dec. 1945		x	
Hungary II	Aug. 1946	x		
Bulgaria I	Mar. 1947		x	
Rumania I	Aug. 1947			x
Austria III[d]	Nov. 1947	x		
USSR	Dec. 1947	x		
France II	Jan. 1948		x	
West Germany	June 1948			x
East Germany	June 1948			x
Poland II	Oct. 1950	x		
Rumania II	Jan. 1952	x		
Bulgaria II	May 1952	x		

[a] The Polish reform was carried out in three phases. In the first, ruble banknotes were exchanged at par for new zloty notes (December 1944); in the second, Cracow zloty notes were exchanged for new zloty notes (January 1945); and in the third, reichsmark notes were converted (February 1945).

[b] The initial Austrian reform was applicable only to those areas of the country occupied by the Soviet army.

[c] However, the Dutch called in and blocked 100 guilder banknotes in July 1945.

[d] The provisions of this program also affected deposits blocked under the previous two programs.

that made use of the monetary reform, with two exceptions, employed the Type Two program. Although a sprinkling of eastern European countries also resorted to this type, for the most part Types One and Three prevailed in this sector of Europe.

The Type One Reform

The Type One reform was first introduced in Greece in late 1944 when that country was in the midst of hyperinflation. About a year later, Hungary adopted the same type of reform to reduce her banknote circulation, and after this failed to halt inflation she repeated the program, this time in a more vigorous and comprehensive fashion, and was successful. Shortly after this, Austria and the USSR undertook to dampen inflationary pressures with this type of program, the latter setting the pattern for the 1950 Polish, and the 1952 Rumanian and Bulgarian reforms. The prevalence of the Type One reform is largely explained by the attempts of two countries (Greece and Hungary) to stabilize economies plagued with hyperinflation, and by the desire (or necessity) of several Soviet-bloc countries to imitate the principal features of the USSR program of December 1947.[7]

Although each of these eight reforms provided for a reduction in the supply of liquid assets at the outset, without the utilization of blocking techniques, there were still many differences among their provisions.

TABLE II.—PRINCIPAL PROVISIONS OF TYPE ONE REFORMS

Country	Rates of Exchange	
	Banknotes	Bank Deposits
Greece	50 billion = 1	50 billion = 1
Hungary I	4 = 1	
Hungary II	200 million = 1[a]	200 million = 1[a]
Austria III	3 = 1	3 = 1
USSR	10 = 1	1 = 1; 3 = 2; 2 = 1[b]
Poland II	100 = 1	100 = 3[c]
Rumania II	100 = 1; 200 = 1; 300 = 1; 400 = 1[d]	50 = 1; 100 = 1; 150 = 1; 200 = 1[d]
Bulgaria II	100 = 1	4 = 1 to 200 = 1[e]

[a] This is in terms of the tax-pengoe. In terms of the so-called flat pengoe, the rate of exchange was 400 octillion-to-one!

[b] Rates applied to following ranges: 0–3,000; 3,001–10,000; over 10,000 rubles.

[c] Presumably only savings deposits were accorded this rate.

[d] Rates applied to following ranges: 0–1,000; 1,001–2,000; 2,001–3,000; and over 3,000 lei.

[e] The most favorable rates were accorded to savings deposits, deposits of private enterprises not exceeding the amount of the wage bill for the last month, and deposits, of state and co-operative enterprises, offices, organizations, and foreign representatives. Other deposits were exchanged at either 100– or 200–to-one.

The principal differences were revealed in (1) the rates of exchange employed between old and new money, (2) the exchange rights accorded to holders of various types of liquid assets, (3) the exchange

[7] It probably would have been impossible for the Greeks and Hungarians to have stabilized their soaring price levels by means of temporary blocking techniques. What was needed, along monetary reform lines, was a fresh start, *i.e.*, a drastic reduction of the means of payment and a complete revamping of the price and wage structures.

Why the USSR chose the Type One reform is not altogether clear. P. A. Baran suggested that the administrative work connected with a blocking program would have been too formidable, and that, anyway, the peasants might not have tolerated such measures. See Baran, "Currency Reform in the USSR," *Harvard Bus. Rev.*, Mar. 1948, XXVI, 205. It is also true, however, that this type of reform had been used in the USSR in 1923. In the official text of the 1947 monetary law, the Soviets mentioned this precedent with much pride.

rights granted to owners of differing amounts of liquid assets, and (4) the rates of exchange applied on the basis of the identity of the owner himself. Table II records the provisions which reflect most of these differences.

The exchange rates employed in the reforms varied all the way from one-to-one (applied only to small deposits) in the USSR to 50 billion-to-one in the Greek reform.[8] The first Hungarian program contained a ratio between old and new banknotes of four-to-one, but in the second reform the rate of 200 million-to-one was adopted (or, 400 octillion-to-one in terms of the flat pengoe), reflecting the degree of inflation which had taken place in that country between the last month of 1945 and mid-1946.[9] In the USSR, the conversion rates ran from one-to-one to ten-to-one, while in the 1950 Polish program they reached 100-to-one, and in the Bulgarian (II)[10] and Rumanian (II) reforms, 200-to-one and 400-to-one, respectively.[11] In almost all cases, coins and small denomination banknotes were exempted from the conversion laws.

Not only were there wide differences among the conversion rates used by these countries, but distinctions were sometimes made on the basis of the type of liquid asset owned by the family or business firm. Thus, the Soviet Union "taxed" all banknotes at ten-to-one, but permitted bank deposits more favorable treatment. The same procedure was adopted in the Rumanian (II) reform in which bank deposits were hit only half as hard as comparable holdings of banknotes. The provisions of the Hungarian (I) reform affected only banknotes, leaving bank deposits untouched, while in Poland (II) and Bulgaria (II) savings deposits were highly favored over banknote holdings. These provisions were sometimes used to strike particularly hard at a certain group known to be in possession of a large volume of one type of asset—such as the banknote-holding peasants in the USSR—or to discourage black

[8] The text of the USSR reform may be found in the *New York Times*, Dec. 15, 1947, p. 6. See also Baran, *op. cit.*, pp. 194-206. and Charles Bettelheim, "La Réforme Moné-taire Soviétique," *Rev. Econ.*, Oct. 1950, pp. 341-53. For information on the Greek reform, see D. Delivanis and W. C. Cleveland, *Greek Monetary Developments 1939-1948* (Bloom-ington, 1949), pp. 110 ff., and the annual *Report of the Bank of Greece* for each of the early postwar years.

[9] For an account of the Hungarian reforms, see N. Kaldor, "A Study in Inflation, I—Hungary's Classical Example," *The Manchester Guardian Weekly*, Nov. 29, 1946, p. 299; *idem.* "Hungarian Inflation, II—Stabilisation," *ibid.*, Dec. 13, 1946, p. 331; B. Nogaro, "Hungary's Monetary Crisis," *Am. Econ. Rev.* (Sept. 1948), XXXVIII, 526-42; and *The Stabilisation of the Hungarian Currency* (Budapest, 1946).

[10] Throughout the remainder of the paper, the Roman numeral will indicate whether it is the first, second, or third reform to which reference is made.

[11] The principal provisions of the Polish program may be found in *Internat. Financial News Surv.*, Nov. 3, 1950, III, 142; the Rumanian reform in *ibid.*, Feb. 8, 1952, IV, 238; and the Bulgarian reform in *ibid.*, May 30, 1952, IV, 368-69.

market activities usually engaged in with large denomination bank-notes, or, finally, to encourage the depositing of currency in savings deposits for the purpose of decreasing the velocity of circulation.

The third distinction was based on the amount of liquid assets owned by individuals and business firms. While, as mentioned above, the Soviets gave more favorable treatment to bank deposits than to bank-notes, they also favored small holders of these deposits over large holders. In Rumania (II), small holders of either banknotes or deposits were favored over large holders, the rates ranging from 100-to-one to 400-to-one for banknotes, and from 50-to-one to 200-to-one for bank deposits. Apparently, owners of small savings deposits in Bulgaria (II) also received special treatment. The progressive rates employed by these reforms were largely designed to bring about a more equal distri-bution of liquid assets, to hit certain capitalist elements with particular severity, or to achieve other social goals.

Finally, the fourth distinction was based on the identification of the owner of the assets. Thus, in Bulgaria (II) all deposits held by private businesses were converted at the highly unfavorable rate of 200-to-one. The Austrian (III) reform granted special treatment to farmers so far as their banknote holdings were concerned and small depositors were hit lightly.[12] In some cases, deposits owned by governmental units, financial institutions, and charitable and religious organizations were either exempted or treated in a special manner.

In most of the Type One reforms, not only were "excess assets" swept away, but also large portions of transactions balances, at pre-reform price and wage levels, were eliminated by the monetary provi-sions. Whenever this occurred, it was necessary for the authorities to lower the price and wage structures in their economies to fit the new, lower level of liquid assets (money supply). Thus, a reduction of liquid assets in the ratio of 50- or 100-to-one did not mean that the *real* value of these assets was reduced to that extent, since prices and wage-rates were lowered simultaneously. Several countries chose this course be-cause their pre-reform inflated price and wage levels were already far out of line with others, and because such a course seemed to offer the best method for "breaking the back" of the inflationary spiral.

In the Bulgarian (II) reform, for example, the *average* conversion rate for liquid assets was about 100 old leva for 2.4 new leva, while most prices and wage-rates were converted in the ratio of 100-to-four. The same reduction in the real value of liquid assets could have been achieved if the assets had been converted in the ratio of 100 old leva

---

[12] For the main outlines of the Austrian reform, see F. H. Klopstock, "Monetary and Fiscal Policy in Post-Liberation Austria," *Pol. Sci. Quart.* (Mar. 1948), LXIII, 122-23.

for 60 new leva, with prices and wage-rates remaining unchanged. The Hungarians (II) also revamped their price and wage structures, and in Rumania (II) these "flow magnitudes" were lowered by about 80 per cent at the time of the monetary reform. On the other hand, the Austrians (III) and the Hungarians (I) converted prices and wages at par, while in the USSR wages and other regular payments were converted at par, but the price system was unified and a general lowering of the price level occurred.

The Type Two Reform

The Belgians were the first to experiment with the Type Two monetary reform, the main features of which were copied several months later by Denmark, the Netherlands, Norway, and Czechoslovakia.[13] Both Finland and France (II)[14] utilized this technique for the temporary blocking of banknotes, and a few of the eastern European countries, before they became allied with the Soviet orbit, introduced reform measures of this type.

There were generally three phases to this type of monetary reform. First, the major portion of banknotes and bank deposits was blocked during the initial days of the program. Second, certain basic allotments and releases were made to individuals and business firms so that normal economic activity might continue. Third, the funds, or part of them, which remained blocked after the primary releases were consummated were gradually deblocked either through individual requests to a deblocking committee, through blanket releases that spanned all deposits, or by other means.

Within this framework, however, each country went about the tasks of first immobilizing and then demobilizing a portion of the liquid asset supply in its own way. In some cases, the formulas chosen were quite simple, but in other instances they were so complex as to defy under-

[13] Descriptions of these programs are found in V. A. deRidder, "The Belgian Monetary Reform," *Rev. Econ. Stud.*, 1947-48, XV (2), 51-69; *idem*, "The Belgian Monetary Reform: An Appraisal of the Results," *ibid.*, 1948-49, XVI (1), 25-40; *Reports and Accounts*, Danmark Nationalbank, 1945, pp. 30-34; *White Paper Regarding the Measures for the Currency Rehabilitation in the Netherlands* (The Hague, 1947); *De Nederlandsche Bank Report for 1946* (Amsterdam, 1947), p. 27, and same *Reports* for later years; Kaare Peterson, "The Monetary Reconstruction Program in Norway," *Norwegian American Commerce*, Feb. 1946, XI, 3-21; and *National Bank of Czechoslovakia Bulletin*, Mar.-Apr. 1948, pp. 1-5 in annex.

For more general accounts, see R. W. Bean, "Results of Monetary Reforms in Western Europe," *Fed. Res. Bull.*, Oct. 1946, XXXII, 1115-22; F. H. Klopstock, "Monetary Reform in Liberated Europe," *Am. Econ. Rev.*, Sept. 1946, XXXVI, 578-95; *idem*, "Western Europe's Attack on Inflation," *Harvard Bus. Rev.*, Sept. 1948, XXVI, 597-612.

[14] See, *Bank of Finland Monthly Bulletin*, Jan.-Mar., 1946, pp. 1-2 and p. 30; A. Snider, "French Monetary and Fiscal Policy," *Amer. Econ. Rev.*, June 1948, XXXVIII, 309-27; and Banque de France, *Compte Rendu des Opérations*, 1948, pp. 7-8.

GURLEY: EXCESS LIQUIDITY AND MONETARY REFORMS   85

standing by the majority of the population; moreover, some of the programs were dragged out for several years after their introduction.[14a] A few of the Type Two reforms initiated in 1945 were still in the process of liquidation as late as the winter of 1951.

The provisions making up the first phase of these reforms varied somewhat from country to country. In most cases, though, the reforms exempted coins, small denomination banknotes, and certain deposits from the initial blocking regulations. The primary reason for exempting coins and small notes was to reduce the volume of administrative work during the currency exchange period. The exempted bank deposits generally included those held by financial institutions, governmental units, other public or semipublic bodies, and charitable and religious organizations. In these cases, all other bank deposits, together with the larger denomination banknotes, were placed in blocked accounts. However, some programs were quite limited in scope. For example, Finland's law hit only 500, 1,000 and 5,000 mark banknotes, leaving the smaller notes and all bank deposits untouched. In France (II), only 5,000 franc notes were subject to the blocking provisions, while the first Austrian reform blocked only bank deposits. In the majority of cases, though, large portions of the liquid asset supplies came under the blocking regulations.

In the second phase of the programs, the basic allotments and releases of funds were made on several bases: (1) per capita; (2) the average monthly wage bills of employers; (3) the date on which the deposit was first opened; (4) the type of liquid asset owned; and (5) the amount of liquid assets owned. The per capita allotments were made so that consumers would have enough to live on until their next pay checks. The releases to employers enabled the flow of wage and salary payments to be resumed. Finally, the partial deblocking of deposits was oftentimes accomplished on discriminatory bases—favoring all deposits opened before the outbreak of war ("good deposits"), treating more harshly those opened during the occupation ("bad deposits"), in a

[14a] The provisions in the Netherlands and Austria were so involved as to be almost beyond imagination. One need only mention that during the life of the Dutch program— it lasted for over six years—there were free deposits, clearing accounts, blocked accounts, option accounts, investment accounts, and several other forms under which funds were tied up. In Austria, after the appearance of the second reform in 1945, there were six different types of deposits in existence. The distinctions were based on the zone in which the individual resided, the date the bank deposit was opened, and the reform under which the deposit was regulated. By the time the third reform came along—the provisions of which cancelled outright some deposits, converted others on a deflated basis, left others untouched, converted a few into forced loans, and blocked still others for a short period of time and the remainder for longer periods—the average depositor was sorely pressed to determine what he fully, only partially, or did not own. The Belgian program also became tangled in many complications, and in Czechoslovakia a Currency Liquidation Fund had to be introduced to administer the final stages of that program.

few cases favoring savings deposits over other types of asset holdings, and usually granting somewhat larger percentage releases to owners of small holdings than to the wealthier owners.

The third and final phase of these reforms—the gradual deblocking of all, or part of, the immobilized funds—was pursued with some marked differences from country to country. These differences were revealed in (1) the methods used to deblock funds, (2) the percentage of funds ultimately returned to their owners, and (3) the rapidity with which the funds were returned. We will briefly consider each of these.

There were generally four types of releases made: (a) releases, on special request, to individuals who had been especially hard hit financially by the war and occupation, or to invalids, oldsters and others; (b) releases for the payment of taxes, the purchase of government bonds, and in some instances for the purchase of insurance policies and other financial and real assets; (c) automatic blanket releases after a specified period of time had elapsed; and (d) discretionary blanket releases in the light of the economic situation as it developed month by month. Many countries relied upon all four methods of releasing funds, but even in these cases the emphasis was often quite different.

There were also differences with respect to the percentage of blocked accounts ultimately released to their owners. In a few instances, all, or almost all, of the blocked funds were returned. This was true in France (I and II), Denmark, Norway, and Finland. In other countries, large portions of these funds were wiped out in one way or another in the later stages of the programs, and in these cases the reforms were, in effect, similar to the Type One programs, in which the total supply of liquid assets was reduced at the outset. In Belgium, for example, after the initial allotments were made, the authorities segregated all blocked deposits into two categories: temporarily blocked deposits (40 per cent of the total), and permanently blocked deposits (60 per cent of the total). The latter portion was largely eliminated by the conversion of these deposits into forced loans and the subsequent redemption of the loan certificates with funds derived from special capital levies. To some extent, this path was also followed in the Netherlands, Czechoslovakia, and Bulgaria (I). In one country, Austria, the authorities simply cancelled a portion of the blocked deposits.

Finally, of the funds ultimately released, a major portion of them was released in a few days or weeks in some countries, while in others the programs continued for years. In France (I) the funds were released almost immediately, in France (II) and Denmark, after only a few months, and in Belgium, the Netherlands, and Norway, only after several years. The percentage of funds released and the rapidity with which they were released depended primarily upon the objectives of the programs. Whenever the principal objective was to contain inflation,

GURLEY: EXCESS LIQUIDITY AND MONETARY REFORMS　87

the funds were usually deblocked slowly and then only in part. In other cases, the bulk of them was released rapidly.

The Type Two programs were, on the whole, quite different from the Type One reforms with respect to their treatment of prices and wages. In the former, the flow magnitudes of the economy were generally left unchanged, while in the latter, as we have seen, they were often drastically altered. The primary purpose of the authorities in carrying out many of the Type Two reforms was simply to skim off the excess liquidity, at prereform prices and wages. Thus, although the average Norwegian had less liquid assets after monetary reform than he had before, the prices he paid for consumer goods and the wages he received were approximately the same a week after the reform as they had been just prior to it.

The Type Three Reform

Enough has been said above to make it unnecessary to delve deeply into the provisions of the Type Three monetary reform, inasmuch as these programs incorporated the principal features of the other two types. In this set of reforms, the liquid asset supply was reduced at the outset by the application of deflated rates of exchange to old currency and deposit holdings, but, in addition, a portion of the remaining supply was frozen in blocked accounts.

The reform carried out in West Germany in 1948 offers a typical example of the measures to be found in this hybrid type of program.[15] In that country, all banknotes were called in and bank deposits were declared between June 20 and 26. Each person then received 60 new deutschemark notes (DM) for 600 old reichsmark notes (RM). Employers were presented with 60 DM per employee for 600 RM.[16] Most bank deposits were converted at the same rate—10 RM for 1 DM—and one-half of the resulting DM balances was freed and the other half blocked. During October 1948, 70 per cent of the blocked balances were cancelled, 20 per cent were transferred to a free account, and 10 per cent were made available for investment in certain securities to be specified later.

The Soviet-sponsored reform in East Germany was quite similar to the program conducted in the western zones.[17] One difference, however,

[15] There is a wealth of material available on this reform. See, for instance, F. A. Lutz, "The German Currency Reform and the Revival of the German Economy," *Economica*, May 1949, XVI, 122-42, and H. Mendershausen, "Prices, Money and the Distribution of Goods in Postwar Germany," *Am. Econ. Rev.*, June 1949, XXXIX, 646-72.

[16] It was at first believed that the initial per capita and employee allotments were made at par. The actual rate of exchange was not made apparent until a week later.

[17] See, Haut-Commissariat de la Republique Française en Allemagne, *Étude d'Ensemble sur la Situation Economique et Financière de la Zone Zoviétique d'Occupation en Allemagne de 1945 à 1950* (Berlin, Mar. 31, 1950).

was that savings deposits were converted at differential rates: one-to-one for the first 100 marks, five-to-one for the next 900, and ten-to-one for all in excess of 1,000 marks. The first Rumanian reform was also patterned along these lines, except that the amount of the initial allotment was more dependent on the economic class in which the individual found himself.[18] For example, farmers were highly favored as to the amount of banknotes that they could exchange for new ones. On the other hand, unemployed persons, military personnel, and individuals in work camps and prisons were permitted to exchange substantially smaller sums. Moreover, certain commercial firms were granted no conversion rights at all. The exchanges were made at the rate of 20,000-to-one, and, in addition, a portion of the new funds was blocked and only gradually released in the later stages of the program.

The monetary reform in West Germany was accompanied by a general decontrol of prices and wages, while in Rumania (I) the price and wage structures were completely revised and lowered. East Germany and Yugoslavia apparently maintained the flow magnitudes at approximately the same levels and kept them under controls.

III. *Objectives of the Monetary Reforms*

The European reform programs had a variety of objectives. There were first those objectives which were concerned with the prevention or the termination of inflationary spirals. Other objectives were concerned with surveys of asset distribution, the redistribution of asset holdings, and the achievement of other social goals.

Anti-Inflationary Objectives

The principal aim of many of the monetary reforms was to dampen without delay the inflationary pressures on prices and wages which appeared in force throughout Europe during the early years of the postwar period. It was generally expected that the reduction or partial blocking of liquid assets would achieve this end by reducing aggregate demand for goods and services, increasing incentives toward work, and decreasing the hoarding of goods.

The monetary reform was expected to reduce private spending in two ways. First, it was anticipated that the loss of liquidity by families and businesses would make them feel poorer, and hence out of a given disposable income less would be spent for consumption and investment goods. The removal of excess liquidity from the economy, accompanied by tight controls over bank loans, would, it was anticipated, render it

---

[18] The basic provisions of this reform may be found in *Bulletin d'Information et de Documentation*, Banque Nationale de Roumanie, July-Sept. 1947, pp. 152-55.

impossible for large-scale private deficit spending to occur. These expectations prevailed even in those cases in which the supply of money was not reduced at the outset, but only partially blocked for varying periods of time. Second, the very act of complying with the provisions of the monetary reforms—*e.g.*, standing in long lines before banks to surrender (permanently or temporarily) the major portion of one's liquid funds—would dampen individuals' expectations of rising prices, and it would induce them to spend less out of disposable incomes. Thus the technical provisions of the monetary reform would reduce (or partially block) the money supply, and the "psychological shock" of the program as a whole, it was thought, would decrease income velocity. In a few countries, special emphasis was placed on the shock effect as the principal virtue to be expected from the monetary reform.

The reform, by suddenly reducing the supply of liquid assets available to individuals, was also expected to increase incentives toward work. The excessive supply of these assets—relative to money national income —that was generated during the war and occupation by government deficits and export surpluses led many workers to take extended vacations after liberation. In a few countries, such as West Germany, the volume of liquid assets owned by a sizeable portion of the population was probably equivalent to one or two years' supply of consumer goods which individuals could reasonably expect to purchase under existing rationing measures. Consequently, many workers in these countries left their jobs, or worked part-time only, since an extra unit of currency from work had a zero or negative net marginal utility, whereas an extra free hour during the day to loaf or scout around for "deals" had substantially more. The monetary reform was expected to send the majority of the vacationers and "non-producers" scurrying back into the labor force as soon as they found themselves without funds.

Finally, it was anticipated that the loss of liquidity by merchants would induce them to relinquish their hoardings of inventories, and that this in turn would halt the price increases and at the same time convince the population that the reform had brought about an increase in the supply of consumer goods. Expectations of falling prices would then become prevalent and would serve, it was hoped, to dampen current spendings. The reforms were supposed to dry up black market activities and make it profitable for merchants to offer, and possible for individuals to purchase, the bulk of consumer goods in legitimate trade channels.

Other Objectives

Not all of the reforms, however, were introduced primarily for anti-inflationary purposes; in several instances, these considerations did not even constitute immediate secondary objectives. The authorities in some countries initiated the reform programs in order (1) to conduct a survey of liquid asset distribution, (2) to redistribute liquid holdings, or (3) to achieve other social goals.

The distributional surveys were expected to serve several purposes. First, they were to prepare the way for subsequent capital levies and capital increment taxes. Capital levies were very popular in postwar Europe, and whatever success some of them had was in no small part due to the data collected during these asset inventories. The pertinent provisions called for the declaration of banknote, deposit, and security holdings, and at times other assets, as we have seen, such as insurance policies and jewelry had to be revealed. The levies were generally not designed as anti-inflationary but rather as burden-sharing measures, and in this sense the monetary reform was an indirect means of redistributing asset holdings.[19]

An aim common to all of the earlier reforms was to prevent the infiltration of old banknotes and other assets that had been carried outside the country during the occupation. This was taken care of in part by the currency provisions which declared all outstanding banknotes no longer legal tender, and which offered the opportunity to each person to exchange his old notes for new ones. By this technique the authorities were able to take stock of the banknotes still within their borders and to make certain that they (the authorities) would not be subject to future competition from potential "monetary authorities" outside the country who held large amounts of the old notes.

Another purpose of the surveys, widely advertised by many of the governments, was to catch black-marketeers and other illegal operators. As old banknotes were turned in for new ones, the authorities made special note of those individuals converting large amounts of high denomination bills—the types generally used for nefarious purposes. In many cases, deblockings were not granted until the sources of funds had been thoroughly investigated by the authorities. Lastly, the survey data were often compared with prewar data on asset holdings in order to locate the large income recipients of the occupation period, the purpose being the collection of long-overdue income taxes.

[19] It was generally recognized that the monetary reform hit only a narrow range of assets, permitting all other assets to escape. But it was sometimes assumed that those who had profited the most during the occupation had had insufficient opportunities to dispose of their liquid holdings. Also, some governments desired to remove a portion of liquid funds from circulation only temporarily. Since these funds were due to be returned to their owners, it was felt that it would be a waste of time to compute the contribution of each person on any other basis. Most of the authorities, however, planned to "equalize the burdens" by means of capital levies at a later date. Almost all countries went through the motions of applying these levies, but in many cases they were weak measures and only in small part corrected the original "inequities."

The second general objective of the reforms, more prevalent in eastern than in western Europe, was to redistribute liquid asset holdings; when the reforms were accompanied by wholesale alterations of the price and wage structures, they were often expected to redistribute incomes, too. The large volume of liquid assets, unquestionably distributed in a more uneven fashion than postwar incomes in many areas of Europe, threatened to swing a heavy share of current output toward the large asset-holding groups if they chose to reduce their holdings. Many governments, especially in eastern Europe, sought to stave this off through the reform provisions. For example, large asset holders were often accorded relatively unfavorable terms upon which their old assets could be exchanged for new ones. Prices and wage-rates were then reset to make it difficult for these same groups to accumulate large asset holdings in the future.

Finally, in some eastern European reforms, other social goals were envisaged by the authorities. These included the suppression of "capitalist elements," the achievement of farm collectivization programs, and the general strengthening of the government's position for the pursuit of future social programs. The attempt to attain these goals was reflected, in part, in the unfavorable conversion rights granted to private enterprisers and independent farmers. Also, in several cases, the reforms were introduced at the end of pay periods, which guaranteed that the workers would be caught with few cash balances, and thus would suffer relatively little from the exchange provisions.

As stated above, the majority of the reforms were intended to combat inflation. All of them, however, were concerned with other objectives as well, while a few in western Europe were initiated almost exclusively for other than deflationary purposes.

IV. *Evaluation of the Monetary Reforms*

Achievement of Objectives

How successful were the monetary reforms in achieving these objectives? Aside from their anti-inflationary aims, they appear to have been successful in the majority of cases. The banknote exchange provisions *did* alleviate several of the currency disturbances arising out of the occupation, and they enabled the authorities to counter, to some extent, black-market activities. The blocking measures presented a breathing spell to governments during which time distributional data were collected. These data were then used to make capital levies more effective. When progressive conversion rates were employed, assets were redistributed in a matter of days. When these and other forms of discriminatory rates were used, certain economic classes were probably rendered impotent, or at least they became more amenable to their government's desires.

The reforms in France (I and II), Denmark, and to a large extent in Norway were primarily designed to achieve several of these objectives, for after the banknote exchanges and the asset inventories had been made, all or most of the blocked funds were promptly returned to their owners. In fact, France (I) did not even bother to block deposits at all, while the Danish law stated that part of the blocked funds would be released a month after the initial blocking, and the remainder three months later. Within three or four months after the introduction of the Norwegian program, the major portion of blocked accounts was released. Since, by and large, these programs accomplished what they set out to do, they must be judged successful. However, considering only the above objectives, most of the other reforms succeeded, too. For example, it appears beyond doubt that several of the eastern European countries were successful in significantly redistributing liquid assets and in furthering other socialist programs via the monetary reforms, even though these reforms were principally conceived as anti-inflationary weapons.

But the majority of the monetary reforms should be judged primarily with respect to their anti-inflationary aims, and from this standpoint the reforms on the whole were disappointing. In fact, several of them were outright failures. It is, of course, extremely difficult, if not impossible in many cases, to separate the effects of the reforms from those of other events and policies occurring simultaneously or shortly afterwards. In Belgium, for instance, only fair success seems to have been attained, but shortly after its monetary program, the Belgian government was compelled to run substantial deficits in order to meet certain expenses connected with the presence of Allied armies within her borders. These deficits almost swamped the initial, favorable effects of the reform, and render it virtually impossible to judge what the full impact of the reform might have been. The same may be stated for the Austrian (II) case, while in several of the eastern European countries the presence of tight controls over prices and wages, the radical changes in political power, the growing proportion of socialized ownership of the means of production, not to mention the lack of available data and the recent dates of three of these reforms, make it especially difficult to appraise the programs.

In a few cases, though, the verdict appears to be clear-cut. In western Europe, the reform that achieved the most impressive results was that of West Germany, and of these results the most dramatic were the return to the work force of many workers from "unproductive" occupations and idleness, and the reduction of absenteeism in the factories.

GURLEY: EXCESS LIQUIDITY AND MONETARY REFORMS   93

As a consequence, real output increased sharply in this country during the half-year following the sudden reduction of liquid assets. In addition, a day or two after the monetary reform the supply of goods in legal channels increased as if by magic. Although this phenomenon was due almost entirely to the diversion of goods from "black" to legitimate channels and to the dishoarding of goods by merchants who had anticipated the currency measures, the fact remains that the shop displays were sufficiently impressive to convince many that the worst was over—that consumer goods would henceforth be easily available at "reasonable" prices. Current spending patterns responded accordingly. To a lesser extent, the same phenomena appear to have taken place in Austria (III), the Netherlands, and a few other countries. In eastern Europe, most facts indicate that the USSR and Hungary (II) had a large measure of success with their reforms. Not enough time has elapsed to warrant any statement about the second reforms in Poland, Rumania, and Bulgaria.

On the other hand, Finland, Greece, and Austria (II) apparently had little or no success in dampening inflationary pressures with monetary reforms. The same may be said for the Polish (I), Rumanian (I), and Bulgarian (I) reforms, and there is no doubt that the first Hungarian program failed miserably to halt inflation. Also, inflationary pressures were not quelled to any significant extent by either the French (II) or Czechoslovakian measures.

Thus, here and there, some dramatic, anti-inflationary results were attained by countries utilizing the reforms, but there were several failures and, it appears, many partial successes only. The persistence of inflation throughout most of Europe during 1946-47, and the necessity of several countries to resort to the monetary reform a second or third time, is evidence that all of these programs did not enjoy complete success. One is forced to conclude that, on the whole, the programs achieved much less than had been expected of them.

Some Causes of Failure

What were the reasons for the complete or partial failure of some of these programs? First, the reforms were not capable of overcoming many of the supply (of goods) difficulties of the early postwar period. Second, in practice they probably did not reduce private spending to any appreciable extent. Third, they were accompanied by inappropriate government policies and other unfavorable events.

In the face of large private demands, real output in many areas of Europe during the early postwar years remained far below prewar levels. This was not due to a large volume of involuntary unemployment, but rather to such factors as the wartime destruction and neglect of capital equipment, the neglect of land fertility, the loss of land area to the USSR, the depletion of inventories, the incapability of many to work at normal speeds for an average workday because of mental exhaustion and undernourishment, and finally to voluntary idleness. In so far as the last phenomenon was caused by excessive liquid holdings, the monetary reforms were capable of affecting work incentives, and hence dampening inflationary pressures. In some countries this was a significant factor and it was here that the reforms achieved some of their most impressive results. But, in other countries, this was not an important element in the inflationary picture, and in all cases the reforms were not designed to cope with the other supply difficulties. However, compared with other anti-inflationary weapons, the monetary reform from this standpoint was not unique; other measures would probably have fared no better and, as we shall observe below, might well have proved less effective in increasing work incentives.

The reforms were also weak anti-inflationary measures because they failed in many instances to reduce appreciably private spending. It is probable that the most serious shortcoming of these monetary programs was that they relied almost exclusively on the liquidity effect to dampen spending, and left untouched real disposable incomes; the latter were not directly affected since prices, wage rates, and other regular payments were either converted at par, or were lowered proportionately.[20] In many instances, it is possible that the liquidity effect would have been weak even if the programs had been carried out in the most effective manner. There is, of course, no way to prove this, but it can be said that, whatever the maximum liquidity effect might have been, in practice this force was probably quite weak in a number of countries for several reasons.

First, even when liquid assets were reduced at the outset of the programs, it was not impossible for families who, in the absence of the reform, would have spent less than their incomes to maintain their same rates of spending if they so desired. Some of the reforms in fact encouraged them to maintain these rates, since funds were blocked only temporarily with the tacit understanding that most or all of them would be returned eventually. It is inconceivable that temporary blocking of this sort could have had much influence on the spending habits of many families.

Second, in many cases, a large number of families probably lost little through the currency exchange provisions. To begin with, liquid assets were undoubtedly so heavily concentrated in the upper-income classes that many families in some of these countries had nothing much to

[20] In a few cases, it appears as though substantial redistributions of disposable incomes took place, which undoubtedly altered spending patterns, too.

lose during the exchange process. Since their current (real) incomes remained approximately constant, these families might well have maintained their prereform spending rates. It should also be recalled that several reforms utilized progressive conversion rates, so that even if low- and middle-income groups held sizeable blocks of liquid assets, they were often hit lightly. Furthermore, some reforms did not affect a large proportion of total liquid holdings in any case. For example, the Finnish program hit only 8 per cent of total currency and deposits. In France (II), only 5,000 franc notes were affected, while in Hungary (I) all deposits escaped the exchange provisions. Moreover, in almost every case, government and private security holdings, life insurance policies, and other forms of liquid wealth were not subject to the conversion laws. Such partial reductions probably had little effect on either consumer or business spending.

In some of the blocking programs, not only was the public under the impression that its funds (or most of them) would be released in time, but large portions of these blocked accounts actually were released so rapidly as to negate whatever favorable effects the reforms might have initially enjoyed. Funds were not only readily deblocked for the payment of taxes, the purchase of government securities, and for emergency expenditures (the latter were sometimes defined as those expenditures which the family was in the habit of making but which it could not make now that its funds were blocked!), but blanket releases were made in such volume as to quickly undermine the reform measures. This was true in varying degrees in Belgium, Czechoslovakia, Austria (II), and the Netherlands.

Finally, in practice, the liquidity effect may also have been weak due to the fact that some of the reforms might have given rise to anticipations of second or third programs. To the extent that this was true, individuals and businesses would be reluctant to hold currency and deposits for fear that these assets would be hit again. To protect oneself against the type of monetary reform conducted in Europe, one had only to consume income or to hold wealth predominantly in either real assets or, in most cases, private securities. There is some evidence that the Austrians and Hungarians reacted unfavorably to their initial reforms, and it would be surprising if families in Rumania, Poland, and Bulgaria were not at this time hesitant to hold the types of assets affected by the two reforms in each of those countries. One monetary reform may not give rise to a flight from money, but it is extremely doubtful that most individuals will remain calm after a second or third program within, say, a five-year period. It is probably true that monetary reforms are also subject to diminishing returns.

Through no fault of their own, several of these measures failed to halt inflation because of inappropriate government actions which accompanied or shortly followed them. These included relatively high government expenditures coupled with inadequate tax receipts, and easy bank credit policies.

Government expenditures in many European countries during 1945-46 were "necessarily" large for a number of reasons. First, several countries were compelled to meet partially the expenses of the Allied armies situated within their borders. Others were required to pay reparations, and all felt obligated to meet partially the costs of reconstruction of homes and factories, the rehabilitation and relocation of large segments of the population, and other social welfare programs. Primarily in eastern Europe after 1947, but also in some western European countries (such as Norway), heavy industrialization programs necessitated large government outlays. These spendings, coupled with large private spendings out of relatively high disposable incomes, soon offset, in some countries, the initial, favorable effects of the reforms.

But, would it not have been possible to boost tax rates to levels sufficiently high to offset the inflationary impact of these governmental outlays? There are simply too many countries under consideration here to permit a general answer to this question. However, a few factors, common to most countries, suggest that an all-out *income* tax program in 1945-46 to accompany the monetary reforms might not have been feasible or possible. Many governments were not able to move rapidly in the income tax field for lack of trained personnel to handle the job. In some instances, it would have required years to gather together and train these personnel.[21] But, even if the administrative set-up had been adequate, it was considered quite likely that higher income tax rates might yield only a small increase in tax revenues. Tax morality was at its lowest ebb immediately after liberation, in large part because the evasion of regulations during the occupation was considered by many as honorable, and these attitudes were carried over into the postwar period. When this factor was linked, in the minds of the authorities, with the longstanding propensity of farmers and other groups, in some areas of Europe, to evade taxes, income taxation as a main weapon

---

[21] Nor was it possible for many of these governments to impose widely based capital levies immediately after the war. The pertinent information of wealth distribution was not on hand, and it would have required months, perhaps years in some cases, to bring together these data. On the other hand, the monetary reform dealt only with those assets whose ownership patterns were known, or could be known in a short period of time. Bank deposits were ideal assets from this standpoint, while banknotes, unlike bathtubs and land, could be recalled and exchanged for new ones on the terms set by the authorities. The major share of the administrative tasks fell on existing financial institutions which had only to increase their staffs to handle the extra loads. These tasks were lightened, of course, by the very nature of the assets affected, which made evasion of the provisions of the law practically impossible.

against inflation did not seem to offer much promise of success. In any case, however, the fact remains that an inadequate tax program, given the relatively high levels of government expenditures, upset the reform's applecart in several of these countries.

The initial effects of a few of the reforms were also negated by credit policies which were incapable of preventing sharp increases in bank loans to businesses and individuals subsequent to the monetary reforms. If funds could not be deblocked, large private spendings were occasionally financed by supplementing current incomes with bank borrowings; sometimes, the collateral used was the blocked deposit! Such was apparently the case in Austria (II), Greece, and one or two other countries. Many governments for social reasons were reluctant to raise interest rates. Higher rates would have had a disturbing influence on house building and on rents of new houses,[22] and would have yielded higher incomes to the rentier class. Debt management considerations, as in this country, sometimes were successful in preventing upward movements in the interest rate structure.

V. Conclusion: Monetary Reforms and Orthodox Measures

The excessive volume of liquid assets in Europe apparently exerted its effects in at least two ways: (1) It increased private spendings out of disposable incomes, and (2) it weakened work incentives. In many of these countries the first phenomenon appears to have largely overshadowed the second. In others, the second phenomenon was particularly potent. Such nonuniformity in the liquidity effect was, to a large extent, due to differences in the volume of excess liquidity existing in these countries. As individuals gained excess liquidity, it is quite likely that their attention was first directed to the possibility of increasing their spending and not to the possibility of reducing their working hours. However, as excess liquidity continued to grow, attention was turned more and more to the second possibility. Some individuals worked fewer hours per day, or fewer days per week, but for many there was little leeway to adjust these hours. The relevant decision, in many cases, was whether to continue work or to quit work altogether, and such a decision was a major one. Therefore, only when excess liquidity had reached very large proportions did a significant segment of the labor force voluntarily give up work for a time to live off accumulated assets. On the other hand, spending probably grew continuously as liquidity grew, even though the total liquidity effect on spending might have been weak.

Thus, the results of the monetary reforms were almost bound to be

[22] See, B. Ohlin, *The Problem of Employment Stabilization* (New York, 1949), p. 23.

more dramatic in some countries than in others, aside from differences in the administrative efficiency and vigor with which the reforms were carried out. For many countries, the most that could be hoped for was some slackening in the rate of spending once excess liquidity had been removed. In those cases in which the liquidity effect on spending proved to be slight, the monetary reform was not a potent anti-inflationary weapon. Moreover, even where this effect might have been potentially large, in practice, as we have seen, various defects in the reforms themselves weakened their impact on spending. On the other hand, in those few countries where excess liquidity had grown so large as to affect seriously work incentives as well as spending, the reforms appear to have been highly successful in spite of several of the same types of defects which were found in less successful reforms. While these defects frequently weakened the liquidity effect on spending, they probably seldom weakened this effect on work incentives. For example, temporary blocking might not have altered significantly the spending habits of individuals who were currently working, but it undoubtedly induced the majority of the voluntarily idle to return to work. Thus, where the monetary reform was least needed it had to be highly efficient to be at all effective, and where it was most needed it could suffer certain defects and still succeed admirably.

Would it have been possible for many of these countries, from the standpoint of inflation control, to have dispensed with the monetary reform altogether? That is, aside from administrative and similar considerations, would it not have been possible for these countries to have dampened inflationary forces with higher income taxes and tighter credit controls, without the utilization of the monetary reform at all? While no general answer to this question is possible, one suspects that in several countries the reforms would have been of no great value as anti-inflationary measures even if they had been carried out with the highest efficiency. For example, in Finland the inflation was largely due to a heavy rate of investment spending which set off a price-wage spiral. Investment spending was heavy because of refugee reallocation problems, the reconstruction of Northern Finland, and the necessity of building new industries to meet reparation demands from the USSR. In the face of this situation, the 1945 monetary reform, which reduced the volume of banknotes in circulation, was a straw in the wind. The introduction of monetary reforms in such cases was due either to factors that had little direct connection with inflation control—such as taking inventory of banknotes still within the country—or to a misplaced emphasis on quantity theorizing which led many authorities to focus their attention on "stocks" to the neglect of flow magnitudes.

But in many countries the reform, or something similar to it, was probably an essential part of any over-all program to control inflation. This was obviously true in such countries as West and East Germany and Austria where excess liquidity had largely destroyed work incentives. But the case for the monetary reform was almost as compelling in the other countries. Consider the alternative measures faced by the authorities in these countries. So far as income taxation was concerned, the impact of excess liquidity on spending meant that, with a given rate of government expenditures, tax receipts had to comprise a larger proportion of national income than they otherwise would if inflation were to be avoided. But since excess liquidity also made individuals less dependent on their current incomes for current expenditures, a given ratio of tax receipts to national income was more likely to kill incentives toward work than if excess liquidity had not been present. Thus, the existence of this liquidity created a dilemma for the authorities in a number of European countries. An excessive volume of liquid assets necessitated an increase in tax rates and at the same time made it especially dangerous, from the standpoint of incentives, to maintain the existing level of rates.

Central bank measures were also probably weak in a number of countries in which liquid holdings were excessive. The presence of these holdings undoubtedly made some families and business firms less dependent on bank loans as supplements to their current incomes, and hence less sensitive to changes in interest rates and in the tightness of the money markets. Furthermore, orthodox monetary policy was not capable of significantly altering the total supply of liquid assets, even though it was capable of altering the composition of that supply. In some countries, excessive liquidity created too many "self-sufficient islands" within the economy for the successful pursuit of conventional monetary measures.

The authorities in some countries also felt that, in the presence of a large stock of liquid assets, the continuance of direct controls over prices and wages—that is, the continuance of the disequilibrium system—would be futile. In many areas of Europe, the termination of fighting brought with it not only a decreased desire to obey regulations but also widespread anticipations of rising prices as part of a postwar inflation. In addition, large segments of the population had little desire to go on accumulating claims to output in the face of an already abundant supply of these claims. Even if work incentives had not been seriously impaired at the time, there was always the danger that the continuance of the disequilibrium system would ultimately lead to a general deterioration of these incentives. The West German case is, of course, an outstanding example of how excessive liquid holdings can destroy a controlled system and lead to a decrease in incentives throughout an entire economy. There is reason to believe that during the past two or three years several of the eastern European countries have found themselves in similar situations, which accounts in part for the repetition of monetary reforms in this area of Europe in recent years.

Thus in a few countries, such as France and Finland, the monetary reform might well have been dispensed with. In others, however, while the monetary reform was not capable of achieving short-run, dramatic results, the sweeping away of excess liquidity was probably essential if the orthodox anti-inflationary measures were to become effective. In a few countries, where work incentives had already been widely destroyed by excess liquidity, there can be little doubt but that the reform was a necessary step along the path of inflation control.

Part IV
The European Payments Union

[10]

THE EUROPEAN PAYMENTS UNION

NEGOTIATIONS AND THE ISSUES

Albert O. Hirschman *

O N July 7, 1950, one week after the expiration of the second Intra-European Payments Scheme, the Council of the Organization for European Economic Cooperation reached full agreement on the establishment of a European Payments Union. This Union represents a radical innovation in the mechanism of intra-European payments and may have important repercussions on the whole system of international financial relations. The following paper does not give a systematic exposition of the EPU agreement.[1] It attempts to trace the rather tormented history of that agreement and to discuss in this connection some of the more important issues that had — and in part remain — to be faced.

Background

Projects for multilateral clearing in Europe have been discussed ever since the European Recovery Program was launched.[2] During the first two years of the European Recovery Program, however, the entrenched position of bilateralism in the postwar trade and payments situation in Europe, and the United Kingdom's unwillingness to permit any transfers of sterling that might result in gold obligations, prevented the successful negotiation of any multilateral clearing arrangement. The intra-European payments schemes which have been operating during the past two years were essentially *ad hoc* arrangements providing some essential finance for intra-European trade, but — among many other shortcomings — they

* Division of International Finance, Board of Governors of the Federal Reserve System. The views expressed in this article are not necessarily those of the Board. The author is indebted to Henry Conrad and George Jaszi for a number of helpful suggestions.

[1] For a good description, see "Mechanics of EPU," *The Economist*, July 15, 1950, pp. 130-32. The agreement is embodied in a 26 page OEEC Document, dated July 7, 1950. The actual convention was signed by the member countries on September 19, 1950.

[2] See, e.g., Raymond F. Mikesell, "Regional Multilateral Payments Arrangements," *Quarterly Journal of Economics*, LXII (August 1949), pp. 500-18, and Robert W. Bean, "European Multilateral Clearing," *Journal of Political Economy*, LVI (October 1948), pp. 403-15.

failed to make any substantial advance toward multilateralization of payments.

In the course of 1949, it became clear that the main European problem had shifted from the area of production to that of trade and payments. The currency adjustments of September 1949 not only improved the competitive position of the devaluing countries with respect to the dollar, but also served to bring about a greater degree of balance in intra-European payments. At the same time, a number of efforts got under way to relax the most irksome restrictions on trade and payments in Europe. Mr. Hoffman's speech before the OEEC Council in Paris on October 31, 1949, in which he advocated the economic "integration" of Europe through the creation of a single market freed from restrictions, crystallized action in the two related fields of trade and payments. With respect to trade, the OEEC countries agreed (with some exceptions) to lift quantitative restrictions to the extent of one half of their imports from each other in 1948. In the field of payments, ECA drew up a blueprint for a European Currency Union (later renamed European Payments Union) which was presented to the OEEC in December 1949.

Principal characteristics of any scheme for multilateral clearing in Europe

As was true of all similar previous plans for multilateral clearing, the EPU project consisted of two distinct parts: (1) an offsetting mechanism and (2) a settlement mechanism.

1. *The offsetting mechanism* is designed to break through the bilateral channels within which intra-European trade has been constricted since the beginning of the war. It aims at permitting one country to offset a deficit in one direction by a surplus in another. This is not expected to be achieved by making European currencies directly convertible into each other and into the dollar, a step considered as premature by many European countries. Rather, each country, while maintaining its present system for controlling foreign exchange trans-

actions, will have an account with a central Payments Union, and the debits and credits accumulated by each country's central bank in its bilateral relations with the central banks of other countries will be transferred at monthly intervals to its EPU account, which will thereby be debited or credited by the combined net result of its intra-European transactions. The great advantage of this method as contrasted with bilateralism lies in the fact that a country does not have to be concerned by deficits with some countries provided that these deficits are offset by surpluses in other directions. It thus eliminates bilateral bargaining and permits an expansion of useful trade. It also means that a country that experiences a serious deficit with another country but remains in over-all balance in Europe will feel no need to resort to quantitative restrictions in order to correct this deficit.

2. *The settlement mechanism.* The settlement of the net balances emerging from multilateral clearing raises a number of important issues. One hundred per cent settlement in gold or dollars would amount to the establishment of one type of full convertibility of European currencies.[3a] It has been generally agreed that such a step would not only be premature in view of the general balance of payments position, but would also interfere with current efforts to liberalize intra-European trade. In a situation in which countries are faced with the obligation to pay gold for any additional import, they probably would be quite unwilling to undertake new risks by lifting existing trade barriers, even though this were done on a reciprocal basis.

On the other hand, there also was agreement that the terms of settlement of the net balances emerging from the clearing should not be too "soft." If countries knew that, as a result of large-scale credit facilities, they could run up a considerable net deficit with the other countries in the group without having to make gold payments, they might be tempted to pursue policies of monetary ease that would lead them straight back into the conditions of inflation from which they were just emerging.

These conflicting considerations led to the

conclusion that the deficit countries should be granted some credit by the Union, but should make gold payments on an increasing scale as their deficit rose. Creditor countries also would finance their surplus partly by credits and would receive gold for the balance. The Union would be endowed with an initial fund in dollars which would serve to make up any differences between gold payments by debtors and gold receipts by creditors.

Launching of the EPU project and first difficulties

In December 1949, the OEEC Council entrusted its Payments Committee to draft the outlines of a European Payments Union that would start operations on July 1, 1950. A general outline was produced and inserted into the second interim report of the OEEC, published in January 1950.[3] In the meantime, however, the project encountered many difficulties. First, there was concern in some United States quarters that the projected Union would in various respects duplicate the functions of the International Monetary Fund; and, more important, it was feared that the arrangement, particularly in view of the inclusion of the whole sterling area, might lead to the establishment of a self-sufficient "high-cost, soft-currency area" characterized by permanent discriminatory restrictions against the dollar.[4]

Once assurances were obtained concerning these points, the EPU project ran into serious trouble as the result of British opposition. During the session of the OEEC Council in January, Sir Stafford Cripps declared that the United Kingdom would be unable to accept substitution of the proposed clearing mechanism for the bilateral agreements involving sterling. He refused to accept an EPU that would supersede the existing bilateral agreements; rather, he favored one that would function only after exhaustion of bilateral credit lines and would thus be superimposed upon the bilateral agreements as a "lender of last resort." At the same time, Sir Stafford declared that the United Kingdom could not agree to restrict its freedom

[3a] See my note on "Types of Convertibility," in this issue of the REVIEW.

[3] *Second Report of the OEEC* (Paris 1950), pp. 228–35.
[4] See Mr. Hinshaw's article below for an analysis of this question.

THE EUROPEAN PAYMENTS UNION 51

of action with respect to quantitative restrictions on trade.

It should be mentioned here that ECA was trying to obtain commitments from the OEEC countries to make further progress in abolishing quantitative restrictions in intra-European trade. Moreover, once these restrictions had been removed, it was deemed important that countries should not easily and unilaterally be able to restore them. It was in this respect that the United Kingdom served notice that it would have to retain its full freedom of action.

The EPU in Congress and the dollar contribution

In spite of these difficulties, ECA went ahead with its project and made it figure prominently in the Congressional presentation of its request for funds for 1950–51. In order to make it possible to provide the Union with appropriated funds, ECA sponsored an amendment of the Economic Cooperation Act so as to permit a transfer of $600 million in free dollars from its appropriated funds to "any central institution or other organization formed to further the purposes of this Act by two or more participating countries, or to any participating country or countries in connection with the operations of such institution or organization, to be used on terms and conditions specified by the Administrator and designed to promote multilateral intra-European trade, to facilitate the transferability of European currencies, and progressively to eliminate the existing systems of bilateral trade, and to liberalize trade among participating countries and between them and other countries." The Congress accepted this amendment and even provided that, unless the $600 million were used for the purposes mentioned in the amendment, they were to be returned to the Treasury (ECA had only asked for *permission* to transfer funds). Through this mandatory provision, the Congress no doubt intended to exert some pressure in favor of the acceptance of EPU by all OEEC countries.

ECA's dollar contribution will serve a triple purpose: (1) to make up any difference between debtors' gold payments to EPU and creditors' gold receipts from EPU that might arise in the course of EPU operations; (2) to provide funds for the redemption under certain conditions (see below) of existing European-held sterling balances; and (3) to constitute a separate fund which will permit ECA to intervene when a country experiences extraordinary and unforeseen difficulties in its intra-European payments relations.

Agreement on the special position of sterling

With favorable action by the Congress, the principal immediate task was to break the deadlock with the British. It was recognized by United States and Continental officials that sterling was indeed in a special position with respect to the EPU project. In the first place, sterling, unlike any other European currency, is widely used as a means of settlement among third countries. Secondly, many countries have traditionally held sterling as part of their monetary reserve. Thirdly, several European countries had, during or after the war, accumulated considerable holdings of sterling. These holdings posed a special dilemma for the EPU: neither Britain nor the countries holding these sterling balances would consent to any blocking; but, in the absence of blocking, the holders of the balances could continue to settle bilaterally with the United Kingdom and would thereby infringe on the principle that all countries had to settle their net over-all position through the EPU.

On their side, the British realized that they could not maintain the negative attitude shown by Sir Stafford Cripps in January. In March, they came forward with a proposal which advocated a limited participation of sterling in the scheme. Without going into its details, it may be affirmed that the proposal constituted considerable progress since, for the first time, the British showed themselves ready to accept transfers of sterling even when such transfers could involve them in losses of gold. The proposal, however, was rejected by both the American and the Continental negotiators since it did not go far enough in the direction of doing away with bilateral payments agreements.

After intensive further negotiations, in the course of which ECA, the Belgians, and the OEEC secretariat each produced tentative proposals, agreement was finally reached in May on the insertion of sterling into the EPU. The agreement provided that Britain would be a full member of the EPU; i.e., that it would establish a net balance with EPU for all the transactions of the sterling area with the other OEEC countries and would settle this balance through the EPU in accordance with the general procedure for settlements (part in gold and part in credits). The United Kingdom also agreed that it would reintroduce previously lifted quantitative restrictions only in the case of a serious drain on its reserves and then only on a multilateral as opposed to a discriminatory basis.

On the other hand, the "special" position of sterling was taken into account as follows:

(1) With respect to the use of sterling as a monetary reserve: it was agreed that, instead of holding EPU credits, creditors could make arrangements to hold in the form of sterling that part of their surplus which would correspond to their surplus in sterling; [5]

(2) With respect to the existing sterling balances of the Continental members of the EPU: it was decided that these balances could be used only if the holders were in a net deficit position with respect to the EPU, but could then be used irrespective of whether the holders were in a deficit position vis-à-vis the sterling area. ECA agreed to indemnify the United Kingdom for any actual losses of gold that might result from such multilateral use of sterling balances.

This solution of the vexing problem of the special position of sterling was generally found quite satisfactory. It was felt that the United Kingdom had indeed come a long way since Cripps' statement in January and that the price paid by ECA for the British concessions was a reasonable one.

Administration of the EPU and the International Monetary Fund

In the meantime, it had become clear that the issue of EPU's relationship to the International Monetary Fund, which had caused much concern at an earlier stage, would be disposed of without too much trouble. By general agreement, the EPU would be governed largely by automatic rules and would function under the supervision of the OEEC, a body that can make decisions only by unanimous vote. This arrangement did not seem likely to result in a powerful supra-national monetary board whose authority would supersede that of the Fund.

An interesting attempt has been made to avoid the paralysis that has often been exhibited by international bodies tied to the rule of unanimity. On a number of important issues that must be deferred for decision to the OEEC Council, the final EPU agreement provides for the procedure of the "Special Restricted Committee." This Committee is to consist of "five persons chosen by lot from a list of persons nominated by each of the members for reasons of competence and standing." When the issue to be decided is a dispute involving one or several specific countries, none of the Committee members may be a national of one of the parties to the dispute. The Committee is to make a report to the OEEC Council on the issue at stake and the Council will then make a recommendation or take a decision "in the light of this report." The intention of this procedure is to invest the Committee with a moral authority which will make for unanimous acceptance of its reports within the OEEC Council.

The terms of settlement of EPU balances

One important question remained to be settled: that of the actual terms of settlement of EPU credits and debits. There was agreement that the gold payments by the debtor should increase as his deficit rose and that the creditor should extend some credit. But exactly what the ratio of gold settlement to credit settlement was to be, had been left undecided pending the solution of the sterling problem. The discussion started around a British proposal that was "soft" in the extreme: it called for a gold-free credit margin for debtors of 10 per cent of each country's total trade turnover (imports plus exports plus invisible current account items) with the other EPU members and, in addition, for another 5 per cent of credits which would go hand-in-hand with increasing gold payments. During subse-

---

[5] This provision has been made applicable to all member currencies, but its practical significance has been considerably reduced by the rules concerning the liquidation of EPU. See *The Economist, op. cit.*, p. 131.

THE EUROPEAN PAYMENTS UNION   53

quent discussions, these figures were whittled down to gold-free credit margins of 3 per cent of total turnover, with gold-accompanied credits for an additional 6 per cent.

With respect to the gold-accompanied credits, the ratio of gold to credit settlement is to increase for debtors in equal installments from 1:4 to 2:3 and 3:2 to 4:1, whereas for net creditors the ratio is to remain fixed at 1:1 after exhaustion of the gold-free credit margin. The *quota* of each member country is defined as that range of its deficit within which it can command any credit from the EPU or, alternatively, as that range of its surplus within which it is committed to credit extension to EPU. This range is thus equal to 15 per cent (3 per cent gold-free credit margin plus 6 per cent credit tied to 6 per cent gold) of its total trade turnover. After exhaustion of the quota, the debtor has to settle fully in gold unless the OEEC specifically decides otherwise. On the other hand, a net creditor who has extended the full amount of credit to which he is committed has no assurance that he will automatically be paid 100 per cent in gold. It is merely provided that, at this point, an attempt shall be made at determining settlement arrangements which are mutually satisfactory to the creditor country, the other members, and the EPU.

The above asymmetries in the settling of debtors' and creditors' balances are only feeble reminders of the original blueprint idea that the EPU settlement mechanism should discourage the accumulation of excessive debit positions by increasing the ratio of gold to credit settlement while it would at the same time discourage the emergence of excessive credit positions by allowing the creditor countries a decreasing proportion of gold settlement as their intra-European surplus would rise. Naturally it proved impossible to obtain the unlimited commitments to extend credit that were implicit in this idea. Nevertheless, the mode of settlement as finally agreed goes farther than any previous international monetary mechanism in placing responsibility to maintain international balance on the creditor as well as on the debtor.

The question of "softness" of the terms of settlement

Even though the quotas and credits are established for a two-year period, it was felt in many quarters that the scheme still resulted in too large an injection of credit into the intra-European payments system. In view of the wide swings that have been characteristic of intra-European payments over the past few years, it is extremely hard to formulate a precise judgment as to the "generosity" of the credit margins provided under EPU. It seems safe to say, however, that the EPU system is, by itself, not "hard" enough to deter countries from following unduly expansionary policies. On the other hand, inflation is far too serious an affair to be started merely because of the existence of sizable credit facilities for the settlement of intra-European deficits. This has been amply shown during the past years when countries have repeatedly failed to utilize drawing rights established for them under the Intra-European Payments Schemes.

With respect to debtor countries, the credit provisions of the EPU mean that *one* of the many punishments for inflation will be mild, at least in the beginning. While this absence of punishment does not appear likely to induce countries to "commit" inflation, it does place more of a burden on their self-restraint than would have been the case with a harder system of settlement. The need for self-restraint will be even greater with the inflationary pressures that are likely to be generated by the additional military expenditures presently being planned.

Special arrangements for Belgium

With respect to the probable creditors, the possible inflationary consequences of wide credit margins are more direct than in the case of the debtors. Whereas it was feared for the latter that the existence of over-generous intra-European credit facilities might fail to check, or might even elicit, inflationary developments, the commitment of the creditors to grant large credits could result directly in an unduly large volume of "unrequited" exports and thereby start inflation in the creditor country. The country that was most concerned with this danger was Belgium. Since Belgium's foreign trade with OEEC countries is particularly high in relation to its national income, the Belgians felt that credit extension by their country according to the general formula would represent a disproportionate contribution which might result in inflation and would thereby compromise the considerable progress Belgium had made toward non-discriminatory trade arrangements and currency convertibility. These feelings led to a last minute crisis in the EPU negotiations. The Belgian Cabinet decided at first to reject the agreement, but the deadlock was broken by a series of concessions to Belgium which considerably reduced its credit commitments.

One of the concessions, later generalized for all countries, provided for repayment of Belgium's outstanding credits within two years unless special agreements providing for longer terms were concluded bilaterally between Belgium and its debtors. Provided that the two-year terms are not widely superseded by such bilateral agreements, this will result in making for somewhat less "softness" in general, since part of the EPU credits will then be used for the repayment of old debts rather than for the financing of current deficits.

Intra-European vs. over-all balance

The EPU arrangement has frequently been attacked on the ground that it appears to place a particular premium on intra-European as distinct from over-all balance of payments equilibrium. It would seem indeed that, in the EPU, debtors and creditors are "penalized" (by having to pay more and more gold or by having to grant more and more credit, respectively) the farther they move away from intra-European equilibrium regardless of what happens to their international accounts as a whole. This criticism calls for the following comments:

(1) It is a strange use of language to say that a debtor is "penalized" when he is only made to pay his debts. It would be far more correct to say that an intra-European debtor obtains the special privilege of not having to settle in gold for a fraction of any intra-European debt he incurs; this privilege is granted primarily to promote the special effort that is being made to reduce trade barriers within

Europe with the intent of creating a strong competitive European economy.

(2) It is true that it would hardly make sense for a country which is a net earner of dollars outside of Europe to receive a credit from EPU rather than to be required to settle its intra-European deficit fully in gold. But the EPU was conceived at a time when all its prospective members [6] expected to continue to run dollar deficits for at least two more years. Should this expectation prove widely off the mark or should the life of EPU be prolonged beyond 1952, it might be well to insert into its mechanism a clause similar to the repurchase provisions of the Fund Agreement.[7]

(3) While in general the EPU account of member countries starts at zero, those countries that are clearly expected to be net debtors or net creditors within Europe have been given "initial positions" in the EPU that take account of this expectation. Countries which are expected to be debtors (Austria, Greece, Norway, Netherlands) start out in the EPU with a certain agreed creditor position, and therefore do not incur any obligation as long as their deficit remains within the scope of this initial credit. Presumed creditor countries (Belgium, United Kingdom, Sweden), on the other hand, start out with a debit which they have to work off before starting to secure any claim on the EPU. However, they receive a full dollar allocation from ECA for the initial debit position with which they are burdened in EPU. In this rather artificial way, certain EPU countries are permitted to earn dollars directly through their European surpluses while others have officially sanctioned and freely financed intra-European deficits; this mechanism, a survival from the drawing rights of the Intra-European Payments Schemes, is no doubt cumbersome, but it at least must be recognized as an attempt at dealing with "structural" surpluses and deficits in intra-European trade which are due to present

[6] The one exception is Switzerland which actually stated that it is likely to prefer paying gold for any EPU deficit to accepting EPU credits that carry interest charges.

[7] Subject to certain conditions, the repurchase provisions oblige Fund members who have purchased foreign currencies from the Fund and have later accumulated monetary reserves to repurchase their own currencies from the Fund in an amount equal to one half of the accumulation.

dislocations or which can be expected to persist after the dollar problem has been solved.

Flexibility and prospective functions of the EPU

The debate over the desirable degree of "softness" or "hardness" in the terms of settlement of EPU balances caused very specific provisions for review to be inserted into the final EPU Agreement. In addition to regular periodic reports, a special comprehensive report is to be made as of June 30, 1951. It will be devoted particularly to the question whether the credit facilities presently provided for will have proven to be excessive or inadequate.

These provisions for review underline the flexible nature of the EPU as a new international financial instrument. With multilateral clearing as its basic operating function, the EPU can indeed be adapted to play a useful role in a great variety of developments. With further progress toward freedom of trade within Europe and toward dollar solvability, the provisions for settlement could be progressively tightened. Such a process is likely to be hastened by the tapering off of ECA aid and would in the end convert EPU into a mere clearing house where income equals outgo. Even in such a situation EPU would still fulfill a useful function, since it would then represent a reliable mechanism for assuring the convertibility of European currencies.[8]

On the other hand, the EPU provides, in the present situation, an excellent instrument for giving precise financial meaning to such phrases as "European solidarity" and "equality of sacrifice." Because of the differences in the industrial and manpower resources of the various OEEC or Atlantic Pact countries, there are

[8] See my note, "Types of Convertibility," in this issue of the REVIEW.

bound to be great differences in their individual contributions to a stronger common defense. The EPU, however, can serve as a ready instrument for equalizing these burdens by the channeling of EPU credits toward those countries shouldering the largest direct burdens, and vice versa. In this way, the total volume of credit in the system need not be increased; but the available credit volume would be used and, if necessary, rearranged so as to provide the countries that devote most resources to defense with some resources of the other countries which would thus participate indirectly in the common effort.

Thus the EPU, whose original and central purpose is to make a contribution to the creation of a single European market, is well suited to play a useful role under conditions of worldwide convertibility as well as in the setting of a large defense effort. Naturally, there is no guarantee that the EPU will actually perform these useful functions. It could well develop into a brake on the progress toward convertibility if it were to refuse to introduce harder terms of settlement as such terms became possible. It could also interfere with a rational common defense effort if it permitted those countries that contribute least to the direct building up of armed strength to suck in additional resources from those countries already burdened by heavy defense expenditures.

To point out such possibilities, however, is merely to say that, like every human institution, the European Payments Union has potentialities for both good and evil. But, endowed with well-defined functions in response to pressing current problems and operating in an area ever more intimately bound together, the EPU at least promises to be that most difficult achievement: a genuinely alive international institution.

[11]

International Currency and Reserve Plans

Introduction.

We shall soon celebrate — unless we forget — the tenth anniversary of the Bretton Woods Conference. The hopeful plans for currency convertibility drawn up in New Hampshire have long been buried under the weight of the so-called dollar shortage which accompanied postwar reconstruction, the Korean crisis and the first years of Western rearmament. The year 1953 witnessed, at long last, a fundamental and spectacular readjustment in the world's payments pattern. From a gold and dollar deficit of nearly $ 11 billion in 1947, foreign countries moved gradually to an actual surplus, before aid, of nearly $ 1 billion in 1953. Their gold and dollar holdings — including United States aid receipts — dropped by nearly $ 6 billion in the three years 1946-1948, but have risen since by $ 8 billion, of which $ 2.6 billion in 1953 alone.

National and international plans for currency convertibility have thus become again, for the first time in many years, a practical policy issue. The problem was raised here, on the initiative of the United Kingdom, a little more than a year ago, but the British suggestions were received with a surprising lack of enthusiasm in the United States, in Europe and even in England. The discussion of the plan soon revealed fundamental disagreements about the very meaning of convertibility under present economic and political conditions.

The Commission on Foreign Economic Policy, under the able chairmanship of Clarence B. Randall, devoted considerable attention to the issues involved. Its report (1), issued last January, has done much to clarify the intimate relationship between the trade

and the payments aspects of international convertibility. In the meantime, the British plan was discussed further in the Organization for European Economic Cooperation (O.E.E.C.) and at the Commonwealth Conference in Sydney. Important steps toward the broadening of currency transferability and the relaxation of dollar restrictions have also been taken in recent months by a number of major countries, particularly the United Kingdom, Germany and the Netherlands.

The United States recession and the pending Congressional debate on the Randall Report have induced a wait-and-see attitude which has slowed down the adoption of even more spectacular decisions, both nationally and internationally. There is little doubt, however, that such decisions will soon be forthcoming, and that they will be vitally influenced by the long overdue clarification of United States policies.

I. - The 1953 British Plan and the Randall Report.

The plan presented by the British last spring rested essentially on a distinction between convertibility for residents and convertibility for non-residents. The United Kingdom proposed to restore the convertibility of sterling earned in current transactions (2) by *non-residents of the sterling area*, but to retain the right, for the United Kingdom as well as for other sterling area countries, to impose restrictions on all foreign transactions of

---

(1) *Report to the President and the Congress*, Commission on Foreign Economic Policy, Washington, 1954.

(2) The exclusion of convertibility for capital transactions has become generally accepted since Bretton Woods as a permanent feature of postwar convertibility plans. The practical wisdom and feasibility of this exclusion raises very complex issues which I shall make no attempt to discuss here. It might be noted, however, that the International Monetary Fund's example was not followed by the Agreement for a European Payments Union, which applies equally to all transactions among members, whether on current or capital account.

their own residents. These restrictions could, of course, be imposed in order to limit the foreigners' sterling earnings and the drain on the area's gold and foreign exchange reserves which might attend the conversion of such earnings into nonsterling currencies, particularly dollars. They could, moreover, be imposed on a discriminatory or even bilateral basis to restrict imports from the countries presenting « excessive » demands for conversion and to favor imports from the countries which retained their earnings in sterling or made use of them to expand their purchases from the area itself.

The proposal was, moreover, made conditional upon a substantial liberalization of United States trade policies and the granting of large stabilization loans or lines of credit to the United Kingdom by the International Monetary Fund and by the United States.

The major criticism levelled against the plan, both here and abroad, was that its adoption might well stimulate a new wave of trade restrictions, discrimination and bilateralism. The Randall report agreed with this criticism and indicated that the Commission « would deplore a merely formal convertibility maintained through trade restrictions. It believes that the removal of restrictions upon trade and upon payments should go hand in hand » (3).

The European countries were particularly fearful of the implications of the British plans for the O.E.E.C. trade liberalization program and the European Payments Union. The Randall Commission expressed a similar concern about dismantling prematurely the most effective instrument for trade liberalization and currency transferability established so far: « The Union has achieved an impressive measure of success — above all, it has shown that freeing trade and freeing payment go hand in hand — and the Commission feels that it should not sponsor any measures that might wreck the Union before there is something better to put in its place » (4).

(3) *Report to the President and the Congress*, Commission on Foreign Economic Policy, Washington, 1954, p. 73.
(4) *Report to the President and the Congress*, Commission on Foreign Economic Policy, Washington, 1954, p. 74.

These criticisms may spring in part from an overpessimistic view of the external position of Britain and of the world's so-called « dollar shortage » (5).

In the absence of heavy balance of payments pressures, the current trend toward trade liberalization might be expected to develop even in the absence of formal commitments, and to be strengthened further by the proposed measures for currency convertibility.

Yet the possibility of renewed balance of payments difficulties — whether in Britain or in other countries — cannot be excluded. Under such circumstances, formal convertibility for non-residents, unaccompanied by parallel commitments with respect to trade policy, might force a relapse into restrictions, discrimination and bilateralism and destroy the progress already achieved toward a multilateral system of trade and payments.

After all, the proposed sterling convertibility already exists for residents of the United States and other « American Account » countries. Sterling earnings accruing to such residents are freely convertible into dollars. Any other country that wishes to is also free to refuse payment in inconvertible sterling, and to demand gold or dollar payment for its exports. Most countries are deterred from doing so by the realization that such a policy would generally expose them to tighter restrictions on their exports to sterling area countries, similar to the restrictions now applied by these countries against imports from the dollar area. Sterling convertibility for non-residents is certainly not regarded as true convertibility by the United States exporters who already « enjoy » this status, and it is certainly not sought by other countries' exporters to whom this « privilege » is now denied.

These considerations explain the coolness with which the British plan was received in Europe, in the United States and even by a large sector of British opinion. While the plan has not been formally amended, there exist numerous indications that opinion is gradually shifting, in Britain and in Europe,

(5) See below, pp. 13 ff.

toward a position fairly similar to that expressed in the Randall report. To be meaningful, convertibility must apply to trade as well as payments, to residents as well as to non-residents. This implies that progress can only be gradual and must depend on the fulfilment of certain prerequisites. « The Commission does... wish to emphasize its view that a strong internal economy, willing and able to control its money supply and its budget as safeguards against inflation, sufficiently mobile to make the best use of its resources, and able and willing to save in order to increase its productivity and improve its competitive position in world markets, is a prerequisite to convertibility; and that the attainment over time of these conditions should be the guide as to how rapidly full convertibility could safely be approached » (6).

These « prerequisites to convertibility » constitute, indeed, an awesome list, especially if they are viewed not only as once-and-for-all prerequisites for the *restoration* of convertibility, but also as permanent prerequisites for the *maintenance* of convertibility after it has been restored. Will any future lapse from internal strength automatically spell the collapse of convertibility for the country concerned? And how will the failure of some countries to reach or maintain convertibility affect the prospects for the achievement or preservation of *international* convertibility? « The Commission believes that the decisions, the methods, the timetable, and the responsibility for introducing currency convertibility should rest on the countries concerned. It recognizes, however, that currency convertibility must be examined in the light of the policies pursued by other countries, particularly the United States » (7). And it clearly thinks also that the restoration of convertibility by Britain would greatly facilitate — or even be necessary for? — its restoration by other countries, and would in turn be greatly eased « if some other of the major trading countries [were] able to make their currencies convertible simultaneously with sterling » (8).

(6) *Report to the President and the Congress*, Commission on Foreign Economic Policy, Washington, 1954, p. 74.
(7) *Report to the President and the Congress*, pp. 72-73.
(8) *Ibid.*, Commission on Foreign Economic Policy, Washington, 1954, p. 74.

The Report thus seems to contemplate the unilateral restoration of convertibility by each country, acting in isolation, while recognizing at the same time the interdependence among the various countries' decisions and policies, particularly the United States, the United Kingdom and other major trading countries. The recognition of this interdependence is in happy contrast with the naive theory which still prevails in academic and business circles, and which long dominated the United States Treasury thinking, *i.e.*, that convertibility merely depends on each country's « setting its own house in order » by stopping inflation, readjusting its exchange rate, abolishing trade and exchange controls and requiring full gold or convertible currency settlement for its exports and other external transactions. Even a country as strong internally and externally as Switzerland still feels unable to adopt such a prescription and run the risk of generalized discrimination against its exports.

International currency convertibility cannot be restored and — even more important — maintained without the active participation and cooperation of the major trading countries. While this participation and cooperation could largely be taken for granted in the nineteenth century, they cannot be ensured today by mere unilateral decisions, but require at least a minimum of collective organization and mutual commitments.

Before discussing the nature of these commitments, we must clarify the meaning of currency convertibility, as an international policy objective. We shall then discover that the necessary commitments are far less formidable than the « convertibility prerequisites » listed in the Randall report, and which, indeed, no international agreement could ever be relied upon to enforce effectively.

II. - Toward a Definition of « Workable » Convertibility.

Currency convertibility used to be defined by the maintenance of a fixed parity or exchange rate with relation to gold or other gold-convertible currencies. It might seem rather paradoxical, therefore, to find the modern proponents of convertibility arguing in favour of flexible or « floating » exchange rates as against fixed or « pegged » rates. The reason for this shift is, of course, obvious. The fixity of exchange rates becomes largely illusory if it is preserved only through trade or exchange restrictions which control arbitrarily the access of traders to foreign exchange for each category of transactions, and may deny them the right to purchase it at any rate whatsoever. Exchange stability has little or no meaning if it is not based on exchange freedom. The latter was taken for granted in all traditional definitions of convertibility. True currency inconvertibility — as distinct from instability of exchange rates — is a relatively modern phenomenon. It might be noted, for instance, that European currencies remained convertible throughout the 1920's even though at a fluctuating exchange rate.

Here again, the Randall report marks definite progress over previous policies, and particularly over the exaggerated emphasis placed on exchange rate stability at Bretton Woods. The Commission expresses itself as « sympathetic to the concept of a "floating rate", which provides alternative methods of meeting trade and exchange pressures » (9).

This seems to leave us with the elimination of trade and exchange restrictions as the modern definition of convertibility. The question arises at once whether any full elimination of such restrictions is conceivable within a foreseeable future, and whether such liberalization can realistically be confined to direct, quantitative restrictions while leaving tariff restrictions to the full discretion of each individual country. There are undoubtedly very important differences between tariff restrictions and other trade or exchange restrictions. Most of these differences relate, however, to the *domestic* impact of such measures upon income and money flows. From the point of view of their *international* impact, the differences between tariffs and trade controls are not so fundamental as to justify the definition of convertibility in terms of a full elimination of the latter without any

concern for the first. High and unstable tariff levels can indeed be as, or more, damaging to international trade as moderate, nondiscriminatory, systems of import or exchange controls.

Shall we therefore be pushed into a definition of convertibility which equates it to the old free trade ideal of classical economists? In this case, progress will indeed have to be gradual, and full convertibility is unlikely to reward our efforts or even those of our children and grandchildren.

Clarity of thought and effectiveness of policy both require a less ambitious definition of immediate convertibility goals. Such a definition can be found in the restoration of a *multilateral system of trade and payments*, rather than in the removal of all protection for domestic production against imports from abroad. This was indeed the meaning of nineteenth century convertibility, which accomodated itself to varying degrees of national protection. The major differences between these age-old techniques of protection and modern inconvertibility techniques lies in the fact that the former extended protection only to the national producers and only within the protecting country's boundaries, while the second discriminate in favor of certain exporting countries at the expense of others, and try to protect domestic producers not only within the country's boundaries but in all foreign markets as well. Once adopted by a major country, such techniques inevitably spread from trading partner to trading partner, each country trying to secure special advantages to itself or being forced at least to defend its exporters against the discriminatory actions of others. International trade is then forced more and more into the strait jacket of bilateral negotiations, relegating increasingly into the background all considerations of price or quality competition and the underlying pattern of comparative costs and advantages.

The key to « workable » convertibility is not free trade — desirable as this would be — but the maintenance of full competition in third markets. Professor MacDougall's study of United States and United Kingdom exports in 1937 showed ample verification for

(9) *Report to the President and the Congress*, Commission on Foreign Economic Policy, Washington, 1954, p. 73.

the classical theory of comparative costs, but found that it depended essentially on *third market competition* rather than on direct trade between the two countries. « Before the war, American weekly wages in manufacturing were roughly double the British, and we find that, when American output per worker was more than twice the British, the United States had in general the bulk of the export market, while for the products where it was less than twice as high the bulk of the market was held by Britain... But while in the normal text-book examples the exports of each country go to each other, the great bulk of the exports of the United States and the United Kingdom in 1937 went to third countries — more than 95 per cent of British exports of all our sample products but three, more than 95 per cent of American exports of all the products but six. It is true that each country was nearly always a net exporter to the other of products in which it had a comparative advantage, but this is of limited interest, since trade between them was in general a negligible proportion of their total consumption » (10).

Thus, the preservation — or restoration — of traditional competitive forces in international trade depends essentially on the equal access of all foreign exporters to each national market, rather than on the elimination of all protection for domestic producers within a country's own territory. The latter objective has never been achieved, and can hardly be expected ever to be fully achieved, without a political as well as economic merger among the countries concerned. Equal access to third markets has always constituted the bulk and the core of international competition.

Convertibility is not incompatible, therefore, with a certain amount of protection and restrictions. The past is, in this case, a guide to the future. The restoration of convertibility depends essentially on the elimination of discrimination and bilateralism — rather than of *over-all* protection or re-

strictions — from the trade and payments mechanism. This implies:

(a) the ability of country A to use its earnings on countries B, C, D, etc. to settle its deficits with countries X, Y, Z, etc., *i.e.*, full currency transferability;

(b) the absence of bilateral or discriminatory trade techniques designed to shift trade artificially from low cost exporters to high cost exporters, thus distorting normal competitive forces not only between domestic and foreign producers, but in all third markets as well (11).

The two problems are largely inseparable, as payments and trade techniques reinforce one another in this respect and can often be used nearly interchangeably to achieve the same result.

The weakness of the International Monetary Fund springs in large part from the artificial separation of these two problems — one of which was entrusted to the Fund, and the other to G.A.T.T. — but even more from basic defects of the Fund's machinery in dealing with currency transferability. Countries may borrow from the Fund, but they cannot use the Fund to convert their earnings on one country into the currency needed to settle their deficit with another. Moreover, the Fund has in practice made little or no attempt to distinguish between exchange restrictions and discrimination. Organized discrimination against a « scarce currency » is theoretically provided for under Article VII of the Fund Agreement, but this provision has never been put to the test by the Fund. On the other hand, Fund members have so far retained the right to currency discrimination — against weak as well as against hard currencies — under Article XIV of the Agreement. Similar discrimination is also contemplated as a permanent feature of the Agreement under Article VIII, although its use under this Article would be subject to Fund approval.

In contrast, the remarkable success achieved by the European Payments Union is largely explainable by its comprehensive ap-

(10) G. D. A. MacDougall, *British and American Exports: A Study Suggested by the Theory of Comparative Costs*, Part I, « Economic Journal », December 1951, pp. 697-724, particularly pp. 697-699. See also below, Table III, p. 18, column 4.

(11) This definition is very close to that proposed in the « Staff Papers » of the Randall Commission, on pp. 467-468.

proach to the problem, encompassing full multilateralism both in trade — nondiscrimination — and in payments — currency transferability. This multilateralism, however, is confined to the relationships among member countries, and does not cover their trade and payments with other countries and particularly with the United States. Partial convertibility with the United States dollar is provided in E.P.U. settlements, but each country is left free to regulate as it wishes its trade and payments with nonmember countries (12).

Most of the difficulties which E.P.U. has had to meet in its four years of operation, and most of the objections raised against it, are closely related to these regional limitations of the Agreement. These were, however, unavoidable at the time the Agreement was negotiated. While they are probably unnecessary and even harmful under present conditions, their elimination might prove dangerous in the event of a renewed dollar scarcity, as it might then contribute to the unnecessary spread of deflationary forces and to ultimate relapse into generalized bilateralism.

III. - The Prerequisites of Convertibility.

Convertibility has been defined above as the absence of discrimination, and particularly bilateralism, with respect to both trade and payments. While indispensable to the maintenance of international competition, such a system is also subject to a major defect. It tends to spread to the world at large any deflationary pressures arising from an economic depression or from trade restrictionism in one of the major trading centers. If each country most heavily and directly affected by the decline in this center's imports adopts *nondiscriminatory* policies — internal deflation, currency devaluation, overall trade or exchange restrictions, etc. — to restore equilibrium in its balance of payments, it will affect unfavorably the balance of payments

of other countries. These may, in turn, be compelled to adopt similar policies — or to reinforce them — thus contributing to the spiralling of deflation, devaluation or restrictions. This process will continue until the first country's surplus is ultimately eliminated, but will involve a multiple restriction of world trade — or an extensive devaluation of currencies — which might have been avoided by direct and systematic discrimination against the surplus country alone. For this alternative to be successful, however, discrimination by the deficit countries must be directed exclusively against the *overall* creditor country, rather than against the contries in *bilateral* surplus with them, since such bilateral creditors may themselves be in overall deficit rather than in overall surplus. If discrimination is left to the discretion of each individual country, acting in isolation, it will inevitably take the form of bilateral discrimination and involve even worse distortions — and, probably, a greater contraction — of world trade (13).

This was recognized in the « scarce currency » clause of the International Monetary Fund, but the practical implementation of such a clause would raise enormous difficulties. Public opinion in the scarce currency country is likely to pay little heed to the intricate economics of the problem and to react violently against the ganging up of other nations against its exports. The danger of retaliatory action will deter many countries from participating in systematized discrimination. This is all the more likely as such discrimination might involve the imposition of tight restrictions against essential imports from the scarce currency country while unessential imports from other countries continue to be imported freely. Countries can hardly be expected to sacrifice their

---

(12) Payments to and from nonmember countries of the sterling area are, however, channelled through the United Kingdom's account, and are subject to the same settlement rules as are applicable among members. The same applies also to all other sterling transfers.

(13) An abundant literature has grown up around this problem and its applicability to the so-called « dollar shortage ». See, in particular:

E. M. BERNSTEIN, *Scarce Currencies and the International Monetary Fund*, « Journal of Political Economy », LIII (1945), pp. 1-14;

RAGNAR FRISCH, *On the Need for Forecasting a Multilateral Balance of Payments*, « American Economic Review ». XXXVII (1947), pp. 535-551;

JOHN H. WILLIAMS, *Trade not Aid: A Program for World Stability*, Harvard University Press, 1953.

own national interests in this manner for the sake of an abstract concept of international equilibrium. Certainly, the exact degree of implementation required from each participant would give rise to endless debate and controversies.

A more practical approach to the scarce currency problem lies in the extension of non-discrimination over the widest possible area, on the basis of mutual agreements and commitments, rather than in any international quarantine of the major creditor country. The E.P.U. experience reveals very clearly the type of commitments necessary for the effective functioning of a multilateral trading area. The creditor countries must facilitate the adoption by the debtors of *nondiscriminatory* readjustment policies:

1. by refraining at least from hampering such policies through unnecessary trade or exchange restrictions over their own imports; definite liberalization commitments were therefore accepted by all members, but exceeded in practice by the surplus countries;

2. by providing fractional financing to cushion moderate deficits of other members with inadequate reserves, thus allowing them to ride out temporary fluctuations in their balance of payments, or to wait for the effect of sloweracting fiscal or monetary readjustment policies;

3. by avoiding retaliatory action against countries which may be compelled to restore restrictions temporarily because of heavier deficits, provided that:

(a) such restrictions remain nondiscriminatory as among members; and

(b) the restricting country submits its case to full discussion by the competent organs of the O.E.E.C.; such discussion may cover not only the external measures adopted, but also the whole range of monetary, fiscal and economic policies of the country concerned.

IV. - From Regional Convertibility to International Convertibility.

Such a close type of cooperation is hardly feasible on a world-wide basis. It is possible only among countries which are highly inter-

dependent (exports to the E.P.U. area account for nearly three fourths of member countries' exports), keenly conscious of their interdependence and able to understand each other's problems and policies. These factors — different in degree, but not in kind, from those underlying a fuller political union — explain the success of, and justify the need for, regional cooperation in trade and payments. The maintenance of freer trade among members constitutes, of course, a form of discrimination. Such discrimination, however, rooted in mutual commitments of the type described above, may be as justified by its broad political and economic results as the discrimination against imports from abroad, and in favor of interregional imports, implicit in present boundaries between nations. The progressive elimination, in the nineteenth century, of internal taxes on the movement of goods between cities or provinces of the same country, or the fact that national tariff walls do not apply to domestic trade, have never been objected to in the name of nondiscrimination. There is no more reason to oppose the efforts to preserve freer trade among countries which are ready to accept, to this end, mutual trade and financial commitments limiting the untrammelled use of their economic sovereignty.

Under the inflationary strains of postwar reconstruction, the sterling area and E.P.U. arrangements provided a practical alternative, not to a better and wider system of international convertibility, but to the infinitely worse alternative of generalized bilateralism in trade and payments. They could not, however, provide a satisfactory answer to the fundamental disequilibria then prevailing between these regions and the outside world, and particularly to their trade and payments problems with the dollar area. In the sterling area, the responsibility for handling these problems centered largely on the United Kingdom, through the administration of the dollar pool and the setting up of different types of sterling accounts — American and Canadian accounts, transferable accounts, resident sterling accounts, bilateral accounts, etc. — subject to different privileges and limitations as to their transferability in payments, and implying at the same time different degrees of tightness in the administration of trade restrictions. In E.P.U., no such centralization was attempted, and each country was left free to handle on its own its trade and payments with nonmember countries. On the other hand — and in contrast to the exclusive use of sterling in settlement among sterling area countries — the partial gold or dollar payments involved in E.P.U. settlements established a direct link between the position of individual E.P.U. countries within and outside the E.P.U. area.

Such a system may tend to stimulate discrimination against an outside scarce currency, but also tends — contrary to a widely spread misconception — to eliminate discrimination if no such scarcity exists in fact.

The stimulus to discrimination arises from both the payments and the trade rules governing the system. E.P.U. creditors are forced to liberalize imports from other E.P.U. members, but are left free to maintain — or liberalize — restrictions on imports from the outside. Since, however, they receive only partial gold or dollar payment for their E.P.U. surpluses, they may be unable to finance large deficits with nonmembers requiring 100 per cent gold or dollar settlements. Even if their gold and dollar position enables them to do so, they may be alarmed by the continued growth of their E.P.U. lending and adopt restrictions on outside imports, in order to force their residents to shift their purchases to E.P.U. sources and thus reduce their rate of lending to the union.

Debtor countries, on the other hand, will normally prefer to incur their deficits with the Union, rather than with other countries, since the first require only partial gold and dollar payment and are, for the remainder, financed by E.P.U. credits. These credits, however are limited in size. When a country remains persistently in deficit with the Union, its ratio of gold to credit settlements rises steadily until the point of 100 per cent gold settlements is reached. When this occurs, the financial stimulus to discrimination disappears, and the deficit country becomes increasingly reluctant to admit freely less essential, or costlier, imports from E.P.U.

sources while continuing to restrict severely more essential or cheaper imports from the outside. On the other hand, such persistent deficits on the part of some members are reflected in persistent surpluses on the part of others. The creditors become increasingly reluctant to continue to extend larger and larger credits beyond their quotas. Since the Union, under these circumstances, is receiving 100 per cent gold settlements from the extreme debtors, its convertible resources tend to increase and to enable it to grant additional payments to the creditors either through a larger ratio of gold to credit settlements, or through some amortization of their previously accumulated claims.

The experience of E.P.U. so far confirms these theoretical deductions. Of the $ 1,350 million of E.P.U. credits initially available to them, present E.P.U. members have used about $ 1,150 million and have therefore only about $ 200 million in all left available. For many months, France, Turkey and Greece have been subject to 100 per cent gold settlements, and have claimed release from their trade liberalization commitments. Restrictions were also restored by the United Kingdom as long as its quota was exhausted or remained perilously close to exhaustion, and it will be remembered that, for a while, the United Kingdom also accepted sterling payment for dollar commodities bought through London. On the creditors' side, substantial amortization payments were granted to Belgium and Portugal in June 1952, and proposals now under discussion envisage both an increase in gold settlements beyond quotas and the regular amortization of long outstanding claims.

This normal evolution of the Union toward convertible settlements and nondiscrimination can only be held in check, in the long run, by a severe and generalized dollar scarcity When this exists, most members will be anxious to preserve their exports against the tighter restrictions applied to dollar trade, and will recognize that this can be done only through mutual trade liberalization and the limited convertibility of intra-E.P.U. settlements. When, however, the dollar position of a majority of members becomes more comfortable, the maintenance of discriminatory trade and payment rules is increasingly regarded not only as contrary to their own selfish interest, but also as unnecessary from the point of view of the group as a whole. It should be noted, for instance, that the E.P.U. management has always prodded excessive debtors to readjust their deficits through monetary and fiscal policies. Exchange readjustments have sometimes been hinted at also, but with a discretion imposed by common sense as well as by the desire to avoid any conflict of jurisdiction with the International Monetary Fund. These pressures had a considerable influence on member countries' policies, particularly in the case of Germany and the Netherlands. They were reinforced in the first case by a special loan negotiated on the basis of an agreed readjustment program, but at no time has the E.P.U. seriously entertained any proposals for further credit extensions to deficit countries which did not take adequate steps to readjust their balance of payments.

We may conclude, therefore, that while *formal* commitments to nondiscrimination and currency transferability are most likely to prove feasible on the basis of regional cooperation, such arrangements will tend *de facto* toward world-wide nondiscrimination and convertibility, except when discrimination against a « scarce currency » becomes the only alternative to the international spread of deflation or of bilateralism.

Even in the latter case, the maintenance of currency transferability and nondiscrimination among member countries preserves powerful competitive pressures upon the higher cost countries. It prevents them from seeking in bilateral trade and payments agreements an escape from basic economic readjustments. They can no longer extract from their creditors bilateral import credits or discrimination in favor of their exports. Moreover, the gradual liberalization of trade restrictions among members opens each market to the competition of the lower cost producers in the area, and exercises a fundamental influence on the readjustment of national price and cost patterns, indispensable to further progress toward world-wide, rather than merely regional, convertibility.

There is little doubt that full competition with Belgian, Swiss, German and other exporters over the whole E.P.U. area has exercised upon higher cost producers a pressure equivalent, or nearly equivalent, in most cases to that of competition from nonmember countries.

Confirmation of this fact can be found in the near elimination of currency discounts and gold premia in the European free markets, and in the ease with which major steps toward trade liberalization and broader currency transferability have been absorbed in recent months. The abolition of rationing, the reopening of international commodity and gold markets in London, the merging of practically all nonresident sterling accounts — outside the dollar area — into a single transferable account system, the adoption of a similar system for Deutsche mark accounts, the liberalization of many categories of dollar imports and other transactions in Germany, Belgium, and the Netherlands, etc. have already narrowed down considerably the gap between regional and international convertibility. There is every indication today that this remaining gap could be bridged if some method could be found to assuage current fears about the existence, or future resurgence, of a world-wide dollar scarcity.

V. - International Inflation and the Dollar Shortage.

A « currency scarcity » condition — i.e., the tendency for many countries to incur convergent deficits toward a single « scarce currency » country — may emerge from many different causes. A number of writers have popularized the view that a higher rate of technical advance in the United States tends to create a chronic dollar shortage. The *possibility* of such a link cannot be flatly denied on purely logical grounds. The *demonstration* of its inevitability or probability depends, however, on highly special assumptions as to the exact nature of such productivity advances, and as to their impact on prices and money wages, terms of trade, the income-elasticity of import demand, etc. It would not be difficult to construct extremely plausible models of United States advances in productivity the impact of which be to reduce, rather than increase, the balance of payments surpluses of the United States, without exercising any generalized deflationary pressures on foreign prices, export levels, economic activity or employment.

A dollar shortage undoubtedly tends to emerge, however, when the United States economy develops lesser inflationary pres-

import levels and export instability than has probably been true at any time in the recorded past (Table I).

The fears of a dollar shortage spring from the special factors underlying the present pattern of the balance of payments of the world with the United States, and particularly from:

(a) the dependence of foreign countries' current dollar earnings on large and « ab-

ESTIMATED GOLD RESERVES AND DOLLAR HOLDINGS OF FOREIGN COUNTRIES   Table I

	In billion dollars				1953 as per cent of:		
	1928	1938	1948	1953	1928	1938	1948
1. Continental Western Europe	4.8	7.3	5.8	10.1	207	138	172
(a) France	2.0	3.0	0.8	1.1	52	35	132
(b) Switzerland	0.2	0.9	1.9	2.1	1,080	230	112
(c) Other	2.6	3.4	3.1	6.9	307	177	220
2. Sterling Area	1.4	3.9	2.9	4.0	288	104	138
3. Canada	0.4	0.4	1.2	2.4	580	610	198
4. Latin America	1.1	0.9	2.7	3.6	320	380	132
5. All Other Foreign Countries	1.0	1.3	2.3	2.9	300	225	126
6. International	. .	. .	3.4	3.3	. .	. .	99
7. Total Outside United States	8.7	13.8	18.4	26.4	300	190	143

Source: *Federal Reserve Bulletin*, March 1954, p. 245.

sures, or greater deflationary pressures, than the rest of the world. This timeworn doctrine still seems to me sufficient to explain the tendency of European countries to run into heavy dollar deficits during a period of intense inflationary pressures associated with war financing and the reconstruction of war damage, or in the course of a world depression marked by steeper price and income deflation in the United States than in most other industrial countries.

I find it extremely difficult, however, to discover any chronic dollar shortage tendency in the current pattern of world payments. Foreign countries' gold reserves and dollar holdings are estimated to have increased by about $ 8 billion in the last five years and $ 2.6 billion in the year 1953 alone. Table I shows that foreign gold and dollar holdings are far higher today than in any previous period. While still inferior to 1938 levels in real puchasing power, they are also far better distributed with relation to most countries'

normal » United States expenditures for foreign aid and military procurement overseas;

(b) the expected increase in their dollar needs if present restrictions and discrimination on dollar transactions were eliminated through the restoration of convertibility;

(c) the possible impact of a United States depression on their levels of reserves, foreign trade and economic activity in general.

A. The Role of « Abnormal » U.S. Expenditure Abroad

The 1953 accumulation of gold and dollars by foreign countries far exceeds their total receipts of United States aid (14). Even the

(14) Other than so-called military-end-use items contributed in kind by the United States under military aid programs. This form of aid and the corresponding United States exports have been excluded throughout from the data presented in this paper, since there is every reason to assume that such items would not be imported in significant quantities by foreign countries under circumstances permitting the cessation of military aic programs.

further exclusion of United States military disbursements overseas would leave Western Europe and the Western Hemisphere in approximate gold and dollar equilibrium, but would leave the rest of the world with a deficit of about $ 1.7 billion (see Table II).

sential imports and by absorbing resources that would otherwise be available for expanding their exports » (15).

The constant reference to Western Europe in these comments lead one to suspect that the Commission was not aware of the fact

GOLD AND DOLLAR TRANSACTIONS OF FOREIGN COUNTRIES IN 1953   TABLE II

(million dollars)

	World	Continental Western Europe	Sterling Area	Canada	Latin America	Other Countries	International Institutions
I. *Estimated Increase in Gold Reserves and Dollar Holdings*	2,720	1,670	860	– 20	250	– 130	90
II. *Through Receipts of U.S. Aid, Exclusive of Military End Items*	1,770	840	400	..	20	420	990
III. *Through All Other Transactions*	950	840	450	– 20	230	– 540	..
A. U.S. Military Purchases of Goods and Services Overseas	2,570	990	280	150	20	1,130	..
B. Civilian Transactions	– 1,620	– 150	170	– 170	210	– 1,670	..
1. Net Outflow of U.S. Capital	590	– 260	90	350	220	140	60
(a) Government	220	– 110	..	..	340	– 20	..
(b) Private	370	– 150	80	350	– 120	160	60
2. Multilateral Transfers and Errors and Omissions	160	200	110	510	110	– 730	– 40
(a) Recorded in U.S. Transactions	– 270	100	– 220	410	130	– 630	– 60
(b) Other	430	100	320	100	– 20	– 90	20
3. Current Account with the U.S.	– 2,370	– 80	– 30	– 1,030	– 130	– 1,090	– 20
(a) Receipts	14,680	3,220	2,520	3,020	4,230	1,650	40
(b) Expenditures	17,050	3,300	2,550	4,050	4,360	2,740	60

Footnote: Data are primarily derived from official estimates of the U.S. Balance of Payments, as presented by Walther Lederer on pp. 22-23 of the March 1954 issue of the *Survey of Current Business*. Differences between total changes in estimated gold holdings as reported in the « Federal Reserve Bulletin », March 1954, p. 240 and the U.S. gold sales and purchases have been entered under « Other Multilateral Transfers » and added to the reported U.S. balance on foreign capital and gold to arrive at the « Estimated Increase. in Gold Reserves and Dollar Holdings ». Unilateral transfers other than aid have been included in « Current Account Receipts ».

Adding to this an estimated $ 0.6 billion for stockpiling purchases, the Randall report discerns in these figures a « concealed dollar gap » of some $ 2 billion to $ 3 billion annually, which would be increased if there were a change in the economic situation, such as a recession here or a deterioration in Western Europe's terms of trade. On the other hand, it should be recognized that major parts of our « extraordinary » expenditure abroad are connected with our defense effort, and that the Western European countries' own defense programs affect adversely their trade position, by increasing their es-

that its « concealed dollar gap » concentrates nearly entirely on the Far Eastern countries — particularly Japan — whose economies have been disrupted by military events and attuned to a high rate of United States military procurement. It is, of course, obvious that these countries are not now accumulating gold and dollar *surpluses* equal to whatever the United States army spends there for procurement of goods and services, plus the amounts of reconstruction or defense support aid to Korea, nationalist China, etc. This

(15) *Report to the President and the Congress*, Commission on Foreign Economic Policy, Washington, 1954, p. 5.

becomes a « concealed dollar gap», however, only if one assumes that such expenditures are likely to be completely eliminated in time, without any corresponding offsets in foreign countries' dollar imports or exports.

Both assumptions would be extremely unrealistic. United States military disbursements overseas are still rising now and will at best taper off gradually, with little or no probability that they will fall down to zero in the foreseeable future. Moreover, such tapering off would simultaneously release for consumption, investment or exports the resources otherwise absorbed in the production of the goods and services contributed under these programs. This trend would be further reinforced by the decline in foreign countries' own military budgets which would be likely under such circumstances.

The absorption of these resources into civilian production will, of course, necessitate difficult economic readjustments. For Western Europe as a whole, the problem is more likely to center on the maintenance of domestic activity and employment than on the balance of payments itself, since its current gold and dollar accumulation is already as large as the total of aid and military disbursements receipts (see Table II, above). In the Far East, however, the readjustments will bear more heavily on the need to reduce imports or increase exports. These readjustments might spread to other areas and recreate generalized balance of payments difficulties with the United States if the decline in United States military expenditures were not offset in part by some increase in United States commercial imports or capital exports. Given the present rate of gold and dollar accumulation by foreign countries ($ 2.7 billion), however, moderate changes in United States export and import levels would be sufficient to absorb any foreseeable reduction in United States aid and military disbursements.

B. *The Role of Dollar Discrimination*

The removal of discrimination against dollar trade constitutes a second factor of

fear and uncertainty in the progress toward convertibility. The Randall *Staff Papers* report that « guesses at the magnitude of the suppressed dollar demand have ranged between $ 1 billion and $ 3 billion a year; the true figure at present is probably much closer to the former than to the latter » (16).

I would myself incline to reduce even further the estimates of the real quantitative impact of dollar discrimination upon the balance of payments.

First of all, we must not forget that more than half of the United States exports flow to such areas as Canada, Central America, the Caribbean Islands, the northern coast of South America, Japan, the Philippines, etc. which either have no exchange controls at all (Canada and most of Central America) or which have no reason to apply discriminatory controls against dollar goods as such.

Secondly, the proportion of United States and Canadian exports in total imports of the rest of the world is now already far larger than before the war. This is true, not only for the world at large, but for all individual areas as well, with the single exception of the sterling area. The proportion is about one third larger than in 1937 for Latin American and continental E.P.U. countries, and 20 per cent larger for the countries outside the sterling area, continental E.P.U. and the Western Hemisphere.

Thirdly, while the elimination of dollar discrimination will tend toward an expansion of United States exports, two other factors are now acting in the opposite direction. The reduction in foreign aid eliminates some elements of discrimination *in favour of* United States shipping and commodities previously purchased under E.C.A., M.S.A. or F.O.A. procurement authorizations. Moreover, the recovery of production and the abatement of inflationary forces abroad reduce foreign demand for other United States goods imported in abnormal quantities in earlier years. It should be noted that the proportion of United States and Canadian goods in the total im-

(16) *Staff Papers*, Commission on Foreign Economic Policy, Washington, 1954, p. 18.

ports of Western Europe and the sterling area has declined substantially over the past year, in spite of greater dollar availability and of the trend toward a relaxation of dollar discrimination abroad. The continuation of this trend, in a noninflationary environment, might well result primarily in price readjustments by soft-currency exporters, rather than in any large diversion in the pattern of trade. This would be all the more likely if progress toward nondiscrimination were undertaken simultaneously by all major trading countries rather than by one or a few countries alone.

For all these reasons, the relaxation of trade and currency discrimination against dollar goods is likely to have a much more moderate impact on the dollar position of foreign countries than is generally feared. In any case, the relatively small order of magnitude of its possible effects should be kept in mind. For instance, a 25 per cent increase in United States exports to the sterling area — where discrimination is most stringent and effective — would amount to about $ 375 million, and a 10 per cent increase in exports to continental Western Europe and the non-dollar countries of Latin America about $ 250 million and $ 100 million, respectively, *i.e.*, a total of about $ 700 million a year.

C. The International Impact of a United States Recession

The international impact of a United States recession could hardly be estimated in advance with any degree of precision. It may be noted, however, that the mild recession experienced since the summer of 1953 has had a far smaller impact on foreign dollar incomes than was generally expected. Gold and dollar holdings continued to rise at a rate of more than $ 2 billion a year throughout the period October 1953 - March 1954. Current and prospective levels of foreign aid and military expenditures — at a rate of $ 4.3 billion a year — will continue for some time to act as a powerful stabilizing influence on foreign countries' dollar earnings. For the next two or three years at least, a United States recession might be expected primarily

to slow down the current accumulation of gold and dollars abroad, but it is highly unlikely to resurrect any large surpluses in the United States balance of payments with the rest of the world.

The international impact of United States recessions, however, is not limited to direct trade between each country and the United States itself. Their major disruptive effects lie in the transmission of contractive forces from country to country, through their own mutual trade as well as through their trade with the United States.

The channels through which these indirect effects are propagated are of several kinds:

1. The demand of each country for exports from other countries — and not only from the United States — may contract automatically as a consequence of the lower income levels resultings from:

(a) the loss of export earnings to the United States;

(b) possibly, the deterioration in its terms of trade associated with a United States recession.

2. This will affect income levels in the supplying countries and react in turn on their own imports from the first, spreading the contraction from each country to the others.

3. This spiral of contractive tendencies may be broken, or on the contrary accentuated, by the economic policies adopted in each country:

(a) some countries may succeed, through compensatory policies, in preventing a decline in national income levels and maintaining their import demand at a higher level; their balance of payments will tend to deteriorate as a consequence, reducing previous balance of payments surpluses or causing a drain on their monetary reserves;

(b) currency depreciation, tariff increases or import and exchange restrictions would, on the contrary, aggravate other countries' difficulties; they may be resorted to:

(1) as the consequence of reserves losses, whether automatic or resulting from the compensatory policies above;

(2) as a substitute for such compensatory policies, in order to offset through increased exports and decreased imports the effects of the recession on economic activity, incomes and employment.

The international propagation and intensification of a United States recession can be considerably reduced by measures which will encourage and enable countries to follow compensatory policies (3(a) above) rather than disruptive policies (3(b) above) in the course of such a recession.

This ratio is substantially exceeded by only a very few countries outside the Western Hemisphere — mainly the Philippines, India, Indonesia and Japan. It varies, however, very greatly among individual Latin American countries, from about 25 per cent in the River Plate countries to more than 80 per cent in Mexico, Guatemala, El Salvador and Colombia.

A thirty per cent decline in exports to the United States would therefore have a very different significance for these various coun-

TABLE III

GOLD AND DOLLAR HOLDINGS, TOTAL EXPORTS AND EXPORTS TO THE UNITED STATES IN 1953
(billions of dollars)

	Gold and Dollar Holdings	Total Exports	Exports to the U.S.	Per cent Ratio of Exports to U.S. to Total Exports	Per cent Ratio of Gold and Dollar Holdings to	
					Total Exports	Exports to U.S.
1. Continental Western Europe and Dependencies	10.06	22.2	2.51	11	45	401
2. Sterling Area	4.05	18.4	1.82	10	22	222
3. Canada	2.42	4.6	2.52	55	52	96
4. Latin America	3.63	7.6	3.58	47	48	101
5. Other Countries	2.90	6.0	1.47	24	48	197
6. All Foreign Countries . . .	23.04	59.0	11.90	20	39	194
7. International Organizations . .	3.34	. .	. .	. .	. .	. .
8. Total	26.39	59.0	11.90	20	45	222

Sources: 1. Gold and dollar holdings: « Federal Reserve Bulletin », March 1954, p. 245; 2. Total Exports: « International Financial Statistics », April 1954, pp. 22 and 24; 3. Exports to the United States: « Survey of Current Business », March 1954, pp. 22-23.

The difficulties of the task will be far smaller if action is taken at an early stage rather than after the recession has already been allowed to spread over a wider area.

The direct impact of a United States recession will be heaviest on the countries which are most dependent on the United States market for their exports. Canada and Latin American countries sell in the United States market about half of their total exports, while European and sterling area countries trade far more extensively with one another and sell only about 10 per cent of their total exports to the United States (see Table III).

tries or areas. It would correspond to only 3 per cent of overall exports and 7.5 per cent of gold and dollar holdings for continental Western Europe, but about 16 per cent of total exports and 31 per cent of gold and dollar holdings for Canada.

There are also very great variations in the cyclical sensitivity of different countries' exports to the United States. Sterling area exports have usually been affected far more severely, and those of Canada substantially less severely, than those of other areas during past United States recessions. Exporters of wool (Australia, New Zealand, Argentina and

Uruguay), minerals (Bolivia, Chile, Mexico) and raw materials in general suffer a far heavier decline than coffee, banana (Brazil, Colombia, Central America), sugar and other food exporters.

TABLE IV

PER CENT CHANGES
IN EXPORTS TO THE UNITED STATES

	1923 1924	1926 1927	1929 1932	1937 1938	1948 1949
1. Continental Western Europe	− 6	..	− 71	− 32	− 12
2. Sterling Area .	− 11	− 18	− 79	− 48	− 18
3. Canada . .	− 4	..	− 65	− 35	− 2
4. Latin America .	+ 1	− 8	− 68	− 32	..
5. Other Countries (*) . . .	− 8	..	− 67	− 34	− 6
6. Total	− 5	− 6	− 70	− 35	− 7

(*) Exluding Eastern Europe.

Taking into account both criteria — ratio of exports to the United States to total exports or G.N.P., and sensitivity of those exports to United States recessions — we should expect the most severe direct repercussions of a United States recession to concentrate on some Western Hemisphere countries — particularly Canada, Mexico, Bolivia, Chile, Argentina and Uruguay — and on Japan, the Philippines, Indonesia and the overseas sterling area.

International policies designed to avoid or moderate the further spread and spiralling of the depression fall into two major categories: monetary policies and trade policies.

Untied loans in convertible currencies — whether from international institutions or from high reserve countries — may be necessary to relieve these countries of severe balance of payments pressures and enable them:

(a) to avoid deflationary or restrictionist policies which will aggravate the depression elsewhere; and

(b) to adopt positive compensatory domestic policies designed to sustain income levels, employment and imports.

The amount of assistance required for this purpose will depend, of course, on the level

of these countries' reserves. Current ratios of gold and dollar holdings to total exports now average 40 to 50 per cent for all major regions except the sterling area (see Column 5, Table III, above). Sterling area and E.P.U. arrangements, however, result in a considerable economy of gold and dollar settlements in intra-area trade. As long as these arrangements continue, the need for external stabilization loans will be considerably less than it would otherwise be for Western Europe and the sterling area. The resources of the I.M.F. in gold and United States dollars — more than $ 3 billion — and in the curriences of other prospective creditors could provide all — or at least a considerable portion — of the residual assistance needed *and actually usable* to overcome the reserve deficiencies *arising from a United States recession*.

The latter qualifications, however, limit considerably the significance to be attached to international monetary cooperation as an anti-recession device. Such cooperation may be more effective in preventing deflationary or restrictionist policies than in stimulating positive compensatory policies. The latter policies would prove very difficult to implement for many of the countries most severely affected by a United States recession, even if large stabilization loans relieved them of any anxiety about their reserve losses and balance of payments deficits. It is by no means easy to provide alternative employment for the men and resources left idle by the loss of export markets, especially in countries highly specialized in one or a few export products, such as tin, copper, rubber, etc.

Moreover, the ability of these countries to repay at a later stage the loans extended to them may very often be questioned by the prospective lenders. The lenders may take the view — rightly or wrongly — that balance of payments difficulties are aggravated during the recession, and will persist long after the end of the recession, as the result of ill-advised or irresponsible domestic policies. Disagreements on such points are likely to prove a stumbling block in many cases, especially when decisions have to be made — as is the case in the I.M.F. — by many countries with diverse geographical, historical and economic backgrounds. They may create far lesser difficulties in more closely knit organizations — such as E.P.U. and the sterling area — grouping countries more highly interdependent economically, more keenly conscious of such interdependence and more familiar with one another's problems and policies.

Without minimizing the role of stabilization loans as an anti-recession device, their limitations should be recognized and should prompt further efforts in other directions as well.

Commodity agreements and buffer stocks designed to reduce excessive instability in agricultural and raw material markets would be of far greater value to primary producing countries than monetary stabilization loans. The difficulties raised by such schemes are enormous, but so are their potentialities for economic stabilization and development (17). One must regret, therefore, the rather cursory dismissal of this approach to the problem in the Randall Commission's report. Some of the Commission's recommendations, and particularly the « avoidance of actions incidental to our own commodity control and stockpile programs that would have avoidably disruptive effects upon world prices » (18) and continued consultation and cooperation with other nations to improve knowledge of world supply and demand for materials and foodstuff, and to explore possible means of lessening instability » (19) are all to the good, but give little hope for concrete action in the near future. This conclusion is clearly shared by the Commission itself, which also recommends « a policy of encouragement of diversification of the economies of the countries now excessively dependent upon a small number of products » (20). The benefits of international specialization must, to this extent, be sacrificed to the objective of domestic economic stability. In practice, however, the

costs and difficulties of diversification policies may well be as or more formidable than those of commodity stabilization.

The above measures will at best reduce, but not eliminate, the direct impact of reduced export earnings to the United States on the monetary reserves and economic activity of the countries affected. They should be coupled with other policy commitments designed to avoid, to the maximum extent, the adoption of beggar-my-neighbor policies of currency devaluation, tariff increases, trade and exchange controls, discrimination and bilateralism, which are a major factor of propagation and intensification of international recessions. The cooperation of the major and stronger nations is particularly vital in this respect. The influence of their policies on other countries, and their ability to use alternative measures to fight depressive tendencies at home, are usually far greater than those of the smaller or less developed economies.

No country, however, can be expected to renounce any means to improve its own domestic activity and employment, even at the expense of others, on the basis of Platonic appeals to international cooperation. While each of them may realize that the cumulative effect of mutual restrictions will be damaging to it as well as to others, none will feel assured that its own restraint, or lack of restraint, in this respect will decisively influence the policies of other countries. Mutual commitments, of a positive as well as of a negative nature, encompassing credit provisions together with trade provisions, remain the most promising way to promote the maximum degree of trade freedom and cooperative anti-recession policies. International agreements, of the I.T.O. or G.A.T.T. type, deserve greater United States support than they have received in recent years. On the other hand, in this field as well as in the monetary field, regional organizations may develop a far closer degree of intimate cooperation among the participating countries than can be anticipated on a world-wide scale. The combination of trade, credit and economic policy commitments and negotiations into a single institution can also contribute

(17) See *Commodity Trade and Economic Development*, United Nations, New York, 1953.

(18) *Report to the President and the Congress*, Commission on Foreign Economic Policy, Washington, 1954, pp. 35-36.

(19) *Idem*.

(20) *Idem*.

to greater success in all three fields, as the O.E.E.C. experiment has amply demonstrated during its brief span of years.

We have just rejoined the conclusions reached in previous sections of this paper, when we discussed the prospects of convertibility and the best means to restore and preserve it in a world of national sovereignties. Regional cooperation should be viewed as a valuable adjunct, rather than a rival, of world-wide agreements.

Conclusions.

The current rate of gold and dollar accumulation in Western Europe and the sterling area, together with prospective rates of United States aid and military expenditure overseas over the next years, provide a considerable cushion against a hypothetical United States depression. We should therefore expect a continuation, and even an acceleration, of the progress already achieved in recent years and months toward currency transferability and trade liberalization.

These, however, are fair weather objectives which can only be pressed forward in an environment of high economic activity and employment. In times of depression, each nation will almost inevitably resort again to trade restrictions and currency inconvertibility in an effort to insulate its own economy from external deflationary pressures. These policies cannot be successful in the end, as each country's actions tend to aggravate the difficulties of others, widening and deepening the contractionist tendencies at work. National anti-depression policies of this character have always proved in the past one of the main factors in the spread and aggravation of international recessions.

This spiral can be broken only by collective arrangements giving operational meaning to the interdependence of the various countries' policies. The avoidance of disruptive action should be made both possible and attractive through adequate access to stabilization assistance in case of need and through reciprocal guarantees against all unnecessary recourse to trade and exchange restrictions.

In cases restrictions become unavoidable, they should be limited in scope and time, and avoid unilateral discrimination against any country participating in the arrangements.

International cooperation of this sort is, however, extremely difficult to negotiate and implement in practice. Moderation in its aims, hopes and promises is indispensable to avoid later disillusionment, disaffection and retrogression. World-wide arrangements are particularly slow and cumbersome to negotiate and implement, and will necessarily remain more limited in their effective content than regional arrangements among countries which are highly interdependent on one another, keenly aware of this interdependence, readier to understand each other's problems and policies and to confide in the commitments and good faith of their partners.

Both types of approach should be developed and encouraged, and the potentialities of each should be as fully exploited as proves possible in practice. Much could be done today to improve the effectiveness of world-wide organizations such as G.A.T.T. or the I.M.F. Much could be done also, under present favorable circumstances, to relax some of the regional limitations of the E.P.U. and sterling area systems. Individual countries — particularly Britain, Germany and the Netherlands — have recently taken important measures in this direction, but drastic revisions in the E.P.U. Agreement are now long overdue to adjust it to the enormous changes which have taken place in the international pattern of trade and payments since the negotiation of the Agreement, four years ago.

Major creditor nations — and especially the United States — will inevitably exercise a profound influence on the progress of other countries and of both regional and international organizations toward currency convertibility and trade liberalization. The United States has a major stake, economically and politically, in the promotion of liberal economic policies abroad and in the strengthening and development of other free nations. These objectives happily coincide with the interests of both consumers and producers in

22   Banca Nazionale del Lavoro

the reduction of tariff and trade barriers here, and with the need to provide increasing outlets for our exports of goods and capital.

The report of the Randall Commission on Foreign Economic Policy is now before Congress. Its obvious shortcomings as a basic document on fundamental, long-term, United States international economic policy have attracted more attention in academic circles than its very real contribution to the clari-

fication of urgently needed, and immediately feasible, United States action in the monetary and trade field. The adoption of its major recommendations would provide the necessary spark for further and considerable advances toward the rebuilding of a workable international framework for economic growth and stability.

ROBERT TRIFFIN
Yale University

[12]

A payments mechanism for the former Soviet Union: is the EPU a relevant precedent?

Barry Eichengreen
University of California at Berkeley, CEPR and NBER

1. Introduction

Since the disintegration of the USSR, trade has spiralled downward in the states of the former Soviet Union (FSU). Intra-FSU trade has been hit especially hard. This is deeply damaging to a set of countries, Russia aside, that are more open and depend more heavily on intra-regional trade than most members of the EC (Figure 1). The contribution of trade to national income is very important for such countries. Trade disruptions reduce purchasing power, disrupt production and hamper investment. Interdependence has driven the EC to undertake far-reaching initiatives on economic integration and exchange rate stabilization: in the FSU the trend is in just the opposite direction.

Part of the decline in intra-FSU trade is a simple reflection of implosion of production. Real GDP in the FSU fell by 10% in 1991 and by a further 20% in 1992 (EBRD, 1993). But intra-FSU trade appears to have declined more dramatically than output: precise figures are not available, but Michalopoulos and Tarr (1993) estimate a decline in trade volumes of more than 50% during 1990–92; Gros (1993a) estimates a decline of 30–50% in 1991–92 alone. Shortages of consumer goods, energy and industrial materials led governments to clamp controls on their export. Chaos in the banking and financial sectors heightened

This paper was written during a visit to the Institute for Advanced Study in Berlin, whose hospitality is gratefully acknowledged. Financial support for this research was supplied by the National Science Foundation and by the Center for German and European Studies of the University of California. Valiant research assistance was provided by Luisa Lambertini, Ansgar Rumler and Graham Schindler. I am indebted for comments and conservations to David Begg, Edward Bernstein, John Black, Peter Bofinger, Michael Burda, Alec Cairncross, Susan Collins, Stanley Fischer, Herbert Giersch, Linda Goldberg, Vittorio Grilli, Albert Hirschman, Michael Jones, Jacob Kaplan, Peter Kenen, Alan Milward, Jacques Polak, Richard Portes, Abrecht Ritschl, Holger Schmieding, Pierre Sicsic, Paul Welfens, Charles Wyplosz and especially Daniel Gros.

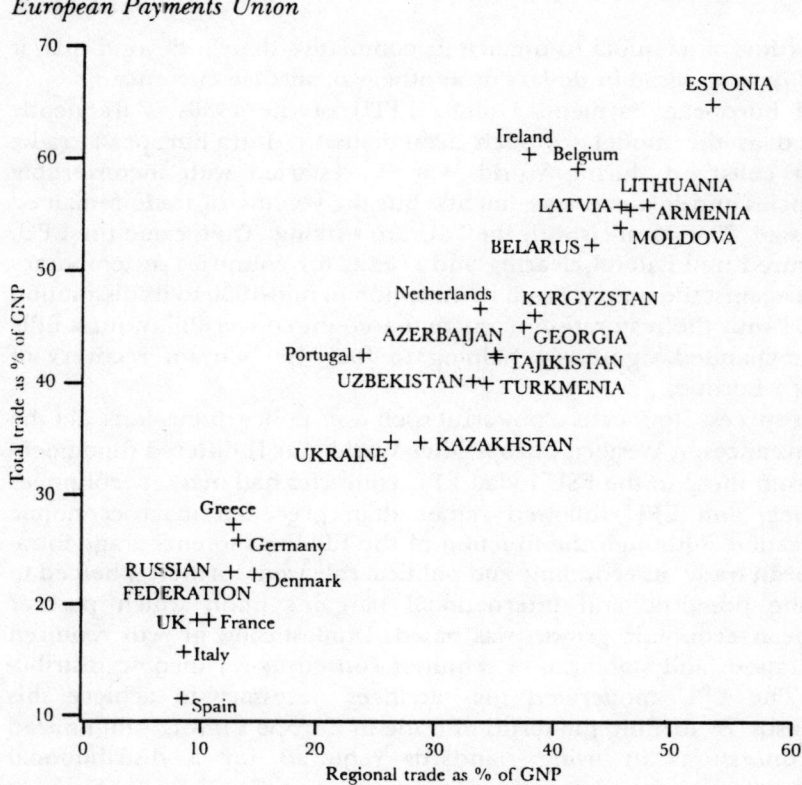

Figure 1. Total and intraregional foreign trade (% of GNP), FSU and EC

Source: IMF, EC Commission.

Note: Data for 1991, except for Greece, Ireland and Portugal, for which 1990.

uncertainty for exporters who did not know how, when or even whether they would be paid. Historical enmities among the successor states resurfaced, provoking governments and enterprise managers to sever trade relationships despite economic costs.

The decline in intra-FSU trade was aggravated further by the absence of multilateral settlements. There has been no mechanism for a republic to use surpluses with some FSU trading partners to finance deficits with others.

Schemes abound to create such a mechanism for the FSU and possibly portions of Eastern Europe as well (Bofinger and Gros, 1992; Dornbusch, 1992; Williamson, 1992). The latest such proposal is for an Interstate Bank (ISB) for the FSU. Each participating country would receive a credit line based on the amount of intra-FSU trade it conducted during a base period. It could draw credits from the union up to some proportion of its quota to finance its cumulative deficit. Beyond that, it would have to settle in dollars or another convertible currency.

The European Payments Union (EPU) of the 1950s is frequently invoked as the model for such arrangements. Intra-European trade, having collapsed during World War II, restarted with inconvertible currencies and bilateral agreements. But the volume of trade remained depressed. The parallels with the FSU are striking. Then came the EPU. It featured multilateral clearing and credits for countries in temporary deficit against the union. From its inception in mid-1950 to its dissolution in 1958 with the restoration of current-account convertibility, intra-EPU trade expanded vigorously, helping to fuel the buoyant recovery of Western Europe.

This success story casts a powerful spell over policy discussions. Yet the circumstances in Western Europe after World War II differed fundamentally from those in the FSU today. EPU countries had market economies in place, and EPU followed rather than preceded macroeconomic stabilization. Although the function of the EPU was to encourage intra-European trade, its economic and political role went further: it helped to seal the domestic and international bargains upon which postwar European economic growth was based. Domestically, growth required stabilization, and stabilization required consensus on income distribution. The EPU moderated the sacrifices necessary to achieve this consensus. By turning the terms of trade in Europe's favor, it minimized the concessions in living standards required for a distributional settlement.

Agreement, once reached, had also to be sustained. The EPU, as a concommitant of the 'social market economy' at the heart of the postwar settlement, was part of the web of institutional arrangements that locked in a cooperative solution to the distributional game. Internationally, the postwar settlement involved a commitment to trade and European integration. But for countries to restructure their economies along export-oriented lines, they had to be convinced that their neighbours' support for trade and integration was permanent. The EPU was an institutional exit barrier that lent credibility to the commitment to trade and integration.

If the EPU operated under special circumstances and played such an historically-specific role, is it really an appropriate model for the FSU of the 1990s? My answer first describes alternative payments mechanisms (Section 2) and existing payments arrangements in the FSU (Section 3). Section 4 analyses what the EPU really did, identifying precisely the economic problem to which the EPU was the solution.

Section 5 considers implications for trade and payments in the FSU. I distinguish arrangements for countries which have stabilized from those for countries still experiencing high inflation. I conclude that multilateral clearing is feasible in both cases, but that trade credits are desirable and feasible only in the first.

This raises an issue neglected in the existing literature: does a clearing union without credits differ significantly from current-account convertibility? As Section 5 explains, the two are similar in key macroeconomic respects. Effectively, the options prior to stabilization are to continue bilateral trade or to adopt arrangements tantamount to convertibility. Put in another way, it is no coincidence that the inability to stabilize has led to a collapse of multilateral settlements: given the difficulty of establishing current-account convertibility and the absence of a feasible half-way house, hyperinflation must lead to bilateralism.

Against these conclusions, Section 6 considers recent proposals for an Interstate Bank, and the final section assesses implications for Western aid.

2. The simple analytics of alternative payments mechanisms

To analyse the welfare implications of different payments mechanisms, one must distinguish static and dynamic gains from trade. I consider first the purely static gains, where each country's trade is continuously in balance.

Each arrow in Figure 2 depicts an export flow (denominated in, say, millions of US dollars). In the example given, Belarus is in surplus with Moldova and in deficit with Ukraine. If multilateral settlements are permitted, Belarus uses earnings from Moldova to finance its payments to Ukraine. The other countries do likewise. Each country's trade balances multilaterally. The combined value of exports is $290 million.

Contrast this with a situation without multilateral clearing. Moldova, earning only the equivalent of $10 million of Belarus's currency, can import only $10 million of goods from that country. Trade balances bilaterally at a lower level. Analogous changes occur in trade between Belarus and Ukraine and between Ukraine and Moldova. Exports decline from $290 million to $200 million.

Though the magnitude of this decline is a function of the numbers chosen, the point is general: the larger the bilateral surpluses and deficits under multilateral settlements, the greater the fall in trade when this payments mechanism is absent. Since bilateral balances between republics were exceptionally large in the Soviet Union, the fall in trade due to the descent into bilateralism has been especially large. Gros (1993b) shows, using 1988 data, that reducing intra-republican trade to the

314   *Barry Eichengreen*

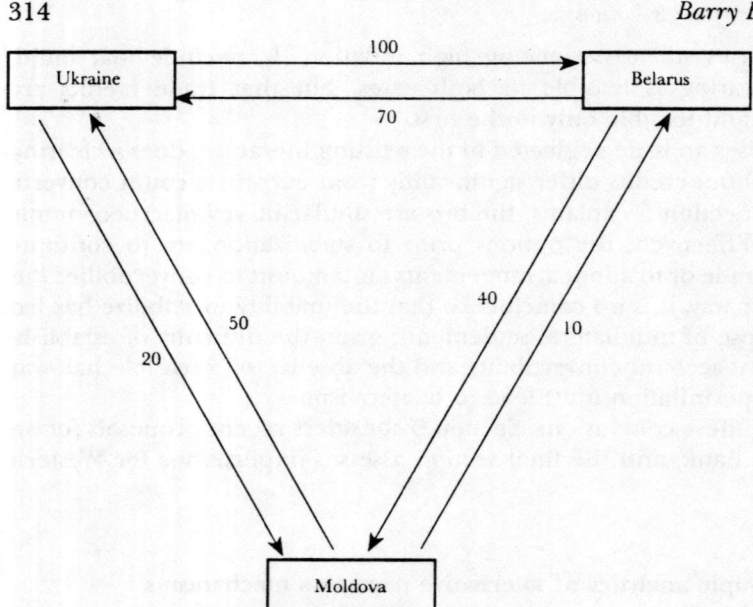

Figure 2. Illustrative pattern of multilateral settlement

smaller of each pair of bilateral trade flows lowers it by 25%, 7% of collective GDP.

One way of multilateralizing settlements is to establish a union to clear inconvertible currencies. The participating countries agree on a common unit of account; for example, by expressing transactions in US dollars at an agreed exchange rate. Each time they exported to (imported from) another participant in the payments union, they would be credited (debited) with earnings in that amount. Credits and debits vis-a-vis all members of the payments mechanism would be summed at the end of each accounting period. Countries in deficit would have to pay into the union a corresponding amount of hard currency.

None of these arrangements provides scope for dynamic gains from trade: for countries to run deficits in one period and surpluses in the next. Combining multilateral settlements with dynamic gains from trade requires either a payments union or a convertible currency. Unlike the clearing union described above, countries participating in a payments union may finance temporary deficits within the union by drawing on a credit line. The union grants them credits to finance their intra-union deficit in the expectation that they will run subsequent surpluses within the union to repay the loan.

A country with a convertible currency can also settle multilaterally. Its central bank simply offers to convert domestic currency into foreign exchange for any resident who can show proof (e.g. an invoice) documenting a need for foreign currency to purchase imports.[1] Such convertibility may be at a fixed or floating exchange rate. It would not matter in which convertible currency earnings accrue and in which convertible currency expenditures are denominated. And, like a payments union, convertibility can deliver dynamic gains from trade. Even if convertibility is limited to current account transactions, foreign investors will be free to repatriate earnings. If this induces the confidence to invest, it may attract the capital flows needed to finance current account deficits that would otherwise be infeasible.[2]

3. Existing payments arrangements

I now contrast these theoretical possibilities with concrete arrangements in the FSU countries. I draw on IMF (1991), Williamson (1992), Goldberg *et al.* (1993) and Gros (1993a).

From the start of 1992, intra-FSU transactions were carried out through 'correspondent accounts' held by each republic's central bank with the Central Bank of Russia (CBR). Bank transfers to and from other FSU republics had to pass through special accounts maintained by the CBR. Purchases from Russia by any other republic drew down that republic's account; its balance increased with each sale to a Russian purchaser.

So long as newly independent non-Russian republics used the ruble as currency, the rationale for this system was to prevent their creation of bank rubles to finance unlimited trade deficits. The correspondent system allowed states to overdraw their accounts only up to a specified credit ceiling.

In practice the ceilings were not enforced. In the first half of 1992, correspondent accounts were used only for *ex post* monitoring of intra-FSU trade balances. Other central banks apparently did not know their balances on a running basis. In July, previously accumulated correspondent balances were frozen, and republics agreed to settle balances bilaterally. The CBR declared it would honor requests for settlement only when correspondent accounts contained sufficient funds, thereby

---

[1] The rationale for limiting convertibility to the current account is to contain the destabilizing effects of capital flight during the early stages of economic transformation. See the literature on the sequencing of liberalization in Latin America, and also Portes (1992).

[2] Convertibility for capital account transactions provides even more scope for reaping dynamic gains from trade, but in transforming economies the potential for capital flight poses problems.

disrupting trade by eliminating the credits by which it was previously underwritten. The CBR and the Russian government, under pressure to grant credits to finance exports from large Russian enterprises to other republics, relaxed CBR credit policy by the end of 1992, allowing large overdrafts on correspondent accounts.

These accounts have been strictly bilateral. Initially, a matrix of intra-FSU accounts did not exist; each republic simply held a correspondent account with Russia. With each republic free to create ruble credits, virtually all of them continuously exhausted their credit limits. There were no surpluses in one republic's account with the CBR to be used to finance purchases from third republics. Even when Kazakhstan exported additional cotton to Russia, accumulating a CBR credit which could theoretically be used to finance Kazakh imports from Belarus, Russia did not permit it. Allowing Kazakhstan to use a CBR correspondent-account credit to finance imports from Belarus would have allowed Belarus to offset part of its deficit with Russian with its surplus with Kazakhstan in circumstances in which Russia was unable to collect from Kazakhstan.

By 1993 a matrix of bilateral correspondent accounts was almost in place, lending transparency to intra-FSU transactions not involving Russia. But any member of the ruble zone could create unlimited bank rubles, so problems of the CBR system of Russian correspondent accounts remain. Uzbeks will not let Kazakhs offset a deficit with Uzbeks against Kazakhs' surplus with Belarus because Uzbekistan cannot collect from Belarus: even a complete matrix of correspondent accounts can only finance bilateral trade.

In January 1993 a new attempt was made to rationalize the system: an Interstate Bank was proposed as for multilateral clearing of inter-republican trade. Russia offered 200 billion rubles to finance its operation. This agreement had to surmount three hurdles: the willingness and ability of the Russian government to underwrite the system; the inadequate credibility of the sanctions to be imposed on countries exceeding their credit ceilings; and the decision to use the ruble as unit of account. (I return to these issues in Section 6 below.) At the time of writing, an organizational committee had been established, but the Interstate Bank is not yet operational.

4. What EPU accomplished

Next I analyse Western European experience after 1945 with an eye to its relevance, if any, for a multilateral payments mechanism in FSU countries today. I examine postwar reconstruction of trade under bilateralism, the obstacles to convertibility, and the European Payments Union (EPU).

4.1. Bilateral trade

During World War II, trade between European countries fell to low levels, mostly conducted outside commercial channels. After the war, imports remained subject to license, and foreign exchange was rationed. Governments were often the sole purchaser of imports, then transferred to public enterprises or resold to private parties.

After a time, the most onerous restrictions on commodity markets were relaxed or removed. But restraints on financial markets remained. Since most European countries still had monetary overhangs and repressed inflation, international capital movements were heavily controlled and currencies remained inconvertible. They could not be exchanged for other currencies except with official permission, granted only under exceptional circumstances.

Given the risk of capital losses, it was rare for one European country to hold significant balances in another's currency. Without this ability to finance trade imbalances, trade reflected bilateral agreements. In the late 1940s, there were 200 such arrangements. Each pair of contracting governments listed commodities for which they would issue import licenses up to agreed limits. In the most restrictive cases, governments guaranteed their ability to settle bilaterally by severely limiting the issue of licenses: if exports to their partner exceeded imports over some period, differences would be settled out of limited reserves of 'hard currency' (gold and dollars).

More typically, temporary deficits were financed by the partner in surplus up to a specified ceiling or swing. Only the bilateral agreements concluded by Belgium, Switzerland and the Allied Zone of Occupation in Germany required settlement in gold or dollars when credit lines were exhausted or the agreement expired. (Belgium and Switzerland anticipated being in substantial surplus with their European trading partners following World War II, while the United States expected to find itself underwriting German production and trade; hence their insistence on hard-currency settlements.) In other cases, notably the UK and Scandinavia, when cumulative net bilateral deficits exceeded the ceiling, the bilateral agreement was typically renegotiated and the ceiling raised (Blancpain, 1964).

Despite adverse connotations, bilateralism helped restart Europe's trade. The credit lines included in bilateral agreements were the grease that allowed the wheels of intra-European trade to resume turning. Even the Bank for International Settlements, no normal trumpeter of the virtues of bilateral agreements, praised their operation (BIS, 1948, p. 143):

'In 1945, during the first phase of their operation, the payments agreements had, indeed, the great virtue of making commercial relations possible on a scale that could not otherwise have been achieved; they got goods moving between countries which, in many cases, had been physically severed from each other for many years. They helped to establish a uniform and smoothly working payments mechanism with a series of reasonable and consistent exchange rates and with relatively flexible controls. They made it possible to economize on the use of gold and international exchange and to develop export capacities. As a result, there was a widespread revival of intra-European trade after the barren years of war.'

The most important intra-European creditor in the immediate post-World War II period was Belgium, which ran persistent surpluses due to its early monetary reform and quick resumption of steel production. The most important debtor was the UK, saddled with an overhang of liquid assets (the 'sterling balances,' on which more later) and capital outflows in anticipation of the abortive restoration of convertibility (Cairncross, 1985).

As time elapsed, this system worked less well. Reciprocal overdraft rights presupposed that surpluses and deficits would not persist. In fact, some countries tended to persistent deficit, others to persistent surplus. Credit ceilings were reached, and additional credits were not forthcoming.

Several factors brought this about. Capacity to supply recovered more quickly in some countries than in others. Fiscal and monetary stabilization, eliminating excess demand, was completed early in some places, late in others. Once the most serious problems were solved, it became apparent that there was no more reason for trade to balance bilaterally than before the war. Switzerland might naturally run a surplus with France, which would run a surplus with Holland, which would run a surplus with Switzerland. There was no mechanism to cancel balances multilaterally.

The various experiments in multilateral clearing are analysed in more detail in Section 5 below. For present purposes it suffices to note that an adequate solution to the problem did not occur until 1950.

4.2. Obstacles to convertibility

These problems had two potential solutions: current-account convertibility or a multilateral payments union. Since they are also available to countries in the East today, it is important to understand why Western Europe opted for the second. I first analyse the rationales for the EPU that dominate the literature and argue that they cannot account for the decision to shun convertibility. I then provide a new interpretation of the EPU.

The dominant explanation for adoption of the EPU is that convertibility was not viable due to the inelasticity of import demands and export supplies. Given the excess demands for traded goods that existed in postwar Europe, freedom to acquire foreign currency and use it to import merchandise would have implied unsustainable current account deficits. It was widely believed that the normal corrective measure – a devaluation designed to raise the relative price of traded goods, stimulating exports and limiting imports – was ineffectual in the circumstances of the period (see for example Balogh, 1949; Kindleberger, 1950). Devaluation, in this view, would not enhance the international competitiveness of the devaluing country. Militant trade unions and the structured character of European labour markets had robbed real wages of their flexibility. Higher import prices would simply be passed through into higher costs, with no improvement in competitiveness.

Even if a country succeeded through currency depreciation in enhancing its competitiveness, the balance of trade still might not improve. Imports were dominated by essential foodstuffs, fuels and capital goods. US exports had a quality advantage in international markets. Consequently, import and export demands were inelastic. Even if devaluation succeeded in altering relative prices, the deterioration in the terms of trade of the devaluing country would swamp the desired movement in import and export volumes (Balogh, 1949; Hirschman, 1949).

Subsequent work (e.g. Orcutt, 1950) suggested reasons why elasticity pessimism might be overdrawn. Table 1 documents that it was. Its regressions explain the change in the volume of imports, the volume of exports and the terms of trade, pooling annual data for a cross-section of countries for the period 1949–55. The sample of countries is the US, Canada and all EPU countries other than Greece, Ireland, Luxembourg, Portugal and Turkey, which are omitted due to lack of data. Data sources are as in Eichengreen and Uzan (1992).

I estimate reduced forms for the change in export volumes, import volumes and the terms of trade. I explain these by the change in the nominal exchange rate, population growth, the rate of CPI inflation, the rate of growth of industrial production of the exporting country, and openness measured as the export share of GNP. I might also have included global economic conditions as a measure of export demand; insofar as this is the same for all countries in a given year its effect should be captured by the vector of dummy variables for years (included but not reported). In addition, since German exports soared during this period (due to monetary reform and price liberalization more than exchange-rate changes per se), a dummy variable for Germany is included in alternative versions of the regressions.

Table 1. Estimated effects of exchange rate changes 1949–55
(Pooled time series and cross sections)

	Change in exports	Change in imports	Change in terms of trade
Change in exchange rate	0.81	−0.27	−0.29
	(5.50)	(2.58)	(3.94)
Change in price level	−0.49	−0.27	0.03
	(1.53)	(1.18)	(1.86)
Output growth	0.64	0.99	0.07
	(2.52)	(4.90)	(0.50)
Population growth	−0.02	−0.68	−0.74
	(0.01)	(0.56)	(0.87)
Openness	−0.01	0.07	0.05
	(0.08)	(0.86)	(0.82)
Constant	−0.78	0.30	1.28
	(5.08)	(2.67)	(16.52)
German dummy	0.18	0.05	0.01
	(2.98)	(1.07)	(0.35)
Standard error	0.12	0.09	0.06
No. of observations	84	83	83

Source: See text.
Note: t-statistics in parentheses. All equations include dummy variables for years.

The 1949 devaluations, whose magnitude differed markedly across countries (Table 2), provide most of the variation in the exchange-rate term. (Simple cross-section regressions comparing 1949 with 1950–51 yield almost identical results.) The pooled analysis in Table 1 indicates that devaluation in fact improved the trade balance.[3] A 30 per cent devaluation, like that of Britain, raised export volumes by 24 per cent, and reduced import volumes by 8 per cent change. The final equation, consistent with assertions in the literature, shows that devaluation worsened the terms of trade. To get foreigners to purchase additional exports, the relative price of exports had to decline, while to get residents to economize on their purchases of imports, their relative price had to rise. Table 1 suggests that the terms-of-trade deterioration induced by a 30 per cent devaluation was about 9 per cent.

These results suggest that devaluation worked. Given the continued prevalence of import controls in many Western European countries, this

---

[3] I tested for possible simultaneity bias using Hausman's procedure, instrumenting the exchange rate with lagged export growth, lagged import growth or the lagged terms of trade, but found little evidence of simultaneity.

European Payments Union   321

Table 2. Devaluations against US $, September 1949–January 1950, (%)

Sterling area except Pakistan	30	Austria	53
		Greece	33
Denmark	30	France	22
Finland	30	Germany	20
Netherlands	30	Belgium	13
Norway	30	Portugal	13
Sweden	30	Italy	8

Source: Tew (1965).
Notes: Austria introduced multiple rates in December 1949; I use an average at Jan 1950. The pre-devaluation rate for the French franc is taken as the mean of the basic and free official rates.

conclusion may seem surprising. By 1950, however, a non-negligible share of Europe's imports was uncontrolled. And the considerably larger size of export elasticities is consistent with the fact that Europe's principal export market, the United States, was essentially uncontrolled. A significant minory of contemporary commentators on the 1949 devaluations (Kent, 1950; UN Economic Commission for Europe, 1951) concurred that devaluation worked.

Before devaluation, Europe's current account deficit (including net flows of factor income) was about 6 per cent of exports. Since the terms-of-trade and import effects roughly cancel out, my results imply that a 30 per cent devaluation, like that actually adopted by Britain and Scandinavian countries, would have eliminated as much as three-quarters of this gap. Slightly larger devaluations would have eliminated this obstacle to convertibility.

This conclusion is subject to a qualification.[4] Even if they had devalued by an additional 10–15 per cent, some countries would have remained in deficit against the US, though a sufficiently deep devaluation could always have allowed convertibility to be restored. If one country devalued and restored convertibility but the others did not, it might run surpluses against Europe but deficits against the United States; it would be unable to settle the latter in hard currency while earning only inconvertible claims from the former. But if all countries restored convertibility

---

[4]An objection voiced at the time was that European countries would have responded to restoration of convertibility by reintroducing draconian import controls. My results suggests this would have been unnecessary. Another objection was that, since in practice all countries would have devalued, little change in competitiveness would have been achieved. However, the US would not have devalued, so Europe would have achieved gains in competitiveness.

simultaneously, it would not matter from which ones they earned convertible credits and to which ones they incurred convertible liabilities. By definition, the dollar problem would have been eliminated along with the balance-of-payments problem.

While this objection does not overturn the conclusion that convertibility was viable, it points up a qualification. Convertibility was feasible for some countries only if it was adopted simultaneously by the others. Reestablishing convertibility would therefore have required an entity to monitor performance and coordinate adjustments. In fact, European countries possessed just such an entity: the Organization for European Economic Cooperation established in 1948 in response to the Marshall Plan.

Another objection to convertibility was that many countries were still saddled with monetary overhangs. Had convertibility been restored, excess liquidity, whose counterpart was an excess demand for goods, would have spilled into excessive imports, whatever the exchange rate. Britain's abortive restoration of convertibility in 1947 led to rapid depletion of its reserves and forced suspension of the experiment within weeks.

For a monetary overhang to exist, there must be binding controls that prevent prices from rising until real balances fall to desired levels. Price controls were still pervasive in many European countries in 1950, especially the UK, Ireland, the Netherlands, Denmark, Sweden and Norway. Less clear is whether the supply of money remained excessive. Some countries (Germany, Austria) had eliminated the overhang through monetary reform. Others (Belgium, Denmark) had blocked money balances temporarily and converted a portion of such funds into forced loans. Still others (France, Italy) used a combination of rapid growth and inflation to ameliorate the problem.

Table 3 reports the ratio of money supply to GNP in the principal EPU countries. By this measure, the UK, the Netherlands and the Scandinavian countries had made considerable progress toward eliminating their monetary overhangs. But the measure is problematic: changes in observed liquidity ratios reflect both changes in the supply of money and changes in the public's willingness to hold it. Toward the beginning of the period, observed ratios are on the money supply curve, demand being in disequilibrium due to price and import controls. Toward the end, following decontrol, observed ratios are on the demand curve as well. A rise in the liquidity ratio may therefore reflect an increased willingness to hold money, due for example to declining inflationary expectations, rather than a growing monetary overhang.

To ameliorate this problem I employed the following procedure. For each country, I estimated money demand functions after convertibility

Table 3. Monetary overhang (money supply relative to GNP), 1938 = 100

	1947	1948	1949	1950	1951	1952
Greece	46	42	49	57	58	64
Italy	85	101	120	121	118	128
France	86	67	69	72	68	66
Norway	197	198	191	173	148	148
Sweden	131	123	123	120	111	112
Denmark	140	125	110	92	86	85
Nether- lands	117	108	101	90	79	80
UK	162		143	138	126	119
Belgium	84	75	77	77	69	67
Switzerland	108	108	115	114	111	110
Austria	156	141	114	102	89	87
Germany	na	na	51	53	49	50

Source: Triffin (1957).
Note: The index for Germany is based on 1938 data for Germany as a whole.
More detailed but probably incomplete data from the League of Nations
Money and Banking 1942–44 would yield a lower estimate of money in 1938
and hence increase (to about double) the postwar German estimate in the
table.

was restored, and applied these parameters to pre-convertibility data to
construct counterfactual forecasts of the level of real money balances
that would have prevailed had convertibility been established in 1950 and
equilibrium restored to the money market. Where actual money
significantly exceeds the simulated values, I conclude that presence of a
monetary overhang would have provoked current account deficits and
reserve losses.

Using quarterly data for 1959–67 (a period roughly matching the life
span of the EPU), I regressed real money balances on a constant, output
and an interest rate.[5] I then constructed counterfactual values for
1950I–1958IV (two pre-EPU quarters and the life span of the EPU). For
Belgium, France, Germany, Norway and Sweden, actual money supply
was within two standard errors of simulated demand at the beginning of

---

[5] I regressed real money (the IMF's narrow measure deflated by the CPI) on a constant, industrial
production, an interest rate, and seasonal dummies, using quarterly data during 1959–67. For Italy,
consistent interest rate data were unavailable and this term was omitted. Data on money, prices and
output are from IMF, *International Financial Statistics*, interest rates from OEEC, *Statistical Yearbook*.
To the extent that the problem overhang was in liquidity (bonds) rather than money, this should
show up in interest rates (large debt issues lower bond prices, raise interest rates, and reduce money
demand) and be adequately captured by my procedure.

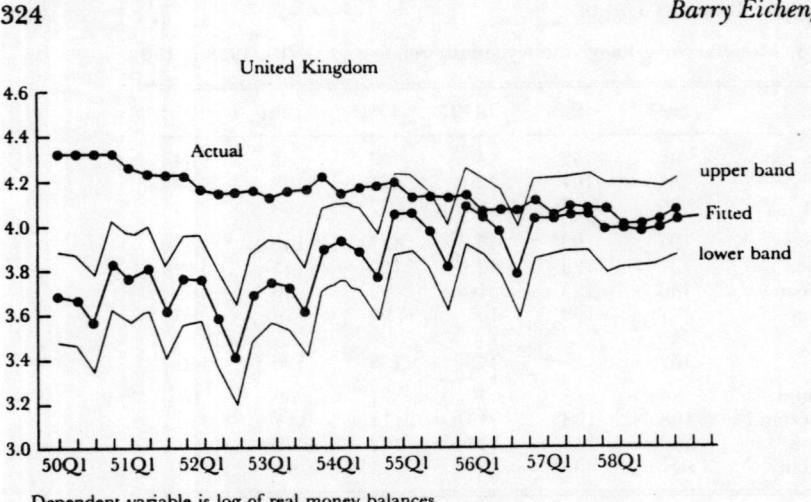

Dependent variable is log of real money balances
Interest rate is average rate for 3-month Treasury Bills

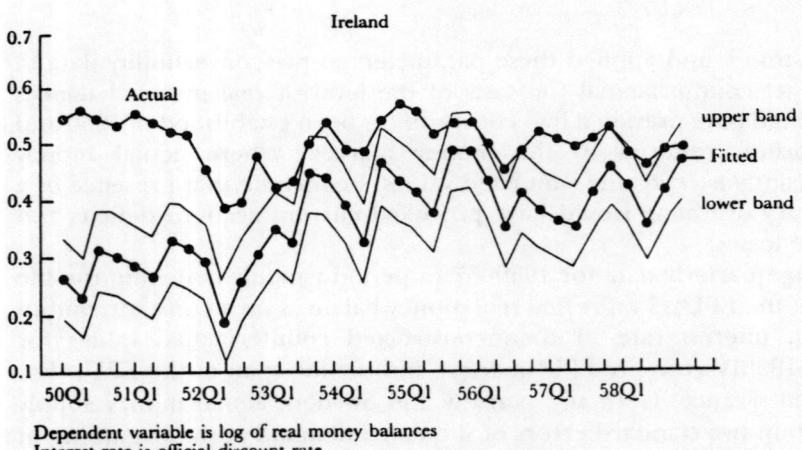

Dependent variable is log of real money balances
Interest rate is official discount rate

Figure 3. Actual money supply and simulated money demand, UK and Ireland, 1950–1958IV

the period. In three countries (Austria, Denmark and Italy) there is some evidence of a monetary overhang at the start of 1950, but money supply moves within two standard errors of simulated demand by the third quarter of 1950, when the EPU commenced. In only two countries, the UK and Ireland, is there evidence of persistent monetary overhang.

Actual and simulated log money balances, along with two-standard-error bounds, are shown in Figure 3 for these countries. In Ireland, actual values remain significantly above the simulation rate as late as 1953. In the UK, the divergence persists even longer.

That Ireland and the UK emerge as countries with persistent monetary overhangs is hardly surprising. In 1950 Ireland was the only EPU country other than Turkey granted a derogation by the OEEC concerning the requirement to remove quotas on 75 per cent of its intra-European trade (Bossuat, 1992). This step can be understood in terms of the excess demand associated with a monetary overhang. In 1948 the IMF, analysing wealth and liquidity overhangs in Europe, placed special emphasis on the UK, concluding that the overhang amounted to a quarter to a half of national income (Bernstein, 1948). At the annual meeting of the IMF and World Bank in Mexico City in 1952, the research staff held a seminar at which it argued that the UK still had substantial excess money balances. The danger that the UK would immediately exhaust its EPU quota was the principal objection to the clearing union scheme voiced by potential creditor countries (Diebold, 1952; Wexler, 1983).

Thus, monetary overhangs remained a problem only for a small minority of EPU countries, the UK and Ireland; even there, they were eliminated by the middle of the EPU years. Monetary overhang can hardly explain Europe's aversion to convertibility.

A final explanation of this aversion might be inadequate international reserves. European countries had spent reserves in pursuit of the war. Germany and Austria had been stripped of reserves after the war. Others had drawn on their remaining gold and dollar holdings to finance imports from the dollar area. However, the US aid partly went into replenishing Europe's reserves, and European current accounts improved after the 1949 devaluations.

For the EPU countries as a whole, evidence of a reserve shortage is weak. Table 4 compares the level of reserves in the early 1950s with reserves in the last prior period of convertibility: the interwar gold standard years 1926–29. The reserves-export ratio, having averaged 35% in 1926–29, was 47% in 1950 before falling back to a postwar low of 34% in 1951. Relative to the trade to be financed, the EPU countries as a group probably possessed adequate reserves.

In sum, inadequate reserves, a monetary overhang, and the impossibility of a market-clearing exchange rate cannot explain why policymakers opted for a clearing union rather than convertibility after World War II.

Table 4. International reserves of EPU countries, 1926–29 and 1950–55

	1925–26	1928–29	1950	1951	1952	1953	1954	1955
% of GNP	6	10	7	6	5	6	7	7
% of exports	29	40	48	34	36	45	44	46

Source: Eichengreen (1993).

4.3. Why the EPU was adopted

Why then was the EPU adopted? I suggest it was to help cement the domestic and international settlements on which postwar European growth was based.

4.3.1. The domestic settlement. As argued in De Long and Eichengreen (1993), postwar Western European growth was based on a distinctive social pact that successfully averted a rerun of the debilitating struggle over income distribution after World War I. In effect, workers agreed to moderate wage demands if management agreed to reinvest the consequent profits in productivity-enhancing plant and equipment. Each side agreed to trade short-term gains for long-term benefits so long as the other side agreed to do the same.

This characterization is illuminating but oversimple. Reality was more complicated, but the large literature that exists on European corporatism after World War II (see Goldthorpe, 1984) suggests that the postwar settlement is not, like Thurber's unicorn, a mythical beast. In the Netherlands, for example, the unions explicitly agreed that the fruits of all productivity increases in the first half of the 1950s should be used to finance investment (Abert, 1969). In Germany, trade unions observed 'significant wage restraint' throughout the 1950s (Maier, 1984). In Austria, German- style wage moderation and investment were secured by close consultation between representatives of labour, management and government (Katzenstein, 1984). Even in Britain, not noted for labour–management harmony, the Trades Union Congress cooperated with management and government to moderate wage demands (Flanagan *et al.* 1983).

Management, for its part, raised investment rates to nearly twice the prewar level. Even in Britain, not one of Europe's high investment countries, management agreed to restrain dividend payout in favor of reinvesting profits (Middlemas, 1986).

There were two immediate conditions for achieving this settlement: first it had to be reached, and then it had to be sustained. Reaching it required minimizing the ratio of short-term sacrifices to long-term benefits, especially since discount rates were high in the immediate postwar years. With incomes and living standards depressed in the immediate aftermath of the war, the marginal utility of consumption was high. Achieving an agreement that involved deferring consumption was exceptionally difficult. Indeed, as Alessandra Casella and I (1993) have argued, it was only with the help of Marshall Plan transfers, which increased the size of the pie to be shared by capital and labour, that it proved possible to strike this bargain at all.

The EPU worked in the same direction by strengthening Europe's terms of trade, which moderated the requisite sacrifices in living standards. Devaluation worsens the terms of trade, reducing the size of the pie to be shared out among competing interest groups. For devaluation followed by convertibility to balance the external accounts, residents of other continents had to be coaxed into purchasing more European exports and Europeans had to be induced to purchase fewer imports. A decline in the relative price of exports (a terms of trade deterioration), was needed to bring this about. Table 1 confirms that devaluation entailed terms-of-trade losses.

Conversely a payments union which restricted imports from extra-European sources had broadly the same effect as a tariff. Europe maintained balance-of-payments equilibrium with the rest of the world (ROW) not by altering relative prices so as to export more but by limiting purchases of non-European goods through the use of import licensing, foreign exchange rationing, and the other administrative devices associated with inconvertible currencies. By reducing the European demand for US goods, this shifted relative prices in Europe's favour. Stronger terms of trade meant that fewer European exports could command more European imports from countries like the United States. As an implicit tax on imports, inconvertibility raised the level of European incomes consistent with balance-of-payments equilibrium with the ROW.

Opting for convertibility rather than the EPU would have shrunk European incomes by 1–2 per cent, an effect comparable to that of eliminating Marshall Plan transfers.[6] This could have threatened the fragile agreements between labour and capital over income distribution in postwar Europe.

Contemporaries emphasized these terms-of-trade effects (Smithies, 1950; Day, 1953). The problem was summed up as follows by the OEEC in 1950: with European productivity growth lagging the American, 'the

---

[6] Imports were 25% of GNP in the participating countries. The standard formula (0.25 × 5%) implies a 1.25% fall in real incomes.

competitive position (terms of trade) of Western Europe would deteriorate . . . .' Attempting to rely on relative prices under convertibility, rather than the discriminatory measures permitted by a clearing mechanism, would lead to 'continuous pressure on the exchanges; a fall in the standard of living would be inevitable.'

Other devices could have achieved the same ends. Western Europe could have violated GATT strictures regarding trade liberalization and nondiscrimination, imposing a tariff on imports from the ROW to improve their terms of trade, rather than violating the IMF Articles of Agreement mandating convertibility after a transitional period of three to five years. The United States, for its own reasons, preferred the second alternative and possessed leverage as a result of the Marshall Plan (Milward, 1984). And, as I describe in the next section, it was easier to append to the EPU agreement safeguards to prevent countries from abusing their resort to import restrictions and to ensure that the measures they took were temporary.

The postwar settlement, once struck, still had to be enforced. In particular, a time-inconsistency problem had to be overcome. Labour had to be convinced to trade lower current income for higher future living standards despite intrinsic uncertainty over whether management would keep its part of the bargain: to reinvest tomorrow the profits accruing from labour's sacrifices today. This was a game with a second-mover advantage. Having obtained concessions from the first mover (labour), the second mover (capital) could renege on its part of the bargain, paying out profits rather than reinvesting. Awareness of this made labour hesitant to agree.

This problem is modelled theoretically by Grout (1984) and van der Ploeg (1987), who show that investment and output will be suboptimally low when it is impossible to negotiate a binding agreement that allows the second mover to precommit. In postwar Europe, to enforce the implicit contract and eliminate the time-inconsistency problem, institutions were designed to disseminate information and monitor compliance. The German system of workplace 'codetermination', in which labour had input into managerial decisions, was only an extreme example of a general trend. In many countries, the representation of interest organizations on advisory and administrative committees of industry and government was made obligatory. Industry-level unions and employers associations exchanged information on the terms of their bargains through government-sanctioned peak associations.

Governments helped to lock in the bargain by adopting policies and programmes which acted as 'bonds' that would be lost in the event of reneging. They agreed to limit rates of profit taxation in return for capitalists keeping their part of the bargain and ploughing back earnings into investment (Middlemas, 1986). They provided limited forms of industrial support (selective investment subsidies, price-maintenance schemes, orderly marketing agreements) to sectors that would otherwise have experienced competitive difficulties. Workers were extended government programmes of maintenance for the unemployed, the ill and the elderly. This web of interlocking agreements functioned as an institutional exit barrier. As a commitment technology it increased the cost of reneging on the postwar settlement.

The EPU was an essential concomitant of these arrangements. Without import licensing and foreign-exchange rationing, which provided limited insulation from international markets, intervention in domestic markets would have been much more difficult. More intense trade competition would have increased the budgetary cost of selective industrial subsidies. It would have made the degree of wage compression across sectors sought by 'solidaristic' trade unions more costly to achieve. Social programmes would have been threatened by pressure to minimize labour costs. The web of institutional arrangements that provided the exit barrier would have been that much more difficult to spin. The domestic settlement might have broken down.

4.3.2. The international settlement. The other element of the postwar growth recipe was trade expansion through European integration. Rather than revert to the pattern of the 1930s, postwar Europe fully exploited trade as an engine of growth. National economies were allowed to exploit their comparative advantage. Expanding the scale of the market allowed them to pursue economies of scale and scope.

This was accomplished, in the first instance, through the liberalization of intra-European trade. Quantitative restrictions were removed more rapidly on intra-European trade. There was a logic to relying on intra-European trade. The countries of Europe were natural trading partners for reasons of proximity and history. To say that Germany was a traditional exporter of capital goods and other European countries of consumer goods is to generalize excessively but to convey the essential point. Without a rapid expansion of trade to permit this pattern of comparative advantage to be exploited, it is doubtful that productivity and incomes could have risen as they did. And slower growth in the international sector would have increased the sacrifices in living standards entailed in the domestic settlement, threatening breakdown there as well.

Restructuring along export-oriented lines was costly. Before undertaking it, policy-makers had to be convinced that Europe's commitment to free trade was permanent. Reallocating resources along lines of comparative advantage entailed sunk costs; sinking them would be an expensive mistake if any of the major European trading nations reneged on its commitment to free trade.

With memories of trade conflict in the 1930s still fresh, European policy-makers had to be convinced that the countries concerned, especially Germany, would make benign use of their productive capacity. The skeptical view was that two wars had proven that Germany should not be trusted to use its industrial capacity benevolently and hence should be pastoralized. Permanently dismantling Germany industry, US State Department officials objected, would punch a hole through the heart of the European economy (Gimbel, 1976), and drag down the demand for the exports of other European countries. Eliminating the continent's principal supplier of capital goods would raise the cost of investment, worsen the dollar shortage, and force other countries to divert resources into capital-goods production.

For Germany, the Wirtschaftswunder (the postwar economic miracle) required consent of the occupying powers to removal of controls on the level of production. In return, postwar policy-makers required that Germany be integrated into the European economy and that credible barriers to exit be created to prevent that commitment from being reversed (Berger and Ritschl, 1993). Given the prominence the Nazis had lent in the 1930s to dependence on foreign supplies, Germany, for its part, required guarantees of its access to raw materials, industrial intermediates and foodstuffs produced abroad.

For those concerned to construct a commitment technology and institutional barriers to exit, the EPU and the arrangements in which it was embedded were preferable to unilateral convertibility. Operating a payments union required a set of institutions (the Organization for European Economic Cooperation, which worked in tandem with the Bank for International Settlements) capable of monitoring compliance and imposing sanctions. EPU membership was linked to trade liberalization. Member countries committed under the terms of the agreement to 'the maintenance of desirable forms of specialization ... while facilitating a return to full multilateral trade...' (Rees, 1963). They adopted a Code of Liberalization mandating a schedule of subsequent liberalizations. By February 1951, less than a year after the EPU went into effect, all existing trade measures were to be applied equally to imports from all member countries. Participants were required to reduce trade barriers, initially by one-half and then by 60 and 75 per cent. The share of quota-free intra-European trade would rise to 90 per cent by the beginning of 1955. Countries failing to comply with this schedule or employing other policies to manipulate the terms or volume of trade in undesirable ways could expect to be denied access to EPU credits.

The Economic Cooperation Administration, which administered the Marshall Plan, supported the EPU, further buttressing the credibility of European countries' commitment to trade. Countries which failed to adhere to the international settlement risked losing their American aid.

5. Implications for the FSU countries

In light of this view of the EPU, is Western Europe's experience in the 1950s relevant for the FSU countries today? A social pact comparable to that constructed in Western Europe after the war is desperately needed in the FSU countries today. The distributional struggle remains intense. An agreement over income distribution that secured wage moderation and high investment would go a long way toward the resumption of economic growth. Can a payments union help to defuse the struggle over distribution that debilitates policy in the FSU today?

Unfortunately, the terms-of-trade benefits that helped the EPU play its conciliatory role are not available to the FSU. Whereas the EPU countries accounted for more than a third of global industrial production in the 1950s, the members of a FSU payments union would account for very much smaller shares. They lack the market power to engineer a significant terms-of-trade improvement. Concentrating on overall trade shares may neglect these countries' market power in individual commodities. The significant exception to the generalization may be Russian exports of petroleum. But an oil-export tax would be sufficient to capture any potential terms-of-trade gains without necessitating a payments union scheme. And Russia currently levies a $5.50 per barrel export tax.

Nor is the rest of the world as prepared to accept terms-of-trade losses as was the United States in 1950. If the republics adopted discriminatory trade policies, other countries might respond in kind. The terms-of-trade justification for the EPU in the 1950s hardly carries over to the 1990s.

Moreover, it is difficult to believe that a payments union could put the finishing touches on a social market economy and thereby lock in a distributional settlement in the FSU countries. Compared to postwar Western Europe, the gulf remains vast between competing distributional claims. Other elements of a distributional settlement are not yet in place, nor even on the horizon. To support a non-existent distributional settlement with a social market economy buttressed by a payments union puts the cart before the horse.

An international settlement among FSU countries akin to that achieved in Western Europe in the 1950s would be highly desirable. A credible agreement to liberalize intra-FSU trade and a commitment technology preventing countries from reneging on that agreement would encourage the FSU countries to restructure along lines of comparative advantage and to continue exploiting the scale economies characteristic of the old system. But after World War II such agreements were locked in by the creation of European institutions whose short-run goal was deeper economic links and whose ultimate objective was political integration. These are precisely the kind of links from which the republics of the FSU are moving away. It seems implausible that a payments union could be embedded in a broader integrationist framework that would enhance its credibility.

Thus, unlike the EPU, the case for a payments union for the FSU countries must rest narrowly on its capacity to provide multilateral clearing. How can such a mechanism best be designed to achieve this effect? I distinguish solutions before and after stabilization has been achieved.

5.1. Post-stabilization arrangements

Assume that monetary and fiscal control are restored prior to establishment of multilateral clearing. EPU-style arrangements then seem quite appropriate. To work, however, they must solve the structural creditor problem and minimize trade, relative-price and capital-market distortions.

5.1.1. Solving the structural creditor problem. If all countries are equally likely *ex ante* to be debtors within the union, they all should be willing to contribute to its working capital. A difficulty (the 'structural creditor problem') arises when some members anticipate being persistent creditors, accumulating inconvertible claims on the union which cannot be used to finance purchases from the ROW.[7] So long as their partners in the union remain in persistent deficit, such claims cannot even purchase goods within the union. Debtors have absorbed the working capital. Creditors have given away a portion of their exports. Anticipating this fact, prospective structural creditors are not inclined to participate.

The structural creditor problem is likely to be severe in the FSU. The Russian Federation has a trade surplus with virtually every republic, due in part to the others' dependence on its energy, traditionally supplied

---

[7] A secondary market in such assets conceivably might develop, with creditors reselling (perhaps at a discount) their claims on the union. Purchases (by convertible currency countries) could be used to finance imports from countries in debt with the union. This is tantamount to current-account convertibility, at a floating rate, and it is likely that union members would refuse to honor such claims for the same reasons they oppose convertibility.

European Payments Union   333

Table 5. Initial schedule of settlements in the EPU
(% of current surplus or deficit)

Cumulative surplus or deficit as % of EPU quota	Country with			
	Cumulative deficit		Cumulative surplus	
	% gold	% credit	% gold	% credit
0– 20%	0	100	0	100
20– 40%	20	80	50	50
40– 60%	40	60	50	50
60– 80%	60	40	50	50
80–100%	80	20	50	50
Overall percentage	40	60	40	60

Source: Kenen (1991).

below market prices. Substitution away from oil imports is possible, but opportunities are limited in the short run. Higher energy prices will translate into still larger deficits for many republics, still larger surpluses for Russia. An FSU clearing mechanism that did not include Russia would have little impact on the volume of intra-FSU trade. What might be done to induce Russia's participation?

It is commonly thought that the EPU provides no guidance on this question: the principal structural creditor, the United States, was outside the system. In fact, EPU experience is relevant since some participants, such as Belgium, were persistent creditors with the union. Why did they participate?

In part, their participation was encouraged by the institutional linkage between multilateral clearing and trade liberalization. Creditor countries were also encouraged to participate by a schedule of hard-currency settlements that escalated more quickly for creditors than for debtors. Table 5 shows the initial schedule of credit and hard-currency settlements. Note the asymmetry in the treatment of debtors and creditors after a fifth of each quota has been utilized. From that point, debtors are able to settle with 80 per cent credit, but creditors receive settlement half in convertible currency.

This asymmetry created the need for a reserve of convertible currencies to finance the difference. The US assigned $350 million of Marshall Plan funds to the EPU. In addition, the recipients of Marshall aid contributed capital subscriptions.

Moreover, drawings on the system were embedded in a mechanism minimizing the likelihood that a country could exploit its partners by remaining a persist debtor. No conditions were attached to a country's drawings on its quota of 15 per cent of its intra-EPU trade. But additional credits could be obtained only if a country agreed to conditions set down by the EPU's Managing Board. Officials of governments receiving exceptional credits were required to appear at the monthly meeting of the EPU Board for questioning and to submit monthly memoranda on their progress. The EPU was underwritten with US aid, which gave this conditionality teeth. European dependence on Marshall aid reduced the likelihood that a debtor would renege on its agreement with the Managing Board and fail to take corrective action to eliminate its deficit.

5.1.2. Solving the trade diversion problem. A payments union is likely to cause trade diversion. Credits would finance intra-FSU trade but not FSU trade with the rest of the world. Member countries would be encouraged to trade too much with one another.

Such trade diversion could have serious costs. One legacy of 70 years of central planning is excessive levels of intra-regional trade compared to trade with the rest of the world (Drabek, 1992; Williamson, 1992). A payments union would simply reinforce this pattern; and, by sheltering large enterprises from Western competition, would allow them to exploit their market power and distort relative prices. This in turn would hinder transformation.

These problems existed also under the EPU. But, as I show elsewhere (Eichengreen, 1993), their effects were relatively mild. By allowing countries to economize on the use of international reserves for settling intra-European trade, the EPU freed up reserves for financing trade with the ROW. The same mechanism is likely to operate in the FSU.

In addition, intra-EPU trade enhanced competition. As noted by Triffin (1957), 'for many categories of goods, the lowest European prices which [domestic producers] had to meet – Swiss prices for some goods, Belgian or German prices for others, etc. – were probably as competitive as those of any third country, including the United States.' Extensive intra-European trade thus allowed efficiency-enhancing arbitrage to operate powerfully, minimizing price distortions. And since the economies of Europe, notwithstanding their troubles, possessed a number of world-class industries, intra-EPU trade drove prices down to the levels established by the least-cost producer.

Clearly, this influence will operate only weakly if at all in the FSU. Even if all the FSU republics were combined into one integrated market, many enterprises would still retain market power; to minimize price distortions, it will therefore be necessary to rely on extra-FSU trade.

This in turn will require minimizing trade diversion. Under the EPU this was accomplished in two ways. The US provided credit to finance trade with the dollar area. The US Export–Import Bank, the Marshall Plan and subsequent US military aid all financed imports from the dollar area. Marshall aid, moreover, was only loosely tied: except for shipping services and certain agricultural goods, the ECA did not require aid recipients to use the funds to import from the US. It financed imports from the whole of the hard-currency world. In addition, many European importers could obtain trade credit from the US market but not from the credit markets of their European trading partners which remained disorganized and depressed.

Product-market distortions under the EPU was also mitigated by rapid liberalization of extra-European trade, partly in response to US pressure. US leverage, derived from its contribution of working capital to the EPU and the provision of Marshall aid generally, was used to enshrine trade liberalization and nondiscrimination in the preamble of the EPU agreement. Moreover, the terms of EPU settlements were progressively 'hardened' (settlement increasingly required in convertible currency). This also mitigated the trade-diverting effects of the system.

5.1.3. Solving the problem of capital market distortions. Along with creating product-market distortions, there is the danger that a payments union will act as a barrier to foreign borrowing. FSU currencies will remain inconvertible. Individuals and enterprises will be able to buy convertible currencies only on the black market and for commercial transactions approved by the government. This poses a risk for Western investors contemplating projects in the FSU. Inconvertibility will create additional uncertainty about whether they will be able to repatriate principal and earnings.

The same danger existed in Western Europe in the 1950s. As the UN (1954) warned:

'Foreign enterprises are bound to feel the impact of such control in connexion (sic) with both the remittance of income (and the repatriation of capital, if desired) and the payment for imports required for operations. Exchange control is usually a symptom of balance of payments pressure; should the pressure increase, control may be tightened or the currency devalued. Either alternative, but particularly the former, may represent a powerful deterrent....'

To some extent this problem was not overcome. Large-scale foreign lending to Western Europe did not resume until after the resumption of current-account convertibility at the end of 1958, which removed remaining barriers to the repatriation of earnings.

The US did however pursue policies designed to offset the capital-market effects of inconvertibility, albeit on a relatively modest scale. It guaranteed American foreign investments against the risk of inability to transfer funds. Pursuant to the Mutual Security Act of 1951 (the successor to the Marshall Plan), the government insured US investments against the risk of inability to repatriate due to currency inconvertibility and loss through confiscation and expropriation. Individuals and companies investing in countries for which aid was authorized by the act (essentially, the former Marshall Plan recipients, plus Taiwan, Haiti, Israel and the Philippines) were eligible to participate. Through the middle of 1954, 67 industrial investment guarantees totaling $47.6 million had been issued to cover private investments. Of the total, $45.0 million insured against inconvertibility of foreign currency assets (US Congress, 1954). This programme surely made some contribution to minimizing capital-market distortions.

Today the US in fact possesses a comparable programme: the Overseas Private Investment Corporation (OPIC). But at the time of writing, OPIC has approved applications for only seven FSU investments, all in Russia, with a face value of only $121 million. To offset the capital market dislocations associated with inconvertibility, more will have to be done along these lines.

5.2. Feasible strategies prior to stabilization

The obstacles to early stabilization in the FSU countries are formidable. If high inflation, large budget deficits and pervasive excess demands persist, is a payments union still feasible? If so, what kind?

5.2.1. Multilateral clearing without credits.
The absence of stabilization poses no barrier to the establishment of a mechanism for multilateral clearing. Enterprises could undertake transactions in whatever currency they prefer, so long as the accounts of the clearing union are denominated in a stable unit of account like dollars, Deutsche Marks or ecu. A Ukrainian enterprise buying oil from a Russian firm could still be charged a price denominated in rubles. The Ukrainian importer would have to submit the contract to the Central Bank of the Ukraine, which would tell it how many hryvna to deposit given the exchange rate between the hryvna and the ruble. The Ukrainian Central Bank would record a bilateral debt in the relevant number of (say) dollars in its account with the clearing union. The Central Bank of Russia would receive a copy of the contract, record a credit on its account with the clearing union, and pay out the specified number of rubles to the exporting firm. The clearing union would determine each country's overall position by clearing all bilateral balances multilaterally.

One aspect of the EPU, temporary credits, would not be feasible prior to stabilization. So long as the excess demand for goods remains ubiquitous, there is no reason why a country, once it utilized its credit line, would subsequently move from deficit to surplus. Imagine that working capital sufficient to fund an EPU-like system (quotas equal to 15 per cent of each country's annual exports to other FSU countries and the original EPU schedule of hard currency settlements) was subscribed. The countries quickest to incur a deficit with the payment union would obtain for free goods equal to 9 per cent (15 per cent times 0.6) of their annual intra-FSU exports. The countries closest to stabilization would 'enjoy' a surplus with the union, but give away 9 per cent of their intra-FSU exports. Absent stabilization, there would be no reason for these positions to reverse subsequently. With the debtor countries having exhausted their quotas, all subsequent transactions would be settled in hard currency.

What would follow is easy to predict. The creditor countries would demand to be compensated out of the union's hard-currency reserves for the exports they had 'given away'. Whether this working capital had been provided by capital subscriptions by each country equal to 60 per cent of its quota or by a donation of Western aid, the implication is the same: the payments union would be liquidated. Multilateral clearing might continue but on the basis of hard currency settlements.

If the hard currency capitalization of the payments union was less then the value of the credit-financed exports of the creditor countries, liquidation of the payments union could not compensate them fully. The recrimination that followed would be a setback to efforts at multi-lateralizing FSU trade. Alternatively, if Western aid provided sufficient working capital fully to compensate the creditors upon liquidation, aid would not be a step toward multilateral clearing but simply one-time compensation of the countries closest to stabilization in return for their having transferred goods of matching value to other members of the FSU. Countries close to stabilization would be no better or worse off, while those furthest from stabilization would have obtained additional goods equal in value to the amount of the aid. Such an arrangement would perversely reward the countries that had made the least progress toward stabilizing.

Finally, if the participating countries themselves subscribed enough hard currency (60 per cent of their quotas) fully to compensate the creditors upon liquidation, the attempt to establish credit-based trade would simply result in a transfer of reserves in the amount of the capital subscribed from those furthest from stabilization and a one-time transfer of goods from those countries closest to stabilization. This, of course, is the same thing that happens when all transactions are settled in hard currency. Thus, setting up a payment union with credits would create a short period when policy-makers might operate under the illusion that things were different. But as soon as the available credit lines were exhausted, the union would be liquidated. The hard work of establishing a credit-based system would have been for naught. Again, recrimination might follow, threatening even multilateral trade on a hard-currency basis.

This point is illustrated by the difficulties Western Europe itself faced in establishing a payments union prior to stabilization. It is no coincidence that EPU negotiations only gained momentum in 1949; prior to that time, high inflation persisted in France, and monetary reform had not yet eliminated the potential for inflation in Germany and Austria. Still other countries faced the same problem to various degrees.

A tentative step toward multilateral clearing took place in November 1947, when Belgium, Luxembourg, the Netherlands, France and Italy concluded the First Agreement on Multilateral Monetary Compensation. They agreed to the multilateral cancellation of existing bilateral balances. The participating countries agreed to offset debts they had incurred through the operation of a bilateral agreement with one country with credits they had incurred through the operation of a bilateral agreement with another. These operations were limited to a reduction in existing credit and debit balances; offsetting operations that would have reduced a country's debt against one partner by increasing its debt against another were not permitted (Triffin, 1957).

In October 1948, all OEEC countries agreed to the multilateral cancellation of debts. This agreement was renewed in June 1949 and ran until the EPU was inaugurated in July 1950. (It is noteworthy that Germany, the country where the inflationary threat remained greatest, was not yet admitted to the OEEC and hence did not participate even in this limited agreement.) Again, no credits were provided. So-called 'second-category compensations' which would have cancelled Country A's debts to Country B by wiping out its credits vis-a-vis Country C to the point where Country A became indebted to Country B were permitted under the 1948–50 agreement but rarely occurred.

As Triffin notes, this agreement made only a minor contribution to financing trade. Fewer than two per cent of the gross surpluses incurred under the provisions of existing bilateral agreements were cancelled multilaterally under the 1948–50 agreement.

By the end of the 1940s, restoration of fiscal balance and monetary reform had eliminated the obstacles to multilateral clearing with credit lines. Stabilization, it would appear, was a prerequisite for the EPU. Stabilization was required to render credible governments' commitments not to exhaust the available credits immediately.

Even following stabilization, the architects of the EPU were careful to limit the incentives for participating countries to relapse into inflation. On the one hand, 100 per cent hard currency settlements would provide no subsidy for the pursuit of expansionary policies. On the other, extensive credits would significantly heighten the temptation to inflate. Hence the decision to adopt the schedule in Table 5 requiring settlement in a combination of hard currency and credit.

The credibility of promises to avoid inflationary policies was further enhanced by conditionality attached to EPU credits. The most notable episode dealt with by the EPU Managing Board was the German crisis. In the initial 5 months of the EPU's operation (July–November 1950), Germany exhausted its quota. Trade deficits were to be expected: postwar reconstruction implied higher levels of domestic investment than saving. (While this was true of most Western European countries, in Germany the investment associated with postwar reconstruction only got underway following monetary reform in 1948.) German deficits were even larger than anticipated. The inauguration of the EPU in June 1950 coincided with the outbreak of the Korean War, which worsened the terms of trade of countries like Germany that imported primary commodities. Simulta-neously, credit restrictions that had been imposed in conjunction the monetary reform were relaxed, and taxes were reduced. Germany suffered cuts in American aid. And the country's EPU quota, calibrated on the basis of its 1949 exports and imports, was soon dwarfed by the rapid expansion of trade that followed once the effects of the monetary reform were felt.

Germany appealed to the Managing Board, which negotiated a $120 million credit, conditioned on the government's adoption of a pro-gramme of financial and economic adjustment. Conditions included commitments to maintain the existing exchange rate, to abstain from any form of deficit financing, and to increase taxes (Kaplan and Schleiminger, 1989). Germany was permitted to reimpose certain quantitative trade controls, but on an explicitly temporary basis. Germany's balance-of-payments deficit quickly evaporated, and the special EPU loan was repaid by May 1951. Germany shifted to perennial creditor status within the EPU.

What brought this result about was the government's compliance with the EPU Managing Board's conditions. Turnover taxes were raised. The structure of income and corporate taxes was modified to restrict domestic absorption. To limit the extension of credit to industry (which had been used largely for the accumulation of inventories), reserve requirements on most banks were increased by 50 to 100 per cent. The discount rate was increased over the objections of Chancellor Adenauer, who feared a delay in reconstruction. That the measure would enhance the prospects for an EPU credit line strengthened the hand of his opposition. As a result of the discount rate increase and related measures, net credits to the economy grew only a quarter as fast in the first half of 1951 as in the second half of 1950.

Clearly, the effectiveness of EPU conditionality rested on special circumstances. The EPU was underwritten by US aid, and the German credit absorbed more than a third of working capital the US had contributed. German reliance on Marshall aid and on the US generally (which had troops on the ground) reduced the likelihood that Germany would renege on its agreement with the Managing Board, to put an understated gloss on the point. It is hard to imagine that an ISB Managing Board could exercise comparable leverage today.

5.2.2. Does clearing without credits differ from convertibility? The preceding arguments suggest that it would be better to set up a clearing union that concentrated on multilateralizing settlements than a payments union with credits. This raises the question of how, if at all, multilateral clearing without credits differs from current-account convertibility.

From a macroeconomic standpoint, the two are in fact very similar.[8] Consider the scope for redressing balance-of-payments problems. If a country with a convertible currency is in deficit with one trading partner and in surplus with another, its central bank loses reserves to the one and gains reserves from the other. Its net reserve position reflects the balance of the two transactions. If its reserves face exhaustion, it has to impose import controls and/or depreciate the exchange rate. (Recall that we are discussing a country unable to stabilize, incapable of adopting more restrictive monetary and fiscal measures to restore internal or external balance.) In the case of inconvertible currencies linked by a clearing union with hard currency settlements, the union cancels reserve inflows and outflows by whichever is smaller, and demands or supplies more reserves to the country's central bank depending on whether it is in overall deficit or surplus. If the country in question lacks the requisite reserves, it will again be forced to impose import controls and/or depreciate its exchange rate. There is no essential difference in the menu of available adjustment measures.

Nor do the two systems differ greatly in scope for segregating current and capital account transactions. Even with convertibility only for merchandise transactions, capital flight can still occur through leads and

---

[8] This point, though curiously ignored in the recent literature, was appreciated by the architects of the EPU (Hirschman, 1951).

lags or by overinvoicing and underinvoicing. An importer wishing to spirit capital abroad can have the foreign exporter overcharge him for the goods purchased and place the excess in a foreign-currency denominated bank account. The central bank, seeing only the invoice for the merchandise imports, has limited ability to curtail this practice. But precisely the same is true under a clearing union with hard-currency settlements: the central banks of the participating countries see only the invoice, permitting importers and exports to shift financial assets between countries and currencies.

Nor does a clearing union without credits necessarily economize on reserves. The literature on the demand for international reserves (Kenen and Yudin, 1965; Heller, 1966; Frenkel, 1974) assumes that rapid adjustments in foreign outlays are costly. Reserves are a buffer stock: they allow foreign outlays to remain stable in the face of fluctuating receipts. The standard payments-union argument is that it allows deficits vis-a-vis participating countries to be financed with credits; a higher average level of trade with the ROW is supported by freeing up reserves to fill the gap created by fluctuations in earnings from the ROW. In the absence of credits, however, no reserves are freed up. Hard currency is needed to settle payments imbalances both within the clearing union and with the ROW. This arrangement is as reserve-intensive as current-account convertibility.

Williamson (1992) argues that a clearing union achieves 'major economies in the need for hard-currency reserves because it is only net imbalances that have to be settled in hard currency, rather than each individual transaction'. Similarly, Bofinger and Gros (1992) assert that a clearing union 'by synchronizing export and import payments ... reduces the fluctuations of its member countries' foreign exchange reserves'. It is not obvious that these conclusions follow *in the absence of credits*. While it is true that, under convertibility, each transaction must be settled in hard currency, it is also true that export payments in hard currency and import receipts in hard currency are synchronized in precisely the same way as in a clearing union. Banks acquiring hard currency can make it available to banks dispersing it via the interbank market. In the aggregate they need only hold reserves sufficient to settle net (as opposed to gross) flows. If competing banks do not trust one another, the central bank can intermediate. Exporters can be required to surrender foreign exchange receipts to a commercial bank which in turn must surrender it to the central bank. Importers can obtain foreign exchange from a commercial bank that obtains it from the central bank. Exactly the same netting of inflows and outflows takes place as under a clearing union, with only net imbalances requiring settlement in convertible currency. A clearing/payments union is less reserve-intensive only when it offers facilities for financing net imbalances with credit.

Perhaps those who argue that a clearing union sans credits is less reserve-intensive than current-account convertibility assume in addition that settlement can be effected more quickly in the first case. If the clearing union nets offsetting transactions daily but banks undertaking transactions in convertible currencies credit their clients' accounts only with a delay (e.g. a week), the latter involves may require additional reserves. But under which arrangement settlement takes place more quickly is ultimately an empirical question, to which I return in the next section.

Finally, there is the issue of whether a payments union scheme will give rise to more macroeconomic and intersectional distortions than current account convertibility. The answer depends on how import licenses are allocated. In the limit they could be auctioned to the highest bidder, in which case resource allocation would be the same as under current account convertibility. In practice, administrative favoritism of some sectors at the expense of others could give rise to important microeconomic distortions, although the macroeconomics of the two arrangements would remain essentially the same.

All this assumes the absence of significant credits. Current-account convertibility and a pre-stabilization clearing scheme would differ significantly if Russia offered to underwrite the provision of credits, as it in fact did at the start of 1993. Given that hyperinflating countries with massive oil-import bills will exhaust available credits almost immediately, this is effectively a subsidy to the other republics. Russian policy makers may feel that subsidies are justified by their foreign-policy ambitions or to compensate other republics for higher oil prices. But the advantages of transparency suggest that transfers should be decoupled from clearing. If Russia wishes to extend transfers, it should do so separately. Once it does, the macroeconomics of strict multilateral clearing and of current-account convertibility is essentially the same.

6. The Interstate Bank

An Interstate Bank for multilateral clearing between FSU countries was proposed at the Bishkek summit in October 1992. Initially, the ISB is to provide clearing services for the 10 founding members, and also possibly the Baltics and Georgia.[9] States with independent currencies (including non-FSU countries) can open correspondent accounts with the

---

[9] Azerbaijan is the one republic likely to remain outside the system.

ISB through which all payments to other member countries will be routed.

This proposal resembles in some respects the recommendations in the previous section for pre-stabilization economies. Transactions will be netted multilaterally on the basis of international payment orders transmitted to the ISB by the central banks of importing countries. Each transaction will be entered on the ISB's books at the exchange rate prevailing on the day the Bank receives the payment order. Netting will occur daily. Countries will have a running tally of their net positions. The ISB may demand hard-currency settlement as soon as a significant deficit emerges. If that settlement is not forthcoming, acceptance orders associated with the debtor country's imports will no longer be processed. Other nations will be notified, allowing them to half exports to the deficit country. Failure to settle can trigger additional sanctions. (For details, see Gros, 1993a: Williamson, 1993.)

Yet there are important differences from the recommendations of the last section. Despite daily netting and tallying, settlement will occur only every 15 days. Countries may incur a cumulative debt with the ISB equal to one month of export receipts. The capital of the ISB will be 5 billion rubles according to the revised March proposal, and the Central Bank of Russia will provide a 200 billion ruble line of credit. This creates an obvious danger, as described above, that countries with high inflation and massive oil-import bills will quickly exhaust their credits, transforming the ISB into a hard-currency settlement system. The fact that accounts are to be denominated in rubles rather than hard currency exacerbates this danger. Being in credit with the ISB is tantamount to holding net balances in rubles; given the rate at which the value of the ruble is eroding, no country will have any incentive to do so. Put another way, the real interest rate on ruble-denominated ISB debts will be strongly negative so long as high Russian inflation persists.[10]

This gives other members of the ruble area an obvious incentive to see that Russian inflation continues. Moreover, as an attempt to hold the ruble area together (by encouraging other republics to continue using the ruble by denominating intra-FSU transactions in that currency), the ISB proposal is an obstacle to Russian stabilization. Russian stabilization has been hindered by the ability of other republics to create bank rubles. Allowing their banking systems to create ruble credits without any regard to reserve requirements gives rise to a free-rider problem in which the benefits of seigniorage accrue to the credit-creating republic but the

---

[10] Ironically, countries such as Ukraine have objected to the ruble as the ISB unit of account not on these grounds (nor should they: they will benefit as prospective debtors) but out of fears that this somehow permits Russian dominance of the ISB (EES-AGIR, 1993).

costs spill over to the rest of the currency area. The ISB, by denominating transactions in rubles and encouraging countries to remain in the ruble zone, perpetuates this problem.

The solution to all these problems is to denominate ISB accounts in hard currency and to hold credits in abeyance until stabilization occurs. As explained above, this is tantamount to current-account convertibility.

If rapid Russian inflation persists, it may soon reduce to negligible levels the value of the capital and credit line available to the ISB. If the credit line is expanded in response, this will perpetuate the perverse incentives described above. If not, the ISB will be transformed into a system of hard-currency settlements tantamount to convertibility, a fact which would be best acknowledged and capitalized upon. An advantage of doing so is that domestic and international payments problems could be solved simultaneously through the agency of Western banks. In December 1992, a consortium of such banks agreed to provide clearing for select financial institutions in Russia, Hungary, Poland, Bulgaria and the Czech Republic (Bray, 1992). The Association Bancaire de Compensation manages the system on a private, not-for-profit basis with a stand-by facility from the ERBD. At latest report, 9 banks participate, of which 2 are Russian (EES-AGIR, 1992).

Participating banks will maintain ecu accounts with their Western partners. These will be drawn on by the clearing bank in accordance with the paying country's instructions. The paying and clearing banks will be linked by the Swift communications system. Transactions will be denominated in a convertible currency. Payments will take up to two days to clear to give the clearing bank time to ensure that funds are available to cover payments.

For example, a bank in Bulgaria operating on behalf of a Bulgarian firm purchasing goods from Russia would route payment to a bank account in Russian through one of the five Western banks. If other FSU republics participated, the same mechanism could clear and settle payments for intra-FSU trade. Thus, abandoning bilateralism for the only feasible pre-stabilization alternative could solve domestic and international payments problems simultaneously.

The use of the Swift system speaks to the question of the relative reserve intensity of current-account convertibility and a clearing union. Rapid clearing via the Swift system will tend to minimize float and further synchronize hard-currency receipts and outlays. While the two days required for clearing via Swift is more than the one day specified in the ISB proposal, it is far from certain that all clearing via the ISB will be successfully completed within a day. Gros (1993a) reports that very large piles of sacks of unprocessed acceptance orders have tended to pile up in the basement of the CBR in Moscow. This bottleneck may not be eliminated once the ISB is established. Furthermore, 'one day' may only refer to the turnaround once the acceptance order arrives in Moscow. In the past, considerable time has been required to transmit the order from other republics to the Russian capital. This problem would presumably be eliminated once commercial banks are linked to Swift, minimizing the need for hard-currency reserves.

7. Conclusions and implications for Western assistance

History is a happy hunting ground for those concerned with economic problems in the FSU. For intra-FSU trade and payments, it seems to offer a compromise between the extremes of bilateral clearing and current-account convertibility, namely a payments union patterned after the EPU. Yet my conclusion is the opposite. The EPU is an inappropriate model for organizing intra-FSU trade and payments. After World War II, the EPU played a historically-specific role: to help seal the settlements on which postwar Western European growth was based. Domestically, it helped lock in a cooperative solution to the struggle over income distribution. Internationally, it cemented commitment to European integration. It was these contributions, not merely the facilitating of multilateral settlements, that made the EPU matter.

Moreover, a central feature of the EPU, credit-based settlements, will not be feasible prior to macroeconomic stabilization. The only multi-lateral clearing union currently feasible is one based on continuous multilateral balance among the participating countries. Such an arrangement is essentially the same as current-account convertibility. The effective choice for the FSU prior to stabilization therefore is between bilateralism and convertibility.[11]

Can Western assistance help rationalize intra-FSU trade and payments in such circumstances? Anything the West can do to promote stabilization will open up further options for multilateral clearing, including EPU-like schemes. Meanwhile, technical assistance to ensure reliable clearing is equally valuable whether clearing is bilateral or with a convertible currency (though in the latter case the private sector can help to solve the problem). But until stabilization occurs, a Western fund to provide working capital for a payments union would be futile.

---

[11] Similarly, the earlier analysis of Eastern Europe in Kirman and Reichlin (1990) concluded that 'an intermediate choice between full convertibility and a very structured system of compensation ... has only a small change of success.'

Discussion

Vittorio Grilli
Birkbeck College, London

Barry Eichengreen concludes his paper by giving a negative answer to the question he posed at the ouset: EPU cannot be used as a model for organizing international payments within the former Soviet Union (FSU). This is certainly a convincing view. EPU was appropriate to a particular set of countries and circumstances that bear little resemblance to the current reality of the FSU.

Nonetheless, lessons can still be drawn from that episode since the basic problem then (the promotion of economic growth by encouraging international trade) is the central issue facing the FSU now. There are two interlinked but distinct issues that a payments union must address. The first is the provision of a medium of exchange, the second the provision of credit facilities.

The first issue concerns transactions that do not have a time dimension – that is, import and export activities that do not involve a balance of trade surplus or deficit, and thus require no international borrowing or lending to finance them. Restricting such trade by requiring continuous bilateral balance is extremely inefficient; multilateral exchange allows trade that can be balanced only by involving several parties. To make multilateral exchange viable, as is well known, what is needed is a globally accepted medium of exchange or international money. Thus this form of trade requires a credible medium of payment, like an internationally established currency or, in short, currency convertibility.

The second issue concerns international transactions involving imbalances in the current account due to a temporal mismatch of imports and exports. An accepted medium of exchange is not sufficient to sustain such transactions; a well-functioning credit system must also be established. The level of credibility needed to sustain this second form of trade is far greater than that required for static multilateral exchange. In the first case, the viability of the system rests entirely on the credibility of the international currency. In the second case, the credibility of the medium of payment (lines of credit) cannot be separated from that of the debtor country.

A 'wide' form of payments union (one involving international credit lines) is clearly superior to a 'narrow' form if it is achievable, since it allows the exploitation not only of static gains from trade but also of intertemporal ones. However, the credibility requirements of a wide form are far more demanding than those of a narrow form payments union; it is therefore much more difficult to set up from scratch. In this respect, the EPU experience is instructive. At the end of World War II, Western Europe certainly lacked the credibility to move immediately to a wide form of payments union. The paper shows us how the system evolved in stages. At the beginning, it was limited to bilateral transactions. It was then gradually extended to multilateral ones and, only later, when relationships amongst countries were established and a minimum level of mutual credibility had been achieved, was a system of trade credits organized. The payments system evolved hand-in-hand with the credibility of its members.

It is clear that a wide form of payments union will be unviable before a full stabilization of the FSU economies is achieved, essentially because of the obvious lack of credibility of the joining countries. In the current state of affairs, the temptation to 'take the money and run' – that is, to default on international trade loans – is too great for the system to be feasible. In the medium run, therefore, the most the FSU can achieve is a narrow form of payments union that could represent an improvement on strict bilateralism.

One of Eichengreen's central propositions is that a multilateral clearing system is substantially identical to currency convertibility. Thus the best hope for the FSU countries is, in the short run, to achieve the convertibility of their currencies. However, while it is true that a multilateral clearing system and convertibility are similar in many respects, I would argue that they are not identical. Convertibility is a decentralized way to implement a centralized multilateral clearing system. Without distortions or informational asymmetries, centralized and decentralized solutions would produce the same outcome. But in the present context, where imperfect information is at the core of the moral hazard problem and the lack of credibility, the two alternative systems can perform quite differently. For example, a centralized system of clearing forces trade among the payment union members, while unilateral convertibility does not. By forcing trade and international relations, a centralized system could foster the building-up of mutual trust. Moreover, a centralized system can be designed to have monitoring functions that, once proven effective, could be used to support a credit system. I would not argue that EPU is the right model for a centralized payments system for the FSU. Nonetheless I believe that it may be premature to dismiss the option of a centralized multilateral payments union in favour of convertibility.

Stanley Fischer
Massachusetts Institute of Technology

The simple answer to the question posed by Barry Eichengreen in the title of his paper is that the EPU is indeed a relevant precedent for the FSU because so many people have turned to the EPU in making the case for a payments union, first to Eastern Europe, and then for the former Soviet Union. But I agree with his conclusion that the success of the EPU does not mean that a payments union of that type – without convertibility, and with quantitative trade restrictions – is the right approach for the former Soviet Union.

In his interesting and challenging paper, Eichengreen argues that the EPU was a success, right for its times, and better than the alternative, a far more rapid return to convertibility and a faster dismantling of trade controls, made possible by larger devaluations of European currencies against the dollar. He disposes of the standard arguments against a rapid move to convertibility – that monetary overhangs were large, and that devaluations would not have worked, and argues instead that the EPU made sense because it prevented the Europeans turning the terms of trade against themselves, and because it was part of a post-World War II social compact that allowed Europe to grow.

I disagree both with the conclusion that the EPU was better than the alternative of a more rapid approach to convertibility, and with the reasons Eichengreen advances for its adoption. Eichengreen is certainly right that the elasticity pessimism of the period was unwarranted, and that devaluations would have worked – and probably did work in 1949. However, the elasticities presented in Table 1 should be treated with some suspicion, since they derive from a period in which trade was controlled. Nor is that evidence, presented in 1993, relevant to the views of the time, which undoubtedly were pessimistic not only about the effectiveness of exchange rate changes, but also about the workings of the price mechanism in general.

The two arguments made for the adoption of the EPU are less convincing. First, even if the EPU prevented the terms of trade deteriorating, that goal could just as well have been attained through the use of tariffs in a liberalized trade regime. Eichengreen does not count among the costs of the EPU the trade distortions with which it was associated. And secondly, the social compact of which the EPU was supposedly a part is a mysterious abstraction: it is clear neither what the compact was, nor why anything in it would have required the use of the EPU rather than the use of tariffs within a less controlled trade regime. The social compact supposedly was an agreement between labour and capital in which labour would accept low wage increases while entrepreneurs would invest; the welfare state was part of the compact. This is an elegant metaphor that describes well the outcome of post-War economic policies, but it is hard to see what intellectual role the social compact plays in accounting for behaviour during this period. Was investment pushed beyond the point of profitability? Perhaps there was some such compact in Germany, perhaps even in the Netherlands, but was there such a compact in Italy or Britain?

There is a much simpler alternative explanation for the adoption of the EPU: at the time, there was widespread distrust – especially in Europe – of the operation of the market system, and the EPU, involving managed trade and a gradual transition to convertibility, was far more in accord with those attitudes than was the alternative. For support, consider the role of the dog that does not bark in the Eichengreen paper, the IMF. The IMF had been set up to deal with problems of postwar payments, but was shunted aside in favour of the EPU. In the debate over the creation of the post-War international institutions, the British had consistently been less enthusiastic about free trade and a rapid return to convertibility than the Americans. In part their concern about convertibility arose from the existence of large sterling obligations to colonies and former colonies; in part it also arose from a lesser commitment to and belief in the price system, especially during a period of transition.

The EPU was certainly a success: convertibility was reattained; Europe recovered and became prosperous; and through the EPU and other institutions, the Europeans learned to cooperate. Nonetheless, it must be emphasized that it took 13 years for Europe to reattain current account convertibility after the end of the war; it could have been done more rapidly, and at lower economic cost.

There is less to disagree with in Eichengreen's analysis of a payments union for the former Soviet Union. Proponents of the payments union support it as a means of slowing the collapse of trade among the republics. They have no doubt that much of that trade should disappear. Thus we are looking at a stopgap institution, one that would depend on and help re-establish the planning systems that have broken down and that should remain broken down. They probably cannot be put together, but in any case they should not be put together.

Eichengreen's discussion emphasizes the role of a payments union in making multilateral rather than bilateral clearing possible. Two points should be made here: first, given the central role of Russia in the FSU, the costs of bilateral trade are smaller than they would be if the republics were of similar sizes; and second, as Eichengreen states, in late 1992 accounts were set up that would in principle make multilateral clearing possible.

The alternative to a payments union has to be kept firmly in mind: it is a system in which currencies become convertible on current account. Eichengreen's paper contains a lengthy discussion of an issue that he says has not so far been discussed: that of the relationship between convertibility and multilateral clearing without credits. Convertibility makes multilateral clearing without credits possible. However, there is an essential distinction: a multilateral system may or may not be one in which individuals have access to foreign exchange for current account transactions; with convertibility, individuals do have that access. The reason the relationship between these systems has not received much attention is that the multilateral clearing systems associated with a payments union would in all likelihood be part of a system of state trading, and a system with convertibility would not. Proponents of the convertibility system are arguing not only for multilateral clearing – which becomes automatic with convertibility – but also for liberalized trade.

Should there be an EPU-style payments union in the former Soviet Union? As Eichengreen argues, the answer is no. Such an institution is unnecessary, especially in the FSU, where convertibility with independent currencies will not only help to make payments possible, but will also introduce international prices and competition into the economy.

What needs to be done then to deal with the problem of international payments? First, as Eichengreen emphasizes, the payments system among the republics needs to be improved, perhaps along the lines of the Share system that he describes. At the same time, it is equally urgent to improve the payments systems within the republics. Second, there should be a relatively quick transition to currency convertibility, associated with both stabilization and the introduction of independent currencies. Even in the event that there is no stabilization in some republics, convertibility with floating exchange rates would permit improved inter-republican payments. That is not to say that stabilization should not be the first priority, just that it may not be easily attained.

Third, there is a real need to provide assistance to the republics most severely affected by the transition to world prices. This means primarily the oil importers of the FSU, who have for long been subsidized by Russian oil pricing. This assistance can come either from the West, which through the IMF and other aid agencies can assist the republics directly, or from Russia. If Russia assists the other republics, it would be better to allow the price of oil to rise and provide loans to cover the increased cost than to subsidize oil prices and encourage its wasteful use. In any case, the IMF should work with all the republics in its traditional way, to identify foreign exchange gaps and ways of closing them.

General discussion

A number of panellists pointed to the dangers of supposing that the current collapse in inter-republican trade was due to the absence of an effective payments mechanism. Dariusz Rosati said it was due at least as much to the absence of internal settlement mechanisms within each republic: reliable contracts and a credible framework of legal and political authority. Until these domestic difficulties were overcome, an external mechanism would make no difference. The EPU, he suggested, was second-hand equipment being touted to the FSU, and should be firmly rejected in favour of early convertibility. This would have additional benefits that had not been present in post-War Western Europe, notably the importation of an efficient structure of relative prices to the highly distorted economies of the FSU. However, he pointed out that it was not full current-account convertibility that was at issue (and indeed, no Eastern Europe country yet had convertibility in this sense); trade convertibility was what mattered, and this was what was equivalent to multilateral clearing.

Richard Portes added to Rosati's diagnosis the presence of a structural creditor problem underlying inter-republican trade: Russia had for long been subsidizing the other republics. He also emphasised that much of the lost trade was distorted in the first place and was not something that public policy should be trying to preserve. The idea of an inter-republican bank was a dangerous one, into which the EC was being urged to put money. However, he warned that the alternative of a rapid move to convertibility, though in principle desirable, had its own dangers. In particular, the risk was that any foreign exchange equilibrium might involve a degree of real exchange rate undervaluation that would condemn the populations of the republics to unrealistically low wage levels.

Paul Hare pointed out that in Eastern Europe, convertibility usually applied only to firms. In the FSU, he suggested, it would probably need to apply to households as well, because of the substantial ethnic minorities present in many of the republics, for whom convertibility would represent an important political guarantee.

Some panellists also disputed the political interpretation of the EPU. Assar Lindbeck wondered of what the welfare state compact cited by Eichgengreen actually consisted. He found it hard to believe that firms had invested, when they did, for any reasons other than simple profit. The welfare state compact sounded to him a highly metaphysical idea for which it would be hard to find any empirical backing.

Guy Laroque pointed out that, in a number of countries of Western Europe, the EPU had been viewed as instrument of American imperialism. Part of the attraction of convertibility had been that it was viewed as an escape from the EPU. He also doubted that much weight could be put on the export elasticities estimated in such a managed trade regime, and pointed particularly to the effect of the Korean War in changing the outlook for European trade.

In reply, Barry Eichengreen conceded that the trade equations could at best be suggestive. However, he was vigorous in defence of the idea that there had existed a welfare state compact of some kind. This phenomenon went under a number of names, including 'corporatism', but the fact that it was difficult to measure precisely did not diminish the weight of historical evidence that some such agreement had existed in many countries. Finally, he agreed with the remarks made by Rosati about the dire environment for internal transactions within the republics, but said that in his view this strengthened the case for early convertibility for the FSU.

References

Abert, J. G. (1969). *Economic Policy and Planning in the Netherlands*, Yale University Press, New Haven.

Balogh, T. (1949). *The Dollar Crisis: Causes and Cure*, Blackwell, Oxford.

Bank for International Settlements (various years), *Annual Report*, BIS, Basle.

Berger, H. and A. Ritschl (1993). 'Germany and the Political Economy of the Marshall Plan', in B. Eichengreen (ed.): *Europe's Postwar Growth, Revisited* (forthcoming).

Bernstein, E. M. (1948). 'Latent Inflation: Problems and Policies,' Staff Memorandum No. 221 (April), IMF, Washington, D.C.

Blancpain, J.-P. (1964). *Vom Bilateralismus zur Konvertibilität*, Buch und Offsetdruck Stanz & Co, Zurich.

Bofinger, P. and D. Gros (1992). 'A Multilateral Payments Union for the Commonwealth of Independent States: Why and How?' CEPR Discussion Paper No. 654.

Bossuat, G. (1992). *La France, l'aide américaine et la construction européene 1944–54*, Imprimerie Nationale, Paris.

Bray, N. (1992). 'East European Banks to Start System for Clearing Payments,' *The Wall Street Journal Europe* (December 16).

Cairncross, A. (1992). *The British Economy Since 1945*, Blackwell, Oxford.

Casella, A. and B. Eichengreen (1993). 'Halting Inflation in Italy and France After World War II,' in M. Bordo and F. Capie (eds): *Monetary Regimes in Transition*, Cambridge University Press, Cambridge (forthcoming).

Day, A. C. L. (1953). 'Convertibility and the European Payments Union,' *Oxford Bulletin of Economics and Statistics.*

De Long, J. B. and B. Eichengreen (1993). 'The Marshall Plan: History's Most Successful Structural Adjustment Program,' in R. Dornbusch, W. Nolling and R. Layard (eds): *Postwar Economic Reconstruction and Lessons for the East Today*, MIT Press, Cambridge, Mass.

Diebold, W. (1952). *Trade and Payments in Western Europe: A Study in Economic Cooperation, 1947–51*, Harper and Row, New York.

Dornbusch, R. (1992). 'A Payments Mechanism for the Commonwealth and Eastern Europe,' unpublished manuscript, MIT.

Drabek, Z. (1992). 'Convertibility or a Payments Union? Convertibility!' in J. Flemming and J. Rollo (eds): *Trade and Payments Adjustment in Central and Eastern Europe*, Royal Institute of International Affairs and European Bank for Reconstruction and Development, London.

Eichengreen, B. (1993). *Reconstructing Europe's Trade and Payments: The European Payments Union*, Manchester University Press, Manchester (forthcoming).

Eichengreen, B. and M. Uzan (1992). 'The Marshall Plan: Economic Effects and Implications for Eastern Europe and the Former USSR,' *Economic Policy.*

EES-AGIR [European Expertise Service – Advisory Group on Inter-State Economic Relations] (1992). 'An Inter-State Payments System for the CIS,' unpublished manuscript, EES-AGIR.

—— (1993). 'Twenty-Third Interim Report,' Centre for European Policy Studies, Working Paper No. EES-AGIR 23.

European Bank for Reconstruction and Development (1993). *Annual Economic Review 1992*, EBRD, London.

Flanagan, R., D. Soskice and L. Ulman (1983). *Unions, Economic Stabilization and Incomes Policies*, The Brookings Institution, Washington, D.C.

Frenkel, J. A. (1974). 'The Demand for International Reserves by Developed and Less-Developed Countries,' *Economica.*

Gimbel, J. (1976). *The Origins of the Marshall Plan*, Stanford University Press, Stanford.

Goldberg, L., B. Ickes and R. Ryterman (1993). 'Departures from the Ruble Area: The Political Economy of Adopting Independent Currencies,' unpublished manuscript, World Bank and NYU.

European Payments Union   353

Goldthorpe, J. (ed.) (1984). *Order and Conflict in Contemporary Capitalism*, Oxford University Press, Oxford.

Gros, D. (1993a). 'The Interstate Bank: An End to Monetary Disintegration in the Former Soviet Union?' unpublished manuscript, CEPS.

—— (1993b). 'Bilateralism versus Multilateralism in the FSU, or What is the Potential Gain from the IB?' unpublished manuscript, CEPS.

Grout, P. A. (1984). 'Investment and Wages in the Absence of Binding Contracts: A Nash Bargaining Approach,' *Econometrica*.

Heller, R. (1966). 'Optimal International Reserves,' *Economic Journal*.

Hirschman, A. (1949). 'Devaluation and the Trade Balance,' *Review of Economics and Statistics*.

—— (1951). 'Types of Convertibility,' *Review of Economics and Statistics*.

International Monetary Fund (various years). *International Financial Statistics*, IMF, Washington, D.C.

—— (1991). *Economic Review: Russian Federation*, IMF, Washington, D.C.

Kaplan, J. J. and G. Schleiminger (1989). *The European Payments Union: Financial Diplomacy in the 1950s*, Clarendon Press, Oxford.

Katzenstein, P. (1984). *Corporatism and Change: Switzerland, Austria and the Politics of Industry*, Cornell University Press, Ithaca.

Kenen, P. B. (1991). 'Transitional Arrangements for Trade and Payments Among CMEA Countries,' *IMF Staff Papers*.

Kenen, P. and E. Yudin (1965). 'The Demand for International Reserves,' *Review of Economics and Statistics*.

Kent, T. W. (1950). 'Devaluation One Year After,' *Lloyd Bank Review*.

Kindleberger, C. P. (1950). *The Dollar Shortage*, Chapman & Hall, London.

Kirman, A. and L. Reichlin (1990). 'L'aide aux pays de l'Est: les lecons du plan Marshall,' in J.-P. Fitoussi (ed.): *A l'Est en Europe*, Presses de la FNSP, Paris.

Maier, C. (1984). 'Preconditions for Corporatism,' in J. Goldthorpe (op. cit.)

Michalopoulos, C. and D. Tarr (1993). 'Trade and Payments Among the Successor States of the USSR,' unpublished manuscript, World Bank.

Middlemas, K. (1986). *Power, Competition and the State, Vol 1: Britain in Search of Balance, 1940–61*, Macmillan, London.

Milward, A. (1984). *The Reconstruction of Western Europe, 1947–1951*, Methuen, London.

Orcutt, G. H. (1950). 'Measurement of Price Elasticities in International Trade,' *Review of Economics and Statistics*.

Organization for European Economic Cooperation (various years), *Statistical Yearbook*, OEEC, Paris.

Portes, R. (1992). 'The Transition to Convertibility for Eastern Europe and the USSR,' in A. B. Atkinson and R. Brunetta (eds): *Economics for the New Europe*, Macmillan, London.

Rees, G. L. (1963). *Britain and the Postwar European Payments Systems*, University of Wales Press, Cardiff.

Smithies, A. (1950). 'European Unification and the Dollar Problem,' *Quarterly Journal of Economics*.

Tew, B. (1965). *International Monetary Cooperation 1945–1965*, Hutchinson, London.

Triffin, R. (1957). *Europe and the Money Muddle*, Yale University Press, New Haven.

UN Economic Commission for Europe (1951). Economic Survey of Europe in 1950, United Nations, Geneva.

United Nations (1954). *The International Flow of Private Capital 1946–52*, United Nations, New York.

US Congress (1954), *Report to Congress on the Mutual Security Program for the Six Months Ended June 30, 1954*, GPO, Washington, D.C.

van der Ploeg, F. (1987). 'Trade Unions, Investment and Employment, A Non-cooperative Approach,' *European Economic Review*.

Wexler, I. (1983). *The Marshall Plan Revisited*, Greenwood Press, Westport, Conn.

Williamson, J. (1992), *Trade and Payments After Soviet Disintegration*, Policy Analyses in International Economics No. 37, Institute for International Economics, Washington, D.C.

—— (1993), 'Alternative Payments Systems for Inter-Republic Trade,' unpublished manuscript, Institute for International Economics, Washington, D.C.

Part V
The Trade Regime

[13]

THE END OF THE I·T·O

WILLIAM DIEBOLD, JR.
Council on Foreign Relations

TROUBLE, violence and discontent marked the close of 1950. New fears swept the United States and its allies as Mac-Arthur's troops retreated before the Chinese forces pouring across the Yalu. A remark by President Truman was misconstrued to mean he was planning to use the atomic bomb in Korea. Prime Minister Attlee flew to Washington to discover American intentions and, if necessary, to counsel caution. Asiatic countries asked the Chinese not to cross the 38th parallel; the American Chief of Staff flew to Tokyo to see General MacArthur who had just publicly questioned the orders that prevented him from bombing the enemy's "privileged sanctuary" in Manchuria. Within the United States, mobilization dominated economic discussion. The House of Representatives voted new taxes. The President asked for still larger military appropriations. A price controller and a civil defense administrator were appointed during the first week of December.

Naturally, in such times, few paid much attention to a State Department press release about the international trade conference under way at Torquay, England. Yet there, almost lost in the long mimeographed sheet, a subordinate clause announced a major change in American trade policy. On the recommendation of the interested federal agencies, said the announcement, the President had agreed that "the proposed Charter for an International Trade Organization should not be resubmitted to the Congress. . . ."[1] In form the decision seemed one of administration tactics; with a crowded Congressional agenda, passage of a bill for customs simplification and the forthcoming renewal of the Trade Agreements Act were more urgent than a long debate on a trade convention that had been pending for several years. The decision meant that the United States was dropping the ITO Charter. Since no other governments wanted to create the trade organization without the United

---

[1] Department of State, *Bulletin*, December 18, 1950, p. 977. The only public harbinger of this action that I have seen is a dispatch from Torquay, England to *The New York Times*, November 10, 1950. The reporter, presumably Michael Hoffman who was covering the tariff conference then in progress, said that after noting the Republican gains in the Congressional elections that had just taken place, "both Americans and non-Americans here have written off any possibility of United States ratification in the next two years. . . . A delay of two years more is likely to mean that the Havana Charter never will be pushed forward again in its present form. . . ."

States, the most ambitious attempt ever made to reach agreement on a comprehensive code of rules for international trade quietly ended in failure.

More than nine years had passed since the Atlantic Charter registered the desire of the countries fighting fascism "to bring about the fullest collaboration between all nations in the economic field." The further formulation of that aim in pledges, commitments and institutions can be traced through the lend-lease agreements, wartime discussions, the Bretton Woods conference, the creation of the Food and Agriculture Organization and UNRRA, the Charter of the United Nations and the British loan agreement. All these acts pointed toward an eventual comprehensive agreement removing barriers to world trade. The Bretton Woods agreements, for instance, and the American act adhering to them, were premised on the forthcoming creation of effective arrangements for cooperation in international trade. Capstone, keystone, cornerstone were the words repeatedly used, but whatever the metaphor, an agreement on trade principles was to be an essential part of the structure of international economic cooperation.

That agreement was the Charter for an International Trade Organization. *Quellenforschung* aside, the Charter's history covers nearly five years of preparation in wartime, over two years of lengthy, laborious, full-dress negotiations that eventually involved over fifty governments, and then nearly three years more of waiting and arguing, ending with what an Italian journal has called a "second-class funeral" in the dying days of 1950.[2] There followed a coda as other governments chimed in and announced that in view of the American decision they would not act on the ITO Charter.

From the first, the ITO was primarily an American idea. Only constant drive from the United States turned sketchy projects into concrete proposals and brought the long negotiations to completion. As late as January 1950, in his State of the Union message, President Truman called for Congressional action on the proposed Charter. He echoed the language with which he had submitted it to Congress in April 1949: "This Charter is an integral part of the larger program of international economic reconstruction and development. . . . An essential forward step in our foreign policy. . . ." Then, at the end of 1950, this favored American project was quietly dropped, and the American public, like the rest of the world, scarcely noticed its fall.

What had happened? How did it come about that this "necessary part" of the "solid foundation of continuous cooperation in economic

---

[2] *Italian Economic Survey* (Rome) January-February 1951, p. 1. The end was so quiet and unceremonious that on April 26, 1951 *The New York Times* was still discussing the effect of the Torquay conference on the Administration's case for the Charter before Congress.

affairs," as the President had called it, should now disappear "not with a bang, but a whimper"? The explanations seem to me to fall broadly into three categories: changes in the world setting between 1945 and 1950, the political situation in the United States, and the defects of the Charter from the point of view of American business. The pages that follow set out some of these explanations. They do not give a documented, play-by-play account of events. Many of the details are still locked away in archives or, in this telephonic age, perhaps only in men's memories. Those that are published are available elsewhere. This is an essay in interpretation, not an historical narrative.

I. THE WORLD SETTING

The ITO appeared on the world stage in preliminary form in December 1945 when the American loan to Britain was negotiated.[8] The war was not long over. The postwar world which had excited so much hope and such thoughtful attempts to foresee its difficulties realistically was at hand. The United Nations was getting under way. The organs and arrangements for postwar international cooperation prepared so carefully while the battles still raged were now to come into their own. Soon, many hoped, they would dominate the scene. Plans for economic reconstruction usually envisaged a "transitional period" in which war damage would have to be repaired and dislocation set right. The United States was prepared to help. The time would be used, too, to create the most favorable possible conditions for the kind of international economic relations prescribed in the Bretton Woods agreements, the *Proposals* and other postwar plans. The economic aims of the recovery plans were well-phrased in Article VII of the lend-lease agreements. There was to be "expansion, by appropriate international and domestic measures, of production, employment and the exchange and consumption of goods, which are the material foundations of the liberty and welfare of all peoples." The victors would move toward "the elimination of all forms of discriminatory treatment in international commerce; to the reduction of tariffs and other trade barriers. . . ."

It would not be any easy task to create this kind of a world, but with good will, care, effort and some luck it could be done; that was the prevalent mood. There were danger signals. Lend-lease had been cut off abruptly, before arrangements had been made to ease our

[8] It was presented in *Proposals for Expansion of World Trade and Employment*, prepared by United States officials after consultation with the British. In September 1946 a more elaborate draft appeared, called *Suggested Charter for an International Trade Organization of the United Nations*, which the United States presented to the Preparatory Committee created by the Economic and Social Commission, which had its first meeting in London in October.

3

European allies, and particularly the United Kingdom, into a position where they could pay for essential imports. The strains and suspicions of the wartime alliance with Soviet Russia were growing; Potsdam had not been a pleasant conference. The ITO itself was very late; negotiations should have been much farther advanced before peace set in. Yet it was an essential part of the structure. Clair Wilcox, chairman of the United States delegation, put the dominant view clearly at the outset of the first ITO negotiations in London in October 1946:

> Of the many tasks of economic reconstruction that remain, ours is by all odds the most important. Unless we bring this work to completion, the hopes of those builders who preceded us can never be fulfilled. If the peoples who now depend upon relief are soon to become self-supporting, if those who now must borrow are eventually to repay, if currencies are permanently to be stabilized, if workers on farms and in factories are to enjoy the highest possible levels of real income, if standards of nutrition and health are to be raised, if cultural interchange is to bear fruit in daily life, the world must be freed, in large measure, of the barriers that now obstruct the flow of goods and services. If political and economic order is to be rebuilt, we must provide, in our world trade charter, the solid foundation upon which the superstructure of international cooperation is to stand.

Few questioned the need for some kind of trade organization. The great differences of opinion were about the powers the international body should have, the practices that were to be outlawed, the extent to which existing trade barriers were to be lowered, and how soon the rules were to come into play for countries whose economic position had been seriously damaged by the war. This last issue became familiar in the ITO negotiations as the question of what exceptions to the general rules should be provided for countries in balance-of-payments difficulties. For Western Europe a large part of the answer—perhaps most of it, according to the thinking of 1945 and 1946—depended on how much financial aid the United States was prepared to give. Unless the help were adequate, the European governments saw no chance of reducing trade barriers and ending discrimination; with substantial aid, and the further protection of escape clauses if their difficulties recurred, they could look forward, with varying degrees of hope and skepticism, to a successful transition period after which an agreement liberalizing international trade could come fully into play. It was no accident that the ITO *Proposals* were launched at the time the British loan was negotiated. Britain and the United States were the key countries, without whose concerted action a world trade agreement would be sadly restricted, if it were workable at all. The loan agreement was a kind of capsule of the prevalent thinking about the postwar world economy. The joint statement on commercial policy, which supported the ITO *Proposals,*[4] stood for the economic world that was to be; the loan was a substantial fraction of the American aid that was to make that world possible.

By March 1948, when the *Draft Charter for an International Trade Organization* was signed at Havana, the postwar world had shown itself to be quite different from that envisaged in 1945. European reconstruction had proved to be a harder task than was expected. Prewar levels of production had been reached in many fields but were proving inadequate to satisfy the postwar expectations of Europeans plus the need for increased exports. The transition period was obviously going to be longer than that contemplated in 1945. What it was a transition to was becoming doubtful. Relations between the United States and the USSR had changed from uneasy alliance to cold war. Communists seized control of the government of Czechoslovakia just a month before the Charter was signed. When the negotiators came home from Havana, Congress was debating the Marshall Plan which registered two major changes in postwar plans: more American aid for Western Europe and a stronger political motive for providing it.

The hopes embodied in the ITO were not dead, but they were dimmed. The Marshall Plan showed that the period during which governments would be in financial troubles requiring the continued use of trade controls was likely to last for a while yet. The ITO negotiations themselves showed how important the exceptions to the rules favoring liberal trade had become. The political alignment of the cold war was not a serious barrier to putting the Charter into effect. Few had expected that Russia would join the organization.[5] Czechoslovakia, which had participated throughout the negotiations, signed the Charter; Poland came to Havana but did not sign. In any case, the Iron Curtain countries accounted for a very small part of world trade; the ITO could work without them. On the other hand, the ITO had little to contribute to the cold war. It could be argued that in the long run international trade on the ITO pattern would strengthen the free world and make it a better place to live in, but that was a distant prospect. For the immediate future the attraction lay in measures, like

[4] The *Proposals* were American; the *Joint Statement* said that the British government was "in full agreement on all important points" and would "use its best endeavors to bring [international] discussions to a successful conclusion, in the light of the views expressed by other countries." There were, of course, some misgivings, especially among the British. And some Americans put more store in the long run political consequences of strengthening Britain than in facilitating a liberal system of world trade. But for most these aims appeared to merge.

[5] However, early drafts of the Charter contained a provision in the state trading section intended to provide a Soviet *quid pro quo* for tariff reductions on Russian exports.

the Marshall Plan, that promised quick political and economic gains. Any immediate benefits from removing trade barriers could be obtained through the General Agreement on Tariffs and Trade (GATT), negotiated in 1947 as an interim arrangement pending adoption of the ITO.

In the circumstances, the ITO lacked urgency. No one could argue that its main principles would quickly take effect and change the face of the free world's economy. The opposition to Soviet policy that had helped pass economically enlightened measures like the British loan and the Marshall Plan did not generate support for the ITO. The Administration had its hands full getting other measures through Congress and could see no gain in loading one more controversial item onto a crowded schedule. As a result, the Charter was held over until the new Congress met in 1949. In April of that year President Truman sent the Charter to the Hill and asked for a joint resolution authorizing American participation. But by then Congress was busy with the North Atlantic Treaty, the Military Defense Assistance Program, and legislation for the second year of ECA. The Administration apparently agreed with Congressional leaders that it was better not to press for quick action on the ITO since these other foreign affairs measures took precedence. The slight recession of mid-1949 brought on a series of complaints about unemployment allegedly traceable to imports, thus helping to create a poor atmosphere for the ITO. Not until April and May 1950 did the House Committee on Foreign Affairs hold hearings on the joint resolution. The Committee did not report, and the matter never came to the floor of the House.

By the end of 1950, when the ITO was dropped, all these factors had intensified. Americans, and their United Nations allies, were fighting in Korea. General Eisenhower was getting ready to take command of a new allied headquarters in Europe. The United States was feeling its way toward some kind of mobilization economy. The aspirations of 1945 seemed more remote than ever. The Charter was adrift in a world for which it was never made.

II. AMERICAN POLITICS AND THE ITO

Depression is traditionally a poor time to get acceptance of trade barrier reduction. Yet the Reciprocal Trade Agreements Act, the most effective step the United States has taken to reduce its tariffs in at least half a century, was put up to Congress in 1933 and passed in 1934, both depression years. Part of the explanation is that the Act was presented largely as a means of fostering exports, and so helping recovery, by breaking down foreign trade barriers. It was presented as a contrast to the Hawley-Smoot Tariff, the retaliations which followed it and the increased use of quotas and exchange controls by foreign countries to close markets to American goods. While Cordell Hull always emphasized that trade was "a two-way street" and stressed the element of reciprocity in the program, it was the prospect of larger exports, not larger imports, that won votes for the bill.

Even more important was the Democratic landslide of 1932 and the composition of the new Administration. In power for the first time since Woodrow Wilson, the victors naturally felt that Democratic policies should be substituted for Republican ones in as many fields as possible. The tariff was an issue on which the tradition of party difference was strong. This may have been something of a myth, at least in the twentieth century, but in some circumstances it could be an effective myth. The traditional Democratic attitude toward the tariff, together with newer ideas for making the policy effective by keeping the tariff out of Congress, were embodied in Cordell Hull, the Secretary of State. Hull's position was particularly strong as an alumnus of Congress and a leading figure in what became the conservative wing of the Democratic party, a key element in the coalition by which Roosevelt kept power. Hull won a sharp fight within the Administration on the kind of trade policy to be advocated and thereafter the field was his. The Trade Agreements Program was not part of the mainstream of economic and social reform of the New Deal. It had a different logic from the NRA, the AAA, and the monetary policy that upset the London Economic Conference, and it clashed concretely with those measures at certain points. Still, its rationale was politically effective, and it is an aspect of the New Deal's pluralism and eclecticism that the break from existing trade policy should have taken this form.

Once enacted, the Trade Agreements Program gained the advantages of inertia that belong to "established policy." The President's power to cut tariffs was used very cautiously. It was concentrated on "excessive protection," the tariff margin that American producers did not need to compete successfully against lower-cost imports. The selective cutting of rates provided a degree of flexibility that could also be used, when necessary, to temper the program to the requirement of votes for renewal every three years. Mr. Hull continued to regard the Trade Agreements Program as a major feature of his foreign policy. Mr. Roosevelt continued to back Hull. The American electorate continued to give Roosevelt large majorities. The Democratic members of the House and Senate continued to follow the leadership of the White House. After war broke out in 1939, the impact of tariff reductions was reduced. Then the Trade Agreements Program became linked to war aims and probably gained a certain amount of support—or at least

7

avoided some overt opposition—on this count. It costs little to vote for an inoperative ideal.

The general pattern of the legislative history of the Trade Agreements Act and its renewals in Hull's and Roosevelt's time was about as follows. The initiative and main drive for the program came from the State Department. Renewal of the Act was regularly a "must" on the President's list of requests to Congress. A minority of the Democrats in Congress opposed the program, for the most part because of protectionist sentiment in their constituencies. The majority that supported the program included men who favored its principles or whose constituencies included an active export or trading interest, and also a number of "doubtful" Senators and Representatives who might well have voted against the Act on one ground or another, or at least remained indifferent to it, had it not been for the arsenal that a strong Administration has at its command when "must" legislation is at issue. To determine how great the otherwise "doubtful" vote was would require careful analysis of the votes at each renewal[6] but there is little doubt that it was sizable and that in some years, at least, the Administration's ability to sway it was decisive in continuing the Trade Agreements Program.

Though there was always some Republican support for the Trade Agreements Program, most of that party's representatives in Congress usually voted against renewal. When the Trade Agreements Act came before a Republican Congress for the first time, in 1948, the President's power was circumscribed by the introduction of "peril points" below which he could not reduce duties without explaining his action to Congress. This provision was eliminated in 1950 but made its reappearance—along with other limitations—in the 1951 renewal, when there was a Democratic majority no longer so strongly under the influence of the White House as in Roosevelt's presidency and when the Secretary of State's status on the Hill was not what Mr. Hull's had been.[7]

This rough sketch of the political pattern on which the Trade Agreements Act depended helps us to understand some of the ITO's diffi-

---

[6] In some years it is hard to say which was the critical vote since the passage of the bill often got the support of men who had shortly before voted for modifications or delaying motions which, if carried, might well have drastically altered the shape of the program.

[7] The Administration's insistence that it never reduced tariffs if that would harm American producers weakened its case against the peril points which, it could be argued, were merely legislative assurance of the same practice. This is a fallacious argument, but I am not here discussing the case for or against the Trade Agreements Program. The point illustrates the difficulty of building up political support for a fairly complex, and to some extent procedural, case, especially when the alternative has the attraction of ambiguity.

culties. The issues were not identical, of course. The Charter covered a broader field and entailed new obligations. One might, therefore, support the Trade Agreements Program while opposing the Charter.[8] Important segments of the business community did just this and thereby played a significant part in bringing about the demise of the ITO.

What these businessmen did not like about the ITO is the subject of the next section. The fact that the merchant and export groups who regularly supported the Trade Agreements Act were split over the ITO removed an important prop on which the Administration's case with Congress would otherwise have rested. It is impossible to say that business opposition meant so-or-so many votes in Congress and thus made passage of the ITO resolution impossible. Only the Administration officials and Congressmen who engaged in the actual head-counting that must have preceded the decision to drop the matter could estimate that. Perhaps we shall someday learn how close the count stood, what the pattern of support and opposition was, who might have been brought around if the Truman Administration had possessed the persuasive forces the Roosevelt Administration used to have. Lacking that, we do not even know for a certainty that the crucial votes may not have been those of a few men whose unwillingness to support the Administration in this matter may have rested on considerations irrelevant to the Charter. Certainly the Republican gains in the elections of November 1950 added to the Administration's difficulties in mustering support for the ITO.

In any case the opposition of certain business groups was undoubtedly a major factor in the defeat of the ITO. The loss of business support worked in two ways. Congressmen close to the business groups and likely to be much influenced by their views became opponents instead of supporters of the ITO. It was not only their votes that were lost but also their help in the intra-Congressional discussion and log-rolling which are so important in putting through a measure of this sort on which there is a sizable doubtful vote. Secondly, the more or less neutral Representatives and Senators, whose convictions and whose constituents' direct interests were not already heavily committed, would be much harder to rally in support of the ITO if they saw that major groups directly affected by the measure were opposed or uninterested.

[8] On the other hand, supporters of the Charter would have to support some kind of Trade Agreements Act so that the United States could carry out its obligation to negotiate in good faith with other members of the ITO for the reduction of tariffs. It could have been argued, however, that a modified form of the Act would be consistent with this obligation. Without reference to the ITO, Senator Vandenberg apparently regarded his co-sponsorship (with Senator Millikin) of the original peril-point procedure as a measure of bipartisan foreign policy consistent with preservation of the spirit of the Trade Agreements Act.

Of course, certain business groups had regularly opposed the Trade Agreements Program but it was kept alive despite them. Not their opposition, but the opposition of merchants and manufacturers who had supported the Trade Agreements Program, marked the difference in the position of the ITO Charter before Congress.

Apart from this shift in business support, the line-up for and against the Charter was similar to that called forth by the Trade Agreements Program in recent years. Except for America's Wage Earners' Protective Conference—the protectionist wing of the AF of L—and certain unions in protected industries, labor generally supported the Charter, but acceptance of the ITO was not a major concern of either the CIO or the AF of L. The American Farm Bureau Federation and the National Farmers Union supported the Charter while the Grange hedged. The farmers' main foreign trade bogey was laid by provisions, introduced into the Charter on American initiative, permitting the use of import quotas in connection with farm programs. Farmers had an interest in the removal of foreign trade barriers on their exports, but the ITO did not promise enough immediate action to stimulate much enthusiasm. Many civic organizations and women's groups endorsed the ITO, and some committees were organized especially to urge American adherence to it, but the Charter's length and complexity, among other things, prevented it from becoming an object of great public interest.

Professional economists and academic people concerned with foreign affairs for the most part favored the ITO, but usually with explicit recognition of its limitations and often with a feeling that it was desirable principally because the other possible alternatives were so unattractive. This somewhat reserved attitude, stemming from the Charter's mixture of high principle with detailed compromises that were distasteful, even if necessary, checked the growth of enthusiastic activity among independent liberals. Even those who had a firm conviction that acceptance of the imperfect Charter was in the American interest admitted that the ITO might not work out as they hoped. Beneath these doubts and reservations was the realization that the Charter was an attempt— a necessary and proper attempt, but one whose chances of success were inevitably uncertain—to bridge a gap between a doctrine of the sound ordering of international trade and a situation in which many of the premises of that doctrine were no longer valid. This was an understanding, and in my opinion correct, view of the matter, but it was not one to generate the kind of political steam needed to pass the Charter.

Two other factors probably played a part in reducing the ITO's chances of success. Great export crops like cotton and tobacco were no longer quite so important as they had been in the South, traditional home of Democratic free trade attitudes. Foreign aid programs were helping to provide current export markets. Peanuts, meat and dairy products were providing a growing share of the South's farm output; industry, especially the manufacture of textiles, was expanding. Some of these new activities, instead of increasing the South's interest in exports, were protected from foreign competition by tariffs and other import controls. So the South could no longer be counted on for solid support on measures aimed at reducing trade barriers. The other factor was that the ITO lacked a backer of the political power of Cordell Hull who could have mobilized more active support for the ITO within the Administration. Nor did any postwar Secretary of State have as great a personal interest in trade barrier reduction as had Hull.

While it is hard to judge how important each of these many factors was, there can be little doubt that business opposition and the Administration's lack of influence with Congress, compared to Roosevelt's day, go far to explain why the Charter was dropped. It remains to explain the business attitudes.

III. BUSINESS CRITICISM OF THE ITO

The men who propounded the ITO were trying to be very realistic. They wanted to avoid the errors which had led to the failure of many efforts to remove world trade barriers in the 'twenties and 'thirties. They were also anxious to produce an agreement that would be acceptable to a large number of countries. These praiseworthy efforts contained the seeds of the ITO's failure.

Thought about the postwar world began early in the Second World War. Those who planned and who thought about plans tried to find guidance in the peace settlement after the First World War and in its unsatisfactory aftermath. They were especially bent on avoiding "the errors of last time." Perhaps they were too much influenced by what they thought of the past and failed to show enough ingenuity and imagination in anticipating some of the less attractive possibilities of the postwar world. However that may be, two conclusions from the interwar experience with international trade policy had great influence in shaping the ITO.

One was that many of the interwar efforts to remove trade barriers had failed because international conferences had limited themselves too much to recommending the endorsement of broad principles, leaving it to each government to act according to the exigencies of its position. As a result, little came of the pledges to reduce trade barriers. This lesson the drafters of the ITO Charter tried to apply by making their document detailed, and including in it specific commitments to avoid particular trade practices except under certain extenuating circumstances, which they also tried to specify.

The second conclusion was that "commercial policy cannot be considered by itself. . . . It must be considered as a part of the more general constructive policies agreed among governments for the prevention (or mitigation) of economic depressions and assurance of social stability."[9] Moreover, in the past the emphasis on tariffs, quotas, taxes, subsidies, etc., slighted the special problems of raw materials that gave rise to private or public commodity agreements and left out of account cartels, monopolies, and private restrictive practices in international trade. Wartime developments stressed and gave immediacy to this view of the weaknesses of the older approach. One after another governments were committing themselves to "full employment" as the primary and overriding aim of national economic policy. Plans abounded for bringing "stability" to the world's raw material markets. Economic warfare and the seizure of alien property were producing reams of material on cartel connections and practices, many of them linked to German aggression.

Therefore, the drafters of the ITO gave their creation a much broader scope than any previous international trade agreement. There were to be detailed rules not only for tariffs, quotas, exchange controls and state trading, but also for international commodity agreements and intergovernmental measures to check restrictive trade practices. Provisions concerning the maintenance of full employment in each country and the avoidance of policies that would create unemployment abroad were left rather general because no one could devise detailed provisions likely to be acceptable to fifty governments.

The desirability of including such a wide range of subjects in the Charter was emphasized by widely-held views in other countries. There, as the American drafters knew, employment policy and raw materials problems were considered much more important than the removal of trade barriers. To make substantial progress in the removal of trade barriers it seemed necessary to show that the United States was not proposing merely to get rid of quotas and reduce tariffs without regard to other conditions affecting international trade. The League report noted above had spoken of "the absolute necessity of adapting commercial policies to the circumstances influencing national balances of payments." Wartime conversations with the British had made it clear that there was no hope of any comprehensive trade agreement's being

---

[9] League of Nations, Economic, Financial and Transit Department, *Commercial Policy in the Interwar Period: International Proposals and National Policies* (Geneva, 1942) p. 157. This report authoritatively sets out a number of views, widely held among economists and officials, which influenced the making of the ITO.

adopted unless there were escape clauses for countries in balance-of-payments difficulties. The Chapultepec Conference of 1945 had emphasized that economically underdeveloped countries were unwilling to talk about removing trade barriers unless it were very clear that their infant industries were exempted. The United States itself was not prepared to accept the logic of a liberal foreign trade policy in all fields, notably agriculture and shipping. How far it would go in the reduction of tariffs remained to be seen.

Casting a shadow on all calculation and discussion was the fear that when the insatiable war demand ended, the United States would plunge into depression. Apart from the special problem of reconversion, it was also widely held that the American economy was inherently unstable and might at any time in the future set off another world depression. Foreign countries naturally wanted to protect themselves, though the means of doing this were far from clear and the chances of success none too good. But the apprehension colored the attitude of many governments, leading them to look for possible safeguards against too close a link with the United States and in any case to demand a free hand to try to protect themselves against an American depression by the use of trade and exchange controls.

Recognizing all this, the drafters of the ITO tried from the first to make their proposals "realistic," by recognizing the limits on governments' willingness to carry out liberal trading principles, and by trying to reach agreement on terms and procedures for applying exceptions to the basic rules laid down in the Charter. This, they felt, was better than proposing a rigid body of principles which would not be carried out by the signatories. Moreover, they wanted to show from the first that the United States understood the difficulties of less favored countries and was prepared to try to accommodate them in the proposed trade organization.

These endeavors—to be specific, to be comprehensive, and to recognize the problems of other countries—explain much of the character of the ITO. The Charter's length, its complexity, and the mixture of general principles with extensive lists of exceptions to them, all stem from these efforts. The American policy that led to these results was understandable, consciously arrived at with a recognition of the risks involved, and seemed to most informed observers at the same time to be the only course feasible if the aim was to get a charter acceptable to enough governments to cover a substantial portion of world trade. But this essay does not aim at re-arguing the case or suggesting whether another course of action would have produced better results (or of

13

judging what "better" results would be).[10] Here the significant point is that the effort to be realistic produced a document that proved to be unacceptable to that reputed arch-realist, the American businessman.

Business opposition to commercial policies that are alleged to go too far in removing trade barriers is an old story. The new element in this case was the opposition the Charter met from businessmen who felt it did not go far enough in removing trade barriers. The people who took this view were not primarily concerned about the effect of the Charter on American trade barriers. Their objection was that the Charter would do little to remove the trade barriers set up by foreign countries and might even strengthen some of them. The essence of this view was that the exceptions to the Charter's general rules, and the escape clauses applicable to special circumstances, were so numerous that most foreign countries could comply with the Charter without actually freeing trade from existing restrictions. Moreover, the businessmen who took this view usually also believed that the Charter went too far in subordinating the international commitments of signatory countries to the requirements—real or imagined—of national economic plans and policies. They believed, too, that the Charter was too heavily laden with the ideological and practical paraphernalia of government regulation and control, so that it would not help, and very likely would hinder, the development of private enterprise. In short, the businessmen who took these views held that the Charter was not "liberal" enough and not "internationalist" enough. Because of their emphasis on these imperfections in the Charter, and their desire for an instrument that approached nearer to their ideals of economic policy, it will be convenient, and not too unfair, to call this group the "perfectionists," in contrast to the "protectionists" who opposed the Charter for quite different reasons, and about whom I shall say a word later in this essay.

There have always been people who felt that the Trade Agreements Program was too modest to make a major contribution to the improve-

---

[10] The American literature for and against the Charter is extensive. The authoritative defense of the ITO, by one of its principal authors, is Clair Wilcox, *A Charter for World Trade* (New York: Macmillan, 1949). See also, W. A. Brown, *The United States and the Restoration of World Trade* (Washington: The Brookings Institution, 1950). A shorter statement favorable to the Charter is Percy W. Bidwell and William Diebold Jr., "The United States and the International Trade Organization," *International Conciliation*, March 1949. An endorsement that emphasizes the difficulties and risks is given by Jacob Viner in "Conflicts of Principle in Drafting a Trade Charter," *Foreign Affairs*, July 1947, 612-628.

The fullest statement of the business case against the Charter appears in the statements and documents presented in the Congressional *Hearings* cited below. See also the writings of Michael Heilperin, especially "How the U.S. Lost the ITO Conferences," *Fortune*, September 1949, 80-82, which argues that a different negotiating technique would have produced a better charter. For an extreme case against the ITO, see Philip Cortney, *The Economic Munich* (New York: Philosophical Library, 1949).

ment of world trade. But they supported it for what help it could be, and because the alternative seemed a less liberal policy. That perfectionist sentiment should be important enough to constitute a major influence on the shaping of American commercial policy, and that it should work *against* a measure designed to remove trade barriers, are something new in American politics.

Protectionists aside, not all business groups took the perfectionist view. The National Council of American Importers supported adherence to the Charter because "the United States and the world have more to gain than to lose by its acceptance. . . ." The Committee for Economic Development recommended that the Charter be adopted if the provisions concerning international investment were eliminated. Other businessmen, acting as individuals or as members of such organizations as the National Planning Association and the Committee for the International Trade Organization, also supported American adherence. But the United States Chamber of Commerce, the National Association of Manufacturers, the National Foreign Trade Council and the United States Council of the International Chamber of Commerce all opposed the Charter. The NAM and the U.S. Chamber of Commerce are the largest of the business organizations; their position on international economic matters is not easily predictable since their membership includes firms benefiting from tariff protection as well as those favoring freer foreign trade. The U.S. Council of the ICC is traditionally internationally-minded. The National Foreign Trade Council, made up exclusively of firms concerned with foreign trade and investment, is generally regarded as the principal spokesman for the foreign trade community as a whole. The Council has been a consistent supporter of the Trade Agreements Program and still maintains that position. The difficulty the Council had in reaching a conclusion about what stand to take on the ITO may be guessed from the remarkable fact that the *Final Declaration* of the Thirty-fifth National Foreign Trade Convention held by the Council in November 1948 said not a word about the ITO, though it contained recommendations on twenty-one subjects, including many suggestions for executive or legislative action and a thirteen-page essay on the conference's theme: Private Enterprise is the World's Best Hope. A few weeks later the Council came out against the Charter. Additional evidence of divided counsels is the presence of some businessmen on the committees or boards of several organizations, some of which endorsed the Charter while others opposed it.

The attitude of the business groups opposing the Charter on non-protectionist grounds varied somewhat in the emphasis given to one argument or another, and in the interpretation of certain parts of the Charter. Nevertheless the common ground was wide enough so that a

15

survey of its main features can stand as a sketch of the perfectionist position without great violence to the views of any one group.[11]

The perfectionists did not seriously object to the principles of trade policy laid down in the Charter. Their complaint was that the principles were not carried out. The exceptions and escape clauses seemed so numerous and extensive that the Charter held little promise of leading to the removal of trade barriers. Objections were particularly strong to the complicated rules sanctioning the use of import quotas—sometimes discriminatory ones—by countries in balance-of-payments difficulties. True, many governments were already engaging in such practices but in the Bretton Woods Agreements and elsewhere most nations had professed their desire to eliminate controls as soon as they could safely do so. The Charter, according to the view of these business groups, made no progress along this road; it was more likely to perpetuate the undesirable practices and so seemed a step toward the restriction of trade, not its liberation.

Two special considerations gave a particular edge to this argument. One was the prevalent view among businessmen that economic difficulties could not be cured by exchange controls and quotas. Convertibility, freer trade and freer play for the profit and price system seemed to them essential for the adjustments that national economies had to undergo; at some point each country would have to take the medicine of such a course; perpetuation of the controls only delayed the day and made the dose harder to swallow. The second consideration arose out of Article 21, paragraph 4(b) of the Charter which appeared to mean that no country could be required to alter policies directed toward the maintenance of full employment or the promotion of economic development even if these created balance-of-payments difficulties. This looked like a perfect loophole for the indefinite retention of controls, especially since most of the businessmen believed that government-sponsored full employment policies were bound, if they worked, to be inflationary and so to exercise pressure on foreign exchange reserves. Moreover, the way to engineer balance-of-payments difficulties seemed not only paved but marked.

In the matter of full employment, the business groups objected to the principles they saw in the Charter. The articles on employment were rather general and somewhat vague because, it will be recalled, the

[11] The survey that follows is based principally on a number of reports issued at various times during the ITO negotiations by committees of the business organizations mentioned. The final positions of all but the United States Council of the International Chamber of Commerce are presented in *Membership and Participation by the United States in the International Trade Organization, Hearings* before the Committee on Foreign Affairs, House of Representatives, 81st Congress, 2d Session (G.P.O., 1950). The U.S. Council's Executive Committee issued a mimeographed *Statement of Position* on May 9, 1950.

negotiators had felt the need to recognize the link between trade and employment but had not found any precise rules acceptable to all governments. When Administration spokesmen pointed out that the language of the ITO Charter's provisions conformed to American legislation and that obligations were carefully qualified to allow each country to find its own way of maintaining a high level of economic activity, the businessmen answered that if the employment provisions meant nothing they had better be left out of the Charter. Otherwise, governments that put faith in them were bound to be disappointed. Furthermore, the provisions might be read as relieving countries of all their obligations concerning trade policy in times of recession, and particularly if the recession occurred in the United States. The businessmen were really concerned about more than the ITO Charter. Their criticisms reflected general uneasiness about the implications of statements that governments were responsible for the level of employment. In part, their attitude was a carryover from the domestic debate at the time of the passage of the Employment Act of 1946 when the proposition that the United States Government should commit itself to maintaining "full employment" had become a symbol of government intervention, the New Deal, the welfare state and all the other large issues that had disturbed American political economy since the depression. To some extent, indeed, the presence of the employment provisions may have stood for the businessmen as an indication that the Charter was not a trade-liberalizing document of the traditional sort, but an instrument linked to planning and government control.

Concern over governmental controls also led the perfectionists to oppose the Charter's chapter on international commodity agreements. The aim of the chapter was to limit the use of such agreements to certain circumstances, to specify what might be done under a commodity agreement, and to establish rules that would insure fair treatment, for instance by requiring equal representation for consumers as well as producers. Prewar commodity agreements had not come up to these standards. Nevertheless, the business groups were inclined to oppose the whole chapter on the ground that it went too far in sanctioning governmental restriction of production and regulation of trade. "Private cartels are bad, . . . government cartels are worse," read a statement by the National Association of Manufacturers.

As to the sections of the Charter dealing with private cartels and restrictive practices, the attitude of the business groups was a little less clear cut. They all abjured restriction and took a stand in favor of competition. But they were dubious of the Charter provisions. On the one hand there seems to have been some feeling that the scope of the provisions was uncertain, so that governments or international agencies might interpret them to ban useful business arrangements as well as undesirable ones. On the other hand, the fact that the Charter's provisions left each government with a good bit of discretion in the enforcement of the ban on restrictive practices suggested to the business critics that the rules would turn out to mean different things in different countries. What one government held to be legal another might ban. The result would be not only confusion and legal uncertainty, but an advantage for one businessman over his foreign competitor. Underlying this concern was the suspicion that an active Anti-Trust Division in the United States would be diligent in the prosecution of cases, while in Western Europe and elsewhere general tolerance of cartels and industrial agreements would result in the acceptance of quite a different standard of business behavior.

One of the greatest stumbling blocks for the business groups was the Charter's treatment of investment. The Committee for Economic Development, which accepted the rest of the Charter, objected to the articles on this subject. The basic complaint was that the Charter did not provide private foreign investments with any firm protection against confiscation or discrimination by governments. The crucial passages were full of adjectives like "just," "reasonable," and "appropriate." Nothing was done to check the freedom of action of countries receiving foreign investment to decide what investment to permit and on what terms. So far as equal treatment was concerned, governments merely undertook "to give due regard to the desirability of avoiding discrimination as between foreign investments."

Such provisions, said the businessmen, were worse than nothing at all. "This article not only affords no protection for foreign investments of the United States but it would leave them with less protection than they now enjoy."[12] By committing itself to the Charter, ran this argument, the United States would give up its right to take independent action to protect American investors. Acceptance of the Charter would weaken the efforts being made publicly and privately to create a proper "climate" for private investment. This would discourage private capital and postpone the day when the governments of underdeveloped countries would come to realize that in their own interests they would have to provide more freedom and security for potential investors.

There was a good bit of irony in this situation. The offensive passages would not have been in the Charter at all if it had not been for the efforts of American business. The first drafts of the Charter had said nothing

---

[12] Statement by the National Foreign Trade Council, *Hearings*, cited, p. 200. Moreover, another article pledged all ITO members to cooperate in helping the economic development of others. The businessmen regarded this as a surrender of American bargaining power and undue emphasis on the role of government capital. Government spokesmen challenged this interpretation.

about investment. American business groups complained to the State Department about this omission. Foreign investment, they pointed out, was an important factor in international trade; moreover, as the main potential source of capital the United States had an interest in seeing to it that a sound legal framework should be constructed that would encourage investment. State Department officials, resisting these suggestions, undoubtedly pointed out that the chances were poor of getting the kind of investment provisions the businessmen wanted. The United States was already having to bargain hard on the trade provisions. Safeguards for investment worked out by a sizable group of nations, many of them underdeveloped, were likely to be much weaker than those that might be arrived at in bilateral negotiations with countries anxious to have American capital for their development. The elaboration of a comprehensive investment code might prove at least as complicated as the working out of the trade charter, which had already taken several years.

However, the business groups stuck to their position, the State Department finally yielded, and the American representatives at the Geneva conference proposed an article on investment. Its final version, reached only after difficult negotiations, "instead of promising to stimulate the flow of private capital, threatened to check it," according to Clair Wilcox, head of the American delegation.[13] So the subject was reopened at the final conference in Havana and, after another round of hard bargaining, new articles were substituted. No one claimed the new provisions went very far toward providing what American business wanted but the representative of the National Association of Manufacturers at Havana called them "the most important gains made by the United States delegation" and said that they "offer foreign investors greater protection than they ever had previously against unjust, arbitrary acts by governments." On further reflection, the National Association of Manufacturers and other business groups rejected this view and made the investment provisions one of their main targets in attacking the Charter.

It is not the purpose of this essay to discuss the validity of the businessmen's criticisms of the Charter, some of which are open to serious objection. Supporters of the Charter maintained that the compromises to which the perfectionists objected were essential to any comprehensive

13 Wilcox, cited, p. 146. Some language about investment had been introduced into the Charter at the first ITO conference in London where the underdeveloped countries pressed for inclusion of an article saying that members would not put "unreasonable impediments" in the way of others' getting the facilities they needed for development. This was matched by a provision that the receiving countries would "take no unreasonable action injurious to" the suppliers of capital. The business groups objected to the inadequacy of the latter provision, but they did not argue that it was positively harmful.

trade agreement. They claimed that within the framework of the ITO the United States could work for improvement of the unsatisfactory provisions and could check the abuse of escape clauses. The business groups disagreed. They saw the whole history of Charter negotiations as a retreat from what the United States wanted (or ought to want) and held that if the ITO were set up the process would continue. Since each government would have only one vote under the Charter, they thought it certain that the United States would consistently be on the losing end of arguments, with debtor countries, or control-minded governments, or underdeveloped countries, or countries in balance-of-payments difficulties, combining to defeat it on major issues.

The businessmen thought the Charter too one-sided to be of any great commercial value to them. Tariff reductions made by the United States would be effective, and this country would be bound by the general provisions of the Charter. But most other countries, being in balance-of-payments difficulties, or underdeveloped, or in need of special measures for economic reconstruction, would be able to take advantage of the exceptions. They would maintain barriers on the importation of American goods and would be allowed to discriminate against exports from this country. Their tariff concessions would mean little because their trade would be held down by quotas and exchange controls. Supporters of the Charter pointed out that the countries in question were doing these things anyhow. Failure to adopt the ITO would not improve matters, while the Charter's exceptions at least laid down rules to govern the application of trade restrictions, provided means of policing them, and gave some hope of eventually getting rid of the restrictions as world economic conditions improved. But the perfectionists would not accept this reasoning. They took the view that by ratifying the Charter the United States would be sanctioning these undesirable trade practices. It would not only have agreed that they were right in principle but would have given up the freedom to use its own economic strength to press for the removal of the foreign controls.

The whole perfectionist case was clearly summarized in one paragraph by the Executive Committee of the United States Council of the International Chamber of Commerce in its *Statement of Position* on the Charter:

> It is a dangerous document because it accepts practically all of the policies of economic nationalism; because it jeopardizes the free enterprise system by giving priority to centralized national governmental planning of foreign trade; because it leaves a wide scope to discrimination, accepts the principle of economic insulation and in effect commits all members of the ITO to state planning for full employ-

ment. From the point of view of the United States, it has the further very grave defect of placing this country in a position where it must accept discrimination against itself while extending the Most-Favored-Nation treatment to all members of the Organization. It places the United States in a permanent minority position owing to its one-vote-one-country voting procedure. Because of that, membership in the ITO based on this Charter would make it impossible for the United States to engage in an independent course of policy in favor of multilateral trade.

This is strong language. It is worth bearing in mind that by the time this and similar statements were written the business groups were actively working against the Charter. Blunt, categorical and rather extreme statements may have seemed more effective than more balanced analyses. Provisions that in other circumstances might have been regarded as dubious but tolerable because they were necessary parts of an acceptable compromise could be denounced as violations of fundamental principles once it had been decided to oppose the Charter. But we cannot be sure that tactical considerations of this sort provide the principal explanation of the all-out condemnation of the Charter by the perfectionists. Many American businessmen—especially when they come together in a group—seem to feel that their constant combat against "government control," "socialism," and the like requires the propagation of basic principles in very clear, simple and absolute terms. Naturally, these statements depict a world in which blacks and whites appear to be more sharply defined than they are in fact. Sore subjects excite extremism; many postwar statements about free enterprise have been heavily freighted with ideology. It is not always easy to tell when these statements are setting out utopian ideals and when they are describing a state of affairs the business groups think is really attainable. Because the drafters and negotiators of the ITO Charter were trying to bridge gaps between different kinds of economic systems and different philosophies of economic organization, their document inevitably diverged considerably from the pure principles subscribed to by many American businessmen. Tactics apart, this taint undoubtedly played its part in stimulating the perfectionist reaction.

Statements made in 1950 were also colored by the hopeful signs the businessmen saw in the improvement in Western Europe's payments position (even before Korea), the defeat of socialist governments in several countries (including Australia and New Zealand), and a widespread relaxation of governmental controls. The devaluations of September 1949 were regarded as a big step toward equilibrium in international trade. The difficulties of low production and dollar shortage that lay behind many of the ITO's exceptions and escape clauses were held to be largely overcome. Therefore, some perfectionists felt, the Charter was "now obsolete." The same evidence could have been used to demonstrate that the Charter as it stood would be less obnoxious than the perfectionists claimed because, as their payments positions improved, governments would lose the right to invoke many of the escape clauses.

The Administration took the view that the Charter would have to be accepted as it stood; reservations would invite similar action by other governments, pulling apart the agreement already reached; renegotiation was impossible. "For better or worse," wrote Clair Wilcox, the Havana Charter "is the only charter that can be considered or adopted by the nations of the world."[14] The perfectionists did not disagree. They felt they had shot their bolt on modifications of the Charter in proposals made during the course of negotiations. Their suggestions as to what the United States should do instead of ratifying the agreement came almost as an afterthought, produced under questioning by their critics. The National Foreign Trade Council simply urged action under the Trade Agreements Act, the negotiation of more commercial treaties, and pushing ahead with Point Four. The other business groups also supported the idea of making more bilateral agreements on trade with countries willing to accept principles the United States could endorse. The National Association of Manufacturers and the U.S. Council of the International Chamber of Commerce suggested that a commercial policy commission under the United Nations Economic and Social Council might provide a means of advancing the interests of multilateral trade on sound principles. The U.S. Chamber of Commerce proposed an agreement limited to strictly trade matters, centering on a simple statement of basic principles, containing a declaration in favor of free enterprise, including no restrictions on domestic freedom of action of member countries, and operating with a system of weighted voting. Such an agreement, they thought, might be negotiated by representative business delegations under the aegis of the International Chamber of Commerce, thus smoothing the way to governmental action.

Opinions about these alternative courses played no appreciable part in the demise of the ITO. The perfectionists opposed the Charter because it was not good enough, not because they were sure they had something better to offer. This is not the place to criticize the alternative proposals or to rehearse the debate about the businessmen's objections to the Charter. Nor need I speculate on the interesting possibility that in this case the businessmen were the "hopeless idealists" while the bureaucrats and college professors who supported the Charter, without being enamored of it, were the "realists." For present purposes, the

14 Wilcox, cited, p. 199.

exposition of the perfectionist point of view is sufficient; it helps explain why the ITO lacked the support needed for American ratification.

Of course, not all the opposition to the Charter came from perfectionists. Protectionists were against it, too. Statements opposing the Charter were submitted to the House Foreign Affairs Committee from a familiar array of protected industries: chemicals, dairy products, livestock and allied industries, nut growers, makers of glassware and glass containers, woolen manufacturers, independent petroleum producers, rayon manufacturers, the paper and pulp industry, the makers of woven wire cloth, and the National Labor-Management Council on Foreign Trade Policy in which a number of protected industries are represented. The American Tariff League was in its accustomed place. The line-up was similar to that on renewals of the Trade Agreements Act, but there were some striking differences in what was said. The protectionist groups presented their familiar arguments warning against the effect on the American economy of permitting freer entry of low-cost foreign goods. But in most of the protectionist statements the emphasis was on the more broadly conceived disadvantages of the ITO—its one-sidedness, its alleged support for governmental control and planning, the freedom of most countries to use escape clauses. In short, the protectionists found it convenient to present much of their position in terms of perfectionist arguments. Observing this, Representative Fulton ironically remarked, ". . . the American Tariff League is the most liberal organization that I have heard before this committee for a long time because they throw the pebble clear out in the pond and say, 'Here is this high level that we want to reach that is even above what the New Dealers ask. And if the charter is not that progressive and so highly moral in principle, we are not going into the charter with its present practical exceptions because it is based on conditions as they now exist.' "[15]

Many of the protectionist groups used other arguments as well, frequently of an "anti-internationalist" sort. They pictured the ITO as a superstate capable of directing American trade policy. Some spoke as if the ITO were going to set tariff levels. There was a certain amount of concern about changes in American laws that would be required by adherence to the Charter and an even greater emphasis—supported by the American Bar Association—on the alleged unconstitutionality of delegating certain powers to an international body.

Whether the protectionists' use of perfectionist arguments was merely "the homage vice pays to virtue" or whether it has some deeper significance as a sign of the times does not concern us here. The fact that groups traditionally in favor of the removal of trade barriers were

[15] *Hearings*, cited, p. 406.

against the ITO enabled those who opposed the removal of import barriers to take the same stand without sharply delineating their real position. The result was to make business opposition to the Charter seem more of a piece than it really was.[16] More important than the appearance was the political reality. In a manner new to the history of American commercial policy, the ITO was whipsawed between the protectionists and the perfectionists.

IV. IS IT THE END?

Nominally, all the President did in December 1950 was to withdraw the Charter from Congress. There was no Congressional action. No one repudiated the American signature. The Charter retained its legal status of an international agreement awaiting ratification.[17] But in 1951, Secretary Acheson testified before a Congressional committee that it was his firm policy that the Charter would never be resubmitted to Congress. Subsequent official remarks on foreign trade policy have referred to the Charter only occasionally, in quick-passing historical reminiscence. United States Government opinion appears to favor putting GATT on a more nearly permanent basis, with the implication that the ITO is dead. No one has suggested that the Charter might be modified to be more acceptable or to fit changed world conditions. Among government officials there is an understandable revulsion from the idea of trying to renegotiate this complex instrument which has had such little political magnetism. Nor can the objective observer who would be spared the grueling grind of negotiation make much of a case for the view that renegotiation would be desirable.

Many suggestions have been made as to how the Charter's chances of passage might have been improved. If businessmen had been on the American delegation from the first, would they have had a better understanding of Washington's point of view? Would they have been more heavily committed to the Charter? Would the State Department have made more headway if it had offered less defense of the weaker parts of the Charter and instead had singled them out as unsatisfactory but unavoidable features that the American representatives would try to

[16] The agreement on the end to be achieved, regardless of a difference about the reasons, probably also helped organizations that included both protected industries and those concerned with increased foreign trade to take clear-cut positions on the Charter. It is interesting to note that the U.S. Chamber of Commerce—which opposed the Charter on perfectionist grounds—was represented at the Havana conference by Elvin Kilheffer who appeared before the House Foreign Affairs Committee on behalf of several protectionist groups in the chemical industry.

[17] Only Liberia ratified the Charter unconditionally. Australia and Sweden ratified it, but made their adherence conditional on similar action by the United States and, in the former's case, also Britain.

change, or at least prevent the misuse of, once the ITO was set up? Could a system of weighted voting have been devised that would have reduced opposition at home and still been acceptable abroad because it reflected the actual bargaining power the United States would have in any trade organization regardless of voting arrangements? Would the Charter have been more acceptable if it had been in two parts: a code of principles toward which the signatories were to work, and an interim "code of exceptions" that would apply in an initial transitional period and in later times of abnormal difficulties? Ought the State Department to have suggested that Congress agree to American adherence to the Charter but at the same time pass a resolution expressing dissatisfaction with some parts of it, directing American delegates to work for its improvement, and stating the principles to which the United States would commit itself?

Any of these questions is good for an argument. But there is little present profit in hypothetical history. None of the devices suggested by these questions holds any serious promise of regaining acceptability for the Charter. The circumstances of world conditions and United States politics that contributed to the rejection of the Charter have not changed in ways favorable to it. There have been no indications of a change of heart among the perfectionists. The protectionists, or at least many of them, appear to be growing more active in the course of 1952. In the election campaign no party has taken a stand on the Charter, and its prospects of revival by the new Administration, of whatever party, seem absolute zero. Nor does there appear to be any force outside the United States pushing for acceptance of the Charter. Early in 1951 several governments withdrew the Charter from their parliaments, explaining that there was no point in going ahead with the project so long as the United States had dropped it. Without American leadership there can be no revival of the ITO or of any reasonable facsimile. The direction of American foreign trade policy is in doubt, but the least likely direction for it to take is the revival or renegotiation of the ITO Charter.

So the ITO is dead. But some of its parts are still alive. Certain of its provisions have acquired a sort of shadow existence by incorporation in other agreements. For instance, the OEEC's Code of the Liberalization of Trade says that state trading should be conducted "in accordance with the general principles laid down" in the Havana Charter. The Code incorporated by reference the Charter's definition of dumping. The Schuman Plan treaty empowers the High Authority to recommend action against countries that do not belong to the coal and steel community if they or their nationals "are engaging in dumping operations or other practices condemned by the Havana Charter." The Charter's

25

definition of an acceptable customs union as one in which the external trade barriers are about midway between those previously applied by member nations turns up frequently.[18] There are several other instances of Charter provisions achieving some kind of legal status even though the Charter itself is dead.

The Charter's provisions concerning intergovernmental commodity agreements have also had a kind of independent existence. In a resolution of March 1947, reaffirmed in September 1951 after the ITO was plainly dead, the United Nations Economic and Social Council recommended that member countries "accept the principles" of the commodity chapter of the Charter "as a general guide in inter-governmental consultation or action with respect to commodity problems."[19] Under the 1947 resolution an Interim Co-Ordinating Committee for International Commodity Arrangements was set up with a chairman representing the Preparatory Committee that was working on the Charter. Later the nominating function passed to the Interim Commission for the ITO and then, in 1951, it was given to the Contracting Parties to GATT. Each year the Co-Ordinating Committee publishes a *Review of International Commodity Problems* that gives particular attention to international consultation on commodity problems, the work of various commodity study groups, and the terms of commodity agreements proposed or adopted. While dropping hints and leaving implications,[20] the *Reviews* have not formally passed judgment as to whether the Charter's principles are in fact being fully applied.

In a somewhat different way, the Economic and Social Council has acted on the Charter's provisions regarding restrictive business practices. On the initiative of the American representative, the Council in September 1951 recommended that member governments take measures "based on the principles set forth in Chapter V of the Havana Charter

[18] This definition is in any case binding on a number of countries because it is incorporated in GATT. For comments on the imprecision and possible meaninglessness of the criterion, see Jacob Viner, *The Customs Union Issue* (New York, 1950) pp. 66-68.

[19] The language quoted is from the 1951 resolution. The earlier version was that governments should "adopt as a general guide" the principles of the commodity chapter. The words "pending the establishment of the International Trade Organization" which had appeared earlier were dropped in 1951. The Economic Commission for Latin America passed a similar resolution (pertaining only to countries that had signed the Charter) at its first meeting in 1948.

[20] For instance, the 1949 *Review* says of the tea agreement of that year, "It will be seen from the text . . . that the present arrangement, although controlling exports, nevertheless does not provide for equal representation of producing and consuming countries." Such equal representation was one of the principal requirements of the Charter; it is applied in the wheat agreement, the most important intergovernmental commodity agreement of the postwar period. In the same *Review* the Committee suggested that somewhat more publicity might be given to discussions in various commodity study groups; this, too, is in line with Charter principles.

. . ." to prevent harmful restrictive practices. A committee was set up to propose international measures that would achieve these purposes and provide for continuing consideration of the problem. At several key points the resolution borrows language from the Charter and in reciting the rationale of the recommendation it states that restrictive practices "may have harmful effects on the . . . aims and objectives listed in Chapter I of the Havana Charter."[21] In the discussion of the resolution there was some objection to inclusion of the ITO principles on the ground that "attempts to resuscitate parts of a dead body" were a "deplorable procedure."[22] Although Isador Lubin, the American representative, had cited examples of how restrictive practices inhibited economic development, spokesmen for a number of underdeveloped countries showed their old suspicion that the United States was trying to impose free competition on the world. However, the Uruguayan delegate explained that he had proposed that the Charter's cartel chapter be taken as a guide just because it did not condemn all restrictive practices, but only those having harmful effects. He interpreted the Charter as sanctioning various government monopolies regarded as essential to Uruguay's development. There was no real challenge to the substance of the Charter's chapter (except from the Iron Curtain representatives, who regarded the whole thing as a fraud), and the Belgian and Canadian delegates maintained that the Charter was the logical starting place because it embodied a satisfactory compromise between those who wanted to check restrictive practices as such and those who condemned them only when they had clearly harmful effects.

Thus, two important chapters of the Charter have attained a limited sort of existence despite the failure of the ITO. There have also been fairly extensive international discussions and proposals in the fields of economic development and international action to check depressions but with much less reference to the Charter. However, the principal survival of the Charter is in the field of commercial policy—GATT, the General Agreement on Tariffs and Trade.

Conceived as an interim measure, GATT was a kind of advance installment of the Charter. It put into effect temporarily most of the provisions of the Charter's chapter on commercial policy and provided

[21] The text of the resolution, as passed, appears in U.N., Economic and Social Council, *Official Records*, Thirteenth Session, 549th Meeting, 13 September 1951, (E/SR549), pp. 645-646. The discussion took place at that meeting and the three previous ones. The original American resolution made no specific reference to the Charter, though it incorporated its gist and some of its language. The paragraph establishing Chapter V as a guide was introduced in a Uruguayan amendment, and the reference to Chapter I by Chile.

[22] Statement by the Chilean representative, 548th meeting, p. 634. The Indian representative took much the same view and the Chinese spokesman doubted the propriety of mentioning the Charter since it had not been widely accepted.

for multilateral negotiations to reduce tariffs, which were carried out at Geneva in 1947, Annecy in 1949, and Torquay in 1950-51. GATT also obliges its signatories "to observe to the fullest extent of their executive authority the general principles" of most parts of the Charter "pending their acceptance of it in accordance with their constitutional procedures." The limitation, "to the fullest extent of their executive authority," applies also to many of the commercial policy provisions since the protocols under which the signatory countries apply GATT exempt them from the need to change existing legislation in many important matters. Indeed, the only articles not included in this exemption are those covering general most-favored-nation treatment, the granting of tariff concessions, the territorial application of the agreement, frontier traffic, customs unions and free trade areas, the joint action of the contracting parties, and a number of provisions essential to carrying out the agreement.

GATT, to which 33 countries now adhere, was originally concluded for three years. During this time, in addition to negotiating tariff reductions, the signatories settled some trade disputes among members and passed on various issues concerning the application of the Agreement's provisions to particular cases. As the failure of the Charter to gain acceptance became evident, considerable energy had to be put into extending GATT, and in particular into preventing extensive cancellation of tariff concessions previously negotiated. These things were done at Torquay, when the agreement was renewed for three years. GATT also lacks a continuing organization and for a secretariat has been relying on the Interim Commission for the ITO, another orphan.

GATT, then, differs from the ITO in covering a narrower sphere of policy, requiring little if any legislative action by signatories, lacking a permanent organization, and committing signatories less firmly (they may withdraw on 60 days' notice). These differences are sources of both weakness and strength.

Because the commitments are less binding, GATT has been more easily accepted than the ITO was. But the counterpart of this advantage is an element of uncertainty, a threat that governments may not stick to GATT if the going gets rough. At the opening of the sixth session of the contracting parties Sir Hartley Shawcross stressed the fact that Britain had only committed itself to GATT provisionally. Since then the wisdom of continued adherence to the agreement has been repeatedly challenged in Parliament and government spokesmen have answered that they were still considering the matter. And in the United States, Congress made it plain that it was not endorsing GATT when it extended the Trade Agreements Act in 1951.

28

The fact that GATT is largely limited to traditional commercial policy subjects protects it from the disputes that arose over other parts of the ITO Charter. But by the same token this limited coverage makes GATT somewhat unsatisfactory to those who are particularly concerned that tariffs and quotas shall not be considered separately from the problems of raw materials, economic development, restrictive practices, and measures to check depressions. The Norwegians have proposed the inclusion in GATT of the Charter's main provisions on the maintenance of full employment. While this proposal, opposed by the United States, has been withdrawn, there is no evidence that it is dead. When the Economic and Social Council was discussing the American cartel resolution in September 1951, the British representative said that his delegation "felt strongly that restrictive business practices could be satisfactorily dealt with only in a body which was equally concerned with tariffs, quantitative restrictions and similar measures affecting trade. . . . His Government believed that in those circumstances the only appropriate body to deal with restrictive practices was represented by the Contracting Parties to the General Agreement on Tariffs and Trade."

There is nothing surprising in these views. They have the same rationale as that followed by the drafters of the Charter. Therefore, they inevitably point to the same result. As one observer expressed it, "If these claims are met in part or fully, a kind of new Charter might be the result which, in turn, would come up against the same strong opposition that has brought the full Havana Charter to its fall. Clearly, if the GATT is to be successful within its narrower sphere it must remain a relatively narrow agreement, retaining, in particular, its present legal characteristics as a multi-nation trade agreement that can be kept in force without ratification by the United States Congress. . . ."[23]

Similarly, there is a widespread opinion that GATT should be given a firmer, clearer juridical status, and there is a general feeling that it requires its own secretariat and some separate organizational existence. But on this matter, too, Sir Hartley Shawcross registered British doubts in the statement already referred to. There is also danger that attempts to strengthen the form of GATT and the national commitment to it will be regarded in the United States as an attempt to slip across the essence of the ITO without benefit of Congress. O. R. Strackbein, a protectionist spokesman, has already transferred to GATT virtually the same attack that was made on the ITO as a super-state. While acknowledging that the Contracting Parties did release the United States from its most-favored-nation commitment to Czechoslovakia

[23] Heinz Heymann, "The G.A.T.T. at Crossroads," Skandinaviska Banken, *Quarterly Review* (Stockholm) July 1951, pp. 58–64 at 63.

under the Agreement, and sanctioned this country's use of the escape clause to withdraw a tariff concession on women's fur felt hats and hat-bodies, he demanded to know, "how it has come about that action of the United States Congress and action of the President in carrying out powers delegated to him by Congress are now subject to review by an international body . . . when such authority of review was never conferred upon it by Congress."[24]

* * * * *

Thus GATT is the ITO *manqué*. There is a constant striving to fulfill the original pattern. If this striving should be satisfied, GATT would risk going over the same precipice as the Charter. So long as the striving is frustrated, GATT's strength is in doubt and it becomes the vortex of many strong and conflicting pressures. These pressures would exist without GATT; GATT may be able to survive them and to help control them, but the issue is in doubt.

V. WHAT NOW?

Much might be said about the ways and means of improving or strengthening GATT. The canvassing of these possibilities is an important part of the reconsideration of American foreign trade policy. But, in order to sketch the problems that face us, let us instead look briefly at the kind of pressures to which GATT and some other multi-lateral trading arrangements are subjected.

American participation in GATT is by executive action under the Trade Agreements Act. When Congress renewed the Act in 1951 it stipulated that the Tariff Commission must investigate all complaints that American producers were being damaged by imports resulting from tariff concessions made under the Act. If it finds the complaints to be justified, the Commission is to recommend remedial action to the President who must explain himself to Congress if he does not order the tariff increased. This virtual invitation to try to counter tariff reductions—what can the producer lose?—has been responded to with a wave of applications for the withdrawal of concessions. At the time of writing, a few have been turned down and a few have been acted on. Some concessions made under GATT have been withdrawn, with the result —as the Agreement provides—that countries affected have withdrawn some matching concessions on American exports. To check imports of products on which there are no concessions, producers have appealed directly to Congress to raise the tariff, as in the case of tuna fish. By a rider to the Defense Production Act, imports of cheese have been re-

[24] Radio address reprinted in the *Congressional Record*, January 14, 1952, pp. A124-A125.

stricted by quotas, in violation of GATT. Other amendments were proposed, but defeated, that would have treated feed grains the same way and curtailed imports of goods made from scarce materials.

There is, then, a new wave of protectionism in the United States. Its material results are not yet clear. Its causes are probably numerous. A contributing factor is undoubtedly the weakening of the Administration's foreign trade policy, accelerated by the events with which this essay has been concerned. Accompanying the drive for higher import barriers is a tendency for Congress to reassert its authority over foreign trade matters, a familiar phenomenon in many fields during the dying months of an Administration.

Along with the attempt to raise new trade barriers has come a resistance to attempts to remove existing ones. The Administration's efforts to get Congress to simplify customs administration have been fruitless, in part because the bill would have reduced what Percy Bidwell named "the invisible tariff." Despite the Secretary of Defense's finding of several years ago that it would be against the national interest to apply Buy American clauses to all military procurement, there is still a marked preference for the domestic product, even at a higher price. Even the provisioning of American troops abroad shows some of the marks of such a policy. As a *New York Times* reporter commented, "An Army that is still hauling canned beer 4,000 miles to be drunk by people living in Heidelberg and Munich presents a formidable psychological problem. . . ."

Of course, the United States was never prepared to accept the pure principles of the ITO in all its own commercial behavior. Loopholes of American design were built into the Charter to permit the use of import quotas in connection with domestic farm programs and the withdrawal of tariff concessions if imports damaged domestic producers. Shipping was excluded from the Charter largely because the United States was not prepared to alter its subsidy policy. But the recent protectionist drive raises the specter of a sharper reversal in trade policy. Events seem to be bearing out a fear expressed by Jacob Viner in 1947. Writing about the ITO he said, "The old schoolmen distinguished between the grace which inspires good resolutions and that other grace which provides the will to fulfill them. There is great danger that the American supply of the latter will fall far short of the State Department's supply of the former."[25]

GATT, and the general approach to trade problems it embodies, have been challenged from other quarters as well. At the tariff-bargaining session at Torquay in 1950–51 the United States was unable to conclude

[25] Jacob Viner, "Conflicts of Principle in Drafting a Trade Charter," *Foreign Affairs*, July 1947, pp. 612–628 at 614.

31

any new tariff agreements with the United Kingdom or with several major members of the Commonwealth because these countries were unwilling to make further substantial reductions in the margins of preference they granted to one another under the Ottawa agreements of 1932. Some American officials interpreted this to mean that Britain was unwilling to go any farther in the making of global multilateral trade agreements and was withdrawing to the shelter of imperial preference-sterling area trading. The return to power of the Conservative Party plus the renewed payments crisis have stimulated a demand in Britain for getting free of the limitations GATT puts on the extension of imperial preference. This attitude, coupled with the building up of a case against recent trends in American trade policy—which to some extent has exaggerated the material effects of the new protectionist drive—may presage proposals for loosening GATT. If the United States remains in violation of GATT as a result of such measures as the cheese import quotas, or if it has to resort more frequently to the escape clause, this country will be in a poor position to defend the agreement against British pressure for change. The outcome might well be steps sanctioning the American actions in return for adjustments to meet the desires of other countries, such as the granting of greater freedom of action for the British on imperial preference. The result would be to leave GATT considerably weaker.

GATT is not the only multilateral arrangement dealing with the conditions of international trade, and the others are also subject to disturbing pressures. The trade liberalization program of the Organization for European Economic Cooperation, and the related provisions of the European Payments Union, led to the removal of quotas on a portion of trade among the European Marshall Plan countries and to the introduction of a considerable degree of non-discrimination among them. Progress in these matters, which began late in 1949, was hampered first by a German balance-of-payments crisis which curtailed the area of liberalized trade and then, more seriously, at the end of 1951 and early in 1952 by British and French measures restoring import restrictions to check drains on their foreign exchange reserves. The French and British actions were in large part a response to economic disturbances caused by the impact of the Korean War, rearmament and the expectation of rearmament.

A third multilateral trade and payments arrangement is the sterling area. Within the group, current payments are free from exchange control and trading privileges are exchanged which are not extended to outsiders. But here, too, there have been disturbances, leading to new trade restrictions within the sterling area and added strains in its relations with the rest of the world. It has apparently come as something of a shock to many Britons to discover that the process of putting each sterling area country's foreign accounts in balance may involve cuts in imports from the United Kingdom as well as from the United States. The recurrence of dollar difficulties raises the specter of a breaking-up of the sterling area, or at least the partial withdrawal from it of members who feel they could make out better in their dollar affairs, and perhaps their external trade and payments generally, if they operated independently of the sterling area dollar pool.

These three arrangements for the removal of barriers to multilateral trade—GATT, the OEEC program, and the sterling area—do not dovetail neatly. GATT, which includes substantially all of the countries in the other two groups as well as the United States and Canada, is based on the most-favored-nation principle. The OEEC quota reductions are for the most part limited to trade among member countries (but a country is not forbidden to extend these concessions to outsiders). So long as the pound is inconvertible the sterling area entails discrimination against payments in hard currencies. The preferential tariff arrangements in the British Commonwealth, largely overlapping the sterling area but not identical with it, introduce still further complications. The absence of a link between quota reductions in the OEEC and tariff reductions in GATT creates trouble for low-tariff countries in Western Europe. The Schuman Plan will create a customs union for iron, coal and steel among the member countries, requiring further derogation of the most-favored-nation rights of outside countries. The discrepancies among these trading arrangements cause some current difficulties and, looking at the long run, both the sterling area and the OEEC trading program raise a basic problem in relation to GATT: How much "regionalism"—a misleading word with its geographic connotations—is compatible with the "globalism" of GATT (and of the ITO principles)? Can trade barriers be removed by both approaches until they merge, or is the inherent exclusiveness of regionalism bound to hamper cooperation in the larger area?[26]

The forces that curtail the area of liberalized trade within each of these trading arrangements may also increase the discrepancies between GATT and the two "regional" groups. The OEEC's trading system and the sterling area are both based on discrimination against American goods and if the troubles that manifest themselves as "the dollar shortage" grow, the severity of the discrimination may grow. But the disruptive forces work within each group as well. It seems illogical that nations should raise trade barriers instead of lowering them at a time

[26] For a fuller discussion of these issues see Howard S. Ellis, *The Economics of Freedom* (New York), 1950, pp. 431-443, 493-507, and my *Trade and Payments in Western Europe* (New York), 1952, pp. 405-417.

when a more effective international division of labor would enable them to carry the burden of rearmament more easily. But unless there is a strong binding force—and even that of the sterling area, the most cohesive of the groups, may not be sufficient—each government is likely to try to deal with its own particular set of problems by the most effective *national* action open to it. To safeguard the balance of payments, import barriers are likely to be the easiest method at hand.

Rearmament not only disrupts trade and checks efforts to remove trade barriers. It substitutes a whole set of different criteria for the principles embodied in multilateral trade agreements such as GATT. The flow of strategic materials must be controlled, not set free. Prices may have to be manipulated, not left to the market. Cost must sometimes be disregarded. In a time of cold war, non-discrimination becomes strategically unwise and insistence on it would be stultifying. When last renewing the Trade Agreements Act, Congress excluded the countries of the Soviet orbit from its benefits by directing that American tariff concessions to them be withdrawn and that they be denied most-favored-nation treatment. In trade terms the consequences were not great or the resulting sanctions very strong. The gesture was largely emotional. But the denial of the principle of non-discrimination goes much further, especially in the matter of export controls. ". . . For if there is anything that strategic considerations demand," says Professor Viner, "it is discrimination in the treatment of different countries, according as they are friends, or foes, or would-be neutrals."[27]

Serious as it is, rearmament is not the main challenge to international trade policy. If it were, the debate would be whether the best course was to put the liberal ideals on ice for the time being or to try to find a way of applying multilateral trading principles within NATO, or some other free-world grouping, while applying the principles of economic warfare to the rest of the world. This is one of the problems we face. Another is how to check protectionist tendencies that conflict with the purposes of programs for strengthening the free world and that increase the need for foreign aid by making it harder for countries to support themselves by exports. But there is another basic problem of continuing importance that exists independently of the present crisis in world politics. If there were no rearmament and no cold war, we should still be confronted by the question: Can the principles on which GATT and the ITO are based be successfully applied in the contemporary world?

Although political tension has increased the economic difficulties of many countries and has made some postwar adjustments more difficult than they would have been in a less threatening world, cold war cannot

---

[27] Jacob Viner, *Rearmament and International Commercial Policies*, Department of State, Foreign Service Institute (Washington, 1951, multigraphed) p. 9.

be considered the primary cause of some major difficulties that plagued the drafters and negotiators of the Charter and that would have continued to plague the ITO if it had been established. Mere enumeration is sufficient to indicate the kind of difficulties I have in mind: the troubles that express themselves in the chronic dollar shortage; extensive government controls over both domestic and foreign transactions; price-fixing and subsidies, whether aimed at keeping prices high or low; widespread inflationary pressures coupled with professed fears of the onset of recession; the contrary pulls of the desire for domestic stability at all costs and the desire for international stability.

Out of each of these circumstances comes a horde of troubles for any attempt to fit the traditional methods of a liberal trade policy to current circumstances. Only a few of these difficulties can any longer honestly be set aside as phenomena of the "transition period"—even if that term retains any meaning. Some of the difficulties arise from practices not covered by the old rules, such as state trading, for which new rules have to be invented, without great success so far. In other cases, the adaptation of old rules produces peculiar results; it has long been plain that allocating shares in import quotas according to the pattern of trade in a base period is a very different kind of "equal treatment" from the avoidance of tariff discrimination among competing suppliers. In still other cases, formal application of old principles in new circumstances produces results contrary to intentions. This is the case, for instance, when "you accept prices as the regulator or allocator of production and the regulator of where commodities should go, even though these prices may reflect nothing more than the arbitrary whim of a dictator or the snap judgment of a petty bureaucrat."[28]

One way of summarizing these difficulties is to say that the trade theory underlying GATT and ITO is largely a nineteenth-century product that does not fit twentieth-century facts. Another is to say that the world can have a flourishing multilateral trade based on national specialization only if free enterprise or the price system are allowed greater roles, internationally and within each country, than they have had for some time. These and other ways of stating the issue all contain part of the truth, but whatever the formulation, the basic fact is that there is a gap between major features of the present world economy and the known means of securing the most economical pattern of international trade. The ITO was an attempt to bridge that gap. How it might have worked we shall never know. Everyone concerned had reservations about the prospects and, as we have seen, the Charter proved unacceptable partly because of lack of confidence in what it could do. It is conceivable that the problem will be largely eliminated

[28] Same, p. 23.

by the freeing of markets and the dropping of policies that conflict with liberal trading principles. But the evidence that this will happen is not very persuasive; the political forces in most countries seem to set more strongly in the other direction. At best only part of the problem is likely to be solved in this way. In any case, we are left with the question of what is to be done if events work out differently.

"The time is out of joint." But we cannot simply suspend trade policy until the world is again orderly and then hope to resume a course based on the old principles. The main end of the principles is certainly valid: an international division of labor that permits maximum production. But, more obviously than ever before, we lack the means of achieving this end. It is not just political support for a wise course that is lacking. We also lack an intellectual reconciliation between multilateral international trade based on a high degree of specialization and the concept of managed and stable national economies. Perhaps there is no reconciliation. Insoluble problems exist. At some points we seem to have come to an intellectual impasse, but there is still much work to be done in clarifying issues before we can say that these problems really defy solution. Meanwhile, men must conduct their affairs and governments their foreign trade policies as best they can, improvising where known methods prove inadequate. And it would not be unprecedented if the intellectual solution followed instead of preceded the evolution of practice.

The ITO was an attempt to find a practicable compromise between the old aims and methods and the new ones. It contained some inventions that may seem worth resuscitating. But the way of the ITO is closed and we face the problem of starting again. In which direction should the United States try to go? We may attempt to keep GATT in as good repair as possible and build on it an adaptation of the multilateral approach. We may seek a liberal trading world by bilateral or even unilateral measures. We may revert to a greater degree of economic nationalism. We may put principles on the shelf and improvise to keep our footing in an unsettled world where the aims of foreign trade policy seem to change frequently. Or we may devise some wholly new line of approach. The new Administration, whatever its party, will have to face these issues, not only because the Trade Agreements Act expires in June 1953 but because a convergence of forces has pushed the underlying trade problems to the surface. Whether or not a consciously elaborated policy is adopted, action will be taken or not taken which will be a policy in fact.

The core of the postwar trade policy of the United States was the ITO, which was in many ways the fusion and highest development of the main elements in the policies that had gone before, since 1934. The

ITO failed in part because the world was not the kind of world on which the Charter was premised. The world has not changed back. The ITO failed in part because of shifts in American politics. Those shifts, and others, are still going on. The ITO failed, finally, because not enough people had confidence in the way it tried to bridge gaps between different concepts of the nature of the economic process, between the supposed interests of the United States and most of the rest of the world, and between faith and practice. The gaps are still there; they may narrow or widen; but a multilateral trading arrangement, covering most of the free world, cannot be successful unless it can bridge them.

The failure of the ITO leaves the United States with only the remnants of a foreign trade policy. It is doubtful that they can survive the buffeting, internal and external, political and economic, that they are now undergoing. The postwar planners were right when they said that an international understanding on trade policy was essential to the success of most other measures of international economic policy, so the whole structure of the free world is affected.

The need for a new foreign trade policy is clear and urgent. But the shape that policy ought to have is obscure. How much can we adapt from past policies? Can we invent new means of attaining old aims? How can we devise a policy that is not only promising but politically acceptable? The dynamics of the world of the 1950's are different from those of the world for which the ITO and its companion international agreements were made. We do not seem to know the commercial policy corollaries of the new propositions; indeed we are not even sure of the new propositions themselves. Our need is for a restatement of what we are after and a fresh analysis of how to get it. The end of the ITO has forced us to face these problems but it has provided no clear guides to their solution.

Part VI
The European Coal and Steel Community

[14]

Richard T. Griffiths

The Schuman Plan Negotiations: The Economic Clauses*

The Treaty of Paris signed in April 1951 brought into existence the European Coal and Steel Community and represents the realisation of an idea conceived by Monnet and Schuman a year earlier. However, the negotiations which spanned the intervening year had dramatically altered the original conception and very few of the original ideas were to survive unchanged in the final treaty. Not only were the sweeping rights of initiative and decision envisaged for the High Authority (henceforth HA) balanced by new institutional checks as the Court and the Council of Ministers, but decisions which had been intended as the preserve of the HA were instead spelled out in meticulous detail as governments fought to defend their perceived national self-interests. This is not to deny the role played by idealism in the original formulation of the Schuman Plan nor in its acceptance by at least some of the partners. Nor is it intended to belittle what was achieved. It was perhaps Monnet's genius to have locked nation states into a process of negotiation which resulted in an international settlement different from all that had passed before, at least in recent European history. Whatever else is said, states did agree to surrender sovereignty over important areas of economic policy to a supranational body, but, equally, they surrendered much less than the authors of the plan had hoped, and in many cases they had prescribed the framework within which the supranational authority was free to exercise those functions which they had conceded. The purpose of this background chapter is to describe, on the basis of newly released governmental archives[1] the process by which this came

* I would like to express my gratitude to the European Communities for the award of a travel grant which enabled me to visit the foreign archives needed for this research and to the Research Council of the European University Institute where my appointment as Visiting Professor allowed me to write the earlier drafts. A special word of thanks is extended to dott. Ruggero Ranieri and Dr. H.J. Küsters for giving me access to some of their archive material. Finally I must acknowledge my debt to the unstinting services of my research assistant Wendy Asbeek Brusse who was closely involved in all the stages of this research.
1 This chapter has been based on research into the following archives:
    Lausanne: Foundation Jean Monnet (FJM)
    Paris: Archives Nationales (AN) Serie 81 AJ and 363 AP (Archive René Mayer);
                    Ministère des Affaires étrangères, Archives diplomatiques (AD)

about as far as the economic clauses were concerned.[2] It is not intended to be an exhaustive account of the negotiations but a description of how and why some of the economic clauses took the form that they did rather than that which Monnet had initially intended. Many important areas have had to be ignored for reasons of space but a number of these are dealt with elsewhere in this volume.[3]

Because this chapter has a thematic structure, the danger exists that the chronology of the negotiations themselves will be lost from sight. This short summary is intended to overcome that to some extent. The delegations first met, in Paris, on 20 June 1950 where they learned for the first time the full scope of French thinking. After a short period to determine their own positions, the negotiations proper began on 3 July and immediately split into a number of working groups. In this period the institutional working group, upon which all the heads of delegation were represented and chaired by Monnet himself, was the most important as far as results were concerned. Nonetheless, in the others the basic battle-lines were drawn. They included a working group on production, investment and prices, chaired by Hirsch, a group on trade policy, chaired by Charpentier, and a group on social questions, chaired by Uri. Hirsch and Uri were members of Monnet's staff,

Bonn:	Politisches Archiv des Auswärtigen Amtes (PAAA) – Information supplied by Dr. H. J. Küsters)
Rome:	Archivo Centrale dello Stato (ACS) – Information supplied by dott. R. Ranieri; Archivo storico del Minestero degli Affari Esteri (AMDAE) Information supplied by dott. R. Ranieri
The Hague:	Algemeen Rijksarchief (ARA) Ministerraad (MR) and Ministerie van Economische Zaken, Buitenlandse Economische Betrekkingen (Min. EZ, BEB); Ministerie van Buitenlandse Zaken (Min.BZ); Ministerie van Financiën, Buitenlands Betalingsverkeer (Min. Fin., BBV)
Brussels:	Ministère des Affaires étrangères (Min. AE Bel)
Luxembourg:	Ministère des Affaires étrangères (Min. AE L)
Kew:	Public Record Office (PRO) Foreign Office (FO), Treasury (T)

It has not been possible, at time of writing, to consult the national delegation reports on the negotiations in the French, German or Italian archives. I have not attributed a source to the conference documents themselves (though I have indicated them with the prefix CD) because most of them are available in any of the archives of the participating countries. However, the most comprehensive and accessible set, are to be found in Lausanne, where there is also a separate series enabling the course of the negotiations to be followed article by article.

2 This distinction between «economic» and «institutional» clauses is essentially artificial. It is true that the negotiations created an institutional framework – the HA, Council of Ministers, Parliament, Court, Consultative Committee – but much of the thrust of the economic clauses involved the distribution of power among them.

3 Among the more glaring omissions are the negotiations on exactly which products were to be included in the Community, the discussions on the harmonisation of freight rates, the inclusion or not of colonies and the associated question of North African ore supplies for Italy, migration, the HA's rights to business information etc.

Charpentier was director-general for economic affairs at the Quai d'Orsay. These groups met until 12 August when the negotiations were suspended for the summer.

When the negotiations resumed on 31 August it was decided to modify the structure. The working groups were no longer to operate as a halfway house between negotiating forum and discussion club but were instead to work under strict guidelines provided by the heads of delegations, meeting in restricted session. This situation continued until 10 October when the working groups were abandoned, as far as the treaty proper was concerned,[4] and in quick succession the heads of delegation themselves held meetings to hammer out compromises to the outstanding points of dispute. From the beginning of November draft versions of the final treaty began to appear with regular frequency[5] and, rather than meeting together, Monnet suggested that the delegations submit their individual objections to the secretariat which would then try to work them into the subsequent draft. By mid-December the treaty, albeit with a number of gaps, was more or less in its final shape, though, of course, those gaps were to hold up progress for another couple of months. In that time the treaty received its final polish from a committee of jurists but, although small changes in the wording could have far-reaching consequences, it is virtually impossible to follow this phase of the negotiations in any detail. It was also in this period that «bilateral» questions such as the deconcentration of German heavy industry and Italian access to Algerian iron ore supplies were resolved.

As the draft treaty began to take shape, the negotiations proper concentrated upon the convention covering the transitional arrangements, a phase which lasted from the beginning of November until the end of January when Luxembourg finally abandoned its resistance to the terms agreed by the rest. The treaty and convention were initialled by the heads of delegation on 19 March and signed by the foreign ministers at their meeting in Paris a month later.

Having looked at the chronological structure of the negotiations, it is worth making a number of observations about their dynamics. In the first place it is possible to argue that Schuman's very success in attracting the participation of other countries in what was originally presented as a Franco-German coal and steel pool killed Monnet's conception before the negotiations even began.

---

4 Experts on coal and steel continued to meet as an integral part of the negotiations on the transition period even after this date.
5 Draft treaty texts for the final period were published on 9 November, 30 November, 9 December and 17 December, and there were a number more in 1951.

What the French had envisaged was that a short legalistic set of negotiations would establish a new framework for the Community and that the treaty would then be signed. The technical details would either be worked out in a separate convention after the Treaty's ratification[6] or left entirely to the HA.[7] Given Germany's weak diplomatic position at the time it is just possible that this may have succeeded but with the Benelux participation it became impossible. Over whatever else they may have disagreed in their attempts to establish a common position before the negotiations began, the Benelux countries were agreed that they would not sign anything until the full economic and social implications were known.[8] As Suétens, leading the Belgian delegation, put it in reply to the French opening statements: «You see the solution to our problems through the High Authority. We see the High Authority through our problems and their solutions.»[9]

A second observation worth making is that a country's negotiating position is relatively strongest at the beginning and at the end of negotiations. At the beginning it can argue that unless its ‹reasonable› demands were met, it would simply withdraw. At the end its position is much the same other than the fact that withdrawal could bring the entire structure falling down. In this respect it is something of a double-edged weapon. Thus at the beginning, it was the Dutch who were willing to take the negotiations to the brink on the question of the Council of Ministers. At the end it was the Italians (over North African ore), the Belgians (over the position of its coal industry), and the Germans. With this in mind, one does not need changes in external economic circumstances (i.e. the appearance of coal and steel shortages after the outbreak of the Korean War) to explain Germany's increasing intransigence after the summer recess. Germany's goals were quite clear as far back as June 1950[10] and they were bound to come out sooner or later. Moreover, they did

6 Schuman's opening speech to the delegations on 20 June. Reprinted in R. Racine, *Vers une Europe nouvelle par le Plan Schuman*, Neuchâtel, 1954, 77–79.

7 CD. *Document de Travail* dd. 24. 6. 1950.

8 Min. BZ, 996.1/1 *Verslag van de bespreking te Brussel op Woensdag 7 juni inzake Schuman-plan* dd. 10. 6. 1950, Min. BZ, 996.1/1 Memorandum from Baron van Voorst to Min. BZ dd. 10. 6.1950. Min. AE (Bel) 5216 *Réunion du Plan Schuman – 7. juni 1950 (Délégations Belgo-Luxembourgeoise et Néerlandaise)*. ARA, Min. EZ, BEB 562 (Verslag van de besprekingen te Brussel op Woensdag 14 juni 1950 inzake Plan Schuman. *Min. AE (L) 11346* Réunion entre fonctionnaires néerlandais, belge et luxembourgeois tenue le 7. 6. 1950 au Ministère des Affaires Etrangères de Belgique en vue de préparer les négociations concernant la création d'un pool international du charbon et de l'acier.

9 *ARA, Min. EZ, BEB 562 Kort verslag van de vergadering die op 22 juni 1950 werd gehouden ten kantore van het Plan Monnet*, CVP 2. FJM, AMG, 3/3/1 *Conversations sur le Plan Schuman*. *Séance restreinte du Jeudi 22 juin 1950*, CPS/CR/2.

10 Min. BZ, 996.1/II *West-Duitsland en het Plan-Schuman* dd. 16/17. 6. 1950. This is a much longer list than that cited in Marlies Steinert, «Un saut dans l'inconnu. La République fédérale

not become apparent before the summer because the negotiations on the economic clauses had yet to reach the stage where agreement had to be reached. Finally, in August 1950, Hallstein, leader of the German delegation, stated before a meeting of the German advisory commissions that it would represent a loss of face if they were to change tactics simply because of an unexpected improvement in the business cycle and this he did not intend to do.[11] What probably did play a role were the demands for German rearmament since this offered an alternative path towards realising Germany's political goal of readmission into the community of nations.[12]

A study of the negotiations also emphasises the curious position of the French. In the first place it is notable that Monnet and his staff seemed to have operated almost independently from the French cabinet which does not appear to have been consulted as a body at all between the end of June 1950 and the middle of December. Massigli, French ambassador to London, was at the time inclined to attribute Monnet's independence to the cabinet crisis which saw Bidault replaced as prime-minister by Queuille[13] but, whatever the reason, the cabinet never appeared to have regained the initiative. Another characteristic of the French position was that they represented at one and the same time a participant in the negotiations and the staff of its secretariat. This ambiguity offered enormous potential in determining the agenda and phrasing the results. Time and again this power was (mis-)used by the French but nowhere more transparently than in the draft treaty of 9 November.[14] This so culpably reinstated so many lost French positions that it was immediately and indignantly rejected by the rest.[15] It is important to bear this in mind because,

d'Allemagne face au Plan Schuman», in *Relations internationales* (1975), no. 4, 162. That list however includes the statement that the question of ownership should not play any role in the application of the Plan – an issue which was to blow up later in the negotiations.

11 PAAA Ref. 213, Verhandlungen über den Schuman Plan (VSP) Akte. Organisation der Ausschüsse, Bildung und Zusammensetzung Vc *Schumanplan-Konferenz. Donnerstag, den 24. August 1950, 15 Uhr.* n.d. Report of a meeting of the German advisory commissions with the delegation.

12 This link was made by Sir Ivone Kirkpatrick, British High Commissioner in Germany in October 1950. PRO, FO 321/85865 I. Kirkpatrick to FO 4. 10. 1950.

13 PRO, FO 371/85853 W. Strong to Sir O. Harvey 27. 6. 1950.

14 CD. *Projet de Traité* dd. 9. 11. 1950.

15 ARA.f Min. EZ, BEB, 340 *Opmerkingen over de met de Franse Delegatie gevoerde besprekingen over hun eerste redactie voorstel met betrekking tot de «Dispositions Economiques et Sociales»* dd. 21. 11. 1950 ARA, Min. EZ, BEB, 563 Onderhoud met de Heren Bauer en Risse van de Duitse delegatie op 10 November dd. 11. 11. 1950. Min. AE (Bel) 5216 *Note concernant le projet de traité relatif au charbon et à l'acier (rédaction du Plan Schuman du 8 novembre 1950)* dd. 16. 11. 1950 and *Note à Monsieur le Ministre Muûls* dd. 21. 11. 1950. Min. BZ, 996.145 *Verslag over de besprekingen te Parijs betreffende het Plan Schuman, van 8–18 November 1950.*

in the reports on the negotiations, the French often tend to remain almost
invisible, while the fact was that from beginning to end it was they who
determined the framework and the parameters within which the rest had to
operate.

Finally, the available accounts of the negotiations themselves, superficial as
they are, are nevertheless distortions of events through a preoccupation with
‹crisis› moments, especially towards the end. The point that is often missed is
that very little of Monnet's original ideas survived unaltered in the final treaty
– and that process of dilution and alteration took place largely in the ‹quiet›
period between July and November 1950. Whilst this chapter, too, will devote
the necessary attention to the final ‹crisis› with Germany, it seeks to redress
the balance by beginning with an examination of four topics which were
resolved in a less dramatic way. Three of them, wages, investment and
production controls and pricing policy involved the core of the relationship
between business policy, national economic policy and the powers of the HA.
The fourth, commercial policy, determined the profile of the new community
to the outside world.

Wages

Given the fact that the Schuman Plan was intended to appeal beyond narrow
business interests, it was inevitable that it should say something about the
benefits to labour. Monnet's original idea was to give the HA wide-ranging
powers in the area of wages but was somewhat ambiguous as to what end
these powers were to be used. On the one hand, it was to prohibit the use of
low wages as a means of artificially maintaining or improving competitiveness
(i.e. to influence nominal wage levels) but, on the other, it was to promote a
standard-of-living comparable with other branches of industry (i.e. to influence
real wage levels). The first was an economic goal, the second a social
one.[16]

Any such powers were inimical to the Dutch, who interpreted them as a
fundamental threat to their newly enforced system of national wage bargaining,[17] and they were supported in this by the Germans. They were not
mollified by Uri's assurance that national wage policy need not be affected
since, if governments were to ignore the HA's recommendations, it could

---

16 CD. *Document de Travail* dd. 24. 6. 1950 (Arts. 17 and 23).
17 ARA, MR, 586 *Nota inzake het Plan Schuman* n.d. (REA 1. 7.1950). ARA, MR, 572 Minutes
    of the Cabinet Economic Committee 1. 7. 1950.

simply impose a levy (prélèvement) on the firms concerned.[18] On the other hand, HA intervention was strongly supported by the Belgians who did not want the common market to come into force until all elements in cost price had been equalized, a position which implied the upward revision of all wage levels to that prevailing in Belgium.[19] This was supported by Luxembourg until it began to threaten an upward adjustment of wages there as well. The Italian position was infinitely more complicated. Because of overmanning, the steel industry was a low-wage sector with high unit labour costs. They, in turn, pushed for an equalization of unit labour costs, a concept so impenetrable and riddled with inconsistencies, that it was virtually ignored by the others.[20] From the start, Uri had held open the possibility that Italy be allowed a compensatory import duty[21] and the Italians virtually retired from the fray. The French were openly divided with Hirsch preferring the more limited Dutch and German interpretation whilst Uri tended far more towards the Belgian and even the Italian standpoints.[22] Upon the resolution of that conflict depended which way the balance within the negotiations would turn.

At the beginning of August, Uri broke the deadlock within the discussions with a dramatic shift in the French position. He argued that the HA should not be needlessly burdened. If the common market were not in danger, it should have no role in wages, whether too high or too low. This was furiously resisted by the Belgians. Miners' wages, they argued, had previously been a purely domestic matter, but the creation of the community would deprive the Belgian government of the various means to compensate for this. To this, Uri replied tartly that high miners' wages meant high coal prices for industrial users and lower living standards for other workers; a situation which the HA could not collude in maintaining.[23] Even after his apparent conversation, Uri still went too far for the Dutch who wanted HA intervention limited to ‹extreme cases› (i.e. when wages in coal and steel were forced below the national level in order to promote unfair competition).[24]

18 ARA, Min. EZ, BEB, 562 *Kort verslag van de tweede bespreking der Sociale Commissie op 22 juli 1950 CVP/WP/Soc 2. FJM, AMG, 4/4/2 Conversations sur le Plan Schuman. Groupe de Travail: Salaires et questions sociales. Réunion du samedi 22 juillet PS/G5/CR2. Min. AE (I.) 11362, Compte-rendu de la réunion de la Vème commission en date du samedi, 22 juillet 1950.*
19 Min. AE (Bel) 5216, *Plan Schuman, Compte-rendu de la réunion de la délégation Belge chez Monsieur van Zeeland, Ministre des Affaires Etrangères, le 29 juin à 14 heures* dd. 30. 6. 1950.
20 Ruggero Ranieri, *Italy and the Schuman Plan Negotiations*, European University Institute Working Paper No. 215, Florence, 1986, p. 21.
21 See note 18.
22 Min. BZ, 996.1/45 *Stand van zaken Schumanplan per 29 juli 1950*.
23 ARA, Min. EZ, BEB 562 *Kort verslag van de zesde bespreking van de Sociale Commissie op 4 augustus 1950 CVP/WP/Soc. 6.*
24 ARA, Min. EZ, BEB, 562 *Kort verslag van de zevende bespreking van de Sociale Commissie op 8 augustus 1950 CVP/WP/Soc. 7.*

41

During the summer recess, the German position shifted much closer to that of the Dutch on this point. In opposing what was seen as a carte blanche for the HA to cream off any extra profits accruing because of low German wages[25] the delegation was instructed to push for a position whereby the HA could only intervene if competitive conditions were ‹seriously› distorted and only then to achieve a ‹gradual reduction› rather than an ‹elimination› of the cause.[26] The Dutch themselves, meanwhile, had decided to reject any powers for the HA to impose prélèvements.[27]

When the heads of delegations reviewed the discussion on 12 September, they immediately decided that the HA was to have no direct powers to achieve an equalisation of living standards (and the much vaunted social purpose was eventually reduced to a few pious platitudes). Belgium and Luxembourg, however, still pressed for the HA to immediately begin to eliminate wage differentials insofar as they distorted competitive conditions – by raising everyone else's, not by lowering their own![28] Indeed, they were not prepared to countenance an ending of the transition period until this goal had been achieved,[29] but the retreat from this position, which was utterly untenable, began almost immediately. Uri, at this stage, reflecting the still latent split within the French delegation, was vacillating between extremes; arguing at one point that the HA should only intervene to prevent «a lowering of nominal salaries which are also a lowering of real salaries»[30] and at another that the HA could publish an ‹avis› recommending higher salaries, which the trade unions could then use in their struggles.[31] With the Italians using the issue as a bargaining counter for a resolution on the migration question and the Dutch and Germans resolute in keeping HA powers to an absolute minimum, it was evident that little had changed.[32] Yet when the heads of

25 PAAA, Ref. 213, VSP, Akte 48, Soust/10, *Protokoll der internen Delegationssitzung am 22. 8. 1950.*

26 *PAAA, Refg. 213, VSP, Akte Organisation Kabinettsausschuß V a, Letter Graf to Bundeskanzleramt and various ministries, 25. 8. 1950, 1A3/6007/50.*

27 *ARA, MR, 587 Nota betreft hervatting besprekingen Plan Schuman dd. 24. 8. 1950 (REA 30. 8. 1950).* ARA, MR, 572, Minutes of the economic committee of cabinet 30. 8. 1950.

28 ARA, MR, 588 *Kort verslag van de vergadering van het Comité Restreint op 12 september 1950 CVP 14 (REA 26. 9. 1950). FJM, AMG, 8/2/23 Summary of meetings of Heads of Delegation.*

29 ARA, Min. EZ, BEB, 562 *Kort verslag van de tiende bespreking van de Sociale Commissie op 27 september 1950 CVP/WP/Soc. 10. Min. AE (L) 11362, Réunion du Groupe des Salaires en date du 27 septembre 1950.*

30 ARA, Min. EZ, BEB, 562 *Kort verslag van de elfde bespreking van de Sociale Commissie op 29 september 1950 CVP/WP/Soc. 11.*

31 ARA, Min. EZ, BEB, 562 *Kort verslag van de twaalfde bespreking van de Sociale Commissie op 9 october 1950 CVP/WP/Soc. 12. Min. AE (L) 11362, Groupe Salaires: Réunions des 9 et 10 octobre 1950.*

32 ARA, Min. EZ, BEB, 562 *Kort verslag van de dertiende bespreking van de Sociale Commissie*

delegations returned to the question again on 24 October, they accepted a clause prohibiting the lowering of nominal salaries much the same as that suggested earlier by Uri, but with the added stipulation that wage-cuts which were part of a general reduction in wages should also be exempted from HA powers.[33] The earlier visionary hopes had been reduced to a limited and highly circumscribed scope for action to outlaw *one* means of distorting competition leaving the Belgians no option but to try to solve their problems by obtaining a better solution in the negotiations on the transitionary arrangements.

Production programme and investment control

The negotiations on controls over production (in the shorter term) and their longer term corollary, investment controls, although often highly technical, struck at the very heart of the new community's identity. Was the community to be a model of free competition, with market forces determining the allocation of production and with HA powers limited to dealing with the effects of downswings in demand? Was it to resemble the enlightened dirigism (in the French view at least) of the *Commissariat du Plan* surplanted on a supranational scale? Or was it to be a camouflaged version of the inter-war steel cartel covered with a sauce of post-war integrationist/federalist verbiage?

Monnet's original ideas seem to have lain in the field that the HA's powers over production and investment would be confined to the transition period only and that thereafter free market forces would be allowed to prevail.[34] Before the negotiations started it seemed unlikely that even this would be acceptable to the rest. Both the Italians[35] and the Dutch[36] were diametrically

op 10 october 1950 CVP/WP/Soc. 13. Min. AE (L) 11362, *Groupe Salaires: Réunions des 9 et 10 octobre 1950.*

33 FJM, AMG, 8/2/12 *Compte rendu de la réunion des chefs de délégation du 24 octobre 1950* no. 9. ARA, Min. EZ, BEB, 557 *Stand van de besprekingen over het Plan Schuman per 28 october 1950.* Min. AE (L) 11362, 11374, *Compte-rendu de la réunion des chefs de délégation du 24 octobre 1950.*

34 Min. BZ, 996.1/11, *Kort verslag van de rede van de heer Monnet die op 21 juni 1950 werd uitgesproken ter toelichting van het Plan Schuman,* CVP No. 1, n.d. FJM, AMG, 3/2/1 *Compte rendu de la seconde séance tenue le 21 Juin 1950,* CPS/CR/1. Min. AE (L) 11347, *Réunion du mercredi 21 juin au Quai d'Orsay. Exposé de M. Monnet.*

35 PRO, FO, 371 V. Mallet to Foreign Office, 4. 6. 1950 reporting a conversation with Grazzi. AMDAE, PARIGI, b478.f1 *Verbale della riunione tenuta al ministero dell'Industria il 27 maggio 1950.*

36 Min. BZ, 996.1/1 *Concept Instructie voor de delegatie die aan de onderhandelingen betreffende het Plan Schuman zal deelnemen* dd. 2. 6. 1950. ARA, MR, 572 Minutes of Economic Committee of cabinet 13. 6. 1950.

opposed to having their own steel modernisation plans put at risk by the HA. The Germans were preparing to argue that, with six separate control agencies already operating in the country, there was no room for any more, at least as far as they were concerned.[37] And Belgium was only willing to concede HA intervention in those cases where the state already had powers, arguing that private investment was a private risk based on calculations of market expectations – a standpoint which effectively meant exempting their own steel interests.[38]

When the delegations met for their first informative meeting on 22 June, Hirsch revealed French thinking in greater detail. As far as production programmes were concerned, the HA would as far as possible act as a coordinating body for programmes drawn up by regional groups. Only in the case of disagreement would it have a decisive say. On the other hand, all investment programmes would be scrutinised. If, despite a negative advice, private business wanted to risk its own capital, that was its own affair. National governments, however, would be bound by a HA decision.[39] The *Document de Travail* further specified that the HA could instruct a modification of production programmes if they threatened a «disorganisation of production» or on grounds of global considerations (powers, thus, which extended beyond the transition phase).[40] These ideas only served to strengthen the Benelux conviction that some national appeals or veto procedure was necessary to control these sweeping powers[41] whilst the Germans saw the way out in a strengthening of the role of the regional groups.[42]

---

37 See note 10.
38 Min. BZ, 996.1/1 W.G. 's Jacob to Min. BZ 8. 6. 1950. This is the best account of the verbal exposition of the Belgian standpoint at the Benelux meeting of 7. 6. 1950. Enclosed as appendix is a Belgian document *Projet de traité réalisant Plan Schuman* n.d. All of these points were later incorporated into the delegates' instructions at the end of June. See Min. AE (Bel) 5216, *Rapport sur les négociations autour du Plan Schuman* dd. 30. 12. 1950. This report also quotes extracts from a number of notes which provided the background to the cabinet's deliberations. See also Min. BZ, 996.1/1. *Verslag van de bespreking te Brussel op Woensdag 7 juni inzake Schuman-Plan* dd. 10. 6. 1950. Min. BZ, 996.1/1 Memorandum from Baron van Voorst to Min. BZ dd. 10. 6. 1950. Min. AE (Bel) 5216 *Réunion du Plan Schuman – 7 juni 1950 (Délegations Belgo-Luxembourgeoise et Néerlandaise)*. Min. AE (L) 11346, *Réunion entre fonctionnaires néerlandais, belge et luxembourgeois tenue le 7. 6. 1950 au Ministère des Affaires Etrangères de Belgique.*
39 ARA, Min. EZ, BEB 562 *Kort verslag van de vergadering die op 23 juni 1950 werd gehouden ten kantore van het Plan Monnet*, CVP 3. FJM, AMG, 3/3/3 *Conversations pour le Plan Schuman. Séance restreinte, Vendredi matin 23 juin 1950* CPS/CR/3. Min. AE (L) 11374, *Réunion restreinte du 23 juin au Commissariat.*
40 CD. *Document de Travail* dd. 24. 6. 1950 (Art. 27).
41 ARA, MR, 536 *Mondelinge toelichting van de Franse Ambassadeur bij de boodschap van Minister Schuman door hem op 28 dezer overhandigd aan Minister Stikker* (REA 1. 7. 1950).
42 PAAA, Ref. 213, VSP, Akte 45, KA61, Delegates' instructions. Confidential document

When these questions were raised in the working group of experts a gap immediately opened between the Dutch and Italians on the one hand and the rest on the question of investment controls. One way out was to weaken HA powers in this area[43], but the other, which was accepted at this stage, albeit with the Italian reserve, was that the Dutch and Italian modernisation plans be exempted from scrutiny as long as they made no claims on community funding.[44] On the question of production programmes, agreement was quickly reached that these were indeed necessary for orientation purposes. However, the idea of giving the HA direct powers, it was argued, was in conflict with the idea of free competition and with the agreement already reached on the reconversion fund stating that the HA could not order an individual firm to close. The dilemma, expressed by Hirsch, was that giving the HA no powers meant exposing coal and steel to unfettered competition with all its heavy consequences, but if it were to intervene too often or in too much detail, it would lead to unnecessary dirigism which was not the intention either. He was prepared to accept giving the HA only indirect powers, which brought him into line with the rest.[45] The question whether that left responsibility with national governments, as the Dutch wanted, or with the regional groups, which the Germans seemed to prefer, was left open. So too was the definition of the circumstances justifying that intervention.

This state-of-play only seems to have given rise to debate in the Netherlands. The concessions on its modernisation plans, which they had no intention of abandoning, had only been obtained by recognising a discrimination against public investment in any future expansion; for example placing Dutch coal mines under HA scrutiny whilst exempting those in Belgium. Cabinet suggested conceding HA control over *all* investment.[46] When this proposal was raised at the heads of delegation meeting on 8 September, it completely dumbfounded the Belgians who complained that it was «as if nothing had been said, written and accepted by the working group», but it was embraced «with

beginning: «Die Delegation hat dem Kabinett anhand des am 25. 6. von Herrn Monnet überreichten Arbeitsdokuments . . .» n.d.

43 ARA, Min. EZ, BEB 562 *Verslag van de vergadering dd. 10 juli 1950* CVP/WP/Prod. 3. FJM, AMG, 4/3/4 *Conversations sur le Plan Schuman. Groupe de travail: Production, Prix, Investissements. Réunion du lundi 10 juillet* PS/G4/CR4. Min. AE (L) 11359, *Réunion du Groupe IV au Commissariat du Plan, le 10 juillet.*

44 ARA, Min. EZ, BEB 562 *Verslag van de vergadering dd. 1 augustus 1950* CVP/WP/Prod. 12. Min. AE (L) 11359, *Groupe IV, Réunion du 1er août 1950.*

45 ARA, Min. EZ, BEB, 562 *Verslag van de vergadering dd. 13 juli 1950* CVP/WP/Prod. 6. FJM, AMG, 4/3/6 *Conversation sur le Plan Schuman. Groupe de travail: Production, Prix, Investissements. Réunion du Groupe IV, jeudi 13 juillet.*

46 See note 27.

satisfaction» by Monnet as a welcome extension of the HA's role.[47] The compromise proposal, by Hirsch, to extend HA competence to mixed financed projects employing less than 50 per cent private capital (thereby including the Société Général) was eventually accepted by all.[48]

The production programmes themselves proved much more troublesome. Having agreed at heads of delegate level that HA intervention was to be restricted to situations of threatened over- and underproduction (first by indirect measures as price manipulation and consultation and, only when that failed, by export, import or production quotas),[49] the experts immediately divided into two camps by reopening the question of the nature of the production programmes. The initial position, that they should be for orientation purposes, was only supported unequivocally by the Dutch delegation and part of the German delegation. The Luxembourg delegation, supported by the majority of Belgians present wanted the regional groups not only to agree production levels but also to allocate that production among enterprises.[50]

At about the same time this tendency towards using the regional groups as a form of a transnational set of cartels was also emerging in the discussions on price formation and the issue of cartels itself was beginning to emerge as a separate question. As a result on 4 October Monnet stated that the nature of the regional groups had been so altered from the original conception, that he wondered whether it would not be better to abandon them altogether.[51] The fall from grace of the regional groups served to reawaken a role for national governments. Any HA intervention on the question of quotas was to be contingent upon a unanimous decision of the Council of Ministers[52], who would also be responsible for determining the national allocation. Only if it

---

47 Min. AE (Bel) 5216 *Plan Schuman: travaux de la Conférence entre les 31 août et le 9 septembre.* FJM, AMG, 8/2/23 *Summary of meetings of Heads of Delegations,* ARA, MR, 588 *Verslag over de besprekingen te Parijs betreffende het Schumanplan van 31 augustus–9 september 1950* (REA 20. 9. 1950.

48 ARA, MR, 588 *Verslag van de besprekingen te Parijs betreffende het Schumanplan van 10 t/m 14 september 1950* (REA 26. 9. 1950). (REA 26. 9. 1950). ARA, MR, 589 *Verslag van de besprekingen te Parijs betreffende het Schumanplan van 17 t/m 23 september 1950* (REA 3. 10. 1950.

49 FJM, AMG, 8/2/23 *Summary of meetings of Heads of Delegations.*

50 ARA, MR (588) *Verslag van de besprekingen te Parijs betreffende het Schuman Plan van 10 t/m 14 september 1950* (REA 26. 9. 1950).

51 Min. AE (Bel) 5216 *Observations sur le mémorandum du 28 Septembre 1950 exposées par M. Jean Monnet au cours de la réunion restreinte des chefs de délégation le 4. 10. 1950.*

52 FJM, AMG, 8/2/9 *Compte rendu de la réunion des chefs de délégation du 15 Octobre* no. 7. ARA, MR, 589 *Nota betreft Plan Schuman* dd. 19. 10. 1950 (REA 25. 10. 1950). ARA, Min. EZ, BEB, 564 *Verslag van de vergadering van de Commissie van Advies voor het Plan Schuman, gehouden op 19 october 1950* (SchV/10).

46

failed, would the HA be charged with the task.[53] It was still entrusted with the preparation of production plans for orientation purposes only and could only consult the enterprises through the medium of, or with permission of, national governments.

Prices

The negotiations on prices were of staggering complexity and it is impossible here to consider them in their «lush fullness».[54] Monnet's original view was to leave decisions on both the level of prices and the method of price determination to the High Authority.[55] The aim, as explained by Uri, would be to fix a band of maximum and minimum prices within which competition, on a non-discriminatory basis, could take place. Sales below the «minimum» would only be permitted if producers could prove to the HA that their costs were genuinely low. The level of prices would be such as to encourage efficient production.[56] However, it was clear from the start that such matters were considered too important to be left to the arbitrary decision of the HA. The decision on the level of prices would determine whether the pool would become an expensive producers' club or whether consumer interests would prevail. Upon the price rules adopted depended the fate of competition within the group and even the ability of some firms to survive at all.

The discussions on price rules were dominated by two opposing concepts. Under the so-called *prix-départ* system the object was to standardise the price paid by consumers throughout the community, the freight costs being paid by the suppliers. The alternative was to standardise prices ex-mine or ex-mill and to allow the consumers to bear the cost of transport. A modified form of this second concept, known as *prix-parité*, whereby a single price was determined within producing regions, entered the discussions at a very early stage. This had the effect of preventing (price) competition within the region but, depending on the rules adopted, it could allow competition between regions. Under the prix-départ system consumers would buy at the closest expedition point (to reduce the remaining transport costs they had to bear). Only if the

---

53 FJM, AMG, d8/2/15 *Proposition relatives aux moyens financiers de la Haute Autorité* dd. 26. 10. 1950 no. 13, FJM, AMG, 8/2/21 *Compte rendu de la réunion des chefs de délégation du 28 octobre* no. 19.

54 Borrowed from William Diebold Jr. *The Schuman Plan – A study in Economic Cooperation 1950-1959*, New York, 1959, p. 238.

55 See note 34.

56 See note 39.

price were high could, for example, a Belgian steel producer sell at expedition point Milan – it had to be high enough to cover his production costs plus freight. If this were the case, however, all Belgian consumers would be penalised by having to pay the same high price, profitable for the steel producers, disastrous for steel users. The prix-parité would allow low cost producers to pass the price benefits on to local consumers and, depending on the margins or the price which high-cost producers were allowed to charge, still left an opportunity for competing in those markets. If the object of a delegation was to protect local producers, its best tactic was to push for a prix-départ system where the prices were high, but not high enough to make cross-hauls from more efficient producers a viable proposition.

The initial government positions were often vague and the real divisions only became clear once the negotiations were taken over by experts. The Dutch, with a relatively efficient coal and steel industry, wanted producer-based prices preferably as low as possible.[57] The Italians favoured the same system though presumably with much higher prices, at least for steel. Those higher prices, plus the cost of freight, were considered sufficient protection[58] (they were later to abandon this stance). The German steel committee initially opposed both ex-mill prices, ironically for fear of French competition, and the prix-parité system, preferring to hang onto the benefits of double-pricing[59], but this was ignored by the cabinet which instructed the delegation to leave matters in the hands of the HA.[60] Since leaving the question to the HA was also the French position, they seemed to have no specific objectives at this stage. The Belgians were in favour of a system of ‹free› producer prices – but only after artificial cost differences (i.e. wage differentials) had been removed.[61] However, by the time the issue had surfaced in the negotiations, that position had been substantially modified.

Within a sub-group investigating coal prices the Belgians had announced that even after the transition period the position of its mines would be «particularly delicate». Thus, as far as coal was concerned, they could not agree to the principle of free price formation. The average price of coal should be taken as

---

57 See note 17.
58 Ranieri, *Italy and the Schuman Plan, p. 19.*
59 *PRO, FO 371/85859 Report on a meeting of the German Ministerial Advisory Committee for the Schuman Plan* dd. 14. 7. 1950. PAAA, Organisation des Ausschusses, Bildung und Zusammensetzung, Vc *Stenographischer Bericht über Gemeinsame Sitzung der vier Ausschüsse für die Schumanplan-Verhandlungen, 28 Juni 1950, 10 Uhr.*
60 See note 42.
61 See note 19.

the new minimum by the HA.[62] This idea was resisted by Germany, Luxembourg and the Netherlands, but the Belgian demands had set thinking in the direction of regional price zones (i.e. prix-parité) which would serve to protect the Belgian market without prejudicing the rest.[63] For Italy this raised the spectre that its steel industry might end up penalized by having to pay high zonal prices plus high freight costs for its coal inputs whilst facing a much more competitive system for its steel. The French remarked that what was needed was to find a system which did not give rise to ‹wild competition›, which did not penalise consumers and which took into account the needs of unfavourably located mines.[64] By the summer recess, that search had yet to begin in any earnest. However the individual delegations had the chance to reformulate their positions in the light of the discussions.

In every country a system of départ prices was accepted as the departure point for any discussions on coal, and a solution along these lines was accepted relatively painlessly early in October.[65] The remaining points of conflict centred on two issues – the system to be adopted for steel and the responsibility for determining prices within whatever system was eventually chosen. The Netherlands played only a minor role in these discussions since its advisory committee was split down the middle on the choice between prix-départ and prix-parité. In the end it was decided that the economy could live with either system as long as HA interferences were reduced to the minimum.[66] Belgium, Luxembourg and Germany favoured a prix-parité system in which the prices in each regional zone were to be determined by the regional groups and approved by the HA. The French, on the other hand, favoured the prix-départ system whilst the Italians wanted a prix-départ system whose operation would be suspended (temporarily) as far as their own steel works were concerned. A somewhat vacuous agreement was reached that prices should be as low as possible.[67] When the working group took up

62 ARA, Min. EZ, BEB 562 *Déclaration des experts de l'industrie charbonnier Belge à la sous-commission des prix. Séance du 20 juillet* Appendix by CVP/WP/Prod. 9.

63 ARA, Min. EZ, BEB, 562 *Propositions du Sous-Comité des Prix du Charbon* dd. 20. 7. 1950.

64 ARA, Min. EZ, BEB, 562 *Verslag van de vergadering dd. 21 juli 1950*, VCP/WP/Prod. 9. FJM, AMG, 4/5/10 *Conservations sur le Plan Schuman. Groupe de travail: Production, Prix, Investissements. Réunion du 21. 7. 1950* PS/G4/CR10.

65 Min. AE (Bel) 5216 *Note pour Monsieur le Ministre des Affaires Etrangères et Monsieur le Ministre du Commerce Extérieur* (Suétens) dd. 16. 10. 1950, ARA, Min. EZ, BEB. 559 *Vraagstukken welke in de week van 23–28 october 1950 door de delegatie te Parijs zullen worden behandeld* dd. 17. 10. 1950.

66 See note 27.

67 FJM, AMG, 8/2/23 *Summary of meetings of Heads of Delegations.* Min. AE (Bel) 5216 *Plan Schuman: travaux de la Conférence entre le 31 aout et le 9 septembre.* ARA, MR, 588 *Verslag over de besprekingen te Parijs betreffende het Schumanplan van 31 augustus–9 september 1950* (REA 20. 9. 1950).

the discussions in mid-September, agreement was reached that the HA should only itself intervene to fix prices at the extremes of the business cycle. It suggested overcoming the split over the eventual price system by leaving the choice to the HA – a return to the Document de Travail. However, with reserves placed by Luxembourg and Italy on this formulation, the compromise was unlikely to survive.[68]

This turned out to be indeed the case and in mid-October the issue flared up again in the heads of delegations' committee. It began as a straight-forward clash between the Belgians and Italians during which Monnet had seemed initially to side with those favouring the prix-parité. However, when the role envisaged for the regional groups came to the fore, his patience appeared to have snapped. He launched into a tirade against the organisation, methods and influence of the French iron and steel federations and explained that, for him, the choice of price system was less a question of economics than one of whether regional groups could be entrusted with the task of price formation. New compromise proposals would be forthcoming.[69] When they arrived, they envisaged a modification of the prix-parité system. It acknowledged that a structure of regional prices would be fixed but it allowed producers to lower that price if they wished in order to be able to match the price prevailing at another region (i.e. if the price in region A plus the freight cost to region B meant a price higher than that in region B, producers in region A could lower the price on such consignments to allow them to compete). As agreed, HA intervention in domestic prices was limited to the extremes of the business cycle, and only then after consulting the Council of Ministers. A last-ditch attempt to give the HA wide-ranging powers over export prices was rebuffed with the result that the only powers were those to fix maximum prices in times of a «hausse» – a traditional cartel weapon designed to prevent other countries setting up competing industries and to maintain market shares.[70] Although the Treaty successfully outlawed national discriminatory pricing policies, it left the conduct of the market as an awkward balance between free competition and protection. Moreover, despite Monnet's fulminations against cartels, the fact that the system was a zonal one virtually sanctioned producers' collusion in

---

68 ARA, MR (589) *Verslag over de besprekingen te Parijs betreffende het Schumanplan van 24 t/m 30 september 1950* (REA 11. 10. 1950).

69 Min. AE (Bel) 5216 *Note pour Monsieur le Ministre des Affaires Etrangères et Monsieur le Ministre du Commerce Extérieur* (Suétens) dd. 16. 10. 1986, ARA, Min. EZ, BEB 559 *Vraagstukken welke in de week van 23–28 october 1950 door de delegatie te Parijs zullen worden behandeld* dd. 17. 10. 1986.

70 FJM, AMG, 8/2/13 *Mémorandum sur les prix et les questions connexes* dd. 24. 10. 1950. Min. *AE (L) 11374, Compte-rendu de la réunion des chefs de délégation du 25 octobre 1950*.

price-fixing at least on a regional scale and it had still to be seen whether this collusion would not become the *de facto* practice throughout the community as a whole.

Commercial policy

Monnet did not originally seem to consider a common external tariff to be necessary but was content to leave the matter with the High Authority along with powers over import quotas, export regimes and negotiating commercial treaties. The HA would, he expected, establish tariff margins sufficient to ensure that trade deflection did not occur and governments would be free to choose a point within those margins.[71] The Dutch, however, were opposed to such a solution since leaving the decision to the HA left wide open the question whether the pool was to going to be protectionist or not. They wanted the common tariff (or tariff margins) clearly stipulated – an average of existing tariffs would be completely unacceptable,[72] a position broadly supported by the other Benelux partners. Monnet's statement that the eventual tariff should be low enough to promote the greatest possible efficiency did little to still their concern.[73] The discussion by the experts scarcely got to grip with the issue at all. The French remaining by the position that the HA should only establish the *margins*, then once the low tariff countries had adjusted their tariffs (upwards), the high tariff countries could move into line. It was argued that if the Benelux tariff remained the bottom level of the tariff band, losses in production from firms which were unviable would be taken up by the UK instead of by another member of the pool.[74]

During the summer recess the Dutch negotiating position hardened. Although the special advisory commission was perfectly happy with an arrangement whereby the Benelux tariff formed the bottom of a tariff band,[75] cabinet was persuaded the tariff band could still leave an unacceptably wide gap. What the

71 See note 39.
72 ARA, MR (586) *Nota inzake het Plan Schuman* n.d. (REA 1. 7. 1950).
73 ARA, MR (586) *Kort verslag van de vergadering die op 3 juli 1950 werd gehouden ten kantore van het Plan Schuman*, CVP no. 4 (REA 18. 7. 1950). See also Min. AE Belg 5216 *Plan Schuman. Déclaration allemande de la séance plénière du 3 juillet 1950*. FJM, AMG, 3/3/17 Conservations sur le Plan Schuman. Séance restreinte. Lundi après-midi 3 juillet 1950 *PS/CR 5. Min. AE (I.) 11374, Compte-rendu de la réunion du 3 juillet 1950–16 heures, compte-rendu sur la réunion du 3 juillet.*
74 ARA, Min. EZ, BEB 562 *Verslag van de bespreking over de handelspolitiek op 3 augustus 1950* CVP/WP/HP 4.
75 ARA, MR, 587 *Nota betreft hervatting besprekingen Plan Schuman* dd. 24. 8.1950 (REA 30. 8. 1950).

delegation was now instructed to push for was a unitary tariff, which was also to be as low as possible.[76] When this was put at the first heads of delegations meeting at the beginning of September it immediately served to destroy an emerging consensus since both the Italians and the French had shifted position to a willingness to accept the Benelux tariff as the minimum,[77] the maximum to be determined after an assessment of freight differentials. As was to transpire later, they had now begun to see the main line of defence in terms of quantitative trade controls. At this point the Germans moved to occupy the other extreme, declaring that under no circumstances would they countenance lowering their tariffs. These, they argued, were aimed at the United States, the United Kingdom and Sweden. Their industry needed to modernise and could not do so with a lower level of protection.[78] The French attempted to argue that competition in steel did not take the form of a continuous struggle for markets but the form of sudden attacks aimed at the very existence of an industry. In such circumstances, what was important was not the level of tariffs but an effective safeguard mechanism. The only concession this brought from the Germans was that if Benelux raised their tariffs, Germany would consider a proportional lowering of its own – a suggestion rejected by the rest.[79]

The issue of tariffs and safeguard clauses now became inextricably inter-meshed. The original French idea had been to leave all powers to control excessive imports in the hands of the HA, but when the issue was first seriously raised in September, the Dutch had demanded a role for the Council of Ministers.[80] A further complication was that the French wanted the HA

76 ARA, MR, 572 Minutes of the economic committee of cabinet 30. 8. 1950.
77 ARA, MR, 588 *Verslag over de besprekingen te Parijs betreffende het Schumanplan van 31 augustus–9 september 1950* (REA 20. 9. 1950). ARA, MR, 588 *Verslag van de vergadering van de Commission Restreinte voor het Schuman Plan op 1 september 1950* CVP 12 (REA 12. 9. 1950). Min AE (Bel) 5216 *Rapport à Monsieur le Ministre. Objet, Reprise, à Paris des pour-parlers au sujet du Plan Schuman. Réunion du 1er septembre 1950.* FJM, AMG, 8/2/23 *Summary of Meetings of Heads of Delegations.* Min AE (L) 11360, *Réunion restreinte du 1er septembre 1950 au Commissariat du Plan.*
78 ARA, Min. EZ, BEB 562 *Verslag van de derde vergadering van de groep van deskundigen voor handels- en tarifaire politiek dd. 13 september 1950* CVP/HP/7. FJM, AMG, 7/2/5 *Groupe de politique commerciale et tarifaire. Réunion du mercredi 13 septembre PS/GII/CR4.* Min. AE (L) 11360, *Réunion du Groupe de la Politique Commerciale le 13 septembre 1950.*
79 ARA, MR, 589 *Verslag van de besprekingen te Parijs betreffende het Schumanplan van 17 t/m 23 september 1950, Verslag van de vergadering van het Comité Restreint op 21 en 22 september 1950* CVP 17 (RFA 3. 10. 1950). Min. AE (Bel) 5216 *Comité Restreint. Compte-rendu de la Réunion du Vendredi 22 septembre 1950.* Min. AE (L) 11374, *Réunion du Groupe Restreint du 21 septembre 1950, Réunion du Groupe Restreint du 22 septembre 1950.*
80 ARA, MR, 588 *Verslag over de besprekingen te Parijs betreffende het Schumanplan van 31 augustus–9 september 1950* (REA 20. 9. 1950).

empowered to act *before* crisis levels had been reached. Moreover, any HA measures would also have to apply to countries in the pool which might not have experienced any extraordinary level of imports at all. Both considerations would place the HA in violation of GATT rules. At this point the French argued that they had compromised on the question of the Benelux tariff and that they now expected some compromise in return.[81] But it was not just the Benelux countries which were proving difficult; the Germans, too, flatly refused to give the HA the powers the French were seeking.[82]

With the situation at an impasse at the experts' level, the question of commercial policy was referred back to the heads of delegation on 21 September. The French repeated their commitment to use the Benelux tariff as a base for the rest of the pool, if safeguards against dumping and a «massive concentrated attack by foreign producers» were recognised. Suétens, acting as the Benelux spokesman argued that these powers should constitute sufficient protection for German industry. He could see no reason why German industry, already working under favourable conditions, should enjoy an extra protection in the form of high import duties. At this point, the Germans shifted position. Hallstein argued that German industry needed high tariffs only in the short term but he was willing to make such protection degressive, eventually reaching Benelux levels. He then introduced a new argument – if the Benelux tariff were written into the Treaty, the group would lose all bargaining power in the GATT negotiations. However, the Benelux countries were unwilling to leave the decision on tariff levels to the uncertain outcome of the Torquay negotiations.[83]

So matters remained until October, the experts meanwhile tightening the definitions and terms of the safeguard and anti-dumping clauses.[84] It was then, at a meeting to discuss a French memorandum describing the state of play,[85] that the Benelux front began to fall apart with the Belgians willing to countenance raising tariffs if negotiations with the UK failed and equally willing to leave an eventual decision to the Council of Ministers, deciding

---

81 See note 78.
82 ARA, Min. EZ, BEB, 562 *Verslag van de vierde vergadering van de groep van deskundigen voor de handels- en tarifaire politiek dd. 14 september 1950* CVP/WP/IIP 8. Min. AE (Bcl) 5216. *Réunion du Groupe politique commerciale (13 et 14 septembre 1950).* FJM, AMG, 7/2/6 *Groupe politique commerciale et tarifaire. Réunion du jeudi 14 septembre* PS/GII/CR5. Min. AE (L) 11360, *Réunion du Groupe de la Politique Commerciale, le 14 septembre 1950.*
83 See note 79.
84 Min. Fin. BBV 1262 Plan Schuman III. *Verslag van de vergadering van de groep van deskundigen voor de handels- en tarifaire politiek dd. 29 september 1950* CVP/WP/IIP 9.
85 CD. *Textes de references sur les institutions et les Dispositions économiques et sociales permanents du Plan Schuman* dd. 28. 9. 1950.

unanimously.[86] The Dutch, now isolated, were forced to accept a situation whereby the convention stipulated a range of tariffs, the decision on the exact point being left to the Council of Ministers. But the agreement was both vague and tenuous.[87] In the end a German compromise proposal succeeded in settling the issue. The Benelux tariff would be stipulated in the convention to the Treaty as a minimum, but so too would a second level, two points higher, to be invoked if international negotiations failed. In order to stop any trade deflection, a tariff quota (equivalent to their needs) at the lowest rate would be determined by the HA until the process of tariff harmonisation (and the penalty of expensive cross-hauls) rendered the system unnecessary.[88]

The transitional arrangements

It was recognised from the beginning that unless the creation of a common market were to be accompanied by violent shifts in the pattern of production and trade, some temporary transitional arrangements would be necessary. However the *Document de Travail* was remarkably vague on the nature of the transition period – leaving its implementation entirely in the hands of the HA (art. 17). At the same time it made provision for the creation of two funds. A reconversion fund (almost immediately renamed adaptation fund) would facilitate the expansion, specialisation or modernisation of existing plant and encourage structural transformation (art. 23) whilst an equalization fund would smooth out the shocks anticipated in the transitional period by temporarily funding exploitation losses (art. 24). The first was to be funded by a mixture of levies and loans, the second by a system of production levies.[89] The two funds needed to be seen together. The equalization fund was needed to postpone the moment of large-scale sackings which might otherwise accompany the immediate introduction of a common market. If firms could adjust to meet the new competitive conditions in time, that moment could be postponed indefinitely. It was at this point that the adaptation fund came into its own since it could help finance that adjustment. But if that adjustment

86 ARA, MR (589) *Verslag van de vergadering van het Comité Restreint op 4 october 1950* CVP 18 (REA 25. 10. 1950).
87 FJM, AMG, 8/2/14 *Compte rendu de la réunion des chefs de délégation du 25 octobre* no. 12. ARA, Min. EZ, BEB 557 *Stand van de besprekingen over het Plan Schuman per 28 october 1950*. Min. AE (L) 11374, *Compte-rendu de la réunion des chefs de délégation du 25 octobre 1950*.
88 ARA, Min. EZ, BEB 563 *Verslag van de vergadering van de Commissie van Advies voor het Plan Schuman, gehouden op 9 december 1950* (SchV/13).
89 CD *Document de Travail* dd. 24. 6. 1950.

were adjudged impossible, it could also create alternative employment for the workers affected by investing in other occupations. At this level it resembled the concept of ‹compensations› embodied in the Stikker Plan. However, article 23 opened the scope much wider and, insofar as it envisaged supranational financing of modernisation schemes, it came closer to the Investment Bank scheme launched by Petsche in the councils of the OEEC.

This ambiguity in conception characterised the initial conflict of views when the adaptation fund was considered by the working group of experts. The Germans hoped to get help from the fund to modernise their steel industry[90] but nevertheless wanted the scale of its operations kept as small as possible. One way to do this was to argue that it should not be used to invest in firms which would be unviable anyway. This immediately created a line-up of Belgium, Luxembourg and Italy. The Belgians argued that firms would not have to close because they were unviable, but because they had sacrificed their protection in the course of forming the common market.[91] To this the Italians had added that if the governments had surrendered their rights of protection to the HA, the least it could do would be to shoulder the responsibility. What they wanted was not only modernisation capital, reallocation and retraining schemes but also an indemnification for all firms forced to close. To this the Germans, with the backing of the Dutch, had replied that it was unwise to specify such a wide scope which might then not be fundable. The Dutch, who were more concerned that production levies needed to finance such a fund would force up the price of coal and steel, argued that if firms attracting modernisation funds were viable any way, there should be no need for community funding since they could also expect to benefit from the results. Only where market imperfections made financing difficult, should the fund be empowered to help. Similarly they also argued that the HA should only intervene to alleviate unemployment if the scale of the problem were such that governments could not cope by themselves.[92] Hirsch, too, distanced

90 See note 42.
91 ARA, Min. EZ, BEB 562 *Verslag van de vergadering dd. 6 juli 1950* CVP/WP/Prod 1. FJM. AMG, 4/3/1 *Conversations sur le Plan Schuman. Groupe de travail: Production, Prix, Investissements. Réunion du jeudi 6 juillet* PS/G4/CR1. Min.AE (L) 11357, *Réunion du Groupe IV au Commissariat du Plan le 6 juillet.*
92 ARA, Min. EZ, BEB 562 *Verslag van de vergadering dd. 7 juli 1950* CVP/WP/Prod. 2. FJM, AMG, 4/3/2 *Conversations sur le Plan Schuman. Groupe de travail: Production, Prix, Investissements. Réunion du 6 juillet, 7 juillet* PS/G4/CR2 and Idem, 7 juillet PS/G4/CR33 (4/3/3). Min AE (L) 11357, *Réunion du Groupe IV, vendredi 7 juillet 1950.* ARA, Min. EZ, BEB, 562 *Verslag van de vergadering dd. 11 juli* CVP/WP/prod. 4. FJM, AMG, 4/3/5 *Conversations sur le Plan Schuman. Groupe de travail: Production, Prix, Investissements. Réunion du Mardi 11 juillet* PS/G4/CR5. Min. AE (L) 11359, *Groupe IV, Réunion du mardi 11 juillet.*

himself from the open-ended commitment being propagated most forcefully by the Italians. On the question of indemnification he simply stated quite bluntly that it fell outside the original scope of the Schuman Plan and was therefore unacceptable. Nor was he prepared to see the fund used to help *any* unemployment in coal and steel. Underemployment in Italian industry, he argued, was an Italian problem and had nothing to do with the HA.[93]

So matters stood when the summer recess intervened. The Dutch cabinet decided, at this point, to accept the installation of the fund provided a definite ceiling were put on the production levies needed to finance it. The remainder of the money could be raised by the HA acting as an intermediary for loans. In fact, so enamoured was the cabinet of this construction that the delegation was instructed to suggest that the fund should be given a permanent character.[94] In Germany, too, opposition to the fund was relaxed in the expectation that, with a more limited definition, the benefits German steel could hope to attract would neutralise much, if not all, of the expected cost.[95] It was in the spirit of the Dutch proposals that the question was eventually resolved. Aid from the fund was tied to strictly limited criteria and was to take the form of a mixture of loans (to industry) and grants (to workers). Without dispensation from the HA, national governments were to contribute half the fund's involved. The cost, however, of limiting the fund's scope was to increase the powers of the HA in its administration.

The resolution of the question of the adaptation fund was relatively painless compared with the other issues related to the transition period where the negotiations dragged on through to January 1951. When it came to the equalization fund, the line-up was much the same as before. The Belgians and Italians, concerned for the eventual survival of their coal and steel industries respectively, pushed for the widest and most generous provisions possible. In fairness it should be pointed out that the Italians were sceptical from the start about such an approach, which they were inclined to think of as one of Monnet's more fanciful inventions. They expected an agreement along the lines of the retention of tariff protection to be a more reasonable solution to the problems of their steel industry.[96] The Dutch and the Germans, who saw

93 ARA, Min. EZ, BEB 562 *Verslag van de vergadering dd. 26 juli 1950* CVP/WP/Prod. 11. Min. AE (L) 11359, *Groupe IV, Réunion tenue le mercredi 26 juillet 1950.*

94 ARA, MR, 587 *Nota betreft hervatting besprekingen Plan Schuman* dd. 24. 8. 1950 (REA 30. 8. 1950). ARA, MR, 572 Minutes of the economic committee of cabinet 30. 8. 1950.

95 See note 25.

96 AMDAE, Affari Economici, Piano Schuman 1950 sc 3 f 2, *Appuntis ulla riunione delle delegazione italiana alla Conferenza del Piano Schuman presso il Ministero degli Esteri,* dd. 24. 6. 1950.

themselves having to pay for this generosity, were determined to limit, as far as possible, the costs they would have to bear. This tactic appeared in the very first discussion on the equalization fund when Germany suggested that its provisions be restricted to helping individual firms in difficulty during the transition period, but this was firmly disposed of by the French who wanted it used as a price equalization mechanism. The latter would obviously be far more expensive.[97] But there were other ways of reducing the costs of the fund, as the Belgians never tired of pointing out. One way was to ensure that the new community price level was relatively high so that the subsidy required to scale Belgian prices down to the community level would be that much less. At one stage they suggested that the existing ‹average price› should become the new ‹minimum price›. Another alternative was that the transition period should see the upward adjustment of everyone else's wage levels to their own.[98] This first idea was resisted by the Dutch and the Germans whilst the second received no support at all.[99] Just before the summer recess, however, the French presented a new set of proposals which, for the first time, opened the possibility of national governments covering part of the costs of the transitional measures.[100]

Within the Belgian government, the fact that the transition to a common market was going to be both painful and costly was grudgingly accepted. The community was not to evolve into a high-wage, high-cost club. On the other hand a foreign ministry report pointed out that the steel industry would benefit from lower coal prices: «It is certain that even in the present regime in our protected economy, the maintenance of the status quo on coal prices is impossible, because of the considerable difficulties experienced by the consuming industries in resisting their foreign competitors.[101] Within the community, Belgium could expect some financial help in meeting the costs of adjustment. Whilst sticking out for a minimum transition period of five years, the government agreed to contributing 50 % of the cost of the price

97 ARA, Min. EZ, BEB 562 *Verslag van de vergadering dd. 7 juli 1950* CVP/WP/Prod. 2. FJM, AMG, 4/3/2 *Conversations sur le Plan Schuman. Groupe de travail: Production, Prix, Investissements. Réunion du 6 juillet, 7 juillet* PS/G4/CR2 and Idem, 7 juillet PS/G4/CR33 (4/3/3). Min. AE (L) *Réunion du Groupe IV, vendredi 7 juillet 1950.*
98 ARA, Min. EZ, BEB 562 *Déclaration des experts de l'industrie charbonnier Belge à la sous-commission des prix. Séance du 20 juillet* Appendix by CVP/WP/Prod. 9.
99 ARA., Min EZ, BEB, 562 *Propositions du Sous-Comité des Prix du Charbon* dd. 20. 7. 1950.
100 CD *Rapport sur les travaux poursuivis à Paris par les Délégations des Six Pays du 20 juin au 10 aout 1950.* Annex IV.
101 Min. AE (Bel) 5216 *Plan Schuman. Note pour le CMCE* dd. 24. 8. 1950.

equalization measures.[102] Agreement now hinged on the willingness of the Netherlands and Germany to shift their respective positions.

That shift in position had indeed occurred in the Netherlands where the cabinet endorsed the recommendation of the advisory committee that the government should accept a levy of fl. 1 per tonne on its coal prices, on the condition that Belgian prices were brought down immediately to the community level.[103] In Germany, however, resistance to paying levies was much greater. At a meeting of the delegation it was suggested that if Belgian coal and Italian steel required protection, it should be achieved by suspending the implementation of the common market in those cases. Should that fail, it was suggested that the French should be manoeuvered into a position where they too would have to pay. That, it was argued, should be sufficient to prize them away from their position of support for the Belgians.[104] These aims were embodied in the instructions drafted by the economics ministry.[105]

When, at a heads of delegation meeting on 4 September, Hallstein advanced the idea of arriving at a common market by stages, he was immediately rebuffed. His point that both levies and prices be kept as low as possible, «to ensure that the period of transition is realized by technical measures and not by financial means» was quietly supported by the Dutch.[106] In another context a German statement that prices should aim for «as much competition as possible, as much discipline as necessary» was interpreted in the Belgian report as «a very grave threat for the Belgian coal industry».[107] The question was obviously so far from a solution that the discussions were deferred until a later date to allow the heads of delegations to concentrate on the draft text for the treaty itself. Behind the scenes, however, Hirsch and the expert from the Belgian coal industry Vinck attempted to formulate a joint Franco-Belgian solution.

The negotiations reopened in November. One important change was that the Germans, having granted miners a 13 % wage increase, were considering

---

102 Min. AE (Bel) 5216 *Rapport sur les négociations autour du Plan Schuman* (Vinck) dd. 30. 12. 1950.

103 ARA, MR, 587 *Nota betreft hervatting besprekingen Plan Schuman* dd. 24. 8. 1950 (REA 30. 2. 1950). ARA, MR, 572 Minutes of the economic committee of cabinet 30. 8. 1950.

104 See note 25.

105 See note 26.

106 Min. AE (Bel) 5216 *Rapport à Monsieur le Ministre. Réunion concernant le Plan Schuman. Séance du 4-9-1950 (Groupe des Présidents), Compte-rendu de la réunion restreinte du lundi 4 septembre.* FJM, AMG, 8/2/23 *Summary of meetings of Heads of Delegations.* ARA, MR, 588 *Verslag over de besprekingen te Parijs betreffende het Schumanplan van 31 augustus–9 september 1950* (REA 20. 9.1950).

107 See note 67.

raising domestic coal prices by 6 DM per tonne which would have the effect of reducing the gulf between existing price levels and, thus, the total sums of money involved in any price equalisation scheme. On the other hand, this potential upward pressure on coal prices served to reinforce the Dutch desire to keep the size of the levy as small as possible.[108] Another important change was that apparent in French thinking. Firstly, the French had concluded that the cost of bringing all Belgian coal down to the community price would be too exorbitant and suggested that this exercise be confined to coking coal destined for the steel industry. On the other hand, they wanted a closure of Belgian production of 1 million tonnes p.a. Secondly, they agreed to waive their own claims to the equalization fund even though there would have to be mine closures in France as well. In return for this gesture, however, they expected to be exempted from levies on French coal.[109] These ideas were incorporated into a memorandum on 21 November. Among other things it specified that the height of the levy would be reduced by 20 % each year, thereby phasing them out totally over a period of five years. The one thing the memorandum failed to mention was the height of the original levy. Evidently unwilling to be embroiled in another potentially interminable wrangle over Italian steel, the memorandum suggested that a special regime of export licences and differential prices should be introduced.[110] This solution to the Italian problem virtually removed the issue from the agenda.

When the delegates met the Germans seized on the opportunity to allow some Belgian prices to remain above the Community level (thereby lowering the total sum involved) to push for a maximum levy of 2 %. The French favoured a greater reduction in Belgian prices and a maximum levy of 3 % (which, note, they themselves had no intention of paying). At this point the Belgians produced their own set of proposals which allowed for national government subsidies to a greater extent than originally envisaged but without conceding the necessity for mine closures.[111] Those closures, however, were considered a *quid-quo-pro* by the Germans and whilst Suétens was prepared once again to negotiate, he advised his government to accept. The coal owners, he added, «wonder if it is worth the trouble to give up our independence for a sum of 3 billion francs. This way of putting the problem is evidently a little simplistic.

---

108 Min. BZ, 996.1 Schuman Plan Algemeen III. Telex Kohnstamm and Blaisse to Spierenburg 16. 11. 1950.
109 Min. BZ, 996.1/45 *Verslag over de besprekingen te Parijs betreffende het Plan Schuman, van 8-18 november 1950.*
110 CD. *Mémorandum sur les dispositions transitoires* dd. 21. 11. 1950.
111 See Min. AE (Bel) 5216 *Etablissement du marché commun pour le charbon* dd. 24. 11. 1950.

The point is to know whether the liberty would allow us to solve the coal problems in a better way ... it is not possible indefinitely to support the burden on our economy of a price of coal 200 francs above the price of our chief competitor, Germany.»[112]

Whilst the Belgian position was drifting towards one of accepting a supranational solution to an acute national problem, the two countries which would have to pay for that solution were also taking stock. In the Netherlands the cabinet had already agreed to paying a levy on coal of up to fl. 1 per tonne. With a bit of guesswork on the future price of coal (fl. 35 per tonne) and the size of the levy (2 %), it looked as though the eventual figure would be lower. Even so, why should they be willing to pay anything at all? The calculation went as follows. The levy would amount to fl. 20–22 million over the five-year period. However, if the full reduction in the price of Belgian coke were to be reflected in a reduction in the price of steel, Dutch import prices could fall by between fl. 15 and fl. 20 per tonne. Since approximately 500.000 tonnes were imported each year, the total saving would be between fl. 37 and 50 millions over the five years – a sum far exceeding the cost to the economy of the levy. That net gain could be greater still if the Germans hardened their position.[113]

And the German negotiating position was indeed hardening ... Erhard informed Adenauer that he was reluctant that Germany should pay any levies at all, but were it to do so he felt that 1 % was the most the balance-of-payments could bear. Nor was he convinced that Germany would gain by being able to take up the gap in the market left by the closure of Belgian mines, partly because he did not believe it would happen and partly because he doubted whether, after satisfying domestic demand and export contracts, there would be sufficient capacity.[114]

In mid-December, when the heads of delegation met again, the Germans had lowered the maximum levy they were prepared to pay to 1.5 %. This had the effect of neutralizing the French suggestion of 2.5 %, but at least it ensured that the compromise figure was likely to be lower than before. The Belgians, in turn, were still insisting that they be continued to subsidize their mines for three years after the end of the transition period.[115] Eventually the figure was

112 Min. AE (Bel) 5216 *Note sur le problème de la péréquation des charbons belges* dd. 5. 12 1950.

113 ARA, Min. EZ, BEB, 559 *De prijsvorming voor kolen en staal gedurende de overgangsperiode van het Plan Schuman* dd. 27 11. 1950.

114 PAAA, Ref. 213, VSP, Akte 45, *Der Bundesminister für Wirtschaft an K. Adenauer: Stellungnahme zum Schumanplan*, 11. 12. 1950.

115 ARA, MR, 591 *Nota betreft Plan Schuman* dd. 28. 12. 1950 (REA 5. 1. 1951).

fixed at a maximum of 1.5 %.[116] Their main delegate, Vinck, was forced to conclude that the Belgians had squeezed out of the negotiations virtually all the concessions they were likely to get,[117] though the Belgian foreign minister Van Zeeland was still less than happy. He confided to the French ambassador that «proponents of the Plan wished to realise their goal by laying upon Belgium a form of dirigism which the country could not accept.»[118]

Cartels and restrictive practices

The issue which threatened to lead to a breakdown of the negotiations, long after the bulk of the Treaty (excepting those constitutional questions held over to the Ministers' conference) and the convention covering the transitional period had been agreed, was the two clauses on cartels and restrictive practices. The conflict which involved primarily, though not exclusively, France and Germany was fought out not only in the context of the Paris negotiations but also in the councils of the Allied High Commission in Frankfurt, where the issue at stake was the implementation of law 27 and the deconcentration of Germany heavy industry. In Paris it was the French who were to make the running, in Frankfurt the Americans. But exactly who was manipulating whom remains unclear.

The original Document de Travail had very little to say on the question beyond some general statements that the community would ensure identical competitive conditions and eliminate artificial impediments to competition. Yet Schuman's initial declaration in May had contained a statement that although the HA would have no say on regimes of ownership, it would recognize the powers of the Allied control bodies and would guarantee the implementation of any obligations imposed on Germany. A clause to this effect was incorporated into the Document de Travail.[119] From the start this had been received with serious misgivings in Germany where it was hoped that acceptance of the HA would imply a relaxation, even abolition, of Allied controls,[120] and in the summer, the German delegation was instructed to press for the modification of this clause using the argument that it was irreconcilable

---

116 ARA, MR, 591, Note Spierenburg to REA dd. 27. 1. 1951 (REA 29. 1. 1951).
117 Min. AE (Bel) 5216 *Note à Monsieur le Ministre (Service d'Etudes Economiques de l'industrie charbonnière)* dd. 22. 1. 1951.
118 AD, Europe 1949–1955, Généralités, Telegramme Hauteclocque to Quai d'Orsay 30. 1. 1951.
119 CD, *Document de Travail* dd. 24. 6. 1950 (art. 34).
120 See note 10.

61

with the principles of equality enshrined in the Schuman Plan.[121] This position
was forcibly conveyed to Monnet by Erhard at the end of September. How, he
asked, could Germany expect to participate in the community on an equal
footing, whilst the Allies were preparing at that very moment to reorganise
the coal and steel industry without any consultation with the German people?
If German industry were forced to enter the community in an unfavourable
position, he warned, it would be difficult to secure parliamentary approval.[122]
What the Germans wanted was a definition of unfair competiton based solely
on questions of the relationship between costs and prices; the HA should have
no powers to interfere in the social, financial or economic structure of the coal
and steel industry.[123]

Within the negotiations themselves the issue had lain dormant until 4 October
when Monnet,[124] «to the great surprise of all . . . in a tone which he did not
usually employ», condemned the existing provisions as totally inadequate and
«launched into a vigorous attack on cartels and agreements in general».[125]
Later, in the negotiations on prices, he returned to the same theme backing
his arguments with the threat that failure to take action on cartels, a point on
which the Americans had chosen to adopt a radical attitude, could jeopardise
chances of obtaining American financial support. He promised a new
document to serve as the basis for further discussion.[126]

The proposals, when they arrived, were sweeping indeed. Without HA
authorisation no agreements, formal or informal, were permitted which
interfered with the free play of market forces by fixing prices, by controlling
production or by sharing markets, products, clients or sources of supply. Not
only had the HA the right to scrutinise all new agreements, it could nullify any
existing ones. As far as ownership was concerned, no fusion (formal or
informal) or any participation of one firm in the share capital of another was
permitted without prior HA approval. Any individual who directly or
indirectly controlled 10 % of a firm's capital was prohibited from participating

121 PAAA, Ref. 213, VSP, Akte 45, *Kurzprotokoll der Sitzung des Kabinettsausschusses für den
    Schumanplan am Montag, dem 28. August, 15 Uhr, im Haus des Bundeskanzlers.*
122 FJM, AMG, 6/6/3 and AN 81 AJ 137 *Note pour Monsieur le Ministre sur l'entretien de J. Monnet
    avec L. Erhard* dd. 28. 9. 1950.
123 FJM, AMG, 8/3/19 *Stellungnahme zur Preishebung im Memorandum über die Einrichtungen
    und die wirtschaftlichen und sozialen Dauerbestimmungen des Schuman-Plans von 28. September
    1950. Entwurf einer Neufassung der Seiten 24. bis 29. einschliesslich des Memorandums vom
    28. September 1950.*
124 FJM, AMG, 17/8/64 *Observations sur le mémorandum du 28. 9. 1950, exposées par M. Jean
    Monnet au cours de la réunion restreinte des chefs de délégation, le 4. 10. 1950* dd. 5. 10. 1950.
125 Min. AE (Bel) 5216 *Note pour Monsieur le Ministre du commerce extérieur* dd. 9. 10. 1950.
126 Min. AE (Bel) 5216 *Note pour Monsieur le Ministre des affaires étrangères et Monsieur le
    Ministre du commerce extérieur* dd. 16. 10. 1950.

in any capacity in another firm. Finally no firm or group was permitted to control more than 20 % of the common market in coal or steel.[127] The virtually unanimous reaction to these proposals was that they went too far. Aimed at preventing monopolies, they had the effect of banning virtually any merger or agreement. This, Monnet admitted, was not his intention; what he wanted to ensure was that no new cartels in the Ruhr would rise and replace the ones being dismantled, once Allied controls had been relaxed. It was agreed that, at the very least, the HA could be allowed to grant exemptions but that still left the HA as the final arbiter in all such cases.[128] The debate then split into two camps. Italy and the Netherlands sided with the French. The Belgians, however, argued that enterprises had the right to conclude agreements among themselves to ensure that free competition did not degenerate into total disorganisation and that such agreements should only be prohibited if they actually went against the essentials of the Plan. In their opposition they received the muted support of the Germans.[129] The amended French drafts changed very little when they arrived at the beginning of December,[130] but they did attract unqualified American support. In a letter to various consular offices in Europe, Acheson disputed whether it was possible to distinguish between a ‹good› and a ‹bad› cartel: *any* cartel would have the effect of devolving economic power away from the HA and would fuel cynical American critics who would see the Plan as recognition of the power of producer groups.[131] The discussions on this question in Paris were virtually suspended for two months. In the forum of the Allied High Commission, however, the issue was coming to a head.

On 14 December Adenauer complained that the American attempts to «deconcentrate» Ruhr industry were turning industrialists against the Schuman Plan. He received little sympathy from the American High Commissioner, McCloy, who pointed out that the Germans should view deconcentration as a benefit rather than a punishment since its ultimate aim was to allow the Germans to enjoy greater efficiency, higher living standards and more employment.[132] Somewhat superfluously the French pointed out that it would

---

127 CD. *Propositions relatives à la mise en oeuvre du plan Schuman en ce qui concerne les accords et pratiques ou tendant à la constitution de monopoles* dd. 27. 10. 1950.
128 Min. BZ. 966.1/45 *Verslag over de besprekingen te Parijs betreffende het Plan Schuman van 8–18 november 1950.*
129 Min. AE (Bel) 5216 *Note concernant les articles 60 (ententes) et 61 (concentrations) du Projet de Traité* dd. 30. 3. 1951.
130 CD. *Mémorandum sur les art. 41 et 42* dd. 7. 12. 1950.
131 *FRUS* 1950 vol 3 762–763.
132 PRO, FO 321/85869 J.E. Killick to A.D. Wilson 19. 12. 1950.

be difficult for the French government to break its own steel cartel if German industry were left in an overwhelmingly favourable position.[133]

The deconcentration issue hinged on three major questions – the number of units into which the Ruhr industry was to be broken up, the number of steel concerns which were to be permitted to own their own mines and, finally, the fate of the German coal-sales organisation (the DKV)[134]. But even in Allied Councils opinion was divided. The official Allied demand was the breakdown of the Ruhr industry into 29 unit companies (reinforced by measures to prevent overlapping stock-ownership and overlapping directorships). Whilst these were backed by the French and Americans, they received only reluctant British support since the British felt that the measures went further than was strictly necessary.[135] On the question of the «captive mines» owned by steel companies, the Germans wanted a figure equivalent to 25–26 % of total coal consumption by the steel industry, the Americans between 10–15 %[136] and the British, who wanted each case examined separately on strictly technical merits, even less.[137] As far as the DKV was concerned, the French and Americans wanted it dissolved whilst the British felt they could side with the Germans who wanted its retention[138]. Eventually an agreed German/American compromise was worked out whereby the number of steel units was reduced to 24, only twelve of which were allowed to own coal mines (supplying no more than 75 % of the needs of each). This amounted to about 16 % of total consumption. These mines, however, were to be separately managed and subject to HA prices (i.e. they could no longer sell at transfer prices) and to any «allocations» policy of the HA in times of shortage (i.e. German steel mills could not continue at full capacity whilst those in France sat idle for lack of coal). The DKV was to be dismantled over a phased period.[139] The fact that the HA now had control over the pricing and, if necessary, distribution of the coal from the «captive mines» served to make the question of ownership much less pressing.

133 FJM, AMG, 10/3/5 *Proposed cable regarding articles 41 and 42* dd. 16. 12. 1950.
134 For the French position at the start of the discussions see AN 81 AJ 137, *Projet d'instructions, profondé par JM à R. Schuman* dd. 22. 12. 1950.
135 PRO, FO 371/93826 A.D. Wilson to D.S. Pitblado 12. 1. 1951.
136 PRO, T 230/182 *Minutes of meeting on Schuman Plan/Law 27 probably held 29. 1. 1951.*
137 PRO, FO 371/93826 Foreign Office to I. Kirkpatrick 13. 2. 1951.
138 PRO, T 230/182 *Minutes of meeting on Schuman Plan/Law 27 probably held 29. 1. 1951.*
139 PRO, FO 371/93826 E. Roll to W. Hayter 5. 2. 1951. FJM, AMG, 13/2/10, AN 81 AJ 137, AN 363AP/17/1 *Mémorandum sur la déconcentration de la Ruhr et la conclusion des négociations sur le Plan Schuman* dd. 8. 3. 1951. FJM, AMG, 13/3/6, AN 363AP/17/3 *Lettre du chancellier Adenauer à la Haute Commission* dd. 14. 3.1951.

64

Whilst this had been going on, Monnet had been trying to drag a response out of the Germans on the proposed draft articles left undecided on 7 December. In January he had informed Hallstein, «if the conference cannot agree upon the provisions in substantially their present form, there is no alternative but to report the failure of the conference to our respective governments».[140] But it was not only Germany which opposed the drafts. The Belgian government, too, accepting in their entirety the arguments of the steel industry,[141] felt that they were altogether too absolute. It stood by the fact that agreements to prevent disorganisation of markets should be permitted and it felt that HA powers on ownership were too sweeping for the achievement of the end-goal (to prevent any group capturing more than 20 % of the market in coal or steel).[142] At the beginning of February, talks on the disputed articles resumed. The Germans, again, remained essentially passive leaving it to Belgium and Luxembourg to make the running. Suétens attempted to put a positive gloss on the matter. Private associations would be able to help the HA in its tasks. At the same time he warned Monnet that his position entailed the risk of turning producers against the Plan.[143] Monnet's reaction remains unrecorded, but in the course of the discussions one important change was made. Whereas the December drafts *permitted* the HA to recognize certain agreements or mergers, the revised texts *obliged* this recognition if certain criteria were met.[144]

Still the Germans refused to budge. On 19 February, Monnet informed McCloy that if the Germans did not reach agreement over deconcentration, they would be confronted not only with the odium of having torpedoed the Schuman Plan but they would also be faced with deconcentration measures harsher than the ones under discussion.[145] But this was exactly what the Germans were afraid of. Would they, after reaching agreement with the Allies, be free from a further round of deconcentration this time emanating from the HA? There was nothing in the draft articles to oblige the HA to interpret the criteria on deconcentration in the same way as the Allied High Commission.[146] Eventually agreement was reached on a draft article which

---

140 FJM, AMG. 11/2/13 *First draft of a letter from JM to W. Hallstein* dd. 7. 1. 1951.
141 Min. AE (Bel) 5216 *Note à Monsieur le Ministre* (A. Biernaux), dd. 22. 12. 1950.
142 Min. AE (Bel) 5216 *Note exposant les principales questions restant à discuter* dd. 9. 1. 1951.
143 Min. AE (Bel) 5216 Suétens to Meurice dd. 6. 2. 1951.
144 Min. AE (Bel) 5216 *Plan Schuman. Note concernant les articles 60 (ententes) et 61 (concentrations) du projet de traité* dd. 30. 3. 1951.
145 FJM, AMG, 12/3/6, AN 81 AJ 137, *Compte-rendu d'une conversation téléphonique de Monnet avec McCloy* dd. 19. 2. 1951.
146 FJM, AMG, 13/2/8 *Note sur l'article 61 et la déconcentration de la Ruhr* dd. 25. 2. 1951.

exempted all *past* concentrations of ownership, as long as they did not impinge on the Plan's ideals, but retained HA control over all future ones. The Belgians were put under enormous American pressure by McCloy who «was of the opinion that the Germans would use the argument of Belgian reserves on this subject to reinforce their resistance . . . in brief he demanded that we be more accommodating».[147] The Belgians complied, so that with both issues settled, the way was cleared for the initialling of the Treaty by the heads of delegations on 19 March 1951.

That left just one small problem – the British. Their dilemma was succinctly expressed in the Foreign Office instruction to the British High Commissioner, Kirkpatrick; «On the one hand we do not wish to be jockeyed into accepting agreements on important aspects of law 27 arrived at as a result of discussions in which we took no part and which appear to be inconsistent with our view that [etc.] . . . on the other hand we obviously do not wish to lay ourselves open to the charge of sabotaging progress towards the initialling of the Schuman Plan at a delicate stage».[148] That dilemma remained unresolved when the High Commissioners met at the end of March to approve the deconcentration agreement. With the added knowledge that the French and Americans would in all probability be prepared to outvote them, the British grudgingly gave their approval, adding only the proviso that the subject should be reopened if the treaty were not ratified.[149] On 30 march, Adenauer was officially informed of the Allies' acceptance. The stage was now set for the Ministers' Conference in Paris the following month.

The Ministers' Conference

The foreign ministers of the six met in Paris from 12–18 April to fill in the gaps still left open in the draft treaty and then to sign it. Were matters to have developed that way, there would have been no real reason to consider it in this chapter since most of those points concerned institutional questions. On the other hand, even though the draft treaty had been initialled by the heads of delegations, the ministers were free to raise any point they wished and to suggest article amendments. Van Zeeland, at last responding to the swelling chorus of protest in Belgium, was the only minister to take advantage of this

147 Min. AE (Bel) 5216 Telegram Gruben to Foreign Affairs 16. 3. 1951.
148 See note 137.
149 PRO, FO 371/93828 Commonwealth Relations Office to various Commonwealth governments
    9. 4. 1951.

opportunity and arrived at the conference armed with a list of treaty amendments which, if discussed, threatened to unravel the entire package. When it became clear that none of the others had the slightest intention of countenancing such a step, he withdrew all but one of his demands.

Van Zeeland's one remaining demand represented a last-ditch attempt to delay as long as possible, even indefinitely, the participation of the Belgian coal industry in the common market. The only undivided support he received was from the Luxembourg foreign minister, Bech. However the others did come some way towards meeting Belgian demands by agreeing to a number of changes in Paragraph 26.4 of the convention of the transition period which permitted the HA to twice postpone for a period of one year Belgium's entry into the common market. Moreover, even after that moment, the Belgian government was to be allowed to continue to subsidize coal production but only insofar as it compensated for the additional costs incurred arising from unfavourable geological conditions. Van Zeeland's demand that this concession should also be extended to compensate for relatively high wages was rejected, though the HA could allow even higher subsidies if the impact of not granting them were considered detrimental to the Belgian economy as a whole. Van Zeeland extracted one further concession which in fact undermined much of the rationale of the transitional arrangements. These had envisaged that unviable Belgian mines would be closed and that coal production would be reduced to 23.5 million tonnes. It seemed logical that, if that were to be the target figure, there was little point in subsidizing the rest. In the face of Van Zeeland's insistence that closures of this magnitude would be a social disaster, the rest gave way and conceded the possibility that subsidies could cover coal production over and above that limit.[150] What the Belgian government had acquired was the right, if it played its cards right, to continue to subsidize its entire coal industry as long as it was considered socially or economically necessary. If, at any time, it chose not to exercise that right, it could transfer the political odium for mine closures to the HA. What it had failed to achieve in months of negotiations, it had obtained at this last moment – a concession by the rest who were unwilling to see the entire fabric of their work collapse on such a ‹minor› point.

The remarkable talent which the negotiations displayed for brinkmanship was shown in yet another area: the question of the Ruhr Authority. As long before as November, the French government had decided that once the treaty were

---

150 ARA, Min. EZ, BEB, 557 *Minister-conferentie Plan Schuman Parijs 12–18 april 1951* dd. 7. 5. 1951.

67

fully implemented, the continued existence of the Ruhr Authority was neither necessary nor even possible.[151] This decision was not communicated to the German government until January 1951, at which time the French suggested that the Ruhr Authority should cease to exist when its functions could be taken over and exercised by the HA.[152] This construction, however, had singularly failed to please the Germans who wanted the Ruhr Authority to cease from the moment the treaty was signed and not from the moment it came into operation, arguing that *Germans* should be allowed to transfer *German* sovereignty to the HA.[153] Eventually Monnet suggested a compromise whereby a note from the French government would commit it to working towards the abolition of the Ruhr Authority when the treaty was ratified and when the transition arrangements had come into operation,[154] a compromise accepted by the French government.[155]

A draft text now lay before the ministers for their approval. This went altogether too far for the British. «To lay it down as an axiom . . . that arrangements which have been tripartitely agreed conflict with proposals under the Schuman Plan to which the other Occupying Powers are not party and the detailed operations of which they are not fully familiar is particularly objectionable as is the statement . . . that the High Commission should give up the exercise *by itself* of functions in the matter of coals and steel». The Foreign Office felt that the letter should only be sent after the other occupying powers had been consulted.[156] Schuman was unmoved by the British protests. He claimed that he had tried and failed to persuade Adenauer to delay handing over the letter until Germany had ratified the Treaty. Similarly Adenauer had turned down a suggestion that the letter be handed over but not published until the British agreed – «an unpublished letter was as bad as no letter at all». Schuman did agree, however, to softening the tone in an attempt to make it more palatable.[157]

The British were not in a position to do much at all. The revised text merely committed the French to acting on the Germans' behalf. The fault was that

---

151 FJM, AMG, 9/5/1, AN 81 AJ 137, *Note de F. Valery sur l'Autorité de la Ruhr et la Communauté charbon-acier* dd. 7. 11. 1950.

152 AN 81 AJ 148 Monnet to Hirsch 8. 1.1951

153 AN 81 AJ 148 *Note objections de la délégation allemande au projet de lettre ci-joint* dd. 19. 2.1951.

154 AN 81 AJ 148 Monnet to Schuman 10. 3. 1951.

155 AN 81 AJ 148 *Projet de lettre au gouvernement de la République Federale Allemande* dd. 11. 4. 1951.

156 PRO, FO 371/93828 Telegram Foreign Office to Paris dd. 17. 4. 1951.

157 PRO, FO 371/93829 Telegrams Paris Embassy to Foreign Office dd. 18. 5. 1951 (nos. 148, 149).

the French had not consulted their partners in advance, and a procedural objection was hardly grounds for wrecking the conference. As the UK ambassador in Paris, William Hayter confided to the Foreign Office, «I confess I am not quite sure why we were so worked up about it». The French had claimed that they were only expressing their own opinion. «In reply to this I asked both Charpentier and Bourbon Busset (Schuman's chef de cabinet) what they would think if the British government in a letter to the Germans expressed their opinion that the Germans ought to have an army of 20 divisions, subject of course to French approval.»[158]

Conclusions

Almost a year had passed between Schuman's initial declaration and the signing of a treaty which embodied his aims. The forty articles in the *Document de Travail* had been expanded to a hundred and it was accompanied by a separate convention on the transition period, a copy of a Franco-Italian agreement on Algerian iron ore supplies, and the French letter on the Ruhr Authority. All of these were the outward signs of the conflicts, struggles and compromises which accompany any negotiating process. And, like all conclusion it is worth examining briefly the governments' reactions to their work.

Ironically, it was the Dutch, originally the most sceptical of the participants, who appeared to be the most satisfied with the end result. In January 1951 the cabinet had concluded that most of its aims and objections had been accommodated in the treaty and praise was lavished upon the negotiating skills of the delegation.[159] Italy, too, once it had obtained protection for its steel plants and guarantees on the question of iron ore supplies, had cause for satisfaction with the treaty itself. The industrial minister, Togni, however, felt that the Treaty still left insufficient safeguards for the Italian steel industry and wanted the sentiment expressed quite clearly at the Ministers' Conference in Paris,[160] whilst Pella was inclined to turn his back on the entire sectoral approach which, he felt, could only damage Italian interests.[161] Moreover, Italy had had to surrender its broader policy goals on matters as migration and

---

158 Ibid., W. Hayter to R.B. Stevens 19. 4. 1951.
159 ARA, MR, 572 Minutes of the economic committee of cabinet 5. 1. 1951.
160 ACS, Archivo Sforza, sc. 6 f.iv. Togni to Sforza 6. 4. 1951.
161 ACS, Verbali del Consiglio dei ministri, dd. 7. 4. 1951 and 9. 4. 1951.

large-scale international finance for this industry.[162] Both of these countries, however, were relatively small producers and whatever resistance there might have been from producer interests, considerations of security of supplies were paramount.

Far more ambivalent were the reactions in the other countries. The Luxembourg cabinet found the draft treaty much too dirigist for its liking, preferring a system «more liberal, more supple and more practical»,[163] but it was more concerned at losing its favoured position within the Belgian market. It complained bitterly that Belgian steel producers would benefit from community-financed subsidies on the coking coal they required whilst those in Luxembourg would pay more for their Ruhr coal,[164] but to no avail. Monnet's position was that Luxembourg was not being discriminated against but was being treated on the same footing as the rest,[165] and since this was true,[166] there was little else to be done other than to be content with a statement recognising the special importance of steel to the economy and the right to appeal directly to the HA for special treatment. The Belgian reaction, as we have seen, was a mixture of satisfaction at having obtained supranational help to solve a national problem, relief at having obtained the right not to solve it, should the government so wish, and a fear for the reaction of organised producer interests who had lost their former privileges. On the other hand, it was argued in an undated note that, from the point of view of security of supplies, if a community was to be formed, Belgium could not afford to be outside it.[167]

Germany could not afford to stay outside the pool either, but for rather different reasons. The Treaty of Paris was an integral part of the peace settlement. The reward for surrendering some sovereignty to a supranational authority was the recovery of national sovereignty over the domestic economy.[168] In this process, French agreement was essential and Monnet's threat during the negotiations on the cartel question which boiled down to saying «accept this or face something much worse» was not an idle one.

162 See Ranieri, *Italy and the Schuman Plan Negotiations*.
163 FJM, AMG 11/2/7 Wehrer to Monnet 9. 1. 1951.
164 FJM, AMG 18/5/4 Note from the Luxembourg delegation 1. 12.1951. FJM, AMG 18/5/5 *Note pour Monsieur le Ministre des Affaires Etrangères* dd. 7. 12.1951. The Luxembourg steel interests felt betrayed by the lack of bilateral consultation by the Belgian delegation. Min. AE (L) 11385, *Plan Schuman. Projet de Rapport Final. Cas de l'acier luxembourgeois* dd. 24. 1.1951.
165 FJM, AMG 11/2/9 Monnet to Wehrer 20. 1.1950.
166 FJM, AMG 11/2/12 Monnet to Schuman 27. 1.1950.
167 Min. AE (Bel) 5216 *Si le Plan Schuman se réalise sans la participation de la Belgique quelle sera sa situation? La Belgique. sera-t-elle assez forte pour resister?* n.d.
168 See Steinert, *Un saut dans l'inconnu*, 176–178.

The reaction of the French cabinet, when at last it was consulted in mid-December, was openly hostile. Nobody apparently disagreed with Monnet's exposition of the macro-economic advantages of the community,[169] but there was deep disquiet over the powers of the High Authority. René Mayer, reacting on behalf of the ministries of finance and economic affairs, raised a whole list of objections to the draft treaty which, he helpfully explained, «are aimed at reducing the risks implied in a transfer of sovereignty to an indispensable minimum.» In much the same spirit was the reply of Bourgès-Maunoury, secretary-of-state to the president of the council, in which he asked Monnet «to inform me precisely how to answer the objections which have been formulated in respect of the powers of the High Authority which surpass enormously those approved by national governments of democratic countries even in war time.»[170] Such sentiments were to be heard far more vociferously expressed when the treaty eventually came up for ratification by the national parliaments.

169 FJM, AMG 22/2/1 *Note relative aux effets du Plan Schuman sur les industries du charbon et de l'acier en France* dd. 9. 12. 1950.
170 AN 363 AP 17/1; FJM, AMG 22/4/2 *Documents relatifs aux observations des ministres* dd. 15. 1. 1951. This includes copies of the ministers' letters and Monnet's replies.

Part VII
The European Economic Community

[15]

Paths to Plenty: Marshall Planners and the Debate over European Integration, 1947–1948

Michael J. Hogan

The author is a member of the history department in Miami University.

THE MARSHALL PLAN is generally regarded as among the most successful peacetime foreign policies launched by the United States in this century. Yet thirty-five years after its inception, we still lack a comprehensive account of this celebrated American initiative. Much of the existing literature is based on limited research in archival and manuscript collections which have only recently become available; and most of the rest focuses narrowly on the developments preceding Secretary of State George C. Marshall's famous proposal, at Harvard University in June 1947; on the Soviet Union's refusal to cooperate in European recovery; and on the anti-Communist motives that infused American policy. But as John Gimbel has pointed out, American leaders had not devised a concrete "plan" for rebuilding Europe at the time of Marshall's speech. Nor had their planning proceeded very far when Soviet officials withdrew from the Foreign Ministers Conference that met in Paris to consider Marshall's proposal in late June and early July. As a result, we know little about the planning process itself or about the negotiations between the United States and its

337

European partners over the nature and purposes of what became the European Recovery Program.[1]

This article attempts to fill part of the gap by describing the planning process in the critical months following Marshall's speech and the collapse of the Paris Foreign Ministers Conference. It argues that American leaders had goals besides Communist containment, goals that would have shaped their diplomacy regardless of the perceived Communist menace and goals that were challenged as often by their European partners as by the Soviet Union. Foremost among them were the interrelated goals of economic integration and enhanced productivity in Europe. Any recovery plan, as the Americans saw it, should seek to eliminate the economic waste, inefficiency, and duplication that had hampered production in Europe and prevented previous American programs of piecemeal assistance from stimulating recovery. Their proposal was to remove the traditional economic and territorial constraints on European enterprise and to forge instead a single, large, functionally ordered and organically integrated economic community. The plan should, in other words, apply the Ameri-

The author would like to thank the Miami University Faculty Research Council, the Harry S. Truman Library, and the Woodrow Wilson International Center for Scholars for financial assistance in the completion of this work. He would also like to thank Kurt S. Schultz for research assistance, Pamela Messer for help with the typing, and Professor Ellis W. Hawley for organizational and stylistic suggestions.

[1] The relevant literature includes Harry B. Price, *The Marshall Plan and Its Meaning* (Ithaca, 1955); Joseph M. Jones, *The Fifteen Weeks (February 21–June 5, 1947)* (New York, 1955); Robert H. Ferrell, *George C. Marshall* (New York, 1966); Louis J. Halle, *The Cold War as History* (New York, 1967); Adam B. Ulam, *Expansion and Coexistence: The History of Soviet Foreign Policy, 1917–1967* (New York, 1968); Joyce Kolko and Gabriel Kolko, *The Limits of Power: The World and United States Foreign Policy, 1945–1954* (New York, 1972); Thomas G. Paterson, *Soviet-American Confrontation: Postwar Reconstruction and the Origins of the Cold War* (Baltimore, 1973); John Gimbel, *The Origins of the Marshall Plan* (Stanford, 1976); Walter LaFeber, *America, Russia, and the Cold War, 1945–1975* (New York, 1976); and Fred L. Block, *The Origins of International Economic Disorder* (Berkeley, 1977). For Gimbel's comment on the state of American recovery planning at the time of Marshall's Harvard speech, see his *Origins of the Marshall Plan,* 6–15. More recent works have begun to break new ground in the study of the Marshall Plan. Hadley Arkes considers the connection between bureaucratic administration and national interest in the recovery program; Armin Rappaport describes the integrationist thrust in American diplomacy toward Europe; and Charles S. Maier analyzes "the politics of productivity" in recovery policy. See Arkes, *Bureaucracy, the Marshall Plan, and the National Interest* (Princeton, 1972); Rappaport, "The United States and European Integration: The First Phase," *Diplomatic History,* V (1981), 121–149; Maier, "The Politics of Productivity: Foundations of American International Economic Policy After World War II," *International Organization* XXXI (1977), 607–633; and Maier, "The Two Postwar Eras and the Conditions for Stability in Twentieth-Century Western Europe," *American Historical Review,* LXXXVI (1981), 327–352.

can idea of federalism in Europe in order to create what John Foster Dulles called a market "big enough to justify modern methods of cheap production for mass consumption."[2] This was the path to increased productivity and recovery on the continent.

Barriers existed to putting this strategy into operation. The Europeans were skeptical of any recovery plan that transcended national sovereignties. There were also disagreements among American officials over the best way to optimize output and integrate Europe. These disputes became clear in the second half of 1947, when the Committee on European Economic Cooperation met in Paris to draft a recovery program. Previous historians have slighted the trans-Atlantic debates over the nature of the recovery plan and the differences within the American government. It seems appropriate to consider them in some detail now. An examination of these developments will tell us more than we now know about American recovery planning and about the different stabilization strategies that would characterize European and American diplomacy during the subsequent history of the Marshall Plan.

Through the spring of 1947, American policy makers had stressed the importance of European initiative and responsibility in drafting a recovery program. But they were willing to provide the Europeans with limited amounts of "friendly aid" in the drafting process and had enumerated a set of planning principles to guide European and American action. These principles included maximum European self-help and mutual aid, joint programming, resource sharing, and German reconstruction. According to Under Secretary of State William L. Clayton and others, these were the keys to eliminating the "small watertight compartments" into which Europe had become divided and to building instead an "economic federation" that could utilize German resources and unleash European productivity.[3] They were also the principles that guided American recovery planning in the months ahead.

---

[2] Dulles, "Europe Must Federate or Perish: America Must Offer Inspiration and Guidance," *Vital Speeches of the Day,* XIII (Feb. 1, 1947), 234–236.

[3] For American thinking in the spring of 1947, see my "The Search for a 'Creative Peace': The United States, European Unity, and the Origins of the Marshall Plan," *Diplomatic History,* VI (1982), 267–285. For Clayton's remark, see his memorandum of May 27, 1947, U.S. Dept. of State, *Foreign Relations of the United States, 1947,* Vol. 3: *The British Commonwealth: Europe* (Washington, D.C., 1972), 230–232 (hereafter cited as *Foreign Relations, 1947,* III).

Following Marshall's speech at Harvard, the State Department's planning for European recovery went forward in George Kennan's Policy Planning Staff and in the new Committee on the European Recovery Program. The Recovery Committee, known informally as the "Board of Directors" or the "Tuesday-Thursday Group," had been organized in late June to consider the proposal which Marshall had recently announced. Chaired by Willard Thorp, the Assistant Secretary of State for Economic Affairs, it met every Tuesday and Thursday evening in the Old State Department Building and was composed of representatives from every departmental office concerned with recovery policy. Among its members there was broad agreement on the need to revive European production and integrate the European economies. To achieve these goals, it was argued, the United States would have to retain a veto over the distribution of its aid and the direction of the recovery program. It would also have to negotiate bilateral agreements binding each of the participating countries to the principles of self-help, mutual aid, and joint programming. The United States also would have to concentrate on providing short-term commodity assistance, leaving the World Bank responsible for long-term modernization loans. This would be necessary in order to limit the financial burden on American taxpayers and make Europe self-supporting in the quickest possible time.[4]

Beyond these points there were important disputes between *traders* and *producers* factions over the best way to enhance production and foster integration. For traders on the committee, expanding intra-European trade was the key to optimizing production; and the way to expand trade was by integrating the European economies. They wanted to replace the present pattern of nonconvertible currencies and bilateral commercial agreements on the continent with a currency clearing scheme and a customs union, both of which, they believed, would liberate European productivity from the constraints inherent in a segmented market. But for

---

[4] For the origins and membership of the Recovery Committee, see Ben T. Moore to Clair Wilcox, July 28, 1947, folder:5.17.10, ERP Subject File, Board of Directors, box 13113, lot 122, Records of the Committee on the Recovery Program, Department of State Records, Record Group 353, National Archives, Washington, D.C. (hereafter cited as RG 353 preceded by folder and box designations); and minutes of the first meeting of the Committee on the European Recovery Program, June 25, 1947, folder: REP minutes, box 26, RG 353. For the agreement on substantive issues among members of the committee, see the sources cited in the following two notes.

the producers faction such measures would not become important until production had revived; negotiating them now would only provoke enervating controversies that could retard recovery. They wanted instead to concentrate on restoring Europe's existing industries and increasing production in such bottleneck areas as coal, transportation, power, and agriculture. Once more, while the traders counted on normal market mechanisms to forge a rational pattern of production and exchange, the producers seemed sympathetic with supra-national planning as a way to coordinate national production and investment decisions, eliminate waste, inefficiency, and duplication, and thus engineer a functional integration of the European economies.[5]

These debates finally resulted in a compromise that favored the producers' approach. In the long run, it was agreed, the United States should encourage the Europeans to abandon statist planning and control, adopt the principles of multilateralism embodied in the proposed ITO charter, and, in this way, permit normal market mechanisms to eliminate uneconomic forms of production and create an efficient pattern of economic activity. In the short term, however, other priorities should apply. To be sure, the United States should attack the most flagrant trade restrictions and bilateral commercial arrangements, look "with favor" on a customs union, and consider support for a currency clearing scheme. But, above all, it should provide basic grants for essential commodities and for those items of capital equipment that would restore existing industries and eliminate the bottlenecks to production. In doing so, the United States should also foster integration in such key sectors as coal, transportation, and power. And during the recovery period at least, it should insist on a supranational organization with authority to allocate scarce resources and surplus production, set production targets in participating countries, coordinate national recovery plans, and thereby further the process of functional integration.[6]

---

[5]This analysis is based on the discussions in the committee's first six meetings, and on several of the many documents which the committee considered. See Committee on the European Recovery Program, minutes of meetings, June 25, July 1, 3, 8, 10, and 15, 1947, folder: REP minutes, box 26, RG 353; Charles P. Kindleberger, "Scope of Secretary Marshall's Suggestion to Europe," July 2, 1947; Willard Thorp to George Kennan, undated memorandum; unsigned and undated memoranda entitled, "Impediments to Intra-European Trade" and "Note on a European Customs Union," all in folder: REP Documents, box 27, RG 353.

[6]In addition to the minutes of meetings cited in the preceeding note, see the Committee

342	PACIFIC HISTORICAL REVIEW

The thinking in Kennan's Policy Planning Staff ran along similar lines. By mid-July the staff had finished a hefty paper on "Certain Aspects of the European Recovery Problem from the United States Standpoint." In this paper it reviewed the cause of Europe's distress and the factors that impeded recovery. The staff paper then went on to note how continued deterioration could imperil American interests, to explain why these interests made a comprehensive aid program imperative, and to offer recommendations that generally paralleled those emerging from the Recovery Committee. In these it drew the same distinction between commodity grants and long-term loans; laid the same emphasis on multilateralizing European currencies and commerce, supporting a European clearing arrangement, and, eventually, promoting a European customs union; and gave the same priority to restoring existing industrial capacity, breaking bottlenecks, and fostering functional integration.[7] The United States, Kennan had explained earlier, should follow the "functional approach" and concentrate its aid on those "key" sectors that lent themselves to treatment on an overall European basis.[8]

Both groups adopted similar positions toward Great Britain and Germany, stressing in each case the familiar themes of production and integration. They agreed that Britain must occupy a "unique" position in the recovery program, partly because of her great dependence on extra-European trade, partly because it would be difficult to reconcile the British system of imperial preference with American designs for an integrated Europe and a multilateral system of world trade, and partly because any shortage of outside assistance might compel the financially beleaguered British to adopt restrictive commercial policies that would retard recovery and wreck American efforts to promote

on the European Recovery Program, minutes of meetings, July 24 and 31, 1947, folder: REP Minutes, box 26, RG 353; and Kindleberger, two undated memoranda entitled, "Problems of Procedure in U.S. Aid to Europe" in folder: REP Documents, box 28, RG 353.

[7] Policy Planning Staff/4, "Certain Aspects of the European Recovery Problem from the United States Standpoint," July 23, 1947, *Reports and Recommendations, 1947*, I, box 3, Records of the Policy Planning Staff, Record Group 59, National Archives, Washington, D.C. (hereafter cited as RG 59 preceded by file and/or box designation). See also Kennan to Robert A. Lovett, June 30, 1947, folder: Chronological 1947, box 33, RG 59.

[8] Kennan to Thorp, June 24, 1947, in *Foreign Relations, 1947*, III, 267–268.

multilateralism. Yet they also agreed that Britain should be held to the principles of multilateralism and incorporated into an integrated *European* recovery program. Special assistance to the British, they insisted, should be considered only if Marshall Plan aid failed to solve Britain's serious balance-of-payments problem.[9]

So far as Germany was concerned, both groups stressed the need for new measures to revive German production and make the Anglo-American bizone self-supporting. A revival would relieve the burden of occupation on American taxpayers and increase the contribution which Germany could make to European recovery. But the United States, they also argued, should avoid treating the bizone as an American "enclave." It should balance recovery there against recovery in the liberated areas, incorporate Germany into an integrated European economy, and adjust its production and trade to the requirements of a European recovery program. As they saw it, this was the key to reconciling Germany's revival with the security and economic concerns of her neighbors and to persuading the Europeans to adopt the "supra-national" approach to recovery planning favored in the State Department.[10]

In line with this thinking, the State Department made a series of successful policy initiatives during the second half of 1947. It won support from the War Department for Germany's inclusion in European recovery planning.[11] It persuaded the British to suspend temporarily their plans to socialize the Ruhr coal mines, placing them instead under a private German management which presumably would be more efficient.[12] It also agreed to

---

[9]Kennan to Lovett, June 30, 1947, folder: Chronological, 1947, box 33, RG 59; Policy Planning Staff/4, "Certain Aspects of the European Recovery Problem"; Committee on the European Recovery Program, minutes of meetings, July 10, 17, and 24, 1947, folder: REP Minutes, box 26, RG 353; and "Special Consideration for Britain under the Marshall Plan," undated memorandum, folder: REP Documents, box 27, RG 353.

[10]Kennan to Lovett, June 30, 1947; Policy Planning Staff/4, "Certain Aspects of the European Recovery Problem"; Committee on the European Recovery Program, minutes of meetings, June 25 and July 17, 22, 24, and 29, 1947, folder: REP Minutes, box 26, RG 353; Kindleberger, "Problems of Procedure in U.S. Aid to Europe"; and Melvin L. Manfull to the Committee on the European Recovery Program, July 2, 1947, enclosing "Questions Concerning the Relation of the US-UK Zones in Germany to the General Problem of European Recovery," folder: REP Documents, box 27, RG 353; and the enclosures in Manfull to the Committee on the European Recovery Program, July 9, 1947, *ibid.*

[11]Gimbel, *Origins of the Marshall Plan,* 249–250.

[12]For this story, see the documents in U.S. Dept. of State, *Foreign Relations of the United States, 1947,* Vol. 2: *Council of Foreign Ministers: Germany and Austria* (Washington, D.C.,

consider sympathetically a French proposal for an international authority to oversee the Ruhr. And in December, it secured French agreement to a revised bizonal level-of-industry plan which the Anglo-American occupation authorities had negotiated earlier.[13] The bizonal plan, it assumed, could help to make Germany self-supporting and enhance its contribution to European recovery. The Ruhr authority, on the other hand, was in line with its efforts to facilitate the kind of supra-national planning and economic integration envisioned in the Marshall Plan.[14]

These successes were tempered by developments in Paris. There, both European and American leaders were taking positions opposed to the State Department's strategy. Under Secretary of State Clayton and other American officials in Europe did not support the statist planning called for in the producers' approach. They put their faith instead in unfettered market mechanisms and, like the traders on the Recovery Committee, were more inclined to stress the importance of reducing tariffs, stabilizing currencies, and creating a European customs union. Among the Europeans, on the other hand, there was great reluctance to accept the principles of self-help, mutual aid, and joint programming or to sacrifice national interest and sovereignty in order to accommodate American plans for reviving production and unifying Europe.

British and French leaders had convened a multinational conference to meet in Paris on July 12, 1947. It was to survey European resources and needs, draft a comprehensive recovery scheme, and present the results to the American government no later than September 1.[15] Altogether, sixteen nations — Austria,

---

1972), 924–925, 927–933, 940–942, 946–966; Gimbel, *Origins of the Marshall Plan,* 207–215; and U.S. Dept. of State, *Bulletin,* XVII (Sept. 21, 1947), 576–584.

[13] For the Franco-American negotiations over the Ruhr and the bizonal level of industry, see *Foreign Relations, 1947,* II, 983–1067; and Gimbel, *Origins of the Marshall Plan,* 225–242, 252–253.

[14] According to a State Department memorandum: "It appears that the basic conception behind the American approach to the Ruhr problem . . . may be realized, at least in Western Europe, through the Marshall Plan which aims at a coordinated and equitable utilization of key industrial resources in the interest of European economic recovery." See the memorandum attached to John D. Hickerson to Lovett, Aug. 23, 1947, *Foreign Relations, 1947,* II, 1050–1054.

[15] Jefferson Caffery to George C. Marshall, telegram #2667, July 3, 1947, *Foreign Relations, 1947,* III, 308–309; and Caffery to Marshall, telegram #2668, July 3, 1947, file: 840.50 Recovery/7-347, RG 59.

Belgium, Denmark, France, Greece, Great Britain, Iceland, Ireland, Italy, Luxembourg, the Netherlands, Norway, Portugal, Sweden, Switzerland, and Turkey — were represented.[16] The occupation authorities provided the conference with information concerning the bizone.[17] The Poles and Czechs, bowing to Soviet pressure, refused to attend; and the Scandinavians were present only on condition that the conference not bypass the United Nations, interfere with their trade in Eastern Europe, or compromise their neutrality.[18]

The harmonious spirit of the conference's first days soon gave way to acrimonious debate over the nature of the recovery program. Following a Franco-British plan, the conferees easily agreed to organize themselves into a Committee on European Economic Cooperation (CEEC). They also agreed to establish four technical committees to investigate the key economic sectors of food and agriculture, coal and steel, power, and transportation, and an Executive Committee to direct the work of the conference.[19] But the British and French dominated the Executive Committee and tried to steer the CEEC toward their version of the recovery program. They urged the conferees to draft a program that would concentrate on modernizing Europe's capital equipment and plant facilities. The Americans, they argued, wanted assurances concerning Europe's self-sufficiency when the Marshall Plan ended, and a comprehensive program of reconstruction and modernization would be necessary to achieve this goal.[20]

---

[16]Caffery to Marshall, July 13, 1947, file: 840.50 Recovery/7-1347. RG 59.

[17]Caffery to Marshall, telegram #2668, July 3, 1947, *Foreign Relations, 1947*, III, 308–309; and unsigned memorandum of conversation, July 25, 1947, file 840.50 Recovery/7-2547, RG 59.

[18]The Polish and Czech stories can be followed in the documents in *Foreign Relations, 1947*, III, 31–327; and in Llewellan E. Thompson, memorandum of conversation, July 11, 1947, file: 840.50 Recovery/7-1147, RG 59. On the policy of the Scandinavian countries, see Caffery to Marshall, July 10, 1947, *Foreign Relations, 1947*, III, 316–317; U.S. embassy, Denmark to the Secretary of State, despatch #234, July 11, 1947, file: 840.50 Recovery/7-1147, RG 59; U.S. embassy, Norway, to the Secretary of State, despatch #1220, July 15, 1947, file: 840.50 Recovery/7-1547, RG 59; U.S. embassy, Norway to Marshall, July 16, 1947, file: 840.50 Recovery/7-1657, RG 59; and memorandum of conversation of July 15, 1947, enclosed in U.S. embassy, Norway to the Secretary of State, despatch #1236, July 22, 1947, file: 840.50 Recovery/7-2247, RG 59.

[19]Caffery to Marshall, July 13, 1947; and Caffery to Marshall, July 14, 1947, file: 840.50 Recovery/7-1447, RG 59; British Chargé to Marshall, July 15, 1947, and Caffery to Marshall, July 20, 1947, both in *Foreign Relations, 1947*, III, 331, 333–335.

[20]Caffery to Marshall, July 18, 1947, file: 840.50 Recovery/7-1847, RG 59; Alexander

The French, in particular, were determined to incorporate their Monnet Plan for industrial reequipment and modernization into any general European recovery scheme. For this reason they objected strongly when the bizonal authorities provided an estimate of German steel production based on the revised level-of-industry plan which the French government had not yet approved. The plan called for increasing Germany's steel production to nearly 11 million tons by 1951, and for production increases, ranging from 80 to 95 percent of prewar levels, in such industries as metals, heavy machinery, and chemicals.[21] In operation, the French complained, this would revive Germany at their expense. It would reduce Germany's reparation transfers and curtail the German coal exports which were needed to meet the steel production targets set in the Monnet Plan. These developments, in turn, would antagonize public opinion in France, strengthen its Communist party, and lessen the chances for French cooperation in recovery planning. Accordingly, the French refused to accept the estimates of bizonal steel, coal, and coke production, halting all work on the conference reports dealing with these commodities until the British and Americans had agreed to tripartite talks on Germany's level of industry. And even when these were scheduled, they refused to abandon their support for a recovery scheme that emphasized industrial reconstruction and modernization or to modify the Monnet Plan in order to match available coal supplies and thus spur Germany's revival.[22]

Opposition to the French plan came from the Benelux delegates and, in varying degrees, from the Swiss, Swedes, and Italians. This plan, they argued, would do little to assist the smaller states in the recovery program or to promote European unity. It

Kirk to Marshall, July 19, 1947, and Caffery to Marshall, telegram #2884, July 20, 1947, file: 840.50 Recovery/7-1947, /7-2047, RG 59; and Caffery to Marshall, telegram #2886, July 20, 1947, *Foreign Relations, 1947*, III, 333–335.

[21] Robert Murphy to Marshall, July 15, 1947, *Foreign Relations, 1947*, II, 988–990; and Gimbel, *Origins of the Marshall Plan*, 225.

[22] For French complaints, see "Conversation Between M. Bidault, Mr. Harriman, and Ambassador Caffery," July 15, 1947 in Caffery to the Secretary of State, despatch #9273, July 21, 1947, file: 840.50 Recovery/7-2147, RG 59. See also Caffery to Marshall, July 11, 1947; Georges Bidault to Marshall, July 17, 1947; Bidault communication to the Dept. of State, July 17, 1947; Caffery to Marshall, July 18 and 20, 1947, all in *Foreign Relations, 1947*, II, 983–986, 991–999. For French policy at the Paris conference, see Caffery to Marshall, July 17, Aug. 6, 8, and 13, 1947, file: 840.50 Recovery/7-1747, /8-647, /8-847, /8-1347, RG 59; and Caffery to Marshall, July 20, 1947, *Foreign Relations, 1947*, III, 333–335.

offered little to those countries that counted on increased trade with a revived Germany, to those that had escaped war damage, or to those that had already achieved a substantial degree of recovery. On the contrary, it would enable France and other states with ambitious modernization programs to monopolize American assistance and to dominate the European economy after recovery had been achieved. It would amount, in other words, to seeking American support for separate national stabilization schemes instead of a comprehensive program.[23]

As a substitute for the French approach, the Benelux delegates urged a program that would make full use of Europe's existing productive capacity, including Germany's idle industry, and would remove the barriers hampering trade expansion and multilateralization. The Dutch pressed for a recovery program that would revive their prewar markets in Germany, and together with the Belgians, they supported the establishment of a committee of experts to explore the means by which participating countries might balance their budgets, establish realistic exchange rates, and make their currencies transferable.[24] In addition, they supported a Franco-Italian customs union and, eventually, a general customs union among all participants. It would be difficult, they recognized, to eliminate trade barriers and forge a single European market. But as a first step, they wanted the CEEC to support those nations that were willing to organize bilateral unions and to begin negotiations looking toward a multilateral system of intra-European trade and payments. Such an approach, they argued, would stimulate recovery by expanding the volume of trade on the continent and by attracting private foreign investment. It would also produce a balanced and equitable revival in Europe and fit with American hopes for an integrated European economy.[25]

---

[23]Kirk to Marshall, July 18 and 19, 1947, file: 840.50 Recovery/7-1847, /7-1947, RG 59; James Clement Dunn to Marshall, July 29, 1947, file: 840.50 Recovery/7-2947, RG 59; Caffery to Marshall, July 20 and 27, 1947, in *Foreign Relations, 1947*, III, 333–335, 338–339.

[24]Caffery to Marshall, July 20 and 31, 1947, *ibid.* 333–334, 341–343; Caffery to Marshall, July 24, Aug. 2, July 31, Aug. 9, 1947, all in file: 840.50 Recovery/7-2447, /8-247, /7-3147, /8-947, RG 59.

[25]For the Franco — Italian negotiations concerning a bilateral union and for the CEEC discussions of a Western European customs union, see Caffery to Marshall, Aug. 9 and 14, 1947, file: 840.50 Recovery/8-947, /8-1447, RG 59; U.S. embassy, Rome to Marshall, Aug. 7, 1947, file: 651.6531/8-747, RG 59; Dunn to Marshall, Aug. 11, 12, and 15, 1947, file:

But if the French declined to modify their Monnet Plan, the British refused to support initiatives that might compromise their trade and payments position. The British economy had deteriorated rapidly during the summer of 1947. The fuel and grain shortages that followed the winter crisis of 1946–47, the worldwide scarcity of dollars, the rising cost of imports from the United States, and the decision to make sterling convertible had all combined to slow the pace of recovery and confront the British Treasury with a major dollar crisis. By early August, Britain's dollar reserves were dwindling at the rate of $176 million a week, a clip that would soon exhaust the balance on the Anglo-American loan of 1946 and force the Treasury to draw down its final reserves.[26]

Under these circumstances, the British were suspicious of the Benelux proposals. They were in no mood to support trade and payments liberalization at a time when their government was considering new bilateral commercial and exchange control arrangements in order to reverse its trade deficit and protect its shrinking reserves. Nor were they anxious to join a European customs union if it meant abandoning their system of imperial preference and compromising their control over domestic economic policies. Technically, they were supportive, but only with a long list of reservations. The development of such a union, they said, would have to be gradual. It would have to be guided by what each country could afford to import and by the principles embodied in the ITO charter then being drafted at Geneva. Its development would have to depend on the extent of American aid. It would have to be preceded by a detailed study of the problems involved. They were willing to collaborate in such a study; but they did not consider its work within the scope of the present conference.[27]

651.6531/8-1147, /8-1247, /8-1547; U.S. embassy, Rome, to Marshall, Aug. 22, 1947, file: 651.6531/8224, RG 59; Caffery to Marshall, Aug. 23, 1947, file: 651.6531/8-2347, RG 59; Dunn to Marshall, Aug. 25, 1947, file: 651.6531/8-2647, RG 59; and Kirk to Marshall, Aug. 20, 1947, file: 651.6531/8-2047, RG 59. There were divisions within the Benelux delegation. The Dutch were particularly interested in the revival of German trade and a European customs union. The Belgians, on the other hand, were more interested in a European clearing arrangement; and they were less enthusiastic about a customs union that would not include Britain.

[26]For the British economic situation and American concern, see *Foreign Relations, 1947*, III, 17–49.

[27]Douglas to Marshall, July 25, 1947, *ibid.*, 43–44; unsigned memorandum of conversation, July 31, 1947, file: 850 Britain, box 1017, Records of the American Embassy, London,

By early August, progress at the CEEC meeting had been disappointing. The Benelux delegates had advanced proposals that came close to fusing the traders and producers strategies discussed in the State Department, and following their lead, the conference had decided to appoint special committees to study the prospects for currency convertibility and a customs union. But these studies would not be finished before the conference adjourned. Once more, the British were dragging their feet on trade and payments policy, and the French were refusing to modify their Monnet Plan. Worse still, the conferees were unable to agree on a comprehensive recovery program and were unwilling to subordinate national interests to European needs. Instead, they were beginning to compile uncoordinated lists of their separate national requirements, and were doing so without careful scrutiny and without regard for American and world availabilities.

Given these developments, Under Secretary of State Clayton and other Americans in Europe began urging the State Department to adopt a more aggressive policy toward the CEEC. Clayton had been on hand for the opening of the CEEC meeting and, in subsequent talks with European leaders, he had urged actions that would boost production, multilateralize trade and payments, integrate the continental economies, and thus put Europe on a self-supporting basis within three or four years. The United States, he said, would help by providing essential commodities and capital equipment to restore existing industries. But the Europeans would have to do their part as well. They would have to seek long-term modernization loans from the World Bank and private investment channels; they would have to balance budgets, control inflation, devise sound production programs, abolish exchange and trade controls, and develop "in broad lines a type of European federation." They should begin, Clayton said, by agreeing to eliminate all tariffs over a ten-year period.[28]

Record Group 84, Washington National Records Center, Suitland, Md; U.S. embassy, London, to Marshall, Aug. 13, 1947, file: 841.50/8-1347, RG 59; Caffery to Marshall, Aug. 15, 1947, file: 841.50/8-1647, RG 59; Dunn to Marshall, Aug. 19, 1947, file: 841.50/8-1947, RG 59; Caffery to Marshall, Aug. 20, 1947, *Foreign Relations, 1947*, III, 364–367.

[28]Clayton to Marshall and Lovett, July 9, 10, and 29, 1947; Caffery to Marshall and Lovett, July 11, 1947; Clayton to Lovett, July 31, 1947, all in *ibid.,* 315–318, 328–330, 339–342. Dunn to the Secretary of State, July 25, 1947, file: 865.50/7-2547, RG 59; and Clayton to Lovett, July 11, 1947, file: 840.50 Recovery/7-1147, RG 59.

At a meeting in Paris in early August, Clayton won support for these views from Lewis Douglas, the American ambassador in Great Britain; Jefferson Caffery, the American ambassador in France; and Robert Murphy, the American political adviser in Germany. At this meeting, Paul Nitze, Deputy Director of the State Department's Division of Commercial Policy and a member of the Recovery Committee, summarized the thinking in Washington and reviewed the Policy Planning Staff's recent paper.[29] Clayton and the ambassadors approved the paper, but also expressed views not fully parallel with it. They placed greater emphasis on the chaotic state of European currencies and commerce, on the possibility that supra-national planning could be used to revive prewar cartels and extend statist controls over the European economy, and on the need for financial and commercial reforms that would expand intra-European trade and enhance productivity. The Europeans, they thought, should "stabilize their money," abandon costly social programs, fix "proper exchange rates," and agree in principle to reduce and eventually eliminate "all tariffs and trade barriers."[30]

Yet clearly the conferees were not doing this. On the contrary, as Clayton and the ambassadors saw it, they were slighting the principles of self-help, mutual aid, and joint programming, unwilling, so it seemed, to transcend national sovereignties and make the "hard-core" adjustments that were needed. They were adopting instead a "pork-barrel" approach and seeking American aid for their separate national requirements. To correct this, Clayton and the ambassadors wanted the State Department to list those production, trade, and payments initiatives it expected from the CEEC and to make these initiatives the *"quid pro quo"* for American aid.[31] For Clayton, in particular, the billions of dollars that the United States

---

[29] Nitze had been sent over as a result of a recommendation by the Committee on the European Recovery Program. See the minutes of its 19th meeting, July 24, 1947, folder: REP Minutes, box 26, RG 353. See also, Marshall to the U.S. consulate, Geneva, for Clayton from Nitze, July 30, 1947, file: 840.50 Recovery/7-3047, RG 59.

[30] Clayton, Caffery, Douglas, Murphy, and Nitze to Marshall and Lovett, Aug. 6, 1947, and Wesley C. Haraldson, memorandum, Aug. 8, 1947, both in *Foreign Relations, 1947*, III, 343–350. See also Nitze's report on his conversations in Paris in the minutes of the 24th meeting of the Committee on the European Recovery Program, Aug. 12, 1947, folder: REP Minutes, box 26, RG 353. For a convenient summary of Ambassador Douglas's views, see Douglas to Lovett, July 18, 1947, file: 841.51/7-1847, RG 59.

[31] See the first three sources cited in the previous note.

was investing in European stabilization gave it the right, even the "duty," to demand the internal adjustments and cooperative action that would lift European trade and production from the "morass of bilateralism and restrictionism."[32]

In Washington, Under Secretary of State Robert A. Lovett did not doubt that European leaders were paying too little attention to the principles of self-help, mutual aid, and joint programming. Nor did he quarrel with Clayton's distinction between commodity grants and long-term loans, or his emphasis on a recovery program that would revive production, make Europe self-supporting in four years, and limit the financial demands on the United States. The American people, he felt, could not be expected to support costly modernization schemes or a grab bag of national "shopping lists."[33] Yet there were important differences between Lovett and his colleagues in Paris, differences that were similar to those between the producers and traders on the Recovery Committee. Lovett doubted that the CEEC should get bogged down in the complicated issues of financial and commercial reform. These must eventually be faced. But since they had the potential of exacerbating political divisions and hampering recovery, it would be better to begin by refurbishing European industry and breaking the bottlenecks to increased production. This was a course on which the Europeans might agree and one that would make long-term reforms more feasible.[34]

Lovett and other policy makers in Washington were also more sensitive than Clayton to the domestic political constraints upon American initiative. They wanted to preserve the appearance of European responsibility and to avoid any impression of dictating to the CEEC, lest this be interpreted as a commitment in advance of congressional action. Behind the scenes they had discussed

[32]Clayton to Lovett, Aug. 15, 1947, file: 840.50 Recovery/8-1547, RG 59.
[33]For Lovett's views, see his telegrams to Clayton and the ambassador, July 10, 1947; to Clayton and Caffery, Aug. 14, 1947; to Douglas, Aug. 20, 1947; and to Caffery, Aug. 24, 1947, all in *Foreign Relations, 1947*, III, 324–326, 356–360, 267–268, 276–277. Lovett, memorandum of conversation, July 25, 1947, and W. Wallner, memorandum of conversation, Aug. 21, 1947, both in file: 840.50/Recovery/7-2547 and /8-2147, RG 59. For Lovett's concern about the cost of the Marshall Plan, see also Walter Millis, ed. *The Forrestal Diaries: The Inner History of the Cold War* (London, 1952), 273, 275–276.
[34]Lovett to Clayton and the ambassador, July 10, 1947, and to Clayton and Caffery, Aug. 14, 1947, both in *Foreign Relations, 1947*, III, 324–326, 356–360.

methods of providing more American direction and were assembling, "as inconspicuously as possible," a small group of economic experts in Paris. But intervention, they felt, could not come without a formal request from the conference. Any discussion of the specific conditions for American aid, or of the reasons that might prompt its termination, must wait until Congress had authorized Marshall funds and the State Department had begun negotiating bilateral aid agreements with the participating countries. After the Greco-Turkish crisis, Lovett warned, congressmen were insisting "that they must not again be presented on a crisis basis with a virtual commitment to any precise course of action." For the time being, therefore, Clayton was simply to reassert American principles and count on Europe's need for outside assistance to produce a "unified" and realistic plan.[55]

The results were disappointing. Clayton, Caffery, and Douglas still worried that a continuing organization would cartelize the European economy. They still wanted to condition American aid on internal and multilateral financial and commercial reforms, and they still complained that European leaders were refusing to transcend national sovereignties and permit the CEEC to examine critically individual national requirements or adjust national production programs to the needs of Europe as a whole. Nor would the Europeans take those measures of self-help that meant reducing living standards below prewar levels and thus risking political difficulties at home. Their work instead amounted to "an assembly job of country estimates" which, as Caffery pointed out, would merely recreate Europe's prewar "economic pattern" with all the "low labor productivity and maldistribution of effort which derives from segregating 27,000,000 people into 17 uneconomic principalities." Once more, the conferees were thinking in terms of a whopping $29 billion in American aid; and according to their own estimates, even this amount would not make Europe self-supporting at the end of the Marshall Plan period.[56]

[55]Lovett and Wood to Clayton and Caffery, Aug. 11, 1947; Hickerson, memorandum, Aug. 11, 1947; and Lovett to Clayton and Caffery, Aug. 14, 1947, all in *ibid.*, 350–360; Committee on the European Recovery Program, minutes of meetings of July 10, 15, and 29, Aug. 7 and 12, 1947, folder: REP Minutes, box 26, RG 353.
[56]Caffery and Clayton to Marshall, Aug. 20, 1947; Clayton to Lovett, Aug. 25, 1947; Caffery to Marshall, Aug. 25, 1947; and Caffery to Lovett, Aug. 26, 1947, all in *Foreign*

The State Department, it seemed, would have to make new efforts to bring both the Europeans and the Americans in Paris into line. This was the conclusion reached at the end of August. With this conclusion in mind, Lovett sent Clayton and Caffery a long telegram reviewing American policy. He also sent his special assistant Charles Bonesteel, along with George Kennan, to discuss outstanding issues with the Americans in Paris. The idea was to forge a consensus that would clear the way for a more forceful presentation of the American "requirements" to the CEEC.[37]

In his long telegram of August 26, Lovett distilled the main points of agreement between all American officials, and then went on to reassert the key features of the producers' approach to European stabilization. The Europeans, he said, should enumerate "concrete proposals for mutual aid," set definite national production targets, and establish vigorous procedures for screening individual country requirements and for "correlating" national production programs on an "area-wide basis." They should also establish a supra-national organization to oversee this work and to coordinate, direct, and modify their plans during the recovery period. Clayton, he intimated, would have to swallow his objections on this score and go slow in pressing for a multilateral clearing scheme, a European customs union, and internal fiscal and monetary reforms. The first two would "contribute little to [the] immediate restoration of production." And as for the latter, Lovett insisted that Europe's chaotic fiscal and monetary structure was really a "symptom rather than a cause" of the continent's distress, that reforms in this area should wait until production had revived, and that any reforms not grounded "in increased production" could actually retard recovery and widen "the cleavages among producer and consumer groups" in the participating countries. To be sure, the importance of securing these reforms

---

Relations, 1947. III, 364–367, 377–383. Caffery to Marshall, Aug. 22 and 26, 1947, file: 840.50 Recovery/8-2247 and /8-2647.

[37] Bonesteel, "Minutes of Meeting on Marshall 'Plan'," Aug. 22, 1947, and Lovett to Marshall, Aug. 24, 1947, both in *Foreign Relations, 1947,* III, 369–375, and footnote #5, *ibid.,* 375. Lovett to Caffery, Aug. 25, 1947, file: 840.50 Recovery/8-2547, RG 59; Caffery to the Secretary of State, Aug. 25, 1947, *ibid.;* and Lovett to Clayton and Caffery, Aug. 26, 1947, file: 840-.50 Recovery/8-2647, RG 59.

would grow "as production expands and economies are stabilized." But for now, production was the first priority.[38]

Kennan and Bonesteel reiterated the same arguments during their meeting in Paris with Clayton, Caffery, and Douglas. The result was a "common position" similar to the one worked out earlier between traders and producers on the Recovery Committee. The goals, in other words, were to be a speedy revival of European production and later "further liberalization of trade." Through the setting and meeting of production targets, the European nations would progressively reduce their requirements for outside assistance, place their economies on a self-supporting basis, and thus clear the way for long-run modernization projects, further trade liberalization, and internal financial reforms. Managing this process would require "concerted action" through a continuing European organization with powers to review national programs, adjust these to European needs, and direct "production, trade, and manpower in the most efficient and economic manner."[39]

On August 30, the Americans communicated these "essentials" to the Executive Committee of the CEEC. So far, they said, the conference results were "disappointing." The expectations of $29 billion in American aid and of a continued deficit at the end of the aid period reflected both an absence of concerted self-help and mutual aid by the conferees and unrealistic ideas about resource availabilities in the United States and consumer needs in the participating countries. They were not interested, the Americans said, in dictating to the conference. But the Europeans should realize that anything short of the American "essentials" would "prejudice the success of the entire Marshall program" in the United States.[40] Similar warnings also came from the State Department's economic experts, known as the "Friendly Aid Boys," who arrived in Paris during the last week of August. They went over the CEEC's technical reports, found the results "unacceptable," and offered the Europeans a good deal of "very blunt criticism."[41]

---

[38] Lovett to Clayton and Caffery, Aug. 26, 1947, *Foreign Relations, 1947,* III, 383–389.
[39] Clayton to Marshall and Lovett, Aug. 31, 1947, *ibid.,* 391–396.
[40] *Ibid.*
[41] Moore to William Phillips and Nitze, Sept. 1, 1947, and William Bray to Phillips, Sept. 9, 1947, folder: ERP Subject File, Paris Conference — Comments and Correspondence,

Nevertheless, the Americans found the conferees as reluctant as ever to take those measures of self-help, mutual aid, and cooperative programming that meant transcending national sovereignties, subordinating national production plans to the needs of a new European community, or accepting standards of living that would reduce their aid requirements to a realistic level. The Scandinavians were opposed to a continuing organization that would circumvent the U.N. or create a Western European economic bloc. The British were opposed to any action that might subject their living standards or trade and financial policies to supra-national control. The French were still refusing to adjust the Monnet Plan in the interest of Europe as a whole. And the conferees as a group were still compiling "individual country statements" with little regard for the kind of coordinated planning that could eliminate waste and low productivity.[42]

In the eyes of American leaders, further reliance upon European initiative and responsibility could not produce the ends desired. The Europeans, as Lovett told the Cabinet, were not being realistic.[43] As the Friendly Aid Boys saw it, the conferees were engaged in actions that would lead to "US rejection" of the recovery program or to a prolonged congressional debate that would "embitter European peoples" and cause untoward "repercussions" on the continent.[44] And as Kennan viewed it, the conferees did not have the political strength or "clarity of vision" to draft a new "design" for Europe. The Scandinavians were "pathologically nervous about the Russians," the British were "seriously sick," and all the other delegations were infected by the same lack of resolve and realism that afflicted the British. The State De-

---

box 38, RG 353. The "Friendly Aid Boys" from the State Department included Moore, Bray, Victor Longstreet, Harold Speigel, and William Terrill.

[42] For developments at Paris, see Clayton to Marshall and Lovett, Aug. 31, 1947, and Department Economic Advisers to Lovett, Thorp, Ness, and Nitze, Sept. 5, 1947, both in *Foreign Relations, 1947*, III, 391–396, 405–408. Department Economic Advisors to Ness, Nitze, and Kindleberger, Sept. 6, 1947, file: 840.50 Recovery/9-647, RG 59; and to Ness and Nitze, Sept. 7, 1947, File: 840.50 Recovery/9-747, RG 59; Lovett to Clayton and Caffery, Sept. 7, 1947, *ibid.*

[43] Lovett, "Notes on Cabinet Meeting, Friday, August 29," file: 811.5043/8-2947, RG 59; and Mathew J. Connelly, notes on cabinet meeting, Aug. 29, 1947, folder: Notes on Cabinet Meetings, Post-Presidential File, box 1, Mathew J. Connelly Papers, Harry S. Truman Library, Independence, Mo.

[44] Department Economic Advisers to Lovett, Thorp, Ness, and Nitze, Sept. 5, 1947, *Foreign Relations, 1947*, III, 405–408.

partment, he concluded, would have to "decide unilaterally" what was best for the Europeans.[45]

This was the position that Clayton had taken earlier, and it was one that Lovett could now accept. Early in September, he helped to establish the Advisory Steering Committee, an interdepartmental group that was to coordinate recovery policy in the executive branch. At its first meeting on September 9, he took the position that the United States could not support the recovery program emerging from the CEEC and must therefore fill the vacuum created by the failure of European leadership. Subsequently, the new group established a number of subcommittees designed to bring the CEEC's work into line with the American "essentials."[46] At the same time, the State Department decided to simply tell the Europeans that greater sacrifices and "some mutual delegation of sovereignty" would be necessary to meet these "essentials" and produce a "workable program."[47] The result was a new phase in recovery planning.

The assumption in Washington was that the Paris conferees were handicapped by restrictive instructions from their Foreign Offices. On September 7, therefore, the State Department appealed directly to the home governments, urging them to accept the American "essentials" and instruct their delegates accordingly. They were also urged to postpone their planned reception of the CEEC's report, originally scheduled for September 15; to continue the conference long enough to bring the general report, if not its technical supplements, into line with American thinking; and then to transmit the results as a "preliminary" document subject to amendations and corrections by economic experts in Washington and Paris. This procedure, the Americans hoped, could avoid the harsh criticism that might otherwise accompany publication of the report in the United States. If followed, the State Department would be able to describe the preliminary report as "correct in principle," blame its shortcomings on the lack of time, and claim

---

[45] Director of the Policy Planning Staff, memorandum, Sept. 4, 1947, *ibid.*, 397–405.

[46] Advisory Steering Committee, minutes, Sept. 9, 1947, folder: ASC Minutes, box 26, RG 353.

[47] The quote is from Caffery to Marshall, Sept. 7, 1947, file: 840.50 Recovery/9-749, RG 59.

that revisions would render the final document acceptable.[48]

In addition, policy makers in the State Department decided to submit the bizonal level-of-industry plan to critical examination by the CEEC. They had been disappointed when the occupation authorities, in responding to questionnaires from the conference, had failed to adjust Germany's recovery plans to the needs of Europe as a whole or to permit the conferees to alter bizonal requirements. This failure, as they saw it, made it difficult for the conferees to consider supra-national approaches, balanced revival programs, or concerted schemes of mutual aid and joint programming. The new initiative, they hoped, would correct this problem. It would encourage the participating countries to submit their requirements to careful scrutiny by the whole conference, to fit their national production plans into a "regional" recovery program that included Germany, and thus to move toward a more efficient system integrated along functional lines.[49]

Opposition to these American proposals came primarily from the British. They did not want the CEEC to review the bizonal plan and determine the rate at which German industry would be reactivated. The plan, so British Foreign Secretary Ernest Bevin declared, had been adequately discussed at Paris, and any further discussion would only permit the participating countries to tamper with Anglo-American policy in the bizone. But as the Americans saw it, British opposition stemmed from a reluctance to submit their own recovery plans to critical review by the CEEC or to subordinate British interests and sovereignty to American designs for a unified European economy. Britain, Secretary of State Marshall complained, wanted to "benefit fully from a European program . . . while at the same time maintaining the position of

---

[48]*Ibid.* Lovett to Marshall, Aug. 31, 1947; Department Economic Advisers to Lovett, Thorp, Ness, and Nitze, Sept. 5, 1947; Lovett to certain American diplomatic officers, Sept. 7, 1947; Lovett to Clayton and Caffery, Sept., 7, 1947; and Lovett to Douglas, Sept. 11, 1947, all in *Foreign Relations, 1947*, III, 396–397, 405–408, 412–417, and 423–425.

[49]Hickerson to Marshall and Lovett, memorandum, Aug. 11, 1947; Douglas to Lovett, Aug. 21, 1947; Kennan, memorandum, Sept. 4, 1947; Marshall to Douglas, Sept. 5, 1947; Caffery to Douglas, Sept. 5, 1947; Lovett to certain American diplomatic officers, Sept. 7, 1947; and Marshall to Douglas, Sept. 8, 1947, all in *ibid.*, 351–355, 368–369, 397–405, 409–412, 415–419. Committee on the European Recovery Program, minutes of meeting, Aug. 19, 1947, folder: REP Minutes, box 26, RG 353; Bonesteel to Lovett, memorandum, Aug. 27, 1947, folder: European Recovery, 1947–48, box 6, Records of Charles E. Bohlen, RG 59; and Murphy to Marshall, Sept. 8, 1947, file: 840.50 Recovery/9-847, RG 59.

not being wholly a European country." And if the United States "sanctions" Germany's exclusion from the European program, it "justifies" the British in "excluding themselves."[50] Despite American pressure, however, the British refused to budge.

As a result, American policy makers were forced to abandon their German initiative in order to concentrate on the larger proposal for extending the Paris conference and revising its general report.[51] The British were opposed to this idea as well. They argued that time did not permit further revisions in the conference report, that prolonging the conference would be tantamount to admitting its failure, and that neither they nor the other participants could make the additional sacrifices required to satisfy American demands. Further pressure from the United States, they insisted, would only "impair national sovereignty," provoke opposition from nationalist and Communist elements across Europe, and threaten the recovery program.[52]

With some support from the French, the British tried to rally the Paris conferees against the American initiative. But the other participating countries were more sympathetic with the State Department's proposal and this fact, together with American threats of congressional opposition if concessions were not forthcoming, led to a "revolt" against British leadership and to a new conference position. While still reluctant to promise an "integrated plan," major changes in the CEEC report, or support for a continuing organization, the conferees agreed to extend the conference for a few days, make whatever changes time and their home governments permitted, and label the results "provisional." They also agreed to "recess" rather than "adjourn," to review the provisional report with officials in Washington, and then, if necessary, to reconvene the full conference and reconsider its report in light of the Washington conversations.[53]

The British were disappointed. Although Bevin agreed to the new procedure, he did so only after an angry attack on American

    [50]Bonesteel, memorandum of telephone conversation with Douglas, Sept. 8, 1947, file: 840.50 Recovery/9-847, RG 59; and Marshall to Douglas, Sept. 8, 1947, *Foreign Relations, 1947*, III, 418–419.
    [51]See Douglas to Marshall, Sept. 9, 12, and 17, 1947, in *ibid.*, 420, 429–430, 434–435.
    [52]Douglas to Marshall, Sept. 9, 1947, *ibid.*, 420.
    [53]U.S. embassy, Lisbon, to Marshall, Sept. 10, 1947, file: 840.50 Recovery/9-1047, RG

"intervention," a fresh warning against further "external pressure," and a plea for renewed expression of American confidence in European initiative and responsibility.[54] No such expression would be forthcoming, since it would imply a commitment to a conference report that still fell short of the American essentials.[55] It might also hamper American leaders at a time when they had decided to scuttle the emphasis on European initiative and play a more aggressive role in recovery planning.

During the last days of the CEEC meeting, American officials worked as full participants in its deliberations. The Friendly Aid Boys labored with their European counterparts to correct details in the technical reports; Clayton, Caffery, and Douglas discussed major policy issues with the heads of the European delegations. With the threat of congressional disapproval hanging like a shadow over the conference, the Europeans bowed to the American "essentials." They agreed to revise the report's preamble, saluting in it the principles of self-help, mutual aid, and joint programming, and using it to proclaim "a new era of European economic cooperation" in which programs of "concerted action" would insure full use of available resources and productive facilities. They also agreed to reduce their estimates of trade deficits during the aid period. They promised as well to cooperate "in all possible steps to reduce the tariffs and other barriers to the expansion of trade," to make appropriate fiscal and currency reforms, to restrain inflation and fix realistic exchange rates, and to finance long-term modernization plans through loans from the World Bank and private commercial channels.[56]

The major stumbling block turned out to be Lovett's demand for a supra-national organization. The Scandinavians still worried that a strong organization would take on the characteristics

59; Caffery to Marshall, Sept. 10, 1947, *ibid.;* Dunn to Marshall, Sept. 11, 1947, file: 840.50 Recovery/9-1147, RG 59; Caffery to Marshall, Sept. 13, 1947, file: 840.50 Recovery/9-1347, RG 59. See also Clayton, Caffery, and Douglas to Marshall and Lovett, Sept. 11, 1947; Caffery to Marshall and Lovett, Sept. 12, 1947; Caffery to Marshall, Sept. 12, 1947, all in *Foreign Relations, 1947,* III, 421–423, 425, 530.
   [55] Douglas to Marshall, two telegrams dated Sept. 12, 1947, *ibid.,* 428–430.
   [55] Lovett to Douglas, Sept. 13, 1947, *ibid,* 430–431.
   [56] Caffery to Marshall, Sept. 14, 1947, and to Lovett and Bonesteel, Sept. 17, 1947, *ibid.,* 431–432, 434. Caffery to Marshall, Sept. 15, 1947, file: 840.50 Recovery/9-1547, /9-1847, /9-1947, RG 59.

of a Western European economic alliance and thus compromise their neutrality. Neither they nor the British wanted a supra-national authority to dictate their trade and production policies. Such an authority, the British continued to argue, would impair national "sovereignty," drive several countries from the recovery plan, and widen the "schism in Europe." Seizing on these European objections, Clayton, Caffery, and Douglas made another pitch for the traders' approach to economic revival and integration. The Europeans, they told Lovett, would never consent to a continuing organization that had the power to allocate materials, distribute production, and design a new European industrial pattern without regard for national boundaries. Even if they did, the result would be a "dangerous degree" of "planned" economic activity and new cartelistic arrangements that would only "frustrate the ultimate restoration of natural market forces." It would be "much wiser," they said, to reduce "trade barriers," fix "appropriate exchange rates," and thus permit "natural economic forces" rather than statist controls to "bring about a community of economic interests and responsibility."[57]

Given such opposition, the State Department backed away from its initial position and settled for a weakly phrased provision in the CEEC's report. Under it, the participating countries agreed to form a joint organization once the recovery program had been launched. But the new organization would not have the supra-national authority for which Lovett and others had called. Instead, it would merely review the progress of the recovery program, make studies, issue reports, and generally "encourage" member states to take those measures of self-help, mutual aid, and joint programming required to meet the broad objectives of the program.[58]

On September 22, the Committee on European Economic Cooperation finished its work and sent its provisional findings to the

---

[57]Caffery, Clayton, and Douglas to Marshall and Lovett, Sept. 15, 1947, Caffery to Lovett and Bonesteel, Sept. 17, 1947; Douglas to Marshall and Lovett, Sept. 17, 1947; and Caffery to Marshall, Sept. 17, 1947, all in *Foreign Relations, 1947*, III, 432–437. See also Caffery to Marshall and Bonesteel, Sept. 8, 1947, file: 840.50 Recovery/9-847, RG 59.

[58]Caffery to Marshall and Lovett, Sept. 19, 1947, file: 840.50 Recovery/9-1947, RG 59. See also the official summary of the conference report in Caffery to Marshall, Sept. 20, 1947, file: 840.50 Recovery/9-2047, RG 59.

State Department. In addition to the various pledges enumerated in the general report and its preamble, the participating countries had appointed special committees to study the feasibility of currency convertibility and a customs union. They had struck a compromise on the German question, one under which Germany's revival was declared essential to European recovery and integration yet was to be carefully controlled so as to protect the economic and security interests of her neighbors. And they had also agreed to the cooperative development of hydro-electric resources, the pooling of freight cars, and the standardization of certain kinds of equipment. And they had established such goals as the rebuilding of Europe's merchant fleet, the restoration of prewar levels of agricultural production, dramatic increases in the output of fertilizers and agricultural machinery, and productive increases, ranging from 33 to 250 percent above prewar levels, in coal, electricity, refined oil, and steel.

To be sure, these pledges and projections were offset by numerous shortcomings in the CEEC report. The report stated that utilization of existing productive facilities must go hand-in-hand with modernizing plant and equipment, that fixing realistic exchange rates would require special stabilization loans from the United States, that achieving internal financial stability had to be balanced against the need to maintain high levels of employment, and that realizing production targets would depend on outside assistance sufficient to cover Europe's four-year trade deficit with the American continent. It estimated the deficit, exclusive of World Bank loans, at $19.3 billion, a sum still larger than Americans considered realistic. Even with aid at that level, it was skeptical that European-American accounts could be balanced at the end of the recovery period.[59]

Despite these shortcomings, the last-minute revisions in the CEEC report were important to policy makers in the State Department. They acknowledged the American vision of an integrated and productive European economy, incorporated the American principles of self-help, mutual aid, and joint program-

[59]Committee on European Economic Cooperation, *General Report,* I, and *Technical Reports,* II (London, 1947). See also the summaries of the reports in Caffery to Marshall, Sept. 20, 1947, file 840.50 Recovery/9-47, RG 59; Dept. of State, *Bulletin,* XVII (Oct. 5, 1947), 681–687; and *International Conciliation* (December, 1947), 803–827.

ming, and set the stage for further consultation between American and European recovery planners in Washington. These consultations opened in the second week of October. During talks with members of the Advisory Steering Committee and other officials, the CEEC delegates sought assurances that American aid would meet their needs without abridging their sovereignty. They wanted promises that the local currency accumulated through their sale of American-provided commodities would not be controlled by the United States. They also wanted the Americans to accept a continuing European organization with "advisory" rather than "executive" authority. They wanted guarantees that American aid would be sufficient to cover their projected deficits with the Western Hemisphere, would be largely in the form of dollars rather than commodities, and would be given without restrictions.[60]

The Americans were not reassuring. American assistance, they said, would consist mainly of commodities. Purchases outside the United States would be limited and restrictions on the local-currency counterpart of American aid would be *mutually* determined by the United States and each of the participating countries. They agreed that the details of European programming and the functions of a continuing organization would have to wait until Congress decided the form and amount of American assistance. But they made it clear that a strong European organization, with some allocation authority, would be necessary during the recovery period. They also whittled away at the CEEC's aid estimate, telling the Europeans that the United States could not cover all of their requirements and that European consumption levels would have to be limited by this fact, by the world-wide shortage of certain commodities, and by the amount of assistance available from other countries.[61]

Both traders and producers in the American camp pressed

[60]Chairman, CEEC Delegation to Lovett, Oct. 22, 1947; CEEC Delegation to the State Department, Oct. 27, 1947, and to participating governments, Oct. 31, 1947, all in *Foreign Relations, 1947*, III, 446–450, 452–461. Mulliken memorandum to Kotschnig and Rusk, Oct. 23, 1947, file: 840.50 Recovery/10-2347, RG 59.
[61]Memoranda of conversations, Oct. 15 and 16, 1947, folder: REP Docmuments, box 28, RG 353; memoranda of conversations, Oct. 21, 22, and 23, 1947, folder: ASC Documents, box 24, RG 353; Nitze to Douglas, Oct. 29, 1947, file: 850 Marshall Plan, box 1018, London Embassy Records, Record Group 84, National Archives, Suitland, Md.; CEEC Delegation to

their strategies on the CEEC delegation. In addition to an allocation authority, the producers wanted realistic production targets,
a bottleneck approach, and the fitting of national recovery plans
into a European pattern of production and exchange — even if it
meant, as Lovett told the CEEC delegation, "some sacrifice of national customs and tradition." For their part, the traders wanted
commitments to monetary and fiscal reform, currency convertibility, and tariff reduction. "American thought," as the CEEC
delegates explained to their governments, was "much pre-occu-
pied with the extent to which the reduction or elimination of
quantitative [trade] restrictions and tariffs might bring benefits
to Europe through the creation of a larger market and concentration of productive effort."[62]

The Washington talks ended without European-American
agreement on many basic issues. The Marshall planners had simply lectured the Europeans on American requirements and had
then proceeded to make the Paris report, as one CEEC official
later recalled, "as attractive as possible for presentation to Congress."[63] Doing so meant reducing the amount of American aid
involved and emphasizing those elements of the traders and producers approaches that would advance the policy goals of greater
production and integration in Europe. This became clear when
President Truman submitted the administration's recovery proposal to Congress in December.

Truman's message, together with the draft bill of the recovery
program and the relevant background information provided by
the State Department, called for $17 billion in American aid over a
four-year period, beginning with an appropriation of over $5 bil-
lion in the first year. This aid was to be conditioned on pledges by
the participating governments to set aside the local currency
equivalent of American assistance for use under terms acceptable
to the United States; to maximize industrial and agricultural production, stabilize currencies, fix realistic exchange rates, and re-

participating governments, Oct. 31, 1947; Lovett to Chairman, CEEC Delegation, Nov. 13,
1947, and record of a meeting between members of the Advisory Steering committee and
the CEEC Delegation, Nov. 4, 1947, all in *Foreign Relations, 1947*, III, 446–470.
   [62]See the documents cited in the preceding note. The quotation is from CEEC Delegation to participating governments, Oct. 31, 1947, *ibid.*, 456–461.
   [63]Ernst H. Van Der Beugel, *From Marshall Aid to Atlantic Partnership: European Integration
as a Concern of American Foreign Policy* (New York, 1966), 93.

364   PACIFIC HISTORICAL REVIEW

duce trade barriers; and to establish a continuing European organization that could make effective joint use of American aid. These and other collective measures aimed at replacing the old "self-defeating" pattern of "narrow [economic] nationalism" in Europe with new forms of economic cooperation and integration.[64]

This was also the major theme in the congressional hearings that followed in 1948. All could agree that the recovery program offered an historic opportunity to foster greater integration on the continent. The "situation is ripe," John Foster Dulles explained, "for a really creative act in Europe."[65] According to Representative John Davis Lodge of Connecticut, it would be a mistake to "put Humpty-Dumpty together again" as it was in 1938.[66] European economic integration, Marshall agreed, was "one of the most important considerations in the entire program."[67] Neither Congress nor the Truman administration wanted to condition American aid on the development of an economic or political union, and provisions to this effect were not included in the Foreign Assistance Act that passed in the spring. But as Dulles noted, the United States could nevertheless "play a very great part" in promoting European economic unity by continuing to insist on maximum self-help and mutual aid by the participating countries, on a cooperative European organization to manage the recovery effort, on resource sharing and joint programming, and on those internal and multilateral currency and commercial reforms to which the Europeans were pledged and which, in operation, would lead to a rational pattern of European economic integration.[68]

Integration, in the language of the Foreign Assistance Act, was the route to "lasting peace and prosperity" in Europe.[69] It could

---

[64] *Ibid.*, 105–107. The administration's recovery bill is printed in U.S. Congress, House of Representatives, Committee on Foreign Affairs, *Hearings, United States Foreign Policy For a Post-War Recovery Program*, 80th Cong. 1st and 2nd sess. (Washington, D.C., 1948), 23–28 (hereafter cited as House, *Recovery Program Hearings*).

[65] U.S. Congress, Senate, Committee on Foreign Relations, *Hearings, European Recovery Program*, 80th Cong. 2nd sess. (Washington, D.C., 1948), 605 (hereafter cited as Senate, *ERP Hearings*).

[66] House, *Recovery Program Hearings*, 155.

[67] *Ibid.*, 108.

[68] Senate, *ERP Hearings*, 108, 208–213, 245, 298, 549–550, 587–588, 605, 756.

[69] U.S. Congress, House of Representatives, Committee on International Relations, Historical Series, *Selected Executive Hearings, Foreign Economic Assistance Programs*, pt. I, *Foreign Assistance Act of 1948* (Public Law 472), 80th Cong. 2nd sess. 1948 (Washington, D.C., 1976), 254–272 (hereafter cited as House, *Executive Hearings*).

correct those "basic" structural difficulties hampering productivity and which arose from the division of the continent into a "multiplicity" of economic sovereignties.[70] This change would follow the precedent set in the United States, where "a large domestic market with no internal trade barriers" had supposedly made possible a remarkable record of growth and abundance.[71] It would also be in line with the interdependent nature of the modern world economy and with the American principles of multilateralism.[72] And by creating a collective framework for controlling contested resources, especially those of the Ruhr, it would help to diffuse the spirit of nationalism that had made Europe the "cockpit" of "power clashes," the "breeder of wars."[73]

By 1948, then, the related ideas of economic unity and greater productivity had emerged as the key concepts in American Marshall planning. Lovett and the advocates of production assigned priority to making the most efficient use of Europe's existing resources and industrial capacity, to breaking bottlenecks, and to integrating national production and stabilization schemes. Clayton and the traders stressed the need for internal and multilateral financial and trade reforms that could expand and integrate the European economy and, by so doing, create a market large enough to stimulate mass production. The former strategy seemed to require temporary statist controls and supra-national planning to achieve its goals; the latter would rely on normal market mechanisms. But both converged on the twin concepts of production and integration.

The Europeans, for their part, resisted both directions in American thinking. They were reluctant to engage in genuine joint programming, to adapt national production plans to European needs, to subordinate national sovereignties to the authority of a supra-national organization, or to make specific commitments to financial and trade reforms. For them the imperatives were national interest and sovereignty; for the Americans they were transnational action and cooperation. While the Europeans

---

[70] Senate, *ERP Hearings*, 587.

[71] *Ibid.*, 208–209, 245, 298, 756, 848–849; House, *Recovery Program Hearings*, 157–159, 322–326, 1442–1444; and House, *Executive Hearings*, 254–272.

[72] House, *Recovery Program Hearings*, 95–96, 322–326, 341.

[73] *Ibid.*, 924; and Senate, *ERP Hearings*, 549. See also *ibid.*, 212–213, 245.

wanted a recovery program that limited the scope of cooperative action, met their separate national requirements, and preserved the greatest degree of national self-sufficiency, the Americans wanted to recast Europe in the image of the United States. In the name of enhanced productivity, of peace and plenty, they urged European leaders to transcend narrow national imperatives and territorial constraints and to replace the old system of national competition and autarky with a functionally integrated and economically productive community. Important differences had thus emerged in European and American recovery planning in the year following Marshall's speech at Harvard University, differences that would continue to plague policy planners and add an element of contention to European-American relations during the subsequent history of the European Recovery Program.

[16]

THE IMPACT OF U. S. ASSISTANCE PROGRAMS ON THE POLITICAL AND ECONOMIC INTEGRATION OF WESTERN EUROPE*

DONALD C. STONE

Mutual Security Agency

World War II left Europe economically bankrupt, politically paralyzed, and spiritually sick. In contrast, we find today—thanks to the leaven of the Marshall Plan and other U. S. assistance, and the self-help and mutual-help measures of Western European countries—a vastly improved Continent of Europe.

First, economic collapse has been avoided. The mills, plants, and shops in most countries are humming as they never did before. The current output of industry in Western Europe is roughly forty per cent larger than in 1938, and sixty per cent above that of 1947. Agriculture has likewise shown encouraging improvement. The volume of intra-European trade which had come to a virtual standstill in 1947 has sharply increased until it is now over one-third higher than that of the pre-war era. The dollar deficit in Europe has been substantially reduced from a peak of $7 billion and, except for the special requirements of the post-Korean rearmament program, it would probably have been brought into manageable proportions by 1951.

Second, the countries of Western Europe have not only achieved this tremendous economic improvement while struggling to raise consumption levels to pre-war standards, but they are now, in the wake of Communist aggression in Korea, engaged in a large rearmament program. This is their demonstration of an ability and a willingness to assume today defense burdens which are more than 60 per cent heavier than those they shouldered in 1949, and significantly higher than in 1938.

Third, European military forces now in being are superior to those in 1947. Supplemented by American divisions, air installations, and naval power, European military forces stand as a warning to any aggressor that force will be met with force.

Fourth, a considerable measure of internal political stability has returned to Western Europe. Governments which in 1947 appeared unable to cope with subversion within and to take positive measures to solve their economic and social disorders, are now on the whole far more vigorous, efficient, and democratic. The possibilities of a Communist take-over, or of the planting of Soviet troops on the edge of the Atlantic through "peaceful penetration" are no longer such imminent threats to Europe or the United States.

Fifth, where there was hopelessness, disillusionment, and self-pity, there has arisen in Europe a new spirit of confidence and a determination to work toward unity and self-support. Despite the clever and diabolical opposition by the Communists and a disturbing amount of neutralism on the part of fellow citizens, many of the people of Europe are rolling up their sleeves to solve their

* Paper prepared for the annual meeting of the American Political Science Association at Buffalo, New York, August 27, 1952.

own problems; they have proof in the massive changes during these five years that a better day is actually possible.

But of most significance to our subject here is the new awareness which the leaders of Europe and the Atlantic Community now have of the reasons for these great accomplishments. People on both sides of the Atlantic are slowly learning that a secure future is dependent upon unity of purpose and unity of conviction and unity of effort.

I do not suggest that serious economic, political, and social problems do not now exist. They are staggering: apathy and malice are all too prevalent, and economic and political weaknesses in some countries generate continuous crisis. But, what gives encouragement that a peaceful world can be, are the new political and economic institutions in Europe and in the Atlantic Community which are both the cause and the result of these changes. Self-help and mutual-help in Europe, buttressed by American aid, are the threads out of which an integrated Europe is being woven. To strengthen those threads is the most challenging of the tasks ahead.

INTERACTING STIMULI

Encouragement of the unification of Europe has in recent years become one of the elements of the foreign policy of the United States—an objective which has been progressively expanded and reflected in legislation. It was implicit in General Marshall's address of June, 1947 at Harvard and in the Economic Cooperation Act of 1948, although no specific reference was made to it. In 1949, however, the Congress set forth "unification of Europe" as an explicit objective of the U. S. in the amendments to the Economic Cooperation Act.

The Mutual Security Act of 1951 stated that the funds authorized for economic and military assistance should be used "to further encourage economic unification and political federation of Europe." In the Act of 1952 the Congress "welcomes the recent progress in political federation, military integration and economic unification in Europe and reaffirms its belief in the necessity of further vigorous efforts toward these ends as a means of building strength, establishing security, and preserving peace in the North Atlantic area."

Too often a politically and economically united Europe has been viewed as an end in itself—a visionary goal. New institutions will prove successful only when they are the consequence of necessity in solving specific problems and have public support. Integrated institutions must be the fruit of concrete needs rather than a theory pressed for its own sake. However, cause and result are interacting, and an institution established to meet one problem will often provide the inspiration and cooperation required to solve another problem.

The fact is that European unity has grown only within the framework of a fast-developing Atlantic Community; and it is impossible to chart the growth of European or Atlantic institutions since 1947 without tracing initiative, action, and inter-action back and forth endlessly across the Atlantic. Both European unity and the Atlantic Community have grown from the same soil: Europe's need for the aid and moral support of an Atlantic Community, and the need of the U. S. for a closely-knit Europe as a strong and defensible sector of the Atlantic Community. The instinctive surge of the West toward unity—impelled by common fears and hopes—has thus simultaneously called into being European and Atlantic institutions intertwined and interdependent.

It was Europe's need and U. S. advocacy of maximum self-help and mutual assistance that called forth the first post-war European institution—the Committee (later the Organization) for European Economic Cooperation—and started the snowball of European hope for security and well-being through unity. Likewise, it was the Brussels Pact, signed in March, 1948, that gave rise to the Atlantic Pact and the North Atlantic Treaty Organization, and led directly to a realization of the century-old dream of a "Council of Europe." It was within the framework of the security of a developing Atlantic Community that the Schuman Plan for a European Coal and Steel Community, purely European in origin, evolved into the "European Community of Six." The Coal and Steel Community provided the principle and the shape for the Pleven Plan which is becoming its military counterpart. It was in the Council of Europe that the idea of a European Defense Force was first projected; but it was the resolution of the North Atlantic Council to integrate forces that made it imperative and furnished the setting for the formal proposal by Prime Minister Pleven of France for a union of the defenses of the six continental countries. The Pleven Plan was pushed toward agreement and reality by inspired European statesmanship and with the aid and encouragement of the executive and legislative branches of the United States government and of General Eisenhower, who regarded it as essential to NATO. And now, to complete the circle, the OEEC, of which the United States and Canada became associate members in 1950, is given new life as an economic arm of the Atlantic Community, and continues to be a fertile breeding ground for further European economic integration.

Many forces and conditions—economic, psychological, political, and military—contributed to these striking achievements. Basic to this progress was far-sighted leadership within Europe and a growing realization that unity of action is indispensable. The post-war policy of the United States to work through international bodies—the United Nations and regional groupings—and to assume international responsibilities thrust upon it have undergirded the whole movement.

The Mutual Security Program is today, as was the Marshall Plan before it, a powerful instrument for aiding the growth of European unification. The United States seeks unity primarily as a means of assuring effective action in protecting freedom—the freedom of men and nations. Financial aid in the execution of these two programs has for the most part been a result, not the cause, of these new organisms.

INSTITUTIONAL PROGRESS

Now that a visible web of European organization exists, it is useful to reexamine the motivations which brought about the creation of each portion and which press for new areas of cooperative action. United States assistance to Europe under the Marshall Plan provided a stimulus acceptable to European

THE IMPACT OF U. S. ASSISTANCE PROGRAMS ON WESTERN EUROPE   **1103**

countries for a unified effort for postwar reconstruction and began a chain reaction of which we still see only the early stages. These initial steps toward European integration are too well known to develop in any detail. However, the interweaving of U. S. and European action is often not fully understood.

Organization for European Economic Cooperation

The first significant step toward European economic unity was the establishment, in 1948, of the Organization for European Economic Cooperation (OEEC) which sixteen Western European countries joined despite the refusal of the Soviet Union to participate itself or to allow any of its satellites to do so. For its part, the U. S. Congress established the Economic Cooperation Administration including the Office of U. S. Special Representative for Europe to work with the OEEC and the participating countries.

The mutual goals of the U. S. and its Western European partners in the crucial experiment were clearly stated in the Convention for European Economic Cooperation signed by all OEEC members in April, 1948:

> Recognizing that their economic systems are inter-related and that the prosperity of each of them depends on the prosperity of all;
> Resolved to create the conditions and establish the institutions necessary for the success of European economic cooperation and for the effective use of American aid, and to conclude a Convention to this end. . . .

The OEEC has subsequently endeavored to carry out these mutual objectives in the closest, day-to-day informal collaboration with the ECA in Washington, and the ECA's European arm in Paris. In the early years of U. S. assistance, the OEEC performed the critical job of recommending the distribution of Marshall Plan funds among the participating countries. Concurrently, this body worked with varied degrees of success to reduce barriers to the flow of trade, facilitate the supply and distribution of essential materials, promote financial stability, and achieve a more effective utilization of European manpower. More recently the OEEC has been assigned the function of making annual studies of the economic and financial performance and capacity of its members which are essential to NATO in drawing up, annually, its military program.

One of the most positive and forward-looking of the goals which the OEEC has established is that of increasing European production and of widening and deepening the market for European produce. An increase in European production by 25 per cent has recently been set by OEEC as a five-year aim. Progress toward this goal was recently given powerful impetus by the United States through an addition to the Mutual Security Act known as the "Moody Amendment" which provides for $100 million worth of counterpart (local currency funds) generated by dollar assistance to be used by the participating countries "with a view to stimulating free enterprise and the expansion of the economies of those countries with equitable sharing of the benefits of increased production and productivity between consumers, workers, and owners."

In addition to these achievements, the OEEC was also responsible for an accomplishment which, although somewhat intangible, was of prime importance to the success of joint recovery, namely, the development of a common European outlook. As each country drew up national recovery plans and submitted them to OEEC for careful analysis and hammering into a joint program, matters that had for centuries been national secrets became common European knowledge. And in the Secretariat, hundreds of the best experts drawn from member countries learned to work together as Europeans rather than as nationals. It is easy to overlook now, four years later, that nothing like this had ever happened before. The method and practice and outlook developed in the OEEC are among the important foundation stones of the growing movement for the unification of Europe.

European Payments Union

In July, 1950, the OEEC created the European Payments Union, a multilateral clearing system for intra-European payments, including transactions with the associated monetary areas of the member countries. The U. S. made an initial capital contribution of $350 million during the first year of the EPU to get it underway.

The Union has already shown in several instances, most notably Germany, the advantages of the collective approach in recommending measures to deal with serious trade deficits. It opened the way for positive and cooperative action to eliminate post-war trade restrictions and discriminatory barriers which obstruct the free flow of goods. Thus the EPU, as the first post-war operating institution, was the initial step taken by Western Europe toward the ultimate goal of a single, large, competitive West European market within which goods and currencies may freely flow.

U. N. Economic Commission for Europe

While of less significance to our subject, note should be taken of the United Nations Economic Commission for Europe (ECE), which was an outgrowth of a U. N. temporary sub-commission on economic reconstruction of the devastated areas in Europe established in 1946. Since the USSR, Poland, Czechoslovakia, and Yugoslavia, as well as the USA, are members of the ECE, it provides a forum for consideration of European-wide economic problems. Despite the effort of the Iron Curtain participants to use some ECE meetings as a propaganda rostrum the ECE has been able to do some excellent research work on such crucial European economic problems as the flow of trade, availability of raw materials, and transportation.

Council of Europe

The moral encouragement which the U. S. gave to European countries through the Marshall Plan provided a new impetus to the age-old urge for structural unity in Europe so admirably crystallized by Winston Churchill at Zurich in 1946. Unity was intensively promoted by a growing number of voluntary organizations with distinguished leaders and large popular followings. In 1948 one organization, officially called the European Movement, assumed the initiative in creating a permanent unofficial agency to guide the many groups striving toward the political union of Europe.

That same year the European Movement called together in The Hague some 800 of the most eminent leaders of Europe whose deliberations set in motion activities which, after agreement by the Brussels Pact countries, resulted in the creation of the Council of Europe in May, 1949. Thus popular will pressed the governments of Western Europe to create the beginnings of an organization of Europe.

The U. S. Congress not only gave encouragement to this development but also, at the invitation of the Council's Consultative Assembly, authorized representatives of the Senate and the House to meet with representatives of that 14-nation body. This is the first occasion when an official delegation from the Congress has participated in discussions of this kind.

The Council of Europe was not all that many leaders of the European Movement desired, for it was not a federal state empowered to act on urgent economic, social, and political problems. But it did provide a forum, partly official, partly semi-official, in which the voice and conscience of Europe could make itself heard and felt in a regular and orderly manner in favor of the harmonization of national policies and actions and in support of further concrete steps toward the unification of Europe.

During the three years of its active life the Council has grappled with the question of how the organizational unity of Europe can be achieved, and in the debates on this issue the cleavage between those who were prepared to yield sovereign powers to a federal Europe and those who were not continued to be the main stumbling block. Perhaps the Assembly of the Coal and Steel Community will receive an adequate mandate to develop a constitution which will bring into being a European political institution capable of reconciling these divergent views.

Meanwhile, functionalism, in contrast to federalism, as a road to European unity gained support with the implementation of the Schuman Plan and the formation of a European army. Yet the voice and the conscience of Europe continue to be heard insistently in Strasbourg, and the efforts to bring about a federal union continue.

Brussels Treaty

During this same period the mounting realization that the Soviet Union was embarked upon an aggressive program of picking off free nations one by one also encouraged concrete steps to build a positive, collective defense structure, operational in peacetime and capable of assuring the security of the free nations of the West. The first step was the signing of the Brussels Treaty early in 1948 by the governments of Belgium, France, Luxembourg, The Netherlands, and the United Kingdom. The U. S., which was already providing assistance to these countries and therefore interested in the effective utilization of all resources, gave active encouragement to the Treaty.

Under the Brussels Treaty the five countries agreed not only to come to each other's aid in the event of armed attack, but also to organize and coordinate and harmonize their economic policies and activities, to develop social and other related services, and to promote cultural exchange. The Brussels

Treaty, as a regional agreement within the context of the U.N. Charter, provided an instrument for collective action which the U. N., because of the Soviet veto, was finding difficult to provide.

North Atlantic Treaty Organization

The Brussels treaty paved the way to still closer forms of joint action on the Continent and to the precipitation of the "Atlantic Community." Recognizing that the collective strength of the Brussels treaty countries might not be sufficient to preserve peace unless the power and influence of the United States and other free nations were brought into association with them, many Americans gave thought to ways in which the United States might help strengthen collective security in Europe as it had in the Western Hemisphere through the Rio Treaty.

Numerous and varied bills were introduced in the Congress, but it was Senator Vandenberg, then Chairman of the Senate Foreign Relations Committee, who, in close consultation with Undersecretary of State Lovett, steered through the Senate a resolution embodying what was conceived to be the prevailing American attitude toward the United Nations and toward regional defense groups. The resultant Senate Resolution 239 declared, as one of six points, that the policy of the United States is to associate itself "with such regional and other collective areas as are based on continuous and effective self-help and mutual aid."

Buttressed by this expression of objectives and a similar statement by the Foreign Affairs Committee of the House of Representatives, the United States began exploratory conversations late in 1948 with the Brussels Treaty countries and others for a collective defense arrangement. The end result was the North Atlantic Treaty with a membership in the organization created by it (NATO) of 12 countries: the Brussels Treaty countries and Canada, Denmark, Iceland, Italy, Norway, Portugal, and the United States. Subsequently Greece and Turkey were admitted.

Several months later, Congress passed the Mutual Defense Assistance Program to implement the Treaty by making aid available for military equipment and materials to member countries in need of such aid. The Act stipulated, however, that U. S. assistance should become available only after bilateral agreements had been concluded between the United States and the countries receiving aid and after presidential approval of a general defense plan prepared by NATO. Such a three-year plan for build-up of armed forces was prepared and the shipments of military equipment to Europe began.

Communist aggression in Korea in June, 1950 caused an immediate reassessment of the danger of Soviet aggression in the Atlantic area and an acceleration in the pace of rearmament in all NATO countries. It likewise caused a shift from reliance on committees in the building of NATO defenses and the coordination of national policies, to the building of a *unified defense force operational in peacetime*, and directed and supported by integrated NATO staff organizations. This clothing of the Treaty with organs in continuous session and with executive arms represents a great step forward in the erection of a strong and effective institution.

These decisive NATO developments brought about a great change in the relationship of the United States to its allies in Europe—a relationship characterized by U. S. participation in the NATO goal of the creation of "an integrated military force adequate to defend Europe" functioning under a single command.

The concerns of NATO are by no means restricted to military matters. Even if Article II of the Treaty had not provided for collective action in the political, economic, and social fields, the consequences of carrying out the joint rearmament program would have required this. The most difficult decisions in mobilizing an integrated defense force with burdens equitably shared are primarily political and economic in nature. This fact is manifested in the foreign policy discussions of the North Atlantic Council and the Annual Review of each member's economic capabilities and contribution to mutual security.

The European Community of Six

One of the signs that NATO can become an effective instrument for collective freedom has been the growth of European unity in the last two years evidenced by some merger of sovereignty as regards certain basic economic and defense functions. Such a merger, inclusive of Germany, provides the hope that a practicable and safe means can be found through which the coal and steel and manpower of Germany can be utilized in the defense of Europe and the Atlantic Community.

The precise form in which institutional unity in Europe could be effectively molded has never been clear. This is one reason why ambitious proposals for an all-embracing federation have floundered. It was only slowly, within the framework of the security and economic assurance of a developing Atlantic Community, and responding to courageous, persistent European leadership, that six countries of Europe came to agree in 1951 and early 1952 to cessions of sovereignty that have laid the foundations for the building of a truly unified "European Community of Six."

The Coal and Steel Community (CSC), the first—and in some respects the most significant—step in this direction, was launched by the Foreign Minister of France, Robert Schuman, in May, 1950. He proposed that the coal and steel industries of France and Germany, together with those of any other European country willing to participate, be merged into a single production and market area and that supra-national institutions be established to carry into effect their collective purposes. Now, scarcely two years later, this proposal, in the form of a treaty, has been accepted by the governments of France, Belgium, Italy, Netherlands, Luxembourg, and West Germany, ratified by the parliaments, and has come into operation.

The U. S. relationship to this new organization was indicated by Secretary of State Acheson when he said that the United States will, insofar as possible, deal directly with the CSC on matters within its sphere.

The European Defense Community

The Schuman Plan paved the way for the suggestion by Pleven of France several months later that a unified European army be created under a single European defense minister, financed by a common budget, and integrated into the North Atlantic defense system. Agreement was reached in February of this year by the six Schuman Plan countries to merge their national armed forces into a single European Defense Force (EDF) in which basic national units of troops (around 12,000) including German troops would be integrated at the army corps level. Moreover, it was agreed to create the supra-national political institutions of a European Defense Community (EDC) empowered to raise, equip, train, command, and finance such a force. When the agreement has been ratified, the EDC will stand as one of the most decisive steps ever taken voluntarily and in time of peace toward institutional unity in Europe. The hopes and fears of many decades are at stake in this ratification.

The benefits that may flow in the future from these developments are as great as imagination will allow. The impoverishment, the wars, the myriad tributary evils that have been inflicted on Europe and the world by nationalist aggression —military, economic, and political—in the heart of the European continent, are the substance of modern history. If the danger of nationalist economic and military warfare could be removed even in Western Europe, then, despite the Russian shadow, the possibilities of peaceful economic and social progress in Europe and the Atlantic area as a whole would indeed be promising.

PRESSURES AND INCENTIVES

When viewed in perspective this progress toward unification of Europe in resolving economic, political, and military problems is most encouraging. Indeed, given all the countless reinforcements of separateness—the heavy inertia of the status quo, national and sectional suspicions, the resistance of vested interests, subversive opposition from within and without—the record is impressive.

For centuries men have dreamed of European federation. As wars in this century have grown in scope and destructiveness, as the techniques of production, commerce, and communication have pressed against national barriers, as man's spiritual and physical needs have outrun the ability of the nation-state to supply, the ideal of a unified Europe has acquired powerful mass support. Today, reason and the vision of a better world are joined with the necessity for survival, and European unification is no longer a remote ideal but a vital and attainable political objective.

With recent progress in mind let us examine more closely the prerequisites for a firm and enduring unity, the pressures which support and obstruct it, and the relation of U. S. participation to further integration.

Importance of Spiritual Perceptions

Unity among people and nations stems from many different forces ranging from fear of destruction by a common enemy to that unity which comes when people believe in and act on the principle of loving their neighbors as themselves. Unity (of a sort) may be achieved by violence and suppression—witness Eastern Europe—but enduring unity can only come from convictions freely arrived at and freely expressed. Indeed, the whole world today faces the choice of unity in freedom or unity in slavery.

Achievement of unity in freedom is the most difficult undertaking to which man can address himself, as it must harmonize two basically different perceptions which govern the social life of man. One is selfishness which ends in man destroying his brother. The other is the "concern" and respect for people as people which leads to unity founded on internal spiritual bonds rather than casual external factors. Inherent in this perception are the advantages which accrue both to an individual and to a nation when narrow "selfism" is submerged into something greater, into the mutual concerns of a common cause. This is why "mutual interest" is a far more positive symbol of our foreign policy rationale than "self interest." The first includes the latter, and if adhered to it affords a mutually acceptable and morally defensible basis for initiative.

Mankind has made enduring social, economic, and political progress only when he has translated the imperatives of this latter perception of concern, equality, responsibility, and brotherhood into his institutional life. This has meant giving up sovereignty of action in the interest of the larger community —license in personal actions which limit the freedom of one's brother; capriciousness on the part of a nation to commit acts of political and economic aggression on another country.

Under the Schuman Plan and the European Defense Community (when the latter is ratified), sovereignty of action is transferred voluntarily from the countries to the new central institutions. The CSC and EDC treaties provide for the exercise of this sovereignty through a CSC executive, an EDC executive, and a common assembly composed of delegates from national parliaments. The establishment of a common Court of Justice with compulsory authority over constitutional and jurisdictional disputes is another significant step toward implementation of the sovereignty of these two institutions.

In contrast, the power of OEEC, NATO, and the Council of Europe is in each instance dependent on the voluntary action of member countries in performing agreed tasks and on their exercise of a full share of social responsibility. It should be noted that a social and moral climate adequate to support responsible performance by participating countries on a mutual interest basis in alliances and other institutions of cooperation is the same kind of climate necessary to the delegation of sovereign authority to the larger community. Since such delegation makes it more difficult at a later date to withdraw from responsibility, the climate itself is favored by every measure that produces unity. Hence the importance of strengthening institutions to the maximum permitted at any time.

The type of sovereignty (a most misunderstood and misused concept) which we should strive to locate in these new institutions is not so much a matter of the transfer of formal authority to them. Rather it is the mutual dependence on these institutions as the form in which countries make decisions and as the instruments for carrying out essential fact-gathering, services, and action. If decision-making in consultative bodies which meet in continuous session can become a fixed practice, fear will be reduced that, when a crisis arises, a country will act in isolation and fail to fulfill its treaty obligations. In other words, the organizational and executive quality of these institutions and the behavior patterns which participation in them engender furnish the most practical test of their vitality. Nevertheless, as history amply illustrates, the failure to provide an adequate charter for an institution usually results in its disintegration as crisis passes.

Unwillingness of countries to take responsible action on a European, an Atlantic Community, or a world basis perforce reflects inadequacies and instabilities in the perceptions governing their social and spiritual orientation. Here we see the extent to which prospects for enduring unity must be founded on permanent institutions which reflect genuine social, political, and economic realities rather than on alliances and other cooperative devices designed for temporary convenience in times of fear or pressed primarily for purposes of self-interest. Without such a foundation dreams of European unity can only be dreams rudely swept away as mankind awakens from repeated nightmares of wars, depressions, and other catastrophes.

Political Imperatives

Aside from these basic perceptions, many other pressures favor or frustrate efforts of the Western World to reform the political and economic patterns of centuries. Dire necessity for survival has been one of the most potent. Aggressive totalitarianism and the failure of national institutions to prevent devastating world wars, world depressions, German occupations, uprooting of mass populations, slave camps, poverty, and violence, leave man—no matter what his perception may be—if he has any interest in survival, with no alternative but to move decisively toward new forms of association.

Two specific dangers in Europe have been most compelling for integration. First, is the fear that a new crop of German militarists, once free of Allied Occupation, might for a third time—with a new wave of irresponsibility— plunge Europe into bloodshed. Second, is the spectre of Soviet imperialism, implemented by communist infiltration and subversion. These dangers grimly attest to the need for heroic measures.

The fear of a rearmed Germany and an untamed Russia has made clear that the countries of Western Europe and the Atlantic Community must not only arm to defend themselves, but must include Germany and in such a manner that the economic and military potential of Germany cannot fly off again on an independent tangent. Thus Western European leaders have sought to so merge the armies and resources and political authorities of Western Europe that aggressive war by any one country cannot be waged against another and that defensive strength against Soviet imperialism can be maximized at the least cost.

A weighty obstacle in the path of these movements toward integration is the position of Great Britain against full participation in any plan—political, economic, or military—which runs counter to the traditional British feeling that they are not in all respects an integral part of Europe. Their worldwide responsibilities, especially in the Commonwealth and sterling areas, and the potential effect of continental involvement on their internal economic and social programs, have all contributed to their refusal to join the Coal and Steel and European Defense Communities. Perhaps the informal but responsible associations which the United Kingdom is now establishing with these two bodies will go part way in reassuring the Continent and lead to closer affiliation.

The situation of the British in relation to European integration is paralleled in part by the role of the U. S. in connection with the broader area of the Atlantic Community. The countries of Europe suspect that the discharge of our leadership responsibilities or even of basic treaty obligations may be impaired by failures in annual appropriations or other vagaries of our political processes or "excesses of youth." To the extent that they lack confidence in the enduring character of our economic and political commitments the European nations will inevitably feel they are making a disproportionate sacrifice of their freedom of action for a mutual purpose.

Other forces are also driving Western Europe toward political integration. There is a feeling among the nations of Western Europe that they are no longer separately able to play that role in world affairs to which their traditions, wisdom, and interests entitle them. United, they would be able to solve more of their own problems without U. S. financial contributions, and to exert greater influence upon the course of world affairs.

Integration an Economic Necessity

Economic imperatives likewise provide compulsions for integration. Technological changes of the last fifty years, and the postwar experience in the recovery effort, have demonstrated clearly the necessity of making more efficient use of economic resources, eliminating waste, and increasing productivity. Among others these are the deficiencies which are retarding the economic development of free Europe: small fragmented production and marketing areas; barriers to the flow of commodities and capital across national boundaries; lack of an integrated transportation system; immobility of labor; difficulties of building balanced military forces on a national basis; efforts to achieve national self-sufficiency; and trends toward monopoly of resources and productive enterprises. Yet the very existence of these economic maladies which make integration imperative seriously complicates the task of integration.

Moreover, there is real difficulty in uniting a part of Europe which has been economically dependent on the other half. The common cultural heritage of the Western European countries, which Eastern Europe shares only to a slight degree, makes it easier for the West to join together for economic survival, but the problem of the economic half-pie is still of formidable proportions.

Genuine unity is not divisible into sectors, although it is always relative.

Experience of the past four years has shown that collective defense calls for the pooling of economic resources. Unified military and economic efforts also require integrated political arrangements capable of supporting specialized endeavor. Successful progress in all three areas—military, economic, and political —depends on the spirit of the people. To the extent that governments and citizens are possessed of totalitarian or other undemocratic perceptions, the structures will falter.

Role of National Strength

We thus see the importance of national strength to the strength of these new institutions. Too often we forget what constitutes national strength. General Eisenhower, speaking at SHAPE last December, summed it up very succinctly:

> The strength that a nation, or a group of nations, can develop is the product obtained by multiplying its spiritual or moral strength by its economic strength, by its military strength. *It is the product, not the sum.*
>
> Consequently, if any one of these factors falls to zero, the whole is zero. There can be no army unless there is a productive strength with a productive power to support it. There can be neither a strong economy nor an army if the people are spiritless, if they don't prize what they are defending.

Where peoples are governed by perceptions which breed privilege, irresponsibility, lawlessness, greed, and ill will, the low quality of national strength provides a weak link in cooperative endeavors, no matter the size of their military forces or richness of economic resources. In international undertakings success depends upon adequate national strength of all geographic elements involved. It is for this reason that the ECA and today the MSA have placed so much emphasis upon the provision of economic and technical assistance in a manner aimed at building situations of strength. Thus, military aid, or economic assistance, or technical cooperation should be conducted in a manner to encourage courageous leadership, concern for the public welfare, integrity in public and private management, and democratic values generally.

Moreover, in any coalition which operates by persuasion rather than coercion, countries will tend to be supercritical of each other when they feel another fails to bear its full share of the burden. Both the U. S. and other members of the Atlantic Community must realize that every country is in a state of relative development. It is naive to expect perfection. The fact that these weaknesses in national strength—these functional ailments—beset each country should encourage the countries jointly and individually to pursue more positive and increasingly resourceful approaches in the promotion of those social and moral values which will mitigate these frailties.

I believe it is true that cooperative action among nations calls for a higher degree of national strength among the participants than action taken on a national basis. Likewise, collective action taken through sovereign international instrumentalities calls for a still greater degree of national strength than action either on a cooperative or national basis. A federation ordinarily encounters greater political and administrative difficulties than a monolithic form of organization. Suspicion, self-interest, inertia, cultural differences, and many other obstacles to cooperative endeavor have a compounding effect as the area of cooperation expands.

This thesis seems inconsistent with the idea that countries often see no need to cooperate when they feel strong, or in the absence of external threat. The prime ingredient of strength referred to here, of course, is not size, resources, or armament, but the sense of responsibility and moral and spiritual stamina of the people. In the words of the prophet Zachariah: "Not by might, nor by power, but by my spirit, saith the Lord."

This aspect of national strength as a foundation for collective action can be seen in the forces which have produced an encouraging measure of integration in Western Europe. The "Community of Six" (coal, steel, defense) could not have progressed this far without favorable political, economic, and social imperatives in the participating countries. Whether a suitable blend of these elements of national strength will develop as future steps are taken and future crises arise in the movement for integration, only time can tell.

These imperatives are equally important in the broader movement toward Atlantic Union. The more culturally diverse and numerically large national participation becomes, the more essential is an adequate common basis of national strength. The extent to which the American people demonstrate patience and courage and a sense of responsibility as key elements in their national strength will be of critical significance to the success of current and future endeavors toward an effective Atlantic Union.

FUTURE ROLE OF THE UNITED STATES

The postwar responsibility which the U. S. has assumed in world affairs, potently expressed in the Mutual Security Program, and the Marshall Plan before it, has been a powerful factor in the growth of these newly integrated organisms of Western Europe. Recent amendments to the Mutual Security legislation referred to above state the U. S. intention to give even more positive support. Of particular significance is the authorization to provide assistance directly to the new European institutions as well as to individual countries.

... the Congress believes it essential that this Act should be so administered as to support concrete measures for political federation, military integration, and economic unification in Europe. Appropriations ... relating to military assistance, defense support, and economic assistance ... may be used ... to furnish assistance to any of the following organizations: (a) The North Atlantic Treaty Organization, (b) the European Coal and Steel Community, (c) the organization which may evolve from current international discussions concerning a European defense community.

In each instance where this new authority is used to give material and psychological assistance directly to the emerging European central organizations rather than to individual countries, the United States will be taking a major step toward the strengthening of these institutions.

The Mutual Security Program for 1952–53 provides for various kinds of aid, all of which may be so administered as to promote the economic unification and political federation of Europe.

First, there is the "end-item" program—the transfer of some $4 billion worth of finished military equipment under the current year's appropriations to our NATO allies in Europe. This form of assistance not only can be based increasingly on the determinations made in consultation with or as a result of agreements reached in these multilateral institutions, but can also be allocated directly to them for assignment and use.

Second, there is the "off-shore procurement" program—funds for the purchase in Europe of military equipment and supplies, and the construction of facilities both for the use of the U. S. forces and for supply to European nations under NATO defense plans. Just as the EDC will be concerned, when fully established, with the assignment of production responsibilities within the Community on the basis of efficiency and capacity of facilities, so too the United States could work through the EDC or through other central channels in the procurement of materiel.

Third, there is "defense support"—the supply of machinery, raw materials, food, and other commodities to Europe to help the European economics sustain the increased defense effort. While this type of assistance is aimed primarily at meeting the needs of individual countries in their defense production commitments under NATO, and, therefore, calls for much direct negotiation on a bilateral basis, strong central institutions will provide opportunities for channeling assistance through them.

Fourth, there is "counterpart"—the deposits of local currencies equivalent to U. S. dollar aid which are used by the European countries with the approval of the U. S. to carry out mutual security purposes. These local currencies could be utilized increasingly by the countries for multilateral projects or as a means of better financial undergirding of the new central structures.

Beyond these specific ways in which U. S. assistance can be administered to encourage European integration, there is a more fundamental question asked by other countries: in what way and for how long will the U. S. develop common policy and conduct operations through these and any new central institutions? What the Europeans need is an assured sense that the U. S. will continue without vacillation to cooperate economically, politically, and militarily; that it will remain interested in Europe, not merely in the sense of carrying out formal commitments but because the American perception is clearly based on the principle of "community."

Financial aid has been one means of American assurance of interest in Europe, and obviously a vital one. Other symbols of American interest which emphasize partnership and mutual concern need to be found. Technical assistance as a cooperative undertaking—not as the export of "know-how"—is an example. Indeed the development and use of suitable symbols can add much meaning and support for mutual objectives, activities, and values.

Especially to be avoided are bewildering shifts in policy, frequent changes in government organizations which administer foreign programs, and short-run appointments of top mission personnel. All of these may lead to an impression

THE IMPACT OF U. S. ASSISTANCE PROGRAMS ON WESTERN EUROPE   1115

that our programs are of a temporary and emergency character, and that when the Soviet crisis is over we will pull back into our shell.

To cement our destiny more firmly with Europe's and Europe's destiny with ours, many thoughtful persons are now searching for additional arrangements pursuant to Article II of the North Atlantic Treaty for cooperation in economic and political, as well as military, spheres. Continuous economic cooperation (in matters of trade and financial policy, production commodity stabilization, etc.) is the best substitute for aid. Additional concrete and permanent (as contrasted with emergency) programs in such areas will give heart to the Europeans as they undertake defense build-up, European unification, and closer association in the Atlantic Community. In this connection, the President has recently requested the Public Advisory Board for Mutual Security to make a study of the foreign trade policies of the U. S. particularly as they affect efforts under the Mutual Security Program to achieve economic strength and solvency among the free nations.

SUMMARY

In this broader context these are some of the forward-looking concepts to which the people and government of the United States must address themselves:

1. The U. S. cannot expect more self-sacrifice and statesmanship on a continuing basis on the part of European countries than the U. S. is itself prepared to contribute. Their problems are our problems; our problems are their problems. One world!

2. Greater appreciation is needed of the effect which the towering economic position of the United States has upon the economics of Europe. Slight changes in our internal economy and external relations have such terrific repercussions abroad that a viable Europe cannot be wrought in the absence of a viable Atlantic Community.

3. The contribution of dollars to meet European balance of payments difficulties is a poor substitute for the desirable alternative of lower tariffs, elimination of trade barriers, and the institution of financial, production, and marketing programs for the Atlantic Community under which Europe can earn dollars. Forthright action here is as essential for our own economic well-being as it is for Europe's.

4. Further development of the principle of computing the obligations of each member of the Atlantic Community on a "burden sharing" basis, helps break down the feeling in some quarters of the U. S. that we are contributing a disproportionate amount. This approach—an approach fundamental to the whole concept of integration—also makes our predominant economic role more palatable to the other partners and gives them a greater sense of participation.

5. There now exists an unstable foundation for Western integration to the extent that the U. S. long-term political and economic commitments or those of any country are of a piecemeal or emergency character. Central cooperative

institutions which flourish under crisis may subsequently atrophy in the absence of permanent political and economic commitments.

6. There is need for a political framework in Europe to provide an umbrella for the recently created functional institutions of the Coal and Steel and European Defense Communities. Further development of the Atlantic Community as an organism through which the members carry out political, economic, and social aims will strengthen European integration, and in turn will receive vitality from it.

7. Since the ultimate source of both national and international strength depends on perceptions that govern attitudes and behavior of people, especially of those in positions of leadership, far more attention is needed in the development and sharing within the Atlantic Community of the moral and spiritual values underlying democracy and in the demonstration that the free world has a far superior answer to human needs than have the Communists or any other totalitarian group.

8. A broad basis of public understanding in this country of these problems and of America's responsibility and opportunity is even more essential for future progress toward European and Atlantic Community than at any previous time. Above all we must learn the art of patience, without relaxing our ideals and endeavors.

If we establish adequate long-term relationships between the United States and the countries of Europe, we can look toward an end of the chronic European financial crises, and the situations that have required large sums of U. S. aid on an annual basis. If we do not make such arrangements, we face the prospect of an indefinite continuation of extraordinary U. S. assistance to Western Europe. In the absence of (1) a satisfactory reconciliation of the U. S. internal and foreign economic policies in relation to our position in the Western Community, or (2) U. S. aid, we would have to anticipate (3) a sharp reduction in the defense efforts of our North Atlantic Allies, a serious deterioration in their economic circumstances, and in all likelihood a decline in their internal political stability. The folly of the latter should be self-evident, but the American people must face the challenge which is embodied in the difference between piecemeal assistance to partners in a common effort and an enduring commitment to remain with them.

Part VIII
The Postwar Growth Process

[17]

Catching Up, Forging Ahead, and Falling Behind

MOSES ABRAMOVITZ

A widely entertained hypothesis holds that, in comparisons among countries, productivity growth rates tend to vary inversely with productivity levels. A century of experience in a group of presently industrialized countries supports this hypothesis and the convergence of productivity levels it implies. The rate of convergence, however, varied from period to period and showed marked strength only during the first quarter-century following World War II. The general process of convergence was also accompanied by dramatic shifts in countries' productivity rankings. The paper extends the simple catch-up hypothesis to rationalize the fluctuating strength of the process and explores the connections between convergence itself and the relative success of early leaders and latecomers.

A MONG the many explanations of the surge of productivity growth during the quarter century following World War II, the most prominent is the hypothesis that the countries of the industrialized "West" were able to bring into production a large backlog of unexploited technology. The principal part of this backlog is deemed to have consisted of methods of production and of industrial and commercial organization already in use in the United States at the end of the war, but not yet employed in the other countries of the West. In this hypothesis, the United States is viewed as the "leader," the other countries as "followers" who had the opportunity to "catch up." In conformity with this view, a waning of the opportunity for catching up is frequently advanced as an explanation of the retardation in productivity growth suffered by the same group of followers since 1973. Needless to say, the size of the initial backlog and its subsequent reduction are rarely offered as sole explanations of the speedup and slowdown, but they stand as important parts of the story.

These views about postwar following and catching up suggest a more general hypothesis that the productivity levels of countries tend to converge. And this in turn brings to mind old questions about the emergence of new leaders and the historical and theoretical puzzles that

Journal of Economic History, Vol. XLVI, No. 2 (June 1986). © The Economic History Association. All rights reserved. ISSN 0022-0507.

The author is Coe Professor of American Economic History (emeritus) at Stanford University, Stanford, California 94305. He acknowledges with thanks critical comments and suggestions by Paul David and Knick Harley. The present paper is the revision of a draft read to the Economic History Association at its New York meeting in September 1985. This, in turn, was a greatly abbreviated version of a longer paper since published. See "Catching Up and Falling Behind," Fackföreningsrörelsens Institut för Ekonomisk Forskning (Trade Union Institute for Economic Research), Economic Research Report No. 1 (Stockholm, 1986).

386   *Abramovitz*

shifts in leadership and relative standing present—matters that in some respects fit only awkwardly with the convergence hypothesis.

The pertinence of all these questions to an understanding of modern economic growth obviously demands their continued study. The immediate occasion for this paper, however, is the appearance of Angus Maddison's new compilation of historical time series of the levels and growth of labor productivity covering 16 industrialized countries from 1870 to 1979.[1] These data enable us to observe the catch-up process in quantitative terms over a much longer span of time than was possible hitherto. At the same time, the evidence of Maddison's tables raises again the historical puzzles posed by productivity leadership and its shifts.

I. THE CATCH-UP HYPOTHESIS

The hypothesis asserts that being backward in level of productivity carries a *potential* for rapid advance. Stated more definitely the proposition is that in comparisons across countries the growth rates of productivity in any long period tend to be inversely related to the initial levels of productivity.

The central idea is simple enough. It has to do with the level of technology embodied in a country's capital stock. Imagine that the level of labor productivity were governed entirely by the level of technology embodied in capital stock. In a "leading country," to state things sharply, one may suppose that the technology embodied in each vintage of its stock was at the very frontier of technology at the time of investment. The *technological* age of the stock is, so to speak, the same as its *chronological* age. In an otherwise similar follower whose productivity level is lower, the technological age of the stock is high relative to its chronological age. The stock is obsolete even for its age. When a leader discards old stock and replaces it, the accompanying productivity increase is governed and limited by the advance of knowledge between the time when the old capital was installed and the time it is replaced. Those who are behind, however, have the potential to make a larger leap. New capital can embody the frontier of knowledge, but the capital it replaces was technologically superannuated. So—the larger the technological and, therefore, the productivity gap between leader and follower, the stronger the follower's potential for growth in productivity; and, other things being equal, the faster one expects the follow-

---

[1] Angus Maddison, *Phases of Capitalist Development* (New York, 1982). Maddison's estimates of productivity levels are themselves extrapolations of base levels established for most, but not all, the countries by Irving B. Kravis, Alan Heston, and Robert Summers in their *International Comparisons of Real Product and Purchasing Power* (Baltimore, 1978) and in other publications by Kravis and his associates.

Catching Up in Growth   387

er's growth rate to be. Followers tend to catch up faster if they are initially more backward.

Viewed in the same simple way, the catch-up process would be self-limiting because as a follower catches up, the possibility of making large leaps by replacing superannuated with best-practice technology becomes smaller and smaller. A follower's potential for growth weakens as its productivity level converges towards that of the leader.

This is the simple central idea. It needs extension and qualification. There are at least four extensions:

(1) The same technological opportunity that permits rapid progress by modernization encourages rapid growth of the capital stock partly because of the returns to modernization itself, and partly because technological progress reduces the price of capital goods relative to the price of labor. So—besides a reduction of technological age towards chronological age, the rate of rise of the capital-labor ratio tends to be higher. Productivity growth benefits on both counts. And if circumstances make for an acceleration in the growth of the capital stock its chronological age also falls.[2]

(2) Growth of productivity also makes for increase in aggregate output. A broader horizon of scale-dependent technological progress then comes into view.

(3) Backwardness carries an opportunity for modernization in disembodied, as well as in embodied, technology.

(4) If countries at relatively low levels of industrialization contain large numbers of redundant workers in farming and petty trade, as is normally the case, there is also an opportunity for productivity growth by improving the allocation of labor.

Besides extension, the simple hypothesis also needs qualification.

First, technological backwardness is not usually a mere accident. Tenacious societal characteristics normally account for a portion, perhaps a substantial portion, of a country's past failure to achieve as high a level of productivity as economically more advanced countries. The same deficiencies, perhaps in attenuated form, normally remain to keep a backward country from making the full technological leap envisaged by the simple hypothesis. I have a name for these characteristics. Following Kazushi Ohkawa and Henry Rosovsky, I call them "social capability."[3] One can summarize the matter in this way. Having regard to technological backwardness alone leads to the simple hypothesis about catch-up and convergence already advanced. Having regard

---

[2] W.E.G. Salter, *Productivity and Technical Change* (Cambridge, 1960) provides a rigorous theoretical exposition of the factors determining rates of turnover and those governing the relation between productivity with capital embodying best practice and average (economically efficient) technology.

[3] *Japanese Economic Growth: Trend Acceleration in the Twentieth Century* (Stanford, 1973), especially chap. 9.

388　　　　　　　　　　　　*Abramovitz*

to social capability, however, we expect that the developments anticipated by that hypothesis will be clearly displayed in cross-country comparisons only if countries' social capabilities are about the same. One should say, therefore, that a country's potential for rapid growth is strong not when it is backward without qualification, but rather when it is technologically backward but socially advanced.

The trouble with absorbing social capability into the catch-up hypothesis is that no one knows just what it means or how to measure it. In past work I identified a country's social capability with technical competence, for which—at least among Western countries—years of education may be a rough proxy, and with its political, commercial, industrial, and financial institutions, which I characterized in more qualitative ways.[4] I had in mind mainly experience with the organization and management of large-scale enterprise and with financial institutions and markets capable of mobilizing capital for individual firms on a similarly large scale. On some occasions the situation for a selection of countries may be sufficiently clear. In explaining postwar growth in Europe and Japan, for example, one may be able to say with some confidence that these countries were competent to absorb and exploit then existing best-practice technology. More generally, however, judgments about social capability remain highly problematic. A few comments may serve to suggest some of the considerations involved as well as the speculative nature of the subject.

One concerns the familiar notion of a trade-off between specialization and adaptability. The content of education in a country and the character of its industrial, commercial, and financial organizations may be well designed to exploit fully the power of an existing technology; they may be less well fitted to adapt to the requirements of change. Presumably, some capacity to adapt is present everywhere, but countries may differ from one another in this respect, and their capacities to adapt may change over time.

Next, the notion of adaptability suggests that there is an interaction between social capability and technological opportunity. The state of education embodied in a nation's population and its existing institutional arrangements constrains it in its choice of technology. But technological opportunity presses for change. So countries learn to modify their institutional arrangements and then to improve them as they gain experience. The constraints imposed by social capability on the successful adoption of a more advanced technology gradually

---

[4] Moses Abramovitz, "Rapid Growth Potential and its Realization: The Experience of the Capitalist Economies in the Postwar Period," in Edmond Malinvaud, ed., *Economic Growth and Resources*, Proceedings of the Fifth World Congress of the International Economic Association, vol. 1 (London, 1979), pp. 1–30.

Catching Up in Growth   389

weaken and permit its fuller exploitation. Thorstein Veblen said it this way:

> There are two lines of agency visibly at work shaping the habits of thought of [a] people in the complex movements of readjustment and rehabilitation [required by industrialization]. These are the received scheme of use and wont and the new state of the industrial arts; and it is not difficult to see that it is the latter that makes for readjustment; nor should it be any more difficult to see that the readjustment is necessarily made under the surveillance of the received scheme of use and wont.[5]

Social capability, finally, depends on more than the content of education and the organization of firms. Other aspects of economic systems count as well—their openness to competition, to the establishment and operation of new firms, and to the sale and purchase of new goods and services. Viewed from the other side, it is a question of the obstacles to change raised by vested interests, established positions, and customary relations among firms and between employers and employees. The view from this side is what led Mancur Olson to identify defeat in war and accompanying political convulsion as a radical ground-clearing experience opening the way for new men, new organizations, and new modes of operation and trade better fitted to technological potential.[6]

These considerations have a bearing on the notion that a follower's potential for rapid growth weakens as its technological level converges on the leader's. This is not necessarily the case if social capability is itself endogenous, becoming stronger—or perhaps weaker—as technological gaps close. In the one case, the evolution of social capability connected with catching up itself raises the possibility that followers may forge ahead of even progressive leaders. In the other, a leader may fall back or a follower's pursuit may be slowed.

There is a somewhat technical point that has a similar bearing. This is the fact, noticed by Kravis and Denison, that as followers' levels of per capita income converge on the leader's, so do their structures of consumption and prices.[7] R.C.O. Matthews then observed that the convergence of consumption and production patterns should make it easier, rather than more difficult, for followers to borrow technology with advantage as productivity gaps close.[8] This, therefore, stands as still another qualification to the idea that the catch-up process is steadily self-limiting.

The combination of technological gap and social capability defines a

[5] Thorstein Veblen, *Imperial Germany and the Industrial Revolution* (New York, 1915), p. 70.

[6] Mancur Olson, *The Rise and Fall of Nations: Economic Growth, Stagflation and Social Rigidities* (New Haven, 1982).

[7] Kravis et al., *International Comparisons*; Edward F. Denison, assisted by Jean-Pierre Poullier, *Why Growth Rates Differ, Postwar Experience of Nine Western Countries* (Washington, D.C., 1967). pp. 239–45.

[8] R.C.O. Matthews, Review of Denison (1967), *Economic Journal* (June 1969), pp. 261–68.

country's *potentiality* for productivity advance by way of catch-up. This, however, should be regarded as a potentiality in the long run. The pace at which the potentiality is realized depends on still another set of causes that are largely independent of those governing the potentiality itself. There is a long story to tell about the factors controlling the rate of realization of potential.[9] Its general plot, however, can be suggested by noting three principal chapter headings:

(1) The facilities for the diffusion of knowledge—for example, channels of international technical communication, multinational corporations, the state of international trade and of direct capital investment.

(2) Conditions facilitating or hindering structural change in the composition of output, in the occupational and industrial distribution of the workforce, and in the geographical location of industry and population. Among other factors, this is where conditions of labor supply, the existence of labor reserves in agriculture, and the factors controlling internal and international migration come in.

(3) Macroeconomic and monetary conditions encouraging and sustaining capital investment and the level and growth of effective demand.

Having considered the technological catch-up idea, with its several extensions and qualifications, I can summarize by proposing a restatement of the hypothesis as follows:

Countries that are technologically backward have a potentiality for generating growth more rapid than that of more advanced countries, provided their social capabilities are sufficiently developed to permit successful exploitation of technologies already employed by the technological leaders. The pace at which potential for catch-up is actually realized in a particular period depends on factors limiting the diffusion of knowledge, the rate of structural change, the accumulation of capital, and the expansion of demand. The process of catching up tends to be self-limiting, but the strength of the tendency may be weakened or overcome, at least for limited periods, by advantages connected with the convergence of production patterns as followers advance towards leaders or by an endogenous enlargement of social capabilities.

II. HISTORICAL EXPERIENCE WITH CATCHING UP

I go on now to review some evidence bearing on the catch-up process. The survey I make is limited to the 16 countries covered by the new Maddison estimates of product per worker hour for nine key years from

---

[9] My paper cited earlier describes the operation of these factors in the 1950s and 1960s and tries to show how they worked to permit productivity growth to rise in so many countries rapidly, in concert and for such an extended period ("Rapid Growth Potential and Its Realization," pp. 18–30).

Catching Up in Growth   391

TABLE 1
COMPARATIVE LEVELS OF PRODUCTIVITY, 1870–1979
MEANS AND RELATIVE VARIANCE OF THE RELATIVES OF 15 COUNTRIES
COMPARED WITH THE UNITED STATES
(U.S. GDP per manhour = 100)[a]

	(1) Mean	(2) Coefficient of Variation[b]
1870	77 (66)	.51 (.51)
1890	68 (68)	.48 (.48)
1913	61	.33
1929	57	.29
1938	61	.22
1950	46	.36
1960	52	.29
1973	69	.14
1979	75	.15

[a] 1870 and 1890. Figures in parentheses are based on relatives with the United Kingdom = 100.
[b] Standard deviation divided by mean.
Source: Calculated from Angus Maddison, *Phases of Capitalist Development* (New York, 1982), Tables 5.2 and C.10.

1870 to 1979.[10] The estimates are consistently derived as regards gross domestic product and worker hours and are adjusted as regards levels of product per worker hour by the Kravis estimates of purchasing power parities for postwar years. I have compressed the message of these data into three measures (See Tables 1 and 2):

[10] The countries are Australia, Austria, Belgium, Canada, Denmark, Finland, France, Germany, Italy, Japan, Netherlands, Norway, Sweden, Switzerland, United Kingdom, and United States.

TABLE 2
THE ASSOCIATION (RANK CORRELATION) BETWEEN INITIAL LEVELS AND
SUBSEQUENT GROWTH RATES OF LABOR PRODUCTIVITY
(GDP per manhour in 16 countries, 1870–1979)

Shorter Periods			Lengthening Periods Since 1870	
	(1)	(2)		(3)
1870–1913	−.59		1870–1890	−.32
1870–1890		−.32	−1913	−.59
1890–1913		−.56	−1929	−.72
			−1938	−.83
1913–1938	−.70		−1950	−.16
1913–29		−.35	−1960	−.66
1929–38		−.57	−1973	−.95
			−1979	−.97
1938–1950	+.48			
1950–1979	−.92			
1950–60		−.81		
1960–73		−.90		
1973–79		−.13		

Source of underlying data: Maddison, *Phases*, Tables 5.1, 5.2, and C.10.

392   *Abramovitz*

(1) Averages of the productivity levels of the various countries relative to that of the United States, which was the leading country for most of the period. (For 1870 and 1890, I have also calculated averages of relatives based on the United Kingdom.) I calculate these averages for each of the nine key years and use them to indicate whether productivity levels of followers, *as a group*, were tending to converge on that of the leader.[11]

(2) Measures of relative variance around the mean levels of relative productivity. These provide one sort of answer to the question of whether the countries that started at relatively low levels of productivity tended to advance faster than those with initially higher levels.

(3) Rank correlations between initial levels of productivity and subsequent growth rates. If the potential supposedly inherent in technological backwardness is being realized, there is likely to be some inverse correlation; and if it works with enough strength to dominate other forces the coefficients will be high.

The data I use and the measures I make have a number of drawbacks. The data, of course, have the weaknesses that are inherent in any set of estimates of GDP and manhours, however ably contrived, that stretch back far into the nineteenth century. Beyond that, however, simple calculations such as I have made fail, in a number of respects, to isolate the influence of the catch-up hypothesis proper.

To begin with, my measures do not allow for variation in the richness of countries' natural resources in relation to their populations. Labor productivity levels, therefore, are not pure reflections of levels of technology. In the same way, these levels will also reflect past accumulations of reproducible capital, both physical and human, and these may also be independent of technological levels in one degree or another. Further, the measured growth rates of labor productivity will be influenced by the pace of capital accumulation. As already said,

[11] In these calculations I have treated either the United States or the United Kingdom as the productivity leader from 1870 to 1913. Literal acceptance of Maddison's estimates, however, make Australia the leader from 1870–1913. Moreover, Belgium and the Netherlands stand slightly higher than the United States in 1870. Here are Maddison's relatives for those years (from *Phases*, Table 5.2):

	1870	*1890*	*1913*
Australia	186	153	102
Belgium	106	96	75
Netherlands	106	92	74
United Kingdom	114	100	81
United States	100	100	100

Since Australia's high standing in this period mainly reflected an outstandingly favorable situation of natural resources relative to population, it would be misleading to regard that country as the technological leader or to treat the productivity changes in other countries relative to Australia's as indicators of the catch-up process. Similarly, the small size and specialized character of the Belgian and Dutch economies make them inappropriate benchmarks.

Catching Up in Growth   393

differences in rates of accumulation may reflect countries' opportunities to make advances in technology, but rates of capital formation may also be independent, to some degree, of countries' potentials for technological advance. Finally, my measures make no allowance for countries' variant abilities to employ current best-practice technology for reasons other than the differences in social capability already discussed. Their access to economies of scale is perhaps the most important matter. If advanced technology at any time is heavily scale-dependent and if obstacles to trade across national frontiers, political or otherwise, are important, large countries will have a stronger potential for growth than smaller ones.

There are many reasons, therefore, why one cannot suppose that the expectations implied by the catch-up hypothesis will display themselves clearly in the measures I present. It will be something if the data show some systematic evidence of development consistent with the hypothesis. And it will be useful if this provides a chance to speculate about the reasons why the connections between productivity levels and growth rates appear to have been strong in some periods and weak in others.

Other countries, on the average, made no net gain on the United States in a period longer than a century (Table 1, col. 1). The indication of very limited, or even zero, convergence is really stronger than the figures suggest. This is because the productivity measures reflect more than gaps in technology and in reproducible capital intensity, with respect to which catch-up is presumably possible. As already said, they also reflect differences in natural resource availabilities which, of course, are generally favorable to America and were far more important to America and to all the other countries in 1870 than they are today. In 1870, the agricultural share of United States employment was 50 percent; in 1979, 3½ percent. For the other 15 countries, the corresponding figures are 48 and 8 percent on the average. The declines were large in all the countries.[12] So the American advantage in 1870 depended much more on our favorable land-man ratio than it did in 1979. Putting it the other way, other countries on the average must have fallen back over the century in respect to the productivity determinants in respect to which catch-up is possible.

In other respects, however, one can see the influence of the potential for catching up clearly. The variance among the productivity levels of the 15 "follower" countries declines drastically over the century—from a coefficient of variation of 0.5 in 1870 to 0.15 in 1979. Not only that: the decline in variance was continuous from one key year to the next, with only one reversal—in the period across World War II. In the same way, the inverse rank correlation between the initial productivity levels in 1870 and subsequent growth rates over increasingly long periods

[12] Maddison, *Phases*, Table C5.

becomes stronger and stronger, until we reach the correlation coefficient of $-.97$ across the entire 109 years.[13] (Again there was the single reversal across World War II when the association was actually—and presumably accidentally—positive.)

I believe the steadily declining variance measures and the steadily rising correlation coefficients should be interpreted to mean that initial productivity gaps did indeed constitute a potentiality for fast growth that had its effect later if not sooner. The effect of the potentiality became visible in a very limited degree very early. But if a country was incapable of, or prevented from, exploiting that opportunity promptly, the technological growth potential became strong, and the country's later rate of advance was all the faster. Though it may have taken a century for obstacles or inhibitions to be fully overcome, the net outcome was that levels of productivity tended steadily to even out—at least within the group of presently advanced countries in my sample.

This last phrase is important. Mine is a biased sample in that its members consist of countries all of whom have successfully entered into the process of modern economic growth. This implies that they have acquired the educational and institutional characteristics needed to make use of modern technologies to some advanced degree. It is by no means assured—indeed, it is unlikely—that a more comprehensive sample of countries would show the same tendency for levels of productivity to even out over the same period of time.[14]

This is the big picture. How do things look if we consider shorter periods? There are two matters to keep in mind: the tendency to convergence *within* the group of followers; and the convergence—or lack of it—of the group of followers vis-à-vis the United States. I take up the second matter in Section III. As to the convergence *within* the follower group, the figures suggest that the process varied in strength markedly from period to period. The main difference was that before World War II it operated weakly or at best with moderate strength. For almost a quarter-century following the war it apparently worked with very great strength. Why?

[13] Since growth rates are calculated as rates of change between standings at the terminal dates of periods, errors in the estimates of such standings will generate errors in the derived growth rates. If errors at both terminal dates were random, and if those at the end-year were independent of those at the initial year, there would be a tendency on that account for growth rates to be inversely correlated with initial-year standings. The inverse correlation coefficients would be biased upwards. Note, however, that if errors at terminal years were random and independent and of equal magnitude, there would be no tendency *on that account* for the variance of standings about the mean to decline between initial and end-year dates. The error bias would run against the marked decline in variance that we observe. Errors in late-year data, however, are unlikely to be so large, so an error bias is present.

[14] See also William J. Baumol, "Productivity Growth, Convergence and Welfare: What the Long-run Data Show," C. V. Starr Center for Applied Economics, New York University, Research Report No. 85-27, August 1985.

Catching Up in Growth   395

Before World War II, it is useful to consider two periods, roughly the decades before 1913, and those that followed. In the years of relative peace before 1913 I suggest that the process left a weak mark on the record for two reasons, both connected with the still early state of industrialization in many of the countries. First, the impress of the process was masked because farming was still so very important; measured levels of productivity, therefore, depended heavily on the amount and quality of farmland in relation to population. Productivity levels, in consequence, were erratic indicators of gaps between existing and best-practice technology. Secondly, social competence for exploiting the then most advanced methods was still limited, particularly in the earlier years and in the more recent latecomers. As the pre-World War I decades wore on, however, both these qualifying circumstances became less important. One might therefore have expected a much stronger tendency to convergence after 1913. But this was frustrated by the irregular effects of the Great War and of the years of disturbed political and financial conditions that followed, by the uneven impacts of the Great Depression itself and of the restrictions on international trade.

The unfulfilled potential of the years 1913–1938 was then enormously enlarged by the effects of World War II. The average productivity gap behind the United States increased by 39 percent between 1938 and 1950; the poorer countries were hit harder than the richer. These were years of dispersion, not convergence.

The post-World War II decades then proved to be the period when—exceptionally—the three elements required for rapid growth by catching up came together.[15] The elements were large technological gaps; enlarged social competence, reflecting higher levels of education and greater experience with large-scale production, distribution, and finance; and conditions favoring rapid realization of potential. This last element refers to several matters. There was *on this occasion* (it was otherwise after World War I) a strong reaction to the experience of defeat in war, and a chance for political reconstruction. The postwar political and economic reorganization and reform weakened the power of monopolistic groupings, brought new men to the fore, and focused the attention of governments on the tasks of recovery and growth, as Mancur Olson has argued.[16] The facilities for the diffusion of technology improved. International markets were opened. Large labor reserves in home agriculture and immigration from Southern and Eastern Europe provided a flexible and mobile labor supply. Government support, technological opportunity, and an environment of stable international

[15] See Abramovitz, "Rapid Growth Potential and its Realization."
[16] Olson, *Rise and Fall*.

396   *Abramovitz*

money favored heavy and sustained capital investment. The outcome
was the great speed and strength of the postwar catch-up process.[17]

Looking back now on the record of more than a century, we can see
that catching up was a powerful continuing element in the growth
experience of the presently advanced industrial countries. The strength
of the process varied from period to period. For decades it operated
only erratically and with weakened force. The trouble at first lay in
deficient social capability, a sluggish adaptation of education and of
industrial and financial organization to the requirements of modern
large-scale technology. Later, the process was checked and made
irregular by the effects of the two world wars and the ensuing political
and financial troubles and by the impact of the Great Depression. It was
at last released after World War II. The results were the rapid growth
rates of the postwar period, the close cross-country association between
initial productivity levels and growth rates, and a marked reduction of
differences in productivity levels, among the follower countries, and
between them and the United States.

Looking to the future, it seems likely that this very success will have
weakened the potentiality for growth by catching up among the group of
presently advanced countries. The great opportunities carried by that
potential now pass to the less developed countries of Latin America and
Asia.

III. FORGING AHEAD AND FALLING BEHIND

The catch-up hypothesis in its simple form does not anticipate
changes in leadership nor, indeed, any changes in the ranks of countries
in their relative levels of productivity. It contemplates only a reduction
among countries in productivity differentials. Yet there have been many
changes in ranks since 1870 and, of course, the notable shift of
leadership from Britain to America towards the end of the last century.[18]
This was followed by the continuing decline of Britain's standing in the
productivity scale. Today there is a widely held opinion that America is
about to fall behind a new candidate for leadership, Japan, and that both
Europe and America must contemplate serious injury from the rise of
both Japan and a group of still newer industrializing countries.

Needless to say, this paper cannot deal with the variety of reasons—
all still speculative—for the comparative success of the countries that

[17] Some comments on the catch-up process after 1973 may be found in Abramovitz, "Catching
Up and Falling Behind" (Stockholm, 1986), pp. 33–39.
[18] If one follows Maddison's estimates (*Phases*, Table C.19), the long period from 1870 to 1979
saw Australia fall by 8 places in the ranking of his 16 countries, Italy by 2½, Switzerland by 8, and
the United Kingdom by 10. Meanwhile the United States rose by 4, Germany by 4½, Norway by
5, Sweden by 7, and France by 8.

Catching Up in Growth   397

advanced in rank and the comparative failure of those that fell back.[19] I focus instead on a few matters that help illustrate the ramifications of the catch-up process and reveal the limitations of the simple hypothesis considered in earlier sections.

The Congruity of Technology and Resources: United States as Leader

Why did the gap between the United States and the average of other countries resist reduction so long? Indeed, why did it even appear to become larger between 1870 and 1929—before the impact of World War II made it larger still? I offer three reasons:

(1) The path of technological change which in those years offered the greatest opportunities for advance was at once heavily scale-dependent and biased in a labor-saving but capital- and resource-using direction. In both respects America enjoyed great advantages compared with Europe or Japan. Large-scale production was favored by a large, rapidly growing, and increasingly prosperous population. It was supported also by a striking homogeneity of tastes. This reflected the country's comparative youth, its rapid settlement by migration from a common base on the Atlantic, and the weakness and fluidity of its class divisions. Further, insofar as the population grew by immigration, the new Americans and their children quickly accepted the consumption patterns of their adopted country because the prevailing ethos favored assimilation to the dominant native white culture. At the same time, American industry was encouraged to explore the rich possibilities of a labor-saving but capital- and resource-using path of advance. The country's resources of land, forest, and minerals were particularly rich and abundant, and supplies of capital grew rapidly in response to high returns.[20]

(2) By comparison with America and Britain, many, though not all, of the "followers" were also latecomers in respect to social capability. In the decades following 1870, they lacked experience with large-scale production and commerce, and in one degree or another they needed to advance in levels of general and technical education.

(3) World War I was a serious setback for many countries but a stimulus to growth in the United States. European recovery and growth in the following years were delayed and slowed by financial distur-

---

[19] The possibility of overtaking and surpassing, however, was considered theoretically by Edward Ames and Nathan Rosenberg in a closely reasoned and persuasive article, "Changing Technological Leadership and Industrial Growth," *Economic Journal*, 72 (1963), pp. 13–31. They conclude that the troubles connected with leadership and industrial "aging" that doom early leaders to decline in the productivity scale are not persuasive. They hold that outcomes turn on a variety of empirical conditions, the presence of which is uncertain and not foreordained.

[20] These arguments are anticipated and elaborated in Nathan Rosenberg's fertile and original paper, "Why in America?", in Otto Mayr and Robert Post, eds., *Yankee Enterprise: The Rise of the American System of Manufactures* (Washington, D.C., 1981).

bances and by the impact of territorial and political change. Protection, not unification, was the response to the new political map. The rise of social democratic electoral strength in Europe favored the expansion of union power, but failed to curb the development and activities of industrial cartels. Britain's ability to support and enforce stable monetary conditions had been weakened, but the United States was not yet able or, indeed, willing to assume the role of leadership that Britain was losing. In all these ways, the response to the challenge of war losses and defeat after the First World War stands in contrast to that after the Second.

Points (2) and (3) were anticipated in earlier argument, but Point (1) constitutes a qualification to the simple catch-up hypothesis. In that view, different countries, subject only to their social capability, are equally competent to exploit a leader's path of technological progress. That is not so, however, if that path is biased in resource intensity or if it is scale-dependent. Resource-rich countries will be favored in the first instance, large countries in the second. If the historical argument of this section is correct, the United States was favored on both counts for a long time; it may not be so favored in the future. Whether or not this interpretation of American experience is correct, the general proposition remains: countries have unequal abilities to pursue paths of progress that are resource-biased or scale-dependent.

Interaction between Followers and Leaders

The catch-up hypothesis in its simple form is concerned with only one aspect of the economic relations among countries: technological borrowing by followers. In this view, a one-way stream of benefits flows from leaders to followers. A moment's reflection, however, exposes the inadequacy of that idea. The rise of British factory-made cotton textiles in the first industrial revolution ruined the Irish linen industry. The attractions of British and American jobs denuded the Irish population of its young men. The beginnings of modern growth in Ireland suffered a protracted delay. This is an example of the negative effects of leadership on the economies of those who are behind. Besides technological borrowing, there are interactions by way of trade and its rivalries, capital flows, and population movements. Moreover, the knowledge flows are not solely from leader to followers. A satisfactory account of the catch-up process must take account of these multiple forms of interaction. Again, there is space only for brief comment.

Trade and its Rivalries. I have referred to the sometimes negative effects of leading-country exports on the economies of less developed countries. Countries in the course of catching up, however, exploit the possibilities of advanced scale-dependent technologies by import substitution and expansion of exports. When they are successful there are possible negative effects on the economies of leaders. This is an old

Catching Up in Growth   399

historical theme. The successful competition of Germany, America, and other European countries is supposed to have retarded British growth from 1870 to 1913 and perhaps longer.[21] Analogous questions arise today. The expansion of exports from Japan and the newer industrializing countries has had a serious impact on the older industries of America and Europe, as well as some of the newer industries.

Is there a generalized effect on the productivity growth of the leaders? The effect is less than it may seem to be because some of the trade shifts are a reflection of overall productivity growth in the leader countries themselves. As the average level of productivity rises, so does the level of wages across industries generally. There are then relative increases in the product prices of those industries—usually older industries—in which productivity growth is lagging and relative declines in the product prices of those industries enjoying rapid productivity growth. The former must suffer a loss of comparative advantage, the latter a gain. One must keep an eye on both.

Other causes of trade shifts that are connected with the catch-up process itself may, however, carry real generalized productivity effects. There are changes that stem from the evolution of "product cycles," such as Raymond Vernon has made familiar. And perhaps most important, there is the achievement of higher levels of social capability. This permits followers to extend their borrowing and adaptation of more advanced methods, and enables them to compete in markets they could not contest earlier.

What difference does it make to the general prospects for the productivity growth of the leading industrial countries if they are losing markets to followers who are catching up?

There is an employment effect. Demand for the products of export- and import-competing industries is depressed. Failing a high degree of flexibility in exchange rates and wages and of occupational and geographical mobility, aggregate demand tends to be reduced. Unless macroeconomic policy is successful, there is general unemployment and underutilization of resources. Profits and the inducements to invest and innovate are reduced. And if this condition causes economies to succumb to protectionism, particularly to competitive protectionism, the difficulty is aggravated.

International trade theory assures us that these effects are transitory. Autonomous capital movements aside, trade must, in the end, balance. But the macroeconomic effects of the balancing process may be long drawn out, and while it is in progress, countries can suffer the repressive effects of restricted demand on investment and innovation.

[21] See also R.C.O. Matthews, Charles Feinstein, and John Odling-Smee, *British Economic Growth, 1856–1973* (Stanford, 1983), chaps. 14, 15, 17. Their analysis does not find a large effect on British productivity growth from 1870 to 1913.

400   *Abramovitz*

There is also a Verdoorn effect. It is harder for an industry to push the technological frontier forward, or even to keep up with it, if its own rate of expansion slows down—and still harder if it is contracting. This is unavoidable but tolerable when the growth of old industries is restricted by the rise of newer, more progressive home industries. But when retardation of older home industries is due to the rise of competing industries abroad, a tendency to generalized slowdown may be present.

Interactions via Population Movements. Nineteenth-century migration ran in good part from the farms of Western and Southern Europe to the farms and cities of the New World and Australasia. In the early twentieth century, Eastern Europe joined in. These migrations responded in part to the impact on world markets of the cheap grains and animal products produced by the regions of recent settlement. Insofar they represent an additional but special effect of development in some members of the Atlantic community of industrializing countries on the economies of other members.

Productivity growth in the countries of destination was aided by migration in two respects. It helped them exploit scale economies; and by making labor supply more responsive to increase in demand, it helped sustain periods of rapid growth. Countries of origin were relieved of the presence of partly redundant and desperately poor people. On the other hand, the loss of population brought such scale disadvantages as accompany slower population growth, and it made labor supply less responsive to industrial demand.

Migration in the postwar growth boom presents a picture of largely similar design and significance. In this period the movement was from the poorer, more slowly growing countries of Southern Europe and North Africa to the richer and more rapidly growing countries of Western and Northern Europe.[22] There is, however, this difference: The movement in more recent decades was induced by actual and expected income differences that were largely independent of the market connections of countries of origin and destination. There is no evidence that the growth boom of the West itself contributed to the low incomes of the South.

Needless to say, migrations are influenced by considerations other than relative levels of income and changing comparative advantage. I stress these matters, however, because they help us understand the complexities of the process of catch-up and convergence within a group of connected countries.

Interaction via Capital Flows. A familiar generalization is that capital tends to flow from countries of high income and slow growth to those

---

[22] The migration from East to West Germany in the 1950s was a special case. It brought to West Germany educated and skilled countrymen strongly motivated to rebuild their lives and restore their fortunes.

with opposite characteristics or, roughly speaking, from leaders to followers. One remembers, however, that that description applies to gross new investments. There are also reverse flows that reflect the maturing of past investments. So in the early stages of a great wave of investment, followers' rates of investment and productivity growth are supported by capital movement while those of leaders are retarded. Later, however, this effect may become smaller or be reversed, as we see today in relations between Western leaders and Latin American followers.

Once more, I add that the true picture is far more complicated than this idealized summary. It will hardly accommodate such extraordinary developments as the huge American capital import of recent years, to say nothing of the Arabian-European flows of the 1970s and their reversal now underway.

Interactions via Flows of Applied Knowledge. The flow of knowledge from leader to followers is, of course, the very essence of the catch-up hypothesis. As the technological gaps narrow, however, the direction changes. Countries that are still a distance behind the leader in average productivity may move into the lead in particular branches and become sources of new knowledge for older leaders. As they are surpassed in particular fields, old leaders can make gains by borrowing as well as by generating new knowledge. In this respect the growth potential of old leaders is enhanced as the pursuit draws closer. Moreover, competitive pressure can be a stimulus to research and innovation as well as an excuse for protection. It remains to be seen whether the newly rising economies will seek to guard a working knowledge of their operations more closely than American companies have done, and still more whether American and European firms will be as quick to discover, acquire, and adapt foreign methods as Japanese firms have been in the past.

Development as a Constraint on Change: Tangible Capital

The rise of followers in the course of catching up brings old leaders a mixed bag of injuries and potential benefits. Old leaders, however, or followers who have enjoyed a period of successful development, may come to suffer disabilities other than those caused by the burgeoning competitive power of new rivals. When Britain suffered her growth climacteric nearly a century ago, observers thought that her slowdown was itself due in part to her early lead. Thorstein Veblen was a pioneer proponent of this suggestion, and Charles Kindleberger and others have picked it up again.[23] One basis for this view is the idea that the capital stock of a country consists of an intricate web of interlocking elements.

[23] Charles P. Kindleberger, "Obsolescence and Technical Change." *Oxford Institute of Statistics Bulletin* (Aug. 1961), pp. 281–97.

402   *Abramovitz*

They are built to fit together, and it is difficult to replace one part of the complex with more modern and efficient elements without a costly rebuilding of other components. This may be handled efficiently if all the costs and benefits are internal to a firm. When they are divided among different firms and industries and between the private and public sectors, the adaptation of old capital structures to new technologies may be a difficult and halting process.

What this may have meant for Britain's climacteric is still unsettled. Whatever that may be, however, the problem needs study on a wider scale as it arises both historically and in a contemporaneous setting. After World War II, France undertook a great extension and modernization of its public transportation and power systems to provide a basis for later development of private industry and agriculture. Were the technological advances embodied in that investment program easier for France to carry out because its infrastructure was technically older, battered, and badly maintained? Or was it simply a heavy burden more in need of being borne? There is a widespread complaint today that the public capital structure of the United States stands in need of modernization and extension. Is this true, and, if it is, does it militate seriously against the installation of improved capital by private industry? One cannot now assume that such problems are the exclusive concern of a topmost productivity leader. All advanced industrial countries have large accumulations of capital, interdependent in use but divided in ownership among many firms and between private and public authorities. One may assume, however, that the problem so raised differs in its impact over time and among countries and, depending on its importance, might have some influence on the changes that occur in the productivity rankings of countries.

Development as a Constraint on Change: Intangible Capital and Political Institutions

Attention now returns to matters akin to social capability. In the simple catch-up hypothesis, that capability is viewed as either exogenously determined or else as adjusting steadily to the requirements of technological opportunity. The educational and institutional commitments induced by past development may, however, stand as an obstacle. That is a question that calls for study. The comments that follow are no more than brief indications of prominent possibilities.

The United States was the pioneer of mass production as embodied in the huge plant, the complex and rigid assembly line, the standardized product, and the long production run. It is also the pioneer and developer of the mammoth diversified conglomerate corporation. The vision of business carried on within such organizations, their highly indirect, statistical, and bureaucratic methods of consultation, planning and decision, the inevitable distractions of trading in assets rather than production of goods—these mental biases have sunk deep into the American business outlook and into the doctrine and training of young American managers. The necessary decentralization of operations into multiple profit centers directs the attention of managers and their superiors to the quarterly profit report and draws their energies away from the development of improved products and processes that require years of attention.[24] One may well ask how well this older vision of management and enterprise and the organizational scheme in which it is embodied will accommodate the problems and potentialities of the emerging computer and communications revolution. Or will that occur more easily in countries where educational systems, forms of corporate organization, and managerial outlook can better make a fresh start?

The long period of leadership and development enjoyed by the United States and the entire North Atlantic community meant, of course, a great increase of incomes. The rise of incomes, in turn, afforded a chance to satisfy latent desires for all sorts of non-market goods ranging from maintenance in old age to a safe-guarded natural environment. Satisfying these demands, largely by public action, has also afforded an ample opportunity for special interest groups to obtain privileges and protection in a process that Mancur Olson and others have generalized.

The outcome of this conjuncture of circumstances and forces is the Mixed Economy of the West, the complex system of transfers, taxes, regulations, and public activity, as well as organizations of union and business power, that had its roots long before the War, that expanded rapidly during the growth boom of the fifties and sixties, and that reached very high levels in the seventies. This trend is very broadly consistent with the suggestion that the elaboration of the mixed economy is a function of economic growth itself. To this one has to add the widely held idea advanced by Olson and many others that the system operates to reduce enterprise, work, saving, investment, and mobility and, therefore, to constrict the processes of innovation and change that productivity growth involves.

How much is there in all this? The answer turns only partly on a calculation of the direct effects of the system on economic incentives. These have proved difficult to pin down, and attempts to measure them have generally not yielded large numbers, at least for the United States.[25] The answer requires an equally difficult evaluation of the

---

[24] These and similar questions are raised by experienced observers of American business. They are well summarized by Edward Denison, *Trends in American Economic Growth, 1929–1982*, (Washington, D.C., 1985), chap. 3.

[25] Representative arguments supporting the idea that social capability has suffered, together with some quantitative evidence, may be found in Olson, *Rise and Fall*; William Fellner, "The Declining Growth of American Productivity: An Introductory Note," in W. Fellner, ed., *Contemporary Economic Problems, 1979* (Washington, D.C., 1979); and Assar Lindbeck, "Limits to the Welfare State," *Challenge* (Dec. 1985). For argument and evidence on the other side, see Sheldon Danzigar, Robert Haveman, and Robert Plotnick, "How Income Transfers Affect Work,

positive roles of government activity. These include not only the government's support of education, research, and information, and its provision of physical overhead capital and of the host of local functions required for urban life. We must remember also that the occupational and geographical adjustments needed to absorb new technology impose heavy costs on individuals. The accompanying changes alter the positions, prospects, and power of established groups, and they transform the structure of families and their roles in caring for children, the sick, and the old. Technical advance, therefore, engenders conflict and resistance; and the Welfare State with its transfers and regulations constitutes a mode of conflict resolution and a means of mitigating the costs of change that would otherwise induce resistance to growth. The existing empirical studies that bear on the economic responses to government intervention are, therefore, far from meeting the problem fully.

If the growth-inhibiting forces embodied in the Welfare State and in private expressions of market power were straightforward, positive functions of income levels, uniform across countries, that would be another reason for supposing that the catch-up process was self-limiting. The productivity levels of followers would, on this account, converge towards but not exceed the leader's. But these forces are clearly not simple, uniform functions of income. The institutions of the Welfare State have reached a higher degree of elaboration in Europe than in the United States. The objects of expenditure, the structures of transfers and taxes, and people's responses to both differ from country to country. These institutional developments, therefore, besides having some influence on growth rates generally, may constitute a wild card in the deck of growth forces. They will tend to produce changes in the ranks of countries in the productivity scale and these may include the top rank itself.

A sense that forces of institutional change are now acting to limit the growth of Western countries pervades the writings of many economists—and, of course, of other observers. Olson, Fellner, Scitovsky, Kindleberger, Lindbeck, and Giersch are only a partial list of those who see these economies as afflicted by institutional arthritis or sclerosis or other metaphorical malady associated with age and wealth.

These are the suggestions of serious scholars, and they need to be taken seriously. One may ask, however, whether these views take account of still other, rejuvenating forces which, though they act slowly, may yet work effectively to limit and counter those of decay— at least for the calculable future. In the United States, interregional

---

Savings and Income Distribution, *Journal of Economic Literature*, 19 (Sept. 1982), pp. 975–1028; and Edw. F. Denison, *Accounting for Slower Economic Growth* (Washington, D.C., 1979), pp. 127–38.

Catching Up in Growth   405

competition, supported by free movement of goods, people, and capital, is such a force. It limits the power of unions and checks the expansion of taxation, transfers, and regulation.[26] International competition, so long as it is permitted to operate, works in a similar direction for the United States and other countries as well, and it is strengthened by the development in recent years of a more highly integrated world capital market and by more vigorous international movements of corporate enterprise.

In the ranking of countries within the group of presently advanced industrial economies, their variant responsiveness to competition may be still another influence making for change in rank and relative level of productivity. As this group competes with the newly industrializing countries of the East and South, however, the pressures of competition on their institutional development, as distinct from their impact on particular industries, should help the older group maintain a lead. There are, however, still more solid grounds for a renewal of productivity advance in both Europe and the United States and for the maintenance of a substantial lead over virtually all newcomers. These are their high levels of general and technical education, the broad bases of their science, and the well-established connections of their science, technology, and industry. These elements of social capability are slow to develop but also, it seems very likely, slow to decay.

Finally, it is widely recognized that the process of institutional aging, whatever its significance, is not one without limits. Powerful forces continue to push that way, and they are surely strong in resisting reversal. Yet it is also apparent that there is a drift of public opinion that works for modification both in Europe and North America. There is a fine balance to be struck between productivity growth and the material incomes it brings and the other dimensions of social welfare. Countries are now in the course of readjusting that balance in favor of productivity growth. How far they can go and, indeed, how far they should go are both still in question.

IV. CONCLUDING REMARKS

This essay points in two directions. It shows that differences among countries in productivity levels create a strong potentiality for subsequent convergence of levels, provided that countries have a "social capability" adequate to absorb more advanced technologies. It reminds us, however, that the institutional and human capital components of social capability develop only slowly as education and organization

---

[26] See R. D. Norton, "Regional Life Cycles and US Industrial Rejuvenation," in Herbert Giersch, ed., *Towards an Explanation of Economic Growth* (Tübingen, 1981), pp. 253–80; and R. D. Norton, "Industrial Policy and American Renewal," *Journal of Economic Literature*, 24 (March 1986).

406   *Abramovitz*

respond to the requirements of technological opportunity and to experience in exploiting it. Their degree of development acts to limit the strength of technological potentiality proper. Further, the pace of realization of a potential for catch-up depends on a number of other conditions that govern the diffusion of knowledge, the mobility of resources and the rate of investment.

The long-term convergence to which these considerations point, however, is only a tendency that emerges in the average experience of a group of countries. The growth records of countries on their surface do not exhibit the uniformly self-limiting character that a simple statement of the catch-up hypothesis might suggest. Dramatic changes in productivity rankings mark the performance of a group's individual members. Some causes of these shifts in rank are exogenous to the convergence process. The state of a country's capability to exploit emerging technological opportunity depends on a social history that is particular to itself and that may not be closely bound to its existing level of productivity. And there are changes in the character of technological advance that make it more congruent with the resources and institutional outfits of some countries but less congruent with those of others. Some shifts, however, are influenced by the catch-up process itself—for example, when the trade rivalry of advancing latecomers makes successful inroads on important industries of older leaders. There are also the social and political concomitants of rising wealth itself that may weaken the social capability for technological advance. There is the desire to avoid or mitigate the costs of growth, and there are the attractions of goals other than growth as wealth increases. A reasonably complete view of the catch-up process, therefore, does not lend itself to simple formulation. Its implications ramify and are hard to separate from the more general process of growth at large.

[18]

REASSESSING THE *WIRTSCHAFTSWUNDER*: RECONSTRUCTION AND POSTWAR GROWTH IN WEST GERMANY IN AN INTERNATIONAL CONTEXT[1]

Rolf H. Dumke

I. INTRODUCTION

Among German economists and economic historians the preferred explanation of the unusually fast rate of growth of the West German economy during the two decades after the Second World War is the reconstruction thesis (Rohwer 1988, pp. 246–48, 286, 300; Abelshauser 1975, pp. 23–31; 1983, pp. 85–102; Abelshauser and Petzina 1981; Borchardt 1982). In this interpretation the primary reason for West German supergrowth is the large gap between existing and potential output after the war-induced shocks to the economy, where potential output is defined by means of a historical long run normal growth path. The end of the reconstruction period is therefore thought to occur in the middle to late 1960s, when the postwar German economy again attains this long run normal growth path and growth slows down to 'normal' rates.

This interesting interpretation of the temporary nature of postwar supergrowth,[2] which may also be applicable to other countries, requires clarification. Can reconstruction be said to have occurred over such a long time span? Which long run German growth path is appropriate? What is the causal mechanism of German growth in the reconstruction story? Is the thesis of reconstruction an alternative to other explanations, or is it a partial explanation which needs those additional explanations — e.g. changes in institutional regimes — to be complete? In particular we ask: how does the reconstruction thesis differ from the productivity gap thesis which has recently been offered to explain growth patterns in an international cross section of countries?

[1] I should like to thank participants of the Warwick Economics Summer Research Workshop (July 1989) and of the CEPR Workshop on European Productivity in London (March 1990) for critical remarks. In particular, I have profited from Stephen Broadberry, Nicholas Crafts, Paul David, Barry Eichengreen, Richard Layard, Vibeke Sorensen. I am also grateful for critique from Knut Borchardt, Charles Kindleberger, Albrecht Ritschl, Richard Tilly, and Georg Ziemes. A *BULLETIN* referee provided helpful comments. The remaining ambiguities and errors are my own.
[2] The term comes from Charles Kindleberger (1967, p. 1).

Clarification of the reconstruction thesis and contrast with the productivity gap thesis are the themes of the Sections II and III.

There are a number of striking similarities between the reconstruction thesis and the newer productivity gap hypothesis (Gomulka 1979, Maddison 1979, Abramovitz 1979, 1986, Baumol 1986, Baumol, Blackman and Wolff 1989) of the long run growth patterns of rich OECD countries.[3] In both stories a gap between potential and actual output drives the growth process. Nevertheless, there are important differences between them in the causal mechanisms and in the definition of potential output. In the productivity gap thesis potential output is a function of the productivity levels and growth rates in the United States, the technologically leading country, from whom innovations are borrowed. International technology diffusion is the fundamental process which is stressed here (a point clarified by Gomulka 1979), whereas in the reconstruction story this explanation, although important, plays a secondary role. In the latter, potential output is defined by a historical 'normal' growth path. Moreover, in the dynamics of reconstruction growth, human capital (or what one could call the social capacity for growth) and the disproportionality between human capital and its complement, physical capital, after war-induced shocks and destruction play a major role in initiating supergrowth by supporting investment in physical capital. The disparity between social capacity for growth and actual output levels, which is greatest after a war, is the reason for fast postwar growth.

The main thesis of this paper is, therefore, that reconstruction and technology gap arguments are complementary explanations; both are needed to explain postwar growth, particularly in countries which were substantially damaged by the war, e.g., Japan, Germany, Austria and Italy. The reconstruction argument, when properly understood, does not suffice to explain the *Wirtschaftswunder*; technological catch-up growth remains a crucial cause. Moreover, the reconstruction process is an additional important argument in explaining growth patterns, especially the convergence process, in an international context.

Aggregate productivity levels in the 1950's and 1960's were influenced by war-induced shocks to the economy (the impact was greatest in the early 1950s). Most empirical tests of the productivity gap or the convergence thesis in the post-WWII period are mis-specified because they ignore the reconstruction impact on growth. 1950 levels of per capita GDP relative to the US not only are indicators of the relative degree of postwar technological backwardness but also indicate relative levels of prewar technology, say of the year 1939, plus a war-induced shock or disturbance. The reaction to the latter is a different cause of growth and one which may result in a much faster rate than that which is due to the international diffusion of innovations in normal times.

[3] See Maddison 1979, 1982 for the main data source.

REASSESSING THE *WIRTSCHAFTSWUNDER*   **453**

In Section IV I present a model of long run growth and apply it to Maddison's (1982) sample of 16 rich OECD countries between 1950 and 1980. Growth in per capita real gross domestic output in the long run is thought to depend on (i) improving technology, (ii) productivity advances due to sectoral labour reallocations and (iii) the reconstruction of the economy from war-induced declines. The level of RGDP per capita in 1950 indexes the productivity levels after the war; the war-induced output gap, the difference in an index of GDP between 1948 and 1938, and the share of the labour force in agriculture in 1960 as an indicator of the order of magnitude of the potential release of labour from traditional low productivity to higher productivity sectors: these are three important reasons for the existence of a large gap between potential output and actual productivity levels after the Second World War. In the long run (here 30 years) potential output is realized. Capital formation is thought to be a function of technical change and is endogenous in the model.

The test of the model shows that both productivity gap and reconstruction effects are economically and statistically significant variables explaining a large amount of the inter-country variation in long run growth rates. Indeed, it is possible to use the estimated coefficients to explain individual country, deviations from the mean rate of growth of all 16 countries in the sample. As expected, the reconstruction effect was the most important source of Japanese and West German growth, in contrast to the two slow growers, the United Kingdom and the United States. In the UK the low share of labour force in agriculture was a relative brake on growth, while in the US the dominant reason for slow growth was the high level of labour productivity already attained in the year 1950.

The same model was re-run to explain growth in later periods, and the resulting coefficients indicate a significant role for the reconstruction effect which persists into the 1960's. However because Japanese reconstruction plays such a dominant role I dropped Japan in a further analysis. The reconstruction effect in the remaining 15 OECD countries is less pronounced and it breaks down after 1960. The average rate of growth of the sample of rich and industrialized OECD countries is thus a useful norm to apply to individual country growth in order to test the length of the reconstruction period in an international setting.

In Section V implications of the empirical results for a full explanation of the *Wirtschaftswunder* are discussed and several interesting possible alternatives to the reconstruction thesis are presented.

II. RECONSTRUCTION IN GERMANY: EXPLANATIONS AND CRITIQUE

(a) Recovery and Reconstruction, Two Somewhat Imprecisely Used Terms

Postwar growth in West Germany has been analyzed by a large and interesting literature which has discussed the contribution of numerous separate causes of growth. Investigations which provide a synthesis of some of this

454   BULLETIN

literature, however, are few (e.g. Abelshauser 1975, 1983, Ambrosius 1986, Borchardt in Stolper 1966, Borchardt 1985, Hardach 1976, Hennings 1982, Rohwer 1988). Among the best is the article by Hennings in which the by now traditional thesis of export-led growth is advanced together with the argument that the establishment of a political consensus for economic growth in the 1950s and 1960s were important contributions to German growth. Following Henry Wallich (1955) this study also keeps the period of 'reconstruction' relatively short: to the years between 1945 and 1950.[4] During this time local sub-economies became reintegrated, structural imbalances and bottlenecks were removed and important economic reforms were instituted. In 1948 three major policies were implemented: the Marshall Plan, currency reform and the dismantling of wartime controls. Hennings argues that together they add up to a 'reform of the economic constitution' which 'changed fundamentally the attitudes and expectations of the population' (pp. 477–78).

Figure 1, from Rohwer (1988, p. 63) illustrates the spectacular recovery of the West German economy from the breakdown in 1944-45. Rohwer's estimates of the year-to-year percentage rate of growth of GDP rise to historically unprecedented levels between 1947 and 1950. It is not surprising that contemporary observers were impressed by the growth rates after the currency reform of June 1948. The UN's Economic Survey of Europe in 1950 (p. 36), for example, found that the pace of recovery from the 1947 trough was 'dramatically fast' in 1948, 'as a result of the impact of the monetary reforms.' And in Germany the economic director of the Bizone, T. Pünder, commented on the remarkable rise of industrial production after the monetary reforms: 'It is almost like a wonder' (see Abelshauser, 1975, p. 60).

There is a dispute among German economic historians about how important these institutional reforms were in initiating West Germany's *Wirtschaftswunder*. Abelshauser (1975, p. 63, 1981, 1983) has tended to de-emphasize the role of institutional change and policy stances in generating early postwar growth, suggesting instead that the reconstruction dynamic started before 1948. In turn he has been criticized by Albrecht Ritschl (1985) and Christoph Buchheim (1988, 1989). This discourse about growth before 1948 need not detain us here.

We are interested in the long run nature of the *Wirtschaftswunder*. It is evidently based upon the dynamics of reconstruction which last much longer than the short postwar recovery (*Wiederaufbau*) that comes to an end in the early 1950s, at the latest. Recovery is usually defined as the return to prewar standards and levels of output, but it can also include further aspects, as Alec Cairncross (1951) pointed out in his still useful discussion of German recovery. According to Maddison's estimates of West German GDP — which have been adjusted to exclude the impact of frontier changes — the 1936 level of output is regained in 1949. The level of GDP in 1938 is surpassed in

---

[4] Both have the concept of recovery in mind, as shall be clarified below.

REASSESSING THE *WIRTSCHAFTSWUNDER*   455

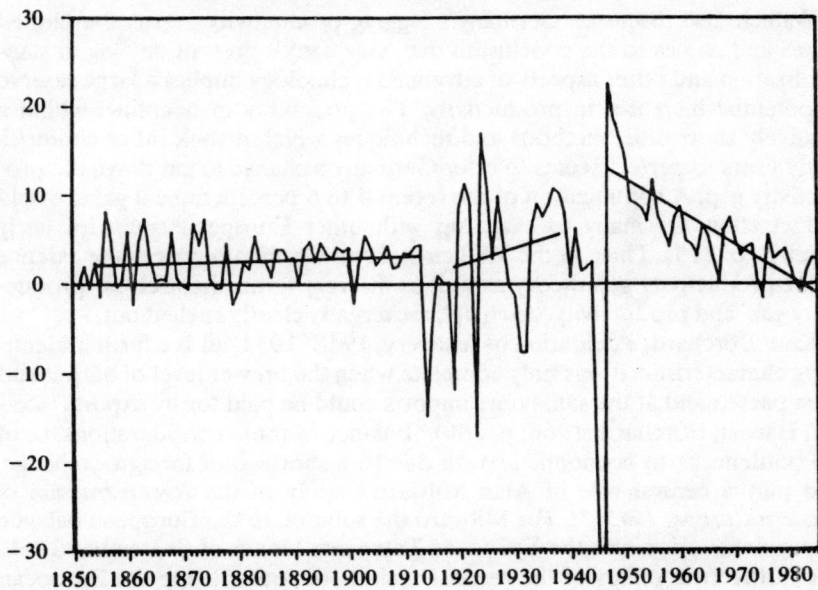

Source: B. Rohwer (1988) Figure 8c.

Fig. 1. Percentage changes in Gross Domestic Product of West Germany, 1850–1984, and linear Trends, 1854–1914, 1919–1938, 1947–1984

1951 (1982, p. 176). The index of industrial production begins to exceed the level of 1936 in 1950 (Cairncross 1951; Abelshauser 1983, p. 64, Table 11). The recovery of labour force in the West German economy was almost instantaneous as refugees from the East fled to the West.[5] The labour force in the Bizone area of West Germany rose by 17.7 percent between 1936 and 1948 (Abelshauser 1975, p. 104, Table 20). Industrial capital stock also grew by 11.0 percent between 1936 and 1948 (Abelshauser 1975, p. 121), notwithstanding the Allied bombing effort during the war and postwar dismantling and disinvestment.

Strangely enough, the recent German reconstruction arguments hardly analyse the recovery of productivity levels in German industries to prewar levels. Here Wallich (1955) is exemplary in a section on productivity (pp. 207–216). Although there is quite a variance among industries, total industrial output per man-hour worked (1936 = 100) re-attains the level of 1936 in 1951 (Table 25. Index of Industrial Productivity).

---

[5] Nevertheless, unemployment was high until the middle of the 1950s. A great number of the refugees fled to the agrarian Länder but the jobs were in the industrial areas. These had been badly bombed. Thus, the shortage of housing in industrial regions prevented the regional reallocation of the labour force and was a cause of structural unemployment.

Wallich also discusses Germany's lagging productivity versus the United States and comes to the conclusion that 'Germany's present-day lag in standardization and other aspects of advanced technology implies a large reserve of potential increases in productivity. The possibility of adapting, within a relatively short time, methods and techniques which it took other countries many years to perfect seems to offer Germany a chance to cut down the productivity gap. A continuation of the recent 4 to 6 percent annual gains would in fact allow Germany to catch up with other European countries fairly rapidly' (p. 215). Thus, in the Wallich story of German recovery the essence of the productivity gap theory as well as the very terms themselves, 'productivity gap' and productivity 'catch up', are already clearly spelled out.

Knut Borchardt's definition of recovery, 1948–1951, adds a further identifying characteristic: it was only complete when the prewar level of output had been passed and at the same time imports could be paid for by exports (Stolper, Häuser, Borchardt 1966, p. 260).[6] Balance of trade considerations, i.e of the bottlenecks to economic growth due to a shortage of foreign exchange, also play a central role in Alan Milward's study of the *Reconstruction of Western Europe, 1945–51*. For Milward the solution to the European balance of payments crisis was the European Payments Union of September 1950, one of the 'twin pillars of the reconstruction', the other being the European Coal and Steel Community of April 1951. Thus, Milward's notion is that of reconstruction in a wider sense, which has to do with the construction of a Western European institutional pattern of 'economic interdependence'.

The concept of reconstruction used in recent German economic history and applied in the following pages, therefore, refers to a period which is longer than the usually discussed period of recovery[7] and has different causes than the currency and other institutional reforms of the year 1948. Reconstruction and its dynamics as used here are based on purely national factors, in contrast to Milward's wider view of the 'political and economic rebuilding' of Western Europe after WWII, which involves international co-operation in the creation of useful international institutions. Length of period and concept of reconstruction in the German literature become clearer with reference to Figure 2, taken from Franz Jánossy (1967).

Jánossy first developed the reconstruction argument to systematically explain the temporary basis of the *Wirtschaftswunder* in a number of European countries after the last great war and the reason for the later declining

---

[6] He is evidently following the path of Cairncross (1951) and other analysts, who pointed out the bottleneck to growth caused by a shortage of foreign exchange. In a later publication Borchardt (1985, p. 193) states that the first phase of the recovery (*Wiederaufbau*) was completed by the mid-1950s. For most commentators this is also supposed to be the end of the *Wirtschaftswunder*. Borchardt warns that the concept of the *Wirtschaftswunder* is badly defined. Thus, there can be no clear beginning or end of the phenomenon. Nevertheless, he himself adopts this conventional date for his analysis of German economic growth after the *Wirtschaftswunder*.

[7] According to Harald Winkel (1974, p. 76; 1982, p. 110) recovery (*Wiederaufbau*) ended with the recession of the year 1967. He seems to be the only German economic historian to posit such a long recovery period. He presumably means reconstruction.

REASSESSING THE *WIRTSCHAFTSWUNDER*   **457**

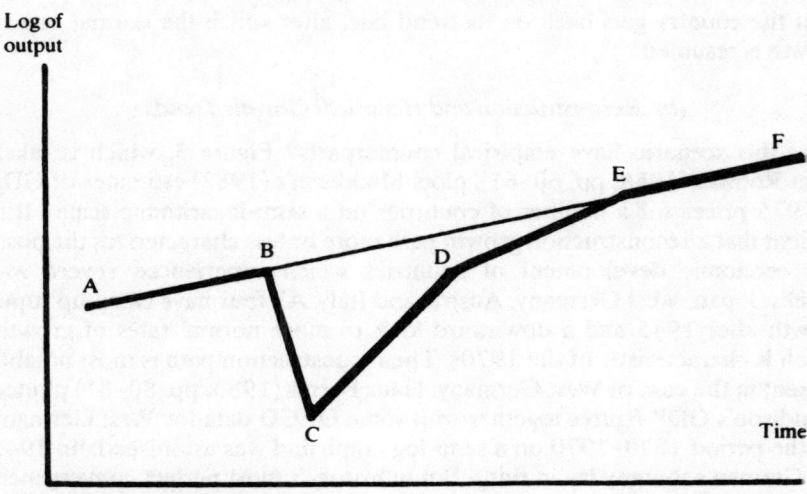

AF, long run trend line
AB, prewar output levels
BC, war induced shocks to output
CE, total length of the reconstruction period
CD, recovery of prewar levels
DE, reattaining the trend line
EF, output levels after reconstruction.

Fig. 2. The reconstruction process according to Jánossy

growth rates, back to a normal growth path. Each country accordingly faces a long run historical normal growth path which is a function of a stable growth of productivity and labour skills in the long run.[8] In the long run capital formation is endogenous and determined or limited by the scarcity of labour skills, or human capital, an exogenous variable in the growth process. The trend line of normal growth is shown by AF. BC illustrates the war-induced decline in output; CD the very rapid growth path towards recovery of prewar levels in D. However, reconstruction does not end here; growth continues at a higher than normal rate on path DE, until the economy rejoins the normal growth path at E. Thence a lower, normal growth rate rules the expansion path, EF, after the *Wirtschaftswunder*.

This general principle for the recovery of countries from wars and other shocks has also been voiced by other observers. For example, Colin Clark (1964, p. 119) observed that 'growth is naturally much more rapid than usual

_____

[8] I present the interpretation of Jánossy as found in Abelshauser 1983, pp. 91–93; and Abelshauser/Petzina 1981, pp. 53–54. See also the interpretation of Altvater, Hoffmann, Semmler 1980. Vol. I, pp. 19–23 and their critique in favour of a Marxist interpretation focussing on the marginal product of capital. Profit rates and investment are seen as the crucial variables influencing capitalist growth.

until the country gets back on its trend line, after which the normal rate of growth is resumed.'

(b) Reconstruction and Historical Growth Trends

Does this scenario have empirical counterparts? Figure 3, which is taken from Rohwer (1988, pp. 60–61), plots Maddison's (1982) estimates of GDP in 1975 prices for a number of countries on a semi-logarithmic scale.[9] It is evident that a reconstruction growth path more or less characterizes the post-war economic development of countries which experienced severe war shocks: Japan, West Germany, Austria and Italy. All four have catch-up super growth after 1945 and a downward kink to more normal rates of growth, which is characteristic of the 1970s. The reconstruction path is most notably present in the case of West Germany. Hans Brems (1983, pp. 80–81) plotted Maddison's GDP figures together with some OECD data for West Germany for the period 1870–1970 on a semi-log graph and was astonished: 'In 1945 the German economy lay in ruins. But in history's most perfect convergence, the 1948–1969 West German curve...swings back to an extrapolated 1870–1913 steady-state growth track.' For Brems the existence of a stable long run growth path of output is an important indicator that neoclassical growth theory is applicable to the long run.

Gottfried Bombach (1985, p. 49), however, has rightly criticized parts of this neoclassical interpretation for a 'period in which the geographical area has changed twice' and in which 'there are new generations of men with a different composition because of these changes, and because of large migration processes'. These are objections which might occur to any historian. He asks, 'Is it imaginable that there exist certain 'iron laws' which determine the path of growth through a full century of (great) change?' only to negate the question: 'I would not be able to find a single argument in favour of such a law.' Likewise, Milward (1984, p. 479) objects, 'the historian is bound to be sceptical about any argument...that over the long run investment and growth tend towards a norm.'[10] He believes that the reconstruction story cannot be applied to Western Europe as a whole, because 'the prolongation of trend lines of growth from the pre-First World War period to the end of the 1960s leaves the growth achieved by Western European economies in the 1960s above the line. Furthermore, the experience of investment or of disinvestment in the world wars and the inter-war period was extremely variable between the separate national economies, too variable to prepare the ground for so similar a common experience after 1945.'

Bombach (p. 49) also correctly argues that 'any trend is arbitrary' because it 'depends (i) on the beginning and the end, and (ii) on the inclusion or exclu-

---

[9] There also seems to be a reconstruction phenomenon — and a convergence vis-a-vis the United States — in the time pattern of labour productivity. See Maddison 1979, Fig. 10.1, pp. 196–197.

[10] Nevertheless, Angus Maddison (1987, p. 681) believes that 'circumstances in the decades before 1913 were more normal than in 1913–50' — a point often made by economic historians.

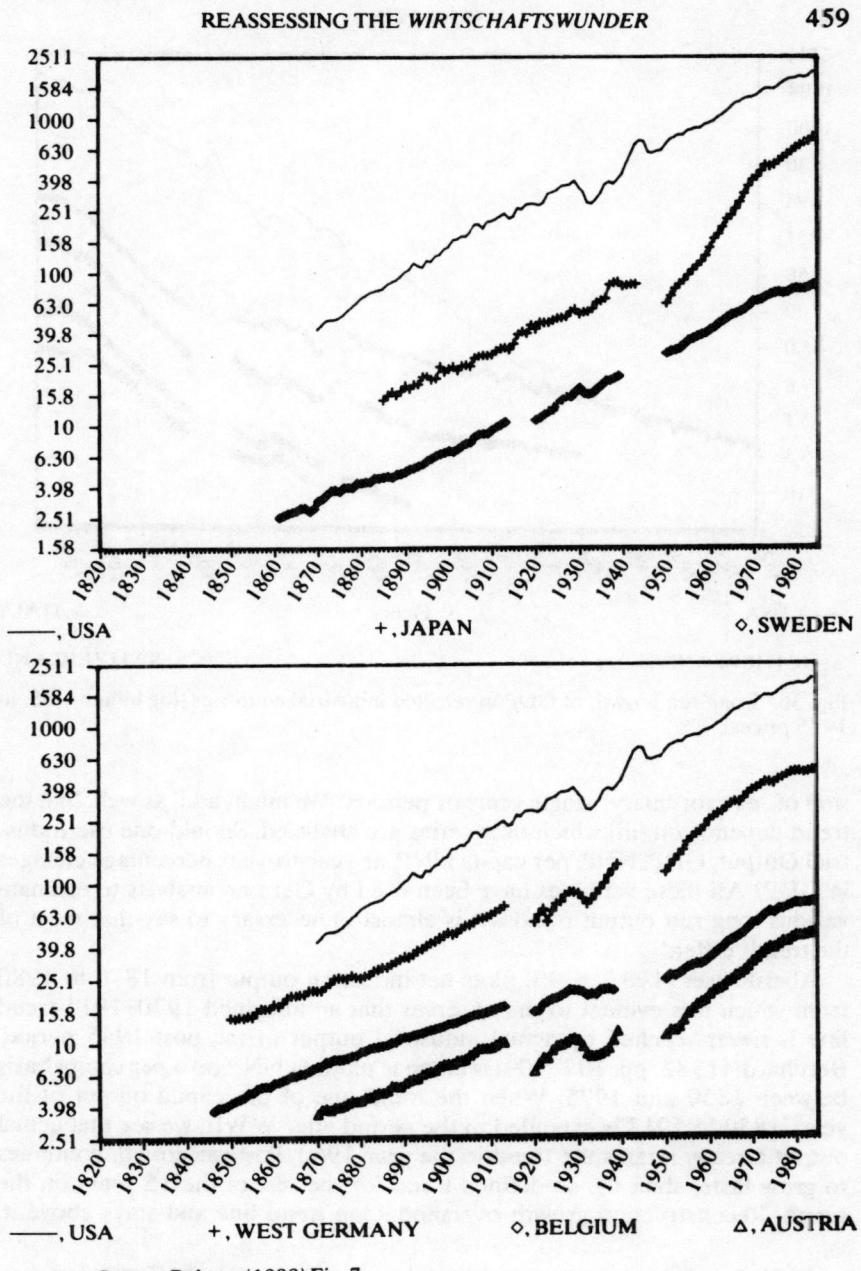

Source: Rohwer (1988) Fig. 7.

Fig. 3a. Long run growth of GDP in Selected Industrial countries (log billion US$, in 1975 prices)

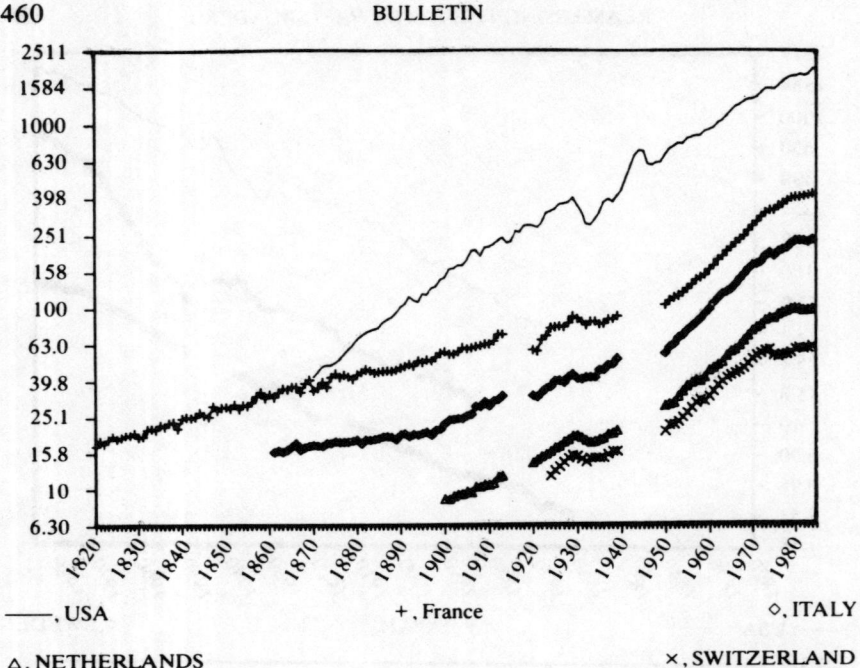

——, USA   +, France   ◇, ITALY

△, NETHERLANDS   ×, SWITZERLAND

Fig. 3b. Long run growth of GDP in selected industrial countries (log billion US$, in 1975 prices)

sion of "extraordinary" single years or periods'. We might add, as well, that the trend depends on (iii) which time series are analyzed. Should one use Industrial Output, GDP, NNP, per capita NNP, or year-to-year percentage changes in GDP? All these variables have been used by German analysts to estimate various long run output trends. It is almost unnecessary to say that most of the trends differ.[11]

Abelshauser (1983, p. 93) plots net industrial output from 1870 to 1980 from which it is evident to the observer that an imagined 1970–1914 trend line is never reached by actual industrial output in the post-1945 period. Borchardt (1982, pp. 107–109) is alone is plotting NNP on a per capita basis between 1850 and 1975. When the trend line of per capita output of the years 1850 to 1913 is extended to the period after WWII, we see that actual output already attains the trend in the year 1960. Postwar growth continues to grow faster than the so-defined trend for the rest of the 15 years on the graph. Reconstruction growth overshoots the trend line and stays above it.

[11] Aside from Rohwer, only log-linear trends have been discussed in the German literature. The concept of a variable or 'stochastic' trend has not yet been applied to the economic history of Germany in the 20th century. Reasons for doing so are spelled out in Section V. of this paper. See Stock and Watson (1988) for a discussion of the concept.

This should not be possible in the reconstruction story.[12] The most detailed analysis, however, was made by Bernd Rohwer (1988, pp. 59ff). When GDP levels are plotted on a semi-log graph, the exponential trend line of the years 1850–1913 lies below actual output for most of the post WWII period. No convergence to the 1850–1913 norm in line with the reconstruction thesis is seen with this particular definition of trend and this measure of output. After 1955 actual output progressively exceeds this trend line (Rohwer, Fig. 8a, p. 62).

Besides the previously discussed 'most perfect convergence' (Brems) which is the result of using a GDP trend between 1870 and 1913, there are only two other trend definitions available in the literature which result in a post-WWII convergence to norm in accordance with the reconstruction story. Both trends were presented in Rohwer's informative study (1988). The first utilizes Glismann's (1980) estimates of NNP in 1976 prices to establish an exponential trend for the years between 1850 and 1913. When this trend is extrapolated into the post-WWII era, there is a convergence of actual output to the norm from below in the late 1960s in support of the reconstruction argument (see Rohwer, Fig. 8b, p. 62). Rohwer prefers to use the average of year-to-year percentage changes of GDP in all the years, 1850–1985, as a linear trend (see Figure 1).[13] With these definitions the decline of postwar supergrowth to more normal levels becomes evident; the reconstruction story is supported. Nevertheless, it is clear that Bombach was basically correct; defining a trend rate of 'normal' growth is tricky business.

Some time ago Wilfried Beckerman (1965, p. 16) stated, 'The view is sometimes taken that international differences in post-war rates of growth reflect deviations, caused by the war and its varying effects, from some longer-run trend. This is very difficult to test, chiefly because of the uncertainty of what is thought to be the longer-run trend.' Beckerman applied four methods to measure interwar trends in GDP per man year for ten countries. But 'the economic disturbances of the inter-war period were so violent that alternative methods of measuring the trend lead to very different results, thereby illustrating the point made above that any concept of an underlying long-run trend is highly dubious (p. 17).' I agree wholeheartedly.

(c) Reconstruction Growth Theory

How are the prolonged and rapid growth rates after the Second World War explained by the reconstruction thesis? According to Jánossy, the potential

---

[12] Borchardt (p. 109) does not see 1960 as the definitive end of the reconstruction period. Such precision in timing seems to him to be unattainable, given the likely range of errors in the historical GDP estimates.

[13] This definition of trend has the advantage that all data points go into the trend and no years have been eliminated on whatever subjective basis, as Bombach feared. Arguably this is the least subjective definition of long run output growth trend available in West German economic history.

for growth continues to expand even in periods of substantial shock to the economy because a backlog of technological innovations made elsewhere continues to accumulate. As well, the quality of the labour force, if it is not decimated in numbers, may remain the same or even continue to rise during a war as long as schools and universities continue to function and on the job training qualifies more of the labour force. In addition, Abelshauser (1983, p. 92) notes, that the endowment of the industrial sector with physical factors of production after 1945 was far better than often assumed. Given the undiminished levels of physical and immaterial inputs and the backlog of technical innovations, potential output far exceeded actual output levels after 1945. This discrepancy is seen as a great potential for development, for rapid catch up growth after the war. According to Abelshauser and Petzina (1981) there was not only a catch up to pre-WWII output levels. Because of the slow growth in the interwar years, a period characterized as incomplete or delayed reconstruction (pp. 65–66) from the shocks of WWI and the Great Depression, the reconstruction boom after WWII could recoup the growth of output lost in the time since 1914. However, the pace with which this potential could be utilized depended upon the rate of growth of physical capital.

Jánossy argued that physical capital formation was the dependent or endogenous variable in long-run normal growth, while human capital was the independent, exogeneous and limiting factor. During a reconstruction phase this is not true; scarcity of human capital does not limit the growth of physical capital. Figure 4 provides empirical support for the notion of a long run constant trend line or of a steady growth of human capital per person over a period of 90 years in Germany, 1871–1959. Apparently this is true even in periods of war, when the growth of physical capital stock (including housing stock) is substantially shocked. The impact of war is, therefore, to be seen only in the destruction of physical capital (including housing) and in the decline of the ratio of physical to human capital.

The implied complementarity of human and physical capital in the Jánossy reconstruction story, however, is not borne out in Figure 5. The ratio of physical capital to human capital falls from about 10 to 1 in 1875 to 2.6 to 1 in 1949 (the data source is Walter Krug, 1967, pp. 36–71).[14] However, during the World Wars and in the interwar period the rate of substitution is notably higher. After WWII, by contrast, physical capital formation is much more rapid than the growth of Krug's 'immaterial capital.'

This does not necessarily mean that human capital already became scarce in the 1950s. Krug only estimated the direct and indirect costs of education and the expenditure for research and development and did not include the human capital of the flow of displaced persons and refugees after the war and the skilled migrants from the GDR in the 1950s. Abelshauser (1983, p. 96) has estimated the value of the human capital imported from the GDR in the

---

[14] Krug believed that he provided evidence for the thesis that human and physical capital were complementary factors of production (p. 70).

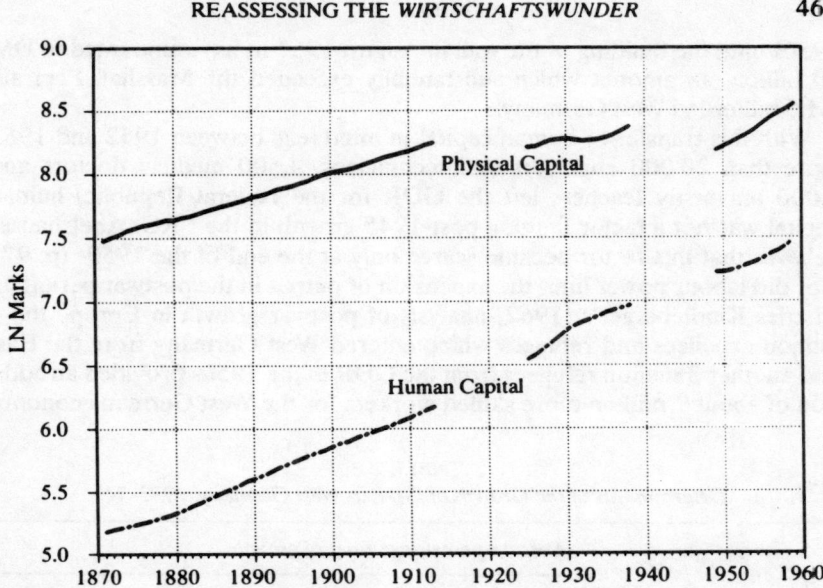

Fig. 4. Physical and human capital per capita, 1871–1959 (1913 prices)

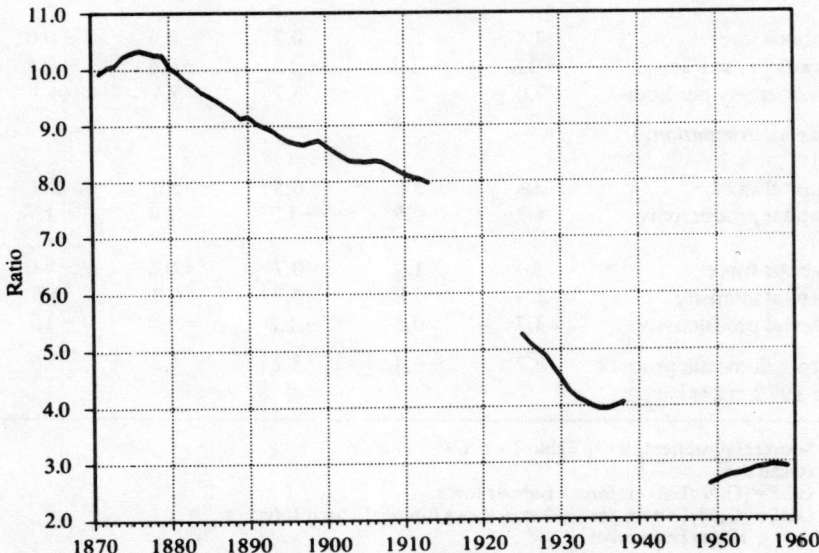

Fig. 5. Physical capital per unit of human capital, 1871–1959

1950s until the building of the wall in August 1961 to have amounted to DM 30 billion, an amount which substantially exceeded the Marshall Plan aid ($1.5 billion) to West Germany.

With this transfer of human capital in mind (e.g. between 1952 and 1963 more than 20,000 engineers and technicians, 4,500 medical doctors and 1,000 university teachers left the GDR for the Federal Republic) human capital was not a factor limiting post-1945 growth in the FRG. Abelshauser believes that this factor became scarce only at the end of the 1950s (p. 97). Nor did labour power limit the expansion of output in the postwar period. In Charles Kindleberger's (1967) analysis of postwar growth in Europe the 9 million expellees and refugees which entered West Germany from the East and another 3 million refugees from the GDR in the 1950s provided an addition of about 7 million more skilled workers for the West German economy.

TABLE 2
Determinants of the Growth of GDP in West Germany, 1950–74

	Average percentage rates of growth				
	1950–54	*1955–59*	*1960–74*	*1965–69*	*1970–74*
Labour orientation:					
(a)					
Labour force	2.4	1.9	0.7	− 0.6	− 0.0
Labour productivity	6.2	4.4	4.5	4.8	3.7
(b)					
Labour force	2.4	1.9	0.7	− 0.6	− 0.0
Hours per worker	− 0.8	− 1.5	− 1.1	− 0.6	− 0.4
Productivity per hour	7.0	5.9	5.7	5.4	4.1
Capital orientation:					
(a)					
Capital stock	3.8	5.8	6.5	5.6	5.4
Capital productivity	4.7	0.5	− 1.2	− 1.4	− 1.7
(b)					
Labour force	2.4	1.9	0.7	− 0.6	− 0.0
Capital intensity	1.4	3.8	5.7	6.3	5.5
Capital productivity	4.7	0.5	− 1.2	− 1.4	− 1.7
Gross domestic product (in 1972 prices)	8.7	6.4	5.2	4.2	3.6

Source: Glastetter (1977), Table 26, p. 69.
Recall that:
GDP = [GDP/Labour force] : Labour force
GDP = [GDP/(Hours per worker : Labour force)] : Labour force:
        Hours per worker

GDP = [GDP/Capital stock] : Capital stock
GDP = [GDP/Capital stock] : Capital intensity : Labour force

REASSESSING THE *WIRTSCHAFTSWUNDER*   **465**

'This excess supply of labour in the 1950s enabled Germany to maintain a high demand for exports, investment, and consumer goods without inflation (p. 33).' It also kept wages down, capital productivity and profits high, and motivated high rates of investment and output growth until labour shortages became notable in 1959 surveys of industrial labour conditions. Kindleberger concluded that the German economy well 'illustrated the Lewis model' of growth with surplus labour up to the turning point when labour becomes scarce (p. 36). The same argument of labour scarcity is used by Abelhauser as an indicator that reconstruction comes to an end in the 1960s: capital productivity and the rate of technical progress declines as a result (p. 98).

(d) Reconstruction and Productivity Growth Patterns

Reconstruction's end in the late 1960s is well indicated by the progressively declining rates of output growth seen in Figure 1 and Table 2. Glastetter's table shows that parallel to the declining rates of GDP growth, labour productivity growth also declines, whether measured by the hour or per worker. Because capital stock grew strongly between 1950 and 1965 and its rate of growth remained high thereafter and because labour force growth was limited to the 1950s, capital intensity is almost continuously on the rise over the period between 1950 and 1974. Not surprisingly, capital productivity growth declines as a result; it even becomes negative after 1960. Kindleberger's and other observers' idea that the labour force becomes a limitational factor by 1960 is corroborated. This is a problem which thereafter can only be partially overcome (because the marginal productivity of capital declines) by high rates of capital formation and a capital intensive mode of production.

Table 3 shows that TFP growth also declines. Besides technical change, or total factor productivity, the main argument for the growth of labour productivity in the neoclassical theory of growth[15] is the growth of capital intensity, weighted by the output elasticity of capital. We assume the latter to be equal

TABLE 3
Total Factor Productivity Growth in West Germany, 1950–74

	1950–54	1955–59	1960–64	1965–69	1970–74
(A)	5.7%	3.1%	2.5%	2.6%	1.8%
(B)	6.2%	4.0%	3.3%	3.0%	2.4%

[15] More precisely, y, the percentage change in output per worker equals the rate of technological progress (or the growth of total factor productivity, t) plus the output elasticity of capital, a, times the percentage change in capital per worker, x. Thus,

$t = y - a:(x)$.

This is derived from a Cobb–Douglas type constant returns production function: $Y = AX^a$, where Y is output per worker and X is capital per worker.

to 0.35[16] Subtracting the weighted growth rate of capital intensity from the growth of labour productivity, we obtain estimates of TFP growth in the five year intervals between 1950 and 1974 in the first line (A) of the table. In the second line (B), TFP growth is derived from the growth of productivity per labour hour less the weighted growth rate of the ratio, capital/labour hours.

The time profile of TFP growth conforms with the notion of reconstruction growth. Although the biggest decline is in the early 1950s, there is almost continuous decline over the whole period, with only a small break in the mid-1960s. Continuity of decline is especially evident in line (B), in the TFP estimate derived from output per labour hour. Above all, the early postwar years, the decade of the 1950s and, possibly, part of the 1960s, show unusually high productivity growth rates, compared with the 1970s and the German experience before WWI.[17] According to Sommariva and Tullio (1987), TFP growth in the period 1921–39 was as high as the above estimates for the decade of the 1960s. From this perspective the 1960s do not experience unusual productivity gains. Rohwer (1988, Figure 68, p. 263) indicates that the contribution of TFP to the growth of GNP declines almost continuously, year by year, from over 6% in the early 1950s to below 2.5% in 1965.[18] These are grounds for restricting reconstruction to the 1950s, or to end it, at the latest, in 1965.

What do Denison's (1970) estimates of the sources of growth of national income, 1950–1962, show in the German case? (See Table 21–11, p. 308.) Here all seems well for the reconstruction story: the contribution of TFP (or the rise of output per unit of combined inputs) to the growth rate (9.93%) in 1950–55 is high (6.74%), and the decline in the growth rate 1955–62 (down to 5.39%) is largely the result of a declining contribution of TFP to growth (2.88%). Denison's attempt to split up TFP is also interesting for the reconstruction thesis. Apparently there are three separate 'sources' of TFP in West Germany in the early 1950s which are affected by reconstruction:

(i) Concerning the contribution of 'changes in the lag of the application of knowledge, general efficiency, and errors and omissions,'[19] Denison remarks (p. 285): 'The residuals obtained for Germany and Italy in 1950–55 are large in comparison with (other countries) or for Germany and Italy themselves in 1955–62. These are two countries

[16] According to Glastetter, Paulert and Spörel (1983) Figure 131, p. 310, the wages share (adjusted for the change in the structure of the labour force) undulates between 55 and 60 percent of income and the share of labour incomes in total incomes fluctuates between 80 and 85 percent in the period 1950–80. I adopt Maddison's (1987) assumption that the output elasticity of capital is 0.35, a figure which lies between the two German estimates.

[17] According to Summariva and Tullio (1987) TFP growth contributes 0.9% to the growth rate (2.9%) of real NNP, 1880–1913: 2.9% (vs. 4.5% NNP growth) in 1921–39; 2.5% (vs. 4.7% NNP growth) in 1950–79; and 1.5% (vs. 2.7 NNP growth) in 1970–79. See Table 1.1, p. 15.

[18] Rohwer presents a graph but unfortunately does not describe his calculations.

[19] This is the residual of the 'residual', i.e., the residual left after Denison has accounted for large parts of the usual TFP 'residual'.

REASSESSING THE *WIRTSCHAFTSWUNDER*   **467**

that were defeated in World War II and had returned least nearly to normal economic life by 1950...(The) strong probability is that the large residuals are picking up an abnormal increase in efficiency in the early fifties that was associated with recovery from wartime disruption and that my techniques are unable to capture...(It) is apparent that the German residual is largest at the beginning of the 1950–55 period. It was in these years that the recovery aspect was strongest.'

(ii) The second source of TFP growth which concerns reconstruction is the 'balancing of capital stock.' Denison discusses the unique problem of an unbalanced and unterutilized stock of capital in Germany after WWII. Between 1950 and 1955 capital utilization rose much more sharply than capital stock. For Denison the story to tell is that 'repair and replacement' of facilities that had been destroyed, damaged, or removed, and small amounts of new investgment, made it possible to bring back into use other complementary facilities that previously were not utilized or fully utilized (p. 150).' For Denison, the declining underutilization of capital stock is an effect of the 'balancing out of the capital stock' after the war and should be considered as an unusual rise of efficiency.

(iii) Another important source of TFP growth which is due to reconstruction in the early 1950s are 'economies of scale' that are dependent upon a rise in per capita consumption and therefore upon 'income elasticities.' This source of growth is especially important in Germany 1950–55 (p. 249). Denison remarks that it may have to do with 'the recovery aspect (from the war).' In any case, 'the 1950–55 period in Germany...is an extraordinarily difficult one to analyze from all standpoints (p. 250).'

The three recovery related sources of TFP add up to a more than 3.6% higher rate of growth of German output in 1950–55,[20] a source of growth which declines to less than 1% in 1955–62.[21] Thus, the Denison growth accounting exercise provides some support for the reconstruction story by finding unusual efficiency gains — and gains that are related to recovery from the war — in the postwar period. Because most of these gains come to an end in 1955 they are really not in operation long enough to support the reconstruction story. They seem to illustrate, rather, the shorter German recovery period.

The results of Maddison's recent (1987) study, however, give more — if qualified — support to the idea of unusual efficiency gains for a longer time

[20] The respective magnitudes of these sources of TFP growth are 1.78% + 0.63% + 1.21% = 3.62% in 1950–55. The improved allocation of resources, the contraction of agricultural inputs, Denison finds, provided an important source of growth in the same period: 1.01%. The sum of all four sources is 4.63%.

[21] For the period 1955–62 the respective magnitudes are: 0.11% + 0.00% + 0.70% = 0.81%. For improved allocation of resources: 0.59%. The sum of all four sources is 1.40%.

span after the war. His estimates of joint factor productivity growth[22] for the average of six rich OECD countries[23] is about three times as high in the years 1950–73 as in the following period, 1973–84. In the case of West Germany the figures are 4.32 and 1.55, respectively. Unusual productivity sources for growth seem to be a general phenomenon characterizing the growth of OECD countries in the postwar period. They are not a specifically German or Japanese war-induced source of growth in line with the reconstruction story. Thus, the growth accounting technique only takes us part of the way in the search of a particular war-induced growth dynamic in Germany.

(e) Some Conclusions about the Reconstruction Thesis

The 'normal' historical growth trend required by the reconstruction thesis is difficult to define empirically. Perhaps an international comparison can provide a better alternative definition of 'normalcy,' as the average development of a number of industrialized OECD countries after 1945. Moreover, is it not really possible, contra Milward, to find a general application of the reconstruction argument to the Western European States or to the OECD?

Is the prolonged time period of reconstruction in West Germany analytically trivial? It could be argued that the war and its dislocations did not end in Germany in 1945. Rather, the postwar flow of refugees from the East and from the GDR in the 1950s was a continuation of the legacy of WWII. If so, then the reconstruction story requires more arguments, e.g. unusual types of productivity advances, to differentiate its explanation from Kindleberger's thesis that the availability of skills and labour supply from the East drove West German growth.

Part of the reconstruction story may confuse growth with mere efficiency gains which occur when moving from a point within a given production possibility curve — the situation after the war — to a point on the PP-curve. Recall, growth should refer only to the shift of the PP-curve. If this movement to the PP-frontier from within characterizes recovery, why is recovery part of a theory of long run growth?[24]

Henry Wallich (1955) was the first analyst of German postwar growth to clearly address this point because he wanted to infer a market-determined growth dynamic from the recovery period: 'Was what happened in Germany

---

[22] Defined as GDP growth minus the contributions of labour quantity, and residential and non-residential capital quantity. See Maddison (1987) Table 11a, p. 665.

[23] France, Germany, Japan, Netherlands, U.K., and the U.S.

[24] This is a fundamental problem only in the case of the traditional (Solow) neoclassical growth theory. Newer models of growth have been proposed by Paul Romer (1986) and others, in which economy-wide increasing returns to scale play an important role. In Richard Baldwin's (1989a, p. 33; 1989b, p. 17) empirical applications of the Romer model to estimate dynamic gains from trade or the growth effects of the European Community programme in 1992, static efficiency gains and dynamic gains are in fact causally linked.

only reconstruction[25] or was it also growth? If both, then in what proportions? Is it at all possible to draw such a distinction in the German experience? (p. 22).' Wallich, in fact, argued 'that while the revival was in good part a recovery it also contained enough of a growth element to permit analyzing it from that point of view. We found that Germany exhibited…the characteristics of a growth pattern that we have called production oriented (p. 33).'

The reconstruction thesis is not an alternative to the explanation of the *Wirtschaftswunder* that is based on institutional reforms. According to Abelshauser and Petzina (1981) reconstruction between the wars was incomplete in contrast to that after WWII. This is so because the beneficial effect of the fundamental international institutional changes after 1945, which were discussed by Milward, and the internal reforms, which created a market economy and a stable currency after 1948, were lacking in the interwar years.

A crucial part of the reconstruction thesis, the technology backlog, also happens to be part of the catch-up growth argument for a number of OECD countries after WWII, where the elimination of a productivity gap vis-a-vis the United States, the technological leader, generates fast growth. It may also be true that the intended role of labour qualifications in the reconstruction story is better described by the concept of a 'social capability' to grow which has been discussed in the recent catch-up literature (see Abramovitz 1986). Is the reconstruction hypothesis then, actually different from the catch-up theory of growth?

The disproportionality between human capital and physical capital after wars in the Jánossy reconstruction story may turn out to be a quite specific new cause of growth. This has been systematically analyzed only in recent theories of growth, e.g. by Lucas (1988), which assume constant returns to a broad concept of capital, including human capital. In these theories, Robert Barro (1989, p. 2) finds, 'if human capital is high relative to physical capital (as in post-war situations where the main wartime destruction applied to physical capital), the subsequent (growth) path may feature high rates of physical investment and per capita growth,' as transitional dynamics from a situation where the initial ratio of human to physical capital does not lie on its steady state value to its return.

The main elements of the reconstruction story of fast and temporary post-war growth which we have discussed so far concern the growth impact of (i) the productivity gap vis-a-vis the U.S., (ii) the disproportionality of the ratio of human to physical capital (H/P) compared with its steady state value after

[25] By 'reconstruction' Wallich actually has in mind what is usually called recovery. This is clear from the following quote: 'During the early period, say through 1951, the recovery element undoubtedly predominated heavily. This is evident…from the extraordinarily high annual increments (to GNP), showing income gains from 13 to 20 per cent…It is confirmed by the very low (marginal) capital-output rations, which were of an order ranging from 1.51 to 2:1…In 1952–54 annual increases (of GNP) amounted to only 7 to 8 per cent, with capital-output ratios of 2.5 to 3.5:1. The 1952–54 figures…could represent…a tapering off of reconstruction or a continuing growth trend (pp. 23–24).'

war destruction, and (iii) postwar labour surplus. All three elements raise the marginal productivity of capital and motivate high rates of capital formation. Nevertheless, it is clear that the kernel of the reconstruction theory, the notion that the shock of war destructions can have a beneficial impact on the long run, is to be found in argument (ii), the other two being auxiliary.[26]

It is possible to measure how far the ratio H/P has been shocked from its steady state value? We can employ a proxy of the extent of this change, based upon the assumption that it is proportionate to the decline of an index of GDP. In Section IV I use several measures of the extent of the shock of the World War to an index of real GDP in West Germany and 15 other OECD countries and investigate the shock's positive impact on long run German growth, 1950–1980, in a comparative setting.

III. RECONSTRUCTION AND THE PRODUCTIVITY GAP THESIS

(a) Productivity Gaps, Social Capacity and War Shocks

In the productivity gap literature (Abramovitz 1979, 1986; Baumol 1986; Baumol, Blackman and Wolff 1989; Dowrick and Nguyen 1989) there are recurring references to the impact of war-induced shocks upon productivity levels in different OECD countries. At times it is hard to distinguish the arguments from the reconstruction story. For example, Abramovitz's first formulation of the productivity gap thesis in 1979 almost sounds as if he was summarizing the German reconstruction argument, but now applied to a group of capitalist countries. His thesis of the postwar growth of ten capitalist economies is that a 'special, but transitory, set of circumstances made the postwar potential for productivity growth strong and enabled developed countries to exploit that potential rapidly, in concert and over a long period. Some of the favouring circumstances arose from the Second World War itself, some from the frustration of normal growth caused by war, political upheaval and depression during a longer period beginning in 1914; some reflected the stage of development which a number of industrialised countries had reached; and some rested on national and international political and economic arrangements which have now broken down (p. 2).'

Abramovitz's initial argument of a greater backwardness, or of a productivity gap, in Europe and Japan is not made in comparison with the United States but with historical achievements in the individual countries themselves: 'When the postwar period opened, the actual levels of labour productivity in Japan, north-west Europe and Italy were especially low compared with those

---

[26] Of course, the experience of a war can also influence productivity levels and the sectoral allocation of the labour force. This does not necessarily have to be viewed as a purely exogenous shock to a country. On the contrary, it can be argued that the policy of autarchy followed by the Axis states before and during WWII contributed to a misallocation of both capital and labour in industries and sectors which were uncompetitive, the lack of competitiveness only becoming clear after 1945. I owe this point to Albrecht Ritschl.

REASSESSING THE *WIRTSCHAFTSWUNDER* 471

which their technological tradition, human skills and governmental, commercial and financial institutions were capable of supporting. This gap between capability and achievement constituted a second source of potentially rapid postwar growth (besides the general acceleration in the advance of knowledge after WWII)' (p. 6). Although this line of argumentation is historical and very much in the spirit of the reconstruction hypothesis, Abramovitz does not carry it further. In the very next paragraph he defines the productivity gap of the individual countries as a gap in their levels vis-a-vis United States productivity levels.

Abramovitz analyzes productivity levels of 10 OECD countries compared with the United States between 1913 and 1970. After 1950 mean productivity levels of these countries rise from about 50 to about 70 percent of the US level. As well, the variance of relative productivity levels for the same group declines by more than five-sixths over the same period: international productivity convergence or catch-up growth is the result. Abramovitz concludes that the productivity gap 'constitutes a strong potentiality for rapid postwar growth in the less advanced countries' (p. 9). A rule of thumb for postwar growth is also spelled out: 'In general, the less productive the country in 1950, the more rapidly its productivity rose' (p. 9).

In the discussion of Abramovitz's (1979) paper Kazushi Ohkawa pointed out that the productivity gap argument is incomplete (p. 32). One also needed to consider a country's 'social capability' for growth. This point was integrated into Abramovitz's later (1986) paper to qualify his argument that followers tend to catch up faster if they are initially more backward: 'One should say, therefore, that a country's potential for rapid growth is strong not when it is backward without qualifications (i.e social capabilities), but rather when it is technologically backward but socially advanced' (p. 388).

This is the precise condition of a country after a war, as Jánossy had argued and Abramovitz himself stated in 1979 (p. 6). While Jánossy and the German authors of the reconstruction thesis identify social capabilities with labour qualifications, Ohkawa and Abramovitz, in contrast, have a wider vision. A country's social capabilities were initially identified by Abramovitz with 'technical competence, for which — at least among Western countries — years of education may be a rough proxy, and with its political, commercial, industrial, and financial institutions (1986, p. 388).'

A yet rougher proxy for human capital (and, implicitly, for 'social capability'), school enrollment rates, plays a remarkable role in Robert Barro's (1989) investigation of the causes of long run catch up growth, 1960-85, for 98 countries. His results could be used to support Abramovitz's (1986 pp. 389–390) notion that a 'combination of technological gap and social capability define a country's potentiality for productivity advance by way of catch-up' in the long run.[27] Barro finds, 'Although the simple correlation

---

[27] 'Could' is the proper word, because Barro, as a matter of fact, never mentions the term technology gap in his paper.

472   BULLETIN

between per capita growth and the initial (1960) level of per capita GDP is close to zero, the correlation becomes substantially negative once initial human capital per person (proxied by school enrollment rates) is held constant. Moreover, given the level of initial per capita GDP, the growth rate is substantially positively related to the starting amount of human capital. Thus, poor countries tend to catch up with rich countries if the poor countries have high human capital per person (in relation to their level of per capita GDP), but not otherwise (1989, p. 22).' Therefore, catch up growth is a function of the disparity between human and physical capital levels (when the latter is proxied by per capita income).[28] Barro pointed out that this disparity is likely to be great after a war and therefore gives rise to high rates of physical capital investment and per capita growth (p. 2). This view is in harmony with the German reconstruction story.

The concept of social capability should depend on more than education and the organization of firms, Abramovitz argued in (1986): 'Other aspects of economic systems count as well — their openness to competition, to the establishment and operation of new firms, (etc)... Viewed from the other side, it is a question of the obstacles to change raised by vested interests, established positions, and the customary relations among firms and between employers and employees. The view from this side is what led Mancur Olson (1982) to identify defeat in war and accompanying political convulsions as a radical ground-clearing experience opening the way for new men, new organizations, and new modes of operation and trade better fitted to techno-logical potential (p. 389).' Widening the definition and the determinants of the social capability for growth in the manner of Olson makes the impact of war a yet more central issue in the Abramovitz catch-up argument.

(b) The Role of Reconstruction in Convergence Growth

Postwar productivity convergence may reflect the dynamics of reconstruction. This point can be readily made by reference to the trends in the coefficient of variation (times 100) of GDP per capita which I have calculated for 16 rich OECD countries between 1950 and 1980.[29] Convergence of income per capita in these industrialized countries is indicated by the decline of the coefficient from 37 to 13 in the full sample. However, this decline is not

---

[28] More or less the same story is told in Baumol *et al.* (1989), chapter 9. A major factor which 'explains an economy's ability to absorb information and new technology is the education of its populace (p. 204).' When school enrollment rates are part of the explanations of catch up growth 'the results were dramatic (p. 205).' With the addition of the education variable, the convergence story applies to large samples (up to 112 countries) in the time periods 1950–81, 1960–81 and 1965–84; without the education variable catch up growth is not discernable for these large samples. 'That is, in effect, countries with similar educational levels were shown quite consistently to be converging among themselves, in terms of (Real Gross Domestic Product per capita), though not catching up with countries whose educational levels were higher (p. 205).'

[29] The data source is Table 1 in the Appendix.

necessarily due to the simple elimination of a productivity gap, as Abramovitz, but especially Baumol (1986) and Baumol, Blackman and Wolff (1989) would have it. Much of the convergence is due to the particular experience of war-shocked economies, e.g., Japan, West Germany, Austria, and Italy. When these countries are excluded from the analysis, the coefficient of variation in this sub-sample no longer declines to one third of its 1950 level, but only by one half. I conclude that part of the convergence story is due to phenomena which apply only to strongly war-shocked economies; i.e. that reconstruction is an important part of the convergence story.

This point is hidden in the appendix to chapter 5 in the Baumol, Blackman and Wolff (1989) volume, the most important of the recent productivity gap studies. The authors acknowledge that their tests of the convergence hypothesis 'entail a problem, because of the heavy weight they assign to the (initial productivity levels) 1950 figures...It can be argued that 1950 was characterized by atypical diversity in (Real Gross Domestic Product per Capita) as a result of the great differences in damage done to various economies by World War II, notably to those of Germany, France, the United Kingdom, and Japan. *Recovery of the most heavily damaged countries would naturally contribute abnormal convergence and would thereby bias the results of our calculations in the direction of our hypothesis* (p. 305) (my *underlining*).'

The only productivity gap analysis which attempts to address this problem is that by Dowrick and Nguyen (1989), the most careful empirical analysis to date. The authors test for parameter stability over decades in their model of productivity convergence: 'The period immediately succeeding the second world war is obviously exceptional in that war-ravaged economies were starting from exceptionally low income levels. If these countries had physical and human capital resources which would enable them to grow exceptionally fast,

TABLE 4

Decomposition of German Relative Growth Rates of per Capita GDP: (Deviations from OECD Average Rates of Growth, Percent per Year)

	(i) 1950–60	(ii) 1960–73	(iii) 1973–85
Actual Growth	3.64	− 0.36	0.36
Less adjustments for			
Cyclical bias	0.33	0.10	− 0.13
Catch-up growth	0.15	− 0.57	− 0.42
Equals adjusted growth	3.15	0.10	0.93
Less contribution for			
Employment deepening	0.80	− 0.28	− 0.22
Capital deepening	0.31	0.35	0.51
Equals unexpected growth	2.05	0.02	0.64

Source: Dowrick/Nguyen, Table 6.

474   BULLETIN

income convergence might be a phenomenon attributable solely or predominantly to postwar reconstruction and the apparent convergence over the
longer time span of 1950–85 might simply be the result of rapid convergence
in the early years with little further convergence occurring in more recent
years (p. 1022).' Excluding Japan from the analysis, the authors find that
'postwar reconstruction does not appear to explain catch-up, which has continued not only beyond 1960, but also beyond the watershed year of 1973
(p. 1028).' This test, to my mind, does not yet rule out all possible roles for
the reconstruction effect; it only rules out a markedly different impact of
reconstruction on catch-up growth between decades. If reconstruction has
such a long run impact on growth, as the German economic historians argue,
then the structural break test may not indicate a pervasive influence.

The authors' decomposition of postwar per capita GDP growth provides
further interesting results for German economic history of the postwar era,
both by defining the terms 'economic miracle' and determining its length.
They argue: 'Certainly Germany's "miracle" — as measured by growth above
our regression predictions — was restricted to the period of 1950–60; it performed quite averagely in the 1960s and its relative success since 1973 is
attributable to a high investment ratio relative to a declining population
(p. 1025).' About two thirds of West Germany's relative adjusted growth rate
in the fifties is due to unexplained growth, i.e. TFP growth which is not due to
catch-up growth (their definition of 'miracle' growth). Accordingly, catch up
growth in Germany plays a surprisingly small role in explaining Germany's
relative growth. Its effect is even negative after 1960 — see Table 4.

For our concerns Dowrick's and Nguyen's most important finding is the
fact that their convergence story does not well explain war shocked economies: 'a large part of the success of Japan, Germany, Austria, and France up
until 1973 is not explained by our analysis. We can only speculate that postwar reconstruction may have played some part in their success (p. 1025).' If
this is true, then the test for structural breaks in catch-up growth over time is
not a sufficient detector of reconstruction effects. They need to be modeled
explicitly. This is the aim of the following section.

IV.   A MODEL OF RECONSTRUCTION GROWTH IN AN INTERNATIONAL
                                    CONTEXT

                  (a) War Shocks and Postwar Productivity Levels

The arguments in the previous sections led to the conclusion that the reconstruction and the catch-up theses overlap. They are partly competing and
partly complementary arguments. For the catch-up thesis, reconstruction
effects may provide a reason for high temporary post WWII growth, while
the empirical test of the productivity gap thesis indicates a way to account for
the rate of improvement of technology in the long run, which the latter could
not explain. One of the aims of this paper is to present an empirical analysis in
which both causes of growth compete.

REASSESSING THE *WIRTSCHAFTSWUNDER*   475

An indicator of how strongly the empirical test of these two arguments may interlock is given by Table 5. Here per capita income levels in 1950 are regressed upon two measures of a war-induced disturbance: "gap" (the Maddison index of GDP in 1948 minus the index in 1938)[30] and 'gap2' (the ratio of RGDP in 1948 to RGDP in 1938) in a sample of 16 rich OECD countries. Apparently, the war shock alone accounts for 72 percent of the variance of the productivity levels in 1950. Countries with high levels of GDP per capita in 1950 were countries whose GDP growth was least disturbed by the war, so e.g. the United States and Canada. Bottom on the productivity list[31] in 1950 were countries with large war damage: Japan, West Germany, Italy and Austria. This war shock continues to influence productivity levels in later years, as the table shows. The magnitude and the pervasiveness of the influence of the war-induced shocks upon postwar productivity levels is surprising. For this reason most of the recent empirical studies of the productivity gap or catch-up thesis (Baumol 1986; Baumol, Blackman and Wolff 1989; Dowrick and Nguyen 1989), all of which use data starting in 1950 or in the early 1950s (Kormendi and Meguire 1985), are ill-specified. They ignore the impact of war-related shocks on those levels in the early 1950s. Possibly the effect of the technology gap on convergence growth in those studies would be diminished when such a shock is included in the model. The pervasiveness of the shock effects may also be one reason why Dowrick and Nguyen did not find a structural break.

A deficiency of the reconstruction argument was that no empirical model — besides, perhaps, the unsuccessful attempt by Beckerman (1965) — has been available to test for the existence of a reconstruction effect on long run growth. In Section II I have argued that the idea of a 'normal' growth path

TABLE 5
Regression of Postwar Levels of Per Capita RGDP on GAP and GAP 2

	R^2				
	1950	1955	1960	1965	1970
Regression of RGDP on GAP...	0.72	0.67	0.55	0.52	0.34
Regression of RGDP on GAP2...	0.74	0.67	0.52	0.51	0.38

Data source: Table 1. Appendix.

[30] The source is Maddison (1982); the index of real gross domestic product is 100 in the year 1913.
[31] Strictly speaking one should use output per employee or per labour hour as productivity measures. Nevertheless, output per capita correlates very highly with them and can be used as a reasonable productivity index.

can be approximated by the average growth trend of a sample of similar industrialized countries since WWII. That is, the perspective of this reconstruction story is comparative, not historical. For this reason data on productivity levels between 1950 and 1980 and on exponential rates of growth of these productivity levels are reported in Table 1 in the Appendix, along with two definitions of the effect of war on an index of GDP between 1938 and 1948.

The measurement of the impact of the Second World War upon the economies of the participating states is a complex topic. The cost of war is a question which was first systematically addressed after WWI, in conjunction with the reparations claims,[32] Broadberry (1988, p. 29) has rightly pointed out that there is a great deal of arbitrariness involved in these calculations.[33] However problematic these calculations are for the costs of WWI, we have nothing equivalent in detail and in the number of nations covered for WWII. Broadberry (1988) provides some rough new calculations of the tremendous costs of WWII for a handful of countries.

Consequently, we can only use an indirect measure of the shock of WWII upon the economy. I accept David Landes' argument (1973, p. 340) that the best measure of material loss due to the war is provided by the comparison of prewar and postwar levels of output.[34] My measure is the change in GDP between 1938 and 1948, dates as close as possible to the beginning and the end of the war available for the greatest number of countries.

There is an advantage to the output measure of the impact of war, in contrast to the cost of war approach. The decline in the level of output due to wartime disruption conforms with the Jánossy model of reconstruction (see Figure 2.) As well, with the output measure an account is taken of all possible disruptions and modernizations during the war. Comparatively indirect, but still significant, disadvantages (e.g. the interruption of market connections) as well as advantages arising from the war (such as the impact of war-time demand for raw materials and foodstuffs on international suppliers) will be indicated. A number of economic historians (Postan, 1967, Rostow, 1978, Pollard, 1981,) also argue that the expansion and modernization of industrial capacity during the war survived war-time destruction and postwar dismantling and contributed to the post-war boom in many countries (see van der Wee, 1984, pp. 23–24). The influence of these effects would be reflected by output levels after the war.

Barry Eichengreen (1986, p. 47) employs another measure of the 'extent of wartime disruptions to productive capacity and organization:' the ratio of industrial production at the beginning of the postwar period (after WWI, in

---

[32] See Bogart (1919) for a discussion of costs: (a) 'direct costs', which are measured by increased indebtedness of governments during the war, and (b) 'indirect costs', which consists of the loss of human life, loss of property, loss of merchant shipping, loss of production, war relief.

[33] For further discussion of the measurement of the cost of war see Milward (1972).

[34] See his Table 55, p. 451, taken from Kuznets (1964). 1945 levels of output are compared with 1937 for about a dozen countries.

REASSESSING THE *WIRTSCHAFTSWUNDER*   **477**

his case) to industrial production in 1913. This is equivalent to our second measure of shock in Table 1, Gap2. However, our measure of output is GDP, not industrial production.

(b) Reconstruction Effects in an International Setting

I have attempted to investigate the influence of so-defined war-induced shocks on postwar growth for a much longer period of time than the five or six years which Eichengreen investigated after WWI. As well, it is possible to find out when the reconstruction variable ceases to influence growth. Thus, growth from 1950 to 1980, growth from 1955 to 1980, growth from 1960 to 1980 and growth from 1965 to 1980 was regressed on the GAP measure (and GAP^2, because there is a nonlinearity in this relationship).

Table 6 shows some of the results of the regressions. The GAP in GDP between 1948 and 1938 (and its square) is an important variable which

TABLE 6
Effect of Reconstruction on Postwar Growth in 16 OECD Countries

Independent variables[a]	Growth per capita RGDP in:			
	1950–80	1955–80	1960–80	1965–80
Equation 1:				
RGDP[b]	− 1.18 E-5	− 1.1 E-5	− 1.1 E-5	− 9.38 E-6
	(− 6.55)	(− 5.63)	(− 4.86)	(− 4.23)
ADJ. R^2	0.754	0.672	0.601	0.530
Equation 2:				
GAP	− 0.000227	− 0.000205	− 0.000176	− 0.0000172
	(− 7.82)	(− 6.55)	(− 4.94)	(− 4.60)
GAP^2	1.148 E-6	1.187 E-6	1.347 E-6	1.242 E-6
	(3.15)	(3.02)	(3.02)	(2.65)
ADJ. R^2	0.800	0.740	0.622	0.580
Equation 3:				
GAP	− 0.000094	− 0.000084	− 0.000070	− 0.000075
	(− 3.34)	(− 2.68)	(− 2.19)	(− 2.15)
GAP^2	1.294 E-6	1.334 E-6	1.381 E-6	1.420 E-6
	(6.52)	(5.58)	(4.98)	(4.4)
RGDP[b]	− 9.230 E-6	− 8.994 E-6	− 9.258 E-6	− 8.32 E-6
	(− 5.70)	(− 4.87)	(− 4.65)	(− 4.01)
ADJ. R^2	0.941	0.904	0.854	0.806

Source of data: Table 1. Appendix.
(*t*-ratios are reported below the coefficients.)
[a]Regression constants are not reported.
[b]Initial levels of Real Gross Domestic Product per Capita in the years 1950, 1955, 1960 and 1965, respectively.

explains a significant amount of the postwar growth in the long run, 1950–80. Equation 2 tells a simple reconstruction story of postwar growth which is more powerful (higher R^2s) than the simple productivity gap story in Equation 1. Countries which experience growth (GAP is large and positive) during the war decade, 1938–1948, apparently grow slower after the war; countries with great war disturbances (when the GAP is large and negative), in contrast, have higher rates of postwar growth. However, the positive coefficient of the squared term of GAP indicates that this relationship is less than proportional. The reconstruction effect in Equation 2 lasts into the 1960s,[35] but breaks down after 1970.

The degree to which the reconstruction and the productivity gap theses compete and complement each other is shown by the comparison of Equations 1 and 2 with 3. In Equation 3 the initial level of Real Gross Domestic Product per capita has been added as a control variable, to monitor the effect of productivity catch up. It is evident that the explanatory power (the R^2s) of this set of variables is substantially higher than those of Equations 1 and 2. Thus, productivity catch up and reconstruction are largely complementary arguments for long run growth; their effects on growth are apparently different and they add up. But they also compete with each other. In Equation 3, which includes the control variable for the catch-up effect, the coefficient of GAP is less than one-half its size in Equation 2. The influence of initial RGDP levels upon following periods of growth remains highly significant, although the catch up effect declines slightly over time. In contrast, when the reconstruction effect has to compete with productivity catch up, GAP loses its significance much faster, possibly already by 1960. In Equation 1 growth is regressed on initial levels of per capita RGDP. Here the estimated coefficient of the initial income level is about 20 percent larger than in Equation 3. Consequently, when catch-up growth has to compete with reconstruction, the size of the catch-up effect also declines, if moderately.

(c) A Model of Long Run Growth in the Postwar Era: Reconstruction Growth, Catch-Up and Structural Change

A more complete model of long run growth can be put together in which a further Denison argument for TFP growth, 'improved allocation of resources,' is included in the list of explanatory variables: the percent of labour force in agriculture in the earliest year available for all of our 16 countries, 1960. (The source of data is World Bank, 1976). Thus, the use of our regressors in Table 6 and Table 7 can be theoretically motivated by recourse to Denison's arguments which pertain to TFP growth. The productivity gap argument is that potential 'advances in knowledge' are determined by labour productivity levels (relative to the technology leader) in the initial year of

---

[35] The impact of GAP upon growth 1965–80 is still statistically significant and the regression explains 58 percent of the variance of the growth experience of these 16 countries.

growth, here 1950. On the other hand, the war-induced disruption variable, GAP, stands for the 'changes in the lag in application of knowledge etc.', the 'balancing of capital stock' and the effect of 'income elasticities' on 'economies of scale.' These are all factors which Denison (1970) associated with recovery and reconstruction and which he found to have played a substantial role in raising TFP in Northwest Europe (especially in Germany and Italy) after the war, particularly in the early 1950s. In effect, I have taken the most important causes of TFP growth in the Denison study and suggest that in the long run their influence on growth is decisive. In contrast to the usual growth models but in accordance with arguments by Dan Usher (1980), capital formation is treated as endogenous; it is completely technology-induced.[36] Because the dependent variable is per capita RGDP, no explicit role for the growth of production and of labour supply is advanced. Long run growth, therefore, equals growth of long run productivity potential. The variables used to explain growth between 1950 and 1980 in our 16 country sample are RGDP50, the level of per capita real gross domestic product in 1950, GAP, and AGLABSH60, the share of the labour force in agriculture in 1960.[37]

Table 7 shows the main empirical results of this study. This basic model explains the growth of labour productivity, or per capita output, in these 16 countries between 1950 and 1980 quite well. Non-linear effects are taken into account by squaring two of the explanatory variables. With this specification the OLS estimate shows an astonishingly high degree of prediction. Ninety-six percent of the variance in the growth rates of these countries is explained by this simple model. The model predicts well at both ends of the range of the growth rates. The significant and negative coefficient of the 1950 level of labour productivity is important. It indicates that convergence is the rule in this sample and model (as in Table 6, Equation 3), where the productivity gap or catch up thesis has to compete with the reconstruction effect. Yet more interesting is the significant effect of GAP and its square on long run growth. Countries which do not experience a war-induced decline in output generally grow more slowly after the war; conversely, countries with important war-induced shocks grow faster after the war. That the re-allocation of low productivity agricultural labour is a good source of productivity growth is indicated by the positive coefficient in Table 7.

The absolute size of the beta values, the regression coefficients of the standardized variables (not reported in Table 7), indicates the relative importance of the variables in the model. The beta of RGDP50 is about the same magni-

---

[36] See Usher (1980), ch. 12, where it is argued that in the long run the nature and magnitude of the inputs are largely determined by changes in technology. Moreover, in contrast to the usual growth accounting, Usher states 'that it is inappropriate to contrast technical change and capital formation as sources of economic growth because the rate of capital formation in any year *t* is itself dependent on technical change in the capital goods industry in all years prior to *t* (p. 278).'

[37] In contrast to Denison, who treats these various sources of TFP growth as separate and additive, our regression model allows these sources of growth to compete against each other.

480   BULLETIN

TABLE 7

Regression of Mean Growth of Real Gross Domestic Product per Capita, 1950–80, on the Level of RGDP in 1950, on the GAP in the Index of GDP 1948–38, and on the Share of the Labour Force in Agriculture in 1960

Dependent Variable: Mean Exponential Rate of Growth of RGDP, 1950–80

Independent variables	2SLS[a]			OLS		
	Coeff.	t-value	sig. level	Coeff.	t-value	sig. level
Constant	0.0432	6.89	0.000	0.0389	6.46	0.0001
RGDP50	− 7.460 E-6	− 3.99	0.002	− 6.336 E-6	− 3.53	0.0055
GAP	− 0.000104	− 4.16	0.002	− 0.000116	− 4.65	0.0009
GAP^2	1.2478 E-6	7.76	0.000	1.2218 E-6	7.12	0.0000
AGLABSH60	0.000676	2.14	0.058	0.000752	2.25	0.0486
AGLABSH60^2	− 0.000012	− 1.67	0.1267	− 0.000013	− 1.66	0.1278

$R^2 = 0.976$ $R^2 = 0.973$

Adj. $R^2 = 0.964$ Adj. $R^2 = 0.959$
Standard error of est. = 0.00239   Standard error = 0.00571
F-ratio = 82.46   F-ratio = 71.1
Probability value = 0.0000   Probability value = 0.0000

[a]As instrument for RGDP50 the following estimate was calculated: RGDP = f(Gap, Gap^2, AgLabSh60, AgLabSh60^2, Working Hours 1950, WorkHrs50^2, Female Participation Rate 1950, FemPartR50^2); $R^2 = 0.969$; F-Ratio = 27.0; Prob. Value = 0.0001.

TABLE 8

Sources of the Average Rate of Growth of Real Gross Domestic Product per Capita in a Sample of 16 Industrialized Countries (Maddison's 1982 Group), 1950 to 1980

Variable	Sample mean (1)	Regress. Coeff[a] (2)	Contribution to growth (3) = (1) *(2) *100
RGDP50	2533.8	− 7.460 E-6	− 1.89
GAP	24.8375	− 0.000104	− 0.26
GAP^2	3294.32	1.2478 E-6	0.41
AgLabSh60	16.6187	0.000676	1.12
AgLabSh60^2	358.838	− 0.000012	− 0.43
Constant		0.04321	4.32
Average rate of growth of the sample			3.27

[a]See 2SLS regression results in Table 7.

tude as the beta of GAP, but smaller than that of AGLABSH60; i.e. all three explanatory variables are about equally important. The betas of the squared terms are large, indicating that nonlinearities are an important part of the explanation.

The net impact of wartime disturbances on the average growth of all 16 countries is small. The opposite sign of the coefficient to the squared GAP variable weakens the effect of GAP on averge growth so that basically little is left in the aggregate. See Table 8 for an analysis of the contribution of the individual variables to average growth (3.27 percent per year) of all 16 countries, 1950–80. Of our set of variables the productivity catch-up effect contributes most (-1.89 percent) to growth. The net effect of the possibility of re-allocating labour is 0.69 percent (1.12, -0.43), and the net effect of GAP on growth is $+0.15$ percent (-0.26, $+0.41$). War disruptions, therefore, have a negligible effect on postwar growth of the sample average.

It is possible to analyze a counterfactual world where the Second World War did not take place. In that instance economic growth in the decade 1938–48 could have been continuous and positive, say, equivalent to the growth record of the US. If we assume that the value of GAP for the average of the counterfactual sample equals 100 index points, then the net effect upon average growth is exceedingly small: GAP contributes -1.04 percent and GAP^2 contributes $+1.25$ percent to average growth. This is a sensible result; without the war there would be no shock to the economy and no reconstruction growth.

However, there would also be a second effect in the counterfactual world. For most of the countries in our sample (possibly with the exception of Canada, Australia and the US) the level of RGDP per capita in 1950 would have been substantially higher without a war and the large inter-country productivity dispersion caused by war would also not have occurred. Thus, there would be smaller productivity gaps in the counterfactual world than in reality, with slower catch up growth after 1950 than took place in reality. A more homogeneous growth record would have characterized the OECD countries.

What, then, does the GAP variable introduce into the analysis? It is a new argument for growth divergence among these OECD countries as a result of different degrees of economic disturbance in time of war. That is, we expect that our explanation of country growth reduces the unexplained variance in the pure catch-up growth model (indeed the R^2 for our basic model is much higher than for catch-up growth alone) and eliminates the unexplained deviations of country growth from the mean of all countries that is found in Dowrick and Nguyen (1989). This is the point of Table 9. Before we turn to it we need to discuss some methodological problems.

It is likely that estimates of GDP soon after the war were beset with greater errors than estimates in more recent times. If so, then an error of measurement of GDP in 1950 causes an error in the opposite direction in the measured growth rate between 1950 and 1980, introducing a spurious negative correlation between levels in 1950 and the subsequent growth rate.[38] Secondly, the existence of measurement errors in an independent variable, x, introduces an unwanted dependency of u, the error term in the regression model, upon x, yielding biased and inconsistent OLS estimates.[39] One way of eliminating the effects of this dependency is to employ a suitable instrument for RGDP50 which is assumed to be independent of u but is highly correlated with RGDP50. This is the reason for the regression of RGDP50 on an instrument set including GAP, GAP^2, AgLabSh60, AgLabSh60^2 etc. (see Table 7) and the employment of the estimated values of RGDP50 of this regression in a TSLS model explaining growth. If the estimated RGDP50 values have been purged from the worst of measurement errors, this will also eliminate the problem of a spurious negative correlation.[40]

Comparing the TSLS with the OLS regression results, we see no substantial changes in the estimated coefficients. This suggests that measurement errors of GDP in 1950 are not a serious problem. The estimated coefficient of RGDP50 in the TSLS model has risen somewhat: that of AgLabSh60 and its square are lower and a bit less significant than in the OLS specification. This suggests that part of the productivity growth effect of structural change, the shifting of labour out of agriculture, is due to productivity catch-up.[41]

Table 9 provides an explanation of individual country growth, measured as deviation from the mean rate of growth of all 16 countries. Several interesting results stand out. Firstly, the model not only explains the growth patterns of Japan and Germany very well, in contrast to other recent cross section growth studies (see, e.g., Dowrick/Nguyen, 1989), where the unexplained residuals are particularly large for these two countries, but it also does well for the slow growers, the UK and the US. For Japan the war shock (GAP) variable is by far the most important of the three explanatory variables in the model; this is also true for Germany. In contrast, the growth rate of the UK has been mostly held back by the fact that it does not have an easy source of productivity growth, the re-allocation of low productivity labour in agriculture to other employments. This also plays a role in the slow growth of the US. However for the latter, its position as the technological leaders puts a relative brake on growth: the US possibilities to borrow technology are limited.

---

[38] This methodological problem is even more urgent in the analysis of productivity convergence between 1870 and 1970, as Bradford De Long (1988) has pointed out in his critique of Baumol (1986).

[39] See Koutsoyiannis (1981), pp. 258ff.

[40] Another way of motivating the TSLS method is to initially consider the equation for RGDP50 and that for gr50to80 as part of a recursive system. However, the error term for the second equation is dependent upon the error term in the first. The measurement error in GDP is part of the first error term, which is obviously not independent of the error term in the growth rates. This system of equations cannot, therefore, be estimated one at a time by OLS without simultaneous-equation bias. See Koutsoyiannis (1981), p. 341. A method of estimation which is admissible in this case is TSLS.

[41] Aggregate productivity change due to the shift of labour from a low productivity sector to one with higher productivity levels is evidently also dependent upon the rising productivity levels in that, say industrial, sector, which is due to catch up growth.

TABLE 9

Factors Explaining Deviations of Country Growth from Sample Mean Growth in Japan, Germany, United Kingdom and the United States, 1950 to 1980

	Japan	Fed. Republic Germany	United Kingdom	USA
$(MGC_j - 3.273)$[a]	3.687	1.116	−1.119	−1.420
Regressors:				
RGDO50[b]	0.967	0.387	−0.091	−1.148
GAP[c]	1.498 ⎫ 2.282	0.885 ⎫ 0.769	0.086 ⎫ −0.273	−0.906 ⎫ −0.106
GAP^2	0.784 ⎭	−0.116 ⎭	−0.359 ⎭	0.800 ⎭
AgLabSh60[d]	1.609 ⎫ 0.379	−0.318 ⎫ −0.013	−1.266 ⎫ −0.681	−1.000 ⎫ −0.462
AgLabSh60^2	−1.230 ⎭	0.305 ⎭	0.585 ⎭	0.538 ⎭
Residual[e]	0.059	−0.027	−0.074	0.296
Explained growth deviations[f]	3.628	1.143	−1.045	−1.716

[a] Mean growth of country j (mean exponential rate of growth of real gross domestic product per capita, 1950–80) less sample mean growth.
[b] Real gross domestic product per capita in the year 1950.
[c] GDP index (1913 = 100) in 1948 less GDP index in 1938.
[d] Agricultural share of the labour force in 1960.
[e] Residual between (a) and (f).
[f] Sum of contributions of all regressors.

The values in this table corresponding to regressor x_i are calculated as $b_i(x_{ij} - X_{ij})$, where X_{ij} is the sample mean over j of x_{ij}, b_i is the coefficient of x_{ij}, and $j = 1, ..., N$ indexes the countries of the sample. The sample mean rate of growth is 3.2728.

484   BULLETIN

Although the high and significant intercept term in Table 7 indicates that we do not have a complete model of growth, these stories are persuasive and reasonable.

Finally the question must be asked, how long is GAP (i.e. reconstruction) effective in influencing postwar long run growth. After re-running the same OLS model (as in Table 7) to explain the growth rate of the 16 countries between 1955 and 1980, between 1960 and 1980, and between 1965 and 1980, the GAP variable remained significant. In some variants of the model (especially when GAP2 is used as the war disturbance variable) a war related shock also helps to explain even later phases of growth, but here the extreme position of Japan plays an important role. Without Japan, the model in Table 7 also works more or less in the same manner, but it is limited to the 1950s. Table 10 provides information on a variety of models tested without Japan,

TABLE 10

The Length of Reconstruction Growth in a Number of Models, without Japan

Dependent variable:
Growth of per capita RGDP, 1955–80

Independent variables	Model 1	Model 2	Standardized variables	
			Model 3	Model 4
Constant	0.0348	0.057		
	(4.54)	(4.25)		
RGDP55	− 5.189 E-6	− 4.640 E-6	− 0.353	− 0.358
	(− 2.72)	(− 2.45)	(− 2.58)	(2.40)
TR13to38				0.012
				(0.12)
War shock[a]	− 6.3 E-5	− 0.0376	− 0.974	− 0.267
	(− 1.95)**	(− 2.08)**	(− 2.20)*	(− 1.80)**
War shock[2a]	6.96 E-7	0.0138	0.874	0.215
	(2.07)**	(1.93)**	(2.03)**	(1.82)**
AGLABSH60	0.00116	0.00118	0.923	0.913
	(3.0)	(3.03)	(3.20)	(2.91)
AGLABSH60^2	− 2.4 E-5	− 2.4 E-5	− 0.773	− 0.769
	(− 2.6)	(− 2.62)	(− 2.76)	(− 2.58)
JapanD			0.477	0.466
			(5.25)	(3.70)
ADJ. R^2	0.837	0.828	0.947	0.942
N	15	15	16	16

*Significant at the 5 percent level.
**Significant at the 10 percent level.
[a]The war shock variable is GAP, GAP2, GAP2 and GAP/GDP38, respectively, in Models 1–4.

or using a dummy variable for the Japanese case. Not only is GAP and GAP2 used as a shock indicator, the percentage change in GDP between 1938 and 1948, (GAP/GDP38), has also been tested together with a measure of the growth trend of RGDP between 1913 and 1938, TR13to38. In all cases the effect of the (however defined) reconstruction variable on growth after 1960 drops in statistical significance to below the usually defined levels, 5 or 10 percent; and in all cases is the reconstruction variable a significant explanandum for growth between 1955 and 1980. With this more complete model, in which the re-allocation of labour between agriculture and industry is allowed to generate productivity growth, the length of reconstruction in the sample of 15 OECD countries can be determined unambiguously.

Consequently, we conclude that our first empirical test of a reconstruction model for the post-WWII era shows that it holds up even when it competes with a clearly specified productivity gap argument. The length of time during which reconstruction forces are in operation is affected in our analysis by the inclusion of Japan. Without Japan the dynamics of reconstruction are limited to the 1950s. Seen in an international context, the *Wirtschaftswunder* or post-war supergrowth for 15 OECD countries (which is not due to simple productivity catch-up) lasts only until the end of the 1950s. Not surprisingly, the three most important causes of TFP growth during that decade, which have been identified by Denison (1970), also provide a convincing story of long run growth in a regression model.

V. CONCLUSIONS

Reconstruction from war is not only a type of growth which characterized West Germany but it can also be seen as a general phenomenon, applicable to OECD countries as a group. Our regression results, therefore, provide information both about the specific nature of West German postwar growth and about economic growth in general. These implications, especially those for German growth, remain to be spelled out.

Jánossy argued that human capital formation determines growth in the long run and that disproportionalities in the ratio H/P capital determine a rapid growth traverse back to the long run growth path. These reconstruction growth dynamics, we have seen, may also characterize newer theories of neoclassical growth, in which human capital plays an important role in generating growth. Thus, elements of reconstruction growth may best be understood by appeal to the mechanics of the newer growth theories.

Turning to growth in West Germany, recall that Dowrick and Nguyen (1989) defined the notion of *Wirtschaftswunder* in Germany as a type of growth which cannot be explained within a catch-up growth framework. If *Wirtschaftswunder* is defined as unexplained growth, a notion with which Borchardt (1966) was unhappy, then our regression model eliminates that wonder. In Table 9, the unexplained residual for West German growth devia-

486   BULLETIN

tions is exceedingly small. In other words, reconstruction growth is the explanation of the German *Wirtschaftswunder*.

Although our comparative model specification cannot discern the precise length of supergrowth in West Germany, reconstruction growth in Germany most probably lasts longer than 1960. Thus, our regression results imply that the German *Wirtschaftswunder* lasts substantially longer than the length of time to recover prewar levels of output.

German economic historians — see Rainer Klump (1985) for a good discussion — have interpreted reconstruction growth as an alternative model to growth which was induced by the introduction of postwar institutions and reforms. The results of the present study imply that reconstruction growth was not only a German phenomenon, that forms of supergrowth also occurred in other countries — e.g. Japan, Austria, Italy — without the introduction of a 'social market economy.' While this questions the beneficial influence of specifically German institutional virtues[42] this finding does not eliminate all influences of institutions on growth. The new *international* order created after WWII was the basis of supergrowth in many different countries, in contrast to the absence of both such growth and institutions in the interwar period.

The reader should therefore be cautioned against interpreting the regression coefficient of GAP as a measure of pure reconstruction growth. The scale of wartime economic destruction measures equally well shocks to political and social institutions in our sample of countries. Thus, obstacles to change by vested interests, Mancur Olson's redistributive coalitions (1982), would also disappear with the disappearance of those interests. By removing social obstacles to growth, war can have a growth effect. Institutional change is an inextricable part of our model of reconstruction, not an alternative to it.

Because both human capital, esp. the ratio of H/P capital, and 'social limits to growth' co-determine reconstruction growth, its micro-foundations are, therefore, even more complex than those of catch-up growth. Conrad and Jorgenson (1985) have demonstrated patterns of sectoral productivity gaps and catch-ups in Germany and Japan vs. the United States which are in congruence with the larger productivity gap story of growth. This type of industrial disaggregation may also be possible for reconstruction growth; its investigation remains an important desideratum of future research.

There remain serious alternative interpretations of German growth outside the reconstruction framework and it is unclear how to choose amongst them. Our model of reconstruction, which includes catch-up growth and the growth effects of structural change as competitive elements, and which endogenizes capital formation in the long run in the manner of Jánossy or

[42] Mendershausen (1955) questioned whether the economic order in postwar West Germany, subsumed under the term 'social market economy,' was all that different from other European countries (pp. 70ff). In his unusual comparison of German postwar recoveries after both World Wars, he further pointed out that the rule of free markets characterized the 1920s much more than the period after WWII. He saw, in the latter, a continuation of the substantial role of the state which had been introduced in the '30s and '40s.

REASSESSING THE *WIRTSCHAFTSWUNDER*   **487**

Usher (1980), can be characterized as supply side oriented. In contrast, Hennings (1982) and Boltho (1982) advance a more Keynesian, or demand side, explanation in which exports, economic policy and capital formation play crucial roles.[43]

A further alternative approach can be found in Sommariva and Tullio (1987). They fit a macro model with neoclassical properties in the long run but one 'allowing for disequilibrium because of the large shocks and long periods of disequilibrium which the German economy experienced in the last one hundred years (p. 194)' to the German economy to explain growth, 1880–1979. The results of a simulation of the model 'validate the hypothesis that the actual high growth rates of output and the stock of capital per capita in the 1950s and early 1960s were a reflection of the destruction of the capital stock during the war and of the inflow of refugees' (p. 211).

Finally, Wilhelm Krelle's (1987) study of 'Long-Term Fluctuations of Technical Progress and Growth' should be mentioned. Krelle suggests that entrepreneurship, which influences the rate of application of basic inventions, the rate of time preference and therefore savings and investment behaviour, comes in long waves. The postwar period of growth can therefore be seen as the upswing of this long cycle. However, whether a long cycle exists, is an empirically problematic issue. The number of observations are too few to be able to permit a statistical test.

In contrast, the questions, whether a long run trend exists, and, if so, whether shocks to the economy result in permanent alterations of this long run trend or in a return to it, can be answered by recourse to the recently developed tests for trend stationarity.[44] Seen in the light of this literature, Jánossy's use of an unvarying historical long run trend in his reconstruction story, if correct, turns out to be an unusual and dramatic case of trend stationarity: in the long run even the largest shocks are dissipated. An empirical test of this notion should be high on the agenda for future research.

Universität der Bundeswehr-München

REFERENCES

Abelshauser, W. (1975). *Wirtschaft in Westdeutschland 1945–1948*, Stuttgart.
Abelshauser, W. and Petzina, D. (1981). 'Krise und Rekonstruktion, Zur Interpretation der gesamtwirtschaftlichen Entwicklung Deutschlands im 20. Jahrhundert', in Schröder, W. and Spree, J. (eds.), *Historische Konjunkturforschung*, Stuttgart, pp. 75–114.
Abelshauser, W. (1981). 'Wiederaufbau vor dem Marshall-Plan, *Vierteljahrshefte für Zeitgeschichte* (*VJfZ*), Vol. 29, pp. 545–78.

[43] Charles Kindleberger has suggested in private correspondence that both catching-up and reconstruction are also dependent on policy.
[44] Nelson and Plosser 1982, Campbell and Mankiw 1987, Stock and Watson 1988, Campbell and Mankiw 1989; for applications in British economic history see Crafts, Leybourne and Mills 1989, and Crafts and Mills 1989.

488   BULLETIN

Abelshauser, W. (1983). *Wirtschaftsgeschichte der Bundesrepublik Deutschland (1945–1980)*, Frankfurt a.M.

Abramovitz, M. (1979). 'Rapid Growth Potential and Its Realization: The Experience of Capitalist Economies in the Post-War Period', in Malinvaud, E. (ed.), *Economic Growth and Resources*, Vol. 1, New York.

Abramovitz, M. (1986). 'Catching Up, Forging Ahead and Falling Behind', *Journal of Economic History*, XLVI, pp. 385–406.

Altvater, E., Hoffman, J. and Semmler, W. (1980). *Vom Wirtschaftswunder zur Wirtschaftskrise*, Berlin.

Ambrosius, G. (1986). 'Die Ökonomie der fünfziger Jahre: Zum Verhältnis von Wachstum, Struktur und Politik', *SOWI* Vol. 15, pp. 17–25.

Baldwin, R. (1989a). 'The Growth Effects of 1992', *Economic Policy*, pp. 248–81, October.

Baldwin, R. (1989b). 'Measuring dynamic Gains from Trade', *NBER Working Paper* No. 3147, October.

Barro, R. (1989). 'Economic Growth in a Cross Section of Countries', *NBER Working Paper* No. 3120, September.

Baumol, W. J. (1986). 'Productivity Growth, Convergence, and Welfare: What the long-run Data Show', *American Economic Review*, Vol. 76, pp. 1072–85.

Baumol, W. J., Blackman, S. A. B. and Wolff, E. N. (1989). *Productivity and American Leadership: The Long View*, Cambridge, Mass.

Beckerman, W. (1965). 'Britain's Comparative Growth Record', in Beckerman and Associates, *The British Economy in 1975*, Cambridge.

Bogart, E. L. (1919), *Direct and Indirect Costs of the Great World War*, New York.

Boltho, A. (1982). 'Growth', in Boltho (ed.), *The European Economy, Growth and Crisis*, Oxford.

Bombach, G. (1985). *Post-War Economic Growth Revisited* (de Vries Lectures in Economics 6), Amsterdam.

Borchardt, K. (1982). 'Trend, Zyklus, Strukturbrüche, Zufälle: Was bestimmt die Deutsche Wirtschaftsgeschichte des 20. Jahrhunderts?' in Borchardt, *Wachstum, Krisen, Handlungsspielräume der Wirtschaftspolitik*, Göttingen.

Borchardt, K. (1985). 'Die wirtschaftliche Entwicklung der Bundesrepublik nach dem Wirtschaftswunder', in Schneider, F. (ed.), *Der Weg Bundesrepublik. Von 1945 bis zur Gegenwart*, München.

Broadberry, S. (1988). 'The Impact of the World Wars on the long run Performance of the British Economy', *Oxford Review of Economic Policy* 4, no. 1, Spring, pp. 25–37.

Brems, H. (1983). *Fiscal Theory, Government, Inflation and Growth*, Lexington.

Buchheim, C. (1988). 'Die Währungsreform 1948 in Westdeutschland', *VJfZ*, Vol. 36, pp. 189ff.

Buchheim, C. (1989). 'Die Währungsreform in Westdeustchland im Jahre 1948. Einige ökonomische Aspekte', in Fischer, W. (ed.), *Währungsreform und soziale Marktwirtschaft*, Berlin.

Cairncross, A. K. (1951). 'The Economic Recovery of Western Germany', *Lloyds Bank Review*, October, pp. 19–34.

Campbell, J. Y. and Mankiw, N. G. (1989). 'International Evidence on the Persistence of Economic Fluctuations', *Journal of Monetary Economics*, Vol. 23, pp. 319–33.

Campbell, J. Y. and Mankiw, N. G. (1987). 'Are Output Fluctuations Transitory?' *Quarterly Journal of Economics*, CII, pp. 857–80.

REASSESSING THE *WIRTSCHAFTSWUNDER*   489

Clark, C. (1964). 'Growthmanship, a study in the mythology of investment', in Prest, *et al.*, *Ancient or Modern?* (Hobart Papers 2), 2nd edn., London.

Conrad, K. and Jorgenson, D. W. (1985). 'Sectoral Productivity Gaps between the United States, Japan and Germany, 1960–79', in Giersch, H. (ed.), *Probleme und Perspektiven der Weltwirtschaftlichen Entwicklung*, Berlin.

Crafts, N. F. R., Leybourne, S. J. and Mills, T. C. (1989). 'The Climacteric in Late Victorian Britain and France: a Reappraisal of the Evidence', *Journal of Applied Econometrics*, 4, pp. 103–117.

Crafts, N. F. R. and Mills, T. C. (1989). 'British Economic Fluctuations, 1851–1913: a Perspective Based on Growth Theory', unpublished paper, July.

De Long, B. (1988), 'Productivity Growth, Convergence and Welfare Comments', *AER*, Vol. 78, pp. 1138–1153.

Denison, E. (1970). *Why Growth Rates Differ. Postwar Experience in Nine Western Countries*, Washington D.C.

Dowrick, S. and Nguyen, D. (1989). 'OECD Comparative Economic Growth 1950–85: Catch-Up and Convergence', *AER*, Vol. 79, No. 5, pp. 1010–1030.

Eichengreen, B. (1986). 'Understanding 1921–27: Inflation and Economic Recovery in the 1920s', *Rivista di storia economica*, Second Series 3, pp. 34–66.

Glastetter, W., Paulert, R. and Spörel, U. (1983). *Die Wirtschaftliche Entwicklung in der Bundesrepublik Deutschland 1950–80 Befunde, Aspekte, Hintergründe*, Frankfurt a.M.

Glisman, H. H., Rodemer, H. and Wolter, F. (1978). 'Zur Natur der Wachstumschwäche in der Bundesrepublik. Eine empirische Analyse langer Zyklen wirtschaftlicher Entwicklung', *Kieler Diskussionsbeiträge*, Vol. 55, Kiel.

Glisman, H. H., Rodemer, H. and Wolter, F. (1980). 'Lange Wellen wirtschaftlichen Wachstums', *Kieler Diskussionsbeiträge*, Vol. 74, Kiel.

Gomulka, S. (1979). 'Britain's Slow Industrial Growth — Increasing Inefficiency versus Low Rate of Technical Change', in Beckerman, W. (ed.), *Slow Growth in Britain*, Oxford.

Hardach, K. (1976). *Wirtschaftsgeschichte Deutschlands im 20. Jahrhundert*, Göttingen.

Hennings, K. H. (1982). 'West Germany', in Boltho, A. (ed.), *European Economy*, Oxford.

Jánossy, F. and Hollo, M. (1969), *Das Ende der Wirtschaftswunder*, Frankfurt.

Kindleberger, G. P. (1967). *Europe's Postwar Growth. The Role of Labor Supply*, Cambridge Mass.

Klump, R. (1985). *Wirtschaftsgeschichte der Bundesrepublik Deutschland*, Wiesbaden.

Kormendi, R. C. and Meguire, P. G. (1985). 'Macroeconomic Determinants of Growth. Cross-Country Evidence', *Journal of Monetary Economies*, Vol. 16, pp. 141–63.

Krelle, W. (1987). 'Long-Term Fluctuations of Technical Progress and Growth', *Journal of Institutional and Theoretical Economics*, Vol. 143, pp. 379–401.

Krug, W. (1967). 'Quantitative Beziehungen zwischen materiellem und immateriellem Kapital', *Jahrbücher für Nationalökonomie und Statistik*, Vol. 180, pp. 36–71.

Landes, D. S. (1969, 1973, German edition). *The Unbound Prometheus*, Cambridge, Mass.

Lucas, R. E. Jr. (1988). 'On the Mechanics of Economic Development', *Journal of Monetary Economics*, Vol. 22, pp. 3–42.

Lützel, H. (1985). 'Entwicklung des Sozialprodukts 1950 bis 1984', *Wirtschaft und*

490 BULLETIN

Statistik, Vol. 6, pp. 433–44.

Maddison, A. (1979). 'Long run Dynamics of Productivity Growth', in Beckerman, W. (ed.), *Slow Growth in Britain*, Oxford.

Maddison, A. (1982). *Phases of Capitalist Development*, Oxford.

Maddison, A. (1987). 'Growth and Slowdown in Advanced Capitalist Economies', *Journal of Economic Literature*, Vol. 25, pp. 649–98.

Mendershausen, H. (1955). *Two Postwar Recoveries of the German Economy*, Amsterdam.

Milward, A. S. (1972). *War, Economy and Society*, London.

Milward, A. (1984). *The Reconstruction of Western Europe 1945–51*, London.

Nelson, C. R. and Plosser, C. I. (1982). 'Trends and Random Walks in Macroeconomic Time Series', *Journal of Monetary Economics*, Vol. 10, pp. 139–62.

Olson, M. (1982). *The Rise and Decline of Nations*, New Haven.

Ritschl, A. (1985). 'Die Währungsreform von 1948 und der Wiederansteig der westdeutschen Industrie. Zu den Thesen von Mathias Manz und Werner Abelshauser über die Produktionswirkung der Währungsreform', *VJfZ*, Vol. 33, pp. 136–65.

Rohwer, B. (1988). *Konjunktur und Wachstum. Theorie und Empirie der Produktionsentwicklung in der Bundesrepublik Deutschland seit 1950*, Berlin.

Romer, P. M. (1986). 'Increasing Returns and Long-Run Growth', *Journal of Political Economy*, Vol. 94, No. 5, pp. 1002–1037.

Sommariva, A. and Tullio, G. (1987). *German Macroeconomic History, 1880–1979*, New York.

Stock, J. H. and Watson, W. M. (1988). 'Variable Trends in Economic Time Series', *Journal of Economic Perspectives*, Vol. 2, No. 3, Summer.

Stolper, G., Häuser, K. and Borchardt, K. (1966). *Deutsche Wirtschaft seit 1870*, Tübingen.

Summers, R. and Heston, A. (1984). 'Improved International Comparisons of Real Product and its Composition: 1950–80', *Review of Income and Wealth*, Vol. 30, pp. 207–62.

Usher, D. (1980). *The Measurement of Economic Growth*, Oxford.

Van der Wee, H. (1984). *Der gebremste Wohlstand. Wiederaufbau, Wachstum, Strukturwandel 1945–1980*, Nördlingen.

Wallich, H. C. (1955). *Mainsprings of the German Revival*, New Haven.

Winkel, H. (1974). *Die Wirtschaft im geteilten Deutschland 1945–70*, Wiesbaden.

Winkel, H. (1982). 'Wirtschaftsgeschichte Deutschlands 1945–1965', in *Handwörterbuch der Wirtschaftswissenschaft*, Vol. 9, Stuttgart.

World Bank (1976). *World Tables*, Washington D.C.

TABLE 1

Growth of per capita Real Gross Domestic Product (Exponential Rates), 1950–80 War-Induced Shocks to GDP (Index of GDP in 1948 less Index in 1938) and the Share of Labour Force in Agriculture, 1960 in 16 OECD Countries (Maddison 1982 sample)

Row	Country	RGDP50	RGDP55	RGDP60	RGDP65	RGDP70	RGDP80	gr50to80	gr55to80	gr60to80	gr65to80	gr70to80	Gap	Gap2	agrilab60
1	Australia	3630	3649	3854	4465	5455	6188	0.01778	0.02113	0.02368	0.02176	0.01261	47.6	1.32782	11.0
2	Austria	1674	2195	2751	3328	4129	5861	0.04177	0.03929	0.03782	0.03773	0.03503	−20.5	0.80000	22.8
3	Belgium	2469	2851	3120	3854	4866	6084	0.03006	0.03032	0.03339	0.03044	0.02234	7.8	1.06235	7.0
4	Canada	3524	3854	4015	4846	5570	7451	0.02496	0.02637	0.03092	0.02868	0.02910	119.2	1.82720	12.0
5	Denmark	2831	2982	3741	4748	5646	6336	0.02685	0.03015	0.02634	0.01923	0.01153	35.0	1.18767	17.5
6	Finland	1908	2514	2880	3600	4525	5657	0.03623	0.03244	0.03376	0.03013	0.02233	22.0	1.11139	36.0
7	France	2209	2600	3179	3964	5091	6679	0.03688	0.03774	0.03712	0.03478	0.02715	5.0	1.04139	19.8
8	W. Germany	1843	2794	3664	4386	5369	6876	0.04389	0.03602	0.03147	0.02997	0.02474	−48.3	0.71437	13.4
9	Italy	1423	1870	2350	2898	3793	4636	0.03937	0.03632	0.03397	0.03132	0.02007	−1.9	0.98716	28.0
10	Japan	809	1165	1711	2630	4355	6527	0.06960	0.06893	0.06694	0.06060	0.04046	−99.0	0.63333	32.9
11	Netherlands	2339	2790	3203	3893	4890	5713	0.02977	0.02867	0.02893	0.02557	0.01556	49.8	1.29021	10.7
12	Norway	2415	2823	3138	3925	4706	7026	0.03560	0.03647	0.04030	0.03882	0.04008	63.0	1.30274	19.5
13	Sweden	3152	3644	4207	5190	6032	6779	0.02553	0.02483	0.02385	0.01781	0.01168	58.8	1.30514	13.8
14	Switzerland	3034	3616	4254	5065	5849	6480	0.02529	0.02333	0.02104	0.01642	0.01024	41.5	1.25523	11.2
15	UK	2696	3108	3459	3906	4345	5145	0.02154	0.02016	0.01985	0.01837	0.01690	17.7	1.13358	3.8
16	USA	4580	5154	5248	6178	6747	7986	0.01853	0.01752	0.02099	0.01711	0.01686	99.7	1.64909	6.5

Source of GDP per capita: Summers and Heston (1984).
Source of GDP Index: Maddison (1982).
Source of Labour Force Data: World Bank (1976).

ERRATUM

Fig. 1 on page 273 of Volume 52 Number 3 appeared incorrectly labelled. The correct version should have been:

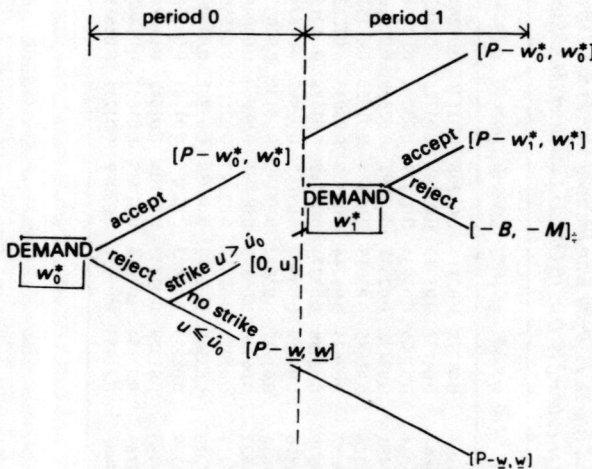

Fig. 1. Game tree with partial payoffs.

On page 289 'of' in line 6 should have been 'or'. Also, the penultimate variable should have read as 'PRIVATE'.

The publishers would like to apologise for these errors.

[19]

AHR Forum
The Two Postwar Eras and the Conditions for Stability in Twentieth-Century Western Europe

CHARLES S. MAIER

BROADCASTING over the BBC in November 1945, A. J. P. Taylor assured his listeners, "Nobody in Europe believes in the American way of life—that is, in private enterprise; or rather those who believe in it are a defeated party and a party which seems to have no more future than the Jacobites in England after 1688."[1] Taylor proved to be wrong, or at least premature, about the end of private enterprise. The question here is why, at least in Western Europe, there was less transformation than he envisaged. Posed in broader terms, how did Western Europe achieve political and social stability by the mid-twentieth century after two great, destructive wars and the intervening upheaval.

Historians often treat stability as a passive coming to rest or a societal inertia that requires no explanation. In fact, stabilization is as challenging a historical problem as revolution. It can emerge dramatically. As one historian who has focused on the process wrote, "Political stability, when it comes, often happens to a society quite quickly, as suddenly as water becomes ice."[2] Stabilization, moreover, does not preclude significant social and political change but often requires it. Certainly the two world wars broadened democracy in Britain and stimulated economic transformation in France. World War II finally removed the contradictions between modernity and reaction in Germany, thereby facilitating a meritocratic pluralism. Yet, despite the transformations, earlier liberal and elitist arrangements that governed the distribution of wealth and power either persisted or were resumed after authoritarian intervals. And at least until

This article was originally drafted during tenure of a fellowship from the National Endowment for the Humanities to pursue research on the United States and European reconstruction after World War II. Previous versions benefited from conversation with Duke University colleagues as well as from discussion at seminars at the University of Wisconsin in Madison, Princeton University, Harvard University, and the European Studies Center at the University of Chicago, and at Werner Conze's seminar for social and economic history at Heidelberg. A semi-final draft was presented as a paper at the Ninety-Third Annual Meeting of the American Historical Association, held in San Francisco, December 1978. I am grateful to Leonard Krieger, Richard Kuisel, and Carl Schorske for their comments at that session. The present version is especially indebted to the suggestions of Professor Kuisel, the subsequent critiques by the anonymous referees for the *American Historical Review*, and the comments of Patrick Fridenson of the University of Paris-X (Nanterre).

[1] Taylor, "The European Revolution," *Listener* (London), November 22, 1945, p. 576.
[2] J. H. Plumb, *The Origins of Political Stability: England, 1675–1725* (Boston, 1967), xvii.

the end of the 1960s the societies of Western Europe seemed more cohesive, humdrum, and routine than either those who feared change or those who longed for it would have predicted.

The key to this stability lies in both postwar eras, the period after World War I as well as that after World War II. Although the years after the first war did not bring enduring stabilization, neither did they produce the radical economic and social change that Left and Right had expected. Outside Russia the first war opened the way only to limited upheaval, conservative reconstruction, or, in some cases, counterrevolution. With the end of the second war, as Taylor's prognosis suggested, many observers again anticipated a major social transformation. This time the postwar years brought not only an ebbing of radicalism but at least a generation of political and economic stability as well. Yet that mid-century stability rested upon the cumulative achievements of both postwar eras. Together the postwar intervals comprised two chapters in a single half-century effort by reform-minded and conservative elites to exploit postwar circumstances for a successful restructuring of the hierarchies they dominated.

GIVEN THE OBJECTIVE OF HISTORICAL COMPARISON, the two periods are usefully envisaged as complementary and parallel alike. Complementary (as is stressed below) in that each made its own distinct but partial contribution to the process of channeling change. Parallel in that key political and economic developments tended to recapitulate themselves. The recurring elements after both wars demonstrate that, although many problems were different, the same underlying political cleavages, enduring class and industrial conflicts, and continuing economic dilemmas remained. As in earlier postwar transitions, each period witnessed a swing from radical challenge to political consolidation. Such a trajectory had marked Europe in the aftermath of the wars of the French Revolution and Napoleon, Russia following the Crimean War, Italy, Prussia, and Austria after the wars of unification, the United States after its Civil War, and France again in the wake of 1870, Spain after 1898, and Russia after 1905. The periods after the two world wars likewise reveal certain parallels.

Consider, first, the comparable political developments. Just as radical or reformist forces of the Left seemed ready to impose extensive changes and then lost their impetus between 1918 and 1921, so the Resistance-born coalitions of Communists, Socialists, Catholics, and liberal democrats initiated reforms but collapsed by 1947–48. In both cases this disarray followed early polarization within the working-class parties and unions. From the viewpoint of the moderates, Soviet-oriented leaders grew ruthlessly opportunistic and sectarian; reverse the perspective and Social Democrats appear preoccupied with Bolshevism or communism. After both wars, too, the respective Catholic parties—the German Zentrum and the Italian Popolari after 1918, the diverse Christian Democrats after 1945—also retreated from their earlier commitments to boldly proclaimed economic reforms. Catholic trade-union leaders and left intellectuals lost out to spokesmen for middle-class stability, the Church hierarchy, or "social-market liberalism."

The Two Postwar Eras and the Conditions for Stability 329

A careful distinction is necessary here. After 1945, plans to supersede capitalism yielded to efforts to reinvigorate economic liberalism. Yet liberal party organizations continued the long-term decline that had originated even before World War I. This attrition hurt both right- and left-wing variants of liberalism, although the Right could fall back upon the economic interest groups it dominated and the Left still controlled influential journalistic outposts. Electoral support, however, was a different story. Voting results were prevailingly disappointing. In 1946 Italian laissez-faire Liberals and the reformist Actionists together polled no more than 8 percent of the electorate. The French non-Marxist, non-Catholic Left had brilliant writers but few voters. Belgian Liberal deputies were returned at roughly half of their prewar strength with about 9 percent of the popular poll, and the revived Liberal Democratic party in West Germany (today's Free Democrats), with its 9.5 percent in Landtag elections and 12 percent of the first Bundestag, remained comparable to voting results of the combined Democratic (Staatspartei) and People's parties in the late Weimar Republic.[3]

Just as striking as the draining of energy on the Left in the respective postwar years was the recapitulation of key industrial and monetary developments. Certainly the economy of the era after 1948 became far more robust than the ephemeral prosperity of the late 1920s. Nonetheless, some of the same dilemmas and solutions marked both recoveries. By the mid-1920s Americans were finally helping ease Europe's postwar balance-of-payments difficulties by the enthusiastic purchase of European bonds. At the same time, leading bankers on both sides of the Atlantic pressed for currency stabilization and monetary convertibility on the basis of the gold-exchange standard: the Reichsmark was anchored in late 1924, sterling in April 1925, the lira in 1927, and the French franc (legally re-established exclusively on a gold base) in 1928. The laboriously negotiated tariff compromises and trade treaties of the latter 1920s along with such interindustry agreements as the Entente Internationale de l'Acier advanced the integration of the major Continental steel and chemical producers. Agreements between industries across frontiers encouraged mergers and concentration within the component national economies. In a similar sequence after World War II, the European Recovery Program of 1948–51 and subsequent Mutual Security assistance provided American credits to compensate for Europe's massive dollar deficit. The European Payments Union, the product of negotiations extending from 1948 to 1951, worked toward renewed currency convertibility. The Coal-Steel Community of the early 1950s reinforced the capitalist revival of the second postwar period.[4]

---

[3] For a useful tabulation of voting results, see Derek W. Urwin, ed., *Elections in Western Nations, 1945–1968*, University of Strathclyde, Survey Research Center, *Occasional Papers*, nos. 4–5 (Glasgow, n.d.).

[4] For the negotiations of the 1920s, see Charles S. Maier, *Recasting Bourgeois Europe: Stabilization in France, Germany, and Italy in the Decade after World War I* (Princeton, 1975), 516–45; and Jacques Bariéty, "Das Zustandekommen der Internationalen Rohstahlgemeinschaft (1926) als Alternative zum misslungenen 'Schwerindustriellen Projekt' des Versailler Vertrages," in Hans Mommsen et al., eds., *Industrielles System und politische Entwicklung in der Weimarer Republik* (Düsseldorf, 1974), 552–68. For the negotiations between coal and steel producers after World War II, the material in the steel trusteeship papers at the Koblenz Bundesarchiv [hereafter, BA], B 109/97, is revealing; these papers are complemented by the memoranda of meetings included in

Obviously, there were crucial differences between the two postwar eras; to discern parallels is not to claim identities. After the First World War, to cite just a first salient difference, the political Right emerged more militant than before 1914. Fascism drew upon a striking force of veterans inured to violence and contemptuous of civilian virtues. After the Second World War, fascism was discredited and even traditional conservative nationalism rejected. The psychological impact of the fighting did not create nuclei of Arditi, Free Corps recruits, or others addicted to paramilitary violence. For most soldiers the second war impelled instead a search for private fulfillment: "the happy obscurity of a humdrum job and a little wife and a household of kids," according to Bill Mauldin, or, a front away, the return to "the mountains of the Caucasus, the exciting blue smoke of the foothills . . . , the sweet faces of loved ones."[5] What analogue existed after 1945 to the *trinceismo*, the glorification of the trenches of World War I, was the partisans' mountain ordeal: a trial that Resistance spokesmen claimed was moral justification for a new elite, although without any encouragement for a continuing cult of violence. Indeed, the distinction in 1914–18 between front soldiers mired down in brutalizing combat and male civilians at home who sometimes enjoyed cushy, protective berths—the so-called *embusqués* or *imboscati*—dissolved in 1939–45 with the rapid movement of troops, the air attacks on civilian targets, and the hardships of occupation. Almost 50 percent of Europe's dead in the second war were civilians, compared to about 5 percent in the first.[6] These factors all contributed to limiting the potential of any veterans-based right radicalism. Except for the recurring but small German nationalist splinters, achieving at best 8 to 10 percent electoral support at the Land level (and about 2 percent in national polls), the search for right-wing movements after 1945 yields only ambivalent possibilities: the Gaullism of 1947 and the Uomo Qualunque of southern Italy, a sort of pre-Poujadism that rejected the moralistic claims of the Resistance Left. This failure of the neofascist Right to emerge in greater strength was a major surprise of postwar European politics.[7]

the archives of the Compagnie de Pont-à-Mousson at La Châtre [hereafter, PAM], boxes 70669, 70671, 70690–91, 77042. Also see William Diebold, Jr., *The Schuman Plan: A Study in Economic Cooperation, 1950–1959* (New York, 1959). For monetary negotiations, see Stephen V. O. Clarke, *Central Bank Cooperation, 1924–1931* (New York, 1967); Sir Henry Clay, *Lord Norman* (London, 1957); L. V. Chandler, *Benjamin Strong, Central Banker* (Washington, 1958); W. A. Brown, Jr., *England and the New Gold Standard, 1919–1926* (New Haven, 1929), and *The International Gold Standard Reinterpreted, 1914–1934,* 2 vols. (New York, 1940); Donald E. Moggridge, *British Monetary Policy, 1924–1931: The Norman Conquest of $4.86* (Cambridge, 1972); and Gerd Hardach, *Weltmarktorientierung und relative Stagnation: Währungspolitik in Deutschland, 1924–1931,* Schriften zur Wirtschafts- und Sozialgeschichte, vol. 27 (Berlin, 1976). For post-1945 negotiations, see William Diebold, Jr., *Trade and Payments in Western Europe* (New York, 1952); J. Kummell, *De Ontwikkeling van het Internationale Betalingsverkeer* (Leiden, 1950); Robert Triffin, *Europe and the Money Muddle* (New Haven, 1957); and Raymond F. Mikesell, *Foreign Exchange in the Postwar World* (New York, 1954).

[5] As quoted in John Morton Blum, *V Was for Victory: Politics and American Culture during World War II* (New York, 1976), 70, 73. For the attitudes and political organization of veterans, only a minority of whom became radically antidemocratic, see James M. Diehl, *Paramilitary Politics in Weimar Germany* (Bloomington, Ind., 1977); Volker R. Berghahn, *Der Stahlhelm, Bund der Frontsoldaten, 1918–1935* (Düsseldorf, 1966); Robert G. L. Waite, *Vanguard of Nazism: The Free Corps Movement in Postwar Germany, 1918–1923* (Cambridge, Mass., 1952); Giorgio Sabatucci, *I combattenti nel primodopoguerra* (Bari, 1974); and Antoine Prost, *Les Anciens combattants et la société française, 1914–1939,* 3 vols. (Paris, 1977), esp. volume 3: *Idéologies et mentalités.*

[6] Gordon Wright, *The Ordeal of Total War, 1939–1945* (New York, 1968), 264.

[7] For the Gaullism of 1947, see Jean Touchard, *Le Gaullisme, 1940–1969* (Paris, 1978), 98–133. On Uomo Qualunque, see Sandro Setta, *L'Uomo Qualunque, 1944/48* (Bari, 1975). And, for post-1945 Germany, see Kurt P. Tauber, *Beyond Eagle and Swastika: German Nationalism since 1945,* 2 vols. (Middletown, Conn., 1967).

Only in retrospect is it discernible that even under the collaborationist regimes conservative elements had to rethink the economic role of the state and the future relationship of capital and labor. To cite just the French situation (although analogues existed in the Netherlands and the Salò Republic), awareness that the Vichy regime was doomed and mass upheaval likely prompted the industrialists summoned by the Conseil Supérieur de l'Économie Industrielle et Commerciale to search for a "factory community" that would provide a "balanced solution" between "yesterday's capitalism" and "collectivism." Such explorations, however, could build upon more than fear of postwar revolution. They carried forward some of the heterodox notions of economic planning that dissenting socialists and conservative intellectuals alike had outlined in the 1930s.[8]

A major condition for a more flexible Right was the fact that the Left too debarked differently after the second war. Between 1918 and 1921 the European working classes had first surged into spontaneous demonstrations, had then waged long, disciplined mass strikes, and had finally retrenched in frustration and divided. Much of their insurrection followed from the intensified labor discipline the war imposed as well as progressive ideological alienation from its national objectives. The second war imposed some of the same ordeals within the factory, but the German occupation made the factory a less central source of oppression. The heirs of the working-class leadership that had come to oppose the first war by 1917 urged active resistance to the Germans after June 1941, so that the second war was less an alien upper-class cause than an arduous wait for liberation. Its conclusion thus brought a different tempo of working-class cooperation and protest. Western Communists played down any radical economic transformation that outran the broad Resistance consensus on purges and the nationalization of key industries or those tainted by their owners' collaboration. Instead Communist leaders stressed anti-Nazi unity (until the final defeat of Germany) and continuing production, even at the cost of harsh industrial discipline. "The bonus per ton is evil," wrote one CGT leader in March 1945 about detested pay differentials, "but coal is necessary." Maurice Thorez insisted to coal miners at Waziers in July 1945 that production itself was a demonstration of solidarity, militancy, and working-class power.[9] "Only by working, only by working hard will we be able to overcome this situation [of hardship]," the secretary of the Milan Chamber of Labor told the factory council of Magneti Mirelli in early 1946. "We all seek socialism. But do you believe that we can

[8] Conseil Supérieur de l'Économie Industrielle et Commerciale, Commission Nr. 4, Procès-Verbal de la séance du 5 novembre 1943, PAM, box 70411; and Report to the Minister, July 17, 1944, *ibid.* Also see Richard Kuisel, "Vichy et les origines de la planification économique (1940–1946)," *Le Mouvement Social*, 98 (1977): 77–101; Jacques Amoyal, "Les Origines socialistes et syndicalistes de la planification en France," *ibid.*, 87 (1974): 137–69; and, on the labor issue, Jacques Julliard, "La Charte du Travail," in Jeanine Bourdin, ed., *Le Gouvernement de Vichy, 1940–1942: Colloque de la Fondation Nationale des Sciences Politiques* (Paris, 1972), 157–210.

[9] L. Delfosse, in *La Tribune des Mineurs*, March 18, 1945, as quoted in Jean Bouvier, "Région et Nation: Inflation, reformes de structures, nationalisation des houillères, et crise sociale," *Actes du Colloque de l'Université de Lille III, 2–3 novembre 1974: La Libération du Nord et du Pas-de-Calais, 1944–1947* [hereafter, *Colloque de Lille*], in *Revue du Nord*, 57 (1975): 609. For Communist policies, see J.-P. Hirsch, "'La Seule voie possible': Remarques sur les communistes du Nord et du Pas-de-Calais de la Libération aux grèves de novembre 1947," *ibid.*, 563–78, which contains an extensive discussion of Thorez's celebrated Waziers appeal, July 21, 1945.

socialize poverty?" Communists, warned Jacques Duclos, as he condemned the 1946 Socialist-supported strikes of French civil servants, had to demonstrate "that democracy is a regime of order, a regime of tranquility and of work."[10]

The open question in France, Belgium, and Italy (to the extent that the Anglo-American occupation would have permitted) was whether an angry and long-repressed working class would explode in a spontaneous radicalism with plant seizures, local "socialization," and summary trials. Communist pressure for carrying through purge procedures probably helped contain grass-roots grievances. In fact, whether in France, Italy, Belgium, Holland, or Bavaria (under American auspices), the purges became more and more restricted. Categories of guilt seemed to blur hopelessly, and moderates came to grasp that trying business leaders for cooperation with the Germans could have radical consequences, or, in the words of one *Esprit* intellectual who advocated it, "The purge of the economic sector entails overturning all property relations."[11] Purges were thus wound down short of any major upheaval, and the emphasis upon sifting individuals probably diverted effort from institutional transformation— although originally the Left had envisaged *épuration* as a mode of collective change.

Perhaps, however, the major force for preventing ideological polarization after World War II was neither the chastened Right nor the tempered Left but the new Christian Democratic parties of the center. For the crucial three years after 1944, left Catholicism with its declared hostility to liberal capitalism seemed ascendant. The appearance was deceptive in the long run, but it served well to contain otherwise radical currents in the flux of the immediate postwar period. Konrad Adenauer could swallow and survive the radical-sounding Ahlen Program of the Westphalian Christian Democrats in 1947, understanding that it kept the CDU from appearing reactionary; Alcide De Gasperi ultimately profited from the mass base organized by Catholic labor leader Achille Grandi; and the French MRP accepted nationalization but, except for collaborators, insisted upon compensation.[12] In Italy and Belgium the prolonged controversy

[10] Milanese secretary of the Chamber of Labor, as quoted in Febo Guizzi, "La Fabbrica italiana Magneti Marelli," in Luigi Ganapini et al., *La ricostruzione nella grande industria: Strategia padronale e organismi di fabbrica nel Triangolo, 1945–1948* (Bari, 1978), 280; and Duclos, as quoted in Alain Bergonieux, *Force Ouvrière* (Paris, 1975), 55.

[11] G. Zérapha, "Le Problème politique français," *Esprit*, December 1944, as quoted in Michel Winock, *Histoire politique de la revue "Esprit"* (Paris, 1975), 260. On the purges, see Peter Novick, *The Resistance versus Vichy* (New York, 1968); Robert Aron, *Histoire de l'épuration*, 3 vols. (Paris, 1967–75); D. Laurent et al., "Sur l'épuration dans le Nord et le Pas-de-Calais," *Colloque de Lille*, in *Revue du Nord*, 57 (1975): 365–80, 623–36; Lutz Niethammer, *Entnazifizierung in Bayern: Säuberung und Rehabilitierung unter amerikanischer Besatzung* (Frankfurt a/M, 1972); and Marcello Flores, "L'Epurazione," in Instituto Nazionale per la Storica del Movimento di Liberazione in Italia, *L'Italia dalla liberazione alla repubblica; del convegno internazionale . . . 26–28 marzo 1976* (Milan, n.d.), 413–67. Also see Guizzi, "La Fabbrica italiana Magneti Marelli," 245–72; and Valerio Castronovo, *Giovanni Agnelli* (Turin, 1971), 671–88. Also see the reports from U.S. diplomats on the slowing of the Belgian and Dutch purges, National Archives, Washington, Record Group 59 [hereafter, NA-RG 59], including the report by Charles Sawyer, May 29, 1945, NA-RG 59,855.00/5-2945; by Theodore Achilles, June 11, 1946, *ibid.*, 855.00/6-1146; and by J. Webb Benton from the Hague, August 15, 1946, *ibid.*, 856.00/8-1546.

[12] For Adenauer's views, see Sozialausschuss der CDU, February 21–22, 1947, in Friedrich-Ebert-Stiftung, Bonn, Hensler Nachlass, 16. Also see Gerold Ambrosius, *Die Durchsetzung der sozialen Marktwirtschaft in Westdeutschland, 1945–1949* (Stuttgart, 1977); and Konrad-Adenauer-Stiftung, *Konrad Adenauer und die CDU der britischen Besatzungszone, 1946–1949* (Bonn, 1975), 46–47, 288–89. On Grandi, see Benedetto de Cesaris, "Cattolici,

over the fate of the discredited monarchs helped the Catholic parties accommodate both Left and Right. As the American embassy reported from Brussels, the Christian Social party, by defending the rights of Leopold III, could retain the allegiance of Belgian conservatives, even while letting its trade unionists champion social reform, and could thus provide "all things to all men who believe in the Roman Catholic religion."[13] This capacity naturally undermined the radical élan of Christian democracy but did allow the movement to serve as an integrating force for moderation.

Domestic party developments obviously took place under the shadow of the great powers. The overwhelming difference between 1918 and 1945 was the continuing intervention of the United States and the Soviet Union in their respective spheres of influence. But in Western Europe, American aid, with its attendant pressure, was only one of many factors abetting liberal reconstitution. The discrediting of the European Right, the fear of Communist motives and the Soviet Union that replaced Popular Front effusions, and the desire on the part of both Christian Democrats and Social Democrats to establish moderate welfare states were powerful impulses on their own. They alone sufficed to make 1945 different from 1918.

DIFFERENT, BUT NOT SEPARATE. Both postwar periods, as noted, formed part of a continuing effort at stabilization, a search that was sufficiently active and persistent (and rewarded finally with sufficient success) to comprise a major theme of twentieth-century Western European history. Stabilization, however, for whom? And of what? Stabilization meant not so much preserving liberal procedures as re-establishing the overlapping hierarchies of power, wealth, and status that can be loosely termed "capitalist." In an age of mass suffrage, these challenged hierarchies had to be defended less in terms of custom than results—that is, their performance for society as a whole. Increasingly, performance included the maintenance of economic welfare. The Depression led voters to shatter the Western political coalitions of the 1920s even when it did not destroy democratic regimes. Distress forced governments in the 1930s to become employers of last resort; by the 1950s they were called upon to assure continuing economic growth as well as high employment at a given level of national income. Stabilization thus entailed a dual task. It meant re-establishing the contested legitimacy of European social and economic elites—buttressing the hierarchies that even in an age of mass voting still presupposed that only small minorities could share the prerogative of directing human labor. Justifying inequality, in turn, required satisfying criteria of economic performance: figuratively and literally delivering the goods. Although they had to broaden their recruitment and recognize new spokesmen for organized labor, by and large the elites superin-

---

eredità 'popolari,' e nuovo stato," in *Problemi del movimento sindacale in Italia, 1943–1973: Annali della Fondazione Giangiacomo Feltrinelli*, 16 (1976): 229–39. For the MRP stance, see the discussions of Bidault and Menthon with Communist and Socialist leaders, January 23, 1945, *Colloque de Lille*, in *Revue du Nord*, 57 (1975): 596–97.

[13] Jefferson Patterson to the Department of State, August 20, 1945, NA-RG 59, 855.00/8-2045.

tending Western society met these related conditions for stability—those of legitimation and those of production. But they did not meet both conditions at once.

Instead, Europe's elites resolved their difficulties seriatim, such that each effort of postwar stabilization overcame one of the two challenges. With the 1920s came not a total, but a nevertheless impressive, response to the ideological attack upon the legitimacy of capitalist hierarchies as hierarchies. That is, the leaders of the 1920s rallied with persuasive justifications of capitalist entrepreneurship. They ended up rejustifying not so much ownership *per se* as a hierarchy of managerial power that preserved the essentials of control. Nonetheless, the 1920s did not solve the economic dilemma of ensuring continuous production and high employment. That task was left to the second postwar period. Only by the 1950s were the afflictions that undermined capitalist stability effectively overcome as a whole. The cumulative achievement required the institutional flux that was left in the wake of not one but two wartime upheavals.

In what sense can it be maintained, however, that developments of the 1920s served durably to reinforce the legitimacy of European capitalism? In light of mass unemployment, the taint of wartime collaboration, and the wave of socialist aspirations incorporated in the Resistance, did not capitalism seem as shaken, vulnerable, and problematic after World War II as ever before—hence A. J. P. Taylor's verdict? In fact, however, the Left's programs after World War II did not often go so far as the challenges of 1918–21.[14] This does not mean that the Left was universally stronger earlier. Although in Germany and Italy social revolutionary outcomes had been more feasible after the First than the Second World War (if only because no occupying forces were present), had it chosen to exploit its power, the French Left possessed a more commanding position in late 1944 than it had controlled in 1918. In Britain the protests of 1918–19 that looked toward a syndicalist socialism were succeeded in 1945 by the more solid, if more moderate, triumph of the Labour party. In short, the relative strength of the Left in the respective postwar periods depended to a great extent upon the particular national situation. The programs of the Left, however, often remained a less clearcut challenge after 1944 than they were after 1918. They aspired less to overturn bureaucratic and economic control than to attain public ownership of key industries. By 1945, however, ownership was a less crucial issue than earlier for many sectors that the Left targeted for nationalization. The earlier socialist challenge that followed in the wake of the Bolshevik Revolution with its innovation of soviets was probably more fundamental. What the participants in the massive strikes and insurrections of 1918–21, the militants at party and union congresses, and the remarkable socialist theorists of the early 1920s urged in aggregate was not merely the centralization of important industries in

---

[14] On this point, see some of the recent surveys of this period, including Francis Carsten, *Revolution in Central Europe, 1918–1919* (London, 1972); Charles L. Bertrand, ed., *Revolutionary Situations in Europe, 1917–1922: Germany, Italy, Austria-Hungary*, Proceedings of the Second International Colloquium of the Interuniversity Center for European Studies (Montreal, 1977); and *Rivoluzione e reazione in Europa, 1917/1924: Convegno storico internazionale, Perugia, 1978* (Rome, 1978).

the hands of the state; this demand came from moderate Social Democrats. Instead, they criticized managerial control of the workplace and of production regardless of ownership; and, by extension, they challenged the chains of command of the Western economies from top to bottom.

These movements failed in the West for many reasons. They were rooted in the shop steward organizations of the Clydeside, the factory grievance committees established during the war to smooth labor relations, which in turn helped generate the *consigli di fabbrica* of Turin and the *Räte* in Germany and Austria. Some spokesmen for these councils envisioned a syndical reorganization of the economy and politics. But often their militancy derived from the more conservative impulses of defending the work skills and artisanal independence still conserved under factory roofs against degrading standardization of tasks and wartime "dilution" (the hiring of unskilled replacements, sometimes women).[15] Moreover, the councils comprised a strong movement only in a few industrial regions, and their revolts exploded out of phase with each other. The movement, moreover, appears to have evoked the least resonance in France, which would still have had to be the keystone of any general West European transformation. In France, reformist socialists as well as industrial leaders restricted the mandate of factory delegates, while after the armistice radicals spilled into street demonstrations that were militant but diffuse and finally settled on a program for nationalization of the railroads.[16] Likewise in Britain, Labour militants came to focus upon takeover of the coal industry. In Germany, the councils emerged during revolution but often just to take charge of factories, regiments, or towns in which central authority crumbled. When German council champions took up explicitly socialist goals, they incurred drastic repression, as in Munich in April 1919 or in the Ruhr after the Kapp Putsch.[17]

Trade-union leaders, moreover, remained cool toward alternative modes of representation, fearing that the new councils would undercut their long, patient

[15] On the resistance of skilled workers, see James Hilton, *The First Shop Stewards' Movement* (London, 1973); Bertrand Abhervé, "Les Origines de la grève des métallurgistes parisiens, juin 1919," *Le Mouvement Social*, 93 (1975): 75–85; and David Montgomery, "The 'New Unionism' and the Transformation of Workers' Consciousness in America, 1909–1922," *Journal of Social History*, 7 (1974): 509–29. Also see Carmen J. Sirianni, "Workers' Control in the Era of World War I: A Comparative Analysis of the European Experience," *Theory and Society*, 9 (1980): 29–88; and Martin Clark, *Antonio Gramsci and the Revolution that Failed* (New Haven, 1977).

[16] Abhervé, "Les Origines de la grève des métallurgistes parisiens"; Nicholas Papyanis, "Masses révolutionnaires et directions reformistes: Les Tensions au coeur des grèves des métallurgistes français en 1919," *Le Mouvement Social*, 93 (1975): 51–73; and Gilbert Hatry, "Les Délégués d'atelier aux Usines Renault," in Patrick Fridenson, ed., *1914–1918, l'autre front: Cahiers du "Mouvement Social"*, 2 (Paris, 1977): 221–35. Also see the older surveys, Roger Picard, *Le Mouvement syndical durant la guerre* (Paris, 1927); and William Oualid and Charles Picquenard, *Salaires et tariffes, conventions collectives, et grèves: La Politique du Ministère de l'Armament* (Paris, 1928).

[17] On Britain, in addition to Hinton's *The First Shop Stewards' Movement*, see Branko Pribicevic, *The Shop Stewards' Movement and Workers' Control* (Oxford, 1959); Arthur Marwick, *The Deluge* (New York, 1970), 56–76, 203–09; and G. D. H. Cole, *Labour in the Coal-Mining Industry, 1914–21* (Oxford, 1923). On Germany, see Eberhard Kolb, *Die Arbeiterräte in der deutschen Innenpolitik, 1918–1919* (Düsseldorf, 1962), and "Rätewirklichkeit und Räte-ideologie in der deutschen Revolution von 1918–1919," in Kolb, ed., *Vom Kaiserreich zur Weimarer Republik* (Cologne, 1972), 165–84; Reinhard Rürup, ed., *Arbeiter- und Soldatenräte im rheinisch-westfälischen Industriegebiet* (Wuppertal, 1975); Peter von Oertzen, *Betriebsräte in der Novemberrevolution* (Düsseldorf, 1963); Erhard Lucas, *Märzrevolution im Ruhrgebiet*, vol. 1 (Frankfurt a/M, 1970), and *Märzrevolution 1920*, vol. 2 (Frankfurt a/M, 1973); and Georg Eliasberg, *Der Ruhrkrieg 1920* (Bonn, 1974).

struggle to speak for labor. Bourgeois politicians such as David Lloyd George in 1919 or Giovanni Giolitti in 1920 deflected protests into cumbersome committees, which finally generated compromise proposals for co-determination that commanded no adherence and were soon shelved (much like the recent Bullock Commission in Britain). Supple industrial leaders, such as Milanese banker and electrical magnate Ettore Conti or Rhenish lignite industrialist Paul Silverberg, similarly exploited such spurious concessions.[18]

Still, given the limitations of the movement, the council episodes suggested that bourgeois concepts of rational economic and political authority were all terribly vulnerable. The dramas staged at Fiat or Renault or the mines of Essen were frightening not primarily because they may have attained an ephemeral success but because they suggested that only force, not consensus, stood in the way of a collectivist alternative. At stake, therefore, was bourgeois legitimacy as well as naked control. Bourgeois response, thus, had to go beyond mere repression. Counterstrategies had to operate on plant and national planes, micro- and macro-levels simultaneously. The need to reassert authority within the factory gave renewed impetus to plans for scientific management, which would further centralize factory authority by differentiating tasks "down to the tiniest detail," as some French sponsors defined their Taylorite efforts.[19]

Acceptance of this technocratic functionalism required conservative flexibility, and business as well as political milieux divided between progressives and reactionaries. The reactionaries distrusted industry-wide organization and insisted on the prerogatives of ownership, asserting what the Germans called their Herr-im-Hause domination. But the more fruitful approach was to build upon the potential for cooptation that wartime labor-management agreements and the unavowed brotherhood of wage-price spirals had encouraged after 1914.[20] As might be expected, the industrial "progressives" were less fixated on ownership, more concerned with managerial expertise; they were multi-divisional foxes rather than single-factory lions. Building upon his wartime organizational efforts, Walther Rathenau forcefully defended entrepreneurial leadership, while outlining complex schemes for capitalist self-government and planning. Later in the decade, Alfred Mond, organizer of the Imperial Chemical cartel and Ernest Mercier, an architect of French electrical networks, pursued related visions (as did Herbert Hoover in the United States).[21] Other spokesmen throughout the

[18] See Charles S. Maier, *Recasting Bourgeois Europe* (Princeton, 1975), chap. 3.
[19] "Concours pour l'application du Système Taylor dans les Mines et Usines de la Société de Pont-à-Mousson: Préamble," PAM, box 18936.
[20] Gerald Feldman, "German Business between War and Revolution: The Origins of the Stinnes-Legien Agreement," in Gerhard A. Ritter, ed., *Entstehung und Wandel der modernen Gesellschaft: Festschrift für Hans Rosenberg zum 65. Geburtstag* (Berlin, 1978), 312–41, and *Iron and Steel in the German Inflation, 1916–1923* (Princeton, 1977), 91; Charles A. Gulick, *Austria from Habsburg to Hitler*, 2 vols. (Berkeley and Los Angeles, 1948), 1: 150–57; and Charles S. Maier, "The Politics of Inflation in the Twentieth Century," in Fred Hirsch and John Goldthorpe, eds., *The Political Economy of Inflation* (Cambridge, Mass., 1978), 49–52.
[21] Walther Rathenau, *Von kommenden Dingen* (1916), and *Die neue Wirtschaft* (1917), volumes 2 and 3 of his *Gesammelte Schriften* (Berlin, 1918); Alfred Moritz Mond, *Industry and Politics* (London, 1927); Hector Bolitho, *Alfred Mond, First Lord Melchett* (London, 1933), 313–18; and Richard Kuisel, *Ernest Mercier, French Technocrat* (Berkeley and Los Angeles, 1967). Also see Martin Fine, "L'Association Française pour le Progrès Social (1927–1929)," *Le Mouvement Social*, 94 (1976): 3–29.

1920s derived from the important interindustry associations—less businessmen than their organizers and lobbyists: François Poncet of the Comité des Forges with his sleek defense of technocratic inequality; Gino Olivetti of Confindustria, who from even before the war was to emphasize that only the industrialist could "technically order the factory according to a pre-established plan"; his successor Antonio Benni, who insisted that industry was "not personified by the capitalist or the stockholder but by its directors, by its chiefs, and by the organizers of the enterprise."[22] Industry, moreover, became the paradigm for political society in general, as, for instance, when Ernest Mercier sought to rally managerial expertise in the above-party Redressment Français or Alfred Mond organized the Mond-Turner talks with trade-union leaders in the wake of the British General Strike.

These initiatives and self-justifying notions were hardly widespread enough to reorder industrial organization, any more than the council movement had revolutionized the workplace. Nonetheless, celebrators and critics alike felt that scientific management represented a decisive economic and social breakthrough,[23] and the economic circumstances of the late 1920s powerfully reinforced this new legitimation of capitalism. The stabilization of currencies on the gold-exchange standard, renewal of intense international competition, and concern about saturation of home markets all made "rationalization" more urgent. Rationalization was a concept that comprised market-sharing agreements across frontiers and within domestic economies plus parallel efforts to lower the burden of wages and other costs through investment, technical improvements, and mergers. At the same time industrial leaders sought legitimation for their power, whether it derived from the right to lay off workers in a cyclical downturn or from their collaboration with an authoritarian regime as in Italy. The managerial mystique evoked widespread enthusiasm, assumed a truly cultic importance precisely because it was a modern and supposedly class-neutral alternative to the immediately preceding socialist attack on industrial hierarchies.

"This Taylorization is connected with the problem of lowering overall costs," noted Marcel Paul, a Pont-à-Mousson manager, when his firm embarked upon the venture in the late 1920s.[24] Scientific management supposedly promised a painless method of cost cutting, although it often just meant speed-ups or extra

[22] André François Poncet, *Réflexions d'un républicain moderne* (Paris, 1925); Olivetti, as quoted in Franklin Adler, "Factory Councils, Gramsci, and the Industrialists," *Telos*, 31 (1977): 79; and Benni, as quoted in Maier, *Recasting Bourgeois Europe*, 567. Also see Franklin Adler, "Italian Industrialists and Radical Fascism," *Telos*, 30 (1976–77): 193–201.

[23] For André Philips's analysis of the central role of scientific management in American economic achievement, see his *Le Problème ouvrier aux États-Unis* (Paris, 1927). For the enthusiasm evoked by what I call the "managerial mystique," see Edmond Giscard d'Estaing, "Le Néocapitalisme," *Revue des Deux Mondes*, August 1, 1928; Paul Devinat, *Scientific Management in Europe*, ILO Studies and Reports, ser. B, no. 17 (Geneva, 1927); and *La Prospérité: Revue trimestrielle de l'organisation scientifique* (1928–), an ebullient magazine that was briefly published by Michelin.

[24] Marcel Paul to Jean Cavalier, May 19, 1928, PAM, box 41595. On the thrust of rationalization, see Robert Brady, *The Rationalization Movement in German Industry* (Berkeley and Los Angeles, 1933); Giulio Sapelli, "L'Organizzazione 'scientifica' del lavoro e innovazione tecnologica durante il fascismo," *Italia Contemporanea*, 28 (1976): 3–28; and Paola Fiorentini, "Ristrutturazione capitalistica e sfruttamento operaio in Italia negli anni '20," *Rivista Storica del Socialismo*, 10 (1967): 134–54.

hours. The unions, however, had already exhausted their capacity for resistance during fruitless labor struggles, in France during 1920, in Italy from 1920 through 1922 and less overtly in 1924–26, in Germany after the inflation and again by 1928, and in Britain during 1921 and 1926. By the late 1920s, moreover, a generation of moderate labor spokesmen emerged who honestly believed in collaboration: trade unionists in Germany and the United States, the aging Albert Thomas at the Geneva International Labor Office, the younger Walter Citrine, and Ernest Bevin, who saw his job of "the large scale organization of labor" as akin to that of the industrial manager.[25]

The Left never again challenged the premise that production was a question for managers and engineers with the same vigor that they had immediately after the first war. Even when the close of World War II seemed to offer renewed opportunity, plans to reorganize the factory and control production remained relatively undeveloped. In France, workers revolted against the coerciveness of the Occupation and sought to oust patrons they identified as both collaborators and exploiters. But their efforts yielded only limited success, and the bitterness of the later strikes in 1947 and 1948 testified to the frustration of aspirations raised at the Liberation. The Communists did support new schemes for a workers' voice in the tripartite management boards (representing management, labor, and the state) for the nationalized industries, urged by Minister of Industry Marcel Paul. But they had to retreat in the face of MRP and Socialist countermeasures to ensure a more technical supervision; nor was it clear that the PC had really wanted more than its own industrial barony.[26] Italian workers were perhaps most consistent in reviving factory representation through the *consigli di gestione*. Communist spokesmen, however, came to define these councils as a structure for giving the workers a stake in production. They were not intended to replicate Gramsci's revolutionary factory councils.[27] And, in Germany, while co-determination as sought in the mining and metal industries may well have represented a creative and innovative demand, it still remained an effort more to share in the control of traditional managerial functions rather than to overthrow them. The left-wing SPD spokesman Viktor Agartz developed the most

[25] "The opposition of leaders of labor to bonafide scientific management has practically disappeared, and during recent years there has been noteworthy cooperation between scientific management leaders and labor leaders"; H. S. Person, "Scientific Management," Industrial Relations Committee Report, February 15, 1928, AFL Papers, Florence Thorne Collection, 117/8A, box 18, State Historical Society of Wisconsin, Madison, Wisc. Also see Milton J. Nadworny, *Scientific Management and the Unions, 1900–1932* (Cambridge, Mass., 1955); Philips, *Le Problème ouvrier aux États-Unis*, 556; Martin Fine, "Albert Thomas: A Reformer's Vision of Modernization, 1914–1932," *Journal of Contemporary History*, 12 (1977): 545–64; Madeline Rebérioux and Patrick Fridenson, "Albert Thomas, pivot du reformisme français," *Le Mouvement Social*, 87 (1974): 85–97; and Alan Bullock, *The Life and Times of Ernest Bevin*, volume 1: *Trade Union Leader, 1881–1940* (London, 1960), 396.

[26] See Etienne Dejonghe, "Les houillères à l'épreuve, 1944–1947," *Colloque de Lille*, in *Revue du Nord*, 57 (1975): 643–66. On nationalization schemes, see Mario Einaudi *et al.*, *Nationalization in France and Italy* (Ithaca, N.Y., 1955), 96–105.

[27] For Emilio Sereni's exhortation, see Guizzi, "La Fabbrica italiana Magneti Marelli," 252; and, on the role of post-1945 councils, see Paride Rugafiori, "La 'Ricostruzione' in una grande azienda IRI in crisi: L'Ansaldo (1945–1948)," in Ganapini *et al.*, *La Ricostruzione nella grande industria*, 428–444; and Giulio Sapelli, "Industriali e lotta di classe a Torino (1945–1947)," *ibid.*, 445–527. Also see Liliana Lanzardo, *Classe operaia e partito comunista alla Fiat: La Strategia della collaborazione* (Turin, 1971). For a good survey, see F. Levi *et al.*, *Il Triangolo industriale tra ricostruzione e lotta di classe, 1945–1948* (Milan, 1974).

extensive concepts of "economic democracy" but quickly declined in influence in his own party once the Federal Republic was constituted.[28] In short, the second postwar era did not resume the fundamental ideological challenge to managerial control of twenty-five years earlier. The first postwar restoration had largely confirmed the premise that the modern industrial order must operate under hierarchical chains of command, like an army or bureaucracy. The presumption of technical rationality legitimized the economic power that ownership alone could not.

SUBDUING LABOR'S BID to control the organization of production and, by extension, to make economic authority democratic was not sufficient, however, to stabilize a political economy that faced great inherent strains after the First World War. If the defenders of interwar capitalism proposed a social bargain—the increasing satisfaction of material wants in return for a restoration of industrial authority—they had to be able to pay up. In the interwar period, however, many difficulties precluded paying up for more than a brief period.

Two interlocking flaws especially undermined sustained prosperity: constraints imposed by the international economy and by domestic conflicts. Once currencies were stabilized under the gold-exchange standard, balance-of-payment concerns, especially in light of the postwar creditor position of the United States, seemed to mandate relatively low European wages so that Britain and the Continent could maintain exports, compete internationally, and preserve their exchange rates. Reparation obligations for Germany and war debts for the Allies just made these constraints more demanding. At the same time, within each country, economic leaders remained preoccupied with potential saturation of the market and limits of profitability—what the Germans term *Rentabilität*. Industry spokesmen felt that profits were faltering, capital accumulation and investment was imperiled, and, in turn, international competitiveness endangered. They sharply attacked what they perceived as the politically determined costs of labor and of new social-insurance obligations.[29]

But, while European businessmen fretted about impediments to accumulation, the relatively high rates of investment in the late 1920s may have outpaced the purchasing power that would sustain the return to capital. Although wages may not have lagged proportionally behind returns to capital,[30] urban and rural disposable incomes did not necessarily grow sufficiently to justify the continued "rationalization" of the 1920s. In formal terms, what had to be attained was a "warranted growth" path of capital and incomes that allowed the expansion of each to call forth and absorb the increments of the others. Only satisfying the

---

[28] Ernst Ulrich Huster, *Die Politik der SPD, 1945–1950* (Frankfurt a/M, 1978), 35–41. Also see Erich Potthoff, *Der Kampf um die Montanmitbestimmung* (Cologne, 1957); and Eberhard Schmidt, *Die verhinderte Neuordnung, 1945–1950* (Frankfurt a/M, 1970), 182–200.

[29] For the best recent discussion of these attitudes in Germany, see Bernd Weisbrod, *Schwerindustrie in der Weimarer Republik* (Wuppertal, 1978).

[30] Peter Temin has insisted on this, for the U.S.-European indices can be read in different ways; Temin, *Did Monetary Forces Cause the Great Depression?* (New York, 1976), 32.

two constraints together allowed each to be resolved in its own right. Only securing the two simultaneously, moreover, was likely to reconcile the major organized interest groups of the European economies.

Reading backward, one can say, of course, that the 1930s did not find the warranted growth path; and the original statements of the difficulty reflected the somber outcome in their pessimistic depiction of a "knife edge" that a dynamic economy had to tread if it was not to falter. Later theory, perhaps reflecting the generation of post-1950 growth, has suggested that in fact equilibrium growth is relatively easy to generate: technological substitutions, public spending, population growth, and income redistribution have all been shown to make ascent of the knife edge far less chancy.[31] Indeed, the dilemma of equilibrium growth at the end of the 1920s was in part self-imposed by the reigning preoccupation with capital shortages and by the brakes placed on national income growth by the neomercantilist policies of the years following currency stabilization. There were dissenters to prevailing policy, such as John Maynard Keynes. But Keynes remained a gadfly and not always consistent in his recommendations. By the 1930s Keynes and like-minded adherents of purchasing-power doctrines pointed to the state as the agency that could assure high aggregate demand. Their intellectual task became simplified when they urged that their societies more or less disconnect from the international market and seek higher employment levels autarkically—that is, that they cease to fret about exchange rates. Indeed, abandonment of old currency parities followed almost by *force majeur* after 1931. In the long run, Keynes also felt, capital accumulation should become a less preoccupying task, for capital would become more plentiful in relation to the need for it.[32]

Today these simplifying premises appear more problematic. Indeed, contemporary Western economic dilemmas suggest partial parallels with the difficulties perceived at the end of the 1920s. United States economic concepts for the postwar international economy largely precluded the welfare-state self-sufficiency that Keynes suggested. This meant further that his vision of satiated investment needs, with its resultant "euthanasia of the rentier," was likewise premature. Industrial societies in a world market arena can hardly allow investment to atrophy without losing real income to new competitors. Even to apply Keynesian macroeconomic stimulus to assure full employment may bring deteriorating balances of trade and, if no foreign subsidies are found, declining welfare. Some

[31] For the "knife-edge view" of the warranted growth path, see R. F. Harrod, "An Essay in Dynamic Theory," *Economic Journal*, 49 (1939): 12–33, 377. Also see Evsey D. Domar, "Capital Expansion, Rate of Growth, and Employment," *Econometrica*, 14 (1946): 137–47. James Tobin and Robert M. Solow allowed for various tenable rates of growth with factor substitutability; see Tobin, "A Dynamic Aggregative Model," *Journal of Political Economy*, 63 (1955): 103–15; and Solow, "A Contribution to the Theory of Economic Growth," *Quarterly Journal of Economics*, 70 (1956): 65–94. For a recent optimistic summary that sees supply normally generating demand (with the 1930s as an exceptional catastrophe), see John Cornwall, *Growth and Stability in a Mature Economy* (London, 1972).

[32] For Keynes's views concerning the decreasing scarcity of capital, see his *The General Theory of Employment, Interest, and Money* (London, 1960), 375–77; and, concerning the advantages of going it alone, see his *Essays in Persuasion* (1931; 2d ed., New York, 1963), 271–96, and "National Self-Sufficiency," *New Statesman and Nation*, July 8, 15, 1933.

of the constraints that vexed the 1920s have thus re-emerged and, with them, the distributive conflicts between the interests of wage earners and the spokesmen for capital. The difference is that, in the 1920s, the difficulties were rooted in too limited a confidence in mass consumption as a force for growth, whereas in the 1970s they may have derived from too excessive a reliance.

What remains historically remarkable is that from the late 1940s into the 1970s the constraints of the interwar period eased as a twin reorientation took place. First, the United States developed a commitment to European prosperity; second, the political and economic calculations of Europeans themselves changed so that they felt less locked into a distributive contest. Both changes together eased the iron framework of wages, profits, state claims, and international payments.[33]

How could this reorientation take place so easily after 1945? For one thing, it was silently underway before that date. The Depression had certainly discredited the old orthodoxies. The war also demonstrated to British and American financial planners that states could impose levels of expenditure far beyond what the budget-balancers of the 1920s or British Treasury officials of the 1930s had imagined was safe and feasible.[34] Certainly the role of the United States was transformed: the credits of the 1920s had been extended via private banks and had remained hostage to the differential rates of return in Europe and New York; the grants of the late 1940s represented political decisions on the part of Washington. The new American policy did not come instantaneously or automatically. Just as between 1922 and 1924 the New York banking community accepted the need to intervene in Europe, so, as the newly opened records of the U.S. National Advisory Council on International Monetary and Financial Policies help show, Washington became increasingly willing to exploit foreign aid for political purposes: from the coy hesitation about extending loans to the Léon Blum mission in early 1946, to the vigorous European Recovery Program and the almost importuning support for noncommunist unions and parties by 1948, to the funds rushed to Yugoslavia after Tito's break with the Cominform.[35]

The Marshall Plan signaled a political decision that the resources of the United States would be available for the reconstruction of a welfare capitalism in Europe. But in quantitative economic terms American aid amounted to little.

---

[33] The conflict between international competitiveness and demand stimulus at home has been brought out especially by the "Scandinavian" models of two-sector open economies. See Odd Aukrust, "Inflation in the Open Economy: A Norwegian Model," in Walter S. Salant and Lawrence B. Krause, eds., *Worldwide Inflation: Theory and Recent Experience* (Washington, 1977), 107–53; and Jeffrey Sachs, "Wages, Profits, and Macroeconomic Adjustment: A Comparative Study," *Brookings Papers on Economic Activity*, 2 (1979): 269–319.

[34] On the fiscal conservatism of the Treasury, see R. A. C. Parker, "Economics, Rearmament, and Foreign Policy: The United Kingdom before 1939—A Preliminary Study," *Journal of Contemporary History*, 10 (1975): 637–47; Robert Paul Shay, Jr., *British Rearmament in the Thirties: Profits and Politics* (Princeton, 1977), 73–79, 136–55, 242–46; and Susan Howson, *Domestic Monetary Management in Britain, 1919–38* (Cambridge, 1975), 120–26. For the transformation of attitudes, see Donald Winch, *Economics and Policy: A Historical Survey* (London, 1972), chap. 12; and Herbert Stein, *The Fiscal Revolution in America* (Chicago, 1969), chap. 8.

[35] Minutes of the Meetings of the National Advisory Council on International Monetary and Financial Policies, meetings 23, 24 (May 6, 1946), 89 (March 18, 1948), 112 (December 3, 1948, on Japan), 115–16 (January 7, 13, 1949), etc., Office of the Secretary of the Treasury, NA-RG 56.

For the major European economies from 1948 through 1951 it probably contributed no more than 10 to 20 percent of capital formation during the first two
emergency years, then tapered off to below 10 percent.[36] Washington's assistance served more as capital-liberating than as capital-transfusing. "The
basic elements in Western Europe's economic crisis . . . ," the staff of the Eaton-
Herter Select Committee on Foreign Aid accurately emphasized, "converge and
appear in their most conspicuous aspect as a deficit in the balance of payments
with the dollar area."[37] By easing balance-of-payments constraints and freeing
key bottlenecks for specific goods, American aid allowed the European economies to generate their own capital more freely, certainly without returning to
the deflationary competition of the 1930s. U.S. aid served, in a sense, like the
lubricant in an engine—not the fuel—allowing a machine to run that would
otherwise buckle and bind.

This calculation suggests that a modulated judgment on the role of American
capital would be appropriate. Ultimately, the real sources of Europe's postwar

[36] The following table provides the ratio of grants and loans made by the the United States to the gross
domestic capital formation of the respective countries. Gross domestic capital formation (converted here into
dollars at current exchange rates) is a more relevant measure for the postwar years than net investment, for
the replacement of depreciated plants meant qualitative improvement. (For Italy in 1948 and 1949, only net
figures are available.) Grants extended during 1948 comprised largely "interim aid" as a stop-gap before Marshall Plan funds strictly speaking came on stream. After 1951, Marshall Plan aid was phased into Mutual
Security assistance with major military components.

Country	1948	1949	1950	1951
UNITED KINGDOM				
$\frac{\text{U.S. Aid}}{\text{GDCF in \$}}$	$\frac{\$\ 937m}{\$10,400m} = 9\%$	$\frac{\$1,009m}{\$9,000m} = 11\%$	$\frac{\$\ 629m}{\$6,400m} = 10\%$	$\frac{\$\ 129m}{\$6,300m} = 2\%$
FRANCE				
$\frac{\text{U.S. Aid}}{\text{GDCF in \$}}$	$\frac{\$\ 781m}{\$\ 5,600m} = 14\%$	$\frac{\$\ 766m}{\$6,400m} = 12\%$	$\frac{\$\ 465m}{\$4,460m} = 10\%$	$\frac{\$\ 421m}{\$5,380m} = 7\%$
WEST GERMANY				
$\frac{\text{U.S. Aid}}{\text{GDCF in \$}}$	$\frac{\$\ 1,130m}{\$\ 3,600m} = 31\%$ (est.)	$\frac{\$\ 948m}{\$4,340m} = 22\%$	$\frac{\$\ 470m}{\$4,400m} = 11\%$	$\frac{\$\ 362m}{\$5,300m} = 7\%$
ITALY				
$\frac{\text{U.S. Aid}}{\text{GDCF in \$}}$	$\frac{\$\ 399m}{\$\ 1,500m} = 27\%$ (net)	$\frac{\$\ 437m}{\$1,300m} = 34\%$ (net)	$\frac{\$\ 257m}{\$2,700m} = 10\%$	$\frac{\$\ 261m}{\$3,000m} = 9\%$

NOTE: All figures in millions of current (1948–51) dollars; only net figures are available for Italy in 1948 and
1949, and only an estimate can be made for West Germany in 1948, since the available statistics do not give
figures for the first half of that year.
SOURCES: Totals of American aid have been taken from *Statistical Abstract of the United States, 1954,* 898–902;
British GDCF, from *Statistical Abstract for the United Kingdom,* no. 87 (1938–49): Table 294, no. 88 (1950): Table
296, and no. 89 (1952): Table 288; and, other 1948–49 statistics, from *Statistisches Jahrbuch für die Bundesrepublik
Deutschland, 1952,* 454–55; *Annuaire Statistique de la France,* 59 (1952): 335; and *Annuario Statistico Italiano,* ser. V, 3
(1951): 590. Non-British GDCF estimates for 1950 and 1951 are taken from United Nations, *Yearbook of National Accounts Statistics* (1957).

[37] U.S. Congress, House Select Committee on Foreign Aid, *Final Report on Foreign Aid* (May 1, 1948), 80th
Cong., 2d sess., House Report no. 1845, p. 24.

growth had to derive from the Continent's own energies. Indeed, some recovery was apparently already underway by late 1946, even for the battered West German economy.[38] Had not the fearsome winter of 1946–47 paralyzed transportation, impeded food and fuel deliveries, and radicalized workers into politically explosive wage demands, recovery might have continued. In that case, without the emergency American response the ongoing European economic performance might well have resembled, say, British growth in the late 1930s: more protectionist and less spectacular than was to be racked up under American auspices in the 1950s, but still respectable.

In this regard, the American economic role in restabilization after World War II paralleled the political role. Europe would probably not have "gone Communist" or collectivist even if the United States had not intervened with the same resolution. The European middle classes remained socially anchored; the German occupation had hardly struck or aimed at them as a group, nor had it attacked their economic values. But both the political and economic development of the 1950s would doubtless have been less resolutely capitalist and market-oriented, less justified by dynamic success. Throughout the first three postwar years, in fact, there was less decisive purpose than confused experimentation and uncertain initiatives. Business recovery was not held back by ideological sympathies for socialism but by the fear of risky venture, the hesitation finally to write off the losses of the war years. Between 1945 and late 1947, for example, the French and the Italians, then the West Germans along with their American occupiers, avoided imposing the deflationary reforms that helped invigorate capitalist growth.[39] Nor were they prepared to abandon the fuzzy political compromises, which found expression in the tripartite Catholic-Socialist-Communist governing coalitions but seemed less and less likely to mandate either socialism or renewed capitalist growth. Only in 1947–48, when ideological and economic threats appeared potentially catastrophic, did the spokesmen for West Europe's middle classes and elites, and their American sponsors, resolve upon the liberal capitalist mandate that might best be described as a new "wager upon the strong."

Economic analysts have proposed several theories for the remarkable growth that followed. Structural explanations include the sharp increase in agricultural productivity achieved by tractors and fertilizers, the resultant supply of labor released for industry (a supply already augmented by the migrants from eastern Germany and the Italian South, among other areas), and the special efficiency

[38] Werner Abelshauser, *Wirtschaft in Westdeutschland, 1945–1948* (Stuttgart, 1975), 167–70.

[39] For the French rejection of deflation, see Richard Kuisel, *Modernization and the Managed Economy: The State and Capitalism in France, 1900–1950* (Cambridge University Press, forthcoming), chap. 7. For the Italians, who in 1947 embarked upon deflation, see George H. Hildebrand, *Growth and Structure in the Economy of Modern Italy* (Cambridge, Mass., 1965), chaps. 2, 8; Marcello De Cecco, "Sulla politica di stabilizzazione del 1948," in his *Saggi di politica monetaria* (Milan, 1968), 109–41; and Camillo Daneo, *La politica economica della ricostruzione, 1945–1949* (Turin, 1975), chap. 7. On the American and German hesitation to impose early currency reform, see Edward A. Tennenbaum, "The German Mark," book draft, chaps. 11–12, Tennenbaum Papers, box 3, folder 5, Truman Library, Independence, Mo. Belgium was the outstanding exception to the general inflationary languor at the end of the war. For the reforms of Camille Gutt, see Léon H. Dupriez, *Monetary Reconstruction in Belgium* (New York, 1947).

of investment in the context of postwar damage and renewal. Monetarist accounts attribute success to rigorous stabilization programs in Germany, Italy, and Japan. The historian can point to the wage restraint that Dutch, German, and Italian workers demonstrated because of labor's commitment to reconstruction and, perhaps, to mere exhaustion after fascist repression and war.[40] On the managerial side, new business confidence and technocratic impulses gradually prevailed. The example of Pont-à-Mousson suggests that once public policymakers, such as Jean Monnet or Robert Schuman, made commitments to supranational institutions, a new generation of expansionist entrepreneurs could find support for pressing vigorous investment plans within their own firms.[41]

The upshot was that both the major restraints that had corseted the economy of the 1920s could be loosened together. U.S. aid helped overcome the deflationary pressures resulting from defense of the balance of payments. But these pressures also remained minimal because a new generation of Keynesian-influenced administrators were willing to take international deficits in stride. Establishment of European-wide clearance schemes and the willingness of intra-European creditor countries, such as Belgium and even Italy, to hold sterling or other European currencies as a *quid pro quo* for American aid also eased the strains on the economies tending toward balance-of-payments deficits. Washington policymakers certainly did not like the impediments to currency convertibility that Europeans kept in force, and they continued to press for the removal of these obstacles to the free circulation of dollars. U.S. Treasury officials and American delegates to the International Monetary Fund insisted stubbornly on convertibility even at the cost of deflationary policies. In contrast, American officials with the Marshall Plan administration (the ECA) tended to accept compromise arrangements that permitted Europeans to prolong shielding their international accounts; and even the stern Treasury disciplinarians had to accept British cancellation of sterling convertibility after the disastrous attempt during the summer of 1947. They likewise were compelled to acquiesce in French creation of a two-tiered currency market in 1948, which allowed scope for floating exchange rates, and they accepted restrictions upon full convertibility in the European clearance unions from 1949 through 1951. Preaching that all currencies should be fully tradable for dollars, Washington officials nonetheless lived with a compromise monetary regime.[42]

---

[40] For examples of structural approaches, see Ingvar Svennilson, *Growth and Stagnation in the European Economy* (Geneva, 1954); U.N. Economic Commission for Europe, *Economic Survey of Europe in 1961*, part 2: *Some Factors in Economic Growth in Europe during the 1950's* (Geneva, 1961); and Charles Kindleberger, *Europe's Postwar Economic Growth: The Role of Labor Supply* (Cambridge, Mass., 1967). For an example of the monetarist approach, see Hildebrand, *Growth and Structure in the Economy of Modern Italy*. Angus Maddison has emphasized policy factors, including a Western internationalism attributed to the Cold War; see his "Economic Policy and Performance in Europe, 1913–1970," in Carlo Cipolla, ed., *The Fontana Economic History of Europe*, 5 (Glasgow, 1976): 442–508. For a general treatment, see M. M. Postan, *An Economic History of Western Europe, 1945–1964* (London, 1967).

[41] See, for example, the debate on expansion of coking facilities and Roger Martin's advocacy of investment, October 16, 1951, PAM, box 70671. Also see Richard Kuisel, "Technocrats and Public Policy: From the Third to the Fourth Republic," *Journal of European Economic History*, 2 (1973): 53–99.

[42] For debates on convertibility, see Minutes of the Meetings of the National Advisory Committee on Inter-

The second major inhibition that had undermined continuing expansion in the 1920s also disappeared: the precarious "knife edge" equilibrium growth path for wages and investment broadened into an easy highway. If policymakers no longer wished to sacrifice living standards on the altar of fixed exchange rates, labor showed sufficient wage restraint such that investment could soar. Rather than relatively high labor costs impelling capital substitution, relatively low labor costs permitted capital expansion. The statistics of the 1950s reveal not only the familiar growth of national income but unprecedented rates of capital formation as well: 30 percent in Japan, 27 percent in Germany, 20 percent in France and Italy, 16 percent in the United Kingdom, 18 percent in the United States.[43] In contrast, the wages share of national income remained stable or even dropped slightly, as in Western Germany: a decade's halting of the slow but otherwise prevailing trend of the twentieth century. The expansion and harmony that businessmen had sought in the 1920s was finally achieved in the 1950s.

This result, of course, required the cooperation of those labor leaders who shared the premises of a growth-organized welfare capitalism—the commitment that I have elsewhere termed the "politics of productivity."[44] "The improvement of productivity, in its widest sense, remains the fundamental problem of Western Europe," declared the Organization for European Economic Cooperation, and it echoed the themes of the managerial mystique of the 1920s as it reported, "Great emphasis is placed in the United States . . . upon public relations efforts by management in acquainting workers with their plant, its problems, and its place in the economy."[45] For society as a whole, the politics of productivity meant simply the adjournment of conflicts over the percentage share of national income for the rewards of future economic growth. As one West German official explained to business and labor representatives in the remarkable Königstein discussions of February 1949 (which, in effect, adumbrated West German economic strategies up to the present day), anyone who could renounce some consumption had to renounce it. "He had to save, whether or not he wanted, because he cannot be permitted to evade the common tasks of reconstruction."[46]

national Monetary and Financial Policies, meetings 70, 79–81, 83–84, 134, 153, 158, 171, Office of the Secretary of the Treasury, NA-RG 56. For the EPU, see William Diebold, Jr., *Trade and Payments in Western Europe* (New York, 1972), 64–69; and Albert O. Hirschman, "The European Payments Union: The Negotiations and the Issues," *Review of Economics and Statistics*, 33 (1951): 49–59.

[43] Simon Kuznets, *Modern Economic Growth: Rate, Structure, and Spread* (New Haven, 1966), 236–37; and U.N. Economic Commission for Europe, *Some Factors in Economic Growth in Europe during the 1950's*, chap. 2, pp. 16–22. For the wage share of national income, see U.N. Economic Commission for Europe, *Incomes in Postwar Europe: A Study of Policies, Growth, and Distribution* (Geneva, 1967), chap. 2, pp. 30–31.

[44] See my "The Politics of Productivity: Foundations of American International Economic Policy after World War II," in Peter Katzenstein, ed., *Between Power and Plenty: The Foreign Economic Policies of Advanced Industrial States* (Madison, Wisc., 1978), 23–49; the articles in this volume were first published in 1977, as the autumn issue of *International Organization*.

[45] Organization for European Economic Co-Operation [hereafter, OEEC], *Europe: The Way Ahead: Towards Economic Expansion and Dollar Balance*, 4th Annual Report of the OEEC (Paris, 1952), 195. Also see Roger Grégoire, "European Productivity Agency," in OEEC, *At Work for Europe* (5th ed., Paris, 1960), 139–52.

[46] Statement of Dr. Troeger, Königstein, January 4, 1949, BA Koblenz, Z 13/63. The labor minister of the Bizone, Halbfell, dissented, arguing against unplanned investment, but was in a clear minority.

As an explicit principle of consensus, economic growth—the notion of continuously higher levels of national product—came into its own at the end of the 1940s. The earliest public celebration of its virtues may well have been Leon Keyserling's speeches as chairman of the Council of Economic Advisers during 1949;[47] but the less precise concepts of sustained high purchasing power or simply "reconstruction" or "production" served to rally labor as well as businessmen from the end of the war on.

Throughout 1945 and 1946 Communist labor leaders themselves seemed ready to accept the trade-off between present consumption and future growth. The increasing hardship of their rank and file during the winter of 1946–47 and the threat of militant unions on their left flank (aside from any guidance that Moscow may have urged as the dispute with the United States deepened) impelled them to abandon their collaborative stance. The French Communists' reluctant sponsorship of the Renault strike, which likewise led to their dismissal from the governing coalition (and, similarly, the Belgian Communists' refusal to accept coal price increases), best revealed their shifting priorities. No less anticommunist an AFL representative than Irving Brown, who felt that the successive strikes revealed the Communists' "complete desire to destroy the government even at the cost of permanently destroying France," understood that a socialist movement could hardly recapture leadership within the CGT if it participated in a cabinet seeking to freeze wages.[48] Despite the admitted difficulty in reconstructing a mass base for the socialists, by 1947–48, American policymakers, AFL emissaries, and European businessmen diligently encouraged the formation of social democratic unions in the Latin countries and pressed for the purge of Communist sympathizers from British, German, and American federations. The moderates of Force Ouvrière, the TUC, or the Italian Catholic union federation (CISL) became all the more essential as interlocutors for labor. "The trend in Europe is clearly toward the Left," noted one of the Department of State's leading European analysts shortly after tripartism collapsed. "I feel that we should try to keep it a non-communist Left and should support Social-Democratic governments."[49] The axis of the politics of productivity thus had to fall

[47] Keyserling, "Prospects for American Economic Growth," Address in San Francisco, September 18, 1949, Truman Library, President's Secretary's File 143: "Agencies: Council of Economic Advisers."

[48] Brown, "Report on Greece, France, and England," July 7, 1947, State Historical Society of Wisconsin, AFL Papers, Florence Thorne Collection, 117/8A, box 17, F. 3A. On the events of 1947, see Wilfried Loth, "Frankreichs Kommunisten und der Beginn des kalten Krieges: Die Entlassung der kommunistischen Minister im Mai 1947," *Vierteljahrshefte für Zeitgeschichte*, 26 (1978): 9–65, and "Die französischen Sozialisten und der Marshall-Plan," in Lutz Niethammer, ed., *Die europäischen Linke und der Marshall-Plan* (forthcoming). Also see Vincent Auriol, *Journal du Septennat*, ed. Pierre Nora and Jacques Ozouf, volume 1: *1947* (Paris, 1970), *passim*; and Alfred Rieber, *Stalin and the French Communist Party, 1941–1947* (New York, 1962), 331–57. On Belgium, see NA-RG 59, 855.00/3-1147 (no. 372), 855.00/3-2147 (no. 1069), 855.00/3-3147 (no. 1097).

[49] John Hickerson to H. Freeman Matthews, June 25, 1947, NA-RG 59, Office of European Affairs, box 3. For European policies of the AFL, see International Labor Committee, Minutes of the Meeting of November 11, 1947, AFL Papers, Florence Thorne Collection, 117/8A, box 17, F. 3C. Also see Matthew Woll to Thorne, April 6, 1948, and the attached "Confidential Report," *ibid.*, F. 4. And see Ronald Radosh, *American Labor and U.S. Foreign Policy* (New York, 1969); Ulrich Borsdorf, "Erkaufte Spaltung: Der Marshall-Plan und die Auseinandersetzung um die deutschen Gewerkschaften," in Niethammer, *Die europäischen Linke und der Marshall-Plan*; Horst Lademacher, "Die Spaltung des Weltgewerkschaftsbundes als Folg des beginnenden Ost-West Konfliktes," *ibid.*; and Lutz Niethammer, "Strukturreform und Wachstumspakt," in Heinz Oskar Vetter, ed., *Vom*

right in the center of the labor movement: "politically speaking the break must come to left of or at the very least in the middle of the [French] Socialist party. Translated into labor terms, the healthy elements of organized labor must be kept in the non-Communist camp. Otherwise the tiny production margin of the fragile French economy would vanish and the ensuing civil disturbances would take on the aspects of civil war."[50]

The economic premises that the "healthy elements" of labor subscribed to remained precisely those of the trade-union leaders who had pioneered collaborative labor relations in the late 1920s. Union spokesmen such as Ernest Bevin had then joined progressive industrialists for talks on enhancing productivity. By the late 1940s they were serving in high office. Their integration testified to the postwar years' fulfilment of the second criterion for stabilizing the welfare capitalist economies of the West. The new cooperation, along with America's underwriting, ensured that capital accumulation and wages and welfare benefits could increase in tandem, thus overcoming the fatal impediments to sustained growth in the 1920s. As Western leaders looked more and more to economic growth, increasingly presupposed, first, as automatic and, second, as the major index of a society's welfare, the stakes of politics narrowed. Communism increasingly became a permanent and sullen opposition, to be analyzed, in the spirit of the 1950s, as inherently pathological. At the same time, the appeal of neofascism or Gaullism remained fitful, largely consigned to the regions that paid for dynamic growth elsewhere with their own relative backwardness. In the political center Christian Democrats (or Tories in Britain) either shared power with Social Democrats or alternated officeholding in a consensual politics that debated only whether the anticipated dividends of economic growth should be devoted to social-welfare consumption or ploughed back into private investment. Residual colonial or religious and ethnic issues—not the baselines of political economy—remained the major sources of passion and controversy.

Repression, cooptation, and the success of the managerial mystique with its vogue of productivity had reconsolidated the bureaucratic organization of industrial work in the 1920s. The economic accomplishments of the period after 1948 completed the second half of the stabilization assignment. They seemed to eliminate the vulnerability of economic life and enhanced legitimacy with output and growth. Despite the tragic waste of the Great Depression, the immense destructiveness of two world wars, and the countless lives scattered like dry autumn leaves throughout Europe, Western leaders recovered more of their prosperity and liberalism, retained more of their privileges and prerogatives, than they would have dared predict.

Sozialistengesetz zur Mitbestimmung: Zum 100. Geburtstag von Hans Böckler (Cologne, 1975), 303–58. On the French unions, see Bergonieux, *Force Ouvrière*; and André Barjonet, *La C.G.T.* (Paris, 1968), 49–51. On Italy, see Daniel L. Horowitz, *The Italian Labor Movement* (Cambridge, Mass., 1963), 208–73; and Adolfo Pepe, "La CGIL dalla ricostruzione alla scissione, 1944–1948," *Storia Contemporanea*, 5 (1974): 591–636, and the works cited in n. 31. Also see the reports from Paris and Rome to the Department of State in *Foreign Relations of the United States, 1947*, 3 (Washington, 1972): 690–91, 695–99 (on the CGT), 847–48, 863–68 (on Italian labor).

[50] Robert Lovett to Ambassador Caffrey, Paris (based on a memo by Hickerson), October 25, 1947, NA-RG 59, 851.00/10-2447.

SUCCESSFUL SYSTEMS OF POLITICAL EQUILIBRIUM must remain isolated (as did Tokugawa Japan) or be international in scope. The notable eras of European stabilization—the generation after Utrecht, for example, or the half-century after Vienna—have been periods of class equilibrium and international compromise simultaneously. The configurations of power among states tend to second those within societies. The Vienna settlement consisted of adjustments between states but also comprised a restoration of old and new landed classes along with a strengthened bureaucracy. *Pax Britannica* assimilated bourgeois elements to this international coalition and added resources outside Europe to equilibrate strains at home. Fully to comprehend the period from 1918 to 1950 as a search for stabilization on the part of old upper and middle classes, now augmented by a reformist working-class leadership, requires looking at the international architecture as well as domestic structures. Obviously, the Cold War had a decided influence on internal outcomes after World War II. But to register this connection hardly reveals the principles of interaction. The Cold War did not, in itself, determine the logic of the international system for domestic stability.

The surprising centers of growth in the 1950s and 1960s were West Germany, Japan, and, though a smaller economy, Italy. West Germany and Japan, above all, became virtual engines of capital accumulation. As such, they played a critical role in U.S. encouragement of an international coalition of liberal polities with mixed capitalist economies. Although, as of 1944, the U.S. Treasury resoundingly rejected the idea that a German economic contribution would be vital for European prosperity, Congressmen, the Harriman mission (to prepare for Marshall Plan aid), and industrial leaders by 1947 viewed German recovery as doubly critical, both for its own sake and for the economic linchpinning of the wider region.[51] If integrated into a West European system of exchange, German skilled labor, technological virtuousity, and coal would benefit all her neighbors. Without German recovery and integration, their economies must operate less efficiently. The same calculation came to hold for Japan and its role in America after the Communist takeover in China and hostilities in Korea.[52] Opponents of a punitive treatment for Germany had emphasized their European economic vision from the outset, and by the summer of 1947 their concept had quickly become the main theme of the influential spokesmen for German recovery. The lesson was not lost on industrial interests in the emerging state: when German firms petitioned to raise their output or rebuild their rolling mills, their directors

[51] U.S. Treasury Memorandum, "Is European Prosperity Dependent upon German Industry?" September 7, 1944, Mudd Library, Princeton University, Harry Dexter White Papers, box 7, F. 22e: "In short, the statement that a healthy European economy is dependent upon German industry was never true, nor will it be true in the future." For the turnabout, see "Records of Conferences," Harriman mission, summer 1947, W. A. Harriman's papers, Washington, D.C. Also see John Gimbel, *The Origins of the Marshall Plan* (Stanford, 1976), and *The American Occupation of Germany, 1945–1949* (Stanford, 1968), 147–58, 163–69, 174–85.

[52] Joyce Kolko and Gabriel Kolko, *The Limits of Power: The World and United States Foreign Policy, 1945–1954* (New York, 1972), chaps. 11, 19; Jon Halliday, *A Political History of Japanese Capitalism* (New York, 1975), 182–90; and John Dower, *Aftermath of Empire: Yoshida Shigeru and the Japanese Experience, 1878–1954* (Cambridge, Mass., 1979), chaps. 9–10, and manuscript essays on "The Reverse Course."

unabashedly pleaded the cause of good Europeans.[53] Nor was recovery only the demand of businessmen. German trade unions and the AFL, which supported them, strongly advocated industrial reconstruction.[54] Rehabilitation of the German economy thus emerged as critical for the United States's wager on productivity.

Was it just an accident that the countries that forged ahead so brilliantly and then came to serve as international poles of growth even beyond expectation were the exfascist powers? This question must be confronted, despite its harsh implications. Did Washington, in effect, reap the final benefit from the discipline and coercion of labor that the Axis states had earlier imposed? Not directly, of course. But the American-sponsored international economy may have ultimately benefited from the fact that the working classes within the defeated countries had been atomized by political repression, wartime sacrifices, and the mere tasks of survival. Labor leaders who returned from concealment, prison, or exile faced sufficient challenge just in rebuilding their shattered movements. Stressing the necessity of production appeared to them less a contribution to restoration than the premise for the patient work of reorganization.[55] In addition, defeat and occupation clearly permitted the United States more direct intervention than was possible elsewhere. Occupation authorities in all three countries could limit the organization of political unions, postpone nationalization, and halt strikes. Allied fiscal control—exerted perhaps most consistently by Joseph Dodge in Japan[56]—ultimately reinforced those who advocated rapid capital formation, although businessmen often resisted at first. Harder to measure, but just as important, was the yearning for private goals in countries where fascists had sought to politicize all aspirations and relationships. The United States, after all, was gambling on the renewed persuasiveness of individual well-being.

Germany, however, had hitherto repeatedly resisted integration into an international productive coalition. Insofar as the international divisions of the period from 1914 to 1950 had an economic dimension, they involved conflict less between capitalist societies and a Bolshevik challenger than among different capitalist alternatives. Anglo-American disagreements over the organization of a global economy persisted and raised bitter recriminations on each side. The issue remained whether the international economy should maximize multilateral

---

[53] See, for example, Akten des Verwaltungsamtes für Eisen und Stahl, BA Koblenz, Z 41/23: "Vorschlag zur Wiedereinschaltung der August Thyssen Hütte in der europäischen Stahlplanung ... 9 Februar 1950."

[54] For example, see the works council of Robert Bosch, AG's protest against decartelization proceedings, March 17, 1948, Deutscher Gewerkschaftsbund Archiv, Düsseldorf: "Wirtschaftspolitik, Dekartellierung 1948–49." For similar objections to controls on German industry, see BA Koblenz, B 109/345: "Stellungnahme der Gewerkschaften zum Ruhrstatut vom 7. Januar 1949." For a specimen of AFL support, see William Green to President Truman, November 24, 1947, AFL Papers, William Green Collection, 117A/11C box 7F (Marshall Plan).

[55] For an example of this organizational effort, see [Hans Böckler] "Bericht der Deutschlandreise, 6. März bis 30. April 1946," Deutscher Gewerkschaftsbund Archiv, Düsseldorf.

[56] Detroit Public Library, Joseph Dodge Papers, Japan Assignment, box 1, F: "Budget: Ikeda Interviews," and Japan Assignment, 1950, box 3, F: "Correspondence, Marquat."

trade and welfare, but thereby reward the most massive and technologically productive economy, or whether as the British desired, it should be based upon regional systems of dominion that guaranteed international markets to the weaker power.[57] Still, the British dominion alternative seemed to be a limited challenge, whereas the German threat to the open international economy had been more ominous and, just as critical, the emanation of an ugly political regime.

This is not to argue that Nazism was menacing because of its international economic policies—the autarky and bilateralism that so angered Cordell Hull. Instead, the connection between politics and economics was central to the very way Nazism was interpreted as a regime. American commentators viewed Nazism as an abusive political economy: a cartel of monopolists who subordinated the public sphere to private forces.[58] Although Hjalmar Schacht's bilateral treaties yoked Eastern Europe into a German-dominated economic bloc, trade access to this area was hardly a crucial stake in itself. Nevertheless, a Germany that was enrolled in a system of international exchange with the West, as the Weimar Republic had been from 1924 to the Depression,[59] naturally appeared a safer and more decent participant in a liberal international order.

Hence the central conflict defining the international political economy from World War I until about 1950 was not that between American and Soviet alternatives, between capitalism and communism. The Soviet-American antagonism after World War II, in effect, imposed a framework on international politics but did not exhaust the issues. Viewed over the whole half century, the American international economic effort of the era of stabilization centered on overcoming British, Japanese, and especially German alternatives to a pluralist, market-economy liberalism. In the case of Germany, these alternatives were incorporated first in Berlin's vision of Mitteleuropa during Ludendorff's regime of 1917–18 and then in Hitler's expansionist Reich. Defeating these German projects, however, could be only the first stage in erecting a stable alternative. To assure liberal, pluralist stability within each West European country, as well as for the Atlantic region as a whole, required the further step of integrating German economic dynamism into an international system of exchange: perhaps the pre-eminent Western diplomatic task in each postwar reconstruction period.

These respective postwar tasks, however, took more than just German defeat; they also required that the United States assume the burden of funding Germany's international deficits—including reparations—after the two wars. Amer-

---

[57] Richard Gardner, *Sterling-Dollar Diplomacy: Anglo-American Cooperation in the Reconstruction of Multilateral Trade* (Oxford, 1956); and Benjamin M. Rowland, "Preparing the American Ascendancy: The Transfer of Economic Power from Britain to the United States," in Rowland, ed., *Balance of Power or Hegemony: The Interwar Monetary System* (New York, 1976), 195–224.

[58] Maier, "The Politics of Productivity," 32–34. Roosevelt's own message calling for the Temporary National Economic Committee investigation on monopoly, April 29, 1938, defined fascism as "ownership of government by an individual, by a group, or by any other controlling private power," an interpretation that linked the attitudes of the "second" New Deal with the concern about Nazi expansionism.

[59] Werner Link, *Die amerikanische Stabilisierungspolitik in Deutschland, 1921–1932* (Düsseldorf, 1970); and Gerd Hardach, *Weltmarktorientierung und relative Stagnation: Währungspolitik in Deutschland, 1924–1931* (Berlin, 1976), 152–62.

ican reluctance to take on this responsibility until 1924 (and then only indirectly) helped produce the impasses of the five years after Versailles. U.S. willingness to take on the burden after 1947 facilitated the stabilization of the 1950s and 1960s. But American readiness was no automatic decision. As one minor Department of State official wrote before victory in Europe, "It seems certain that Germany has lost the war; but it appears that Dr. Schacht has a very good chance of winning the peace."[60]

In light of these developments, the international corollary of the era of domestic stabilization may be viewed as a German-American (or perhaps a trilateral German-American-Japanese) association achieved only after two world wars. Success for this policy was registered not by the rubble of Berlin but by the frustration of such postwar German leaders as Jakob Kaiser of the CDU and Kurt Schumacher of the SPD, both of whom sought unsuccessfully to maintain under democratic auspices a less capitalist and less exclusively Western-oriented German society.[61] Their very setbacks testified to the triumph of stabilization in West Germany, Western Europe, and the noncommunist countries as a whole. Just as the end of the second war against Germany resolved the international issues left undecided after the close of the first, so the strengthening of Western pluralism after the second war completed the European domestic institutional restructuring begun after the first. Stabilization meant an end to the German problem. It likewise meant winning the adherence of a large enough segment of the working classes to preserve the scope for private economic power and hierarchy that defined liberal capitalism. The achievement was not simply restorative, for the new, very real guarantees of social welfare and social-democratic political participation contributed change even as they purchased continuity.

This suggests that the major sociopolitical assignment of the twentieth century paralleled that of the nineteenth, which saw the incorporation of the middle classes and European bourgeoisie into the political community. The international corollaries of the earlier development were the paralysis and reduction of Metternichian Austria within Europe and the extension of overseas empire. The international corollaries of the new development were the linking to the West of at least part of Germany and the recession of overseas empire: the trajectory from grandeur to welfare. The institutional device for the nineteenth century was parliamentary representation; the institutional foci for the twentieth-century achievement included trade unions, ambitious state economic agencies, and bureaucratized pressure groups—the components of what I have termed elsewhere "corporate pluralism."

Observers have often failed to note the magnitude of the twentieth-century

---

[60] Joseph Fuqua to Woodrow Willoughby, December 21, 1944, NA-RG 59, International Trade Papers, box 19, F: "Article VII: United Kingdom—General."

[61] Hans Peter Schwartz, *Vom Reich zur Bundesrepublik: Deutschland im Widerstreit der aussenpolitischen Konzeptionen in den Jahren der Besatzungsherrschaft, 1945–1949* (Berlin, 1966), 297–344; Werner Conze, *Jakob Kaiser: Politiker zwischen Ost und West, 1945–1949* (Stuttgart, 1969); Lewis J. Edinger, *Kurt Schumacher: A Study in Personality and Political Behavior* (Stanford, 1965); and Ernst Nolte, *Deutschland und der Kalte Krieg* (Munich, 1974), 208–14, 322–23.

accomplishment because the costs were so distressing. Certainly this essay should not be read as an argument that, because stability resulted, the intervening tyranny, warfare, sacrifice, and resistance lose their historical significance. Still, to ask about significance is to search for meaning, which is just one task of history. To trace the structural principles of collective life must remain an equally valid historical enterprise; and that pursuit compels us to admit that even catastrophic events do not always durably alter the trajectory of institutions any more than the constant slow renewal that procedes in the absence of disaster. Indeed, that continuing change best facilitates the analysis of earlier patterns. If now the institutional solutions of the second postwar era show signs of wear and tear, if the social compromises of the welfare state become precarious as economic growth falters, if the stability of the past generation appears perhaps to have rested on exceptional and transitory advantages, such as the consensus on postwar reconstruction or the ease of securing resources from outside Europe, then we can better begin to understand the recent era not merely as events but as history.

Part IX
Retrospect and Prospect

[20]
The Bretton Woods-GATT System After Fifty Years – A Balance Sheet of Success and Failure*

Richard N. Gardner

In Washington Lord Halifax
Once whispered to Lord Keynes:
It's true they have the money bags
But we have all the brains

This mischievous little verse, written on a yellowing piece of paper left over from the first Anglo-American discussions on the postwar monetary system, stirs memories of one of the great adventures of economic diplomacy in our time. It recalls an effort of creative statesmanship that has seldom been equalled – an effort to construct an international economic order capable of serving the two overriding goals of world peace and the general welfare of nations.

A great gulf of years now separates us from this scrap of paper and from the American and British negotiators, half of whom, at least, it presumably delighted. As this essay is written, it is half a century since the charters of the International Monetary Fund (IMF) and the International Bank for Reconstruction and Development (IBRD) were completed at Bretton Woods, New Hampshire. Nearly the same time has passed since the first discussions leading to the General Agreement on Tariffs and Trade (GATT).

In this half century, the international setting has radically changed. The United States and Great Britain – the two main protagonists in this history – no longer hold a virtual monopoly on international economic policy-making. Continental European countries that at the time of Bretton Woods were occupied, enemy or neutral – France, Germany, Italy and Spain – have emerged as major participants in economic diplomacy, either through the developing European Union or in their own right. Japan has become an economic powerhouse and an

*From the new Spanish edition of *Sterling-Dollar Diplomacy: The Origin and the Future of the Bretton Woods-GATT System* published by Circulo de Lectores in September 1994 in connection with the commemoration in Madrid of the 50th anniversary of Bretton Woods.

essential participant in trade, monetary and aid negotiations. The nations of Asia, the most dynamic part of the world economy, are now major economic actors, including a China whose trade and income are growing at unprecedented rates. Latin America, after years of uneven and inward-looking development, is now embarked on rapid growth and hemispheric integration. And with the end of the Cold War, Russia and the countries of its former empire are rejoining a world economic system from which they deliberately excluded themselves at the end of the Second World War. Today the 'money-bags,' the 'brains,' the economic weight and the political influence are all better distributed than they were half a century ago.

Yet the old and difficult issues that confronted the 'founding fathers' of the Bretton Woods-GATT system are still with us: how to reconcile the freedom of international trade and payments with high levels of domestic employment and growth, how to balance the need for effective international economic institutions with still-powerful demands for national economic sovereignty, and how to relate regional and bilateral economic arrangements to a global economic order.

An introductory explanation is necessary to warn the reader of what this essay is and what it is not. It is not a study of economic theory in which one can find an original discussion of the principles of international trade. Still less is it a statistical analysis of the postwar pattern of international trade and payments. It is rather an essay about the making of international economic policy and the shaping of institutions to implement that policy during and immediately after the Second World War. It places special emphasis on the interaction between official policy and public opinion – particularly on the difficult problem of explaining complex economic policies to a democratic electorate. It is thus a hybrid work straddling the boundaries of history, international relations, political science and even international law. Perhaps it can best be described as 'a study in international economic diplomacy.' The question which this essay endeavours to answer is the following: How well did the architects of the postwar economic order succeed in providing us with international institutions to promote the general welfare of nations? What new requirements for action should be on our agenda as we contemplate the next fifty years of international economic cooperation? I shall endeavour to answer the first question in this essay.

My evaluation of the successes and failures of the Bretton Woods-GATT system is somewhat different today than it was when *Stirling-Dollar Diplomacy* was originally written during my post-graduate years at Oxford in the early 1950s. A short time after the first edition was published in 1956, I joined the administration of President John F. Kennedy and served for four years in the Department of State. Many years later, I was appointed by President Jimmy Carter to be U.S. Ambassador to Italy. Currently, I have the privilege of serving as U.S. Ambassador to Spain (although this essay remains an unofficial and personal work). This experience in government has had an inevitable effect. Once the critic turns actor, he does not write criticism in quite the same old way. After testifying on dozens of occasions before Congress, one becomes rather more understanding of the problems that others faced in obtaining Congressional approval for the Bretton Woods agreements and the International Trade Organization. One becomes more acutely aware of the difficulties of diplomatic negotiation between democratic countries – particularly of the severe constraints imposed by one's own and other countries' political systems. One sees more clearly that the choices available to the policy-maker are often limited by past commitments and by contemporary public attitudes, and that those choices are often risky and disagreeable. One realizes that policy must sometimes be made piece by piece – the pieces not always fitting very neatly together – and that the interplay between officialdom on the one hand, and parliaments and the public on the other, often results in promises which cannot be delivered.

In the light of this subsequent experience, I now regard the work of the 'founding fathers' in designing the postwar economic order as an extraordinary accomplishment. It could fairly be described as a 'political miracle' because the postwar institutions they bequeathed us were in considerable degree created, as this historical account demonstrates, against powerful political and intellectual currents on both sides of the Atlantic. Today, when political realities impose severe constraints on new efforts of constructive internationalism, it is worth recalling for a moment how great the obstacles were for the 'founding fathers' fifty years ago.

On the British side, there was profound scepticism throughout the establishment that a system based on open multilateral trade would be in Britain's interests. The Federation of British Industries and the London Chamber of Commerce were hostile. Many felt that the tide of the future was barter trade, managed markets, discriminatory arrangements, currency controls. Many believed that the United States was destined to go into a deep depression after the war, dragging Britain into the abyss and destroying its postwar commitments to the welfare state and full employment. To these people it seemed folly to lie down with the U.S. in an international system based on liberal economic principles. There were also doubts whether Britain's postwar balance of payments would be strong enough to permit it to operate successfully without exchange and trade controls. And, of course, there were those on the right who wanted to make Imperial Preference and the sterling area the basis for a postwar order.

Those two pillars of establishment opinion in Britain, *The Economist* and *The Times*, looked at the postwar planning with deep misgiving. As *The Times* put it:

We must . . . reconcile ourselves once and for all to the view that the days of *laissez-faire* and the unlimited division of labour are over; that every country – including Great Britain – plans and organizes its production in the light of social and military needs, and that the regulation of this production by such 'trade barriers' as tariffs, quotas, and subsidies is a necessary and integral part of this policy.

One member of parliament warned that acceptance of the American postwar monetary proposals 'will be the end. The end of all our hopes of an expansionist policy, and of social advance. It will be the end of the Beveridge Plan, of improved education, of housing reconstruction, the end of the new Britain we are fighting to rebuild. It will lead again to world depression, to chaos, and, ultimately, to war.'

The U.S. Ambassador to Britain, John Winant, cabled Washington in 1944 that 'a majority of the directors of the Bank of England are opposed to the Bretton Woods program. . . . It is argued by those in opposition that if the plan is adopted, financial control will leave London and sterling exchange will be replaced by dollar exchange.'

A leading financial journalist said that in the view of many Members of Parliament he had talked to, 'it would be preferable to have two international systems, a dollar bloc and a sterling bloc. It is argued that conditions, interests and mentality within the two groups differ fundamentally, and that for this reason any attempt to lump them together is foredoomed to failure.'

One of the things that inflamed British opinion was the American emphasis on nondiscrimination, the insistence that Imperial Preferences would have to be eliminated. Lord Croft described this demand as 'the Boston Tea Party in reverse,' and an 'interference with the freedom of our own country to manage its affairs that I regard as unparalleled in the history of the world.' On the other end of the political spectrum, Lord Lindsay of Birker was no less incensed: 'When I heard Americans making snooty remarks about that poor little preference of ours, I thought it was the limit, and I still think so.' One MP rose in the House of Commons and solemnly declared: 'If the Government tries to eliminate Empire Preference a number of us will conduct such a nationwide campaign in this country as will light the very beacons on the hills. We will attack them in the marketplace, in the towns and the cities, we will rouse this whole country against them in such a crusade as will overcome this Government, because we will not have it.'

The postwar economic plans had no smoother reception on the American side. The *Wall Street Journal* called the Keynes plan 'a machine for the regimentation of the world.' The *New York Times* considered the Bretton Woods proposals unnecessary – it favoured going back to the gold standard, 'the most satisfactory international standard that has ever been devised.' The American Bankers Association said that 'a system of quotas or shares in a pool which gives debtor countries the impression that they have a right to credits up to some amount is unsound in principle, and raises hopes that cannot be realized.' The Guaranty Trust Company, progenitor of Morgan Guaranty, called both the British and American plans for Bretton Woods 'dangerous' on the grounds that they would 'enable nations to buy merchandise without being able to pay for it.' Senator Robert Taft, leader of the right wing of the Republican Party, denounced the Bretton Woods agreements, charging that the United States was 'putting all the valuable money into the Fund,' and would be 'pouring money down a rat-hole.' A Senator from Utah rose in indignation on the floor of the Senate, brandished a fistful of foreign currencies, and defied any one of his colleagues to 'go downtown in Washington and get his shoes shined with this whole bunch of bills.' And, again, the American Bankers Association objected to the founding of the International Monetary Fund because 'we should be handing over to an international body the power to determine the destination, time, and use of our money' – abandoning, without receiving anything in return, a vital part of American bargaining power.

The postwar trade arrangements were also bitterly opposed by many in the United States. In their final form, free traders found them too protectionist and protectionists found them too liberal. When the International Trade Organization (ITO) was completed in 1948, the U.S. Congress wanted no part of it. The National Foreign Trade Council, the National Association of Manufacturers, and the U.S. Chamber of Commerce were strongly against it. Even the General Agreement on Tariffs and Trade, which survived the demise of the ITO as a multilateral trade agreement, lived for years in a kind of political limbo. Congress was so sceptical of being restrained in the use of its tariff and other foreign commerce powers that, in successive renewals of the trade agreements programme, it inserted a clause stating that renewal of the legislation 'shall constitute neither approval nor disapproval' of the GATT.

It is in the light of such attitudes in the two countries that the creation of the postwar institutions deserves to be called a 'political miracle.' The 'miracle' was only possible because it was undertaken at the end of a war when public opinion could be mobilized in the hopeful enterprise of building a better world, and because both countries were led by men of great vision surrounded by dedicated internationalists of outstanding ability. The great leaders were Franklin D. Roosevelt and Winston Churchill, who saw the need to provide firm economic underpinnings for the postwar world even though, preoccupied with the problem of winning the war, they left the details to others. The job of constructing the postwar international organizations was overseen by Cabinet and sub-Cabinet level officials like Secretary of State Cordell Hull, Secretary of the Treasury Henry Morgenthau, and Undersecretary of State Will Clayton on the American side, and Sir Kingsley Wood, Sir John Anderson and Richard Law on the British side. But the critical choices in the complex and technical negotiations were made by career civil servants together with professional economists and lawyers on temporary leave from their universities and law firms. The key figures in the Bretton Wood negotiations, of course, were John Maynard Keynes of the U.K. and Harry Dexter White of the U.S. Among the most important trade architects were British negotiators Sir Percivale Liesching, James Meade and Lionel Robbins and American negotiators Myron Taylor, Dean Acheson and Harry Hawkins.

These 'founding fathers,' a relatively small group of men, were united by a common commitment to practical and constructive internationalism. They conceived of a postwar economic system ruled by law. They wanted it to be a universal system, if possible, including the Soviet Union and communist countries but, failing that, at least a single multilateral system including everyone else, rather than a collection of trading blocs. They wanted permanent international institutions to promote cooperation on monetary, trade and development problems. And they wanted somehow to reconcile the concept of maximum possible freedom in trade and payments at the international level with the domestic pursuit by governments of progressive economic and social policies.

The fact that the 'founding fathers' underestimated the requirements of postwar reconstruction or that they designed postwar institutions marked by compromises and inconsistencies I now see as less important than their achievement in building durable structures for cooperative international problem-solving. Their handiwork represented a victory over the economic nationalism and 'beggar they neighbour' policies of the interwar period.

Perhaps most importantly, the 'founding fathers' averted the very real danger that, after victory in the war, the United States would revert to isolationism as it did after the First World War. They managed to establish a framework for U.S. cooperation in the solution of the international economic problems of the future. They thus laid the foundations for the Marshall Plan and a host of other cooperative enterprises that have supplemented and reinforced the postwar institutions down to the present day.

Beyond the experience of the author as a critic-turned-actor, there is a more fundamental reason for a changed evaluation of the economic diplomacy of the wartime and early postwar years. We now have the advantage of a longer historical perspective. *Sterling-Dollar Diplomacy* first appeared in 1956; most of the research and writing was done in 1953–54. In those years, the results of the wartime and early postwar efforts at international economic cooperation looked very different from the way they do today. The International Monetary Fund was then largely inactive, bypassed by belated efforts of postwar reconstruction. Sterling and the other major European currencies were still inconvertible; the provisions of the International Monetary Fund, permitting exchange restrictions for a 'transitional' period, looked as if they might apply indefinitely. The Charter for an International Trade Organization had just been withdrawn from the Congress and the General Agreement on

Tariffs and Trade seemed too weak to organize an effective attack on trade barriers. The recipients of Marshall aid were preoccupied with removing quantitative restrictions among themselves; the U.S. was beginning to undermine its commitment to liberal trade with a variety of protectionist practices; the outlook for substantial reductions in trade barriers on a global basis seemed highly uncertain. International economic cooperation was obstructed by a huge American trade surplus – the supposedly chronic 'dollar shortage' – and by divergent U.S. and European approaches to domestic planning and full employment.

Today, as we look back across half a century, the picture looks very different. For the world economy as a whole, the years since Bretton Woods have been a period of prosperity and growth unprecedented in history. In very round numbers, world production has soared from $300 billion a year at the end of World War II to nearly $30,000 billion a year today. World trade has grown from $30 billion a year to well over $3,000 billion a year. Even allowing for inflation and population growth, these hundred-fold increases represent an extraordinary increase in the welfare of the common man. The past five decades have seen more progress in improving living standards than any previous time in recorded history. Life expectancy has increased by 50 percent. Infant mortality has been halved. Average per capita incomes worldwide have doubled. In the industrialized democracies and in some of the more successful Pacific Rim nations, per capita income has grown considerably more than that – by three to six times in some cases.

Western Europe survived the challenges of Fascism and Communism and enjoyed the benefits of political and economic freedom. Japan rose from the ashes of defeat to become a prosperous democracy. Asian countries like Korea, Taiwan, Hong Kong and Singapore achieved income levels approaching those of established developed countries like Australia and the U.K. Latin America, led by Mexico, Chile and Argentina, finally began to take off into economic growth after years of stagnation. Only Africa and a few die-hard Communist countries like Cuba and North Korea remain exceptions to this economic success story.

While it would be an oversimplification to give all the credit for this economic success to the international economic institutions established during and after World War II, it is clear that the postwar planners must have done *something* right. The institutions they created – the International Monetary Fund, the World Bank, the General Agreement on Tariffs and Trade – have demonstrated an extraordinary ability to adapt themselves to the changing needs of the world economy. This is particularly remarkable when one considers the handicaps under which each of them was founded (see *Sterling-Dollar Diplomacy* for details).

To be sure, the balance sheet of international economic cooperation contains its full measure of debits as well as credits. For the United States and Western Europe, the rapid growth of income registered in the first quarter century after Bretton Woods was not matched in the most recent quarter century. For reasons we shall explore in a moment, the Bretton Woods system of fixed parities collapsed in the early 1970s, and since then the world has experienced both volatile exchange rates and currency misalignments. The interrelated energy and debt crises raised further questions about the adequacy of international economic arrangements, as have recent years of sluggish growth and rising unemployment. Successive GATT rounds of tariff reduction have been accompanied by the growth of non-tariff barriers. And despite the multiplication of international aid institutions, more than a billion people in developing countries still live in abject poverty.

But if the recent record is less than satisfactory, the fault may lie more with the policies of governments than with the deficiencies of the international agencies. Moreover, it is hard to imagine how the world today could deal with its many challenges without the help of the institutions we have inherited from the early postwar years.

To form a balanced judgement on the Bretton Woods-GATT system, it is necessary to look in more detail at the record of the international institutions in accomplishing their objectives in the three areas for which they were originally established – monetary, trade and development cooperation.

The International Monetary Challenge

As this historical account makes clear, the 'founding fathers' saw the creation of a new international monetary system as an essential foundation for a just and stable postwar political and economic order. It was therefore no accident that the Bretton Woods Conference of 1944 was held even before the San Francisco Conference of 1945 that created the United Nations – as well as before the conferences of 1947–48 that created the GATT and the ill-fated International Trade Organization. Monetary questions had to be dealt with before trade questions, in the view of the 'founding fathers', because countries would not be willing to commit themselves to tariff reductions if the conditions of competition could be completely altered by large and unforeseen changes in exchange rates.

In their early thinking about the postwar monetary order, the British and American governments had a supranational design. The postwar planners saw fluctuating and misaligned exchange rates, completely free capital movements and totally autonomous national monetary and fiscal policies as incompatible with an open trading system and the achievement of high levels of employment and growth. They wanted collective intergovernmental management of the quantum of international liquidity, of international capital flows, and of exchange rates and national adjustment policies. The following statement by the Chancellor of the Exchequer eloquently summarized the original concept shared by both John Maynard Keynes and Harry White:

We want an orderly and agreed method of determining the value of national currency units, to eliminate unilateral action and the danger which it involves that each nation will seek to restore its competitive position by exchange depreciation. Above all, we want to free the international monetary system from those arbitrary, unpredictable and undesirable influences which have operated in the past as a result of large-scale speculative movements of capital. We want to secure an economic policy agreed to between the nations and an international monetary system which will be the instrument of that policy. This means that if any one Government were tempted to move too far either in an inflationary or deflationary direction, it would be subject to the check of consultations with the other Governments, and it would be part of the agreed policy to take measures for correcting tendencies to disequilibrium in the balance of payments of each separate country.

The collective intergovernmental management of money envisaged in early postwar planning proved impossible to realize. The ambitious Keynes Plan for overdraft facilities in 'bancor' in a clearing union was set aside in favour of White's more modest conception of a system based on gold and IMF drawing rights. But in the postwar world of rapidly growing trade and inflation, neither gold nor IMF quotas could provide sufficient international reserves. The world thus ended up on a dollar standard, in which the quantum of international reserves was determined mainly by the balance of payments deficits of the United States – which is certainly not what Keynes or White or the other postwar planners had in mind.

The creation of Special Drawing Rights in the first amendment of the Fund Articles at the end of the 1960s was meant to signal a return to a truly international reserve system. Yet this has not worked out either. SDRs represent only a tiny fraction of world liquidity today, and although some developing countries continue to press for SDR issues as a form of development aid or as a means of improving the distribution of world liquidity, neither Britain, the U.S., nor any major developed country now favours moving toward an international reserve system based on SDRs. The idea of a limited form of reserve consolidation, with national holdings of dollars being placed in the Fund in exchange for SDRs, proved non-negotiable during the Carter administration and has been set aside indefinitely. Today, interest in London, Washington and other financial capitals is no longer in the collective management of liquidity, but in a more modest and achievable objective – the gradual movement toward a multi-currency reserve system in which the yen, the mark and perhaps eventually a European currency unit can join the dollar as international reserve assets. Whether such a multi-currency reserve system can be managed so as to ensure the international monetary stability sought at Bretton Woods is an open question.

The original ideas of the 'founding fathers' for collective international monetary management proved no more feasible for capital movements than for liquidity creation. The IMF Articles approved at Bretton Woods provided for freedom from exchange controls only on current transactions; significantly, the postwar planners envisaged that countries would need the latitude (and, in extreme cases, should be required) to control disequilibrating movements of short-term capital. In those days there was a strong belief in both London and Washington that governments would have to protect the system against the uncontrolled activities of private bankers. Secretary of the Treasury Henry Morgenthau went so far as to describe the purpose of the Bretton Woods Conference as 'to drive the usurious money lenders from the temple of international finance.'

It is precisely here, of course, that the world of today contrasts most dramatically with that envisaged at Bretton Woods. The 'money lenders' are very much with us. We have developed a highly sophisticated, 24-hour-a-day global capital market which facilitates instantaneous transfers of funds on a scale that the 'founding fathers' could not have imagined. We are now in a world in which capital flows have displaced trade flows as the principal determinant of currency relations; some $1 trillion of exchange transactions take place every day, only about 2 percent of which are linked to transactions in goods and services. As the postwar world evolved, both the British and the American governments, like those of most countries, came to attach a high priority to freedom from controls on capital as well as current transactions. Moreover, few people have much confidence that international capital movements could be effectively limited, even if this was our aim.

All of this brings us to the last respect in which the original design for international monetary management proved inoperable – the international adjustment process. The postwar monetary order was to be based on fixed exchange rates which could be adjusted only to correct a 'fundamental disequilibrium' through a process of international consultation and agreement. In their original versions, the American and British currency plans envisaged that such a regime would be made possible by far-reaching international control over the economic policies of deficit and surplus countries.

Under the first (unpublished) draft of the White Plan, members were obliged 'not to adopt any monetary banking measure promoting either serious inflation or serious deflation without the consent of a majority of member votes of the Fund.' The published version omitted this far-reaching (and politically unrealistic) provision, but authorized the Fund to make recommendations for changes in the economic policy of countries going too far toward deficit or surplus. Moreover, recommendations could be reinforced by sanctions – either the denial of the use of Fund resources beyond a certain point for a deficit country or the rationing of the 'scarce currency' of a surplus country by means of exchange restrictions employed against it. Under the Keynes plan, the Clearing Union could require a deficit country that drew more than half of its overdraft facilities to deposit collateral, depreciate its currency, control outward capital movements or surrender liquid reserves in reduction of its debit balance. It could recommend to that country internal economic measures needed to restore equilibrium. It could require a surplus country whose credit balance exceeded half its quota to carry out such measures as the stimulation of domestic demand, the appreciation of its currency, the reduction of import barriers and the making of international development loans.

With the notable exception of the 'scarce-currency' clause, most of these references to international supervision of the economic policy of deficit and surplus countries were eliminated during negotiation of the Fund Articles. In the course of the negotiations leading to Bretton Woods, it proved impossible for the British and the American negotiators to agree on the appropriate balance between deficit and surplus country responsibilities; references to international oversight of domestic economic policies were watered down to facilitate approval of the IMF by Parliament and Congress. By the time of the Bretton Woods conference and its aftermath, national autonomy was being emphasized instead of supranationality. Keynes went so far as to assure the House of Lords that, under the IMF, the external value of sterling 'would be altered if necessary so as to conform to whatever de facto internal value results from domestic policies, which themselves shall be immune from criticism from the Fund.'

Thus the Bretton Woods compromise left a good deal of ambiguity about the responsibilities for adjustment of surplus and deficit countries. It ruled out adjustment through freely fluctuating exchange rates or by controls on payments for current transactions – since exchange stability and multilateral trade were two primary Bretton Woods objectives. But it said very little about how adjustment was to be achieved. The architects at Bretton Woods apparently hoped that, with the aid of Fund resources, deficit and surplus countries could be relied on to restore a balance within a relatively short time by reasonable domestic policies and by occasional changes in exchange rates to correct any 'fundamental disequilibrium.' Unfortunately, however, this system simply failed to work out.

The inadequacies of the Bretton Woods adjustment mechanism were camouflaged in the early postwar years when the United States was in surplus and the rest of the world was in deficit. Nobody paid much attention to the problem of how the Fund would 'police' surplus and deficit nations to ensure their good behaviour. In effect, during these years the U.S. 'policed' the economic policies of deficit countries unilaterally, using the leverage of postwar aid to encourage the adoption of internal and external policies which it regarded as appropriate. It also, in a sense, 'policed' itself – adopting liberal aid and trade policies appropriate to a surplus nation, quickly recognizing that, if it failed to do so, the rest of the world would go broke. This was not so much a question of American altruism as of enlightened self-interest.

The United States was the economic giant among nations; there was no one with whom to share responsibility; it alone had the power to save the wartime multilateral dream and ensure the survival of freedom in the West. The political costs of failure being unacceptable, it was consequently willing to pay the price in terms of the Marshall Plan, in other measures of postwar aid, and in non-reciprocated trade concessions providing liberal access to the U.S. market. Nobody had to invoke the principal IMF sanction envisaged for 'policing' the creditor – the 'scarce-currency' clause considered so important by Keynes. It was unavailable, in any case; since the Fund was inactive during the period of U.S. reconstruction, aid and dollars in the Fund were not technically 'scarce.' But for the reasons mentioned above, the sanction wasn't needed.

When the 'dollar shortage' gave way to 'dollar glut' and when the U.S. -centred system was replaced by a more balanced distribution of economic power, the shortcomings in the Bretton Woods design became apparent. The countries of Continental Europe and Japan did not 'police' themselves to undertake creditor-country responsibilities following the earlier American model. It was not that they were more 'wicked' than the United States; but because none of them was big enough to be decisive, they did not assume the same responsibility as the U.S. had for 'saving the system'. The 'scarce-currency' clause was now a dead letter; nobody, least of all the U.S., wanted to use exchange controls on current transactions as a sanction against surplus countries. It was becoming uncomfortably clear that a system of fixed exchange rates, in which gold and the dollar (supplemented by the possibility of international credits) were the main components, was rather asymmetrical in its pressures for adjustment. Deficit countries were under pressure to adjust when they ran out of reserves and had to go to the Fund or to the central bankers for aid; but there was no similar pressure on creditors to reduce their surpluses.

The deficiencies of the system were also evident on the deficit side, particularly where the U.S. was concerned. To begin with, there were some difficulties in applying conventional balance of payments accounting concepts to the U.S. in its role as central banker to the world. There was very little agreement as to the relevance of the concept of payments equilibrium for a country such as the United States which, in its role as world central banker, had to supply a large part of world liquidity needs. When dollars are the principal instrument available to increase world reserves, are U.S. deficits benign or malignant? Given the desire of the Europeans to run surpluses in the early postwar years and the slow growth of the stock of monetary gold, how would it have been possible for the U.S. – at least before 1967 when its record of price stability compared favourably with that of Western Europe – to have achieved equilibrium without taking measures both destructive of its own and the general welfare and inconsistent with IMF and GATT rules?

Was there also some measure of truth in the view that a modest U.S. payments deficit was an appropriate reflection of the 'financial intermediation' performed by it as central banker to the world and the world's most highly developed capital market? Or were those Europeans right who claimed this was but a sophisticated rationale by which the U.S. was trying to spend beyond its means at Europe's expense – refusing to accept the discipline it urged upon Europe when the situation was reversed? Perhaps all we can say here on this difficult conceptual problem is that, while U.S. payments deficits were in the general interest in the 1940s and

1950s, given the responsibilities of the U.S. in the international monetary system, its deficits were too large during most of the 1970s and 1980s to be acceptable to its allies in Europe and Japan.

In practice, therefore, as far as developed countries were concerned, the postwar international monetary system permitted a large degree of national autonomy. Despite the original concept of international oversight of domestic policy, there was no adjustment process worthy of the name. Yet the system still provided for fixed (though adjustable) exchange rates. The system might indeed have functioned if countries had proved reliable in managing their affairs voluntarily with due regard for the requirements of international adjustment in a regime of stable currency relationships. This was to prove an impossible dream. The two great English-speaking democracies themselves set no good example. In the first postwar decade, Britain tried simultaneously to run a welfare state, maintain a world currency and continue a world military role. This led to sterling devaluations and to sluggish domestic growth. More serious for the international system, the U.S. began in the 1960s to overreach its resources just as Britain had done, refusing to trim the 'Great Society' in the face of the Vietnam War; it thus inaugurated an era of high inflation and large U.S. balance of payments deficits, leading to the suspension of dollar convertibility into gold in 1971 and the final collapse of fixed currency relations in 1973.

The world of the 1980s and 1990s has been characterized by a high degree of exchange rate volatility and by periods of substantial overvaluation and undervaluation of the dollar in relation to the yen and the mark, which replaced the pound sterling as major international currencies. Recent years have also been marked by large and chronic U.S. current account deficits and by large and chronic Japanese current account surpluses that have proved both difficult to reduce and a continuing source of international friction. These imbalances have been a reflection of the U.S. inability to control its domestic budget deficits and of the Japanese propensity to over-saving and under-importing. In the last year, progress has been made on the U.S. side toward greater fiscal responsibility; but whether Japan is willing or able to discharge its economic responsibilities to the rest of the world is still an open question.

With the increased interdependence which exists today, including the high degree of capital mobility between nations which was unforeseen at Bretton Woods, it is essential that countries adjust their domestic economic policies with a view to maintaining a mutually beneficial world economic system. It is simply impossible to have complete national policy autonomy and also maintain an open international system of trade and capital flows. If we wish to preserve the latter, we shall have to accept some limitation on the former.

It was in recognition of this fact that the 1978 amendment to the IMF Articles of Agreement legitimizing floating rates also provided for 'firm surveillance' by the Fund over the exchange rate policies (and by implication the domestic monetary and fiscal policies) of member countries. This surveillance is exercised through the so-called Article IV consultations between the Fund and its members. But to date these consultations have had little influence on the policies of the U.S., Japan, Germany and other major industrialized countries. Unlike most developing countries, these nations can finance their deficits by borrowing from the international capital market, so they have no need for IMF assistance and its accompanying conditionality. In fact, no major industrialized country has borrowed from the IMF since 1977, the year when the U.K. and Italy both entered into standby arrangements.

During recent years the search by industrialized countries for a more structured international monetary system with greater exchange rate stability and a more effective adjustment process has taken place outside the IMF through meetings of the Group of Seven (the U.S., the U.K., Germany, France, Italy, Canada and Japan). The G–7 process involves not just annual Summits at the head of government level, but periodic meetings of Treasury Ministers and Central Bank Governors. Beginning with the Plaza Agreement in 1985 and the Louvre Agreement in 1987, efforts have been made toward greater international management of the floating rate system. The G–7 have gone so far as to experiment with a set of economic indicators designed to provide a framework within which countries could coordinate their monetary and fiscal policies. So far the practical results of these efforts have been limited because of an obvious fact of international economic life: the governments of the major economic powers are reluctant to subordinate their domestic policy objectives to the goal of keeping their currencies in some agreed international alignment. As long as this is the case, world leaders will continue to call for a new international monetary system while refusing to adopt the concrete measures to bring it about. Probably the best we can achieve in the foreseeable future is a deepening of the G–7 consultative process, so that 'peer pressure' is exercised on the major countries to take greater account of the international consequences of their domestic economic actions.

Given the difficulty of achieving more stable currencies and more effective adjustment on a world-wide basis, it was only natural that hopes for greater monetary stability should focus on limited regional arrangements. The European Monetary System and its Exchange Rate Mechanism (ERM) did for many years provide a zone of relative monetary stability. Yet the ambitious plan for European Monetary Union (EMU) provided for in the Maastricht Treaty suffered a major setback in the fall of 1992 when the pound sterling and the lira abandoned the fixed exchange rate parities of the ERM in favour of unilaterally managed floating. For Britain and Italy the high German interest rates triggered by the massive fiscal requirements of German unification were transmitting, through the ERM, an unacceptably depressing effect on their economies. Forced to choose between domestic growth and employment on the one hand and international monetary stability on the other, the two countries understandably gave priority to their internal economic requirements. When Germany digests the costs of unification, progress toward an EMU may well be resumed. But the lack of convergence in inflation rates and budget deficits between EMR members, as well as unforeseen future cyclical developments, make it unlikely that the EMU will be realized within anything like its original timetable for more than a core group of European countries.

If the Fund's original purpose as supplier of liquidity and monitor of sound adjustment policies has been largely frustrated with regard to the industrialized countries, it has nevertheless found a compensating role in relation to the developing nations that the 'founding fathers' could not have imagined. For many of the latter, the Fund has become the international arbiter of those sound domestic policies that qualify a country for external aid. Its financial assistance to these countries has tended to certify the credit-worthiness of the borrower and has thus made it easier to obtain credit from private lenders as well as governments. The Fund's capacity to mobilize not just its own resources, but those of central banks and commercial banks, was of critical importance in enabling the international community to cope with the debt crisis of the 1980s.

The Fund's usefulness to developing countries has increased significantly with the growth of its resources and with the creative devices developed over the years in the way these resources can be made available. At the outset the Fund's quotas totalled less than $8 billion. Successive increases have brought these resources to about $182 billion today (130 billion SDRs). Equally important have been innovations like the stand-by arrangements developed during the Fund's early years that assured countries that they could make drawings on the Fund up to a certain amount provided they carried out economic programs agreed to in consultation with the Fund. More recently the Fund established the structural adjustment and enhanced structural adjustment facilities to provide loans on concessional terms to low-income developing countries. In these and other ways, the Fund transformed itself from a rather tight-fisted short-term lender at near market interest rates to finance temporary balance of payments difficulties, to a more generous and policy-based lender financing structural adjustments over longer periods at nominal interest rates. For this evolution of the Fund, a large share of the credit should go to successive far-sighted Managing Directors – Johannes Witteveen, Jacques de Larosiere and Michel Camdessus.

The Fund has been criticized in many parts of the world for the harsh economic medicine it forces upon borrowing countries, sometimes with explosive political consequences. It has been said – only half in jest – that the Fund has 'toppled more governments than Marx and Lenin combined.' The Fund itself has admitted that it needs to pay more attention to the impact of its adjustment programs on social spending and on the welfare of the poorest segments of the population.

Still, much criticism of the Fund's policy-based lending has been misplaced. The Fund cannot be faulted when a developing country is obliged to make sacrifices in order to live within its means after years of over-borrowing and over-spending. The reforms it asks of borrowing countries, on the whole, have been sound: minimization of unproductive expenditures, particularly military spending and over-generous subsidies; a firm anti-inflation policy and a realistic exchange rate; opening up the economy to international trade and investment; price liberalization and the reform of public enterprises; the improvement of labour markets and the creation of social safety nets; and better governance, meaning participatory forms of government, a transparent legal framework, and the elimination of corruption. While progress in those directions still leaves much to be desired in the developing world as a whole, it has certainly been greater than it would have been without the Fund.

Perhaps the greatest challenge to the Fund since the end of the Cold War has come from former Communist countries in transition to market economies. The Fund has created a systemic transformation facility which permits disbursement of aid to deal with the special problems of these countries once it is assured that a satisfactory program of reform is in place. The experience with this new function of the Fund is still too brief for us to submit an unambiguous judgement on its success or failure. In Central Europe, where progress is being made in controlling inflation and re-starting economic growth, one can perhaps say that Fund resources, combined with its useful policy oversight, are making a positive contribution. For Russia, on the other hand, where economic prospects are bleak as of this writing, the Fund is blamed by some for failing to do more to help the economic reforms in Boris Yeltsin's critical first two years. Yet a good case can be made for the proposition that Russia's poor economic management in those same years, due mainly to the inflationary policies of its central bank, would have wasted Fund assistance and undermined the credibility of its lending standards. It remains to be seen whether the Fund can find a useful role to play in Russia and in other republics of the former Soviet Union where so little exists in the way of effective institutions or policy consensus.

According to the very first purpose laid down in its Articles of Agreement, the IMF was 'to promote international monetary cooperation through a permanent institution which provides the machinery for consultation and collaboration on international monetary problems.' Keynes hoped that the Fund might be the embryonic economic government of the world. He feared that the decisions taken when the Fund was inaugurated at Savannah meant the destruction of this ambitious aim. Certainly the Fund is an international, not a supranational, organization. In accordance with the Savannah decisions, its directors serve full time rather than part time at the headquarters of the Fund and act as representatives of the governments that choose them. Yet over the years they have also developed the 'world, objective outlook' for which Keynes had argued. The Board of the Fund, like the Board of the Bank, has developed a large measure of solidarity and 'team spirit.' The directors can bring this common approach to bear on their respective treasuries, thus assisting accommodations in national policies.

No less important is the fact that senior government officials, both in treasuries and central banks are to an increasing extent alumni of the Fund board or Fund staff. Even where this is not true, they are in frequent contact at annual meetings and periodic consultations. They all know one another better because of the Fund and have a degree of shared experience and outlook that otherwise would have been hard to achieve. Add to this the fact of 1700 officials a year from member countries attending IMF training institutes and hundreds of Fund experts working in the banking systems and Treasury Ministries of those countries. In the long run, the Fund's influence on a rising generation of policy-makers from developing countries and former Communist countries in transition may prove to be one of the institution's most lasting contributions to a better world economic order.

The International Trade Challenge

The postwar Anglo-American design for a reasonably free and non-discriminatory world trading system has fared somewhat better than the original design for a postwar monetary system. The refusal of the U.S. Congress to approve the International Trade Organization was an initial setback, but substantial progress in reducing trade barriers has been achieved through the General Agreement on Tariffs and Trade. Successive rounds of trade negotiations have brought the average level of tariffs in industrial countries down to about 4 percent. GATT has also managed to deal with many of the non-tariff barriers which emerged as the most significant obstacles to trade, with the reduction of tariffs to modest levels. And with the conclusion of the Uruguay Round in 1993, the world has finally established a comprehensive set of rules covering virtually all trade barriers, as well as a World Trade Organization to assist in its enforcement. In addition, half a century of trade negotiations has produced two huge areas of free trade that were not remotely foreseen by 'the founding fathers' – the single market of the European Union and the North American Free Trade Area.

This record of achievement is surprising when one considers the uncertain prospects for international trade cooperation in the early postwar years. Unlike the Bretton Woods institutions, which had the advantage of being negotiated by a relatively small number of countries in the midst of wartime idealism, the ITO had to be negotiated by a larger and more diverse group of governments who were struggling with the hard postwar realities of reconstruction and development. Its Charter attempted to cover too many controversial areas on which consensus did not exist – trade and employment, commodity agreements, foreign investment and restrictive business practices. The U.S. Congress recoiled from the complex provisions designed to deal with these subjects. More fundamentally, Congress was not yet ready to approve a full-fledged international organization that seemed to impinge upon its own Constitutional powers to regulate U.S. foreign trade.

Drawn up as a trade agreement pending the creation of the International Trade Organization, GATT had to live on as an organization when the ITO was withdrawn from Congress. Its legal basis as an organization was insecure. It had no adequate secretariat or budget. For nearly a decade visitors to GATT headquarters were greeted with a sign reading 'Interim Commission for the International Trade Organization'.

That GATT was obliged to live for years in a state of legal obscurity and institutional undernourishment was due mainly to the facts of political life in the United States. It was bad enough that the Congress was unwilling to approve the ITO; to add insult to injury, it disclaimed approval or disapproval of GATT in successive renewals of U.S. trade agreements legislation. The Eisenhower administration's attempt to give GATT a firm legal and institutional underpinning with the Organization for Trade Cooperation negotiated in 1955 suffered the same fate as the ITO Charter: refusal of the Congress to act. U.S. contributions for the support of the GATT Secretariat had to be smuggled through the Congress each year under a category in the State Department budget entitled 'international conferences and contingencies'. Some members of the Congress deeply resented the restraints that GATT seemed to place on American freedom of action in the trade field, particularly since U.S. participation in GATT had never received Congressional approval. Not until 1968 did an Administration dare to ask the Congress for permanent authorization for contributions to the GATT Secretariat – an acknowledgment of legitimacy enjoyed by every other major international agency. U.S. coolness to GATT was a major limitation on its effectiveness since, in the absence of American leadership, not much could be done by others to strengthen GATT as an instrument of liberal trade.

In light of these handicaps, GATT's accomplishments have been rather extraordinary. Much of the credit for this must go to the United States since, in spite of its antipathy to a world trade organization, it was willing to open its domestic market to the products of Europe and Japan during the early postwar years even though these countries were still severely restricting their imports of U.S. goods. This one-way act of trade liberalization had at least as much to do with the remarkable postwar recovery of Europe and Japan as did the Marshall Plan and other measures of U.S. aid. One must also be impressed at how, under the skilful leadership of Eric Wyndham White, GATT's chief executive for its first twenty-one years, the institution survived its initial difficulties and became a vital instrument for trade expansion for countries which account for more than 80 percent of world trade. Despite the absence of a formal organizational structure, the Contracting Parties established a permanent Council to operate between meetings, a network of specialized committees, and a small permanent secretariat. Quietly but perceptibly, GATT developed authority in a threefold role – as a forum for trade negotiations, as a body of principles governing trade policy, and as a centre for the settlement of trade disputes.

As a forum for trade negotiations, GATT has promoted an unprecedented amount of tariff disarmament in eight major bargaining rounds: Geneva, 1947; Annecy, 1949; Torquay, 1951; Geneva, 1956; Geneva, 1960–61 (the 'Dillion Round'); Geneva, 1964–67 (the 'Kennedy Round'); Geneva, 1975–79 (the Tokyo Round') and Geneva 1986–93 (the 'Uruguay Round'). In the Kennedy, Tokyo and Uruguay Rounds, which dwarfed all the others in importance, the average height of tariffs in industrial countries was brought down to about 4 percent. The U.S. has reduced its average tariff to this level from the 60 percent that prevailed before the Trade Agreements Program began in 1934.

These achievements, to be sure, were the result of commitments undertaken by national governments, but they would not have been possible without GATT. In each of the difficult bargaining rounds, GATT – or more precisely its chief executive – was an indispensable element in laying the groundwork for the negotiations and guiding them to a successful conclusion. This function was reinforced in the Dillon and Kennedy rounds when Eric Wyndham White became chairman of the Negotiating Group. Indeed, when differences between the U.S. and the E.E.C. seemed irreconcilable, it was his last-minute intervention that saved the Kennedy Round from collapse and provided the basis for a final settlement. More recently, GATT Directors General Arthur Dunkel and Peter Sutherland have played equally decisive roles in bridging national differences that threatened to derail the Uruguay Round. Both from the standpoint of results achieved and of GATT's role in producing them, the wartime goals for the bargaining down of tariff restrictions have enjoyed a considerable measure of realization.

The role of GATT in dealing with non-tariff barriers has been much more difficult, but since its failures in this field have been so widely publicized, it may be useful to recall some successes that are often forgotten. We need only remember, for example, the bitter differences over quantitative restrictions (QRs) in the postwar negotiations described in *Sterling-Dollar Diplomacy*. The compromises reached in the negotiation of GATT worked out much better than the sceptics believed possible. To some American critics, the exception which permitted QRs to protect the balance of payments and a country's domestic employment policy constituted an 'economic Munich.' Yet by the 1960s, QRs had been largely eliminated among developed countries on trade in industrial goods (with the notable exception of textiles). To some British critics, the limitations on the use of QRs threatened to frustrate full employment policies and postwar recovery. Yet in not a single instance did they actually do so. That other explosive issue in the GATT negotiations – Imperial Preference – has also gradually faded from sight. Successive rounds of tariff reductions together with inflation have reduced the preference margins to insignificance.

The really difficult non-tariff barrier issues have turned out to be quite different from the ones that preoccupied the British and American negotiators at the time of GATT's creation. Substantial non-tariff trade barriers arose in the form of 'grey area' restrictions – voluntary export restraints and bilateral orderly marketing arrangements whose existence was not foreseen when GATT was negotiated. The proliferation of anti-dumping actions forced trade negotiators to seek new rules in this area. Government procurement practices and domestic subsidy programs emerged as major trade-distorting measures that were not adequately dealt with in the original GATT rules. Moreover, these rules turned out to be totally inadequate to deal with agricultural protectionism. Ironically, this was mainly due to the desire of the U.S. to ensure the maintenance of its agricultural import restrictions in pursuance of New Deal price support programs on behalf of American farmers. When the U.S. began to suffer from the impact of Europe's Common Agricultural Policy in the 1960s, it had occasion to regret its earlier success in carving out such a generous agricultural exemption in the GATT rules.

Decades of postwar experience also revealed the necessity of broadening the scope of GATT regulation to cover three other areas whose importance was not anticipated by the 'founding fathers.' One was trade in services – banking, insurance, securities, construction and the like – which grew dramatically in relative importance to merchandise trade. A second was the protection of intellectual property – copyrights, patents and trademarks – where the lack of universal rules and their enforcement has proved increasingly costly to business in advanced industrial countries. The third area was that of trade-distorting requirements placed by governments on foreign investors, including domestic content requirements and minimum export requirements.

By the middle 1980s, a widespread conviction had developed that GATT had to 'grow or die'; it needed to extend its regulation to cover all these areas or slip into increasing irrelevance. It was this conviction that led to the Uruguay Round, certainly the most ambitious trade negotiation in world history. After seven years of arduous negotiations, which stalled repeatedly and at times seemed close to collapse, the U.S., Europe, Japan and their trading partners were able to put forward new or improved rules in all the trade areas mentioned above. These rules, to be sure, are replete with exceptions and ambiguities in deference to divergent economic interests, but they provide a framework on which GATT can build and become stronger in the years ahead.

To be really useful, any set of principles requires effective procedures for interpretation and enforcement. In its early years, GATT made a courageous beginning at developing such procedures. Its panels of experts, drawn from member countries with no direct interest in the subject matter, managed to resolve a number of dangerous trade disputes that could have unravelled painstaking accomplishments in trade liberalization. In 1963–64, for example, a GATT panel helped to bring a truce in the famous 'chicken war' between the U.S. and the Common Market, resulting from the latter's system of variable levies. Unhappily, this early record of success in dispute settlement was not matched in GATT's later years. Too often, a country found in violation of its obligations by a GATT panel availed itself of GATT's unanimity rule to prevent the Contracting Parties from confirming their decision. The whole dispute-settlement process was too slow and became fragmented after the Tokyo round, with different procedures for the different non-tariff barriers dealt with in the various Tokyo Round codes.

Fortunately, the Uruguay Round has produced an historic breakthrough in the system for the interpretation and enforcement of the international trade rules. The process is now subject to strict timetables. In place of a variety of dispute settlement procedures under different GATT codes, there is now an integrated system for the settlement of all trade disputes, with only minor exceptions. A country that loses its case before a GATT panel will no longer be able to block the decision. If it does not bring its laws into conformity with its GATT obligations within a specified period of time, it must compensate the affected countries with equivalent trade concessions, otherwise trade retaliation will be authorized against it.

The creation of a new World Trade Organization (WTO) to supplement the GATT is another historic achievement that belatedly fills the vacuum left by the failure of the ITO. By bringing together under one constitutional umbrella the rules and disciplines on government practices affecting trade in goods and services and the protection of intellectual property, the WTO facilitates cross retaliation in an integrated dispute-settlement mechanism. Thus a country that violates its obligations to respect intellectual property rights, for example, can be subject to WTO-authorized retaliation in the form of higher tariffs on its exports of manufactured or agricultural goods by countries that are injured by its action.

In addition, the WTO will help resolve one of the serious weaknesses of GATT – the 'free rider' problem. In the past, a GATT member could claim the benefits of most-favoured-nation treatment from GATT codes or GATT-sponsored tariff reductions without making comprehensive commitments itself. Now the benefits of the WTO will be available only to countries that are contracting parties to the GATT, that adhere to all of the Uruguay Round agreements, and submit schedules of market access commitments for both industrial and agricultural goods and services.

The world has thus taken a major step toward an enforceable system of international trade law. But it remains to be seen how the system will actually work in practice. It is already apparent that the U.S. and some of its trading partners disagree on whether WTO members will be free to employ their trade remedy laws in unilateral fashion. The U.S. has asserted that it will continue to apply Section 301 of its trade legislation. For matters covered by the Uruguay Round agreement, this Congressional authorization to retaliate against foreign trade practices considered unfair will be exercised in conformity with the new dispute-settlement procedures. For matters not covered by the Uruguay Round agreement, the U.S. will continue to reserve the right of unilateral action. Even if this U.S. claim is not challenged by other countries as a matter of principle, disputes are likely to arise over what matters are covered and what not covered by the Uruguay Round agreement.

The conclusion of the Uruguay Round and the creation of a World Trade Organization have certainly remedied some of the major weaknesses of the international trading system, but there are more than enough new challenges remaining to keep the fraternity of international trade experts busy for the foreseeable future. One of the major challenges is posed by the worldwide trend towards regional arrangements. Customs unions and free trade areas are specifically authorized by Article XXIV of GATT, provided they meet certain conditions of openness to ensure that they will be more trade-creating than trade-diverting. Unquestionably, the European Union and NAFTA meet these tests, but other regional trade arrangements developing in parts of Latin America and Asia will require careful scrutiny from the new WTO. Moreover, the likely evolution of the European Union and NAFTA into much larger trading areas in their respective regions during the decade ahead will introduce a new level of complexity in the continuing effort to reconcile global and regional trading rules.

Another unresolved issue occupying the trade experts will be the special problem of Japan. Despite years of negotiations aimed at opening up the Japanese market, Japan continues to run a trade surplus with the rest of the world that has averaged about $100 billion a year. Japan's imports of manufactured goods remain at the low level of 3 percent of its GDP compared with 7 percent in the U.S. and 8 percent in Europe.

The difficulty of penetrating the Japanese market is the result of many factors – Japanese industrial policy, the discriminatory policies of its Keiretsu industrial groups, restrictions on inward foreign investment, and impediments in distribution channels for imported products. Even the new WTO and the expanded GATT rules are not likely to provide answers to the special kinds of barriers that Japan presents to the world. This has led the U.S. to its controversial demand that Japan accept objective criteria, either quantitative or qualitative, to assess progress in opening its market. Some denounce this as 'managed trade'; however, could this not be regarded as a results-oriented set of benchmarks to open up a market where trade is already managed? Some compromise in this controversy must be found if disputes between the world's two most powerful trading nations are not to disrupt the entire trading system.

One last challenge that requires special mention derives from the growth of the GATT to near universality. In one sense, this represents a triumph for the goals of the 'founding fathers,' since 'Third World' and former Communist countries that used to denounce the GATT as a nefarious capitalist club are now clambering to get in. But this victory for trade openness is also a new challenge, since it takes place at a time when the worldwide spread of capital and technology has created a true global marketplace. In 1970 the poor countries of the world sold just $3 billion worth of manufactured goods to their wealthy counterparts; today that figure is in excess of $150 billion.

The opening up to world trade of formerly closed economies in Asia, in Latin America and in countries of the former Soviet empire has brought well over 2 billion new people into the global marketplace. As well as potential new consumers, they are also producers, many of whom are prepared to work at one-fourth or one-sixth of wage rates in the U.S., Western Europe and Japan. Even as the Uruguay Round was being concluded, we began to hear second thoughts from leaders of the industrialized democracies about the dangers that low-wage foreign competition might pose for the jobs and living standards of their people. Is it possible that, with the achievement of near universality for the GATT system, we have planted the seeds of its eventual destruction?

The International Development Challenge

The effort to promote the economic development of the less developed countries is another major challenge of our time. The most important international financial institution engaged in this effort in terms of the size of its resources and the weight of its influence is the International Bank for Reconstruction and Development. We take this for granted now, but in early planning for the postwar economy, the Bank came almost as an afterthought. Virtually all the attention of the British and American governments was focused on the International Monetary Fund. When, on the eve of Bretton Woods, the negotiators finally considered the Bank, they were in a conservative mood: the British did not expect to be beneficiaries; the Americans were afraid of the Congress. The Bank's lending capacity was limited almost entirely to what it could raise by bonds issued on the private capital market. There was simply no conception of the vast needs of the less developed countries and of the role the Bank should play in meeting them. Indeed, the Bank was conceived mainly as an institution for reconstruction. Incredible as it seems today, the word 'development' did not even appear in Harry White's first draft circulated within the U.S. Treasury Department.

As it turned out, the Bank played only a marginal role in the accomplishment of its primary purpose – the reconstruction of a war-devastated Europe. The financial requirements of reconstruction were far beyond the Bank's comparatively modest resources. In 1946–47 two great Americans – Dean Acheson and Will Clayton – persuaded President Harry Truman that a special effort of enlightened U.S. statesmanship was required. The result was Secretary of State George C. Marshall's famous address at Harvard University in June 1947.

In the light of history, there are three aspects of the Marshall Plan that particularly deserve to be remembered. First, the U.S. pumped $16 billion (the equivalent of about $100 billion today) into the European economies over a four-year period – half of it on a grant basis – thus laying the essential foundation for the 'economic miracle' of the Continent in the 1950s and 1960s.

Second, the Marshall Plan was not conceived as a Cold War instrument; on the contrary, the Soviet Union and its East European satellites were invited to join. As Secretary of State Marshall declared in his Harvard address: 'Our policy is not directed against any country or doctrine, but against hunger, poverty, desperation and chaos.' The postwar division of Europe was sealed when Stalin refused to join a Europe-wide recovery effort and prevented the participation of other East European countries as well.

But it is the third aspect of the Marshall Plan that is most relevant to this history: the entire programme was conditioned on a cooperative recovery effort by the European countries themselves. Indeed, in the Marshall Plan legislation, the U.S. Congress made steps toward European unity a requirement for American aid. The Organization for European Economic Cooperation (OEEC), established to manage American assistance, worked effectively to increase trade and financial cooperation among the aid recipients. The dismantling of intra-European trade barriers, the European Payments Union, the Treaty of Rome itself – all can be traced back to the Marshall Plan initiative. After years during which the U.S. has been denounced for 'imperialist' and 'hegemonial' designs on Europe, this is worth special emphasis. It is, after all, a strange kind of 'imperialism' that urges weak and divided countries to unite so that they may become strong political and economic rivals.

No doubt the Marshall Plan was motivated not only by U.S. altruism and enlightened economic interest, but by the fact that Europe's free institutions were vulnerable in the face of Soviet-led Communist movements unless economic conditions improved. Nor is there any doubt that, in later years, a resurgent and self-confident European Community came into conflict with the U.S. on many trade and financial questions. But neither of these facts can obscure the objective benefits of European recovery and integration that are now enjoyed, not only by Europeans themselves, but by the U.S. and the rest of the world. And it is a source of satisfaction that successive U.S. administrations have continued to support the great historic movement toward European unity, even while wishing to be sure that it proceeds as far as possible in harmony with the global institutions that emerged as liberalizing forces after World War II. As these lines are written, the U.S. is giving its full encouragement to the process of political and economic unity in Europe in the belief that this process serves the enlightened interest of the U.S. in terms of greater global stability and welfare.

The Bank, like the other Bretton Woods twin, took some years to overcome its initial handicaps. As a reconstruction agency, it was inevitably overshadowed by the Marshall Plan. In the 1950s, when it at last began to focus on the less developed countries, its dependence on the private capital market restricted it to a rather conservative banker's role. It financed only specific projects that promised profits sufficient to repay the initial investment, covered only foreign exchange (not local currency) costs, and concentrated on traditional 'public utility' investments in power and transportation. Equally important, it lent only on commercial terms, with market interest rates and repayment schedules of ten to twenty years.

Yet even in these early years, the Bank's contribution was by no means unimportant. After the disastrous experience of defaults in international bond issues during the interwar period, it is doubtful whether the U.S. capital market could have once again been tapped on such a large scale, particularly for the less developed countries, without the International Bank as intermediary. World Bank bonds, representing a diversified package of investments undertaken by an experienced and prudent management and backed by guarantees of borrowing governments as well as by the U.S. capital subscription, were soon regarded in Wall Street as a first-class investment. Gradually, the Bank diversified its borrowing operations as Europe recovered and the U.S. slipped into balance of payments deficit. By the middle and late 1960s, European capital markets were providing substantially more of the Bank's new money than the U.S. capital market.

Moreover, the Bank's role in stimulating the flow of private capital was enlarged with the creation of two Bank affiliates. The first – the International Finance Corporation – put government money to work in equity investments in private enterprises in less developed countries. The second – the International Center for Settlement of Investment Disputes – created a centre of arbitration for the resolution of disputes between foreign investors and governments.

These achievements in mobilizing and stimulating the flow of private capital for development can be credited in large part to two experienced figures from the U.S. financial community – Eugene Black and George Woods. But the Bank's evolution under their presidencies was not limited to the area of 'bankable' investment. The really big breakthrough was the launching of the International Development Association as the Bank's 'soft-loan' affiliate for the granting of very long-term loans at nominal rates of interest. It was with the creation of IDA in 1960 that the member governments, responding to U.S. leadership, finally recognized the inadequacy of the original Bretton Woods conception which made the Bank almost entirely dependent on the private capital market. Today Bank lending of more than $10 billion a year on near-commercial terms is supplemented by some $5 billion annually in interest-free IDA loans repayable over forty years with ten-year grace periods.

By the middle and late 1960s, the Bank and IDA were making programme as well as project loans, were financing local as well as foreign exchange costs, and were moving into new fields such as agriculture and education. Later the Bank extended its activities to embrace projects in health and family planning. To carry out projects in these fields, the Bank began to work closely with such agencies of the United Nations as UNESCO, the Food and Agriculture Organization, the World Health Organization, the UN Development Program and the UN Population Fund. In these and other ways the Bank altered its original attitude of splendid isolation from the United Nations system.

During the Presidency of Robert S. McNamara in the 1970s, the character of the Bank changed even further. Its focus became not just economic development, but poverty reduction and basic human needs and the access of the poor to education, health care and family planning services. More recently, under Tom Clausen, Barber Conable and Lewis Preston, the Bank has financed projects to protect the human environment in such areas as forestry, water resources management and energy efficiency. It now manages a Global Environmental Facility (GEF) in cooperation with the UN Development Program and the UN Environment

Program. The GEF, replenished recently with $2 billion to be committed over three years, is serving as the centrepiece of global efforts in support of the international conventions on climate change, biodiversity and the protection of the ozone layer, as well as of efforts to combat marine pollution.

The Bank's historic contribution – like that of the Fund – cannot be measured by its financial operations alone. It has served as an inspiration and model for the establishment and growth of regional development banks in Latin America, Africa and Asia, and, more recently, in Europe. Its consortia and consultative groups have brought donor countries together and coordinated their aid in support of internationally-approved development plans. This 'multilateral-bilateralism' (or multilateral coordination of bilateral aid programs) is now an important element in international financial cooperation – a vital supplement to the discussions of bilateral aid policy among donor countries in the Development Assistance Committee of the Organization for Economic Cooperation and Development, the successor to the original OEEC.

When all of this is taken into account, it is clear that multilateral cooperation in development lending has come a long way. At the present time the U.S. is conducting much of its development lending through the multilateral development banks. All in all, about one-third of total world development assistance is being disbursed by multilateral agencies, while much of the rest is being transferred pursuant to arrangements worked out by consortia and consultative groups. The multilateral banks, like the IBRD, now have hard-loan windows lending on near market terms to the most advanced developing nations, and soft-loan windows lending on concessional terms to the poorest and least credit-worthy developing countries. The hard loans are financed by borrowing on the world's capital markets, the soft loans mainly by donor contributions. The total annual lending commitments of the banks have reached over $40 billion a year.

The World Bank's ability to mobilize increasing amounts of capital, together with its prestige and experience, have given it a growing influence on both the aid policies of the rich and the development policies of the poor. Its Presidency is becoming one of the world's most influential platforms for improving the aid efforts of the developed countries. Its role in training, advice and technical assistance also enables it to shape profoundly the development efforts of the poor countries. Its Economic Development Institute, the visiting Bank Missions, the Bank's assistance in project preparation and execution – all of these help encourage those sound internal policies without which no amount of external assistance can possibly bear fruit. It should also be added that, in response to criticism, the Bank has become a more open institution, willing to provide information and engage in dialogue with non-governmental organizations. No doubt, as we shall suggest in a moment, aid is still insufficiently large, while the economic performance of many developing countries continues to be disappointing. But the Bank's achievements since Bretton Woods represent a quite spectacular advance in international collaboration for development over anything that went before.

Perhaps the most eloquent measure of the success of the development efforts of the last fifty years has been the growth of private capital flows to the developing world. In 1993, of $177 billion in total capital flows to these countries, $113 billion, or about two-thirds, came from the private sector. Some $56 billion of this amount was in the form of foreign direct investment, $13 billion in the form of portfolio investment, and $43 billion in lending from commercial banks and other sources. It is clear that Henry Morganthau's 'usurious money lenders' – far from being 'driven from the temple of international finance' – are providing an indispensable and rapidly growing source of finance for world economic development.

Yet we cannot end this survey of fifty years of effort in international development on an entirely sanguine note. Two debit entries must be entered on this balance sheet; these concern the development policies of the poor and the aid policies of the rich.

What used to be called the 'Third World' now comprises a highly differentiated development universe. China, Hong Kong, Taiwan, Singapore, Korea and a number of Asian countries have registered phenomenal growth. Mexico, Chile and Argentina and a few other countries of Latin America have begun to take off after years of disappointment. In contrast, Africa south of the Sahara, with the exception of South Africa and one or two other countries, is a continent in agony. Per capita income has been declining, on the average, for over a decade. The World Bank has estimated that, if present trends continue, it will take Africa forty years to recover the income levels it achieved in the 1970s. These examples of development success and development failure serve to remind us that no amount of help from the international financial institutions can solve the development problem without the right set of conditions in recipient countries.

Paul Hoffman remarked at the beginning of the Marshall Plan that 'only the Europeans can save Europe.' In the final analysis, the developing countries' progress will depend on their own efforts. Only their own commitment to putting their houses in order, to wealth-creating strategies, to realistic foreign exchange and interest rates, to providing incentives to domestic and foreign investors, to family planning and environmental protection, and to less corrupt and more responsive government can ensure them a better future. How to help the poorest of the developing countries to tackle these issues remains a major challenge for the international community.

The other major source of concern lies in the growing 'aid fatigue' of the rich countries. After years of impressive growth, the total amount of 'official development assistance' – aid supplied by the developed countries on concessional terms – has begun to stagnate. It is now at 0.35 percent of GDP as compared with the target of 0.7 percent approved some years ago by the UN General Assembly. Whatever one thinks of the UN target, it is clear that current aid levels will not be sufficient to achieve the goals of 'sustainable development' – assisting economic growth in developing countries while preserving the human environment – that were agreed to in Rio at the 1992 UN Conference on Environment and Development.

The United States, which demonstrated such exceptional leadership in world development efforts for most of the last fifty years, is now a major part of the problem. Its aid level as a proportion of GDP is 0.15 percent, at the bottom of the OECD ranking of developed countries. Its funding for the multilateral development banks has fallen by 40 percent since 1978 and its arrears in contributions to those banks now exceed $800 million. This falling off of U.S. commitment has resulted mainly from Congressional and public demands that the government cut back on foreign spending and devote more resources to neglected domestic needs. These demands are understandable, but if sustainable development fails on a global scale, U.S. economic and environmental goals will be undermined as well.

It would seem that the challenge to political leadership in the U.S. to make a convincing case to Congress and public opinion on behalf of policies of enlightened internationalism may be just as great today as when the 'founding fathers' laid the groundwork for the postwar economic order half a century ago.

Economism, Universalism, and Legalism Revisited

The final chapter of *Sterling-Dollar Diplomacy* emphasizes three 'errors' which underlay wartime and postwar economic diplomacy – Economism, Universalism and Legalism. In the light of fifty years of history, however, these 'errors' do not seem as serious as we originally thought.

We said that the postwar planners were guilty of Economism in building a set of postwar economic institutions before the political setting could be clearly foreseen. But they had to start somewhere. If the British and American governments had not used the period of their wartime collaboration to establish the Bretton Woods institutions and chart the main outlines of what became the GATT, these institutions might never have been created. From the perspective of half a century, we can be grateful that the economic foundations of a decent world order were laid while the fighting was still in progress, even if those foundations might otherwise have been better shaped to postwar political realities. Also it would have been difficult to hold a successful Bretton Woods conference after the war. Not only would the wartime spirit of idealism and solidarity have been dissipated, but it might have been necessary to contemplate closing the exchange markets until the conference reached a successful conclusion.

We said that the postwar planners were guilty of Universalism in sometimes considering universal institutions as a substitute for cooperation on a bilateral or regional basis. It is certainly true that they failed to supplement these institutions soon enough with measures to deal with the special problems of the pound sterling and of European reconstruction. To say that they were guilty of Universalism, however, does not mean that they made a mistake in founding universal institutions in the financial and trade field. Quite the contrary. Precisely because of their universal character, the Bretton Woods institutions and GATT have been indispensable vehicles, not only for cooperation between North America, Europe and Japan, but also for assistance to the nations of the less developed world and to the former Communist countries. Indeed, the role of these institutions in promoting economic reforms in China and in the countries of Central and Eastern Europe may one day be judged among their most important achievements. None of these possibilities could have been realized had the British and American governments sidetracked the International Monetary Fund in favour of a bilateral financial agreement, as was urged by the opponents of Bretton Woods in the 'key currency' proposal.

We said that postwar planners were guilty of Legalism in exalting agreement in form over agreement in substance. Certainly some agreements were negotiated in excessive detail, without any real meeting of minds and without adequate procedures for adjustment in the light of changing circumstances. One notorious example was the Anglo-American Financial Agreement, with its inflexible timetable for sterling convertibility and its camouflaging of divergent intentions with respect to the funding and writing off of wartime sterling balances. A second example was the ITO Charter, so encumbered with rules and exceptions that it collapsed from its own weight even before it could take effect.

Yet the Bretton Woods institutions and GATT are also legal instruments and, as this history reveals in abundant detail, they certainly were subject to very different interpretations on the two sides of the Atlantic. However, most of the differences that seemed so important half a century ago have disappeared, removed by changes in American and British policy or simply overtaken by events. Perhaps these institutions have succeeded (where the Anglo-American Financial Agreement failed) because they have provided a framework for continuing consultation and adjustment of policy. This history suggests that the self-serving statements negotiators made to please domestic opinion may have been a price worth paying, given their common interest in enabling the institutions to work in practice. Whether they do, in fact, work depends not only on this measure of common interest, but also on the leadership of the international staff, the evolution of national policies, and the procedures by which original ambiguities can be clarified in changing circumstances.

'There is,' Keynes warned at Savannah, 'scarcely any enduringly successful experience yet of an international body which has fulfilled the hopes of its progenitors. Either an institution has become diverted to be the instrument of a limited group, or it has been a puppet of sawdust through which the breath of life does not blow'. One cannot escape the conclusion that Keynes, perfectionist though he was, would have been the first to acknowledge the service to the general interest, as well as the continuing vitality, of the institutions in whose conception he played such a leading part.

Name Index